thinking about

SOCIOLOGY

thinking about
SOCIOLOGY
a critical
introduction

Karen L. Anderson

OXFORD
UNIVERSITY PRESS

OXFORD
UNIVERSITY PRESS

Oxford University Press is a department of the University of Oxford.
It furthers the University's objective of excellence in research, scholarship,
and education by publishing worldwide. Oxford is a registered trade mark of
Oxford University Press in the UK and in certain other countries.

Published in Canada by
Oxford University Press
8 Sampson Mews, Suite 204,
Don Mills, Ontario M3C 0H5 Canada

www.oupcanada.com

Library and Archives Canada Cataloguing in Publication

Anderson, Karen L.
Thinking about sociology : a critical introduction / Karen L. Anderson.

Includes bibliographical references and index.
ISBN 978–0–19–543787–4

1. Sociology Textbooks.
2. Sociology Methodology. I. Title.

HM586.A54 2012   301   C2011-908070-2

Cover image: © iStockPhoto.com/Bertlmann

Printed and bound in the United States of America

2 3 4 — 15 14 13

Contents

Part III Early Sociological Theorists   107

5. The Beginnings of Sociology   108

6. Karl Marx and Max Weber   136

7. The Social Interactionist Perspective   164

Part IV Core Concepts   189

8. Socialization and the Young Child   190

PART V Core Topics of Difference and Inequality   317

PART VI New Topics, New Directions   443

Preface

FROM THE PUBLISHER

There is more to society than meets the eye, yet while most people know this, they continue to view the world with a largely uncritical, everyday perception of the way things are. Sociologists are committed to delving deeper, applying a sociological imagination to the study of society in order to gain a better understanding of the way that social institutions such as school, work, and home affect every individual's life course and life chances.

Thinking About Sociology: A Critical Introduction focuses on developing critical thinking and problem-solving skills in sociology through a lively survey of the core topics, concepts, and applications widely identified by sociologists as being central to an introductory sociology course. The goal is to encourage students to challenge their everyday thinking about the world around them without sacrificing the focus on the issues fundamental to the discipline, including social change, inequalities and power, social institutions, and socialization.

To that end, *Thinking About Sociology* contains a great deal of both foundational and current content. By pairing classical examples with current, often Canadian examples—in

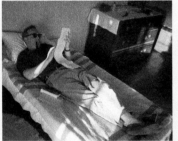

highlight boxes as well as in numerous visual examples presented with thought-provoking captions—this textbook aims to offers students and instructors something different: an introduction to core skills and concepts that at the same time challenges readers to rethink their own assumptions about their role in society and the social institutions with which they interact.

This book is designed to give introductory students a useful, compelling, and timely introduction to the study of sociology, with the hope they will come away with an appreciation of the field's pioneering theorists and studies and a better understanding of the application of sociological theories in the Canadian context. To that end this book takes an accessible approach:

- Theories, concepts, and applications are presented in a straightforward writing style that respects the intelligence of the student reader.
- Carefully chosen examples present some of the discipline's landmark studies, while current examples and thought-provoking photographs featuring the life situations of ordinary people challenge students to think critically about their own experiences.
- Biographical information on some of sociology's founders is highlighted in Profiles in Sociology boxes, giving students insight into the lives and work of some of the discipline's major figures—Comte, Durkheim, Marx, Mills, Porter—as well as others who have made important, though perhaps less celebrated, contributions to the discipline, such as Margaret Bourke-White.
- Studies in Social Research boxes present case studies and current research on topics ranging from men's unpaid domestic work to street art as a form of cultural expression.
- The text's critical perspective invites students to think like sociologists, encouraging them to re-evaluate their assumptions about themselves and their social world.
- Strong coverage of Canadian issues and examples, examining such topics as inequality, sexuality and gender, popular culture, and the Internet and social media, helps students better relate to the theories and concepts presented.

In June 2011 Toronto became the first city outside of India to host the Indian International Film Academy awards. What do you think that indicates about the changing ethnic composition of Canada's cities, and Toronto in particular?

Members of Carleton University Students' Association gather on Parliament Hill to rally against reopening the equal marriage debate in December 2006. Do you think the debate surrounding same-sex marriage in this country is over, or is there a chance it could be reopened?

Facilitating Student Learning

A textbook must be accurate, current, and comprehensive, but it must also speak to the needs and interests of today's students, providing them with an accessible introduction to the discipline of sociology, and so numerous features to promote student learning are incorporated throughout the book. They include the following:

- *Chapter Outlines* allow students and instructors to see how the material within a chapter fits together and relates.
- *Learning Objectives* at the start of each chapter provide a concise overview of the key concepts to be covered.
- *Chapter Summaries* at the end of each chapter ensure understanding of key concepts is complete and help students refresh their recollection of key themes and concepts when reviewing for tests and exams.
- *Discussion Questions* at the end of each chapter draw out key issues while encouraging readers to draw their own conclusions about sociology.
- A *running glossary* of key terms provides definitions in the margin alongside the text where the terms are used. All marginal definitions—expanded, in many cases—are compiled in a comprehensive *end-of-book glossary* that serves as a valuable review tool and reference.

18 Popular Culture and Mass Media

CHAPTER OUTLINE

Introduction
Popular Culture
  1. 'Well Liked by Many People'
  2. 'Inferior Kinds of Work'
  3. 'Work Deliberately Set Out to Win Favour with the People'
  4. 'Culture Actually Made by the People Themselves'
Popular Culture and the Industrial Revolution
The Communication of Popular Culture: Many-to-One and Many-to-Many Relations
  One-to-One
  Few-to-Few
  One-to-Many
  Many-to-One
  Many-to-Many

Mass Media and the Communication and Consumption of Cultural 'Goods and Services'
  The Three Screens
Mass Media and Social Behaviour
  Mass Media and Violence
  TV Violence
  Onscreen Violence: Seven 'Research Strands' and Inclusive Results
  Canadian Children's Views About Onscreen Violence
Summary
Discussion Questions

LEARNING OBJECTIVES

In this chapter you will:

- distinguish between popular culture, one-directional mass media, and two-directional user-produced participatory media
- gain a clearer understanding of popular culture
- learn about popular culture and the Industrial Revolution
- examine how popular culture is communicated and shared
- reflect on the role of mass media in communicating entertainment and information
- seek to understand the effects of mass media on consumer behaviour
- think critically about the relationship between onscreen violence and real-world violence.

Supplements

Today's textbook is no longer a volume that stands on its own—it is but the central element of a complete learning and teaching package. *Thinking About Sociology* is no exception. The book is supported by an outstanding array of ancillary materials for both students and instructors, all available on the companion website:

 www.oupcanada.com/Anderson

For the Instructor

- An ***Instructor's Manual*** includes comprehensive outlines of the text's various parts and chapters, and additional questions for encouraging classroom discussion.
- A ***Test Bank*** offers a comprehensive set of multiple-choice, true/false, short-answer, and essay questions, with suggested answers, for every chapter.
- ***PowerPoint slides***, summarizing key points from each chapter and incorporating figures, tables, and photos from the textbook, are available to adopters of the text.
- ***A comprehensive companion website*** includes a selection of additional resources to benefit instructors using this textbook.

Instructors should contact their Oxford University Press sales representative for details on these supplements and for login and password information.

For the Student

The ***Student Study Guide*** offers self-testing study questions, annotated links to useful resources, and much more. Go to www.oupcanada.com/Anderson and follow the links!

| COMPANION WEBSITE | Karen L. Anderson
Thinking About Sociology
ISBN 13: 9780195437874 |

About the Book

Thinking About Sociology: A Critical Introduction is intended for introductory sociology courses for first-year university students. The book helps students start to think like sociologists, to question their taken-for-granted assumptions about their place in society, and to evaluate critically how they interact with other individuals and social institutions. To this end, Anderson takes a critical perspective when discussing the core concepts, skills, theories, and applications used in the study of sociology, giving students the skills they need to understand and confront the challenges they will face in life. Anderson presents examples that are diverse, topical and relevant to Canadian students, covering such areas as education and training, immigration and integration and social networking and mediated interactions.

Inspection copy request

Ordering information

Contact & Comments

 Instructor Resources

You need a password to access these resources. Please contact your local Sales and Editorial Representative for more information.

 Student Resources

FROM THE AUTHOR

Introduction: Thinking Sociology

If we could use just two words to describe the social climate of the last 50 years, they would have to be *change* and *uncertainty*. The last five decades have seen unprecedented growth in the use of new technologies, including computer-based communications, social media, and information processing. 'Artificial intelligence', robots, new reproductive technologies, including cloning, and other technological advances no longer surprise us.

The political map of the world has changed substantially in this 50-year period as well, with the breakup of the Soviet Union and THE demise of many communist states in eastern Europe, the reunification of East and West Germany, the phenomenal growth in economic power of China, and the shake-up of the economies of most Western nations that followed fast on the heels of the American prime mortgage crisis of 2008. The election of a black American president in that same year, something that few would have dreamed possible even a year earlier, galvanized people around the world.

All of this change and uncertainty might lead us to believe that we are living in unique and turbulent times—times uniquely fraught with danger and uncertainty, times uniquely filled with hope for a better and safer future for ourselves and future generations. But concern about threats from social, economic, political, cultural, and religious crises has been a constant in the life experiences of most people living in industrialized Western societies since at least the end of the eighteenth century.

An Invitation and a Caution

The primary goal of this textbook is to get you thinking as a sociologist. Thinking as a sociologist requires the ability to identify and work through problems that are of interest to sociologists using the techniques of observation, evidence gathering, discussion, analysis, and reporting. It also demands the ability to understand (and think critically about) sociological concepts, principles, theoretical perspectives, and methods of research and their applications.

Learning to think as a sociologist can change how you understand yourself and the world that surrounds you; it can lead you to rethink previously taken-for-granted ways of understanding yourself and your society. It can even help you to become aware of new issues or to consider old issues from a very different perspective.

Ignorance, contrary to the popular saying, is not bliss. The purpose of a liberal education, including the study of sociology, is to become better equipped to deal with troubling questions such as:

- What does it mean to be human?
- How is society possible?
- Why are people unequal in society?
- Why can't everyone be just like us?
- Why is there misery in the world?
- Does the individual really make a difference? (Charon, 2010)

Most people rarely think about these questions; when they do think about them, it is usually in the most casual of manners. We are born into a society with a long history. We are given a rank and multiple roles, told what to do and how to think. As Peter Berger has pointed out in his now classic book *Invitation to Sociology* (1963), the first insight of a sociologist is that things are not what they seem. Social reality, Berger tells us, 'turns out to have many layers of meaning. The discovery of each new layer changes the perception of the whole.' Berger likens this discovery to experiencing 'culture shock', but without having to leave home to discover 'the sudden illumination of new and unsuspected facets of human existence in society'.

Learning to be a sociologist is not for the complacent or the faint of heart. If you are deeply attached to your taken-for-granted world, if you do not have a curiosity about yourself and others, do not wonder about why you hold the beliefs you do, why you feel more comfortable with one group of people and not another, why there is inequality, discrimination, oppression; if you have never been curious about what goes on in the homes of the people on the other side of town, or the other side of the continent, or the side of the world, then becoming a sociologist is not for you.

A sociologist *is* 'interested in looking some distance beyond the commonly accepted or officially defined goals of human actions' (Berger, 1963). She *is* interested in what goes on behind the scenes and in what lurks beyond 'official interpretations of society' (Berger, 1963). Sometimes this is uncomfortable. It can be unsettling to realize that those whom you previously regarded as deviant or undesirable are simply different, or that those whom you hate are the 'products of social circumstances that should be understood more carefully and objectively'. At its best, sociology enables its practitioners to 'confront their ideas, actions, and being. We are never the same once we bring sociology into our lives,' says Charon (2010, p. 325). 'Life is scrutinized. Truth becomes far more tentative.'

I invite readers to learn to think as sociologists, and to explore the connections between formal learning, citizenship, and service to your community. In so doing I hope that readers will better understand the challenges they face in life, and be better positioned to confront those challenges. I am convinced that learning to think as a sociologist better equips students to understand, and to shape, history. At the end of this course of study you should be able to:

- apply sociological principles and concepts to your own lives and to understanding the lives of others
- demonstrate an understanding of the relationship between the individual and society
- show skill in asking relevant sociological questions
- undertake and evaluate basic sociological research
- understand how sociological theory is used to explain research findings
- recognize the importance of historical and cultural contexts
- look critically at your own taken-for-granted assumptions about the social world
- subject your own claims and those of others to critical examination
- better articulate a sense of social responsibility
- know how to use sociological inquiry and insights to help create a more just society
- identify and explain the structural impediments preventing some groups in our society from fully participating and sharing equitably in the resources available to other members of the community.

Additionally, you should understand:

- the fundamentals of rigorous scientific inquiry into social phenomena, including the role of evidence and how to evaluate evidence

- that historical, cultural, environmental, and social processes are both direct and indirect causes of the diversity of human experiences, and of the social inequalities and differences extant in society today (e.g., racism, sexism, poverty)
- how social institutions and cultures produce shared experiences 'which can lead people in similar circumstances to develop similar attitudes, values, beliefs and behaviours, (Hironimus-Wendt & Wallace, 2009, p. 76)
- the potential of sociology for addressing, reducing, and/or resolving social inequalities and injustices.

What Do Sociologists Study?

Sociologists study everything from such seemingly individual and personal matters as love, sexual orientation and sexuality, family life, and parenting, to large-scale, social-structural issues such as the way in which nation-states govern their citizens and how international financial capital affects globalization. As Berger (1963) writes, nothing is 'too sacred' or 'too personal', 'too distasteful' or 'too commonplace' or mundane for sociological investigation.

Sociologists often make a distinction between macro-level and micro-level orientations in their analyses. Micro-level orientations focus on individuals and their interrelations, especially on the face-to-face interactions that occur between individuals in specific social settings. For example, a sociologist with a micro-level orientation might be interested in how racism or prejudice is expressed between two or more social actors. That sociologist might also study how poverty affects the lives of individuals.

By contrast, a sociologist with a macro-level orientation studies and interprets large-scale social phenomena that affect society as a whole. A sociologist interested in macro-level issues might look at the ways in which racism and prejudice are institutionalized in society today. Or the focus might be on the rise and development of capitalism and the effects this form of social organization has had on the creation of a class of impoverished and/or unemployed persons.

Few, if any, sociologists would claim to be expert in all aspects of human social interaction, in all possible settings. Rather, sociologists tend to specialize in one or a few fields of study. A recent undergraduate calendar from a large Ontario university indicates a wide range of fields of study in sociology, including course offerings in the following areas: urban life, education, gender, sexuality and sexual orientation, deviance, the family, ethnicity and race, religion, work and occupations, health and illness, social class, social change, social organization, and social movements. As well, some sociologists specialize in devising theories of society, while others specialize in refining the methods by which social research is carried out. This is by no means a complete list of everything that makes up the discipline of sociology, but it does give some indication of the wide variety of topics that sociologists might study.

All conscious, thinking individuals continually strive to make sense out of the social world in which they live. One of the most difficult challenges faced by any sociologist is how to reconcile her own common-sense and deeply familiar understandings of the world with more formal and often counter-intuitive 'scientific' understandings. After all, not only the people sociologists study but also the sociologist herself perceive, understand, interpret, and explain their own actions and the actions of those around them in ways that are familiar, comfortable, and 'natural'.

As a member of a given community, a sociologist inevitably attributes commonly understood and taken-for-granted meanings to his own actions and to the actions of others. Yet, as a sociologist, he must be willing to acknowledge the extent to which personal experience is influenced by larger social factors. The sociologist draws on the core knowledge base of sociology in order to achieve a less 'me'-focused picture of his own and others' experiences. This is the paradox that Max Weber perceived lying at the heart of sociology. It is a paradox that C. Wright Mills dealt with, too, when he coined the term the 'sociological imagination', defined as the ability to transcend common-sense understandings of the world, and to develop instead a deeper comprehension of the relation between the private and the public, the individual and the social.

For any discipline to have a core knowledge base, its practitioners much share a set of core concepts, topics, and skills. Concepts are the 'basic building blocks in a discipline' (Wagenaar, 2004, p. 5); they are the expressions that point to 'key disciplinary ideas'. Topics refer to 'broad areas of interest', while skills encompass what practitioners can accomplish with their concepts and topics (Wagenaar, 2004, p. 5).

Many strands make up the discipline of sociology as it is practised today. Given that the topics of interest to sociologists cover almost everything that humans do and the ways in which they organize themselves to do those things, and given that sociologists employ an equally extensive repertoire of concepts, methods, and theories to study those topics, sociology is often portrayed as a discipline still in development, whose practitioners continue to search for a unifying direction and purpose.

The Structure of this Textbook

This textbook introduces readers to the concepts, skills, topics, and tools that make up the core of the discipline of sociology. It shows you how to use those concepts, tools, and skills to gain insights into the everyday world. It offers a range of sociological perspectives on life's challenges that are different from the ones offered by common-sense understandings, and it suggests ways to use those insights in order to better meet life's challenges and shape history.

Part I, comprising Chapter 1, introduces students to the field of sociology by examining how sociologists view and interpret their world. This chapter introduces the core concepts of the sociological imagination, and the social construction of reality. Part II, comprising chapters 2 through 4, introduces some of the foundational concepts, critical-thinking skills, and research tools that constitute the 'core' of the discipline of sociology and that make up the sociological perspective. Chapter 2 takes up critical sociological thinking, while chapters 3 and 4 cover sociological research as an empirical undertaking. Together, the chapters that make up parts I and II provide enough of an introduction to the discipline's core concepts and skills to start you on the road to asking good sociological questions and to thinking as a sociologist.

The chapters that make up Part III present some of the background to sociological thought and introduce the work of the founders of sociology. Chapter 5 introduces the work of the first sociologists, including Comte, Saint-Simon, and Durkheim. In Chapter 6, the work of two of the 'founding fathers' of the discipline—Karl Marx and Max Weber—is surveyed. Chapter 7 looks at George Herbert Mead and other early social interactionsts. All three chapters incorporate discussions of the work of present-day sociologists to illustrate how the ideas and work of the early founders are used by sociologists today.

The chapters in Part IV take up several additional core concepts, including socialization (chapters 8 and 9), culture (Chapter 10), social structure and social agency (Chapter 11), and finally inequality and social class (Chapter 12).

Chapters 13 through 17, which make up Part V, each deal with a core sociology topic—social stratification, sex and gender, gender differences, sexuality and sexual orientation, and race and racism. Part VI looks at new and recent areas of sociological inquiry, beginning with popular culture and mass media (Chapter 18). Chapter 19 picks up the discussion of mass media by looking further at the ways we communicate with each other, and the effects that social media and networking have on human social interaction. Are we becoming more individualized or do the new social media promote social interaction and cohesion? Chapter 20, on public sociology and activism, closes the text by asking if a public role for sociologists is advisable and if sociologists should set themselves a goal of influencing large-scale societal directions.

The message I hope to convey throughout this textbook is that nothing about human behaviour is inevitable and, in the same vein, that the future is emergent and susceptible to change and new directions. I hope that the approach I have taken to introducing sociology will encourage you to become an active participant in your own learning and help you to think as, and become, a sociologist.

ACKNOWLEDGEMENTS

This book could not have been written without the help of many people, and I would like to thank them here. One person in particular, Gary Woodill, deserves special thanks. Gary read and commented on each draft of the manuscript. His help and support greatly contributed to the final shape that this book has taken. I am especially grateful to Dave Stover, president of Oxford University Press Canada, for taking on this project in the first place. Patti Sayles, developmental editor, worked with me during a crucial, formative part of the project and I thank her for her steadfast support. I could not have asked for a better copy editor than Eric Sinkins, whose suggestions, comments, and corrections have added so much to the textbook. Eric, many, many, thanks—I had a great time working with you. Thanks also go to production co-ordinator Steven Hall and the design team at OUP. The skilled layouts and overall design convey the meaning of the text in a wonderfully clear, understandable way.

The manuscript of this work was reviewed at various stages of its development by a number of my peers across Canada, and I thank those who shared their insights and their constructive criticisms. In particular I would like to thank Susan Miller at the University of Manitoba and Joseph Galbo at the University of New Brunswick, whose thoughtful comments and suggestions, together with those of several anonymous reviewers, have helped to make this a much better book.

Karen Anderson
November 2011

thinking about

SOCIOLOGY

Part I
The Sociological Perspective and Its Core Knowledge Base

All conscious, thinking individuals strive to make sense of the social world they live in. One of the most difficult challenges for any sociologist is how to reconcile common-sense, deeply familiar understandings of the world with more formal, often counterintuitive, 'scientific' understandings. After all, everyone—not just those the sociologist studies but the sociologist herself—perceives, interprets, and explains their own actions and the actions of others in ways that are familiar and seem to be 'natural'.

As a member of a community, a sociologist inevitably attributes her own and others' actions to commonly understood and taken-for-granted causes. The child next door struggles at school; perhaps he should spend less time hanging out at the playground and more time doing his homework. Yet as a sociologist, she must be willing to acknowledge the extent to which personal experience is influenced by larger social factors. The boy's mother is a single parent who works an evening job; society doesn't provide sufficient resources to help children who don't get help at home with their schoolwork. The sociologist draws on what we call the core knowledge base of sociology in order to achieve a less 'me'-focused picture of her own and others' experiences. This is the paradox that the German sociologist Max Weber perceived at the heart of sociology; it is the same one the American sociologist C. Wright Mills addressed when he expounded the 'sociological imagination'— the ability to transcend common-sense interpretations of the world to develop a deeper understanding of the relationship between the private and the public, the individual and the social.

For any discipline to have a core knowledge base, its practitioners must share a set of core concepts, topics, and skills. *Concepts* are the discipline's basic building blocks: they are the expressions of what Wagenaar (2004, p. 5) calls 'key disciplinary ideas'. *Topics* are 'broad areas of interest', while *skills* encompass what practitioners can accomplish with their concepts and topics. Becoming a sociologist involves acquiring a new knowledge base, one that is different from the familiar, everyday worldview we regularly use.

This introduction to sociology begins with a close look at what constitutes knowledge about the world and how a sociological perspective might be applied to the study of society. The entirety of this book, in fact, is an extended explication of the sociological perspective—that all knowledge is based on unique experiences and invariably reflects some point of view. But the social constructedness of knowledge— the way our understanding of things is shaped by the world around us—is, for the most part, invisible. Few of us recognize that our worldview—the way we understand everything we experience in the world— is not 'natural' or common to all people. Our own worldview makes such good sense to us because everything we see through it appears to be a perfectly reasonable reflection of 'the way things really are'.

By asking you to learn to think like a sociologist, I hope to provide you with a new way of understanding your own and others' behaviours, and with an awareness that the social world you live in, including what you know about all forms of social interaction and social practices, is neither inevitable nor shared by everyone.

1

The Sociological Perspective

CHAPTER OUTLINE

LEARNING OBJECTIVES

In this chapter you will:

- learn about the common core knowledge base of sociology
- become familiar with core sociological concepts, including the sociological imagination, the social construction of reality, and society as the product of human social interaction
- gain insight into sociology as both a subversive and a conservative undertaking
- understand that sociologists rely on three interconnected skill sets—thinking skills, research skills, and theorizing skills
- learn about several core topics considered important to sociologists.

INTRODUCTION: THE SOCIOLOGICAL PERSPECTIVE AND ITS CORE KNOWLEDGE BASE

core sociological knowledge base
A set of fundamental concepts, skills, and topics, available to all sociologists, that enables sociologists think differently about the world.

Becoming a sociologist involves learning that the taken-for-granted perspective we use every day to understand the world around us is neither natural nor common to everyone. It also entails adopting a different **core knowledge base** that will equip us to think differently about the world and better confront challenges. While there is much that separates sociologists in terms of theoretical orientation and research areas of interest, contemporary sociologists share a common core knowledge base.

Core Concepts

Sociological concepts, like the concepts we use on a daily basis and out of which we form our taken-for-granted understandings, draw heavily on the cultural context in which they appear and are used. What sets sociological concepts apart from our everyday, common-sense ones is that they are deliberately constructed as tools to help sociologists reflect on the meaning and significance of the social world in which we live. These concepts act as

An Indonesian boy sleeps on the street of a Jakarta slum. Can you imagine how your interpretation of this scene using an everyday perspective might differ from your interpretation from a sociological perspective?

shorthand descriptors for complex social phenomena or for complex ways of understanding human social behaviour.

Sociology as a discipline is simultaneously conservative *and* potentially subversive. On the one hand, sociologists are concerned with gathering and analyzing data—empirical evidence they draw on to define, describe, and explain or theorize social existence as it is experienced in a given society at a particular point of time. It is the job of sociologists to gather those data as accurately as possible in order to produce a clear and reliable understanding of whatever they study. This is what makes sociology *conservative*.

On the other hand, many sociologists recognize that whatever the members of a given society experience, those experiences (and the way those experiences are interpreted and understood) are *socially constructed*. As such, experiences and understandings are capable of being challenged and changed (or *subverted*). Not only do sociologists study social phenomena in order to gather empirical evidence, many often use that evidence to address and provide solutions to social issues and problems.

Core sociological concepts that we will take up in this and later chapters include the following:

- the social construction of reality
- the sociological imagination
- social institutions
- society and social facts
- social class
- socialization
- culture.

Core Skills

All sociologists rely on three inter-connected skill sets:

- complex and critical thinking skills
- research skills
- theorizing skills.

The last of these includes the ability to develop and apply appropriate theories and the ability to explain the outcomes of research.

Core Topics

Issues of difference and inequality hold top place among topics considered important to address in an introductory sociology course. Among the most significant aspects of difference and inequality that sociologists study are:

- race and ethnicity
- social class and stratification
- gender
- sexuality and sexual orientation
- popular culture and mass communications
- social media.

The first four items of this list probably won't surprise you; the last two, however, might. Later in this textbook, we will look at the ways sociologists study difference and inequality from these vantage points.

Finally, many sociologists are concerned that students be shown ways in which sociology can offers insights relevant to their own lives. I share their concern that students in the process of becoming sociologists should learn how sociological insights can be applied to help improve their own lives, as well as the lives of others (Schweingruber, 2005; Berger, 1963).

A CORE SOCIOLOGICAL CONCEPT: THE SOCIAL CONSTRUCTION OF REALITY

social construction of reality

A concept introduced by Berger and Luckmann (1966), who argued that human experience—the way we understand 'reality'—is shaped by the society in which we live; our experience of reality may therefore be challenged and changed.

One of the core concepts that make up the sociological perspective is the **social construction of reality**'. *Reality*, in everyday usage, means 'everything that exists'. In its most inclusive sense, the term refers to everything that *is*, whether or not it is observable, accessible, or understandable by science, philosophy, theology, or any other system of analysis.

Addressing the questions *What is reality?* and *Where is reality found?* is a complex endeavour, and trying to answer such questions in an all-encompassing way would pull us into philosophical debates that are well beyond the scope of this textbook. Instead, we are going to look at the notion of reality only from the perspective of a sociologist. But to do that, we begin our inquiry into the social construction of reality, rather far from sociology proper, with the northern leopard frog (*rana pipiens*).

In the second half of the last century the American government—more specifically, the army and navy—put a fair bit of money into funding research on vision and other senses in a variety of non-human species. Among the work funded was research on frog vision. Just how, and what, do frogs see? (For those of you interested in some of the details of this research, I suggest you start with the study of frog perception and cognition by Lettvin, Maturana, McCulloch, and Pitts [1968]). It turns out there is a world of difference between what a frog 'sees' and what a human 'sees'. A frog can visually distinguish:

- light from dark
- up from down (i.e. a horizon)
- small, dark objects that move
- larger objects that cast shadows.

Unlike humans, a frog does not see the details of the stationary world around it—it will starve to death if surrounded by flies if the flies don't move. A frog flees his enemies only by leaping toward areas that are darker. A frog can remember something that moves only if the object stays within his line of vision and he is not distracted.

The visually rich world that is available to sighted humans is simply not there for frogs. The trees, flowers, birds, bulrushes, lily pads that are 'there' for humans, are not perceived as being 'there' by frogs. Reality for a frog is a product not of what is 'out there' but of the extraordinary interaction between the individual frog (with a frog's embodiment, including a frog's eye and a frog's brain) and the 'not-frog'—the environment, the external world.

Humans are like frogs in that we are biological entities that interact with an environment, and the nature of that interaction is shaped (in part) by our physical embodiment. But we are also not at all like frogs. Human beings cannot exist for long in isolation, in a world that

Chances are, this leopard frog wouldn't even see you unless you were moving. Could you survive with such a limited perception of reality?

is self-reflexive only. To be a human being means to be oriented to an external world that contains other human beings. In that sense, we can say that there is no such thing as a single reality across all species. Reality is species-specific.

What constitutes reality for us as individual humans is not just the product of our embodiment and the physical environment in which we exist (as it is for a frog); it is also a product of the fact that we are social creatures, with a wide variety of socially mediated experiences. So, for humans, reality is an even less immediate thing than it is for the frog. The reality that humans experience is strongly shaped by the social world in which we are raised and live.

One of the clearest statements of this perspective—at least as it can be applied to humans—comes from American sociologists Peter Berger and Thomas Luckmann. In 1966 the two collaborators published *The Social Construction of Reality: A Treatise in the Sociology of Knowledge*. There are two propositions from this text that are important to consider.

Proposition 1: Society Is a Human Product

Berger and Luckmann argue that 'society' is very much a product of men (and women) working together. The social environment is not the immediate result of our biological constitutions. To be recognizable as a human being means that we are, first and foremost, social beings. In fact, an existence in a 'state of nature', without social influences or contact, is impossible. Human existence is always existence in the context of order, direction, and stability. And that order, direction, and stability, which are social constructs, precede the existence of any given human. We are all born into a society that is itself a product of human activity. Moreover, our biological makeup requires that this be so. A newborn infant, left to his own

PROFILES IN SOCIOLOGY

Peter L. Berger and Thomas Luckmann

Peter Berger (b. 1929) and Thomas Luckmann (b. 1927) both emigrated to the United States from Austria following the Second World War. Both men studied at the New School for Social Research in New York. Berger went on to become professor of sociology and theology at Boston University, while Luckmann taught sociology at the University of Constance in Germany. Both sociologists have focused their research, writing, and teaching on the sociology of knowledge and the sociology of religion. Both men, separately, have written many books examining the sociology of religion and sociological theories. Together, Berger and Luckmann wrote *The Social Construction of Reality* (1966), which has become a classic study in sociological thinking. In that text Berger and Luckmann develop their theory of society as both an objective and a subjective reality. They explain how an individual's understanding of what constitutes day-to-day reality is the product of her interaction with her society. Humans produce new ideas and new social institutions that then become part of the everyday, taken-for-granted reality and are often no longer recognized as human creations; this process is known as *reification*.

devices, cannot survive on his own. Unlike the frog, we have no inherent internal mechanisms that would allow each of us to produce, out of our biological resources alone, a stable environment for our individual existence.

Proposition 2: All Human Activity Is Habitualized, and this Habitualization Is the Groundwork for Institutionalization

Humans form social groups, and these groups learn to do certain actions in specific ways. Once a human activity is repeated over and over again it becomes habit—well established, regularized, and adopted widely across groups of social actors. When this happens, patterns of behaviour take on an objective status and become institutionalized (Berger & Luckmann, 1966/1987, p. 70). Social institutions always have a history—they are not created instantaneously. Once established, though, they control human behaviour by setting up predefined patterns of conduct.

Social institutions channel and control our behaviour through a variety of social control mechanisms. For example, most first-year sociology students will come to the first day of classes at their university or college already well versed in how to behave in a classroom. From very early on in their lives, they have learned to take a seat and, unless otherwise instructed, to remain in it during the class period. Students also know that a certain amount of deference and politeness should be paid to the teacher. There are social control mechanisms in place to make sure that students conform (more or less) to these standards of behaviour. In a large lecture hall, for example, professors will resort to a few mild forms of social control if they feel it necessary: they may stop lecturing, look directly at students who might be causing a disruption, and ask them a question, for example. Rarely does a professor invoke the sanction of having disruptive students kicked out of class, or out of the course, in order to maintain control over what is going on in the classroom. So, behaviour in a lecture theatre is not controlled by the actual expulsion of disruptive students—that may never occur.

Behaviour is controlled by the institutionalization of education, which gives professors the authority to invoke certain sanctions.

Are you now beginning to see how complex 'reality' is for humans? How much 'reality' is shaped not only by what humans are as *biological* beings, but also by what we are as *social* beings? It's a lot simpler to be a frog that has no social world with which to contend! As humans, not only are we confronted with a biological reality, we also have to contend with a social world. On a day-to-day, moment-by-moment basis, the reality we perceive is considered by each of us to be nothing less than the world as it actually is. From our first moments of life we learn how to make sense out of the world we encounter in ways that are consistent with the perceptions of others around us. As children we are taught how things are and how things are done.

Most of us never really question this. We simply accept that the 'reality' that we are born into and that we experience as we grow up is an 'objective reality'—that it is simply the way things are. And why, in the normal course of our lives, should we ever question this? All reality appears to us like the air we breathe: it is just always *there*. But, as Berger and Luckmann remind us, 'It is important to keep in mind that the objectivity of the institutional world, however massive it may appear to the individual, is a humanly produced, constructed objectivity' (Berger & Luckmann, 1966, p. 48). Berger and Luckmann also point out that that humans and their social worlds interact and co-produce each other. As children we are all taught about the social world we live in. We learn to make that world a part of ourselves. But we also act back on that world, and sometimes, in co-operation with others, we alter it significantly.

THE SOCIOLOGICAL IMAGINATION

At the beginning of this chapter, I suggested that sociology, as a discipline, was both conservative and radical. Nowhere are these two faces of sociology better represented than in the work of the American sociologist C. Wright Mills, author of another of the core sociological concepts, the **sociological imagination**.

In 'The Promise', an essay first presented to the American Political Science Association in 1958 and later published as the first chapter of *The Sociological Imagination* (1959), Mills famously writes: 'Neither the life of an individual nor the history of a society can be understood without understanding both' (Mills, 2000 [1959], p. 3). Mills goes on to point out that for ordinary people, the task of coping with the 'larger worlds' they confront requires both 'skills of reasoning' and a 'quality of mind' to help them to cogently understand what is going on in the world, and how it affects their lives. It is this 'quality of mind'—the capacity to relate history to biography, the personally experienced milieu to larger social structures, or one's personal troubles to public issues—that Mills calls 'the sociological imagination':

sociological imagination
As defined by C. Wright Mills, an orientation adopted by a sociologist to recognize and understand the connections between individual experience and larger social structures.

> The sociological imagination enables its possessor to understand the larger historical scene in terms of its meaning for the inner life and the external career of a variety of individuals. It enables him [sic] to take into account how individuals, in the welter of their daily experience, often become falsely conscious of their social positions. Within that welter, the framework of modern society is sought, and within that framework the psychologies of a variety of men and women are formulated. By such means the personal uneasiness of individuals is focused upon explicit troubles and the indifference of publics is transformed into involvement with public issues. (Mills, 2000 [1959], p. 3)

PROFILES IN SOCIOLOGY

C. Wright Mills (1916–1962)

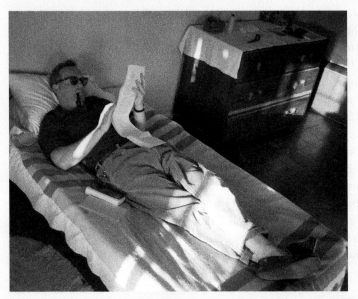

In the introduction to this textbook I suggested that sociology, as a discipline, is both conservative and radical. Nowhere are these two faces of sociology better represented than in the work of the American sociologist Charles Wright Mills, author of one of two core concepts—the sociological imagination—that together make up the sociological perspective. Mills, who died in 1962 at the age of 43, has been described as 'a bundle of paradoxes' by American sociologist and culture historian Todd Gitlin (2000, p. 229):

> He was a radical disabused of radical traditions, a sociologist disgruntled with the course of sociology, an intellectual frequently skeptical of intellectuals, a defender of popular action as well as a craftsman, a despairing optimist, a vigorous pessimist, and all in all, one of the few contemporaries whose intelligence, verve, passion, scope—and contradictions—seemed alive to most of the main moral and political traps of his time. A philosophically-trained and best-selling sociologist who decided to write pamphlets, a populist who scrambled to find what was salvageable within the Marxist tradition, a loner committed to politics, a man of substance acutely cognizant of style, he was not only a guide but an exemplar, prefiguring in his paradoxes some of the tensions of a student movement that was reared on privilege, amid exhausted ideologies yet hell-bent on finding, or forging, the leverage with which to transform America root and branch. (Gitlin, 2000, p. 229)

Mills was born in 1916 in Waco, Texas, the son of an insurance broker father and a stay-at-home mother. He earned his PhD in sociology in 1941 from the University of Wisconsin and in 1946 took up a teaching post at Columbia, where he was popular with students but clashed frequently with colleagues. He married three times and had a child with each of his wives. Along the way he published many influential studies focusing on social class and its political impact, including *The New Men of Power* (1948), *White Collar* (1951), and *The Power Elite* (1956). *The Sociological Imagination* was published in 1959, a year before Mills travelled to Cuba, where he interviewed Fidel Castro, Che Guevara, and other Latin American revolutionaries. Mills died of a massive heart attack following a trip to Europe in 1962.

Mills's brilliance lay in his understanding that we live in small worlds, whether as children or as adults. Because of this, it is usually difficult to understand the larger social forces affecting us. The more powerful these social forces are, the less equipped we are to comprehend them without some significant extra work—hence the role of the sociological imagination. A champion of egalitarian political principles, Mills saw the sociological imagination as being for everyone, not just the purview of trained sociologists. As a pragmatist, Mills believed it necessary that we all take action to confront both 'personal troubles' and 'public issues' in order to achieve 'the all-around growth of every member of society'. (For a short biography of Mills, see www.sociological-imagination.org/short_biography_of_c_wright_mill.htm.)

'The Promise', quite possibly Mills's most famous essay, challenges us to use our sociological imagination to connect our individual, personal biographies with the larger history and structure of the society/community in which we live (Marullo, Moayedi, & Cooke, 2009). This, Mills tells us, is the first 'terrible' but 'magnificent' lesson of sociology: 'the idea that the individual can understand his own experience and gauge his own fate only by locating himself within his period, that he can know his own chances in life only by becoming aware of those of all individuals in his circumstances' (Mills, 2000 [1959]). It is the 'task and the promise' of the sociological imagination to enable its possessor to 'grasp history and biography and the relations between the two within society' (Mills, 2000 [1959], p. 6). Developing a sociological imagination also challenges us 'to develop ethical, moral, and intellectual skills that we can use to critically understand the complexity of society and reflect on how society has influenced our "personal history"' (Hoop, 2009, p. 48).

When, as sociologists, we use our sociological imagination, we do so in the context of constructing an understanding of, or knowledge about, human experiences as seen in a larger context. The sociological imagination helps us to distinguish between, on the one hand, bad circumstances that an individual might experience as a result of poor behaviour or poor choices, and, on the other hand, bad circumstances that result from structural forces that are beyond the individual's control (Hironimus-Wendt & Wallace, 2009, p. 76).

Mills suggests that the sociological imagination is particularly useful in times of great social disruption, when the relationship between the individual and society is unsettled. For example, during the Great Depression of the 1930s, which followed the stock market crash of 1929, about 30 per cent of the Canadian labour force was unemployed, and one in five Canadians was dependent on government relief (Struthers, 2011). Instead of turning to taken-for-granted understandings about job loss and personal responsibility, and therefore blaming themselves for not being able to find work, many people came to understand that their own personal troubles were, in fact, part of a public issue affecting people across the country (see Table 1.1). Unemployed workers staged numerous strikes and public protests, many of which ended in violent confrontations with police. Out-of-work citizens came to view and respond to the personal trouble of being unemployed as a public issue, not the result of bad choices made by a group of poorly motivated or otherwise misguided individuals.

A public issue can be said to arise when existing social arrangements 'limit the range of choices available to individuals into either a subset of primarily bad choices, or no good choices at all' (Mills, 2000 [1959]). Mills went so far as to argue that sociology should never be some sterile and inconsequential enterprise, detached from the daily experiences of all people. Rather, sociology should be a vital undertaking, one that allows everyone to become engaged in understanding and changing the social world in which he or she lives. In this way, Mills hoped, a critical and sociologically aware populace would be able to transform its society, making it more equitable for all members.

'Reality' and the Sociological Imagination

Mills's concept of a sociological imagination focuses on the interplay between our common social history and the kind of thinking we must do and awareness we must gain if we are to reveal and transform our socially acquired beliefs, understandings, and behaviours. But just what is required to produce knowledge about the social world we live in using a 'sociological imagination'? For most of us, the use of our imaginations seems to contradict everything we

TABLE 1.1 Change in average annual per capital income, 1928–9 to 1933, by province

Province	Average per capita income 1928–9	1933	Decrease (%)
British Columbia	$594	$314	47
Ontario	549	310	44
Alberta	548	212	61
Saskatchewan	478	135	72
Manitoba	466	240	49
Quebec	391	220	44
Nova Scotia	322	207	36
New Brunswick	292	180	39
Prince Edward Island	278	154	45

Source: Canadian Centre for Policy Alternatives, www.policyalternatives.ca in Stapleton, 2009.

have been taught about neutrality, rational thought, and objective, dispassionate observation. In short, the phrase 'sociological imagination' seems to be antithetical to good, objective scientific inquiry, the very thing that sociologists claim to be part of the sociological perspective.

To many, rational scientific inquiry and imagination are diametrically opposed. Scientific inquiry produces true knowledge of events and things, while imagination results in fantasy and fiction. While science is an undertaking that produces 'real' material benefits, imagination is ethereal and non-concrete.

objective knowledge
Knowledge that is purported to be free of bias.

Now, modern scientific inquiry can hardly be criticized for a lack of results, or for producing useless categories of knowledge. Indeed, modern natural sciences are compelling precisely because they have been able to achieve a certain mastery over nature. In spite of all the recent criticisms of the natural sciences, North Americans and Europeans continue, for the most part, to be enthralled by the promises science holds. The taken-for-granted view of science in North America is that it is a means—the best and only true means—of gaining **objective knowledge** about the world around us. If we wish to produce true knowledge (i.e. objective knowledge as opposed to fiction or fanciful knowledge, or knowledge based on superstitions and misguided beliefs), then we must use scientific methods for collecting and interpreting information.

The proponents of this taken-for-granted understanding of science often refuse to give careful attention to how scientific researchers are actually locked into a specific kind of relationship with whatever it is that they are researching. Their taken-for-granted understanding is that scientists can be objective because they are able to become independent of the very world they are studying. However, what scientists seek to discover is intimately connected to whatever worldview and assumptions they bring to their investigation. As many sociologically influenced thinkers have pointed out, objectivity, based on the total separation of observer and observed, is impossible to achieve. 'Human beings', says moral philosopher Mary Midgley, 'direct their enquiries to things that strike them as important.' As humans we ask questions that matter to us. What matters is 'what brings things together, what shows a pattern, what tends to make sense of the whole' (1992, p. 65).

Once we realize this, we see that any object of scientific study may actually be viewed from many different perspectives or standpoints. Moreover, the same object can be interpreted through a wide range of **value systems.** When we understand that knowledge is relative rather than absolute, we can also see that knowledge is a set of claims that are socially constructed. What gets presented as 'true knowledge' ultimately depends on the researcher and the social and cultural conditions in which the researcher operates.

The sociological perspective shows us that if we really want to understand how we go about producing knowledge about the world we inhabit, we must pay serious attention to the metaphors and cultural images that underlie the everyday interpretations of truth and reality available to us in this society (Midgley, 1992). A critical sociological approach to knowledge abandons the search for universal measures of truth or authority. Instead, critical-thinking sociologists look for diverse ways of understanding the same set of events.

The nineteenth-century German philosopher Wilhelm Dilthey (1833–1911) noted that the subject matter of all the human sciences, including sociology, is 'mental objects', which are different from the physical objects that form the subject matter of the natural sciences. Knowledge produced by social scientists is an understanding of the shared meaning given to social behaviour rather than simple observation of social behaviour.

Self-knowledge, Dilthey went on to explain, is acquired through a circuitous route of understanding that is historical and that always refers back to the larger social group of which we are members. Our personal knowledge about life is always shaped by the beliefs and values that emerge out of the social groups to which we belong. Assertions about the passage of life, judgements of value, and rules of conduct—definitions of goals and what is 'good'—are all products of social life. Our minds, Dilthey tells us, can understand only what they have created.

The arguments of Mills, Berger and Luckmann, and Dilthey about the relationship of the individual to the social are underscored by the work of many contemporary philosophers. In his analysis of the historical structure of understanding, Hans-Georg Gadamer has shown that we cannot understand things unless we approach them from a point of view that is consistent with our own mental history (1986, pp. 220–34). This means that there is no neutral point from which we can understand things with absolutely no presuppositions to guide our thought.

Gadamer's findings also echo in the work of the German philosopher Edmund Husserl, who has shown that all experience and understanding of experience is developed out of the communal system of meanings that underlies everyday life. Husserl calls the entire communal system of meanings, the **'lifeworld'.** There are significant differences between these taken-for-granted understandings and sociological ones: the former are based on unexamined assumptions about the 'lifeworld' and all that it contains, while the latter bring all assumptions forward for examination.

value system
A set of beliefs about what is important in life and what kinds of conduct or behaviour are appropriate.

lifeworld
German philosopher Edmund Husserl's term for the entire communal system of meaning that underlies everyday life.

APPLYING A SOCIOLOGICAL PERSPECTIVE: THREE EXAMPLES

As we have seen, the sociological perspective upholds the proposition that human interaction is socially based and systematically organized. This proposition is potentially useful to all of us because it supports critical thinking about our own lives and the society we live in, as well as about other societies distinct from our own. But adopting a sociological perspective can be disturbing, as it often raises challenges to the beliefs and assumptions that most members of Western society share about themselves and the world they inhabit. These beliefs and assumptions are based on our immediate experiences and are rarely, if ever, reflected upon or reasoned out.

individualism
A moral stance that stresses the importance of individual self-reliance and independence.

The ancient Greeks called these shared beliefs, customs, and traditions *nomi*, or 'laws'. These laws constitute the foundational traditions and values of a given society or culture. They may be written or unwritten. They are primal beliefs and understandings shared by the society's members concerning right and wrong. The examples that follow present common-sense, taken-for-granted views on **individualism**, race, warfare, and love and contrast them with views from a sociological perspective. The sociological perspective views these things as existing in specific historical, social, and cultural contexts that together shape how each specific issue is understood by those who experience it.

Example 1: Individualism

For most Westerners, individualism, a moral stance that stresses the importance of individual self-reliance and independence, serves as a kind of lens through which most other beliefs are seen and evaluated. The taken-for-granted belief in individualism operates in much the same way as a mathematical theorem; that is, it acts as a rule that substitutes for direct evidence. Thus, in Western societies, individualism is not a proposition that must be supported by evidence and proofs; it is something most people consider to be self-evidently true. Yet critically motivated research into the concept suggests that this was not always the case. Contrary to everyday understandings, individualism has not always been universally understood as a natural and therefore highly desirable state of human affairs.

When we consider the writings of sixteenth- and seventeenth-century social theorists such as Thomas Hobbes, John Locke, and Niccolo Machiavelli, all of whom contributed to our appreciation of individualism, and we compare their work to that of authors from antiquity, we begin to understand the problematic origins of our modern understandings of this concept. Hobbes, Locke, and Machiavelli were among the first Western writers to argue in favour of individualism. But they did so in explicit opposition to the writings of philosophers of classical antiquity, whose ideas up to that point had dominated Western philosophy.

Today, propositions about individualism that Hobbes, Locke, and Machiavelli all favoured have become part of our everyday frame of reference and no longer appear in need of defence. Thus a concept that was once hotly contested has become part of our everyday belief system. If we take the time to inquire into the history of other examples of our society's most cherished beliefs and understandings, a new and potentially critical standpoint from which to question them emerges. Taking a sociological perspective allows us to think in new ways about the everyday beliefs and understandings that we use to make sense of our lives.

Example 2: Racial Prejudice

Canadians pride themselves on their appreciation of diversity and lack of prejudice against those seen as different. But we do not need to look very far into our history to find examples of commonly held understandings that have led to discriminatory and prejudicial treatment of some ethnic and national groups. Historically, certain segments of the Canadian population were classified as undesirable and thus as unwanted or undeserving outsiders. The treatment of Aboriginal peoples in Canada is a familiar example. Less familiar, perhaps, is the example

What feelings does this image arouse in you? Pity? Contempt? Mild disgust? To what extent do you think your feelings are conditioned by our taken-for-granted assumptions about the importance of individualism and self-reliance?

of non-European immigrants to Canada. As Figure 1.1 shows, prior to 1961, Europeans made up over 90 per cent of all immigrants to Canada. This fell to 69 per cent between 1961 and 1970, then to 36 per cent between 1971 and 1980, and to 26 per cent between 1981 and 1990. Between 1991 and 2001, just 20 per cent of those immigrating to Canada were Europeans. Why is the situation today so different from what it was just over a century ago?

During the late nineteenth century, when well over 90 per cent of persons immigrating to Canada were European, the Canadian government also promoted the immigration of a relatively small number of Asian labourers. These men, most of them Chinese, worked on the construction of the transcontinental railway. But the arrival of even a few Chinese-born labourers disturbed many of this country's European-born citizens.

The decision to bring in Chinese workers to build the rail lines in British Columbia was made by prime minister John A. Macdonald over the emphatic opposition of the people of that province. To make his decision more acceptable, Macdonald conceded that Chinese

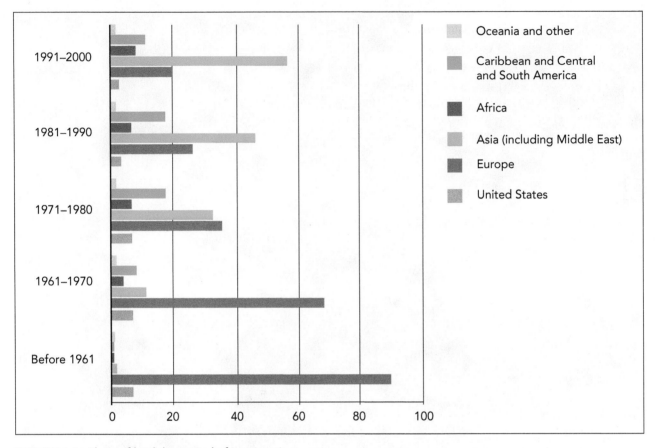

FIGURE 1.1 Place of birth by period of immigration

Source: Statistics Canada, Update on Cultural Diversity, *Canadian Social Trends*, 11-008-XIE2003002, Fall 2003, no. 70, September 2003; http://www.statcan.gc.ca/bsolc/olc-cel/olc-cel?lang=eng&catno=11-008-X

immigrants would reside in British Columbia only temporarily. In the debates of the House of Commons, Macdonald reassured Canadians:

> At any moment when the legislature of Canada chooses, it can shut down the gate and say, No more immigrants shall come here from China and then no more immigrants will come, and those in the country at the time will rapidly disappear. They have not their families with them, and leave nobody behind them, but according to their system, religion or superstition, . . . they will not even leave their bones behind them. They are sent back to China either alive or dead; and therefore there is no fear of a permanent degradation of the country by a mongrel race. . . . (Canada, 1883, vol. 2, p. 905)

Concern about the 'non-assimilating race', as these immigrants were called, was widespread among Canadians. In a submission made to the Royal Commission on Chinese Immigration, 1885, members of the Knights of Labour, LA (Local Assembly) 3017 of Nanaimo, wrote a memo in which they maintained that the Chinese labourer, being without ties or family, was therefore 'able not only to live but to grow rich on wages far below the lowest minimum on which we can possible exist'. The memo went on to declare that the Chinese labourers:

are thus fitted to become all too dangerous competitors in the labour market, while their docile servility, the natural outcome of centuries of grinding poverty and humble submission to a most oppressive system of government, renders them doubly dangerous as the willing tools whereby grasping and tyrannical employers grind down all labour to the lowest living point. . . . [T]he Chinese live, generally, in wretched hovels, dark, ill-ventilated, filthy and unwholesome, and crowded together in such numbers as must utterly preclude all ideas of comfort, morality or even decency. . . . (as cited in Meyers, 2004 [1914], p. 307)

Members of British Columbia's Sikh community line the street to attend the annual Khalsa Day parade in Surrey. Do you think this sort of expression of national culture should be celebrated in Canada?

Even a hundred years later, in the 1990s, sentiments similar to these continued to form part of the taken-for-granted understandings of a number of Canadians. In 1993, a turbaned Sikh was prevented from entering a Royal Canadian Legion hall in Surrey, British Columbia, to attend a commemorative service. The stated reason for refusing to admit the man was that he was wearing a head covering, something that is explicitly prohibited by Legion rules. Legion members are expected to enter Legion premises with bare heads as a way of showing honour to the Queen and to those who have fallen in war. But practising Sikhs, who fought alongside Canadian soldiers in the Second World War, must wear their turbans as a sign of religious commitment. In the ensuing debate over the refusal to allow turbaned Sikhs to enter Legion premises, some disturbing evidence emerged: Legion members who had voted against allowing their turban-wearing compatriots into the hall had no problem with other members wearing more Westernized headgear, such as baseball caps.

Often, then, unexamined understandings that emerge as racist or prejudicial behaviours are reflections of deeply felt fears and biases harboured by some (or most) members of society against those identified as 'others'. These 'others' might even be members of the same society, as in the case of the Sikh veteran in BC, but are considered to be sufficiently different from, or inferior to, the 'real' insiders to warrant differential treatment. Or the 'others' might be members of another society (like the Chinese workers brought into Canada to work on the rail lines) who are perceived as undesirable or inferior, or as a threat to the way of life of the 'true' or 'legitimate' members of the society. Using a sociological perspective allows us to unmask prejudices.

Example 3: Romantic Love

Some of the most deeply rooted beliefs held by North Americans concern their personal experiences. One such belief is that romantic love is a natural and possibly instinctual part of the human makeup. It is found in all societies, and throughout human history.

But is this the case? Certainly most North Americans and Europeans expect to fall in love at least once in their lives. They also expect to subsequently set up house with their chosen loved one and to find emotional and sexual satisfaction with that person. While most North Americans are privately skeptical that love will last forever, most nevertheless tend to hold strongly to the conviction that falling in love is a natural and universal experience, and that 'being in love' is a prerequisite for marriage. Yet the experience of falling in love and the expectations that go with it are not as widespread as most North Americans believe.

In many societies, decisions about when and whom to marry are rarely left up to the individuals involved, who often have very little say in the matter. In countries such as India, where more than 90 per cent of marriages are arranged (Gautam, 2002, cited in Madathil and Benshoff, 2008, p. 222) marriage is considered by many people far too important to be left to the whims of the individual. The majority of marriages in that country are arranged by parents and other relatives. Romantic love, while it is acknowledged to exist, is considered a temporary infatuation and even a barrier to a happy marriage.

Sociologists have long understood that cultural norms of individualism or collectivism have significant impact on marriage practices. North American culture, with its emphasis on individualism, treats marriage and the family as existing in order to maximize the needs of the individual. Falling in love and selecting a mate is considered a normal developmental task of adolescents and young adults and is highly valued in Western societies. By contrast, in Indian society as in the majority of world cultures, group identity and cohesiveness are emphasized. Marriages tend to be arranged by family members and are viewed as agreements between two families, and not between two individuals as in North American culture (Madathil & Benshoff, 2008 p. 223; Medora, Larson, Hortacsu, & Dave, 2002, p. 165). How does all this affect marital satisfaction? North Americans, who usually base their marriages on romantic love and free choice of marriage partner, feel strongly that free mate selection is fundamental to marriage satisfaction.

American sociologists Jayamala Madathil and James Benshoff (2008) conducted a study comparing marital satisfaction for three groups: Asian Indians in arranged marriages living in India, Asian Indians in arranged marriages living in the United States, and Americans in marriages of choice. They found significant differences when they compared the overall marital satisfaction scores of the three groups. Asian Indians in arranged marriages living in the United States reported higher marital satisfaction than those of the other two groups (Madathil & Benshoff, 2008, p. 228).

Even in Western cultures, romantic love has not always been experienced as it is today. Two movements concerning love—courtly love and romanticism—have influenced our present-day practices. According to Ann Swidler (1980), the cultural ideal of courtly love in Western societies can be traced back to the twelfth century. Heralded by the troubadours of the time, this tradition was begun in medieval France, where it was linked to the courage of a knight in his quest for moral heroism and for the love of his chosen lady. The practice of courtly love was complex and focused not on the actual relationship but on a complicated, mutual idealization between two people who rarely had any physical contact with each other. Unlike the Church's conception of love, which it challenged, courtly love promoted the ideal that, under certain highly codified circumstances, sexual love between a man and a woman was well worth striving for. Moreover, sexual love between a man and a woman could be ennobling for both (and not degrading, as the Church insisted).

But the expression of that ideal love was encumbered by an elaborate system of ethical and aesthetic rules connected with ideals of courtesy and courtship, and decidedly *not* with the institution of marriage. It was a widely accepted belief that one could never love a marriage partner. Instead, love was an intense, passionate relationship, a holy unity between one man and one woman who never married and who rarely had any contact. In the ideal situation, a gallant knight performed heroic deeds to win and keep the love of his lady, to whom he rendered years of faithful service. At the same time, this gallant knight was most likely married (as the lady herself usually was), with several children, and had numerous sexual affairs. Although sexual contact between the two was permitted in some parts of Europe, the relationship often went unconsummated, guided by rules of decorum and the pursuit of ideal, not sexual, love (Hendrick & Hendrick, 1992, pp. 38–9).

Around the late eighteenth century a new movement emerged in Europe, called romanticism. With it came an emphasis on the *feeling* of love, as opposed to the correct and decorous behaviour that had characterized courtly love. Sexual love also emerged as a state that all men and women, regardless of class origin, could strive for. According to Singer (1987), romantic love in this period came to mean

> . . . oneness with an alter ego, one's other self, a man or woman who would make up one's deficiencies, respond to one's deepest inclinations, and serve as possibly the only person with whom one could communicate fully. If the world were properly attuned to the value of love, this would be the person one married, establishing a bond that was permanent as well as ecstatically consummatory.

> The sexual bond would participate in a social order constructed out of loving relationships that united all people to one another and mankind to nature as a whole. (Singer, 1987, p. 4)

But romanticism gave way to a new set of values during the Victorian era. From the second or third decade of the nineteenth century to the early part of the twentieth century, a progressive devaluation of the worth of women took place. Men became paid wage workers, and women, confined to the home, were considered weak and in great need of men's protection and economic support. Women were also thought to be of a delicate constitution with minds not quite able to stand up to the rigours of a great deal of education. Women became 'the weaker sex'—nurturing, tender, made solely for child-bearing and child-rearing.

The devaluation of women brought extensive changes to the ideals of love. One ideal to emerge was that women were, by virtue of their delicate natures, disinclined toward sex. Their role was to resist sex prior to marriage and then, after marriage, to succumb to the sexual advances of their husbands. Men, on the other hand, were viewed as being charged with sexual energy. The man's role was to take the lead, to woo his intended, and to persuade her to submit. Summing up love in the Victorian era, Hendrick and Hendrick write:

> It is perhaps difficult for us to imagine today the limits within which couples lived in the Victorian era, with respect to their sexuality and feelings of love they experienced for each other. It appears that in addition to the hardness of life in simply earning a living there was poverty of the spirit in terms of people's ability to communicate their most intimate desires and needs to each other. . . . These conditions of the Victorian era, the disjunction between communicating about love and sex and the ongoing natural desires of men and women, set the conditions for the creation of sexual dysfunctions and disorders of love and desire that opened the twentieth century. (Hendrick & Hendrick, 1992, pp. 42–3)

By about 1880, romantic love had become even more romantic; the common view of love was that it was a strong magnet pulling together two people who were 'just made for each other'. The customs of courtship had become quite formal. Young women and men of 'good breeding' (meaning of middle- or upper-class backgrounds) were not to speak to each other until formal introductions had been made (Waller, 1938 1951). Once that happened, the mother of the young lady was then at liberty to invite the young gentleman to call on her daughter. Later, the young lady herself could extend an invitation (Bailey, 1988). In this era, most courtship took place in the home of the young woman, and sexual restraint was important. In spite of this, sex and marriage were strongly connected, and sexual fulfilment in marriage was the ideal. As well, outside of the genteel parlours of the middle and upper classes, a great deal of sexual behaviour that did not meet the cultural ideals was already happening.

According to American sociologist L.M. Terman, who published his findings in 1938, while 87 per cent of women born before 1890 were virgins at marriage, only 30 per cent of those born after 1910 (and prior to the publication of his study) 'waited until marriage'. By the first decade of the twentieth century, a 'virtuous woman' was one who had had sex only with the man she was going to marry (Cate & Lloyd, 1992, p. 22). By 1920, dating, the main focus of the present-day North American courtship system, was in place. Dating— the informal, unchaperoned interaction between two people with no specific commitment to each other—followed rules established by local peer groups. The rise of dating has been attributed to a variety of cultural phenomena and events, including the recognition of adolescence as a distinct period in the life cycle, the rise of mass culture, the emancipation of

Is romantic love an old-fashioned concept? Not according to the majority of North Americans. How would you characterize romantic love today? How does that differ from the same concept 50 years ago? What about 500 years ago?

women, widespread ownership of cars, the motion picture industry, and the decline of the community as a means of social control.

Dating, though, meant spending money, and this in turn shifted the locus of power out of the hands of the young woman and her mother and into the hands of the young man himself. With the introduction of dating as the courtship ritual of preference, a young woman (or her mother) could no longer expect to be able to invite a young man to call on her in the family's front parlour (Bailey, 1988). Ideally, dating would lead to a steady relationship between a man and woman, with the woman still expecting to exercise sexual control and the man expected to pay for all expenses. At the same time, romantic love remained the only basis on which to marry. Mate selection, in popular ideology at least, continued to rest on the presence of a mysterious attraction felt between two people destined to spend their lives together.

Although the particulars involved in the rating and dating system of the first half of the twentieth century have changed in the twenty-first, the cultural ideal that love is the most important factor in mate selection continues to be emphasized. Coontz (1988) has pointed out that the importance of love in mate selection even increased over the course of the twentieth century. According to her, '[the] degree of emotional satisfaction . . . demanded from husband–wife . . . relations in the twentieth century would have astounded previous generations' (Coontz, 1988, p. 356).

Today, there is a large body of popular literature, including a plethora of articles in women's magazines, devoted to the theme of 'finding and keeping a man', often through the use of what might euphemistically be called the 'wiles of femininity'. As Cate and Lloyd (1992) comment, 'The vision of the perfect relationship now emphasizes the importance of balancing togetherness, and individuality, other-orientation and self-fulfilment, and communicating openly while protecting the partner's feelings' (Cate & Lloyd, 1992, p. 31). Meanwhile the still-present threat of HIV/AIDS and other sexually transmitted diseases has caused a rethinking of the free-love ideals promoted by the hippie generation of the 1960s. As a result, we are witnessing a strong cultural emphasis on chastity and lifelong monogamous relations between members of a couple who are forever in love with each other.

By using a sociological perspective to trace out the different ways that love in its various courtly and romantic guises had been expressed and experienced over the past eight centuries, we can gain an understanding of our own 'romantic' experiences today—an understanding that relates personal experiences to historical, social, and cultural events. Instead of being a natural outcome of the human condition, the experience of romantic love appears to be socially constructed. As difficult as it might be to accept, the way we fall in love, the emotions we feel, the people we choose to be the objects of our affection (as well as of our desire and lust)—the very things that make up the most intimate aspects of our personal biographies, even including the ways we choose to express our most intimate feelings—are all understandable as being shaped by our society and culture.

SUMMARY

Becoming a sociologist entails acquiring a core knowledge base that consists of core concepts, skills, and topics that are different from the taken-for-granted perspective used in day-to-day living. Taken together, the elements of this core knowledge base constitute a unique sociological perspective that recognizes that human interaction is socially based and systematically organized. Core sociological concepts are deliberately constructed as tools to help sociologists reflect on the world around them. These concepts refer to complex social phenomena or to ways to approach understanding human social behaviour.

In this chapter I have drawn on the work of C. Wright Mills, Peter Berger, and Thomas Luckmann. Foremost among the core concepts shared by sociologists are the following:

1. *The sociological imagination.* An orientation or way of thinking about the social world and human behaviour that focuses on the ever-present link between individual experience and larger social structures.
2. *The social construction of reality.* An orientation or way of thinking about the social world and human behaviour that maintains that the reality experienced by members of any given society is shaped or constructed by human social experiences. Human experiences are social accomplishments.
3. *Society as a product of human social interaction.* Society is produced through the social interactions of individuals. As several prominent nineteeth- and twentieth-century German philosophers, including Wilhelm Dilthey, Hans-George Gadamer, and Edmund Husserl have shown, our personal knowledge is always shaped by the beliefs and values that emerge out of the social groups to which we belong.

To become a sociologist you must learn to be a critical thinker who can deal with ambiguity. You must also become both a researcher who is skilled enough to choose wisely among many research designs and methods, and a theoretician capable of devising convincing explanations for research outcomes.

Finally, becoming a sociologist and adopting a sociological perspective can be a challenging undertaking. As a sociologist you will often be called upon to question or even challenge your personal beliefs and assumptions based on your own immediate experiences. I challenge you to keep an open mind as you start out on your journey to becoming a sociologist.

DISCUSSION QUESTIONS

1. What does it mean to say that knowledge is 'socially constructed' or 'sociologically produced'?
2. What skills does critical thinking involve?
3. What are some of the ways that you can apply a 'sociological imagination' to help you better understand your everyday life?
4. What value does critical thinking bring to everyday life?
5. If taken-for-granted understandings serve us so well in our daily lives, why would we want to question them or subject them to critical scrutiny?
6. What is individualism? What are some everyday examples of individualism?
7. Are Canadians fundamentally prejudiced and bigoted? Or are they among the least prejudiced people in the world? Explain.
8. How central is the ideal of romantic love to the lives of most Canadians?

Part II
Core Skills: Critical Complex Thinking and Research

The core skills of critical and complex thinking and research are two fundamental components of the sociological knowledge base. Basic assumptions about what we can know and how we can know it separate the taken-for-granted thinkers among us from those who use critical thinking. People who believe that all knowledge comes from authoritative sources usually believe that any solution to a problem comes directly from that authority, too. Taken-for-granted thinkers expect that there is a strong correlation between what they personally believe to be true, what an accepted authority has told them is true, and what is 'actually' true. In the minds of taken-for-granted thinkers, most problems can have only one correct solution, one that is ultimately justified by reference to some authority. Their typical line of reasoning is influenced by thoughts like, 'It's in the textbook, so it has to be true,' or 'If the Church says that homosexuality is a sin, it must be so.'

Critical thinkers, by contrast, question epistemological assumptions (assumptions about the nature of knowledge, and what constitutes justified belief as opposed to opinion). They recognize that all knowledge is contextual and subjective, that it is filtered through personal perceptions. A critical thinker constructs knowledge on the basis of what appears to be the most reasonable assessment of existing evidence. He or she is willing to re-evaluate conclusions when new evidence, perspectives, or tools of inquiry become available (King & Kitchener, 1994, p. 15).

Research capability is another core skill cultivated by sociologists. There are many ways of 'knowing' something: belief or faith, the opinions or pronouncements of experts and leaders, common-sense understandings, and science. Science, as a way of knowing about the world, is based on *empirical evidence*—that is, on evidence that is gathered, and verified, using our senses. Sociologists generate knowledge about the social world by systematically observing human social behaviour and by recording their observations to be used as evidence, which they then analyze. Sociological research skills include

- the ability to do research using appropriate research methods,
- the ability to use and assess research results, and—importantly—
- the understanding that sociology is a scientific endeavour.

2 Critical Sociological Thinking

CHAPTER OUTLINE

LEARNING OBJECTIVES

In this chapter you will:

- learn the difference between critical thinking and everyday or common-sense thinking
- examine critical thinking in historical perspective
- learn the characteristics of a critical thinker
- study examples of critical sociological thinking
- find out who goes to university and why
- learn about Canadian multiculturalism and why it is in crisis.

INTRODUCTION

critical thinking
Thinking that is purposeful, deliberate, and self-regulatory, and that arrives at judgements based on well-defined criteria and evidence.

Complex **critical thinking** skills make up one of the three core skill sets (alongside research skills and theorizing skills) that all sociologists must acquire. To many introductory sociology students the word *critical* has a negative connotation: to find fault with something or someone. Applied to the task of becoming a sociologist, this taken-for-granted understanding of the word *critical* might lead you to think you should try to find fault with what you are asked to read or what you hear about in lectures. To be critical in this common-sense view means to be harsh or judgemental, to look for all the faults you can find.

But if we look at the history of the English word *critical*, it appears to have two roots in the Greek language: *kriticos*, meaning 'discriminating judgement', and *kriterion*, meaning 'criterion'. Thus, a critical thinker is someone who makes 'discriminating judgements with reference to criteria' (Van Gyn, et al., 2006, p. 25). In general, critical thinking skills include skills in 'applying, analyzing, and evaluating information' in a way that can be recorded and justified (Ruminski & Hanks, 1995, p. 5). A person engaged in critical thinking will make a judgement only when there is sufficient evidence, will suspend making judgements in the face of insufficient evidence, and will change a judgement when the evidence warrants such an action (Green & Klug, 1990).

Van Gyn and associates (2006) define critical thinking as follows:

> A quality of thinking that is characterized by *self-regulated use of intellectual habits and deliberations* on a challenge situation or task that involves *exploring and generating alternatives, and making evaluative judgements. These judgements are based on criteria*, which *provide justifications* for the conclusion, and are applied to meaning, relational, empirical or value claims. (Van Gyn, et al., 2006, p. 36)

Similarly, The American Philosophical Association (APA) provides this definition:

> Critical thinking is purposeful, self-regulatory judgment which results in interpretation, analysis, evaluation, and inference, as well as explanation of the evidential, conceptual, methodological, criteriological, or contextual considerations upon which that judgment is based. (Facione, 1990, p. 3)

Both definitions emphasize self-regulation, deliberation, and arriving at judgements based on well-defined criteria, especially evidence. The skills necessary to arrive at reasoned judgements include interpretation, analysis, evaluation, inference, and explanation (Keesler, Fermin, & Schneider, 2008, p. 346). A critical thinker must possess the ability to identify value judgements, the predisposition to seek out evidence, and a commitment to fairness. For the most part, those who address the general issue of critical thinking emphasize thought that enables thinkers to 'avoid conventional misunderstandings, misleading notions, and literalism' and that encourages thinkers to 'challenge conventional suppositions and positions' (Van Gyn, et al., 2006, p. 26).

Critical thinkers are mindful of the ways in which they accept or reject information, and then use that information to support a position. They are aware, too, that the status of knowledge is not constant: with further inquiry, a position taken now may be changed later (Van Gyn, et al., 2006, p. 26).

CRITICAL THINKING IN HISTORICAL PERSPECTIVE

In one sense, then, critical thinking is the same for all times and places and across all disciplines. Ancient Greek philosophers, medieval theologians, and contemporary sociological theorists all have examined and challenged the established beliefs of their times. But critical thinking also differs from discipline to discipline, and even from one historical time period to another within a given society. For the ancient Greeks, critical thinking meant actively questioning the everyday, taken-for-granted beliefs that were commonly held by the members of different city-states. To replace these non–critical thinking beliefs, the early Greek philosophers sought out universal truths that were independent of any untested assumptions or opinions. This search for universal truths, they believed, was the highest activity to which any human could aspire. It afforded knowledge-seekers the ultimate answers to questions that were traditionally (but inadequately) answered by everyday beliefs and understandings. Thus, beginning with Aristotle, Greek philosophers looked for universal knowledge of the nature or 'essence' of all things. They believed knowledge could be very precise and therefore applicable to all similar cases.

The School of Athens, by Italian Renaissance painter Raphael. What are some of the situations that demand your critical thinking skills on a day-to-day basis?

Philosophers of the early modern period, in their turn, questioned the authority of the Greek philosophers. In doing so, they cast doubt on a conceptual system that had been used for over two thousand years. They believed that Aristotle and his followers had based their thinking on erroneous principles and, because of this, had produced uncertain work with no practical results. For seventeenth-century philosophers like René Descartes, reasoning had to produce absolute certainty, which could be achieved only if it was freed from opinion and if thinkers followed a universal method that had no presuppositions as its basis. Descartes was convinced that scientific inquiry was that universal method. While the ancient Greeks had used their critical thinking skills for the philosophical attainment of happiness and the good of all human beings, early modern philosophers strived for ideals of survival and comfort. They restricted themselves to discovering what could be tested by the new scientific method of inquiry (Talaska, 1992, pp. 256–64).

Since the mid-twentieth century, philosophers and social scientists have been able to show that all traditions in philosophy and science are rooted in systems of pre-established and unexamined assumptions. It isn't just our moral and political beliefs and laws but also our scientifically achieved and therefore supposedly 'objective' truths that are part of this worldview composed of traditional values, beliefs, and ways of thinking. So-called objective scientists think about the world and everything in it, often without examining the basic assumptions and ideas of their particular traditions of thought. Being a scientific thinker does not guarantee that you are also a critical thinker! To be a critical thinker also requires you to challenge established understandings.

CHARACTERISTICS AND HABITS OF A CRITICAL THINKER

Van Gyn and associates (2006) use the term *habit* for each of the attributes that critical thinkers must, as a matter of course, come to display in their work. Richard Paul (1990), Van Gyn and associates (2006), and others have identified several habits characteristic of a critical thinker today. Among them are the following.

1. Independence of Mind

A commitment and disposition favourable to autonomous thinking, i.e. thinking for oneself.

Most of the beliefs we hold today were acquired when we were very young when we tended to form beliefs merely because we wanted to believe something, or because we were rewarded by significant adults in our lives for doing so. To develop as critical-thinking adults, we must now learn to question what has been presented to us as 'the truth'. We must learn to judge for ourselves who or what constitutes a legitimate, justified authority, and who or what is not legitimate.

2. Intellectual Curiosity

The disposition to wonder about the world.

Critical thinkers must be curious about the world they live in and want to know more about that world. Where others might simply take things for granted, a critical thinker is

Every religion has its own set of values and beliefs that is presented to its members beginning at a very early age. What are the rewards a young child can expect for accepting these values and beliefs? Are there any dangers?

curious and asks questions: How many other ways can we look at this problem or phenomenon? Why do people react this way? What do their reactions mean? Critical thinkers must seek to explain apparent discrepancies in the world, and wonder about how they became who they are and where their own ideas came from. A critical thinker must be perplexed about how we deceive ourselves, and about how we fail to perceive our contradictions and inconsistencies while we seemingly know so much about ourselves. To do this, a critical thinker must be willing to go beyond readily available information, and to seek out other information that will support sustainable judgements.

3. Intellectual Courage

The willingness to evaluate all ideas, beliefs, or viewpoints fairly, and the courage to take a position.

Critical thinkers must have the courage to recognize that even their most deeply held convictions and beliefs may be questioned. They also must have the courage to address the possibility that some seemingly absurd or even dangerous ideas may be justified. Often critical thinkers must go against taken-for-granted opinions, although the pressure to conform can sometimes be great, and penalties for not conforming can be severe. Intellectual courage is called for if a critical thinker is to reassess all that he or she has been taught to believe. Forming and holding convictions is important; the danger lies in believing those convictions to be infallible and therefore not submitting those convictions to review and reconsideration. A critical thinker must have the courage to be fair-minded and open-minded—that is, to recognize that familiar views may seem superior when they are not; to be able to consider the merits of other, divergent or conflicting, views of the world; and to be able to change one's position. A critical thinker must have the courage to take a position, even if it is not one that is popular, if it is the most defensible position or if it is the morally right thing to do.

4. Intellectual Humility

Awareness of the limits of one's knowledge.

Critical thinkers must be sensitive to the biases and limitations of their points of view. They should strive for insight into the foundations of their own beliefs. Socrates' well known admonition 'Know thyself' is accompanied by a less familiar one: 'I know nothing except the fact of my ignorance.' A critical sociological thinker must constantly evaluate his or her own 'ignorance'. It is much easier to be aware of others' thoughts and ideas than it is to be aware of one's own. A critical thinker directs his or her analytical mind toward self-evaluation in an attempt to understand, and control, his or her own biases, predispositions, and 'triggers to irrationality' (Ruggiero, 1996, p. 26). As Ruggiero notes, self-evaluation

> helps you resist the three major forms of manipulation—the exploitation of gullibility (e.g. people selling you things you don't need); the societal pressure to think, speak, and behave according to the latest fashion; and unrelieved self-congratulation, entertaining only thoughts that flatter and soothe your ego. This last kind is the worst because it deceives you into thinking that your opinions enjoy official status and expecting that others should pay them homage. (Ruggiero, 1996, p. 26)

5. Intellectual Empathy

Being conscious of the need to put oneself in the place of others in order to understand them.

A critical thinker must be able to construct the viewpoints and reasoning of others. A critical thinker is willing to remember the occasions on which he or she was wrong and can imagine the possibility of misunderstanding someone in a current situation. Critical thinkers recognize the tendency in themselves to value those whose views accord with their own while disparaging those who hold contradictory views.

6. Intellectual Perseverance

The willingness to pursue intellectual insights and truths in spite of difficulties, obstacles, and frustrations.

A critical thinker is prepared to struggle with confusion and unsettled questions over a long period of time with a view to achieving a deep understanding or insight. A critical thinker has learned to tolerate ambiguity and complexity and to work with a fairness and open-mindedness to arrive at the best possible understanding. A critical thinker perseveres even when faced with difficult challenges.

7. Reflexive Disposition

Awareness that one's own approach is fallible.

A critical thinker who possesses a reflexive disposition plans ahead for, and monitors, his or her thinking by reflecting on its strengths and weaknesses and by reflecting on the limitations of the judgements he or she arrives at. The possessor of a reflexive disposition is willing to consider both the strengths and the shortcomings of any given way of thinking (his or her own current way of thinking included), and is willing to consider other perspectives, outcomes, and consequences (Van Gyn, et. al., 2006).

Aristotle once wrote, 'The unexamined life is not worth living.' Perhaps the simplest reason for becoming a critical thinker is to be able to expand one's horizons. Critical thinking also allows one to become actively engaged with life rather than merely reacting to what is presented. Constructing a critical sociological analysis of an event, or social institution, or social practice is a creative undertaking that involves bringing together information from a variety of sources.

CRITICAL SOCIOLOGICAL THINKING

While the attributes associated with critical thinking are general enough to apply to all disciplines, critical sociological thinking can be said to have characteristics that are specific to the discipline of sociology (Beuchler, 1998; Geertsen, 2003; Grauerholz & Bouma-Holtrop, 2003). Grauerholz and Bouma-Holtrop (2003) suggest that what makes critical sociological thinking unique is that its practitioners possess not only 'sociological knowledge and skills' but also 'the ability to use this knowledge to reflect upon, question, and judge information while also demonstrating a sensitivity to and an awareness of social and cultural contexts' (2003, p. 485). Many sociologists point to the connection between the practice of critical thinking and the use of the sociological imagination, introduced and defined in the last chapter (Baker, 1981; Bidwell, 1995; Buechler 2008; Green & Klug, 1990; Thompson & Tyagi, 1993, as cited in Grauerholz & Bouma-Holtrop, 2003). Using a sociological imagination allows sociologists to 'perceive and understand that their individual life choices, circumstances, and troubles are shaped by larger social forces such as race, gender, social class and social institutions' (Grauerholz & Bouma-Holtrop, 2003, p. 493).

What unique contribution can a sociological perspective bring to the critical thinking exercise?

1. The sociological perspective gives us the best possible perspective on the complexity of social life, its history, and its potential future. It is the best perspective available to us from which to 'understand clearly, decide rationally, and act wisely' (Buechler, 2008, p. 219).
2. A sociological perspective requires us to examine and question taken-for-granted understandings. 'To be a sociologist is to assume that things are not what they appear to be, that hidden interests are at work, and that claims cannot be taken at face value' (Buechler, 2008, p. 219).
3. Sociology examines relations of domination and exploitation between social groups. Many sociologists who are dedicated to progressive change require both a vision of a better society and the conviction that such a society is attainable (Buechler, 2008, p. 219).

In short, sociology provides a unique perspective on the social world, a perspective that supports the critical thinking enterprise (Buechler, 2008, pp. 320–1). In the previous chapter we considered two of the core concepts making up the sociological perspective. To review:

1. *The social construction of reality.* From Berger and Luckmann (1966) we learned that society is a human product—a social construction—and that the reality we perceive is a reality that is mediated by the society in which we live. Certainly, as individuals we experience that reality in a subjective way—we have intentions, and we act on those intentions. Yet others around us also experience similar intentions, and also act on those intentions. When this happens, as Berger and Luckmann (1966) have shown, social patterns, or social institutions, emerge. These social institutions take on lives of their own, quite independent of the individuals belonging to them. When this happens, it is often difficult to perceive that society is a human product. The institutions and patterns of social behaviour that inform our decisions are neither 'genetically or biologically given, nor are they God-given, naturally occurring, or predestined' (Berger & Luckmann, 1966).

2. *The sociological imagination.* Seeing society as a social construct means that we cannot make sense of the individual without understanding her in the context of her society. The sociological imagination (Mills, 1959) is a perspective unique to sociology that allows sociologists to make sense of how individual troubles relate to public issues. As Mills (1959, p. 19) has said, 'personal troubles' become 'public issues' when 'both the correct statement of the problem and the range of possible solutions require us to consider the political and economic institutions of the society and not merely the personal situation and character of a scatter of individuals.'

In future chapters we will consider additional core insights/concepts that make up the sociological perspective and that contribute to critical sociological thinking. For now, these two core concepts—the social construction of reality and the sociological imagination—provide us with a base from which to apply critical sociological thinking, as the four examples that follow illustrate.

Example 1 of Critical Sociological Thinking: Corporate Crime

For many Canadians, crime is a result of the actions of individual wrongdoers. The commonly held view is that, once caught, all wrongdoers are (mostly) treated equally before the law. But critical sociological thinkers have shown that race, social class, and gender can make a difference to the rights of the accused or the sentence of the convicted. Inequalities of power and social position based on race, class, and gender influence not just who commits crimes but how the criminal justice system responds to those crimes.

One area of particular interest to critical sociological thinkers is corporate, or 'white-collar', crime. **Corporate crime** is 'the conduct of a corporation, or of employees acting on behalf of a corporation, which is proscribed and punishable by law' (Braithwaite, 1984, p. 6). Corporate crime includes acts that violate criminal law, as well as civil and administrative violations. Both the corporation—which exists in law as a 'legal person'—and any individual representative or employee of that corporation may be selected as a 'sanction target', able to

corporate crime
Any conduct of a corporation, or of its representatives/ employees acting on the corporation's behalf, that is a criminal, civil, or administrative violation.

The world's largest television screen replaces the sky over this outdoor street in a commercial block in Beijing known simply as 'The Place'. The screen has been used to project a wide assortment of images, including scenes of ocean life, giving a good illustration of how society can turn our perception of reality upside down.

be charged and convicted under the law, depending on the 'kind of act committed, rules and quality of evidence, prosecutor preference, and offending history' (Simpson, 2002, p. 7).

When most people think of criminals and criminal activities, they do not think first of corporations and their CEOs, nor do they think of the presidents of banks or other financial

No harness, no hard hat, no safety netting. If this worker falls and dies, his death would be treated as a corporate crime, his employer criminally responsible. How would you compare this to a gun homicide, or a death caused by a drunk driver? Why are they (or aren't they) the same?

institutions. Yet corporate offences actually cause more death, injury, and economic loss than the top eight 'street crimes' taken together (Kappeler, Blumberg, & Potter, 2000, as cited in Hartley, 2008, p. 1).

Corporate crimes can range from polluting the environment to committing financial fraud, engaging in price fixing, creating hazardous working conditions, or producing and selling unsafe products (Kappeler, Blumberg, & Potter, 2000, as cited in Hartley, 2008, p. 1). These crimes are usually committed in order to build or maintain profits, manage uncertain markets, or put a rival corporation out of business (Simpson, 2002, p. 7). Sociologists have remarked on the seeming lack of effort displayed by the criminal justice system to prosecute corporate executives whose companies have broken laws. Nor does the 'average citizen' seem to be overly concerned that the social cost of corporate crime far exceeds that of crimes committed by individual members of society.

In analyzing corporate crime, critical sociological thinkers usually start with a careful empirical study of what kinds of corporate crimes are committed, who commits them, and how the perpetrators are treated within the justice system. Rather than accept the taken-for-granted understanding that most members of society believe to be true, critical-thinking sociologists try to establish what the situation really is like. To do this they often begin by looking for discrepancies between what is commonly understood to be the case and what their research tells them is actually the case.

For example, most critical-thinking sociologists who have studied the criminal justice system agree that the economic costs to society of corporate crimes far exceed those of street crimes. By searching out comparative data on Canadian crime rates, criminologists have been able to estimate that while the average economic loss for a street crime such as a break-and-enter during the 1980s was between $700 and $900, the average loss for a corporate crime in the same period was in the neighbourhood of $8,000 (Cullen, Maakestad, & Cavender, 1987). American data from the same period show that the average monetary harm per burglary was $1,000, while the average loss per corporate offence was $5,650 (Cohen, 1989; FBI, 1988; Simpson, 2002). More recently the FBI has estimated that white-collar and corporate crime in the US costs over $300 billion a year, while Reiman (2007), using Chamber of Commerce data, estimated the loss to be $418 billion in 2003 alone. The latter is roughly 24 times the $17 billion that the FBI estimates was the cost of all property crimes committed by individuals during the same period (as cited in Hartley, 2008, p. 184).

Yet while these statistics are readily available, critical-thinking sociological researchers also note that owing to shifts in government policies, the prosecution of corporate crimes is declining (Cohen, 1989). The criminal justice system appears to be reluctant to focus on corporate crimes, preferring instead to follow common-sense understandings by focusing on neighbourhood and domestic crimes committed by individuals. In Canada, for example, there were 610 homicides in 2009, and everyone agrees that homicide is a serious criminal act (Statistics Canada, 2010). But in 2002–4, 'acute injuries occurring on the job resulted in an average of 465 deaths annually, and close to 300,000 compensated time-loss claims' (Wilkins & Mackenzie, 2007. p. 1). Yet these deaths—even those occurring as a result of unsafe working conditions—are not considered homicides, and corporate executives usually go unprosecuted. Even when corporate offenders are prosecuted and convicted, their sentences seem disproportionately light.

Critical sociological thinkers believe they have evidence that the criminal justice system is far from blind to social class differences, treating upper- and middle-class offenders more leniently than it does those who hold less powerful positions in society. Recently, questionable corporate policies have produced spectacular economic crises on a global scale. Yet despite bringing many national economies to their knees (only to be rewarded with multi-billions of dollars in debt bailouts from governments around the globe), many CEOs and high-level corporate executives continue to receive enormous salaries, huge bonuses, and 'golden parachutes' upon retiring. Consider the case of the American corporation General Dynamics: in 1991, it cut its workforce by 18,000 employees while at the same time paying 23 top executives $35 million in salaries, bonuses, and stock options—three times what they had earned in 1990 (Holtzman, 1992, and Vise & Coll, 1991, as cited in Simpson, 2002, p. 14). Indeed, if we consider pay for corporate executives compared with pay for workers, we discern some stunning differences. In the US, the ratio of CEO salaries to workers' salaries in 2004 was 431 to 1, up from a ratio of 301 to 1 in the previous year and 107 to 1 in 1990 (Anderson, Cavanaugh, Klinger, & Stanton, 2005, as cited in Hartley, 2008, p. 184).

These examples of corporate crime illustrate the benefits of critical sociological thinking by drawing attention to the true costs of corporate crime and by pointing out the need for changes in legislation and government policy dealing with corporate crime.

Example 2 of Critical Sociological Thinking: Aboriginal People and Criminal Justice

Crime rates in Canada are not evenly distributed across the country; they vary by province. The eastern provinces record the lowest rates, while Manitoba and Saskatchewan have the highest (see Figure 2.1).

In addition to wide fluctuations in the distribution of crime across Canada, there are also wide differences in the ways in which race and gender are connected to any individual Canadian's likelihood of appearing before the courts. **Overrepresentation** is a term used by Canadian researchers and commissions of inquiry to characterize situations in which members of a particular group defined by class, ethnicity, gender, and so on, are disproportionately implicated in a particular crime or in crime generally. It's the appropriate term to refer to the situation described by Fitzgerald and Carrington (2008, p. 550) when they report that 'Aboriginal people are more highly represented as offenders in the criminal justice system relative to their numbers in the population than is the case for non-aboriginals'. In the American literature, the term used to refer to the phenomenon of minority overrepresentation in the criminal justice system is *disproportionate minority contact*, or *DMC* (see Huizingea, et al., 2007, for example).

In Canada, **Aboriginal peoples** 'occupy a distinct social, cultural and political status within Canada as bearers of constitutionally protected Aboriginal and Treaty rights' (Kong & Beattie, 2005, p. 7). The overrepresentation of Aboriginal people as offenders within the Canadian criminal justice system is well documented (Royal Commission on Aboriginal Peoples, 1966; La Prairie, 2004). In 2006, approximately 4 per cent of the adult population of Canada identified themselves as Aboriginal (Statistics Canada, 2006b). However in 2006–7, 20 per cent of adults admitted to provincial or territorial custody, 18 per cent of adults admitted to federal custody, and 18 per cent of adults admitted to custodial remand were Aboriginal. In Canada, custodial remand occurs

> when a person is ordered by the court to be held in custody while awaiting a
> further court appearance. . . . While rates of crime and sentenced custody have

overrepresentation
A situation that occurs when a disproportionately large number of people of a particular class or ethnicity, etc., is included in a group that is meant to represent the larger population.

Aboriginal peoples
In Canada, the Inuit, Métis, and First Nations (including status and non-status Indians) collectively.

been generally decreasing, the use of custodial remand has been increasing steadily, progressively comprising a larger share of the incarcerated population. (Johnson, 2003, p. 2)

Moreover, while the total number of adults admitted to remand from 2001–2 to 2006–7 increased by 14 per cent, the total number of Aboriginal people admitted during the same period increased by 23 per cent (Babooram, 2008, p. 8) (see Table 2.1, Table 2.2).

While Aboriginal people in general are overrepresented among offenders admitted or remanded to provincial/territorial or federal custody, the problem of overrepresentation is even greater among Aboriginal women. Data from 2005 indicate that 30 per cent of all women (compared to 21 per cent of all men) serving sentences in provincial or territorial institutions are Aboriginal. Federally, the representation of Aboriginal women serving sentences has grown from 15 per cent in 1997 to 25 per cent in 2006 (Kong & AuCoin, 2008, p. 12).

As with crime rates in general, however, there is considerable variation in Aboriginal incarceration across provinces and territories—a variation that has been relatively stable over the past decade. For example, of those adults admitted to provincial custody in Saskatchewan, 80 per cent were Aboriginal people, though Aboriginal people make up just 10 per cent of the province's total adult population (Rugge 2006: 2). While, as La Prairie (2004) notes, there is virtually no overrepresentation of Aboriginal people in provincial correctional institutions in Prince Edward Island and Quebec, the situation is markedly different in Nova Scotia and Newfoundland and Labrador, where it is 1.5 to 2 times higher than expected, in BC (5 times higher), Manitoba (7 times), Alberta and Ontario (9 times), and Saskatchewan (10 times higher than expected) (Rugge, 2006, p. 187). Moreover, once incarcerated, Aboriginal offenders are more likely than non-Aboriginal offenders to serve a higher portion of their sentences

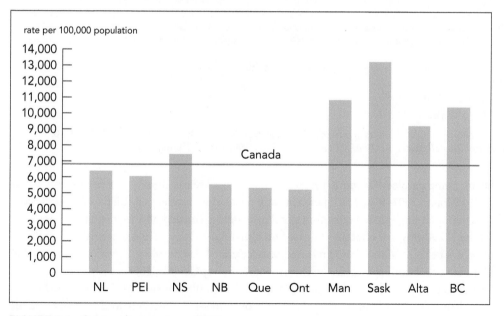

FIGURE 2.1 Crimes, by province, 2007

Note: Total *Criminal Code* offences, excluding traffic.

Source: Statistics Canada, *Canada Year Book*, 11-402-XIE 2010000, October 2010; http://www.statcan .gc.ca/bsolc/olc-cel/olc-cel?catno=11-402-X&chropg=1&lang=eng.

TABLE 2.1   Number and proportion of adults admitted to remand and identified as Aboriginal, by province/territory, 2001–2 and 2006–7

Province/territory	Number		Proportion (%)	
	2001–2	2006–7	2001–2	2006–7
Newfoundland and Labrador[1]	n/r	128	n/r	29
Prince Edward Island	10	n/a	6	n/a
Nova Scotia[1]	151	218	8	9
New Brunswick	107	189	8	11
Quebec	1,063	964	4	3
Ontario[1]	4,389	5,771	8	10
Manitoba	4,822	6,151	63	65
Saskatchewan[1]	3,802	4,338	78	79
Alberta[1,2]	n/a	8,473	n/a	36
British Columbia	2,139	2,724	20	20
Yukon	241	281	75	75
Northwest Territories	213	245	90	90
Nunavut	n/a	n/a	n/a	n/a
Total provinces and territories[3]	**16,927**	**20,881**	**15**	**18**

Note: Calculations for proportion distribution are based on total custody admissions excluding those where the Aboriginal identity is not known.

1   Data for these respondents are from the new Integrated Correctional Services Survey and have been tabulated from micro data for the years commencing as follows: Newfoundland and Labrador, 2001–2; Nova Scotia, 2002–3; New Brunswick, 2002–3; Ontario, 2003–4; Saskatchewan, 2001–2; Alberta, 2005–6. For these respondents, percentage calculation is based on sentenced custody totals excluding intermittent sentences. Accordingly, comparisons to data from previous years should be made with caution.
2   Alberta has been excluded due to a system change that occurred in 2005–6, which altered the methodology by which admissions to custody were calculated.
3   Due to missing data for some years, totals and percentage calculations exclude Newfoundland and Labrador, Prince Edward Island, Alberta, and Nunavut.

n/r = data are too unreliable to be published

n/a = data are not available for the given period

Sources: Statistics Canada, The changing profile of adults in custody, 2006/2007, *Juristat*, 85-002-XIE2008010 vol. 28 no. 10, December 2008; http://www.statcan.gc.ca/bsolc/olc-cel/olc-cel?catno=85-002-XIE&lang=eng#formatdisp.

before being paroled. Of the 104 Aboriginal offenders released on a first federal full parole supervision in 2007–8, just 55.8 per cent were released on accelerated full parole supervision; the corresponding rate for non-Aboriginal offenders is considerably higher, at 70.3 per cent. Of the 251 Aboriginal offenders released on a first federal day parole supervision in 2007–8, only 31.9 per cent of them were released on accelerated day parole supervision, compared to 51.4 per cent of non-Aboriginal offenders (Public Safety Canada, 2008, p. 87).

Why is that the case? To find an explanation for a situation such as this, a critical sociological thinker must look beyond the details of individual situations to the broader public issues. In this case, she would begin with the fact that over half of all Canadians who identify as Aboriginal now live in cities, and over half of those who live in cities reside in one of the country's 10 largest census metropolitan areas (CMAs). In a city-by-city analysis of nine urban centres, La Prairie (2004) found that 'disadvantage' factors (including low levels of income,

TABLE 2.2 Number and proportion of adults admitted to sentenced custody and identified as Aboriginal, by province/territory, 2001–2 and 2006–7

Province/territory	Number		Proportion (%)	
	2001–2	2006–7	2001–2	2006–7
Newfoundland and Labrador[1]	n/r	154	n/r	20
Prince Edward Island	19	n/a	3	n/a
Nova Scotia[1]	102	150	7	8
New Brunswick[1]	116	228	8	10
Quebec	266	241	2	3
Ontario[1]	2,777	2,452	9	10
Manitoba	2,090	2,486	69	69
Saskatchewan[1]	2,480	2,703	79	81
Alberta[1,2]	n/a	7,283	n/a	35
British Columbia	1,900	2,055	21	22
Yukon	214	129	76	68
Northwest Territories	504	396	90	90
Nunavut	n/a	n/a	n/a	n/a
Total provinces and territories[3]	**10,449**	**10,840**	**16**	**20**
Total Federal[4]	**n/a**	**938**	**18**	**18**

Note: Calculations for proportion distribution are based on total custody admissions excluding those where the Aboriginal identity is not known.

1 Data for these respondents are from the new Integrated Correctional Services Survey and have been tabulated from microdata for the years commencing as follows: Newfoundland and Labrador, 2001–2; Nova Scotia, 2002–3; New Brunswick, 2002–3; Ontario, 2003–4; Saskatchewan, 2001–2; Alberta, 2005–6. For these respondents, percentage calculation is based on sentenced custody totals excluding intermittent sentences. Accordingly, comparisons to data from previous years should be made with caution.
2 Alberta has been excluded due to a system change that occurred in 2005–6, which altered the methodology by which admissions to custody were calculated.
3 Due to missing data for some years, totals and percentage calculations exclude Newfoundland and Labrador, Prince Edward Island, Alberta, and Nunavut.
4 Warrant of committal admissions only. Prior to 2005–6, the federal jurisdictions did not supply the number of adults admitted to custody and identified as Aboriginal, only the proportion.

n/r = data are too unreliable to be published

n/a = data are not available for the given period

Sources: Statistics Canada, The changing profile of adults in custody, 2006/2007, *Juristat*, 85-002-XIE2008010 vol. 28 no. 10, December 2008; http://www.statcan.gc.ca/bsolc/olc-cel/olc-cel?catno=85-002-XIE&lang=eng#formatdisp.

employment, and education, high mobility, and single parenting) and 'vulnerability factors' (age distribution proportion of the population) were different for Aboriginal people than for non-Aboriginal people. The results of her analysis, in which she compared the distribution of 'disadvantage' factors and 'vulnerability' factors to the overrepresentation phenomenon, are striking:

- Cities of the Prairie provinces had the largest percentage of Aboriginal people living in extremely poor neighbourhoods, notably Winnipeg (41.2 per cent), Saskatoon (30.2 per cent), and Regina (26.9 per cent).

- Toronto (15.8 per cent), Vancouver (17.1 per cent), and Edmonton (19.4 per cent) had the smallest percentage of Aboriginal people living in extremely poor neighbourhoods (2002: 197).
- The cities making the highest contribution to overrepresentation are Thunder Bay, Winnipeg, Saskatoon, and Regina.
- The cities making the lowest contribution to overrepresentation are Toronto, Montreal, and Halifax.

There appears to be, among urban Aboriginal residents, a strong correlation between poor socioeconomic living conditions and overrepresentation in the criminal justice system. Consider, as an example, the situation in just one of these cities: Winnipeg. Winnipeg has both the greatest number of Aboriginal residents (55,755 in 2001) and the highest concentration of Aboriginals of any Canadian city (roughly 8 per cent of Winnipeg's citizens identify themselves as Aboriginal—Statistics Canada, 2003a, p. 10, as cited in Fitzgerald & Carrington, 2008). Moreover, Aboriginal people living in Winnipeg are nearly seven times more likely than non-Aboriginals to appear as offenders in police-reported crime data (Fitzgerald & Carrington, 2008, p. 547).

As Fitzgerald and Carrington (2008) observe, in concurrence with La Prairie, a significant portion of the high crime rate among Aboriginal peoples can be explained by the characteristics of the urban neighbourhoods where they live. There is a strong association, they argue, between indicators of social disorganization and neighbourhood crime rates:

> Specifically, we found that a substantial part of the reason why Aboriginal people are more likely to be identified as offenders is the socially disorganized and therefore criminogenic nature of the neighborhoods in which they tend to live. This result confirms La Prairie's suggestion that the structural conditions of cities contribute to Aboriginal overrepresentation among identified offenders in the criminal justice system. . . . The findings presented here are consistent with other Canadian research indicating that Aboriginal people tend to live in very different urban environments than their non-Aboriginal counterparts. As well, in this study, the socially disorganized nature of these places explained a substantial part of the variation in Aboriginal and non-Aboriginal crime rates across the city. Together, these results point to the importance of examining the problem of the high rate of involvement of Aboriginal people in the criminal justice system from an ecological perspective that incorporates information about community structures and processes. This approach has implications for policy and program development as it 'leads away from a simple "kinds of people" analysis' toward an examination of how the structural and social features of communities may contribute to crime (Sampson & Wilson, 1995, p. 54). (Fitzgerald & Carrington, 2008, p. 548)

Example 3 of Critical Sociological Thinking: Who Goes to University and Why?

Most first-year university students believe they are in university as a result of their own efforts. While individual effort is certainly necessary to gain admission to university in Canada, an examination of the characteristics of university students raises questions about what other requirements—and barriers—exist.

Most Canadians, when asked to consider the barriers to a university education apart from the personal effort involved, will think first of economic barriers. Certainly in Canada, as in many other Western countries, the likelihood of attending a university or college is connected to family income. Students from lower-income families have been shown to be less likely to attend university than students from more well-to-do families, as Figure 2.2 illustrates.

These large differences in university participation rate by parental income **quartile** are of concern to students and their parents, as well as to governments. Common-sense understandings of the reasons behind these gaps focus on access to credit: youth from economically disadvantaged families do not have the economic resources to attend university and must, therefore, rely on government and bank loans. The prevailing common-sense understanding is that students are often unable to secure enough loan money to cover their costs. Hence, we see far fewer children of first- and second-quartile parents attending post-secondary institutions.

In 2007 Marc Frenette, an analyst working for the Business and Labour Market Analysis Division of Statistics Canada, published a report in which he set out to account for this large gap. The discussion that follows is based largely on his report.

Although the common-sense understanding of the attendance gap between children of lower-quartile parents and children of higher-quartile parents focuses on the inability of the former to gain access to sufficient loans to pay for post-secondary education, Frenette was not satisfied with the obvious answer. With the publication of new data, generated from the Youth in Transition Survey (YITS), Cohort A, Frenette was in the position to link university

quartile
In descriptive statistics, each of four equal groups into which a population can be divided according to the distribution of values of a particular variable.

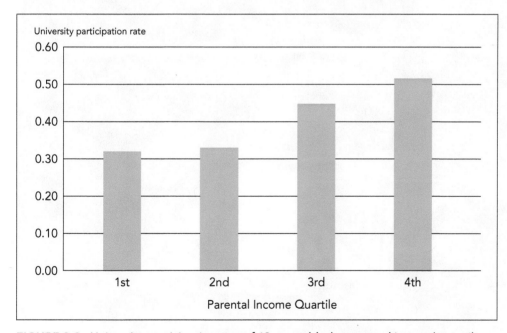

FIGURE 2.2 University participation rate of 19-year-olds, by parental income[1] quartile

1 Adjusted for family size of youth at age 15.
   For each quartile of parental income, the threshold levels of equivalent income are $20,409 (25th percentile), $30,531 (50th percentile), and $41,000 (75th percentile).

Source: Statistics Canada, *How Long Do People Live in Low-income Neighbourhoods? Evidence for Toronto, Montreal and Vancouver.* Analytical Studies Branch Research Paper Series, 1F0019MIE2004216, no. 216, January 2004; http://www.statcan.gc.ca/bsolc/olc-cel/olc-cel?lang=eng&catno=11F0019M2004216.

attendance of 19-year-old Canadians to a 'plethora of information on these youth when they were aged 15, including results from standardized tests, high-school marks, feeling control (or mastery) over one's life, self-esteem, parental income, parental education, parental expectations, peer influences, high school attended, and financial constraints, among others' (Frenette, 2007, p. 9).

The YITS project was carried out by the Organisation for Economic Co-operation and Development (OECD). Students born in 1984, who were 15 years old as of 31 December 1999, were surveyed in 2000, 2002, and 2004. In addition to overall Grade 10 marks, four measures of academic abilities were taken to assess reading, math, and science skills. Two measures of 'non-cognitive' abilities were also used: feeling control or mastery over one's life, and self-esteem. Students were also asked:

- how many of their friends were planning to pursue their education after university
- to what extent they agreed with the notion that getting a good job later in life depends on their success in school now
- their region of residence
- their sex
- whether or not they wanted to attend university but were unable to do so because of lack of finances.

How would you have answered the bulleted list of questions in the YITS project? What barriers to post-secondary education, if any, have you overcome?

The parents of these youths were also administered a questionnaire in 2000 asking for information on:

- the quartile of total income in 1999
- the presence of parents in the home
- the highest level of education attained by either parent
- parental expectations around the educational outcome of the child
- the threshold levels of equivalent income.

Finally, the differences in quality of the education provided at the students' high schools were taken into account. In an attempt to quantify these differences, the researchers created an index of schools ranked according to their propensity to generate university-bound students.

Equipped with the new data, Frenette was able to assess whether lack of access to credit was the main reason preventing the children of low-income parents from attending post-secondary educational institutions, or if other factors such as their 'performance on standardized tests, overall marks, parental influences, peer influences, etc.' were the cause (Frenette, 2007, p. 9).

Figure 2.2 above shows that some students have a distinct advantage in terms of attending university, and that this advantage is indeed linked in some way to parents' income. But Frenette's analysis of the data reveals that while university participation increases with parental income, so does the likelihood of possessing characteristics that may foster higher educational attainment. Among Frenette's findings were the following:

- In terms of reading abilities, students in the highest income quartile (Q4) were far more likely to be at the top of the reading distribution compared to students in the lowest income quartile (Q1).
- Youth from families in the highest income quartile generally performed better on standardized mathematics and science tests, and generally reported higher marks than students from the bottom of the income distribution. The same pattern was evident when Frenette looked at the distribution of marks overall.
- Differences in the mastery/self-esteem scores across the income distribution were much smaller, although they were not negligible.
- In terms of parental presence, only 5.0 per cent of students in Q4 had just one parent in the home, compared to 30.3 per cent of youths in Q1. Among families with two parents present, students in Q4 were also far more likely to have both *birth* parents present.
- Not surprisingly, parental education was very unequally distributed across income quartiles. Students in Q4 were almost five times as likely as students in Q1 to have at least one parent with a graduate or professional degree than students in Q1 (21 per cent versus 45 per cent). Slightly more than half of all students in Q4 (50.6 per cent) had at least one parent who possessed a university degree; among students in Q1, only 16.3 per cent had at least one parent with a university degree. At the other end of the spectrum, 46.9 per cent of students in Q1 did not have a parent with a post-secondary certificate, compared with just 17. per cent of students in Q4.
- Given the large differences in parental education, it is not surprising that parental expectations vis-à-vis university education tended to rise with family income. In fact, 79.4 per cent of students in Q4 had parents who expected them to obtain a university degree. Among students in Q1, only 62.0 per cent of parents expected them to obtain a university degree.

Analyzing the data, Frenette found that 96 per cent of the total gap in university attendance between youth from the highest and lowest income quartiles could be accounted for by differences in observable characteristics. Eighty-four per cent of the gap was accounted for by a combination of these factors:

- differences in long-term factors such as standardized test scores in reading obtained at age 15
- school marks reported at age 15
- parental influences
- quality of high school.

Frenette also found that family income might pose different barriers to attending university. First, differences in academic performance across the income distribution could themselves be the result of differences in family income. Why? Families with more financial resources might spend more money on books for children, take their children to museums, spend more on daycare in the early years, locate in neighbourhoods with better schools, and so on. These actions, Frenette concluded, could result in higher performance on standardized and scholastic tests, and thus, in a higher probability of attending university in the future. As we can see from Frenette's analysis, the seemingly individual decision to attend or not attend university is very much influenced by academic performance, which in turn is strongly influenced by social and not individual factors.

So what about the expected role of credit constraints? It is certainly the case that upon deciding to attend university, students may be faced with another barrier that is related to their family's financial position: an inability to secure the loans necessary to pay for post-secondary education. However, the evidence Frenette considered casts doubt on the *widespread* existence of credit constraints in Canada. Frenette calculated that only 12 per cent of the gap was related to financial constraints (2007, p. 23). It is interesting to note that Carneiro and Heckman (2002), in a review of comparable data gathered in the United States, likewise found very little evidence of credit constraints.

What the findings of the study suggest is that, given the weak evidence of widespread credit constraints, we should shift our focus to the question of why students from lower-income families—as a group, and not as individuals—tend to perform more poorly on standardized and scholastic tests than do students from higher-income families.

Example 4 of Critical Sociological Thinking: Canadian Multiculturalism in Crisis?

multiculturalism
The peaceful co-existence within a state of different ethnic and cultural groups. In Canada, multiculturalism is a federal policy, supported by numerous social programs designed to promote and accommodate ethnocultural diversity.

Beginning in the early 1970s, the ethnic, cultural, and linguistic composition of Canada changed significantly as a result of the immigration of peoples from eastern Europe, Africa, Central and South America, and Asia (see Table 2.3). Recognizing the growing diversity of the Canadian citizenry, the federal government under Prime Minister Pierre Elliott Trudeau in 1971 adopted a policy to promote 'multiculturalism', initially by financing a number of social and cultural programs that were intended to accommodate the growing diversity of the Canadian population. **Multiculturalism** became an official policy of the Canadian government when it was enshrined in section 27 of the Canadian Charter of Rights and Freedoms as part of the Constitution Act of 1982. Six years later, Canadian cultural diversity was further guaranteed with the passing of the Act for the Preservation and Enhancement of Multiculturalism in Canada, also known as the Canadian Multiculturalism Act (1988). Part of the preamble to that act states that:

> [T]he Government of Canada recognizes the diversity of Canadians as regards race, national or ethnic origin, colour and religion as a fundamental characteristic of Canadian society and is committed to a policy of multiculturalism designed to preserve and enhance the multicultural heritage of Canadians while working to achieve the equality of all Canadians in the economic, social, cultural and political life of Canada. . . . (Canada, Minister of Justice, 1988, p. 2)

The Canadian Multiculturalism Act has remained largely unchanged since 1988 with the exception of some minor amendments.

Toronto

At the end of World War II there were about 650,000 people, mostly of British descent, living in Toronto. A few others from eastern and southern Europe also called Toronto home, but Torontonians were so overwhelmingly 'British' and Anglo-Protestant values and traditions so predominant in the city that Toronto was sometimes described as the 'Ulster of the north'. By the mid-1990s, Toronto was a city of approximately 3 million people, recognized as

TABLE 2.3 Top 10 birth countries/regions of recent immigrants to Canada, 1981–2006

Rank	1981 Census	1991 Census	1996 Census	2001 Census	2006 Census
1	United Kingdom	Hong Kong	Hong Kong	People's Republic of China	People's Republic of China
2	Vietnam	Poland	People's Republic of China	India	India
3	United States	People's Republic of China	India	Philippines	Philippines
4	India	India	Philippines	Pakistan	Pakistan
5	Philippines	Philippines	Sri Lanka	Hong Kong	United States
6	Jamaica	United Kingdom	Poland	Iran	South Korea
7	Hong Kong	Vietnam	Taiwan	Taiwan	Romania
8	Portugal	United States	Vietnam	United States	Iran
9	Taiwan	Lebanon	United States	South Korea	United Kingdom
10	People's Republic of China	Portugal	United Kingdom	Sri Lanka	Colombia

Note: 'Recent immigrants' refers to landed immigrants who arrived in Canada within five years prior to a given census.
Source: Statistics Canada, Census Snapshot – Immigration in Canada: A Portrait of the Foreign-born Population, 2006 Census, *Canadian Social Trends*, 11-008-XIE2008001, Summer 2008, no. 85, June 2008; http://www.statcan.gc.ca/bsolc/olc-cel/olc-cel?catno=11-008-X&lang=eng.

the hub of Canada's financial, communications, and English-language cultural life. Largely as a consequence of immigration, Toronto had gone from being the preserve of an Anglo-Protestant majority to a city of ethnic and racial minorities. Today, Toronto has more people of Roman Catholic heritage than of any other religious tradition. Over ninety different languages are commonly spoken in the city, and tens of thousands of children who enter school each year do not speak English as their mother tongue.

By the turn of the twenty-first century more foreign-born people immigrating to Canada had settled in Toronto than in any other Canadian metropolitan area. In 2006, Toronto's population stood at 5,072,100, of whom 2,320,200—or 45.7 per cent—were born outside of Canada. About 447,900 foreign-born people (40.4 per cent of all immigrants arriving in Canada) settled in and around Toronto in the five-year period between 2001 and 2006. During that time, Toronto's foreign-born population grew by 14.1 per cent. The neighbouring cities of Brampton and Markham saw their foreign-born populations increase by 59.5 per cent

In June 2011 Toronto became the first city outside of India to host the Indian International Film Academy awards. What do you think that indicates about the changing ethnic composition of Canada's cities, and Toronto in particular?

and 34.1 per cent over the same time, while three other municipalities in the Greater Toronto Area—Ajax, Aurora, and Vaughan—experienced increases to their foreign-born populations of more than 40 per cent (compared with a rise of 4.6 per cent for the GTA's Canadian-born population). More than two-thirds (68.5 per cent) of Toronto's newcomers were born in Asian countries, with the top five source countries being the People's Republic of China, India, the Philippines, Pakistan, and Sri Lanka.

In December 2007, the arrest of 57-year-old Toronto resident Muhammad Parvez and his 26-year old son Waqas for the murder of their daughter and sister, 16-year-old high school student Aqsa Parvez, sparked enormous interest among the local media, which were quick to characterize the crime as an 'honour killing'. In an article discussing tolerance and the limits of multiculturalism in Canada, Eve Haque, professor in the Department of Equity Studies at Toronto's York University, notes that the newspaper articles reporting on the arrest contained 'all the elements of an increasingly familiar narrative about gender, religion and multiculturalism in the West' at the heart of which is a 'simplistic bifurcation between the liberal tolerance of the West, and the pre-modern barbarism of Islam' (Haque, 2010, pp. 79–80).

The media's fascination with the case went beyond the details of Aqsa's murder, including the alleged motive—her refusal to wear the **hijab**, an act of disobedience that supposedly brought shame and embarrassment upon the family. The media brought other issues surrounding the oppression of Muslim women to the fore, making Aqsa's murder an exemplar of the difference between Western behaviour (held to be 'civilized', modern, and secular) and Muslim behaviour, characterized as pre-modern and governed by outdated values rooted in religious fundamentalism (Haque, 2010, p. 80). The incident also provided the media an opportunity to recall previous episodes in the clash of Western and non-Western values concerning the treatment of women, including the treatment of women under traditional Islamic Sharia Law, the controversy with Elections Canada over the right of Muslim women to vote while wearing the **niqab**, and the exclusion of Muslim girls from school and sporting events when they refused to remove their hijabs.

In light of all this, Eve Haque asks how the media's publically expressed concerns about 'Canadian' Muslim women fit with the twin ideas that Canada is a secular, tolerant nation, open to all regardless of origin, and that all newcomers can be integrated into a multicultural, bilingual framework that reflects the culture of the two 'founding nations'. To answer her own question, Haque takes a close look at how Canada's policy of multiculturalism first emerged and how it established a hierarchy of national belonging based on the division of all comers to Canada into two broad categories: those whose culture fits, broadly, with the culture of the two founding nations, French and English, and those who can be identified as the 'cultural Other'. Haque's objective is to help us rethink our 'understanding of violence against Muslim women' by challenging this powerful tendency to divide Canadians into the categories of 'culturally similar' and 'culturally different'. This division, Haque argues, sustains an implicit racial hierarchy that Canadians can well do without (Haque, 2001, p. 81).

Two products of the Royal Commission on Bilingualism and Biculturalism, which ran from 1963 to 1970, were the Official Languages Act (1969) and the Multiculturalism Policy (1971). Although the Royal Commission had officially denied 'racial and ethnic exclusions', the two pieces of legislation that resulted from its work did not acknowledge the founding status of Canada's Aboriginal peoples and referred to all non-English and non-French immigrant groups as 'Other ethnic groups'. While disavowing 'racial distinctions' between the two founding groups and other ethnic groups, the Commission framed these distinctions in terms of 'language and culture', and it limited the extent to which the languages and cultures

hijab

Either the head covering traditionally worn by Muslim women or (generally) a modest style of dress that involves covering everything except the face and hands in public.

niqab

A veil worn by some Muslim women, especially in Pakistan and parts of India, as part of hijab.

of 'Others' would be officially recognized. In this way, Haque tells us, language and culture were used to establish a new national identity—one based on multiculturalism and English/ French bilingualism—into which all citizens should be integrated. English and French were designated the 'two founding nations', while everyone else belonged to 'Other ethnic communities', peripheral to the two founding nations. It is in this context that Haque discusses how violence against Muslim women has been made into a problem of culture.

In Canada's secular society, religious tolerance shapes the way Canadians should cohabitate with each other (Brown, 2006, p. 11). Religion is not banished from the public sphere; rather, its expression is regulated. In Canada, tolerance is to be exercised by autonomous, liberal individuals. Those who are intolerant are also designated as 'intolerable'. The autonomy of the state from both religious and cultural authority is the essential ingredient in the promotion of the liberal, tolerant individual. Today, and especially since 9/11, individuals belonging to what are identified as 'traditional cultures' are, as a group, presupposed to have identities that were shaped entirely by the cultures into which they were born (Mamdani, 2002, p. 767, as cited in Haque, 2010). In this way, a division between the 'civilized, autonomous, individual subject' and the 'non-liberal, fundamentalist' subject, shaped by traditional culture, has emerged.

Since September 11, Islamic culture has been held as the best representation of a non-liberal fundamentalist culture, and the question of how Muslim women are treated has become the measure of 'this culture's barbarity' (Haque, 2010, p. 84). In Canada, Aqsa Parvez's death and the subsequent arrest of her father and brother in December 2007 have been portrayed in both local and national news media as illustrating the 'dangers of Islamic culture' and the threat that such an intolerant, fundamentalist culture presents to a 'secular and tolerant multicultural society' (Haque, 2010, p. 86). Instead of framing Aqsa's death as an instance of domestic violence, the media framed her death as a question of cultural violence, choosing to focus especially on Aqsa's lack of freedom to adopt 'normal' Western dress codes and behaviour. But, as Haque points out, the repression of daughters and wives by patriarchal fathers crosses virtually *all* religions (see for example the site ChristianDomesticDiscipline.com). Yet when men who are *not* Muslims kill their daughters or wives, it is not blamed on their culture, or religion, but on the 'rage' of the individual perpetrator.

Haque concludes that the media accounts of Aqsa's death have been written in a way designed to confirm the national narrative that we are a tolerant nation with equal opportunities for all and that Aqsa's death is an example of the failure of multiculturalism and integration, especially with regard to Muslim women. Aqsa was portrayed as a 'home-grown girl' who was thwarted in her attempts to become 'a normal Canadian girl' by the 'barbaric cultural practices of her religious culture'. But as Haque argues, domestic violence against women is an issue within all communities in Canada. It is not something that is reserved for or confined to women within Muslim communities. As Haque also notes, the stories about Aqsa's murder appeared at the same time as stories about Robert Pickton's conviction for murdering six women in British Columbia. Addressing violence against women as a merely cultural issue does not address the roots of violence in Canadian communities or how state policies serve to perpetuate racial and cultural hierarchies of exclusion. For instance, how, asks Haque, did it happen that it took so long for police to finally begin investigating the deaths of so many Aboriginal women in BC?

Almost 20 per cent of Canadians today are 'visible minorities'. At what point do we begin to understand that we, as Canadian citizens, are all 'minorities', and that there are no special privileges to be accorded to those of us who have English or French origins? Haque concludes:

If we begin here, then perhaps, for example, we might be able to read Aqsa's death and life not as a tragedy in which she was merely a thwarted victim of her religious culture (i.e. 'hijab teen') but as a citizen subject valiantly involved in the negotiation of the terms of her minoritized belonging in the nation. (Haque, 2010, p. 98)

SUMMARY

Most sociologists are strongly committed to questioning the mechanisms and processes that underpin social interactions. In doing this, they often challenge deeply engrained taken-for-granted or common-sense understandings and stereotypes. Critical sociological thinking is an inherent part of the discipline of sociology and is one of the three essential tools of a sociologist's core skill set (the other two being research and theory). Critical-thinking sociologists 'effectively analyze, infer, and evaluate information from primary sources and synthesize that information' to produce new and often counterintuitive understandings of the social world. The four examples presented above show how critical-thinking sociologists work at observing, gathering data, making inferences, and analyzing that data to arrive at non–common-sense understandings on widely different topic areas. What the work of these and other sociologists has in common is the application of critical sociological thinking in general, and the sociological imagination in particular. In the next three chapters we will take a closer look at two other related core skills for sociologists: research and theorizing.

DISCUSSION QUESTIONS

1. In what ways does critical thinking for the ancient Greeks differ from critical sociological thinking today?
2. In what ways does critical thinking today challenge the kind of critical thinking done by seventeenth-century philosophers such as René Descartes?
3. In what way does a sociological imagination help us to understand the relationship between individuals and their society?
4. How might one apply a sociological imagination to the analysis of poverty in Canada?
5. Why is it important to understand the meanings we, both as individuals and as members of a particular society, give to social behaviour?
6. Why do you think people generally are far more aware of the social costs of street crimes—drug trafficking, prostitution, violent crime, and so on—than of corporate, or 'white-collar', crime? Do you believe there is any crime that is truly 'victimless', as corporate crime is sometimes described?
7. What are the characteristics of a critical thinker?
8. Is being able to expand one's horizons a reasonable or defensible justification for becoming a critical sociological thinker?

3 Quantitative and Qualitative Research

CHAPTER OUTLINE

LEARNING OBJECTIVES

In this chapter you will:

- explore the general factors influencing sociological research
- learn about sociological research as a scientific endeavour
- become familiar with research processes used by sociologists
- differentiate between qualitative and quantitative research strategies
- gain an understanding of value relevance and value neutrality
- learn about Durkheim's research on suicide.

INTRODUCTION

Like most people, sociologists ask questions about the social world, and carefully observe that world in search of answers to their questions. But unlike those whose personal research is guided by a hunch or an immediate need, sociologists' research must follow a highly disciplined logic in order for their work to have scientific value. A sociologist must know how to design and conduct her study: she must formulate good, researchable questions, and know enough to be able to choose the most appropriate research method(s) with which to collect her data. She must follow strict procedures when gathering and analyzing her data. Finally, as sociologists do not generally keep the results of their research to themselves, she must seek out ways to present her findings to her peers and the general public.

Sociological research, then, is a **scientific** endeavour: the knowledge it produces about the social world is supported by **empirical** (or **tangible**) **evidence**. Sociological research is undertaken with the objective of describing, understanding, and even influencing or improving the social world in which we live. The results of sociological research can often be used to develop remedies for social problems, strategies for social projects, or plans for bringing about social change (Bouma, Ling, & Wilkinson, 2009).

All sociological research begins with a **research strategy**. A research strategy is the general orientation a sociologist takes to how she conducts her research. There are two main research strategies or general orientations used by sociologists: quantitative and qualitative. This chapter discusses the general factors that influence all sociological research, as well as the specific factors that affect qualitative and quantitative research strategies.

A quantitative research strategy differs from a qualitative one in a number of ways. A researcher using a **quantitative research strategy** focuses on collecting and processing data using statistical procedures. By contrast, a researcher using a **qualitative research strategy** collects data that are rich in description and not easily handled using statistical procedures. Quantitative data are usually expressed in numbers, percentages, or rates, answering questions such as: *How much? How many? How often?* A qualitative research strategy is less concerned with numbers and more concerned with what people say or have said. Qualitative data are usually expressed in words and reveal how research subjects feel about something, or the ways in which they understand something.

GENERAL FACTORS INFLUENCING SOCIOLOGICAL RESEARCH

When most people think about doing sociological research, they think first about choosing a **research method**. But as sociology research methods specialists Alan Bryman and James Teevan correctly point out, 'the practice of social research does not exist in a bubble, sealed off from the various philosophical allegiances of their practitioners' (Bryman & Teevan, 2005, p. 2). Instead, they note, there are four general factors that influence all sociological research, regardless of which research strategy is used. These factors are: *theory, epistemology, values,* and *ontology* (see Figure 3.1).

When a sociologist undertakes a research project and chooses a research strategy, she isn't just making a choice between gathering quantitative or qualitative data. She is also making a

scientific
Based on or rooted in science, the systematic study of empirical evidence through observation and experiment.

empirical (or **tangible**) **evidence**
Evidence that has been acquired through direct observation, and that can be verified or disproved by direct or indirect observation by more than one person.

research strategy
The general orientation or approach a sociologist takes in conducting research. A **quantitative research strategy** is an approach in which the researcher collects data that can be quantified and expressed in terms of numbers, percentages, or rates, and that are amenable to statistical manipulation. A **qualitative research strategy** is an approach in which the researcher collects data that are rich in description and not easily measured using statistical procedures.

research method
The actual technique a researcher uses to collect data.

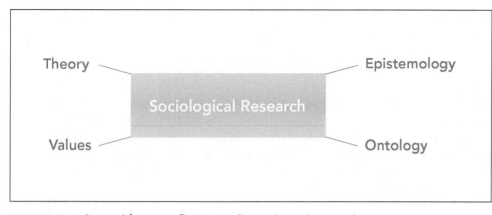

FIGURE 3.1   General factors influencing all sociological research

choice about how she will use theory, which epistemological and ontological orientations will shape her research, and what role her values will play in her work.

1. Theory

Data are empirical facts, meaningless in and of themselves: they become meaningful when they are presented or considered in relation to a theory. At the most basic level, a **theory** is an explanation of some observed regularity—for example, why women are less likely than men to be CEOs of large corporations, or why Canadians of Aboriginal origin are overrepresented in prison populations.

When we, as common-sense thinkers, try to understand something new—a person, a thing, or an event—we usually do so by comparing it with something familiar. Suppose, for a moment, that someone you know is suddenly unemployed through no fault of his own. At first, employment insurance (EI), along with savings and possibly financial assistance from family and friends, might help alleviate the situation. But unemployment remains a fact: it has happened regardless of whether your acquaintance wanted it or not, and it is by no means immediately apparent why it happened. Faced with this situation, your acquaintance starts looking for an explanation: 'I'm still unemployed because cheap immigrant labour has taken away a job that is rightfully mine,' or 'I've lost my job because the austerity measures adopted by the current government are ruining the economy.'

Suppose that this acquaintance becomes despondent after several months of unsuccessful searching for a new job. He might explain that despondency in simple terms such as, 'I'm unhappy because I've never gotten a decent break in life.' Or the explanation could become more complicated: 'Relationships in my early childhood with an unloving mother and an absent father, along with unresolved sibling rivalries, have resulted in my inability to deal with the current difficulties that I am now facing.'

In this example, your unemployed acquaintance has used everyday or common-sense thinking to explain his situation. He has drawn on previous experiences, general ideas commonly shared within the society, and his own emotional states to explain being unemployed.

All theories, whether they are common-sense or carefully worked out sociological ones, work in a similar way. Like a metaphor, any theory both reveals and conceals certain aspects of human experience (Ricoeur, 1970; Sullivan, 1984). A theory directs our attention to certain

data (*sing.* **datum**)
Known facts or statistics, gathered and used as the basis for reasoning, reference, or calculation.

theory
The perspective or template a researcher uses to organize how she views the world; it provides a guide for explaining any regularity she observes in the data.

aspects of people's behaviour, or to certain events or things, and suggests a framework by which we can understand what we observe.

Grand Theories, Theories of the Middle Range, and 'Working Hypotheses'

research design

The framework for collecting and analyzing data.

A theory, as we have seen, serves as a template that helps us make sense of observed regularities. Sociological theories differ from common-sense, everyday theories in that they provide the sociological researcher with guidelines she can use for thinking *in a disciplined manner* about the kinds of research questions to pose, and how she must proceed in order to answer those questions. Sociological theories shape both the research strategy and the **research design** that a sociologist will adopt, the kinds of data that she will collect, and how she will go about analyzing the data once she has collected it.

The American sociologist Robert K. Merton (1910–2003) made an important distinction between three levels of abstraction in theorizing. At the least abstract level is what he called 'working hypotheses', which he considered the 'minor but necessary' components of 'day to day research'. At the most abstract level can be found the 'grand theories', described as 'the all-inclusive systematic efforts to develop a unified theory that will explain all the observed uniformities of social behaviour, social organization, and social change'. And in the middle

Rioters or protesters? This scene from the 2010 G20 summit was an unfamiliar one for most Torontonians. How might you make sense of it by drawing on more familiar experiences?

is what Merton labelled 'theories of the middle range', the theories that 'lie between the two extremes' (Merton, 1949/1968).

There are many 'grand theories' in sociology: Marxist theory, structural-functionalist theory, symbolic interactionism, structuration theory, to name a few. We will consider these and others in subsequent chapters. But Merton, famous for his research on the socialization of medical students at Columbia University in New York, felt that grand theories were 'too remote from particular classes of social behaviour, organization and change to account for what is observed' or to offer researchers much in the way of useful guidelines for conducting **empirical** research. Middle-range theories, by contrast, worked admirably in that role:

> Middle-range theory involves abstractions, of course, but they are close enough to observed data to be incorporated in propositions (hypotheses) that permit testing. Middle-range theories deal with delimited aspects of social phenomena, as is indicated by their labels. (Merton, 1949/1968, p. 51)

Merton goes on to state that middle-range theories include theories 'of deviant behaviour, the unanticipated consequences of purposive action, social perception, reference groups, social control, [and] the interdependence of social institutions' (Merton, 1949/1968, p. 51).

In spite of Merton's dismissal, highly abstract grand theories *do* have connections with 'observable reality' and *can* be used to influence middle-range theories. Consider, for example, the work of another American sociologist, Harry Braverman (1920–76), on the deskilling of labour during the twentieth century. Braverman's *Labour and Monopoly Capital* (1974) was strongly influenced by one of the 'grand' theories, Marx's analysis of the inherently conflictual nature of class relations in capitalist society. Far from being 'too remote' from observable social processes to be of any use to researchers, Marx's grand theory actually inspired Braverman's research, which, in turn, has inspired an extensive body of work on the ways in which the deskilling of workers—and the increased control over their labour by capital—has occurred since the nineteenth century.

Other researchers have built on Braverman's seminal work on monopoly capitalism to generate what Merton would call a 'middle-range' labour process theory, which argues in part that:

- the labour process entails the extraction of surplus value
- capitalist enterprises constantly need to transform the production process
- capitalist enterprises must always seek ways to exercise control over labour
- under capitalism there is an ever-present conflict between capital and labour (Bryman, 2004, p. 6).

Inductive versus Deductive Theory

There is one more important consideration in understanding the role of theory in sociological research: theory may be used either *deductively* or *inductively*. When a theory guides the research—when data are collected and analyzed in order to answer the questions raised by an existing theory—then the theory is said to be **deductive**. However, when the theory is not formulated until after the data have been collected and analyzed—in other words, once the researchers have drawn generalizable inferences from the results of their research—then the theory is **inductive.** A deductive use of theory is typically part of a quantitative research strategy, while an inductive use of theory is characteristic of qualitative research.

empirical
Based on, guided by, or verifiable by observation and experiment rather than theory or logic.

deductive
Denoting research informed by a quantitative research strategy, in which a theory is used to generate a hypothesis and guide the collection of the data needed to confirm or reject it.

inductive
Denoting a theory is the outcome, rather than the starting point, of research.

2. Epistemology

Epistemology is a branch of philosophy that deals with the nature, scope, and limitations of knowledge. Epistemology addresses such questions as:

- What is, or what should be, regarded as 'acceptable' knowledge in a discipline?
- How is knowledge acquired?
- How do we know what we know?

Epistemological questions concern the validity of our knowledge, including what methods should be used to arrive at an explanation and what proofs are required to establish something as known.

Historically, a major epistemological concern among sociologists has been whether or not the social world can be studied using the same principles and procedures used in the natural sciences (Bryman & Teevan, 2005, p. 8). Those who argue that the social sciences should imitate the natural sciences—particularly in their use of deductive research to test hypotheses—support an epistemological position known as **positivism**. Those who hold that research in the social sciences must be guided by an inductive approach while respecting the differences between people and the kinds of research subjects and objects studied by the natural sciences adopt an epistemological position known as **interpretivism**.

3. Values

A **value** is an attitude, belief, or opinion that a person holds and that affects or influences his or her behaviour. Until recently, conventional wisdom stated that the scientific method of inquiry, if properly pursued, affords a value-free, objective way of obtaining information about both the social and the natural worlds. For example, another of the founders of sociology, Émile Durkheim (1858–1917), argued that a sociologist must suppress all 'preconceptions' (including his or her values) when conducting research (Durkheim, 1938, p. 31). Implicit in his stance was the belief that suppressing one's preconceptions or values is even possible.

Today, however, many social scientists question the belief that any scientific research (whether about the natural or the social world) can ever be value-free. There is a growing sense that scientific inquiry is never completely value-free because researchers are incapable of totally excluding the influence of social and cultural values in their attempts to establish knowledge. The values of a researcher can intrude at any number of different points in the research process including:

- choice of the research area
- formulation of the research question
- selection of the research method
- formulation of the research design and data-collection techniques
- implementation of data collection
- analysis of data
- interpretation of data
- conclusions. (Bryman, 2004, p. 22)

Questions about of the role of a researcher's values along with her moral and ethical stance and her commitment to making her research relevant to others are all hotly contested issues in sociology. Should the sociologist step back from issues of values, ethics, and morals when conducting research, or should she let her values be the very thing that leads the way? As readers might suspect, the research strategy a sociologist adopts strongly reflects the answers she gives to these questions.

4. Ontology

Ontology is the study of what there is 'out there'—in other words, the study of what can be said to constitute 'reality'. Ontological questions include the following:

- What is there to know about?
- What is the nature of the objects that we study?

In the social sciences, ontological questions about the nature of the social entities we study take one of two forms:

1. *Are the social entities we study 'objective entities'?* In other words, does a group, community, or organization have an existence that is independent of the social actors involved, either as subjects of observation or as observers? An affirmative answer to these questions is associated with an ontological position known as **objectivism**.
2. *Should the social entities we study be considered as social constructions?* That is, are the entities that sociologists study to be treated as things that have been constructed out of the actions (and perceptions) of the social actors, whether they are the subjects of the study or the scientists conducting the study? An affirmative answer to these questions is associated with an ontological position known as **constructionism (or constructivism)**.

By now you should have noticed that there are two different positions for each of the four influences on sociological research. Theory is either inductive or deductive. Values are considered to be held in abeyance (i.e. a value-neutral approach is preferred) or they reflect the aims and interests of the researcher (marking a value-relevant approach). An epistemological orientation is either interpretive or positivistic, and an ontological orientation can be either objectivist or constructionist. Most sociological research is closely tied to one of two main research strategies: qualitative and quantitative. Now that we've surveyed the four factors that influence social research, we will look at how they play out in both quantitative and qualitative research.

QUANTITATIVE RESEARCH STRATEGY

When a sociologist decides on a quantitative research strategy, he usually proceeds as follows:

- *In terms of theory, he adopts a deductive approach.* That is, he chooses to move from the general to the particular, inferring ideas and hypotheses from a general theory which he will attempt to prove or explain with his research findings.
- *In terms of epistemology, he takes a positivist orientation.* The sociologist accepts that he can best know things through experiments and the collection and analysis of numerical data.
- *In terms of ontological orientation, he espouses objectivism.* He accepts that the objects he can study have an objective existence independent of himself or of any other researcher.
- *In terms of the role of values, he adopts a value-neutral or objective stance.* The sociologist acknowledges that he can and must refrain from imposing his own values on the research process.

In this section we will see specifically how each of these factors plays out in quantitative research (see Figure 3.2).

ontology
The study of what there is 'out there'; in other words, the study of what is said to constitute 'reality' or the nature of being.

objectivism
An ontological position that asserts that the meanings attached to social phenomena are independent of the will or ideas of individuals involved in them.

constructionism
(or **constructivism**)
An ontological position that asserts that the meanings attached to social phenomena are constructed out of the acts and perceptions of social actors involved in them.

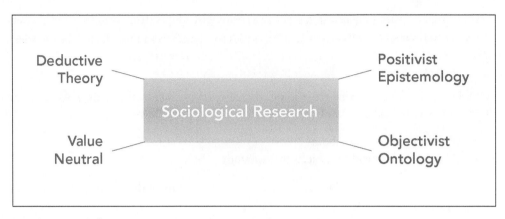

FIGURE 3.2 Influences on quantitative research strategies

1. Deductive Theory

hypothesis
A speculation, usually informed by an existing theory, about the relationship between two or more variables.

When a researcher begins a research project following a quantitative research strategy he usually begins by formulating a research topic and choosing one or more theories that have already been developed by other researchers to explain their research findings on that topic. Either he uses the theory loosely to identify a set a concerns around which he will gather data, or, more formally, he infers a testable **hypothesis**—a hunch about relationships between the variables he has identified. Hypotheses should not be confused with theories, which are more general explanations that have been developed based on repeated testing of hypotheses (see Figure 3.3).

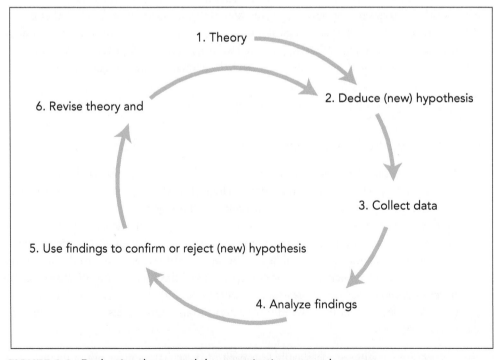

FIGURE 3.3 Deductive theory and the quantitative research process

Scientists are said to create knowledge when they gather facts in a manner that is free of the influence of values, and then generate theories (or 'laws') from those facts. The theories/laws generated in this manner are held to be different from the everyday, common-sense views of the same phenomena—including myths and religious beliefs—that are held by the general population.

2. Positivist Epistemological Orientation

Positivism is the epistemological orientation that supports a deductive approach to generating hypotheses. This orientation, used extensively in the social sciences, dominates research in the natural sciences, where the highest level of interest is in prediction and control. Over four centuries ago, scientists such as Francis Bacon (1561–1626) began developing a method of scientific inquiry that would effectively establish control over nature. A good theory, from this point of view, is one that successfully predicts events and their outcomes and that can thus be used to gain mastery over those events.

American sociologist Joyce McCarl Nielsen (1990) outlines five assumptions of a positivist epistemological orientation that are applicable to both the natural and the social sciences:

1. The social world is knowable in the same way as the natural world is knowable. The most advantageous way to explore the social world, therefore, is by using the same principles of investigation used to study the physical world. The social world is studied best through observation and the recording of those observations by a neutral, independent, and, above all, objective researcher.
2. There is an objective, independent reality, completely detached from and external to the researcher.
3. Empirical observation based on the use of the senses is the only way to gather data about the real, external world. Data are considered objective if they can be either verified or refuted by independent observers exposed to the same phenomenon. Verification of one observer's findings by another independent observer is essential for the verification of conclusions.
4. The social world, like the natural world, is ordered in a predictable way. Events don't just happen; there is a pattern to them that follows a predominantly cause-and-effect form. The overall goal of social science research is to construct universal laws about the social world and human behaviour that hold true across time, place, and culture.
5. There is a certain unity to all sciences, including the social sciences. All sciences share the same methods of acquiring knowledge about the world. These methods are the best—if not the only—way of uncovering legitimate knowledge. (Nielsen, 1990, pp. 4–5)

Rationalism and empiricism are considered the 'twin pillars' of positivist epistemology. **Rationalism** has its basis in the work of the ancient Greek philosophers and can best be characterized by the statement, 'What is, is; what is not, is not.' The seventeenth-century French philosopher, mathematician, and scientist René Descartes (1596–1650) made the famous rationalist statement, 'I think, therefore I am.' This statement is considered to be true because the first part, 'I think,' makes any negation of the second part, 'I am,' illogical. In making this statement, Descartes grounded his sense of existence in the process of thinking and not in his feelings or emotions. He did not say 'I love' or 'I feel and therefore I am'. Descartes put his trust in rational thought (Nielsen, 1990, p. 2).

rationalism
An approach to reality that can best be characterized by the statement, 'What is, is; what is not, is not.'

empiricism
An approach to reality that holds that the only valid knowledge is knowledge gained through the senses by directly observing, recording, or monitoring social and natural phenomena.

Empiricism, the other foundation of positivist epistemology, is an approach to reality that holds that the only valid knowledge is knowledge gained through the process of using the senses to directly observe, record, or monitor social and natural phenomena. In the words of British philosopher Karl Popper, 'only observation and experiment may decide upon the acceptance or rejection of scientific statements, including laws and theories' (Popper, 1969, p. 54).

A positivist epistemological orientation offers explanations that are capable of being falsified with reference to sensory experience. What is taken as evidence must be observed: all other ways of knowing are considered incapable of such falsification (Popper, 1969, p. 54). Popper states that 'a system is to be considered as scientific only if it makes assertions which may clash with observations; a system is, in fact, tested by attempts to produce such clashes, that is to say, by attempts to refute it' (Popper, 1969, p. 59). Most other epistemological approaches to knowledge, such as religion or myth, are not scientific because they are not testable; they cannot be refuted by reference to empirical reality.

To sum up, researchers who use a positivist epistemological orientation to research argue that genuine knowledge comes to us only through the senses. As scientists, they say, we must work deductively: we must use theory to generate hypotheses that we then test; the results of our research must be used to assess our theory. We create knowledge when we gather facts in a manner that is free of the influence of values, and we then generate theories (or 'laws') from those facts. The theories/laws we generate in this manner are different from the everyday, common-sense views of the same phenomena, as held by the general population. What is held to be true by the general population, including religious beliefs and myths, cannot be confirmed by the senses (Bryman, 2004, p. 11).

Cause and effect, right? Everyone knows that giving kids sugar will make them hyper. That's precisely the sort of everyday belief a positivist researcher might aim to refute. Indeed, a recent study carried out to test the theory showed no relationship between children's activity levels and sugar consumption.

3. Objectivist Ontological Orientation

A quantitative research strategy supports the ontological position of objectivism. Objectivism asserts that 'social phenomena confront us as external facts that are beyond our reach or influence' (Bryman, 2004, p. 16). Objectivism holds that all social organizations are independent of the will or ideas of individuals in them. For example, a production plant that builds cars has rules and procedures for getting cars through the assembly line. The plant has a hierarchy of authority, a production process, and rules of conduct that must be followed. The division of labour in the plant assigns workers to different types of jobs. These jobs are hierarchical: the plant owner has a certain kind of authority and role; the manager, another; the foreman, yet another. The assembly line workers, who are near the bottom of the hierarchy, have yet another type of job that comes with its own authority (or lack of authority) and performance requirements.

In this type of organization, what is required of a floor supervisor, to take one example, is independent of any individual who might occupy that position. While each individual supervisor brings her own experiences, personality, and other individual characteristics to the job, the role of 'floor supervisor', when that individual leaves the organization, does not leave with her.

Moreover, the organization—in this case, the automotive production plant—exerts a great deal of pressure on individuals who work there to conform to its organizational requirements. Workers, managers, foremen, and owners alike all learn what the rules and procedures are, and how to follow them. They do the jobs they were hired to do; if not they can expect to be reprimanded, or even fired. The organization itself acts as a kind of 'constraining force' that structures and inhibits its members' actions (Bryman & Teevan, 2005, pp. 12–13).

4. Value Neutrality

As far as it is reasonably possible, a researcher should strive to achieve value neutrality when conducting and analyzing the results of quantitative research.

Max Weber on Value Relevance and Value Neutrality

Max Weber (1864–1920) was a German sociologist who wrote on social theory and social research. Weber thought that while the choice of subject matter in social research was the result of an investigator's value orientation, the interpretation of whatever data were generated must be subjected to the laws of evidence. From Weber's point of view, what isn't value-free—i.e. what has **value relevance** for sociologists—is the problems that attract them to do the research in the first place. But the findings of research must be reached independently of a researcher's values. So for Weber, it was important to distinguish value relevance from **value neutrality.** *Value relevance* means that a social scientist chooses a problem to research on the basis of that problem's relevance to his values. But then he must take a value-neutral position when he analyzes the data he collects. Here the sociologist cannot impose his values on the data—he must proceed in a value-neutral way, regardless of whether or not his findings are consistent with the values he holds dear.

In the same manner, Weber felt, it is possible to make objective, value-neutral comparisons between two or more social systems once a particular perspective, end, or purpose has been settled upon. To put it another way, Weber believed that ultimately the values a researcher brings with him to a research project cannot be evaluated objectively. But once a value is subjectively chosen, a sociologist can make his study and arrive at an analysis of the data

value relevance

The extent to which a social scientist's values affect her approach to investigating a social problem. According to Weber, it is all but impossible for a social scientist to prevent her values from affecting her choice of research topics.

value neutrality

An approach to investigating a research problem that is unaffected by the social scientist's values. According to Weber, social researchers must not allow their personal values to influence the collection and analysis of data or the dissemination of research findings.

he collects in an objective manner. Weber himself took several different value stances in his own work. For example he sometimes adopted a nationalistic perspective, at other times he championed individual liberty, and in still other instances he shaped his research according to existing cultural norms.

Weber advocated that sociologists openly acknowledge their values, and he warned against the delusion that they might be able to work completely independently of those values. He called this a delusion to which we all too frequently succumb and claimed that acknowledging a value orientation is the prerequisite to making an objective evaluation (Weber, 1994/1895, p. 19). When a sociologist fails to consciously acknowledge and clarify his values, it is unlikely that he will conduct the subsequent analysis impartially.

By drawing the distinction between value-relevant choice of research subject and value-neutral analysis of the data, Weber was able to uphold the position that value neutrality is at the core of science, and that a researcher must proceed in a neutral way when analyzing the evidence, regardless of what the outcome might be.

Consider a hockey team as a type of organization: it has a hierarchy (management, coaches, players), a fixed set of positions (goaltenders, defencemen, forwards), and assigned roles (third-line checking centre, designated enforcer, etc.). What other organizational requirements are there on a hockey team? How are these enforced?

Moral and Ethical Issues

Weber felt that a social scientist must never advise others on what they should or should not do with the results of her research. She can offer a critique of a policy or practice, based on what her research shows; she can point out internal inconsistencies between the desired ends of a policy and 'the facts', the actual results as reflected in her data; she can provide an evaluation of the probable consequences of taking a specific course of action. But she must leave the final decisions about what to do with the results of her research up to others. In Weber's opinion, a sociologist searches only for truth; she leaves the moral and ethical issues and how to resolve them up to others.

Many sociologists today disagree with Weber on this point. They argue that sociologists have a responsibility to intervene with policy-makers and to work to actively advance the interests of the people they study, especially if they are disadvantaged or oppressed.

The American sociologist Howard S. Becker, in an article entitled 'Whose Side Are We On?' (1967), makes the point that it is impossible for sociologists to be value-neutral. Therefore, he argues, sociologists should do research that deliberately favours society's less powerful groups, who have no one else to speak for them. Becker calls this 'siding with the underdog' (Becker, 1967). But the opposite sentiment is just as possible: researchers can and sometimes do find the people they are studying repugnant. The British anthropologist Colin Turnbull, for example, was appalled by what he found to be enormous cruelty towards children and old people among the Ik, an African tribe he studied (Turnbull, 1972). In the introduction to his book on the Ik, Turnbull wrote, 'The reader is entitled to know something of the aims, expectations, hopes and attitudes that the writer brought to the field with him, for these will surely influence not only how he sees things but even what he sees' (1972, p. 13).

Questions about of the role of a researcher's values along with her moral and ethical stance and her commitment to making her research relevant to others are all hotly contested issues in sociology. Should the sociologist step back from issues of values, ethics, and morals when conducting research, or should values be the very thing that leads the way? As readers might suspect, the research strategy a sociologist adopts strongly reflects the answers she gives to these questions.

THEORY, ONTOLOGY, EPISTEMOLOGY, AND QUANTITATIVE RESEARCH

A deductive approach to theory, the use of positivism as an epistemological orientation and objectivism as an ontological orientation, and the adoption of a value-neutral or objective stance—these, as we have seen, are the trademarks of quantitative sociological research. They are also exemplified in Émile Durkheim's pioneering work on suicide, the influences of which can be seen in the work of some contemporary sociologists, including some notable Canadian studies described below.

Émile Durkheim on Suicide

French sociologist Émile Durkheim (1858–1917), who is considered one of the 'founding fathers' of the discipline (along with Karl Marx and Max Weber), produced a large body of groundbreaking work that included a study of the social influences on suicide. At first

social fact

Any of the values, norms, beliefs, practices, and social structures of a society that are external to individual members of a society but that nonetheless influence their behaviour or attitudes. Durkheim stated that social facts are to be treated as 'things'.

consideration, the decision to commit suicide—and, thus, to end one's own life—seems to be an entirely personal one. Durkheim (1897/1952), however, was the first to show that this was not the case and that even at this most seemingly personal level of action, there were **social facts** at work, acting independently of the conscious will of the person considering suicide. Suicide rates, Durkheim demonstrated, varied strongly by country, and by group affiliation.

Durkheim began his research to test the theory that an individual committed suicide because of some psychological disorder. He originally hypothesized that suicide rates would be highest where rates of psychological disorders were also high. He expected that the data he was about to gather would confirm that individual psychological disorders were at the root of an act of suicide. However, his analysis of the statistics provided to him by hospitals and governments throughout Europe did not support his original hypothesis.

Fans of the late singer Amy Winehouse lament her death in July 2011. One would think that the life of a celebrity would bring a high degree of social solidarity, and yet Winehouse is but the latest of a long line of musicians— Kurt Cobain, Michael Hutchence, Sid Vicious, Jimi Hendrix, Janis Joplin, to name just a few—to suffer drug- and alcohol-related deaths, possibly suicides. What conclusions might we draw about social solidarity and fame?

Instead, Durkheim found that while there were more female than male inmates in the asylums of Europe, more men than women (by a factor of 4 to 1) committed suicide. And while Jews had the highest rate of psychological disorders amongst members of identifiable religious groups, they also had the lowest rate of suicide. Age also seemed to play a role: psychological disorders were more frequent among older persons, while it was young people who most frequently committed suicide. Why?

To answer this question, and explain his findings, Durkheim had to revise his theory. He now theorized that suicide rates vary with something he called 'the degree of social solidarity'. He speculated that the more beliefs that members of a given social group shared in common, and the more frequently they interacted with each other, the less likely they were to commit suicide. Social solidarity, Durkheim theorized, serves to anchor individuals and to provide them with a solid base so that they are less likely to take their own lives when faced with difficulties.

From his revised theory Durkheim now deduced a new hypothesis that suicide rates decline when there is a high degree of social solidarity and rise when there is a low degree of social solidarity. He was then able to collect new data in order to demonstrate that married adults were half as likely to commit suicide as unmarried ones, arguing that marriage creates strong social ties that bind the individual to society. In an effort to account for his earlier findings, he reasoned that women commit suicide less often than men because they are more closely bound to the strong social relations generated in the family. Jews, meanwhile, are less likely to commit suicide because centuries of religious persecution had made them into a tight-knit, defensive group, according to Durkheim.

Durkheim and Suicide Today

Durkheim, brilliantly, was able to show that even something as seemingly personal and private as the decision to take one's own life was a public issue in that the decision is strongly susceptible to social influences. His work underlines the usefulness of applying a sociological imagination within the context of a quantitative research strategy, and it provides a foundation for the kinds of analyses that sociologists are doing today.

Durkheim's influence goes beyond his methods and choice of subject; indeed, some of his actual findings are consistent with recent data gathered on suicide in Canada. For example, Table 3.1, which shows suicide rates in Canada by sex and by age, indicates a strong variation by sex, and a weaker one by age.

While Canadian men are far more likely than Canadian women to succeed in taking their own lives, owing in large part to their use of more lethal methods, female hospitalization rates for attempted suicide are far higher than corresponding male rates. In 1998–9, the age-standardized hospitalization rate for attempted suicide was 108 per 100,000 females aged 10 or older, and just 70 per 100,000 of their male counterparts (Langlois & Morrison, 2002, p. 13).

Canadian suicide rates also vary by place of residence, as Table 3.1 shows. Rates are highest in Nunavut (83.5 for males, 20.8 for females per 100,000 population), Quebec (21.7 for males and 6.1 for females), and Nova Scotia (18.8 for males and 3.7 for females). Young people in Aboriginal communities in Canada have suicide rates 5 to 6 times higher than those of non-Aboriginals (Canada 2003). Suicide rates among Inuit youth are among the highest in the world, at 11 times the Canadian national average.

TABLE 3.1 Suicide rates by sex, provinces, and territories, Canada, 2006

Place of residence	Sex	Suicide rate (per 100,000 population)
Canada	Both sexes	10.0
	Males	15.6
	Females	4.6
Newfoundland and Labrador	Both sexes	9.7
	Males	17.0
	Females	2.5
Prince Edward Island	Both sexes	4.9
	Males	9.1
	Females	0.9
Nova Scotia	Both sexes	11.1
	Males	18.8
	Females	3.7
New Brunswick	Both sexes	11.2
	Males	18.5
	Females	4.5
Quebec	Both sexes	13.8
	Males	21.7
	Females	6.1
Ontario	Both sexes	7.7
	Males	11.8
	Females	3.9
Manitoba	Both sexes	11.8
	Males	18.1
	Females	5.5
Saskatchewan	Both sexes	11.3
	Males	17.1
	Females	5.4
Alberta	Both sexes	11.0
	Males	16.5
	Females	5.8
British Columbia	Both sexes	7.9
	Males	12.6
	Females	3.3
Yukon	Both sexes	7.4
	Males	10.6
	Females	3.7
Northwest Territories	Both sexes	10.6
	Males	16.2
	Females	4.1
Nunavut	Both sexes	52.5
	Males	83.5
	Females	20.8

Source: Statistics Canada, *Mortality, Summary List of Causes*, 84F0209XWE2006000, July 2010; http://www.statcan.gc.ca/bsolc/olc-cel/olc-cel?lang+eng&catno=84F0209X.

QUALITATIVE RESEARCH STRATEGY

Qualitative research differs from quantitative research in how it stands with regard to the four factors that influence sociological research—theory, ontology, epistemology, and values (see Figure 3.4). Characteristically, qualitative research is:

- guided by wide-ranging, complex research question(s)
- rich in detail
- intended to contextualize a situation, not demonstrate a relationship between two variables
- designed to provide a holistic account of a social phenomenon or social problem.

When a sociologist decides on a qualitative research strategy, he usually proceeds as follows:

- *In terms of theory, he adopts an inductive approach.* That is, he chooses to begin with research and to generate his theory out of that research.
- *In terms of epistemology, he takes an interpretist position.* The sociologist endeavours to understand the subjective meaning of the social action he observes.
- *In terms of ontological orientation, he espouses constructionism.* He asserts that the meanings social actors attach to social phenomena are constructed by those actors.
- *In terms of the role of values, he is aware that research is influenced by the researcher's values.* Research can never be totally value-free.

In the section that follows, we will look at what each of the four main influences on qualitative research means in the context of a qualitative research strategy.

1. Inductive Theory

As you have learned by now, in research informed by a quantitative research strategy, theory is generally used deductively to generate hypotheses and to guide and influence the collection of the data needed to confirm or reject a hypothesis. Depending on the conclusions that can be drawn from the data collected, an existing hypothesis is either confirmed and the theory is demonstrated, or the existing theory is revised and a new hypothesis is deduced.

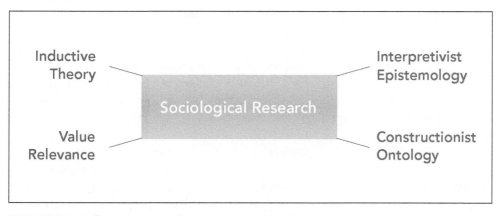

FIGURE 3.4   Influences on qualitative research strategies

However, many researchers prefer to take an inductive stance towards theorizing, making theory the outcome, and not the starting point, of research. Often researchers cannot know ahead of time all of the questions they will want to investigate, which theories will be the most useful to them, and what methods will result in new discoveries (Becker, 2009). With an inductive approach to theory and research, theory is the outcome of, rather than the impetus for, research. Theory is derived from the data collected, rather than existing prior to the collection of data, as in the case of deduction (see Figure 3.5).

2. Interpretivist Epistemological Orientation

Interpretivism is an epistemological position associated with qualitative research strategies. Sociologists who adopt this position argue that what is studied in the social sciences—people and they way in which they are organized socially—is very different from what is studied in the natural sciences. This requires a very different approach to research, one in which the social scientist tries to understand the meaning that his subjects impute to their own actions.

An interpretivist (also called a *hermeneutical*) epistemological orientation is based on the assumption that we can learn about the meaning of the actions of people who are separated from us by time or physical space because all humans communicate with one another using some symbolic medium. The usual medium of symbolic communication between people is

STUDIES IN SOCIAL RESEARCH

Hockey, the Stanley Cup, and Suicide

Durkheim's theoretical insights into suicide reverberate in the work of Canadian sociologist Frank Trovato. Trovato, in his 'The Stanley Cup of Hockey and Suicide in Quebec, 1951–1992' (1998), draws on Durkheim's work to formulate and test the hypothesis that suicide rates might be lower during periods of ceremonial occasion, such as a major holiday or sporting event. Occasions of this sort provide otherwise alienated and lonely people—those who are most at risk of committing suicide—with a reason to communicate and interact with others and thus to experience social solidarity with them.

The Montreal Canadiens' performance in the Stanley Cup playoffs was an excellent subject for testing the hypotheses Trovato derived from Durkheim's theory about suicide and alienation. Many players from the Canadiens' illustrious history—Maurice 'Rocket' Richard, Bernie 'Boom Boom' Geoffrion, Guy Lafleur, Yvan Cournoyer, and Ken Dryden, to name just a few—are heroes in Quebec and household names throughout Canada. Quebecers have a passionate love of hockey and the team they call 'Les Glorieux', and 'the Habs', as they are nicknamed in English, have won the Stanley Cup 24 times—more than any other team—most recently in the 1992–3 season.

Trovato conducted his research to test the hypothesis that the Stanley Cup playoffs in Quebec constitute a ceremonial occasion, and that as such, they provide a surge of social solidarity and a resulting drop in suicide rates across the province. Trovato further hypothesized that the performance of the team during the playoffs might also have an effect on suicide rates.

Using a variety of statistical techniques, Trovato tested data on all suicides occurring in Quebec between 1951 and 1992. According to Durkheim's research, the most alienated members of society are single or divorced men over the age of 35 years. Yet Trovato found no sign of decrease in suicide rates among this group, or among any other group in Quebec society during the Stanley Cup playoffs. It would appear that the playoffs do not create a ceremonial event that provides alienated people with a deterrent to suicide.

What Trovato did find, though, was an increase in the suicide rate among young men between the ages

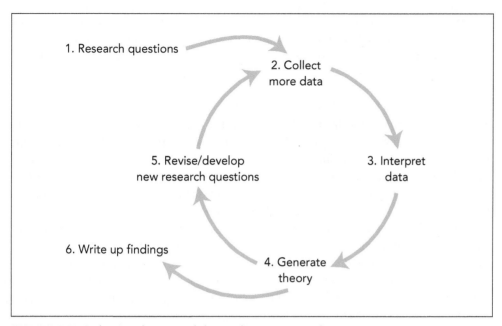

1. Research questions

2. Collect more data

3. Interpret data

4. Generate theory

5. Revise/develop new research questions

6. Write up findings

FIGURE 3.5 Inductive theory and the qualitative research process

of 15 and 34 in seasons when the Montreal Canadiens were eliminated from the playoffs. Young males, according to this research, do not commit suicide when the Canadiens lose but do commit suicide more frequently when the club is eliminated early from the playoffs.

Trovato makes sense of these findings by turning, once again, to Durkheim's theories. The loneliest people, the ones most likely to commit suicide, are socially isolated, lacking in social solidarity. Among young men aged 15 to 34, the most vulnerable and socially isolated are given a chance to experience social solidarity during the playoffs when they become part of the social rituals that accompany the games. Most often, drinking alcohol is an important part of the rituals that young Quebec men engage in while watching the playoffs. But this ritual has a very poor outcome for the most vulnerable, especially when the period of ritualistic social activity is cut short by the Canadiens' elimination from the playoffs. This can exacerbate feelings of alienation and loneliness, and lead, ultimately (as Trovato observed), to a higher suicide rate among the young men.

Twice in the team's history, the Vancouver Canucks reached Game 7 of the Stanley Cup finals and lost. On both occasions, fans took to the streets, vandalizing downtown stores and cars to express their disappointment. What role might social solidarity have played in this hockey-related violence?

language. Communications that pass between people are structured and are made meaningful in terms of social rules. An interpretivist approach to knowledge is an attempt to understand human action and behaviour by interpreting the symbolic meanings of human communicative interaction.

Max Weber and *Verstehen*

Max Weber described the interpretivist approach to sociological research as **Verstehen**, which translates literally as 'human understanding'. For Weber, *Verstehen* was an integral part of sociology, which he defined as 'that science which aims at interpretative understanding of social behaviour in order to arrive at a casual explanation of its course and its effects' (1915/1947, p. 88). As sociologists we exercise *Verstehen* through empathy, through our ability to imagine what it would be like to relive the experiences of our subjects.

Weber held that the difference between what a natural scientist does and what a social scientist does lies not in inherent differences in the methods of investigation that both use, but in the fact that the aims and interests of a natural scientist are different from those of a social scientist. A natural scientist is interested in observing natural events and eventually formulating abstract laws to explain those events. A social scientist may be interested in observing events in human social interaction, and in deriving abstract laws to explain them, but she also has to be concerned with particular qualities in the human actors she observes, and in the meaning that those actors, themselves, ascribe to their actions.

3. Constructivism as an Ontological Orientation

In contrast to the ontological orientation of objectivism is *constructivism*, a position consistent with a qualitative research strategy. This position derives from the belief that social phenomena and their meanings are social accomplishments, produced through social interaction. Such phenomena are, therefore, also in a state of constant becoming, or 'emergence'. We have encountered constructivism before in our discussion of the work of Berger and Luckmann (see Chapter 2). The view expressed by Berger and Luckmann in their classic work *The Social Construction of Reality* (1966) is that the categories we use to make sense of the world do not have built-in essences; instead, their meanings are constructed in the process of social interaction.

Fish is Fish (1970) is a wonderful children's book by Leo Lionni that offers an easily understood example of the constructivist perspective. In this book, Lionni tells the tale of Fish, who is curious about what happens on land but who can't go exploring himself because he can only breathe in water. Being a clever sort of fellow, Fish soon makes friends with Tadpole. Tadpole becomes Frog, who, unlike Fish, *is* able to go exploring outside the pond. Frog has many adventures on land, where he meets all sorts of creatures. When he returns to the pond he tells his friend Fish all about what he has seen—birds, cows, people, and such. With no experience of the world outside his pond, Fish imagines each of the creatures, but of course from his own point of view. He imagines cows as fish with udders, people as fish walking upright on their tails, and birds as fish with wings.

Lionni's tale resonates strongly with the constructivist position that reality is not just something 'out there' that can be perceived directly and objectively. How we perceive reality, how we interpret what we experience, is always filtered through what we already know. As researchers, and equally as members of society, we always use our existing experience to build new knowledge.

There are creative opportunities, as well as dangers, inherent in the fact that we all construct new knowledge based on our current understandings and perceptions. If we want to know something as simple as 'how many women attend my university?' or as complicated as 'why have women's participation rates at university and college increased over the last five decades?' we can either do the research ourselves or, like Fish, consult an 'authority' for the answer. In either case, from a constructivist ontological perspective, our experiences shape not only how we go about doing our research but also how we interpret or understand the results of our inquiries.

Consider another example, the concept of masculinity. A concept is a name given 'to a category that organizes observations and ideas by virtue of their possessing common features' (Bryman & Teevan, 2005, p. 381). Social scientists and historical researchers have been able to show that the concept of masculinity does not have the same meaning across all cultures, or even within a single culture over a long timespan. Instead, the meaning of masculinity is something that 'emerges' through social interaction. It is ephemeral in that it varies according to time and place. In short, the social world and its categories are not just facts that exist apart from social actors, exerting a pressure on them to conform; rather, they

Fish is Fish

Leo Lionni

Leo Lionni's *Fish is Fish*. Imagine describing a social setting you're very familiar with—the classroom, a hockey arena, the local dog park—to someone with no knowledge at all of the setting. How would you describe it? What categories would you use? What would you use as a frame of reference?

are constructed out of those very social actors' own interactions over a period of time (Bryman, 2004, p. 18). In this way, the circumstances that Durkheim thought of as external social facts actually have a history and are intimately connected with, and sensitive to, the behaviour (and especially changes in the behaviour) of the members of a given society.

To sum up, a qualitative research strategy is informed by a constructivist ontological orientation and an epistemological orientation of interpretivism, and uses theory inductively. Adopting a qualitative research strategy means that it is difficult for researchers to know ahead of time all the questions they might want to ask and investigate, the theory or theories they will ultimately find relevant to explain their discoveries, or even the exact methods that they should use to produce information or to solve problems (Becker 2009). The objective of a qualitative research strategy is more often than not to work inductively to generate theory as an outcome of the research.

STUDIES IN SOCIAL RESEARCH

The Breast Cancer 'Epidemic' from a Constructivist Ontological Perspective

A good example of approaching research from a constructivist ontological orientation is found in the work of Lantz and Booth (1998, as cited in Bryman, 2004) on the popular media depiction of breast cancer as an epidemic caused by women's use of birth control pills. In their research, Lantz and Booth (1998) analyzed articles published in a variety of popular magazines. They found that many of the articles ascribed blame to women who were portrayed as victims not just of a terrible disease but of their own behaviours, many of them involving what these women did to control their own fertility by taking birth control pills (Lantz & Booth, 1998, p. 915). In these magazines the breast cancer epidemic was constructed as a social fact. Moreover, it was ascribed a particular meaning: the consequence of the lifestyle choices made by the very women who were its victims. Yet fewer than 20 per cent of the cases of breast cancer are in women under the age of 50, who would be the ones likely to use, or to have used, birth control pills (Lantz & Booth, 1998, p. 915).

Breast Cancer $5.95 (Paperback)
Its Link to Abortion and the Birth Control Pill
By Dr. Chris Kahlenborn

Based on six years of study and a meticulous analysis of hundreds of scientific papers and other sources.

Learn More About This New Resource!

Download

The book above is advertised on a number of websites, including those of some Catholic bookstores. What are some possible motives for promoting the depiction of breast cancer as tied to use of the birth control pill?

4. Value Relevance

Qualitative social inquiry, which acknowledges the influence of social and cultural values on research, often has an emancipatory interest in empowerment and is informed by social ethics based on such principles as justice, beneficence, non-malfeasance, and autonomy (Beauchamp & Childress, 1989). Such emancipatory interests are behind most feminist critiques of traditional sociology, for example. Canadian feminist and sociologist Dorothy Smith (1990) describes conventional social science research as practices 'that convert what people experience directly in their everyday/everynight world into forms of knowledge in which people as subjects disappear and in which their perspectives on their own experience are transposed and subdued by the magisterial forms of objectifying discourse' (D. Smith, 1990, p. 4). That is to say, 'conventional social science' is little concerned with the needs or interests of the people being researched and is rarely concerned with the people behind the research.

Others interested in using their research to benefit those whom they study note that calls have come from governments of developing countries to change the way in which information is gathered, processed, and released. Literacy workers and popular educators like Paulo Freire, for example, have used use the context of popular education as a means of transforming consciousness and social relations (Kirby & McKenna, 1989). In place of traditional research, some researchers, influenced by **standpoint epistemology**, argue in favour of research that is done by people who are 'on the margins of the production of knowledge'—in other words, research done by researchers who are not trained sociologists but who are regular people coping with the challenges of their day-to-day lives. These people can use

standpoint epistemology
The view that all research and knowledge production is directly related to the vantage point or social location of the researcher.

their unique experiences to help them design and carry out their own research projects and to 'create knowledge that will describe, explain or help change the world in which they live' (Kirby & McKenna, 1989, p. 17). From a standpoint epistemology perspective, even graffiti messages like 'If voting could change the system it would be illegal' or 'We're poor and we know why' come from individuals who are analyzing their experience. Making sense in this way, it is argued, can lead people to take action and claim space to express their analysis (Kirby & McKenna, 1989, p. 17).

This point of view has much in common with the one expressed by those social scientists who argue that all research and knowledge production is directly related to the vantage point or social location of the researcher. According to Joyce McCarl Nielsen, 'standpoint epistemology', as this view is known,

> begins with the idea that less powerful members of society have the potential for a more complete view of social reality than others, precisely because of their disadvantaged position. That is, in order to survive (socially and sometimes even physically) subordinate persons are attuned to or attentive to the perspective of the dominant class (for example, white, male, wealthy) as well as their own. This awareness gives them the potential for . . . 'double vision', or double consciousness—a knowledge, awareness of, and sensitivity to both the dominant world view of society and their own minority (for example, female, black, poor) perspective. (Nielsen, 1990, p. 10)

Feminist researcher Nancy Hartsock (1983) argues that a standpoint epistemology is based on the following premises:

1. The material life of the researcher—what she does for a living, what her standard of living and the quality of her material surroundings are like, and so on—structures and limits that researcher's understandings. Being an administrative assistant produces a different standpoint to being the same company's chief executive officer.
2. Powerful members of society and less powerful members of the same society often have opposing understandings of or standpoints on the social world.
3. Accepting the premise that one's everyday life has epistemological consequences, standpoint theorists argue that the standpoint of the less powerful group has more potential for providing a good analysis than that of the more powerful group. It is in the interests of the members of the more powerful group to maintain and legitimize their position. Thus their understanding of the social world is limited to what is needed to accomplish that legitimizing.

Research conducted from a particular standpoint is based on the premise that the point of view of both the researchers and the researched is shaped by their social positioning and material activities. This, of course, is consistent with Weber's views. However, contemporary feminists and other researchers influenced by standpoint epistemology part ways with Weber on the issues of the necessity (or even the possibility) of ever leaving behind one's values, or epistemological orientation, to conduct a value-free analysis. Nor would they agree on the desirability of the researcher's ending his participation once his research has been completed. Many contemporary researchers now feel that it is incumbent on the researcher to make sure that his research is used to help the people he studies.

STUDIES IN SOCIAL RESEARCH

Theory, Ontology, Epistemology, and Qualitative Research: Memorializing the Stonewall Riots

An inductive approach to theory, the use of an interpretivist epistemological orientation and a constructivist ontological orientation, and the adoption of a value-relevant stance are the trademarks of qualitative sociological research. Research questions best answered by a qualitative research strategy are those requiring deep investigation, usually into the ways in which the research subjects understand their own social worlds. The following example—a study of the commemoration of the Stonewall riots—illustrates the use of a qualitative research strategy.

The Stonewall riots, which took place in New York City's Greenwich Village in 1969, are enshrined in the collective memory of the gay community as a defining event that started the gay rights movement in the US and around the world. Annual 'Gay Pride' parades, held in cities around the world, celebrate these riots as the start of the gay rights movement. Yet four other events similar to the Stonewall riots, which took place in San Francisco, Los Angeles, and New York in the 1960s, are not so well remembered. Sociologists Elizabeth Armstrong and Suzanna Crage (2006) set out to answer this question: Why are the Stonewall riots remembered—and, indeed, commemorated—as the start of the gay rights movement, while other equally significant riots do not receive the same treatment? To find an answer the two social researchers took an inductive approach to theorizing, and, accordingly, developed an explanation to their question only after they had conducted their research.

The Stonewall riots took place around the Stonewall Inn, a gay bar in Greenwich Village, when that bar was raided by police in the early hours of 28 June 1969. During the 1960s, government-sponsored persecution of sexual minorities was commonplace, and often included police raids on gay bars. Few establishments in the US openly welcomed gay patrons in the 1950s and 1960s; the Stonewall Inn was one of the exceptions. Owned by people with ties to the Mafia and located in a densely populated, pedestrian-friendly neighbourhood, it catered to

The Stonewall Inn. The sign in the window reads: 'We homosexuals plead with our people to please help maintain peaceful and quiet conduct on the streets of the Village.'

some of the poorest and most marginalized members of the gay community living in New York City.

In spite of the acknowledged significance of the 1969 riots (US president Bill Clinton designated the Stonewall Inn and the area around it a national historic landmark in February 2000), the episode does not mark the first time that gays fought back against police. Nor was the raid on Stonewall the first to foment political organizing (Armstrong & Crage, 2006, p. 725). Yet other similar events in the US failed to achieve the stature of Stonewall, and have been almost forgotten. Why did the events at Stonewall take on such significance, while others were completely lost to collective memory? To answer this question Armstrong and Crage adopted an *interpretivist epistemological orientation* and sought to understand how the gay activists in New York came to understand their own position and to rebel against their treatment as 'deviants' and against the police oppression that accompanied that designation.

Armstrong and Crage describe collective memories as 'images of the past' that have been selected, reproduced, and commemorated by a social group via memorials, publications, statutes, and parades (Olick & Robbins, 1988, p. 106; Wagner-Pacifici, 1996, p. 203, as cited in Armstrong & Crage, 2006). Taking a *constructivist ontological approach* to their research, they examined the gay riots and their meaning as social accomplishments—that is, as products of people's social interactions. Stonewall became a defining, commemorable moment not because it was the first gay riot but because it was the first such event 'to occur at a time and place where . . . gay activists had adequate mnemonic capacity to institutionalize the gay pride parade as a commemorative vehicle' (Armstrong & Crage, 2006, p. 725). In other words, Stonewall became memorable as a result of the way that the people who participated in the riots were able to interact with each other and to make lasting memories about the riots that became institutionalized. By the mid-1960s, gay activists had already successfully blocked police use of mass arrests and entrapment and had forced the New York Liquor Authority to acknowledge that liquor licences could not be revoked merely because known gays frequented a bar (Armstrong & Crage, 2006, p. 736). At the same time, movement members pursued efforts to get mainstream media coverage in newspapers with national distribution. In early 1969, well before the riots, gay activists in New York City had already founded a radical group in Greenwich Village and were discussing 'gay power' in their publications (Carter, 2004, p. 122; Rodwell, 1968, as cited in Armstrong & Crage, 2006, p. 736).

By June 1969 the gay movement in New York had grown in strength and militancy. The Stonewall Inn, with its ties to the Mafia and its customer base of 'homeless teens, queens, and others not welcome elsewhere', was being raided about once a month. But during the raid of 28 June, which took place in the early hours of the morning, an angry crowd formed and trapped the police inside the bar. The riot escalated, eventually involving over a thousand rioters and several hundred police (Leitsch, 1969a, as cited in Armstrong & Crage, 2006, p. 737). The rioters included people from many different backgrounds and included both 'marginalized and more privileged elements of the homosexual community' (Armstrong & Crage, 2006, p. 737). When the activists called their contacts in the local media, reporters showed up, giving the 'event' extensive coverage in the following day's newspapers. Although the coverage was largely homophobic, the result was that a crowd turned up to see the ruined bar, giving activists an opportunity to distribute gay liberation flyers. When the riot police made a second appearance, another night of rioting followed. Participants felt that something of historic significance had happened, and accounts of the riots continued to be published over the next several months.

New York activists now had the task of persuading fellow activists in other cities across the country to participate in the commemorative events. Gay activists had to be persuaded that 'gay commemoration was appropriate, that Stonewall was commemorable, and that hosting a public event was the way to do it' (Armstrong & Crage, 2006, pp. 739–40). By 1972, gay rights activists in a few cities were holding commemorative events. 'Gay Pride Week' was a success, and it continues to be celebrated with large crowds and boisterous parades around the world. As Armstrong and Crage observe, 'Activists discovered that bringing homosexuals together in public had a magical emotional impact—the ritual created collective effervescence by visually and experientially counteracting the view that homosexuality is private and shameful' (2006, p. 742).

Police raids on the gay community continued in the late 1960s and early 1970s. By studying the responses to these raids, Armstrong and Crage were able to advance a complex analysis of the events and to offer an explanation of why the Stonewall riots became known as the start of the gay liberation movement. Their research strategy was clearly value-relevant, as it was influenced by concerns for the interests and well-being of the people behind the research. As an example of inductive research, Armstrong and Crage's study shows how research can be used to develop a generalizable theory, in this case about how specific events become memorable. The researchers showed that no event is inherently commemorable; it is *made* commemorable through the actions and intentions of those involved.

SUMMARY

This chapter introduced the four common factors that influence all sociological research: values, epistemology, ontology, and theory.

In and of themselves, raw data are meaningless. Empirical facts become relevant in relation to a theory—an explanation of some observed regularity that directs our attention to certain aspects of whatever it is we are currently studying. Sociologists use theory *deductively* to guide the collection of data, or they arrive at theory *inductively*, when they draw generalizable inferences after the data has been collected and analyzed. Theory is typically used deductively in conjunction with a quantitative research strategy. It is arrived at inductively most frequently in conjunction with a qualitative research strategy.

Epistemological questions about the limitations of knowledge are treated differently in qualitative and quantitative research strategies. Most often, those who adopt a quantitative research strategy take an epistemological position known as *positivism*, arguing that the social world can be studied using the same methods and proofs used in the natural sciences. Those who adopt a qualitative research strategy often hold that sociologists should adopt an *interpretivist* epistemological orientation, arguing that there is an important difference between people (the research subjects of sociology) and the kinds of research objects studied by the natural sciences.

Ontological questions about what sociologists should or can expect to be able to study also receive different answers depending on whether a qualitative or quantitative research strategy is adopted. With a qualitative research strategy, sociologists generally accept that the social entities we study can be considered as social constructions (*constructionism*). With a quantitative research strategy, the entities under study are considered to be independent of the social actors who are involved (*objectivism*). When a sociologist decides on a quantitative research strategy, it usually means he has chosen to take a *value-neutral* stance, and believes that he can and must refrain from imposing his own values on the research process. By contrast, adopting a qualitative research strategy usually entails taking a *value-relevant* stance, meaning that the researcher holds that it is not possible to keep personal values and beliefs in complete check and independent of the research.

DISCUSSION QUESTIONS

1. What are the main factors influencing all sociological research?
2. Summarize the role of theory in sociological research. Explain the difference between inductive and deductive use of theory.
3. What are the main differences between 'grand theories', 'theories of the middle range', and 'working hypotheses'?
4. To what extent does a quantitative research strategy differ from a qualitative research strategy? What are some of the similarities? What are the benefits and drawbacks of each?
5. List some of the areas where the values of a researcher can have an influence over the research process. Is it possible for sociological research to maintain a position of value neutrality?
6. Max Weber believed that a sociologist should never advise anyone about what should or should not be done with that sociologist's research. Do you agree or disagree? Explain.
7. Do Durkheim's insights into suicide have any relevance for sociologists today? Why or why not?
8. The work of feminist researchers is often informed by principles of social justice and an interest in the empowerment of women. Their research is influenced by standpoint epistemology, and they argue in favour of designing research that will help those on the margins to change the world in which they live. Describe some of the premises of standpoint epistemology. Should research be done specifically to help bring about the emancipation of oppressed groups? Are there any drawbacks to conducting this kind of research?

4 Research Design and Research Methods

CHAPTER OUTLINE

LEARNING OBJECTIVES

In this chapter you will:

- learn how a research design is chosen
- differentiate between simple case studies, longitudinal studies, comparison studies, longitudinal comparison studies, and experiments
- understand the difference between independent and dependant variables
- learn about a variety of research methods that sociologists use to collect data
- gain a better understanding of how sociologists conduct surveys, questionnaires, and interviews
- discover how sociologists have used content analysis and participant observation as research methods
- become familiar with the role of ethics in sociological research.

INTRODUCTION

research design
The framework for collecting and analyzing data.

research methods
The actual techniques for collecting and analyzing data.

As a researcher in sociology, deciding on a qualitative or quantitative research strategy is just the first of three key decisions you will have to make before you begin your research. You must also decide on a **research design**—the framework you are going to use for collecting and analyzing data—and choose one or more research methods, the actual techniques you will use to collect data. Sociologists have developed three main **research methods** or techniques for collecting data.

RESEARCH DESIGN

Five different research designs are used in sociological research:

- case study
- longitudinal study
- comparison (or cross-sectional) study
- longitudinal comparison study
- experiment.

In this section we will look, in turn, at each of these designs, whose differences are summarized in Figure 4.1.

The Simple Case Study

case study
A type of research design that focuses on a detailed analysis of a single case or situation, usually a community or organization, in a specific location.

participant observation
A research method in which a researcher is immersed over a period of time in the social setting under study in order to observe, listen to, and gather information on the social life and culture of the people she or he is studying.

longitudinal study
A research design in which data is collected on the same unit of analysis, on at least two separate occasions.

As a research design, a simple **case study** answers the question *What is happening?* In sociology, a case study is a detailed analysis of a single case, usually focused on a community or organization in a specific location. There have been many famous case studies done in sociology. One example is William Foote Whyte's *Street Corner Society* (1955), a classic case study of social relations, social structure, and politics in a poor Italian community ('Cornerville') in Boston during the late 1930s. In carrying out this research, Whyte helped pioneer the technique of participant observation, a research method often used along with a case study research design. **Participant observation** involves a researcher immersing himself over a period of some time in the social setting he wishes to study. During that time the researcher observes, listens to, and gathers information on the social life and culture of the people he is studying. We will discuss this and other research methods later in the chapter.

Another example of a simple case study is Paul Willis's *Learning to Labour: How Working Class Kids Get Working Class Jobs* (1977), a now classic case study of working-class youth in Great Britain. Willis and his co-workers studied the transition from school to work experienced by white, non-academic, working-class 'lads' in an industrial town ('Hammerstown') in the West Midlands of England. (This study is discussed in greater detail later in this chapter, in the section on research methods.)

The Longitudinal Study

A **longitudinal study** involves two or more case studies of the same units of analysis (e.g. individuals, families, organizations) with a certain amount of time between the studies, conducted in order to answer the question, *Has there been any change over a period of time?* (Bouma, Ling, & Wilkinson, 2009, p. 102). Longitudinal studies occur in a number of circumstances:

- When the researcher remains a member of, or participant in, the community under study, over a period of several months or even several years.
- When a case that has been studied at one point in time is returned to at a later point in time.
- When archival materials are used and compared to contemporary situations.

A classic example of a longitudinal case study is Robert Lynd and Helen Lynd's study of 'Middletown'. Their early work, done in the 1920s, is documented in *Middletown: A Study in Contemporary American Culture* (Lynd & Lynd, 1929); Robert Lynd presented the results

TYPE OF RESEARCH DESIGN	QUESTIONS ASKED
1. Simple case study (A)	What is happening? Is there a relationship between variables X and Y in entity A, where entity A is a group, a social situation, text, or other focus of research?
2. Longitudinal study (A) Time 1 (A) Time 2	Has there been a change in A? Is the relationship between variable X and Y in the entity A the same or different at time 1 and time 2?
3. Comparison study (A) (B)	Are A and B different? Is the relationship between variables X and Y the same in entities A and B?
4. Longitudinal comparison study (A) (A) (B) (B) Time 1 Time 2	Are A and B different through time? Has there been a change over time in the relationship between X and Y in entity A compared to entity B?
5. Experiment Experimental Group (A) (A) Control Group (B) (B) Time 1 Time 2	Is the difference between A and B due to a change in the independent variable? Is the difference in Y (dependent variable) between Group A and Group B due to a change in X (the independent variable)?

FIGURE 4.1 Five types of research design and research questions asked

Source: Adapted from Bouma, Ling, & Wilkinson, 2009, pp. 97–8.

of a follow-up study, conducted in the 1930s, in *Middletown in Transition* (R. Lynd, 1937). 'Middletown' was in fact Muncie, Indiana, and the Lynds were hired to do the first study by the Rockefeller Institute of Social and Religious Research. During the 1920s there had been a great deal of labour unrest in the United States, and the institute's founder, John D. Rockefeller, Jr, felt that religion might have an important role to play in bridging the divergent interests of capital on the one hand and organized labour on the other.

What the Lynds discovered was a Muncie divided along simple class lines—lines marked geographically by the White River that runs through town. There was a working class, whose members lived on the south and east sides of town and who held wage jobs in manufacturing, small business, and commerce. There was a business class, whose members lived on the north and west sides of the city, and who included managers, doctors, lawyers, educators, and business owners. This pattern of class division has continued even into the twenty-first century.

When Robert Lynd returned to 'Middletown' by himself in 1935 to do his follow-up study, he discovered that while the economic climate had changed—it was the height of the Great Depression—many of the social and cultural patterns he had noticed previously had not. For example, the themes and messages of sermons delivered by ministers to their congregations in 1933 were scarcely different from those Lynd had heard in 1924. Indeed,

Dated 1941, this postcard shows some of Muncie's landmark edifices, from the courthouse and various places of learning to the monument named 'Appeal to the Great Spirit'. What do you think of the way the town's Aboriginal origins have been represented?

Caplow and associates (1982), in a follow-up study done over forty years later, reported that sermon topics of 1977 were about the same as they had been in 1924. One important difference that Caplow noted, however, was the nature of religious chauvinism. In 1924, most

PROFILES IN SOCIOLOGY

Margaret Bourke-White (1904–1971)

Photojournalism is not considered a branch of sociology. However, photojournalists such as Margaret Bourke-White and Jacob Riis (profiled in the next chapter) have provided sociologists with artifacts that are invaluable to social research as they document, in a way that words cannot, the customs, manners, and living conditions of people serving as subjects of sociological inquiry.

American photographer and photojournalist Margaret Bourke-White was born in 1904 in The Bronx, New York, the daughter of a Polish-Jewish father and an English-Irish mother. Bourke-White received her degree from Cornell University in 1927. Although her interest in photography began as a hobby (she attended a one-week course at Columbia University, using a $20 camera), she quickly turned it into a career. She got her start as a professional industrial photographer in Cleveland, Ohio, at the Otis Steel Company, when she was in her early twenties. She helped found photojournalism as a profession, and was the first women to be hired as a photojournalist. In a career of 'firsts', she was the first photographer hired by *Fortune* magazine (1929), the first Western photographer allowed into the USSR (1930), the first female photojournalist for *Life* magazine (1935—in fact, she shot the cover photo for the magazine's inaugural issue in 1936), the first female war correspondent, and the first photographer allowed into combat zones during World War II, when she flew in American bombers to document the destruction caused by their bombing raids; she was also among the first photographers to document the Nazi death camps.

Taken by Margaret Bourke-White in 1937—the year of Robert Lynd's second study of 'Middletown'—this photo of men at a Muncie pool hall suggests the town's acceptance of the 'New Deal' economic measures introduced by Franklin Delano Roosevelt in 1933 to combat the Depression. Do you think an establishment like this would attract patrons from both the working and business classes? What is the value of such an image to Lynd's study?

In 1936 Bourke-White toured the American South, taking pictures for Erskine Cladwell's book, *You Have Seen Their Faces*, which documented the rural poor. After the Second World War she covered Pakistan and India for *Life*, and photographed Mahatma Gandhi for the last time, just hours before he was assassinated. During the 1950s she covered the Korean War and the infamous South African gold mines, also for *Life*.

For those who are interested in learning more about Margaret Bourke-White's life and work, a short but insightful documentary is available on YouTube: www.youtube.com/watch?v=iAkBu63H8H0&feature=youtu.be.

people in 'Middletown' felt that their own religion was the only 'right' religion, and that everyone else should convert. By 1977, that sentiment was no longer expressed. Rules about what could or could not be done on Sundays, strictly enforced in 1924, were no longer in force in 1977. But answers to questions about religion and personal faith given in 1924 remained similar to the ones given in 1977, and church attendance in 1977 was actually higher than it was in 1924, especially because in 1924 working-class members could not afford to go to church, either because of the cost of paying into the collection or because they could not afford 'Sunday' clothes.

comparison (or cross-sectional) study
A research design that studies the relationship between two or more variables involving two or more cases at the same point in time.

The Comparison Study (or Cross-sectional Study)

A **comparison** (or **cross-sectional**) **study** examines patterns of relationship between two or more variables in two or more cases at the same point in time. A researcher who uses this type of research design is interested in variations at a single point in time between people, social

STUDIES IN SOCIAL RESEARCH

Jennifer Hook's Study of Men and Unpaid Domestic Work

Jennifer L. Hook (2006) used a longitudinal comparison research design when she studied men's housework and childcare behaviours in 20 countries over the period 1965–2003. Hook undertook the study in order to test hypotheses about the relationship between national context and men's unpaid work behaviours. Is the extent of a man's involvement in family life entirely attributable to his individual characteristics or does the national context in which he lives help or hinder his behaviour with respect to family life?

During the mid-1900s, women's participation in the labour force increased significantly in the West. As a result, new family models emerged, and the roles of men and women were altered from the traditional male breadwinner/female caregiver division of labour. Today, women's labour force participation rates have reached parity with men's. However, men have not responded to this in predicted ways: while the amount of time men spend on housework and childcare has increased from mid-twentieth-century levels, it has not reached parity with the time women spend on those activities (Bianchi, et al., 2000; Gershuny, 2000; Gershuny, Godwin, & Jones, 1994, as cited in Hook, 2006, p. 639). Moreover, nations with very different national employment practices

and social policy configurations show similar trends in unpaid domestic work unevenly divided between men and women.

In researching her topic, Hook drew on data from the *Multinational Time Use Study*, a collection of over 50 harmonized time-use datasets from over 20 countries. She used 44 surveys from this collection, spanning the period 1965–2003. This data provided background and time expenditure statistics for 98,780 respondents aged 20–59 (Hook, 2006, p. 644).

Hook's research showed that the 'effect of living with a child on men's unpaid work time is contingent on national employment practices and policies', including women's labour force participation rate and national parental leave provisions (Hook, 2006, p. 644). In countries with lengthy parental leave, men's participation in unpaid family labour actually decreased. For example, in countries offering parental leave of 42 weeks, men's unpaid labour was three minutes less per day than in nations offering no parental leave, as, for example, the United States and Australia in the early 1990s. Moreover, in many nations women's labour force participation is part-time, thus removing demands that men do more household work.

classes, age groups, in terms of whichever dependent variables have been chosen for study. The benefit of this design is that comparing the occurrence of the same social phenomena in two or more cases—be they organizations, community groups, families, etc.—helps us to better understand those phenomena. Cross-cultural research and cross-national research, which involve studying the same social phenomena as they occur in different cultures or parts of the country, are typical forms of comparison studies.

The Longitudinal Comparison Study

Combine the comparison and longitudinal approaches, and the result is a **longitudinal comparison study**, a research design that can be used to answer the general question, *Have the differences between X and Y in groups A and B changed over time?* (Bouma, et al., 2009, p. 109). Bouma, Ling, and Wilkinson use the following example to illustrate the longitudinal comparison research design:

longitudinal comparison study
A research design that measures the same variable in two or more groups and compares the changes in that variable over time.

It is clearly not the case that all women want to avoid unpaid family work and to coerce men into doing more. Nor is it the case that all men want to avoid doing unpaid family work and to leave it all up to women. Some women are reluctant to give up their role as maternal gatekeepers; some men want greater paternal rights and more involvement in the home. But what Hook was able to demonstrate was that gender relations involve not just individual but also household and national-level factors. By using a longitudinal comparative research design, Hook was able to observe how variations in the effect of living with children on men's unpaid domestic labour are contingent upon national context, including women's work hours, length of parental leave, and availability of paternity leave (Hook, 2006, p. 644). In fact, she uncovered a number of national factors that bear on men's and women's work arrangements, both paid and unpaid. The results of her research have implications for national policy debates, as they help us to understand the role of federal social policies on work and parental leave in maintaining, or altering, persisting gender inequalities. Her work thus helps to shift the focus away from the behaviours of individual men and women, and toward the national-level policies that have an effect on maintaining or changing gender inequalities.

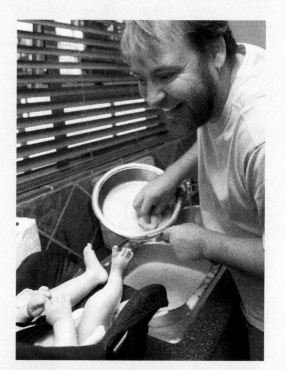

What independent variables do you think might influence a man's willingness to take on an equal share of the domestic chores? Age? Ethnic background? Employment status? Level of income? Level of education attained?

A good example of this type of research would be a study of two groups of babies: one group bottle-fed and the other breast-fed. Each group would be measured at the same interval—weekly for eight weeks beginning one week after birth.

STUDIES IN SOCIAL RESEARCH

Stanley Milgram's Experiment: Obedience to Authority

In the early 1960s, Stanley Milgram, a psychologist at Yale University, conducted a series of social psychology experiments to measure the extent to which a research subject could be induced to cause harm to another research subject. The findings of that research were published by Milgram in a 1963 issue of the *Journal of Abnormal and Social Psychology*, and discussed more thoroughly in his book *Obedience to Authority: An Experimental View* (1974).

Milgram was interested in answering this question: Under what conditions will a person comply with the orders of someone else that they perceive to be in authority? Conducting his experiments just after the start of the trial of Nazi war criminal Adolf Eichman, Milgram was interested in obedience to authority that had serious consequences, such as the obedience shown by soldiers who carry out orders from superiors to massacre civilians during wartime. In writing about his experiment, Milgram noted that obedience is a basic part of social life: all communal living requires some system of authority. 'For many people,' Milgram tells us, 'obedience is a deeply ingrained behaviour tendency.' It is 'a potent impulse' that often can override an individual's 'training in ethics, sympathy, and moral conduct' (1974).

Milgram wanted to find out how 'average people' behaved in real-life situations when confronted with commands from an authority figure to carry out actions that would most likely come into conflict with their ethical and moral training. To do this, he designed an experiment to test 'how much pain an ordinary citizen would inflict on another person simply because he was ordered to by an experimental scientist' (1974).

Milgram's experiment involved duping a naive volunteer—the real subject of the experiment—into thinking that all others involved in the project were either genuine researchers or uninformed participants who were likewise volunteering to aid in the project. The naive volunteer was assigned the role of teacher, and then asked by an actor posing as a research scientist to administer shocks to another actor posing as a learner every time the learner made a spelling mistake. The naive research subject was told the experiment was about learning. What he or she did not know was

Public Announcement

WE WILL PAY YOU $4.00 FOR ONE HOUR OF YOUR TIME

Persons Needed for a Study of Memory

*We will pay five hundred New Haven men to help us complete a scientific study of memory and learning. The study is being done at Yale University.

*Each person who participates will be paid $4.00 (plus 50¢ carfare) for approximately 1 hour's time. We need you for only one hour: there are no further obligations. You may choose the time you would like to come (evenings, weekdays, or weekends).

*No special training, education, or experience is needed. We want:

Factory workers	Businessmen	Construction workers
City employees	Clerks	Salespeople
Laborers	Professional people	White-collar workers
Barbers	Telephone workers	Others

All persons must be between the ages of 20 and 50. High school and college students cannot be used.

*If you meet these qualifications, fill out the coupon below and mail it now to Professor Stanley Milgram, Department of Psychology, Yale University, New Haven. You will be notified later of the specific time and place of the study. We reserve the right to decline any application.

*You will be paid $4.00 (plus 50¢ carfare) as soon as you arrive at the laboratory.

TO:
PROF. STANLEY MILGRAM, DEPARTMENT OF PSYCHOLOGY, YALE UNIVERSITY, NEW HAVEN, CONN. I want to take part in this study of memory and learning. I am between the ages of 20 and 50. I will be paid $4.00 (plus 50¢ carfare) if I participate.

NAME (Please Print)..

ADDRESS ....

TELEPHONE NO.................. Best time to call you ....

AGE .... OCCUPATION .... SEX ......

CAN YOU COME:
WEEKDAYS .... EVENINGS .... WEEKENDS ....

... This study is longitudinal in that it involves a series of measures of the same variables in the same groups over time. It is also a comparison because it compares two separate groups. (Bouma, et al., 2009, p. 109)

that the learner was deliberately making mistakes and that no real electric shocks were being delivered.

Throughout the experiment, whenever the 'teacher' hesitated to administer the next level of shock to the 'learner', the 'research scientist' gave the 'teacher' one of four verbal prompts:

1. Please continue.
2. The experiment requires that you continue.
3. It is absolutely essential that you continue.
4. You have no other choice, you *must* go on.

Aside from the presence of the 'research scientist' and his verbal encouragement to continue, 'teachers' were free to stop administering shocks at any point during the experiment. Most of the 'teachers' showed anxiety and concern, especially when the 'learner' began exclaiming that he had heart trouble. Yet in his first set of experiments, Milgram found that 40 per cent of the 'teachers' in his research were willing to administer the full 450-volt shock, with only one 'teacher' refusing to continue past the 300-volt mark. What Milgram found was stunning: '[t]he extreme willingness of adults to go to almost any lengths on the command of an authority constitutes the chief finding of the study and the fact most urgently demanding explanation' (Milgram, 1974, p. 8).

Milgram's experiments are even more remarkable for their thoroughness: Milgram conducted at least 21 variations of this basic experiment to see which, if any, modifications in the experiment might have consequences for the extent to which 'teachers' were willing to administer shocks. For instance, he found that when two or more 'teachers' were present in the room—one of them a naive volunteer, the other an actor—and the actor/'teacher' refused to continue, the vast majority of the 'naive teachers' also refused,

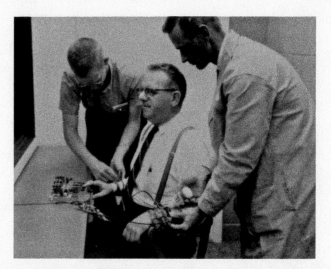

Electrodes are attached to the wrist of a learner in the Milgram experiment. How do you think you would behave placed between a supposed research subject crying out in pain at the shocks you're administering and an authority figure commanding you to continue?

with just 4 out of 40 continuing to administer the highest shock. When the research scientist left the room and gave orders via phone instead of in person, only 9 of 40 'teachers' were fully obedient (Milgram, 1974, p. 207, as cited in Blass, 1991, p. 398).

In commenting on the results of his research Milgram concluded that 'ordinary people, simply doing their jobs, and without any particular hostility on their part, can become agents in a terrible destructive process. Moreover, even when the destructive effects of their work become patently clear and they are asked to carry out actions incompatible with fundamental standards of morality, relatively few people have the resources needed to resist authority' (Milgram, 1973).

Experimental Research

An experimental research design is used to determine what (if any) effect a change in one variable has on another (Bouma, et al., 2009, p. 113). An experimental research design, by specifying that a change in one variable causes a change in another, is said to provide the most rigorous way of testing a hypothesis. Experiments are held as the touchstone against which to compare all other forms of research. Yet although experimental research is considered the strongest of all research designs in terms of producing robust and trustworthy results with internal validity, true experiments are rarely conducted in sociology. They are more frequently used in the related areas of social psychology, organizational studies, and social policy (Bryman, 2004, p. 34).

There is an important distinction to be made between *laboratory experiments*, which take place in the controlled environment of a university or hospital lab, and *field experiments*, which take place in real-life settings. While the majority of experiments that social scientists are likely to conduct are field experiments, lab experiments are often conducted by social psychologists, as we saw in the box beginning on page 92, which details a very famous example of one such experiment.

Once you have settled on your research question, chosen the appropriate research strategy and research design, and selected your research site and the participants for your study, you still must decide on the variables you are going to study and the methods you will use to collect your data. It is to these very important aspects of the research process that we now turn.

VARIABLES

variable
A concept or feature of something that is capable of varying in amount or quality, e.g. income (amount) or social class (quality).

independent variable
A variable that affects, but is not affected by, the variation or occurrence of another variable (the dependent variable).

dependent variable
A variable that is caused or affected by an independent variable.

In general, the objective of all sociology research, whether it is carried out using a qualitative or a quantitative research strategy, is to collect data on the 'observed' changes in one or more variables. A **variable** is a type of concept that is capable of varying in amount or quality. For example, the concept 'social class' may be treated as a variable; one can be a member of the upper class, the working class, the capitalist class, and so on.

A variable is something that it is possible to have more or less of; it may also be something that exists in different 'states' or 'categories' (Bouma, Ling, & Wilkinson, 2009, p. 49). Income is an example of a variable: it can be measured in the number of dollars an individual earns in a year. It is an attribute of a given unit of analysis—in this case, an individual—that is under study. Religion is another example of a variable; being Catholic, Protestant, Muslim, or Jewish is an attribute that distinguishes individuals from one another (Bryman & Teevan, 2005, p. 26).

All variables are considered to be either independent or dependent. An **independent variable** is a variable that has been determined to have a causal impact on a dependent variable; as it varies, so does the dependent variable. A **dependent variable**, then, is a variable that is caused or influenced by an independent variable. For example, we have learned that an individual's decision to attend university is influenced by his or her parents' education level and income; it is also influenced by whether or not the individual's friends are planning to go to university. In this example, the decision to attend university is the dependent variable; parents' education, parents' income, and friends' university choices are all independent variables.

In the natural sciences, there is usually agreement among researchers about the units of analysis to be studied, the kinds of variables to be measured, the units by which those variables will be measured, and the instruments with which to measure those units. If a paleontologist wants to measure the height of a skeleton, he can measure it in inches or metres using a tape measure. A kinesiologist can measure a person's reaction time in seconds using a stop watch, while an electrical engineer can study electric current in terms of its variable strength, which can be measured in amps using an ammeter.

When it comes to sociology, however, there is little agreement about the nature of commonly studied variables such as social class, social status, and even race. Sociologists hold different opinions about how these and other variables are to be measured. It is hardly surprising, then, that they also hold widely varying opinions about what instruments to use to do the measuring. Here are a few of the more common social variables that sociologists examine in their research:

• social class	• sexual orientation	• race
• social status	• education level	• ethnicity
• age	• occupation	• income level
• gender	• marital status	• employment status

While sociologists study a wide variety of social variables and have a dizzying variety of ways to **operationalize** and measure those variables, they only have a few methods that they use to collect their data.

operationalize
A concept is operationalized when it is defined in a way that can be measured through empirical observations.

RESEARCH METHODS

Research methods are the actual techniques used for collecting data about the variables you have chosen to study. Sociologists have developed three main methods or techniques of collecting data:

- *Surveys, questionnaires, and interviews.* Sociologists use face-to-face, online, or self-administered questionnaires to capture respondents' responses to questions.
- *Observation.* Sociologists observe and record what is happening.
- *Content analysis.* Sociologists examine and analyze the content of documents, texts, and other recorded materials such as films, voice recordings, and photographs.

For a quantitative research strategy, the main methods for gathering data are content analysis of documents, surveys, structured interviews and questionnaires; and structured observation. The main methods for collecting data within a qualitative research strategy include fieldwork, participant observation, focus groups and less-structured interviews, and content analysis of documents. These methods will be discussed in the sections that follow.

RESEARCH METHODS USED WITH A QUANTITATIVE RESEARCH STRATEGY

A quantitative research strategy involves the collection of numerical data, and a deductive relationship between theory and research. This approach to research, which takes an objectivist stance towards the conception of social reality, has a lot in common with the approach

survey

An investigation of the opinions, characteristics, or experience of a group of people, based on a series of questions designed to generate quantitative data on two or more variables. The data collected are examined for any patterns of relationship between and among the variables.

questionnaire

A set of questions with a choice of answers, devised and administered to respondents for the purposes of a survey or statistical study.

interview

A conversation, usually face-to-face, guided by a series of questions and conducted in order to discover the opinions or experience of someone.

taken in the natural sciences (Bryman & Teevan, 2005, p. 50). Quantitative research generally follows a conventional series of steps, outlined in Figure 4.2.

Surveys, Questionnaires, and Interviews

A **survey** is a research technique that entails the collection of (usually quantifiable) data from a number of people (always more than one person, and usually many more than one person) at a single point in time. Surveys are usually used in conjunction with a comparison or cross-sectional study. The objective of a survey is to collect quantitative data from respondents about two or more variables and then to examine those data in relation to one another to discern any patterns in their relationship.

Data are most frequently collected using either a self-administered **questionnaire** (typically either mailed or online) or via an **interview** (administered over the phone, in person, or via the Web). There are three varieties of interview: structured, semi-structured, and unstructured. In a *structured interview*, an interviewer reads the same questions, in the same way and in the same order, to all the people chosen to be part of the survey. The questions are specific, and respondents are usually offered a limited and fixed range of answers from which to choose their responses. In a *semi-structured interview* the interviewer may vary the order of the questions she asks, and may ask additional questions if she thinks the situation

1. Theory
    ↓
2. Hypothesis
    ↓
3. Research design
    ↓
4. Research methods/devise measures of concepts
    ↓
5. Select research site(s)
    ↓
6. Select research subjects/respondents
    ↓
7. Administer research instruments/collect data
    ↓
8. Process data
    ↓
9. Analyze data
    ↓
10. Findings/conclusions
    ↓
11. Write up findings/conclusions

FIGURE 4.2 **The process of quantitative research**

Source: Bryman & Teevan, 2005, p. 51. Copyright © Oxford University Press Canada 2005.

warrants. In an *unstructured interview* the interviewer uses set topics as a guide, and adopts a more informal style of questioning. A questionnaire, in many ways, is a structured interview without the interviewer. Because the respondents must read and answer the questions by themselves, the research questionnaire must be short, easy to follow, and easy to answer.

In all cases, whether using questionnaires or structured, semi-structured, or unstructured interviewing techniques, the sociologist collects data that are measures of the variables under study. The goal of all survey research is to aggregate and summarize the replies of all respondents in order to paint a picture of the group under study. This means that each question asked must be relevant to one of the variables being studied and not simply there to satisfy the curiosity of the interviewer (Bouma, et al., 2009, p. 73).

Questionnaires and interviews both have strengths and weaknesses as data-collection methods. Some advantages of questionnaires over structured interviews include the following:

- *Cost and ease of distribution/collection.* A mailed questionnaire is cheap, easily prepared and distributed, and straightforward to translate into numerical data when (and if) it is returned. However, mailed questionnaires are not necessarily filled out and returned quickly, necessitating follow-up requests.
- *Interviewer effects.* The personal characteristics of an interviewer—everything from race and gender to voice quality—may affect responses. More importantly, interviewees have a greater tendency to respond to questions with 'politically correct' answers, or to under-report activities about which they are sensitive. With a mailed questionnaire the problem of interviewer effects is eliminated.

Have you ever been asked to complete a survey online? How likely are you to fill in an Internet survey versus a mail-in or face-to-face survey?

Some advantages of interviews over questionnaires include the following:

- *Clarity.* With a questionnaire there is no interviewer to help respondents with questions they have difficulty understanding.
- *Completion rate.* Respondents are less likely to skip a question, or to answer a question only partially, if an interviewer is present.

The example that follows illustrates how the survey research method is used as part of a quantitative research strategy that employs a comparison (or cross-sectional) research design.

A Survey Example: Ethnic Differences and University Education Attainment

Canadian sociologists Teresa Abada, Feng Hou, and Bali Ram (2009) used the 2002 *Ethnic Diversity Survey* (Statistics Canada, 2003b) as their main source of data in researching this question: *How do 'ethnic differences' affect 'university education attainment' among the children of Canadian immigrants?* Until the 1960s immigration to Canada from non-European countries, including Asia, Africa, Latin America, and the Caribbean, was greatly curtailed by barriers that had been set up to control immigration. With those barriers now removed, Statistics Canada projects that by 2017, 'visible minorities' will constitute 20 per cent of Canada's total population (Statistics Canada, 2005, as cited in Abada, Hou, & Ram, 2009, p. 2).

Differences in the educational attainment of the children of these new immigrants—a pattern that immigration scholars call 'segmented assimilation'—have important implications for the relative position of the children of immigrants in the Canadian ethnic hierarchy, and for the 'different modes of reception' that they will encounter (Abada, et al., 2009, p. 2). Until Abada and colleagues conducted their study, there had not been a systematic attempt to identify and examine the factors contributing to differences in university education attainment among the children of immigrants (Abada, et al., 2009, p. 4). To conduct their study Abada, Hou, and Ram used a quantitative research strategy and a comparison (or cross-sectional) research design. They collected their data using a survey.

Theory

In their study, Abada and associates chose to use the theoretical framework of 'parental human capital, social capital and modes of incorporation'. The *parental human capital framework* posits that 'highly educated parents have the financial and nonmonetary resources to invest in their children's abilities early on' (Abada, et al., 2009). The children of parents with high levels of human capital benefit from 'good schools, safe neighbourhoods', and abundant resources from 'formal and informal organizations'. These advantages accumulate over many years, such that the children of parents with high human capital acquire both the skills and expectations for university attendance (Corak, 2001; Portes, et al., 2005; Zhou, 1997, as cited in Abada, et al., 2008, pp. 4–5).

The children of immigrants from some ethnic groups, however, unexpectedly 'show clear advantages' in spite of the fact they have parents with lower human capital. This suggests that in addition to parental human capital, other resources play an important role. Such resources include *social capital*—resources that belong to individual families—and *ethnic capital*, resources that belong to the ethnic community as a whole. Social and ethnic capital, according to Abada's team, can play an important role in accounting for differences in educational attainment among the children of immigrants from different ethnic groups (p. 5).

Finally, additional studies reviewed by Abada and colleagues (2008) suggest that factors such as the presence of a father in the household, the bilingual background of the children, and the settlement experiences of parents and grandparents may also be relevant to university completion among the children of immigrants. Immigrants who were favourably received and did not encounter discrimination are expected to 'experience a faster socioeconomic advancement and a smoother adaption process regardless of the human capital they possess' (Portes & MacLeod, 1999, p. 257, as cited in Abada, et al., 2008, p. 6). By comparison, both native-born and foreign-born black men and immigrant women from the Caribbean and Philippines 'faced severe devaluation of their foreign credentials'. In some instances, when parents endure such disadvantages, their children's perception of what is attainable can be affected, thus lowering their future achievements (Helly, 2006; Simmons, 1998, Zhou, 1997, and cited in Abada, et al., 2008, p. 7). On the other hand, the experience of exclusion from certain career paths (e.g. sports, politics, or entertainment) may spur the children of discriminated-against parents to pursue careers that are dependent on education achievement, such as science and engineering, and thus have a positive effect on post-secondary achievement for visible minority youth.

Hypotheses

On the basis of their preliminary analysis of the literature, and guided by their choice of theory from that literature, Abada and colleagues deduced the following hypotheses to test in their research:

1. Immigrant parents' level of educational attainment will account for the educational differences among their children: children with the lowest levels of educational attainment will have parents with lower levels of education.
2. In cases where parental educational level does not adequately account for differences in educational attainment, 'the average skill level of the ethnic group in the father's generation is critical in intergenerational mobility'(Borjas, 1994, as cited in Abada, et al., 2009, p. 8). In other words, in cases where parents' educational attainment did not predict their children's level of attainment, Abada, Hou, and Ram found that greater skill levels among the ethnic group of the father's generation did correspond to the level of educational attainment of the children.
3. Rural–urban differences in resident locations of parents prior to immigration to Canada may affect children's educational attainment (Abada, et al., 2009, p. 9).

Research Design and Data Collection

Abada's team chose a cross-sectional (comparison) research design that drew on quantitative data gathered in the 2003 Statistics Canada *Ethnic Diversity Survey* (EDS). As Abada, Hou, and Ram explain, this national survey of over 42,000 non-Aboriginal Canadian residents aged 15 years and over

> . . . was designed to provide information on how Canadians of different ethnic backgrounds interpret and report their ethnicity and how people's backgrounds affect their participation in the social, economic, and cultural life in Canada. . . . [T]he survey covers a wide range of topics including ethnic ancestry, ethnic identity, place of birth, visible minority status, religion, religious participation, knowledge of languages, family background, social networks, civic participation, interaction with society, attitudes, satisfaction with life, trust, and socio-economic activities. (Abada, et al., 2009)

Concepts (Variables) and Their Measures

The research team used six different sets of independent variables to explain ethnic differences in university attainment (the dependent variable). The first set of independent variables comprises basic demographic data, including:

- *age* (25–34 years)
- *gender* (male/female)
- *family structure* (lived mainly with biological parents until age 15; lived mainly with birth mother until age 15; lived mainly with birth father until age 15; lived with neither birth mother nor father until age 15)
- *place of residence* (large metropolitan areas, small metropolitan areas with a population of 100,000+, and non-metropolitan areas)
- *generational status* (for the purpose of compiling and sorting the data, Abada, et al. assigned numerical codes of 1.5 to those whose age at immigration was 6–12 years; of 1.75 to those who immigrated before age 6; of 2.0 to those who were born in Canada with both parents who were immigrants; and of 2.5 to those who were born in Canada with one immigrant parent and one Canadian-born parent).

A second set of independent variables measured father's and mother's level of educational attainment—university degree, some post-secondary education, high school graduation, less than high school graduation. A third set defined mother tongue and language environment—mother tongue is English or French; mother tongue is neither English nor French but English or French was spoken with parents until age 15; mother tongue is neither English nor French and neither language was spoken with parents by age 15.

For the fourth set, Abada, Hou, and Ram aimed to devise a measure of each subject's ethnic network and their 'sense of belonging or exclusion while growing up in Canada'. One way they chose to measure this was by asking 'whether the respondents reported that at least half of their friends were from the same ethnic group by age 15'. A second measure was 'whether the respondents ever felt uncomfortable or out of place because of their ethnicity, culture, race, skin color, language, accent, or religion by age 15'. A third measure of the strength of ethnic networks was 'whether the respondents reported a strong sense of belonging to their ethnic or cultural group' (Abada, et al., 2009, p. 11).

A fifth set of variables, which the researchers called 'ethnic capital', measured 'the average socioeconomic resources among respondents' parents' generation'. To generate this measure, Abada, Hou, and Ram used data from the 1991 Canadian census to calculate, for each birth country, the average number of immigrants who had completed a university degree and the mean earnings for male immigrants aged 35–50. They then merged these two variables with the EDS-sourced data on the birth country of each respondent's father (or mother, if the father was not an immigrant).

The final set of independent variables was the percentage of people among each respondent's father's generation living in rural or small-town (fewer than 5,000 residents) communities.

Research Site(s), Research Subjects/Respondents

Abada's team focused its study on 'group differences in attaining university degrees' among second-generation Canadians. This group included Canadian-born children of at least one immigrant parent and those children who immigrated to Canada with their parents at age 12 or younger. The researchers chose a subset of 330 young adults aged 25–34 from seven visible minority and eight ethnic groups with a minimum sample size of 50 persons each. Visible minority groups are defined in Canada's Employment Equity Act as 'persons, other than Aboriginal peoples, who are non-Caucasian in race or non-white in color'. The groups identified in the Employment Equity Act include:

- Chinese
- South Asians
- Filipinos
- Arab/West Asians
- other East Asians (e.g. Koreans, Japanese)
- other visible minorities (Renaud & Costa, 1999, as cited in Abada, et al., 2009, p. 9).

Ethnic groups with European background included British, French, German, Italian, Dutch, Polish, Portuguese, and other European groups.

Findings/Conclusions

There are large group differences in university education attainment among the children of immigrants to Canada. Children of Asian and French immigrants show the highest levels of educational attainment; children of Filipino and black immigrants lag behind other groups and generally do not exceed their fathers' levels of education (Adaba, et al., 2009, p. 20).

Parental attainment in education—and especially father's educational attainment—is a strong predictor of children's university completion. Parents with higher education attainment have financial and other resources to help their children develop the abilities that will eventually lead to their attainment of a university degree. Growing up in a two-parent household also is associated with higher academic achievements, while having a father who grew up in a small town or rural area is associated with a lower likelihood of obtaining a university degree.

Having a sense of belonging to one's ethnic group played an important role in giving educational advantages to visible minorities, but not to European groups, Abada's team found. Growing up with friends of the same ethnic background was also positively correlated with university completion, as was growing up with feelings of exclusion because of one's race or ethnicity (Abada, et al., 2009, pp. 20–1).

As a further move to analyze their data, Abada, Hou, and Ram performed a statistical procedure known as the 'Oaxaca decomposition', which is used to identify the presence of discrimination. While the intricacies of this analysis are beyond the skills required in an introductory sociology course, the findings are worth noting. They include the following:

- Differences in demographic factors, parental education, and social and ethnic capital account for part of the advantages in university completion rates among some Asian groups.
- Visible minorities generally benefit from the fact that their fathers' generation tends to be more concentrated in metropolitan areas.
- Social capital (measured by a strong sense of belonging to one's own ethnic group and by a larger network of friends of one's own ethnicity) and a sense of isolation increase visible minority groups' university completion rates.
- When parental human capital (measured by average earnings among the father's generation) is low among visible minorities, it tends to reduce their university completion rates.
- High levels of parental education contribute largely to youths' university completion rates among Filipinos, other East Asians, and South Asians.

- High concentrations in rural areas and small towns among the father's generation contribute to the relatively low levels of completion rates among Dutch and German youth.
- Low levels of parental education are the most important variables contributing to low university completion rates among Portuguese and Italian youth (Abada, et al., 2009, pp. 19–20).

Abada and colleagues surmise from the results of their investigation that higher educational attainment may be seen as a means of counteracting and challenging anticipated disadvantages attached to race and ethnicity. Cultural explanations may account for the advantages of Asian groups. For example, a greater sense of obligation to one's parents and a cultural orientation towards self-reliance and achievement are possibilities to be considered in further studies, as are considerations about the cohesiveness and availability of resources to aid new immigrants within specific ethnic communities.

RESEARCH METHODS USED WITH A QUALITATIVE RESEARCH STRATEGY

A qualitative research strategy is distinct from a quantitative research strategy in a number of ways, as discussed in Chapter 3. To review, a qualitative research strategy:

- is concerned more with words than with numbers
- maintains an inductive relationship between theory and research—theory is generated out of research
- stresses an interpretivist understanding of respondents' worldviews
- sees social life as the outcome of the interaction between people, and not as an independent reality, external to those involved in its construction.

Qualitative research methods include the following:

- participant observation, in which a researcher becomes immersed in the social life of the people she is studying, observing what people do and say with the objective of coming to understand a culture
- focus groups
- discourse and conversation analysis
- analysis of texts and other documents.

The steps typically followed in qualitative research are summarized in Figure 4.3.

The next two examples illustrate research methods that can be used with a qualitative research strategy.

Interview, Group Discussion, and Observation: Learning to Labour

Case studies are often conducted using interviews, group discussions, and participant observation as these research methods generate data that allow the researcher to examine the case under study in intensive and detailed ways. In interviews, the researcher poses questions and records the respondents' answers. In group discussions, the interviewer poses predominantly open-ended questions, and asks interviewees to respond to those questions that are relevant to them. Observation involves the extended participation of the researcher in the social life of the people he is studying. In this case, research takes place 'in the field' where the researcher is immersed in the lives of the people under study. The researcher observes his subjects going about their daily lives over an extended period of time in order to understand their behaviour in the context in which it occurs.

An Example of Participant Observation: How Working-Class Kids Get Working-Class Jobs

In his now classic study of British working-class 'lads' in 'Hammertown', in the West Midlands of England, Paul Willis (1977) used a qualitative research strategy, a case study research design, and a number of research methods including unstructured interviews, group discussions, and participant observation. Willis wanted to explain why the working-class youths of Hammertown settled for working-class jobs instead of striving for the higher-paying, higher-status jobs of their middle-class counterparts. For Willis, the informal culture shared by the working-class youths in his study was not merely transferred from adults to passive children.

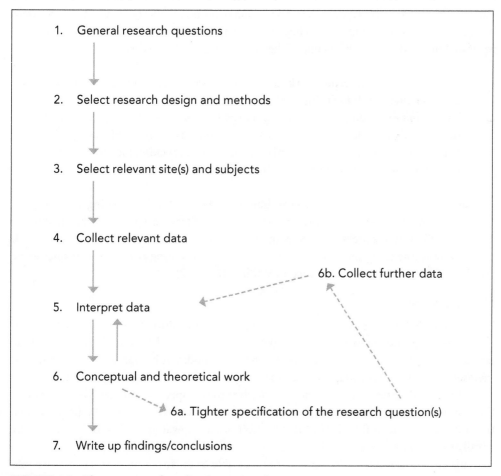

FIGURE 4.3   The process of qualitative research

Source: Adapted from Bryman & Teevan, 2005, p. 146.

Rather the 'lads' actively participated in creating their own informal culture and in socializing newcomers into its belief systems, values, and rules of conduct (Willis, 1977, p. 4).

Research Site and Subjects

Willis's research concentrated on a group of 12 teenaged boys attending a working-class, all-boys high school twinned with an all-girls school in the same area. Willis observed the 12 'lads' in all school settings—halls, classrooms, lunchrooms—as well as outside of school. In addition, he conducted regular semi-structured group sessions with them and semi-structured one-on-one interviews with individual boys, their parents, teachers, and school officials. All interviews were recorded, so at the end Willis had a very rich and deep data set to analyze and interpret.

Willis found the 'lads' to be in constant rebellion against the school system and very disdainful of the 'ear-oles', the name they gave to their conformist, working-class peers. As well, the 'lads' actively expressed their disregard for girls, teachers, minorities, and middle-class values. In the course of his research, Willis became convinced that together the 'lads' developed and enforced on each other a cultural project of apparent opposition or resistance to the middle-class values and norms that dominated the lives of their teachers, school officials, and members of the society at large. These were the very values that the despised 'ear-oles' accepted. In developing their oppositional culture, Willis contends, the 'lads' were trying to go beyond the rules of the school and society and to thwart the school's main objective of making students 'work'. As one of the 'lads', named 'July', told Willis:

> I don't think the school does fucking anything to you. . . . It never has had much effect on anybody. I don't think [after] you've learnt the basics. I mean school, it's fucking four hours a day. But it ain't the teachers who mould you, it's the fucking kids you met. You're only with teachers thirty percent of the time in school, the other fucking two-thirds are just talking, fucking pickin' an argument, messing about. (as cited in Willis, 1977, p. 26)

Asked midway through the school term about when he last did some writing, another 'lad', 'Fuzz', responded: 'Oh, er, last time was in careers 'cos I writ yes on a piece of paper, that broke me heart.' When Willis pressed 'Fuzz' about why it had broken his heart, 'Fuzz' responded: '. . . 'cos I was going to try and go through the term without writing anything. 'Cos since we've cum back, I ain't dun nothing' (as cited in Willis, 1977, p. 27).

Theory and Conclusions

Willis contended that the 'lads' developed a working-class culture that was distinctive from the middle-class one that the schools try to instill. Their intent, he argued, was 'to defeat the formality of the dominant culture through informal modes of interaction'. They identified themselves as a cohesive group through their opposition to learning, to girls, and to ethnic minorities. In all three cases, they held themselves to be superior, and they actively resisted the dominant values of the system in which they were forced to take part. At the same time they were well aware of their lack of real possibilities for upward mobility, or of ever having a really satisfying job.

Willis also observed that the 'lads' were never able to do anything more than move into uncreative, highly controlled manual-labour jobs once they left school, and that they were divided among themselves, as well as alienated from women and from the ethnic minorities who shared their class position. In securing their own positions, the 'lads' overvalued manual labour, their gender, and their ethnic origins, and made these badges of distinction from others they considered to be even lower than themselves in the social hierarchy. They associated despised effeminate traits with mental work, which they then discredited as being passive and 'lacking robust masculinity' (Willis, 1977, p. 105).

Content Analysis

A researcher using content analysis as a research method may examine media of all types, including printed documents (e.g. diaries, government and other reports, novels, magazines), video and/or audio materials (e.g. films, documentaries, television programs, radio programs, YouTube videos), and virtual texts (e.g. websites, blogs, Twitter posts). Content analysis can be used in a quantitative research strategy by coding the data into predetermined categories so that it can be tabulated. It can also be used with a qualitative research strategy by analyzing the materials in order to reveal a deeper and often hidden meaning. The five W's of journalism and news reporting—who, what, when, where, and why—are the most salient questions asked in content analysis along with questions about what is not being reported or covered. The latter often reveals a lot about what is and is not considered important by the person or people who have created the materials being researched (Bryman & Teevan, 2005, p. 332).

Discourse analysis is a form of content analysis that is specifically applied to the analysis of texts such as newspaper articles. The work of French social philosopher Michel Foucault (1926–84) helped to popularize discourse analysis during the 1970s and 1980s. For Foucault, a discourse is a system of thought that systematically constructs the world in a specific way. In the social sciences, 'discourse' has come to mean established categories that shape the way we think about, understand, and depict specific topics or objects. In this understanding, any given discourse forms an 'acceptable' (i.e. acceptable to a group of people with similar interests) version of a topic or an object. Thus, discourses are much more than just 'talk' about an object or a topic. For example, the policies of a conservative government towards public healthcare may be portrayed by supporters as fiscally responsible and by opponents as cruel and likely to result in inhumane treatment of those who do not have the resources to pay for their own treatment. Thus, while there is one topic, healthcare policies, there are two very different 'discourses'.

Sociologists who undertake discourse analysis note that the discourses they analyze are not merely neutral means of conveying reality to readers or listeners. Rather, they are used to accomplish certain ends, or to create certain effects. Sociologists are often concerned with uncovering the intent behind the way in which the originator of a particular discourse defines reality. This is certainly the case with our next example.

An Example of Content Analysis: Gender Discourse and the 2002–3 Iraq War Debate

Sociologists Wendy M. Christensen and Myra Marx Ferree (2008) undertook a content analysis of the gender images and metaphors used in the public debate in the United States surrounding the declaration of war on Iraq. The debate began in the spring of 2002 and continued for a year, up until the time the Bush administration decided to launch an invasion against Iraq in the spring of 2003. In their research, which focused on a sample of national news discourses from 2002 to 2003, Christensen and Ferree were able to demonstrate that both pro-war and anti-war speakers drew on 'binary images of gender to construct their cases for or against the war'. While pro-war speakers characterized the Bush administration's arguments for the invasion as a 'correct "macho" stance, anti-war speakers characterized them as inappropriate, out-of-control masculinity', otherwise known as 'cowboy diplomacy' (Christensen & Ferree, 2008, p. 287).

Data Collection

Christensen and Ferree carried out their research by sampling news sources with political positions that varied from moderate right to moderate left in terms of their support for the Bush administration's position. They chose *The New York Times,* National Public Radio, *USA Today,* and Fox News Network to represent these positions. From these sources they selected articles that went beyond just reporting on events, but that had 'at least one speaker who expressed at least one viewpoint regarding the pros and cons of going to war with Iraq'. Once they had identified sources that met these requirements, they randomly drew a 20 per cent sample (370 articles) stratified by source and month. They also drew an additional sample of 84 news items not already in the representative sample in order to 'locate additional war debate articles'. They selected these additional articles on the basis of keyword searches for gendered images, including 'masculine, macho, cowboy, wimp, sissy/sissies, Mars/Venus'. Further, they examined a non-random sample of about 150 US and European editorial cartoons that represented Bush and Iraq in a gendered fashion, and from that sample chose four cartoons 'to graphically represent this contest over gendered imagery' (Christensen & Ferree, 2008, p. 293).

Christensen and Ferree found that in the argument about whether to go to war, gendered symbols were used by both pro- and anti-war speakers to frame the political debates. Both sides aligned themselves with specific, albeit different, images of masculinity and the cowboy, and used these images to support their position. Anti-war speakers characterized the cowboy as a 'gunslinger', evoking images of 'lawlessness, crudeness, and isolation'. For pro-war speakers, by contrast, the cowboy figured as the 'sheriff', a 'plain-spoken American, enforcing the law, and spreading civilization' (p. 298). For the latter group, the sheriff-cowboy took it upon himself to bring civilization to 'rougher, more savage parts of the

How would you interpret this cartoon, which appeared on the cover of the German news magazine *Der Spiegel*? How would you compare it to the cartoon on page 108?

world' and to deal with 'outlaws' using simple speech and quick action. But what is interesting is that whether characterized positively as the plain-speaking sheriff or negatively as a gunslinger, the cowboy image was used as a metaphor for America by speakers on both sides of the debate. What differed, of course, were the two sides' intentions for mobilizing public sentiment.

Christensen and Ferree maintain that the gender images and metaphors used in the debate 'impoverished the quality of media coverage of the issues'. The organization of the debate in gendered terms 'encouraged binary thinking and so lowered the quality of war debate' (p. 288). It did so by placing 'the voices for peace, both in the US and in Europe, on a devalued, feminized footing and by casting the Administration's posture of masculinity as the multivalent, but quintessentially American, "cowboy"'(p. 288). Thus, the debate serves as 'an excellent example of the symbolic power of gender to frame issues and constrain alternatives' (p. 298).

Findings/Conclusion

Overall, the *New York Times* and National Public Radio were more likely to publish articles with an anti-war stance, while *USA Today* and Fox were more likely to publish articles promoting a pro-war position. All four sources had approximately the same probability of publishing articles that used gendered language. They differed, however, in the meaning the speakers gave to gender, and how the speakers used gender to legitimize or discredit a point of view.

A cartoon by Swedish political cartoonist Olle Johansson.

The use of gendered metaphors, such as the cowboy in the debates over the Iraq invasion, illustrate the power of gender to 'organize policy discourse', according to Christensen and Ferree (2008, p. 303). These images 'naturalize' male power, yet they remain contested in that both sides of the debate used the image of the cowboy to support their views of how to deal with Iraq. But whether viewed positively or negatively, the cowboy metaphor was typically used to depict a masculine image, attributed to the US as the dominant actor, while assigning Europe the feminine and subordinate position, either as grateful woman or as a whining date or potential conquest.

Christensen and Ferree believe their data show that 'gendered language both encourages and reflects a frame of mind in which the alternatives are narrowed to binary choices. Rather than giving reasons for assertions, speakers make character—readily exemplified by gender—part of the good/bad frame.' Because both pro- and anti-war speakers shared a common metaphor of the cowboy and framed their preferred alternatives in terms of different representations of that cowboy, it was difficult for either side to question whether the metaphor of masculinity they were using was 'at all appropriate as a frame for political decision-making' (p. 303). This contributed greatly to rendering the debate ineffective and explains why, in the year leading up to the invasion of Iraq, media commentators were 'not more critical of the Bush Administration's war plans' and why the 'reservations about going to war expressed by some of the US's closest allies' were not taken more seriously (Christensen & Ferree, 2008, p. 287).

RESEARCH ETHICS

Researchers at Canadian universities today must conduct their research according to guidelines set by their university's research ethics boards. University researchers must submit their research plans to their university's research ethics board for approval prior to carrying out any research involving human subjects. Ethics boards commonly require that:

- research participants must give informed consent to be part of the research
- the identity of research participants must be protected (unless the participant gives written permission to be identified)
- research participants must not be coerced either into participating or into divulging information
- researchers must store their data in a secure place, for up to seven years (Bouma, Ling, & Wilkinson, 2009, p. 42).

Many professional organizations, such as the Canadian Sociology and Anthropology Association (CSAA), have established codes or statements of professional ethics. The CSAA's code was established to protect participants from any harm that might occur as a result of the 'intervention of researchers into their lives and cultures' (CSAA, 1994). In following this code, researchers are asked to 'guard against the uncritical promotion of research, which . . . furthers the power of states, corporations, churches, or other institutions over the lives and cultures of research subjects. . . .' Researchers are also enjoined not to 'exploit individuals or groups for personal gain' (CSAA, 1994).

Researchers must not expose participants to the risk of personal harm, nor should researchers deceive their subjects about the nature of the research 'if there is any reasonably anticipated risk to the subjects or if the harm cannot be offset or the extent of the harm be reasonable predicted'. Researchers have an obligation to openly disseminate results of their research, except those results likely to 'endanger research participants or to violate their anonymity or confidentiality'. Research participants have the right to feedback on the results of the research, and to be consulted (when practicable) over the content of publications.

Finally, the CSAA's code specifies that:

> Sociologists and anthropologists have a responsibility to speak out publicly, both individually and collectively, on issues about which they possess professional expertise. They have a professional responsibility to contribute to the formation of informational ground upon which public policy may be founded. They should be candid about their qualifications and should make clear the limits of their expertise. Particularly in their relations with the media, members should have regard for the reputation of the discipline and refrain from offering expert commentaries on material which as researchers they would regard as comprising inadequate or tendentious evidence. (1994)

As a researcher dealing with human participants, sociologists must always be aware that there are ethical issues involved in doing research and strive to be considerate of their research participants' needs and feelings. For sociologists, as for other social scientists, this means gaining informed consent, respecting the privacy and confidentiality of participants, not exposing research participants to harm, not deceiving research participants, keeping the data collected accurate, secure, and correctly recorded, and openly sharing research findings with research participants and with members of the public.

SUMMARY

Like other scientists, sociologists do research in order produce knowledge that is supported by empirical evidence. This chapter is an introduction to the sociological research process. You have learned that all sociological research begins with a research strategy or general orientation and includes both a research design and one or more research methods or techniques for collecting data. There are only two research strategies used by sociologists: qualitative and quantitative. A quantitative research strategy focuses on collecting measurable data and analyzing that data using statistical procedures. A qualitative research strategy means the researcher focuses more on what people say about how they think or feel about something—information that is usually expressed in words and is not easily analyzed using statistical procedures.

In this chapter you have been introduced to five research designs used by sociologists to ensure that the data generated by their research provides the best possible answers to the research questions being asked: case study, longitudinal study, comparison study, longitudinal comparison study, and experiment. A case study research design is used when a sociologist wants to answer the question *What is happening?* to a community or organization in a specific location, while a longitudinal study involves two or more case studies of the same organization conducted at different points in time. The longitudinal study is used in cases where a sociologist wants to know if changes have occurred in an organization over time.

Sociologists use a comparison design when they want to examine the same social phenomena in two or more cases. A comparison design is typically used in cross-cultural research. A longitudinal comparison research design is used when a sociologist wants to learn if the differences that exist between two organizations or entities at one point in time continue to exist or change over time. Finally, sociologists sometimes adopt an experimental research design in a field or (more rarely) a lab setting in order to determine if a change in one variable (for example, the gender of the research subject) has an effect on another variable (for example, political preference).

Research methods are the actual techniques that sociologists use for collecting data. This chapter reviewed three main methods or techniques of data collection: surveys, questionnaires, and interviews; observation; and content analysis. Surveys, questionnaires, and interviews are used to capture respondents' answers to questions, while observation is used to record actual occurrences. Content analysis allows sociologists to examine and analyze the content of all kinds of recorded materials, including texts as well as audio and visual recordings. The chapter ended with a discussion of research ethics—the guidelines set by university research ethics boards and professional associations such as the Canadian Sociology and Anthropology Association.

DISCUSSION QUESTIONS

1. Which research strategy, design, and method(s) would you use to research the effects of an individual's ethnicity on his or her educational attainment? Explain your choices.
2. Which research strategy, design, and methods would you use to find out about the attitudes of Canadian university students towards a national identity? Explain your choices.
3. Design a research project that uses a qualitative research strategy. Then approach the same topic again, this time using a quantitative research strategy. Compare the research design and methods as well as the research questions and conclusions that each strategy might yield.
4. What are some of the most important ethical issues to be considered by sociologists?
5. The most famous of the experiments in social psychology, Stanley Milgram's experiments on obedience to authority, involved duping a naive volunteer. Was this research ethical? Why or why not?

Part III
Early Sociological Theorists

In Part III we consider another core skill essential to sociological inquiry: theorizing. Theories are perspectives, templates we use to explain the world. They guide us in the kinds of questions we ask and interpretations we make.

Like other scientists, sociologists are concerned with constructing and validating theories about the world. But the notion of 'doing science' is controversial in that all theories carry a set of value judgements about how research 'ought' to be done. Most sociologists recognize that by choosing a theoretical framework and a set of methods to guide their research they are making judgements about what is an acceptable practice of inquiry into social life.

Because the topics of interest to sociologists cover almost everything that humans do, and given that sociologists use an equally extensive repertoire of methods and theories to study those topics, sociology is often portrayed as a discipline still in development, whose practitioners continue to search for a unifying direction and purpose. The pioneers of the discipline—notably Karl Marx, Émile Durkheim, and Max Weber—did their most influential work in the late nineteenth century, a time of great political, economic, and social upheaval. They were affected by these revolutions and made them the focus of their work. Marx, Durkheim, and Weber all sought to develop theories to explain the speed and direction of social change taking place in Europe. And in spite of their differences in theoretical perspectives, they shared a common devotion to studying and theorizing about the problems inherent in capitalism and the Industrial Revolution.

Karl Marx was both a social theorist and a political activist who actively supported the overthrow of capitalism as the only real solution for eliminating the misery experienced by the majority of nineteenth-century Europeans. Marx wrote extensively on the subject of capitalism; at the same time, he engaged in political activities he hoped would bring about a socialist revolution.

Marx's theoretical positions and his activism were strongly opposed by Durkheim and Weber. Both recognized that there were serious problems with capitalism and capitalist society, but unlike Marx, they sought to reform society from within. Durkheim and Weber both feared socialism, and their ideas about what constitutes society and how it should be analyzed have dominated mainstream sociology much more than the theories of Marx.

The theories of American psychologist, philosopher, and sociologist George Herbert Mead and the symbolic interactionists, developed during the first part of the twentieth century, helped to shift the sociological focus from large-scale social processes (where it had been, exclusively, in the work of Durkheim, Weber, and Marx) to theories of how the mind, self, and society emerge out of social interaction and of how social reality is a product of the collective efforts of individuals organized into social groups. The symbolic interactionists treated the individual and society as being mutually constituted through an ever emerging process of social interaction.

Taken together, the ideas of Marx, Weber, Durkheim, and Mead have been responsible for generating the theoretical frameworks that have inspired several generations of sociologists. New approaches to the study of society call into question many of the basic assumptions underpinning the work of the discipline's founders. But sociologists today still draw on the work of these early contributors to help them understand the complex interaction between the individual and society.

5 The Beginnings of Sociology

CHAPTER OUTLINE

LEARNING OBJECTIVES

In this chapter you will:

- gain an understanding of the social conditions that were significant in the development of sociology
- learn about the contributions of sociology's early founders, including Comte, Saint-Simon, and Durkheim
- become familiar with basic sociological concepts such as 'social facts'
- understand Durkheim's approach to the study of sociology and the sociological method
- discover the contributions of some early Canadian sociologists.

INTRODUCTION

Academic disciplines taught in today's universities and colleges have been shaped by the social, economic, and political circumstances in which they emerged. The discipline of sociology was developed by thinkers who wanted to understand and control the direction of social changes taking place in eighteenth- and nineteenth-century Europe and North America. It was one among several 'social' or 'human sciences' (including economics, political science, and psychology) to emerge during the late nineteenth and early twentieth centuries in response to the 'problem of social order' (Donzelot, 1979; Foucault 1970; Hazelrigg 1989). As Abrams explains,

> The generation that gave birth to sociology was probably the first generation of human beings ever to have experienced within the span of their own lifetime socially induced change of a totally transformative nature—change which could not be identified, explained and accommodated as a limited historical variation within the encompassing order of the past. (Abrams, 1972, p. 55)

In order to act effectively, the thinkers of the late eighteenth and nineteenth centuries needed a frame of reference that would allow them to identify and contemplate the structure of the situation they were in and also to anticipate the consequences of their attempts at changing that structure. Such a frame of reference could not be derived from contemporary models; social conditions at the time offered nothing but confusion. Nor could it be derived from the past, because conventional categories of historical thought were also in question—how could conventional categories of thought be used to make sense out of something entirely without precedent in human history? Remember: at the time, the kind of organized protest that we see so often today had not been established (and was thus not available) as a tool to lobby for and realize changes to social and labour conditions. The solution, these intellectuals realized, was that the conditions of rapid change then occurring were themselves amenable to scientific study. It is in this context that the principles of sociological inquiry were first articulated (Abrams, 1972).

American sociologist George Ritzer (2000) has identified six social conditions of the nineteenth and early twentieth centuries that were of the utmost significance in the development of the discipline of sociology in Europe and North America.

1. Political Revolutions

Beginning in 1789, with the French Revolution, and carrying over into the nineteenth century, a long series of political revolutions made an enormous impact on western Europe and North America. Social thinkers of the nineteenth century were greatly affected by the chaos and disorder that were occurring in their midst. They were intent on doing everything possible to restore order to society, and some of the most conservative among them even advocated a return to feudalism. Those less conservative, however, realized such a return was not only impossible but highly undesirable. They sought to organize society from a new foundation, one based on equality of all humans, and this search directly influenced their interest in its study. For others, including Comte and Durkheim, whose work we will cover in this chapter, the issue of social order was foremost.

2. The Industrial Revolution and the Rise of Capitalism

By the start of the twentieth century, the Industrial Revolution had transformed the economies of most western European countries from an agricultural to an industrial base. Thrown off the land or unable to survive as agriculturalists, people abandoned farms in ever-increasing numbers to seek work in factories, which were constantly changing owing to the invention of new and more 'efficient' technologies.

At the heart of this new production system was an equally new economic system—capitalism—powered by the free-market exchange of goods and services. But while the new economy meant huge profits for a few, the majority of people were forced to work long hours in appalling conditions for low wages. As a reaction, labour movements, movements to abolish slavery, and other radical social movements emerged in several countries. These movements were aimed at ending social injustices or, even more radically, at overthrowing the capitalist system and establishing in its place an economy controlled by workers. Although their theories had rather different objectives and outcomes, thinkers such as Karl Marx and Max

CAPITAL AND LABOUR.

This cartoon, which appeared in a 1943 issue of the British weekly magazine *Punch*, was inspired by a British government report on the horrific state of workers in coal mines. How is it a critique of capitalism?

Weber, whose work we will cover in Chapter 6, are considered to be among the founders of sociology. Both men spent much of their lives studying and confronting the problems inherent in capitalism and the Industrial Revolution.

3. The Rise of Socialism

Socialism, as an economic, political, and social ideal, emerged during the nineteenth century as a means of coping specifically with the excesses of industrialization and capitalism. Karl Marx actively supported the overthrow of capitalism as the only real means of alleviating the misery of the majority of nineteenth-century workers throughout the world and, especially, in western Europe. Marx wrote and developed his theories about capitalism as one of several 'modes of production' that were typical of human evolutionary progress. He felt that the capitalist mode of production was the penultimate stage in human evolution, to be followed by advanced communism as the final stage. Marx personally engaged in several political activities that he hoped would help bring about a worldwide socialist revolution.

Marx's view about the desirability of a final, communist stage in the evolution of human societies was not, however, shared by either Durkheim or Weber. Although both early sociologists recognized that there were serious problems with capitalism, they sought to reform society from within rather than to support the kind of revolutionary activity advocated by Marx. Weber and Durkheim actually feared socialism, and their ideas have dominated sociology much more so than those of Marx. Especially in the United States, the way the discipline of sociology developed during much of the twentieth century was in reaction to Marx's ideas, particularly the advocacy of socialism and advanced communism as the natural evolutionary step to follow capitalism.

4. Urbanization

During the industrialization of Europe, vast numbers of people were uprooted from their rural homes and forced to migrate to urban areas in search of work. The rapid expansion of some cities, such as Manchester and Glasgow, produced an almost endless list of urban problems—overcrowding, noise, pollution, poverty, crime, public health crises, unemployment, and alcoholism. During the nineteenth century the nature of urban life under an industrialized and capitalist system attracted the interest of many sociologists, including Marx's collaborator and friend, Friedrich Engels. Later, in the early twentieth century, American sociologists at the University of Chicago focused on the city of Chicago as a kind of laboratory for studying urbanization and its attendant problems.

Martin Scorsese's Academy Award–winning film *Gangs of New York* (2002), a story about the urban underworld of nineteenth-century Manhattan, was set in an area known as Five Points. A more realistic though no less compelling picture of that infamous neighbourhood was given by Charles Dickens, who in 1842 reported on what he called 'a world of vice and misery', filled with tenements, hovels, brothels, stinking outhouses, and pigs running in the streets. Photographic crusader Jacob Riis's work, especially his photographs of tenements, child labourers, and places such as 'Bandit's Roost', were instrumental in getting much of Five Points razed between 1885 and 1895 as part of the city's slum clearance efforts.

5. Religion

As the foundations of Europe's feudal society were rocked by political and economic revolutions, its religious underpinnings were also threatened. Some of the early sociologists were concerned about the fading influence or outright disappearance of religion in people's lives.

A narrow alley off the main street of a Glasgow slum, photographed in 1868 by Thomas Annan, who was among the first photographers to document the deplorable living conditions of Scotland's poor. The Scottish call this kind of alley a 'close'—can you imagine why?

PROFILES IN SOCIOLOGY

Jacob Riis (1849–1914)

Born in Denmark, Jacob August Riis immigrated to the United States when he was 21 years of age. On his arrival he first worked as a carpenter, but he soon found himself out of work and spent much of his early years in the US destitute and living in very poor conditions. A chance meeting, however, led to a job with the New York News Association, which was followed by stints with the *Brooklyn News* and then the *New York Tribune*, where he worked as a police reporter. In the latter role Riis worked in the poorest of New York City's slums and began using photography as a way of illustrating his stories. He did much of this work late at night and was able to document many of the worst aspects of life in these poorest of neighbourhoods.

Riis published several books, among them *How the Other Half Lives: Studies among the Tenements of New York* (1890), *Out of Mulberry Street: Stories of Tenement Life in New York City* (1896), *The Battle with the Slum* (1901), *Children of the Tenements* (1903), and *Neighbors: Life Stories of the Other Half* (1914). Through his photography, public speaking, and journalism Riis was able to convey to well-to-do New Yorkers the horrific conditions of the tenements,

Bandit's Roost, a notoriously dangerous and run-down section of Manhattan's Little Italy, as photographed by Jacob Riis in the 1890s. Could you argue that Riis's photography represents a kind of qualitative sociological research?

flophouses, and alleyways so often hidden from their view—scenes that were the daily reality for many immigrants to the city. His work as a social reformer was recognized by US president Theodore Roosevelt.

Durkheim wrote one of his most important works on religion. Comte went so far as to propose that sociology be transformed into a new kind of religion (with himself as high priest). Max Weber made a point of studying religion from a cross-cultural perspective. Even Karl Marx had strong views on the social role of religion, although his famous description of religion as 'the opiate of the masses' gives us an idea of the critical perspective he took on the subject.

6. The Growth of Science

Early sociologists were preoccupied with science. By the end of the nineteenth century, science had acquired authority as the main means of producing true knowledge about any subject. The scientists associated with physics, chemistry, and biology were accorded enormous prestige. Comte and Durkheim, whose work we will take up later in this chapter, sought to model sociology after the highly successful natural sciences. Marx, too, was impressed with scientific research, especially the work of Charles Darwin. Others, though, including Weber, thought that human social life was distinctive enough that a wholesale adoption of the models used in the natural sciences was difficult and unwise (Ritzer, 1992).

Taken together, then, these six factors set the parameters for sociology's emergence as a separate academic discipline. As you have already learned, from the beginning of its development, there have been strong disagreements among sociologists about how to make sense of the social world. As a result, there are many different theoretical and political orientations toward social life that vie for sociologists' support. Early sociologists promoted numerous different perspectives. The work of Durkheim, for instance, exemplifies a positivist theoretical perspective connected to a conservative political orientation; that of Weber, an interactive theoretical perspective connected to a liberal political orientation; and that of Marx, a positivist and historicist perspective tied to a radical, activist, political orientation.

As unrelated as these three orientations appear, common ground can be found in two aspects: in the stability-seeking motives of the discipline's founders, and in their commitment to using scientific methods of research and reasoning. Comte and Durkheim, along with the French social reformer Henri de Saint-Simon, were troubled by the French Revolution (1789–1802) and its aftermath. With Marx and Weber they shared a strong concern about industrialization and its implications for Western society. All of these early contributors to the discipline of sociology saw how dehumanizing industrialized society could be; all but Weber thought that a better world for future generations was possible.

HENRI DE SAINT-SIMON

As one of the first to recognize the emergence of a new social order out of the decline of feudalism, Henri de Saint-Simon was concerned with explaining how the new society would work. It was Saint-Simon who, in writing his promotional papers and pamphlets, introduced the term 'industrial society' into European social theory. He argued that industrialism heralded the beginnings of a new society, one that would bring about a new era of human history. The outgrowth of a declining feudalism, this incipient industrial society would provide the basis for solving all the problems inherent in feudalism.

Saint-Simon proposed the term **social physiology** as the guiding principle by which the new society should be studied. The premise of social physiology was that society was like a living organism and could be examined by studying its social organization, including its growth, order, stability, and any abnormal pathologies. Social physiology involved a three-part program, beginning with close observation of the 'course of civilization'; this would eventually yield 'laws of social organization', which would in turn become the basis on which humans could construct the best of all possible forms of social organization (Turner, Beeghley, & Powers, 2007, p. 19).

Saint-Simon naively believed that he had identified and developed a law of human history, according to which ideas moved from a polytheistic stage, through a stage of Christian theism, and on to a final, positivistic stage. With each stage, he proposed, came both a desire to maintain social order and the inevitable transition to the next stage, entailing disruption and crisis. All that anyone could hope to achieve was to know the laws of any given stage, adapt to the demands of these laws, and do everything possible to support their course of development.

social physiology
The notion that society may be studied as if it were an organism, demonstrating growth, order, stability, and pathologies.

PROFILES IN SOCIOLOGY

Claude Henri de Rouvroy, Comte de Saint-Simon (1760–1825)

Born in Paris, into a poor but aristocratic family, Henri de Saint-Simon was by all accounts a wild and uncontrollable youth who spent long portions of his early years imprisoned by his family as a way to control his behaviour. He ran away from home at the age of 19 and later became an officer in the French army. His king, Louis XIV, supported the Americans in their struggle for independence from the British, and Saint-Simon was sent to America to fight in the American Revolution.

Upon his return to Europe, Saint-Simon tried unsuccessfully to promote canal building schemes in Central America and Europe. When the French Revolution broke out in 1789, Saint-Simon gave it his full support, renounced his title, made revolutionary speeches, proposed reforms, and befriended the peasants. He continued, however, to promote his private affairs, buying up the confiscated lands of aristocrats and the Church at a fraction of their value. He acquired, then lost, a fortune and was confined to a mental asylum for a time.

At first Saint-Simon believed that scientists would become the theologians of the new social order, while industrialists would be the 'engineers' who performed the task of reconstructing society. Later, as his mental illness progressed, he became even more committed to the idea that, ultimately, scientists and artists would become the priests and spiritual leaders of the new secular religion of positivism, while industrialists would be the 'temporal' leaders, implementing the new spiritual program by applying scientific methods to production and to the organization of labour (Turner, et al., 2007, p. 20).

Saint-Simon's contribution to sociology is important not, of course, for his 'odd' or naive views about religion but for his attempts to apply scientific thinking to the analysis of social organization. He attacked the ideas of the conservative Catholic scholars of his day, many of whom argued that economic and political revolution had destroyed the fabric of society, and that the way to recover was to return to the social organization of the old feudal order. Saint-Simon was committed to moving forward, to using science to understand and improve upon social organization. He shunned the call to reinstate the Catholic Church and other social hierarchies of feudalism, and he advocated for the role of industrialists in the establishment of a new social order based on the principles of positivist science. But with his off-the-wall ideas about a religion of positivism, he lost credibility and followers.

In his book *Industrial Systems* (1821) Saint-Simon argued that the new industrial society should be organized on scientific principles with the economic and political systems working in harmony. Politics, in his view, had to become the 'science of production' (Turner, Beeghley, & Powers, 2007, p. 37–8). Because it used the principles of prediction and verification, science would form the basis for all social practices in the new industrial society as envisaged by Saint-Simon. Decision making would be given over to those institutions that were associated with science and technology. The state would be replaced by those men most able to manage the affairs of the nation—that is, by a council of scientists, artists, financiers, and industrialists who would plan and coordinate for the good of all.

One of the more interesting aspects of Saint-Simon's work is the influence he had on the development of both conservative sociological theorists such as Comte (see below) and radical theorists like Karl Marx (discussed in the next chapter). On the one hand, Saint-Simon wanted to preserve society, and strongly supported using the same methods for studying social and natural phenomena. On the other hand, he saw a pressing need for social reforms, especially ones leading to the central planning of the economy. Unlike Marx, though, he did not believe that the working class would one day supersede the capitalists (Ritzer, 1992, p. 14).

Can you imagine a society run by scientists and artists? Who in society would you say plays the biggest role in how 'the affairs of the nation' are run? What impact would that have on Saint-Simon's vision?

AUGUSTE COMTE

Auguste Comte is usually credited with being the founder of sociology, a term that he coined. Among the very first to reflect on the nature of 'society' itself, Comte's major work, the *Course of Positive Philosophy* (1830–42), stands as a classic sociological interpretation of modernity. Comte sought to reconcile the aftermath of the French Revolution—including the social disruption and the 'reign of terror'—with the counter-revolutionary, conservative forces that together laid the basis for French industrialism during the period of the Restoration (Delanty, 2000, p. 32).

Like many of his contemporaries, Comte believed that European society was in a state of crisis brought about because one form of society was disappearing while another was struggling to replace it. But unlike the Enlightenment thinkers who preceded him, Comte did not think that something new, exciting, and hopeful was happening to society; instead, he had an anguished sense that the old system, as it was breaking down, was being gradually engulfed by anarchy. Far from being the herald of a new era, as it had been for the Enlightenment thinkers, Comte saw the French Revolution as little more than 'social disorganization presided over by political tyranny' (Nisbet, 1966, p. 51).

PROFILES IN SOCIOLOGY

Isidore Auguste Marie François Xavier Comte (1798–1875)

Born to conservative, middle-class, Catholic, monarchist parents in Montpellier, France, Auguste Comte enjoyed a comfortable childhood. In Paris as a young man, he eked out an existence as a private instructor. So poor that he could afford only two meals a day, he nevertheless managed to attend public scientific discussions and debates. It was at one of these that he met Henri de Saint-Simon, 40 years his senior. Comte served for several years as Saint-Simon's secretary, student, and collaborator, finally leaving his employer in 1824 after a bitter dispute over ownership of ideas. Comte went on to develop a number of Saint-Simon's ideas about science, technology, and society, although he often did not credit his former mentor. He never held a secure academic position, and although he taught courses from time to time, he remained on the fringe of French academic circles (Swingewood, 1984, p. 40).

Like Saint-Simon, Comte suffered from bouts of insanity. He was confined for a time to a sanatorium for depression, and twice attempted suicide. In 1825 he married Caroline Massif, a registered Paris prostitute. It was not a happy marriage, and they separated several times before parting for good in 1841. After his marriage ended, Comte lived for a while on subsidies from English social theorist John Stuart Mill and others who admired his work.

In 1844, at the age of 46, Comte fell in love with Clotilde de Vaux, a 36-year-old unpublished novelist and descendant of an aristocratic family, whose husband had abandoned her several years before (Ashley & Orenstein, 1990, p. 69). When they met, Clotilde was already terminally ill. On her death in 1846, Comte erected an altar to the memory of 'my saint Clotilde' and visited her grave every Wednesday. He then dedicated himself to formulating a new religion, which he called the 'religion of humanity'. He assigned himself the title 'Great priest of Humanity' and lived an austere existence, giving up wine, tobacco, and coffee.

Comte's work can be divided into two phases. In the first, marked by his anxiety over the chaos that followed the French Revolution and his criticism of the Enlightenment thinkers he blamed for the disintegration of society, Comte proposed a new scientific approach that he called 'positivism' (or 'positive philosophy') to answer the question: *What are the criteria by which we can distinguish scientific from non-scientific knowledge?*

Comte, like others who were influenced by positivism, including Spencer and Durkheim (whose work we will examine later in this chapter), reasoned that by examining the structure of societies found in times and places other than his own, he might derive the laws of the social universe, including variations in the forces and effects of those laws on patterns of social organization. Comte wrote about this new approach in a five-volume work, *Course of Positive Philosophy*, which was published between 1830 and 1842. Here he developed what he first called 'social physics' and only later renamed with the Latin–Greek hybrid 'sociology', as the science by which the laws of the social universe would be discovered. In fact, Comte detested the term *sociology*. He was forced to use it because the Belgian statistician Adolphe Quetelet had already adopted the term *social physics* to refer to his particular version of descriptive statistics (Comte, 1830–42/1896; Turner, 2006, p. 451).

Comte was among the first to make clear reference to society, the object of sociology, as something more than a sum of the individuals that made it up. According to Comte, 'society . . . can no more be decomposed into individuals, than a geometric surface can be resolved into lines or a line into points' (1854/1966, vol. 2, p. 153). Just as Newton had uncovered laws about underlying dynamics of, and fundamental relations between, the forces of gravity,

Comte wanted this new science of the social to formulate the laws that underlay and drove social relations. Once formulated and tested, these laws could be used as tools to modify the social world (Turner, et al., 2007, p. 30).

Along with Saint-Simon, Comte maintained that every society was the embodiment of the system of ideas that characterized its specific epoch. Any given society was an organic whole, and not just the aggregation of the individuals who made it up. Sociology, then, should be the science of the whole of the social organism—in other words, society. Comte concurred with Saint-Simon in viewing society as an organic whole, whose component parts, or organs, stood in interdependent relationship to each other. Because it was an organic whole, Comte felt it necessary to study all of society, and not just some of its parts. He wrote that 'there can be no scientific study of society, either in its conditions or its movements, if it is separated into portions, and its divisions are studied apart' (Comte, 1896/1830–42, vol. 2, p. 225).

In drawing the analogy between a biological organism and a society, and in modelling sociology after the biological sciences, Comte was the first to develop a model of sociological analysis that later became known as **functionalism**. Comte's concerns with both the normal and the pathological operation of society and his comparison of the organs and tissues of biological entities to the various parts of social entities are all examples of the way in which biological analogies were imported into sociology. Comte was particularly concerned with social reform, especially with correcting the social ills that the French Revolution had introduced. But he did not urge another revolution (as Marx would later do). Instead, Comte believed that only reforms were needed to encourage the natural evolution of society towards something better.

Comte believed that 'sociology', as the science of the social world, would eventually come to dominate all other sciences. Sociology, as he conceived it, would be the study of both '**social statics**' (existing social structures, social order) and '**social dynamics**' (the process of social change). These two concepts were governed by two categories of social law that Comte saw as important for sociologists to uncover:

- laws of succession—the laws governing the movement from one stage of human development to another (social dynamics)
- laws of coexistence—the laws governing the relations between the elements of a given society (social statics).

Comte was an elitist: he believed that sociology would eventually dominate all of science because of its ability to uncover and interpret social laws and to develop programs of reform to help ameliorate the problems within the system. Comte's social theory was in fact the articulation of a political project that was a rather uneasy combination of both aristocratic and bourgeois points of view. Strongly influenced by developments in biology, Comte was particularly concerned with analyzing societies in terms of the functional relationship of the part to the whole. He was convinced that when positivism—knowledge based on experimental science—gained complete domination, all social revolutions and upheavals would cease. He also believed that there was no need to for anyone to actively engage in making a social revolution. He believed that positivism was part of a natural, evolutionary process that would inevitably come to dominate the thinking of the entire world. Moreover, he believed that the changes that were needed were intellectual ones, so there was little reason to support social or political revolutions. For him, society was strongly characterized by consensus rather than conflict. Later in his life Comte went so far as to advocate a 'religion of humanity', complete with a priesthood of sociologists to ensure that the new science of sociology achieved its full political potential.

functionalism

A general theoretical orientation to the study of society that focuses on large-scale social structures and their role in maintaining or undermining social stability.

social statics

Comte's term for social structure and/or social order.

social dynamics

Comte's term for the process of social change.

LITTRÉ AND THE SOCIÉTÉ DE SOCIOLOGIE (1872–4): SOCIOLOGY AS POLITICAL PRACTICE

Following the publication of *Cours de philosophie positive* (1830–42), other French thinkers and academics took up Comte's ideas about positive philosophy and his program for sociology as a new science of society. Prominent among Comte's earliest followers was the journalist, publicist, and politician Émile Littré (1801–81). Although little known today, Littré was one of the most renowned intellectuals of mid-nineteenth-century France, whose work included the four volume *Dictionnaire de la langue française* (1877), a work that took him 30 years to complete.

Littré was instrumental in founding the short-lived Société de Sociologie (1872–4), the first known sociological society in the world (Heilbron, 2009, p. 31). A disciple of Auguste Comte, Littré was a staunch proponent of Comte's ideas about the direction of history and evolution of humanity. Like Comte, Littré believed that the French Revolution heralded the end of the revolutionary phase of human history and the beginning of a new 'organic phase' in which order and progress could be reconciled (Heilbron, 2009, p. 35). For this reason both Comte and Littré had eschewed revolutionary doctrines in favour of a limited kind of socialism informed by the teachings of positivism (Littré, 1879, p. 160, as cited in Heilbron, 2009, p. 31). But whereas Comte began to dedicate himself to sociology as the religion of humanity, Littré chose another path: politics.

Littré believed that all sociological research should be designed to achieve some practical outcome. Societies, he claimed, changed only gradually, and it is the role of those who practise sociology to make sure that whatever change occurs is change in the direction of improvement. Political practice was nothing more or less than the sociological method in action with the practical aim of improving society (Heilbron, 2009, p. 46). Few members of the short-lived Société de Sociologie were academics or career scholars. Instead, most were committed to republican politics, and nearly one-third of them held a high political office. While they did help to introduce the term 'sociology' to a wider audience, there is little evidence that their ideas contributed much to academic sociology as it later developed (Heilbron, 2009, p. 55).

HARRIET MARTINEAU (1802–1876): METHODS OF SOCIOLOGICAL RESEARCH

Considered by many to be the first woman sociologist, Harriet Martineau (1802–76) was born in Norwich, England, the sixth of eight children. Her father was a manufacturer, and so Harriet grew up in reasonably comfortable surroundings, even receiving (unlike most women of her generation) a good education. Taught both at home by her siblings and private tutors and in school, Harriet learned classics, languages, literature, history, composition, mathematics, religious studies (she was raised as a Unitarian), music, philosophy, and poetry. Barred from attending university because of her gender, she augmented her formal education with extensive self-directed study (Hill & Hoecker-Drysdale, 2003, p. 6). When she was in her early twenties her father died; the family business failed, and she and her younger sisters were forced to earn their own living. Martineau then embarked on a literary career, gaining notoriety for a series of publications (1832–4) illustrating the principles of political economy.

A caricature of Littré by the nineteenth-century French cartoonist André Gill in the newssheet *L'Éclipse* shows the well-known lexicographer and disciple of Comte sitting in the 'tree of science'. The reading monkey is a small parody of Darwinism, reflecting the skepticism felt by many French citizens of the time about scientific positivism and evolutionary theory. How do you think Gill intended us to view Littré?

In 1834 Martineau set sail for America. There, a two-year 'holiday' provided her with enough material for two books—and with a new, lifelong commitment to the abolition of slavery. As a result of her American trip, Martineau published the three-volume *Society in America* (1837), in which she identified the moral principles to which Americans claimed

A portrait of Harriet Martineau. How would you compare this depiction with portraits, photographs, and caricatures of some of the other sociologists discussed in this chapter?

allegiance, and compared those principles to her own observations of social patterns. She demonstrated a wide gap between the values prized by Americans—democracy, justice, equality, and freedom—and the young republic's actual institutionalized practices, including racism, which she decried. Although Alexis de Tocqueville's *Democracy in America* was written at the same time as Martineau's *Society in America* and has certainly become more famous, several sociologists now contend that Martineau's book, and not de Tocqueville's, made the most acute observations of American society (McDonald, 1994, p. 171).

Martineau's arrival in America followed a month-long ocean voyage (Hill, 1989), during which she prepared a set of methodological guidelines for observing American society. These guidelines, which were strongly positivist in nature, focused on the observation of things—physical artifacts, official records, and other material indications of institutional organization (Hill & Hoecker-Drysdale, 2003, p. 65). *How to Observe Morals and Manners* (1838) can be considered the first systematic treatise on methods of sociological research. In it Martineau examines such issues as social class, religion, types of suicide, national character, delinquency, and penology (Hill & Hoecker-Drysdale, 2003, p. 18).

In 1853, Martineau capped her contributions to the founding of sociology by publishing an English translation of Auguste Comte's *Cours de philosophie positive*. Martineau's work in sociology was largely ignored until it was abridged and presented in the 1960s by the American sociologist Seymour Martin Lipset. A decade later, sociologist Alice Rossi designated Martineau the 'first woman sociologist'. In 1994 feminist sociologist Lynn McDonald made the claim that, compared to de Toqueville's *Democracy in America,* Martineau's work *Society in America* is 'wiser' and more 'astute', especially around issues of racism and the discrimination experienced by freed blacks (McDonald, 1994, p. 17).

As a sociologist, Martineau achieved three major accomplishments (Deegan, 2003, p. 300):

- She wrote the first book on sociological methodology (*How to Observe Morals and Manners,* 1838).
- She completed an 'insightful and methodologically advanced analysis of American society' (*Society in America,* 1837).
- She translated into English, and condensed, Comte's *Cours de philosophie positive* [1830–42] (1853).

THE CONTRIBUTIONS OF ÉMILE DURKHEIM

Émile Durkheim, who held the first academic chair in sociology, thought of sociology as 'the science of institutions, their genesis and their functioning' (Durkheim, 1895/1982, p. 45), and did much to establish 'society' as the legitimate object of sociological analysis.

During his career as a sociologist Durkheim published over 500 articles, books, and reviews, including *The Division of Labour* (1893), *The Rules of the Sociological Method* (1895), *Suicide,* (1897), and *The Elementary Forms of the Religious Life* (1912). He also founded a respected—although controversial—sociology journal, *L'Année sociologique* and served as an 'advising editor of the *American Journal of Sociology* from its first year of publication to the outbreak of World War I' (Tiryakian, 1975, p. 10). Durkheim contributed many important concepts to sociology, including the concepts of society, social facts, the sociological method, and anomie and normlessness.

Émile Durkheim (1858–1917)

Born in Lorraine, France, in 1858, Émile Durkheim was encouraged to follow the rabbinical calling of his father, grandfather, and great-grandfather. He was given a thorough secular and religious education by his parents. However, as a young student, Durkheim was strongly influenced by a form of Catholic mysticism and turned away from the rabbinate toward more secular interests.

Durkheim studied philosophy and history at the prestigious École Normale Supérieure in Paris and read Comte's texts on sociology. It was here that he broke from Judaism and dedicated himself to academic studies, especially philosophy (Lukes, 1985). Another significant influence on Durkheim's ideas about society was the political circumstances of mid- and late nineteenth-century France. Throughout his life Durkheim witnessed repeated political changes and upheavals. His professional concern with stability and his abhorrence of sudden change may be directly linked to his personal anxiety over the fragility of the French republic and his desire to see the French state preserved. Durkheim hated social disorder, a subject to which he devoted most of his work. In his view, social disorder was not a necessary part of the modern world. Like Comte, Durkheim believed that all social disorders could be greatly reduced through the introduction of social reform.

Society

society
A broad grouping of people who live together and who have developed, through interacting with one another, common interests, institutions, and collective activities, typically demonstrating a unique pattern of social relations and shared norms, values, and beliefs.

Society, for Durkheim, has no material existence, and its existence is independent of the individuals who are affected by it. He argued that society is best understood as a synthetic, higher-level reality that must be 'accorded its own level of experience' (Gafijczuk, 2005, p. 19). Individuals, in the course of their day-to-day activities, do things that are not purely individual; that is, they do things that are the result of some mix of their individual psychological makeup, their personal life experiences, and external social forces (or 'society'). While social forces exist outside of the individual, they impinge on the individual's daily experience, and they structure that experience in certain ways. Durkheim assigned to the newly established discipline of sociology the special task of uncovering the ways in which external forces (i.e. society) impinge on and shape the experiences and behaviours of individuals.

Durkheim believed there are many levels of reality manifested in the universe, including social, physical, chemical, biological, and psychological levels. Each level emerges out of a previous, simpler one. He further believed that the social level of reality was the most complex of all. The social level of reality emerges from the interactions of individuals who possess the capacity for symbolic communication and reflection. But it has unique properties that extend beyond those available to any one individual. For Durkheim, 'society' is *sui generis*—that is, society is a higher-order reality that must be granted its own level of existence (Gafijczuk, 2005, p. 19). By using the Latin phrase *sui generis* ('of its own kind', i.e. unique) to refer to society, Durkheim meant to convey the understanding that 'society' could not be reduced to or explained in terms used to describe any other level of reality; the properties used to define 'society' could not be borrowed from expressions of other realities, such as biology or psychology.

In *Rules of the Sociological Method*, Durkheim made a strong case for giving society ontological status, in other words status as a new and emergent object of study. Without being granted ontological status, Durkheim suggested, sociology was not possible because sociological laws could be 'only a corollary of the more general laws of psychology' and 'the ultimate explanation of collective life will consist in showing how it emanates from human nature in general' (1895/1978, p. 98). Two years later, in his study of suicide, Durkheim reinforced this line of thinking, arguing that 'there can be no sociology unless societies exist' and that 'societies cannot exist if there are only individuals' (1897/1952, p. 38).

What Durkheim proposed ran counter to the dominant mode of thinking at the time, in the sense that it went against the primacy of the individual. In place of individual motives, needs, and beliefs, Durkheim proposed granting causal priority to a new ontological object—society. As a result, he produced arguments explaining human behaviour that defied or denied the common-sense assumptions of his day (Turner, 2006, p. 135).

Social Facts

Durkheim's concept of '**social facts**' is central to his argument about the autonomy of sociology as a discipline distinct from biology or psychology. First, 'social facts' are to be considered as 'things' that are external to the individual and that are capable of exercising coercive power

social facts
'Things' that are external to the individual and capable of exercising coercive power over him or her, independent of, and resistant to, the will of any given individual.

Consider smoking as a behaviour that may proceed from a mix of individual psychological makeup, personal life experiences, and external forces. In what ways might each of these influence smoking behaviour? Which do you think has the greatest influence?

over him or her. In other words, 'social facts' are independent of, and resistant to, the will of any given individual. They constrain the individual and, as Durkheim held, 'it is impossible to free ourselves of them.' It is 'social facts' that exercise power over the individual, not the other way around. Durkheim further stated that 'the presence of this power may be recognised . . . either by the existence of some specific sanction or by resistance offered against every individual effort that tends to violate it' (Durkheim, 1978, pp. 10 & 20, as cited in Benton, 1977, pp. 90–1).

Is personal hygiene a social fact? Think about it: there's no written rule that says you have to brush your hair before you leave the house. But what if you went for a week without showering or bathing? What kinds of pressure might you feel—at school, at work, on the bus—to clean up your act? Could you just ignore these sanctions? What other agents exist in society to condition us to believe that cleanliness is next to godliness?

Each individual acts according to customs, moral rules, and legal criteria. Each individual exercises his rights and duties in a way that is consistent with the laws and customs of his society. But these laws and customs exist independently of him. If he chooses not to comply with the laws or conform to customs, his choice does not change the existence of the laws or customs; they continue despite his individual nonconformity. Moreover, the moral laws and customs of his society exist prior to his birth and continue after his death—they were not created by him, and he is subject to them whether or not he is consciously aware of what they are, or even of their existence. They are in evidence every time he speaks or otherwise attempts to interact with others. If he wants to be understood by others he must use a language that others understand. If he wants to purchase an item he must use a currency that others accept as valid. Although he is not usually conscious of the coercive power of social facts, he is made aware of them if, for example, he breaks a law or transgresses a custom and is faced with a repressive sanction (Benton, 1977, p. 92).

The externality of social facts implies that they are not spontaneously understood by the very people subjected to them; social facts are not amenable to common-sense understanding. Like a chemist who researches chemical reactions or a physicist who studies physical forces, a sociologist studies social facts. To understand chemical reactions, physical forces, or social facts requires 'data from outside the mind'—that is, data gathered 'from observations and experiments'. Durkheim is clear that the causes of a chemical reaction, a physical force, or a social fact equally cannot be 'discovered by even the most careful introspection'. Durkheim goes on to propose that, in order to study social facts, the sociologist must put himself

> in the same state of mind as the physicist, chemist, or physiologist when he probes into a still unexplored region of the scientific domain. When he penetrates the social world, he must be aware that he is penetrating the unknown; he must feel himself in the presence of facts whose laws are as unsuspected as were those of life before the era of biology. (Durkheim, 1978, p. xlv).

Taken together, all social facts consist of representations of 'supra-individual' (i.e. beyond the individual) social phenomena. Durkheim explains these supra-individual phenomena through analogy. If we think of an individual in the same way we think of a single chemical compound, then when individuals combine together we get something that is distinctive, or 'emergent', something that is different from any of the individuals involved but that derives from their association. This is analogous to the way two chemical compounds combine to produce something entirely different from either of them—a new compound with properties deriving not from the component compounds alone but from their association (Benton, 1977, p. 85).

Durkheim concluded that not only do social facts exist, but they make up a distinct field of reality with its own properties and laws that can be studied by sociologists. Durkheim thus rejected the claim that all explanation in the human sciences must be in terms of the actions, intentions, or will of individual social actors. Durkheim accepted that there are ideas or representations—the 'psychological facts'—that constitute the 'conscious states of the individual'. But these psychological facts are of little concern or interest to sociologists. There are, however, external 'social facts' that are the result of the association of many individuals. It is these facts that are the proper subject matter of sociology. Social facts, according to Durkheim, are to be recognized by the power of external coercion they exercise over individuals.

The Sociological Method

The defining task of the discipline of sociology, Durkheim argued, is to discover and interpret what is external to the individual. Moreover, the approach that a sociologist might use to do this is similar to the approach used to discover laws in other sciences (Lukes, 1985, p. 68; Swingewood, 1984, p. 107). But, Durkheim claimed, sociology is an autonomous science, different from all other sciences, because it has the ability to discern a new level of reality— social reality—and to intelligently grasp the social facts indicative of that level of reality. The skills to achieve this kind of understanding are vital to the sociologist, and can be acquired and honed only through distinctly sociological training and the application of the sociological method of inquiry.

We have already discussed one of Durkheim's key theoretical concepts, the social fact. Durkheim developed this concept, together with the sociological method by which social facts may be studied, in *The Rules of the Sociological Method* (1895/1978, 1982) and *Suicide* (1897/1952). The first point Durkheim makes is that the sociological method must be strictly empirical, represent positive science, and have nothing to do with what he called 'philosophy'. Second, the sociological method must be objective. 'Society' and other 'social facts' are 'things and must be treated as such'. In short, the subject matter of sociology must be treated in the same way used to treat the subject matter of physics or chemistry. To demonstrate this, Durkheim drew an analogy to chemistry:

> . . . [I]t is true that society has no other active forces than individuals. . . . Of course, the elementary qualities of which the social fact consists are present in germs in individual minds. But the social fact emerges from them only when they have been transformed by association since it is only then that it appears. Association itself is also an active factor productive of special effects. In itself it is therefore something new. (1897/1951, p. 310)

Here we can see that Durkheim considered the relationship between an individual and society to be interactive: while social facts constrain individual actions, social facts also emerge from the actions and interactions of those very individuals (Sawyer, 2002, p. 238). Social life, Durkheim wrote, is much like a ritual, in that it moves in a circle: 'On the one hand, the individual gets from society the best part of himself . . . but, on the other hand, society exists and lives only in and through individuals.' Societies, Durkheim concluded, can no more do without individuals than individuals can do without society (Durkheim, 1912/1915, p. 389, as cited in Sawyer, 2002, p. 238). Social facts constrain the individual, and in turn the individual's mental states are reflections of social facts.

Durkheim's idea about the way social facts emerge is instructive. He made a distinction between what he called 'social currents' and the 'crystallization' of those currents as 'social facts'. In the everyday collective life, people express themselves symbolically and interact with each other in ways that are often 'incapable of being mentally fixed by the observer' (Durkheim, 1895/1978, p. 45). These ways of interacting he calls 'social currents', which are very much like social facts, with the exception that they have not obtained enough force and consistency to become fixed. Once that happens—that is, once a social current becomes stable and repeatable—it has crystallized into a 'social fact'. Sociologists, he maintained, use scientific methods to study these materialized facts.

In studying materialized social facts, Durkheim helped pioneer the use of statistics by sociologists. In *The Rules of the Sociological Method* (1895/1982), Durkheim developed his conception of the proper subject matter of sociology: the study of materialized 'social facts'. In *Suicide* (1897/1952), as we saw in Chapter 3, he tested his ideas in an empirical study. Durkheim reasoned that if he could demonstrate that a seemingly individual behaviour like suicide was actually linked to social causes (i.e. social facts), he could make a persuasive case for sociology as the science of society.

Social norms are generally accepted ways of doing things—the rules that govern all of social interaction. Social norms can be prescriptive (they can tell us what to do) or proscriptive (they can forbid us to do certain things). Following Comte, Durkheim argued that the major problem facing modern society was the absence of a morality appropriate to the new social conditions. Old traditions and practices (social norms) had gone, but there was nothing to replace them. The result was a pathological condition or state that Durkheim called **anomie**, or 'normlessness', which he defined as 'the state of normative or moral deregulation which afflicts modern society'. Included among its consequences are 'unbridled economic appetites which undermine the integrative tendencies of the modern division of labour, as well as pathologies of individual conduct, such as suicide' (Tiryakian, 1975, p. 9). Anomie produces social instability. Durkheim believed that it was the role of sociology to assist in the project of social reconstruction by scientifically deriving a new moral system to act as the anchor of modern society (Tiryakian, 1975, p. 9).

social norms

A set of rules governing social interaction. Social norms can be prescriptive (they can tell us what to do) or proscriptive (they can forbid us to do certain things).

anomie

Durkheim's term for the weakening or absence of the usual moral standards governing social life, which allows free rein to destructive (or self-destructive) exercises of will in pursuit of expanding or unrealistic personal goals

Most jurisdictions have policies and programs in place to encourage recycling, yet how often have you seen a pop can tossed into a regular garbage bin, or a plastic wrapper thrown into a blue box? Would you reprimand someone—friend, family member, or stranger—for mixing garbage with recyclables? In other words, is recycling a social current or a social fact?

A Critique of Durkheim

By the end of the nineteenth century, the organic model of society and the notion of using an organic analogy to liken society to a biological organism were losing ground. After all, the individuals who made up society could be separated from each other and were not bound together like the organs and other parts of a body. Moreover, mature individuals were often quite capable of surviving if cut off from society. Even more troublesome was the issue of boundaries: it was easy to know where the boundary of one body left off and another began, but societies were an entirely different matter. Societies merged, pieces broke off to form independent units, and the limits of any one society were hard to define.

These problems, however, had not stopped Durkheim from using the organic analogy in his earlier work. Durkheim was concerned with establishing the reality of society. He believed it to be a complex, natural entity and, as such, an appropriate object for scientific study. He argued that society was not amenable to being changed by individuals at will, and instead that society existed independent of individuals who made it up and that it exercised powerful constraints over them. Key concepts in Durkheim's analysis of society—organ and function, morphology and physiology, the normal and the pathological—all derive from biology. As sociologist Daniela Barberis (2003) writes:

> Indeed, we now take 'society' for granted, but a considerable amount of work was necessary to constitute it as an obvious and almost irresistible way to think about the world. Organicism played a pivotal role in this process. (Barberis, 2003, p. 66)

When Durkheim published *Rules of the Sociological Method* in 1895, he was widely attacked for reifying or hypostatizing society (in other words, attempting to treat an abstract concept as if it were a real, material object). This is important, for in response to those criticisms, Durkheim seemed to back down from his position that society was a separate entity that existed apart from individuals and that could be taken as a legitimate object of study by the new discipline he championed (see, for example, 1897/1952, p. 391).

Durkheim argued that the individual was a product, and not a cause, of society (1893/1964a, p. 286; Sawyer, 2002, p. 243). At the same time he also knew that the individual played a significant role in the development of 'society', and he tried to solve the problem of the relationship between the individual and society by arguing that humans have a dual nature: one part 'purely individual', the other 'social' (1914/1964b, p. 337). But he did not provide an account of the 'mechanisms and processes' by which individuals create society and by which society, in turn, creates individuals (Sawyer, 2002).

Durkheim perceived that the individual was the indispensable substrate of the social world (Marshall, 2006, p. 132). He also perceived that humans are first and foremost social beings, and that the social abilities of humans precede their ability to reason. Biologically, the ancestors of present-day humans were social creatures long before they were able to reason in the ways contemporary humans are able to reason. Being social is indeed a necessary prerequisite for the kind of cognition human beings display today.

By 1910 Durkheim had done much toward securing the legitimacy of sociology in France. But while the discipline had a fairly coherent line of development in that country from the Enlightenment, through the French Revolution, and on to the ideas of Comte, Saint-Simon, and Durkheim, what happened in Germany was rather different. There, a split emerged between, in one camp, Karl Marx and his supporters, who remained on the fringes of mainstream sociology, and in the other, Max Weber, another of the early giants of the discipline.

The split is interesting, and worth considering for a number of reasons, including the unresolved issue left from Durkheim's work: do social facts exist as things? Does 'society' exist as an external reality that exerts coercive or causal powers over individuals? Or are social facts merely the collected actions of all those individuals who participate in social interactions?

Do we best understand social life from the point of view of the subjective mental states of individuals, a position that Weber championed? Do we best understand it from the point of view of the causal power exerted by external social structures, a position consistent with the work of Karl Marx (and, interestingly, of Durkheim)? Or, do we require a different approach altogether, one that draws on the new theories and research techniques of the twenty-first century to elaborate a theory of society and social life that has a place both for individual agency and subjectivity and for the causal powers of social phenomena (Sawyer, 2002, p. 245)?

THE BEGINNINGS OF CANADIAN SOCIOLOGY

Although sociology first appeared as an institutionalized discipline in Europe and the United States in the late 1800s, it wasn't until the early 1920s that sociology courses were first offered in a number of academic departments at universities across Canada. In 1924 the first academic department of sociology was established at McGill University. McGill remained the only university in Canada with a sociology department until the 1950s and 1960s, when several other universities across Canada established their own departments of sociology. For example, the department of sociology at the University of Toronto wasn't established until 1963. This was seven years after Canadian sociologists received a boost with the founding of their first professional organization, a sociology chapter established as part of the Canadian Political Science Association.

Unlike American sociology, Canadian sociology has reflected the social reality of a country with two major cultural and linguistic communities. The launch within a 15-year span of two professional English-language sociology journals—*The Canadian Review of Sociology and Anthropology* (1964) and *The Canadian Journal of Sociology* (1975)—and two French-language journals—*Recherches sociographiques* (1960) and *Sociologie et sociétés* (1969)—further established sociology as an independent academic discipline in Canada.

French-Canadian sociology was at first strongly influenced by the Catholic Church, and by the intellectual traditions of Europe and especially of France, where sociologists were concerned with economic and political trends. Sociologists in Anglophone Canada were, at first, strongly influenced by the work of American sociologists (especially those sociologists who taught at McGill) and British sociologists (who exercised a strong influence over the sociologists at the University of Toronto). But Canadian sociologists quickly began to fashion their own brand of sociology, strongly influenced by the unique Canadian context. Among the most important aspects of Canadian sociology is the commitment Canadian sociologists have made to understanding a changing national society.

Carl Addington Dawson (1887–1964), a student of Robert Park's at the University of Chicago, taught at McGill University, where in 1922 he founded the first full-time sociology department at a Canadian university. In his role as chairman of the Canadian Social Science Research Council, he sponsored additional studies of Canadian communities, including Horace Miner's

St Denis: A French Canadian Parish (1939) and Everett Hughes's *French Canada in Transition* (1943). Dawson himself published an extensive series of studies of immigrant settlement in western Canada. Another prominent member of McGill's Department of Sociology was Aileen Ross (1902–95), who was among the very first women sociologists to hold a teaching position at a Canada university. Ross wrote on the structure of social philanthropy (1953) and on the socialization process (with the publication of *Becoming a Nurse*, in 1961). She was instrumental

PROFILES IN SOCIOLOGY

Early Influential Canadian Sociologists

Harold Innis (1894–1952)

Born near Hamilton, Ontario, Harold Innis graduated from McMaster University just before World War I and saw frontline duty in France, an experience that made him a committed and lifelong pacifist. Following the war, Innis studied political economy at the University of Chicago, earning his PhD with a dissertation on the Canadian Pacific Railway. He became interested in how the economies of colonized nations such as Canada developed. His first book, *The History of the Fur Trade in Canada* (1930), and subsequent books on the cod fisheries, the dairy industry, and wheat industry all developed the staples thesis, his best-known contribution to the study of Canadian political economy. The staples thesis argues that the Canadian economy depended on the extraction and export of single, unprocessed commodities. This reliance, in turn, put Canada in a vulnerable and dependent relationship with other, more developed nations that focused their economies on manufacturing rather than resource extraction. Innis spent the latter part of his academic career writing *Empire and Communications* (1950) and *The Bias of Communication* (1951), massive studies of the social history of communications media over a period of 4,000 years. Innis's theories on communication had an undeniable influence on the work of his younger University of Toronto colleague, the 'media prophet' Marshall McLuhan.

Marshall McLuhan (1911–1980)

Born in Edmonton, Alberta, Marshall McLuhan earned his bachelor's degree from the University of Manitoba in 1933 and a PhD in English literature from Cambridge University in 1942. His first book, *The Mechanical Bride: Folklore of Industrial Man* (1951), together with *The Gutenberg Galaxy: the Making of Typographic Man* (1962), helped to pioneer the field now known as popular cultural studies. McLuhan was interested in how changes in technology brought about cultural and cognitive changes, arguing that print culture, first made possible by Johannes Gutenberg's invention of the movable type printing press in the fifteenth century, brought about a cultural revolution that helped visual culture gain ascendancy over aural/oral culture. His most widely read books, *Understanding Media: The Extensions of Man* (1964) and *The Medium Is the Massage: An Inventory of Effects* (1967) (with graphic designer Quentin Fiore), are landmarks in the field of media theory, earning him worldwide notoriety both in academia and in the broader public.

John Porter (1921–1979)

John Porter was born in Vancouver, British Columbia, but moved to England with his family when he was 15. During the Second World War he served in the Canadian Forces as an intelligence officer, before completing his studies, following the war, at London School of Economics. Returning to Canada in 1949, he took a teaching post at Carleton College, teaching political science for two years before becoming the school's first appointment in the nascent discipline of sociology. His most famous book, *The Vertical Mosaic: An Analysis of Social Class and Power in Canada* (1965), started out as his doctoral dissertation. This book, a study of social stratification and the barriers to success in this country, helped establish sociology as a legitimate discipline taught in Canadian universities. It stands today as a foundational and influential study of inequality in the Canadian context.

is initiating comparative sociology as a field of study at McGill, publishing *The Hindu Family in Its Urban Setting* (1961) and *Student Unrest in India: A Comparative Approach* (1969).

At the University of Toronto, political economist Harold Innis followed the British model of sociological inquiry to address important questions about Canadian economic development. Innis developed what became known as the 'staples thesis', arguing that, historically, Canada's economic and social development depended on the extraction and exportation of natural resources, rather than on manufacturing. This situation made Canada dependent on other more developed nations and resulted in a kind of branch-plant approach to economic development. Innis also studied the vital role of communications and communication technologies in the development of Canadian society and culture. This theme was elaborated on by another University of Toronto professor, Marshall McLuhan. Although McLuhan taught in the university's English department, he was in fact a social theorist who articulated important insights into the impact of electronic communications on thought, behaviour, and the structure of society. McLuhan gained a worldwide reputation for his groundbreaking work on media and culture, and is famous for declaring that 'the medium is the message' and for coining the term 'global village'.

John Porter is one of Canada's most influential and important sociologists. In his most famous work, *The Vertical Mosaic* (1965), Porter used Canadian census data from 1931, 1951, and 1961 to argue that while Canada is an 'ethnic mosaic', it is also hierarchically structured. Porter found that wealth and power were unequally distributed among the ethnic groups that make up Canadian society, drawing on the theoretical work of Max Weber to demonstrate that different ethnic groups were unequally represented in a variety of occupations.

Porter was the first Canadian sociologist to make the link between ethnicity and social class. Porter found that in the period between 1931 and 1961, the 'charter groups' (Canadians

STUDIES IN SOCIAL RESEARCH

Some Landmark Works of Canadian Sociology

1930	*The Fur Trade in Canada*, by Harold Innis (1894–1952)	**1951**	*The Mechanical Bride*, by Marshall McLuhan (1911–80)
1934	*The Settlement of the Peach River Country: A Study of a Pioneer Area*, by Carl Dawson (1887–1964)	**1953**	'The Social Control of Philanthropy', by Aileen Ross (1902–95)
1936	*Group Settlement: Ethnic Communities in Western Canada*, by Carl Dawson	**1957**	*The National Policy and the Wheat Economy*, by Vernon Fowke (1907–66)
1937	*Canadian Frontiers of Settlement*, by Carl Dawson	**1959**	*The Presentation of the Self in Everyday Life*, by Erving Goffman (1922–82)
1939	*St Denis: A French Canadian Parish*, by Horace Miner (1912–93)	**1960**	*Negroes in Toronto: A Sociological Study of a Minority Group*, by Daniel Hill (1923–2003)
1940	*The Cod Fisheries: The History of an International Economy*, by Harold Innis	**1965**	*Lament for a Nation: The Defeat of Canadian Nationalism*, by George Grant (1918–88)
1947	*The New North West*, by Carl Dawson		*The Vertical Mosaic: An Analysis of Class and Power in Canada*, by John Porter (1921–79)
1948	*Church and Sect in Canada*, by Samuel Delbert Clark (1910–2003)	**1968**	*Introduction to the Mathematics of Population*, by Nathan Keyfitz (b. 1913)

of British and French ancestry) held social, economic, and political advantage over 'less preferred' groups, who were typically employed in lower-status jobs and who were often blocked from achieving upward social mobility. Using occupation as a rough measure of social class, Porter determined that Canadians of Jewish and British origin were at the top of the hierarchy, consistently overrepresented in the professional and financial occupations that conferred both a high income and high status. By contrast, Greeks and Portuguese were near the lower end, consistently overrepresented in agriculture and unskilled jobs that provided them with low income and a lower status.

Today, Canadian sociologists continue to be concerned with issues of economic development, inequality, ethnicity, communications, and diversity, as well as cultural expression and survival.

SUMMARY

The discipline of sociology was first established by eighteenth- and nineteenth-century thinkers who wanted to both understand and exercise some control over the direction of social change that was occurring in Europe and North America. Sociologist George Ritzer (2000) has identified six social conditions that were key to the development of sociology as an academic discipline: (1) the social chaos that followed the French Revolution of 1789; (2) industrialization and the rise of capitalism; (3) the rise of socialism; (4) the displacement of rural inhabitants and mass migration to the cities; (5) challenges to society's religious basis; and (6) the growth of science.

Early French sociologists, including Saint-Simon, Comte, and, later, Martineau and Durkheim, were motivated by a desire to understand and control the new social order that they perceived emerging. Saint-Simon, in addition to coining the term 'industrial society', introduced the metaphor of society as an organism—characterized by growth, order, stability, and abnormal pathologies—subject to laws of social organization that could be discovered by social scientists. Comte introduced the term 'sociology' and proposed that the object of sociological analysis should be 'society'. Sociologists, he further proposed, should follow a new scientific approach, which he labelled 'positivism', in order to understand the structure of society and to formulate the laws that could be used as tools to modify the social world. Comte developed a model of sociological analysis that later became known as functionalism, and he conceived of sociology both as the study of social order (he called this 'social statics') and the process of social change (which he called 'social dynamics').

The work of Émile Durkheim, who was the first to hold an academic chair in sociology, did much to establish 'society' as the main object of sociological analysis. For Durkheim, 'society' was special as an object of analysis because, unlike the objects of analysis examined by, say, physics, the object of sociological analysis has no material existence and is independent of the individuals who together make up a society. Individuals in society, Durkheim argued, are affected by social facts that are external to them and that can be recognized by the power of external coercion they hold over individuals. Social facts—the laws and customs, moral rules and regulations of a society—exist independently of the will of any given individual and constrain the individual's actions. We need only think about the sanctions we would face if we violated one of these constraints to recognize their power. The most important task of sociology, Durkheim believed, is to discover and interpret the social facts that are external to and that constrain the individual.

Sociology as an academic discipline was established later in Canada than in Europe and the United States. The first Canadian sociologists were concerned with issues of political economy and communications—not surprising, given Canada's vastness combined with its sparse population and its history of economic development based on resource extraction. Later Canadian sociologists placed their focus on the intersection of ethnicity and social class, themes that pervade the work of Canadian sociologists today.

DISCUSSION QUESTIONS

1. What social conditions precipitated the development of the discipline of sociology?
2. What contributions did Saint-Simon, Comte, and Durkheim make to establish the discipline of sociology?
3. What are some of the social conditions today that might lead to a further revolution in thinking about society?
4. Discuss Durkheim's concept of a 'social fact'. How did this concept help shape the way in which he viewed 'society'? What is the relationship between a 'social fact' and a 'social current'?
5. Discuss what Marshall McLuhan might have meant by the statement, 'the medium is the message'. McLuhan was writing at the time about television. How might 'the medium is the message' be applied to our modes of electronic communication today?
6. John Porter characterized Canadian society during the 1960s as a 'vertical mosaic' made up of different ethnic groups hierarchically arranged in terms of status and access to wealth and income. Is that term still applicable today?

6 Karl Marx and Max Weber

CHAPTER OUTLINE

LEARNING OBJECTIVES

In this chapter you will:

- learn about some of the social and intellectual influences on the founders of sociological inquiry
- become acquainted with the sociological thinking of Max Weber and Karl Marx and their different approaches to the study of society
- come to understand the basic concepts used by Karl Marx in his analysis of capitalist society
- reflect on Max Weber's approach to the study of society
- discover why the work of Karl Marx and Max Weber is still relevant to sociologists today
- think about the role of objectivity in the social sciences.

INTRODUCTION

In this chapter we will follow two strands of sociological thinking that are woven into the tapestry of contemporary sociology: the interpretative sociology of the German sociologist Max Weber and the dialectical materialism of Karl Marx.

Max Weber is best known for his work on the history, economy, and religion of Western societies, as well as for his theoretical work on comparative economies, political legitimacy, social class, the development of modern law and world religions, and the rise of capitalist society, bureaucracies, and the modern state. Unlike the sociologists who preceded him, Weber focused on determining how cultural values and beliefs (as well as 'social norms') helped social actors shape their subjective understandings of their own behaviour. Weber wanted to know what the subjects of sociological study actually thought, believed, and understood about the way they behaved. Karl Marx, in contrast, developed a historical-materialist method that allowed him to focus on the exterior, material world; this, he believed, held the key to understanding the social life of members of any given society.

Weber believed that the subjective motives, judgements, and understandings that social actors hold about own behaviour are legitimate focal points of a value-free sociology. Individuals, Weber determined, act in the social world and understand the social world, through 'interpretive acts'. It is the role of the sociologist to discover how social actors assign meaning to the world in which they live and act. Marx, on the other hand, thought it was the legitimate role of the intellectual to change society in ways that would make it more equitable for everyone.

KARL MARX

Of all the thinkers and writers of the last two centuries, Karl Marx has probably affected more people than any other. His writings have inspired thousands of books and articles on subjects ranging from social and economic relations in hunting-and-gathering societies, to detailed treatises on the operations of capitalist economies, to fomenting revolutions. Major political and economic revolutions have been made in Marx's name—the Russian and Chinese revolutions of the past century are just two examples. In many countries, Marxism became institutionalized, as political parties and state administrations promoted and developed their own versions of Marxist theory and politics. In countries where Marxism took hold as the basis for state organization, it was supported by many who were attracted to Marx's ideas concerning an ethical denunciation of inequality and exploitation and his celebration of universal human unity (Worsley, 1982, p. 14). In other countries, specifically the United States, entire governments devoted themselves to combating Marxism and communism, both at home and throughout the world.

His political activism, combined with his role as a social scientist, make Marx unique amongst the early sociologists. As a revolutionary, Marx sought the overthrow of capitalism, which he believed to be based on the oppression of the many (the working class, or *proletariat*) by the few (the owners of productive property, or *bourgeoisie*). He and his close friend and collaborator, Friedrich Engels, looked forward to the day when capitalism would be replaced by a new social order—advanced communism—in which all individuals would be free to realize their full potential. In *The Manifesto of the Communist Party* (1848), commonly

PROFILES IN SOCIOLOGY

Karl Marx (1818–1883)

Karl Marx was born on May 5, 1818, and grew up in the small Prussian city of Trier, located in the southern part of the German Rhineland. His father, Heinrich, was a lawyer who had converted from Judaism to Lutheranism shortly before Karl's birth in order to escape the social difficulties suffered by Jews living in Germany. Both of his parents came from rabbinical families, and with a moderately successful lawyer father, Karl grew up in a comfortable, middle-class environment.

He first attended university as a law student in Bonn, where he distinguished himself by running up debts, drinking too much, fighting (he was once wounded in a duel), and being arrested for carrying a deadly weapon. His father, who had hoped that Karl would follow in his footsteps by becoming a lawyer but was worried that his son was becoming a spendthrift and a 'slovenly barbarian', had him transferred to the University of Berlin. But prior to his departure, Karl became secretly engaged to his next-door neighbour, Jenny von Westphalen, the daughter of the Baron von Westphalen, a follower of Saint-Simon.

While at the University of Berlin, Marx encountered the work of G.W.F. Hegel, which was to have a profound influence on all his thinking. When Marx submitted his doctoral dissertation on Greek philosophies of nature, he had hoped to win a post as a university lecturer. But he soon learned that he had been blacklisted by the Ministry of Education because of his radical tendencies. He then turned to journalism as a way to support himself. As a journalist, he met his lifelong friend and collaborator, Friedrich Engels, the son of a wealthy German manufacturer with interests in textile factories in both Germany and England. Throughout the rest of his life, Marx would depend heavily on monetary support from Engels, who managed his father's textile company in Manchester, and who was periodically able to help support Marx and his family while Marx did his research and writing.

In 1844 Marx was charged with high treason by the Prussian government. He was expelled from Paris,

A monument to Karl Marx in Sichuan province, China. What is the significance of this apparent work in progress?

where he had been living and writing, and moved first to Brussels and later to London. By 1847, he and Engels were actively involved in the Communist League, and together they wrote the *Communist Manifesto* (1848). In 1849 Marx was involved in promoting a workers' revolution in Cologne, Germany. Put on trial for insulting authorities and inciting rebellion, he was acquitted by a jury but was now bankrupt, having spent his inheritance on arms for the failed workers' revolution. In 1849, Karl and Jenny Marx moved again to London, where they lived in a set of rented rooms in Soho, a poor district in the centre of the city, where they lost three of their six children in early infancy.

Marx became the London correspondent for the *New York Daily Tribune*. He also spent a great deal of his time at the British Museum, reading government statistics and the reports of factory inspectors, which described in detail the horrible conditions in which most of the working class laboured. In London he remained active as a political revolutionary and was responsible for putting together the rules and statutes of the International Working Men's Association, which supported workers' rights. The first volume of his book *Das Kapital*, in which Marx analyzed the capitalist mode of production, was published in 1867; it was later translated into Russian and enjoyed brisk sales. Marx died at home in 1883, after a lengthy illness.

known as the *Communist Manifesto*, Marx and Engels wrote of the inevitability of a society in which 'the free development of each is the condition for the free development of all'.

As American sociologist George Ritzer (2000) remarks, 'there has long been an uneasy and often bizarre relationship between sociological theory and the work of Karl Marx.' In certain countries (the former Soviet Union, for example) prior to the late 1960s, sociological theory was virtually identical to Marxist theory. At the same time, in North America (and especially in the United States) Marx's theories were dismissed as the work of an ideologue, with little to contribute to a scientific understanding of society. But by the end of the 1960s, with the participation of North American students in the civil rights movement, the women's liberation movement, and in anti–Vietnam War protests, the West's appreciation of Marx had changed. From the 1960s through to the early 1980s there was a serious effort to integrate Marx's theories into sociology. Yet by the beginning of the 1990s, Marx's work was once again out of favour in academic circles. A scan of articles published in major sociological journals, and of sociology titles published in the last two decades, indicates that very little in the way of Marxist scholarship was published during the 1990s (Smith, 2004, p. 237). However, it now appears that there is yet another revival in interest in Marx's work on the horizon, especially in the area of political economy (Jenkins, 2003, p. 30, as cited in Smith, 2004, p. 237).

Many North American students are surprised to find Marx mentioned as one of the founders of sociology. Some believe, to quote Ritzer, that 'Marx was a bloodthirsty radical whose ideological commitments prohibited him from producing a serious scientific theory' (Ritzer, 2000, pp. 147 & 149). Marx's approach to studying and theorizing the social world was, indeed, strongly influenced by his political beliefs—beliefs that were vilified in North America, especially in the US, where Marx's brand of communism was demonized as a threat to everything America stood for. But Marx was no 'bloodthirsty radical'. Rather he was a humanist, who was affected by the suffering and exploitation that he witnessed among the working class under capitalism. It was his humanism that led him to call for revolution and the overthrow of capitalism (Ritzer, 2000, p. 149).

Intellectual Influences

philosophical idealism
The philosophical position, espoused by Hegel and rejected by Marx, that thought creates reality and that physical things lack 'veritable being'—that they are, essentially, not real.

Marx's theories about social organization are rooted in his reaction to the writings of the great German philosopher Georg Wilhelm Friedrich Hegel (1770–1831). Hegel espoused a form of **philosophical idealism** in which he denied that physical things—for example, trees, houses, people, animals—had 'veritable being' (were real, in other words). Instead, following a philosophical tradition that begins with Plato, Hegel emphasized the important role of thought in creating reality. Marx, however, rejected Hegel's idealist assertion that only

A protester makes his views on communism known in New York's Times Square, 1965. Note the anti-violence demonstrators in the background.

philosophical categories were real and, therefore, that material objects were, ultimately, not real. Marx, saw misery, poverty, and oppression everywhere around him, and had little inclination to ignore the material conditions of peoples' lives.

The physical needs and requirements of humans, Marx felt, are so central to human life that they come before any intellectual needs; moreover they can be fulfilled only by direct productive activity. The objects essential to meeting the physical needs of each individual exist 'outside' of that individual and are 'indispensable to the manifestations and confirmation of' that individual's 'essential powers'. An individual can only 'express his life in real, sensuous objects' (Marx, 1964, p. 181). In and of themselves ideas do not live, or act. Nor do they have 'needs'. These are characteristics of living, physical, sensuous humans, and they make material wellbeing the single most import aspect of human existence.

While Marx rejected the idealism of Hegel's philosophy, he retained some aspects of the dialectic method of analysis that Hegel had used. But Marx 'stood Hegel upright' by having his own dialectic method focus not on ideas but on the actual material conditions of peoples' existence—hence the term **dialectical materialism**. Marx's dialectical materialism is couched in terms of patterns of opposition in class conflict. All societies, for Marx, are made up of integrated classes of people, and no one class can be understood abstracted from

dialectical materialism
Marx's term for historical materialism, his theoretical perspective for understanding history, society, and social relations.

Who in this photo needs social change? Who's in the better position to realize it? Are such conflicts of interest inevitable in a class-based society?

its relationship to the other classes. Certain classes within any given society invariably come into conflict with each other, and through this conflict, changes occur.

Marx felt that members of different social classes are ultimately enemies because they have opposing, or contradictory, interests. This is so not because individuals from different classes consciously want to oppose each other but because the structure of society makes their conflict inevitable. Under capitalism, it is difficult for a whole class of people—the proletariat (working class)—to meet their subsistence needs, control their own activities, or achieve their full human potential. They are clearly in a subordinate position, and regardless of whether or not they are conscious of the fact, they have an interest in changing society. If, on the other hand, there is a whole class of people—this time the bourgeoisie (the owners of the means of production)—who have their needs satisfied, are in control of their own activities, and are able to devote themselves to realizing their human potential and achieving most of their goals, then as a group the bourgeoisie will have little natural interest in changing society.

Marx was fully convinced that these opposing qualities of life-based interests could not be reconciled and that class conflict is always inevitable under such material conditions. He set himself the task of discovering the exact conditions, in capitalist societies, under which freely acting, individual members of a given social class (the proletariat) would finally recognize their common class interest, unite together, and bring about the next social revolution.

Friedrich Engels (1820–1895)

Friedrich Engels was Marx's close friend and collaborator for over 40 years. He was the author of two important works—'Outlines of a Critique of Political Economy' (1844) and *The Condition of the Working Class in England* (1845)—that deeply influenced Marx's thinking. After reading Engels' work, Marx began a period of intensive study of political economy that lasted for more than 20 years (Turner, Beeghley, & Powers, 2007, p. 111). In his written work, Engels developed the argument that, because it is based on private property and trade competition, industrial society is the most inhuman and exploitive form of social organization in human history. Capitalism is enormously productive, Engels argued. Yet it forces people to distrust and exploit each other because marketplace competition leads everyone to try their best to charge high prices while buying cheaply. At the same time, overproduction leads to a cycle of misery and starvation, followed by the next cycle of overproduction.

Engels led something of a double life. His father, with whom he had a strained relationship, had him leave school before he finished his final year, and so Engels never went on to university. In 1842, at the age of 22, Friedrich was sent by his father from Germany to Manchester, England, to oversee the textile mills in which his father had a part-ownership interest. At that time, Manchester was the most industrialized city in the world, a model city for capitalism and the Industrial Revolution. Its population had grown from 24,000 in 1773 to over 400,000 in 1840, and it lacked sewers, police, and city government.

If the elder Engels had hopes that his son's stay in Manchester would de-radicalize him, he was to be disappointed. Shortly after his arrival in that city, Friedrich met Mary Burns, a young working-class woman with whom he began a common-law relationship that lasted until Mary's death in 1862. With Mary acting as his guide, Friedrich was introduced to the impoverished, working-class people of Manchester. The result of Friedrich and Mary's collaboration was Engels' study *The Condition of the Working Class in England* (1844). Engels' stinging indictment of capitalist society has the distinction of being the first urban ethnography ever published. In outlining the atrocities characteristic of industrialized urban life, Engels described how workers, including children, were forced to labour for long hours, were in chronic poor health, and lived in horrific conditions. After Marx's death in 1883, Engels devoted his time to editing Marx's two unfinished volumes of *Capital*. Engels died of throat cancer in 1895.

Engels certainly agreed with Marx that social revolution, led by the working class, was inevitable in England and in other capitalist countries. But whereas Engels was content with describing the horrors of industrialization and predicting the demise of capitalism, Marx set about developing a social theory that would both explain social relations in capitalist societies and justify the social revolution that both he and Engels believed inevitable. Marx's simultaneous commitment to science and social revolution makes him unique among the founders of sociology.

In *The German Ideology* (completed in 1846, when Marx was 28 years old) Marx and Engels laid out the ideas that would underpin all of Marx's subsequent social theory:

- Above all else, humans must be able to obtain their subsistence—whatever they need in order to survive, such as food, shelter, and clothing. The first and most important act, therefore, is producing the means to satisfy human needs.
- How people live tends to 'coincide with what they produce and how they produce, and the nature of individuals depends on the material conditions of their production' (Marx & Engels, 1846/1947, p. 20).

Historical Materialism

historical materialism
The term used today to describe Marx's theoretical perspective for understanding history, society, and social relations.

Historical materialism is the term used today to describe Marx's theoretical perspective (he called it 'dialectical materialism') for understanding history, society, and social relations. In *A Contribution to the Critique of Political Economy* (1859) Marx wrote this incisive summary of the theory we now label historical materialism:

> In the social production which men carry on they enter into definite relations that are indispensable and independent of their will. These relations of production correspond to a definite stage of the development of their material forces of production. The totality of these relations of production constitutes the economic structure of society, which is the real foundation on top of which arises a legal and political superstructure to which corresponds definite forms of social consciousness. It is not the consciousness of men, therefore, that determines their existence, but instead their social existence determines their consciousness. At a certain stage of their development, the material forces of production in society come in conflict with the existing relations of production, or—what is but a legal expression of the same thing—with the property relations within which they had been at work before. From forms of development of the forces of production these relations turn into their fetters. Then occurs a period of social revolution. With the change of economic foundation the entire immense superstructure is more or less rapidly transformed. (Marx, 1859/1970, pp. 20–1)

mode of production
The characteristic way in which human labour is organized and carried out in a given era.

Marx believed that all the societies that have existed throughout all of human history can be classified into one of six economic stages, which he called **modes of production**:

- primitive communism
- ancient societies
- feudalism
- capitalism
- advanced communism.

(The sixth stage, 'Asiatic societies', could also exist in the same time frame as primitive communist and ancient societies).

Any given mode of production is made up of a combination of the **material forces of production** and the **social relations of production**. In all societies, Marx said, there are certain tasks that must be accomplished—producing food, making clothing, building shelter, raising children, healing the sick, placating the gods, and so on. These tasks are divided among the members of any given society. For Marx, the social relations of production are the relationships that exist among individuals with respect to ownership of, and access to, the material forces of production.

In class-based societies, when private interests own or control the material forces of production, society becomes stratified into two main classes: the owners of the **means of production** form the dominant group, while non-owners experience varying degrees of exploitation at the hands of the more fortunate owners. Marx devised his social theory to focus on who benefited from, and who was exploited by, existing ownership arrangements in all class-based societies. He developed his concept of modes of production as a way of categorizing and describing different types of society characterized by different structural arrangements with respect to the ownership of the forces of production. He did this in order to understand the types of social classes that were characteristic of each mode of production and the nature of the class conflict that was inherent in each mode of production. It was this inevitable class conflict, he believed, that would lead to social transformation, whether it was from feudalism to capitalism or from capitalism to socialism.

MARX'S ANALYSIS OF THE CAPITALIST MODE OF PRODUCTION

Marx presented his analysis of the **capitalist mode of production**, and the reasons for its inevitable transition to communism, in his three-volume opus, *Capital*, published between 1867 and 1894. While Marx and Engels had written *The Manifesto of the Communist Party* (1848) as a call to the 'workers of the world' to unite and 'lose their chains', Marx wrote *Capital* as an empirical analysis of the capitalist mode of production and as a rationale to explain its inevitable transformation. For the most part, Marx based his analysis on data gathered from records published by the British government. In *Capital*, Marx demonstrated that the most salient feature of the capitalist mode of production is the accumulation of capital by using exploited, alienated labour and by constantly revolutionizing production processes. In the long run, Marx predicted, the instability caused by the constant revolutionizing of the production process, and the degradation of people through their **alienation** and exploitation would serve to unite the proletariat, who would bring about a revolution.

material forces of production
Everything needed for production to take place, including labour power and the means of production.

social relations of production
The social relations through which control over the productive forces is established and maintained. In their legal form, the social relations of production take the form of property laws.

means of production
Everything, apart from labour, needed for production to take place. In the capitalist mode of production, the means of production include energy, raw materials, tools, facilities, and expertise.

capitalist mode of production
The mode of production, typically industrial in nature, in which productive property is held privately and used for private gain.

alienation
A loss of control over, or connection with, some aspect of one's being or activity, especially as a result of the organization of wage labour.

The Value of Commodities

Marx began the first volume of *Capital* (1867/1967) with a discussion of the nature of *commodities*. A commodity, he wrote, is 'an object outside of us, a thing that by its properties satisfies human wants of some sort or another'. What, Marx asked, makes a commodity valuable? Every commodity, he answered, is produced to be consumed. As such, it has two sources of value: its *use value*—essentially a measure of its usefulness to humans—and its *exchange value*, the quantity of other goods that something can be exchanged for. Marx also noted that commodities differ from each other in terms of their use values. For example, people produce bread to eat, and clothing to wear. They produce shampoo to wash their hair and blankets to keep themselves warm. Some things, too, Marx noted, are not produced by humans but are there to be taken freely by all—the air, for example.

In light of their different use values, Marx asked how it might be possible to compare the value of a blanket with the value of a loaf of bread. After all, bread and blankets are made in very different ways using very different materials, and they fulfil very different human needs. The answer, Marx tells us, is to be found not in the respective use values of these two commodities but in their exchange values. The exchange value of something is not 'natural', in that it does not simply emerge directly from the natural world (Barbour, 2003, p. 200). But every commodity that is produced is produced using human labour time, whether that time is spent baking a loaf of bread or weaving a blanket. Thus, the exchange value of each and every commodity is determined by the labour time that is 'socially necessary' to produce it. As exchange values, Marx concluded, all commodities should be considered as 'definite masses of congealed labour-time'.

When Marx referred to 'socially necessary labour time', he noted his understanding that some workers are more skilled, or differently skilled, than others, and he argued that skilled labour could be considered as a multiple of unskilled labour in calculating the value of a commodity. Marx also understood that technology could be used to reduce the amount of labour time necessary to produce a commodity. Thus, for example, the mechanization of bread making significantly reduces the amount of labour time 'congealed' in any single loaf of bread when it is produced in a factory, compared to when the bread is made by hand in an artisanal bakery.

Labour and the Commodity of Labour Power

Under the capitalist mode of production, workers sell their *labour power*—their capacity to work—to capitalists who own the means of production. The cost of food, clothing, shelter, and all the other sundry things that are necessary to keep a worker alive and able to perform labour for a set period of time each day, as well as the cost of doing the same to support a family (which contributes to the next generation of workers), are included in the cost to the capitalist of this 'peculiar commodity'.

labour power
The physical or mental capacity for work that an employee sells to an employer in return for a wage or salary.

The capitalist realizes his profit, in the form of *surplus value*, when the cost to him of purchasing **labour power** is less than the exchange value of the commodities produced by the labour he has purchased. Marx used the *rate of surplus value* as an exact measure of the degree of exploitation of any given labourer, explaining that 'the rate of surplus value is therefore an exact expression of the degree of exploitation of labour power by capital, or of the labourer by the capitalist' (Marx, 1867/1967, p. 218). Exploitation, for Marx, was not injustice; it had a precise meaning, focusing on the extraction of surplus value by one segment of the population—the capitalist class—from another, the proletariat.

Which groups are represented in this 'Pyramid of Capitalist System', which appeared in a 1911 issue of the *Industrial Worker*, the newspaper of the Industrial Workers of the World? How well does it capture Marx's concept of the capitalist mode of production?

STUDIES IN SOCIAL RESEARCH

Ruling Ideas and Ideology

An ideology can be defined as an integrated system of ideas that is external to, and coercive of, people (Lefebre, 1968; Ritzer, 2000, p. 175). Later in his life, Engels used the term *ideology* to refer to a dominating systematic view of the way the world ought to be—the sort of view found in religious doctrines or political values, something akin to 'illusions'. From this perspective, ideological thinking leads to distorted thought or false consciousness, which in turn mystifies real social relations in order to defend and perpetuate the interests of the dominant social class (Swingewood, 1984, p. 72). Under capitalism, for example, the ruling or dominant ideologies function to foster the exploitation of the proletariat by the bourgeoisie.

Marx called labour 'man's [sic] self-confirming essence' (Marx, 1964). All that humans produce, including their beliefs, religion, arts, literature, and science, is the result of human labour. Marx believed that work should be an end in and of itself. Work done for any other purpose—especially work done in order to generate a profit for an employer—is always 'alienated work'. But under the capitalist mode of production, workers are forced to sell their labour power and are subsequently alienated from the products of their own labour. Instead of owning themselves and what they produce, workers labour to produce commodities that they neither own nor (usually) can use.

The End of Capitalism?

Marx's commitment to dialectical materialism meant that he was convinced the capitalist mode of production contained within itself the seeds of its own destruction. The capitalist mode of production, he noted, requires a certain cycle to be repeated over a period of time and without variation in order to ensure capitalism's continued existence. First, workers must produce commodities that are sold on the market and converted into wages for themselves and profit (surplus value) for the capitalists. With their wages, workers then purchase the necessities of life, in the form of commodities, thus giving back their wages to the capitalists. The capitalists then use some of their profits to purchase more labour power, and other commodities that go into the productive process. This, in turn, results in the production of more commodities, which are then sold on the market in order to realize the next round of wages and surplus value. After consuming their subsistence needs, the workers are ready to go back into the market for the next round of sale of their labour power, and the expenditure of that labour power as labour to create the commodities that the capitalist, once again, takes to market. It was Marx's view that the capitalist mode of production works as long as the workers produce the commodities that can be sold by capitalists, their own wages, and surplus value. In so doing, workers also reproduce the social relations on which the capitalist mode of production depends: the exploited proletariat on one side, and the capitalist bourgeoisie on the other.

After making his analysis of the inner workings of the capitalist mode of production Marx arrived at the following conclusions.

- The proletariat will always remain workers who own nothing but their labour power, and who are thus compelled to sell their labour power to the owners of the means of production, i.e. the capitalists. As owners of the means of production, the capitalists will always be in a position to extract surplus value from the workers. Lacking access to surplus value, workers will never be in a position to purchase or control private property; they can get only enough to survive and to reproduce the next generation of workers.

- The proletarians will be increasingly impoverished as capitalists use more and more technology and machinery in order to drive down prices to become more competitive in the marketplace.
- As fewer and fewer workers are needed to produce commodities, and as technology is increasingly used to replace skilled labourers, an industrial 'reserve army of labourers' will be created. The main characteristic of the members of this 'reserve army of labourers' is that the specific skills of its members are rendered superfluous. Any one labourer can be used to replace any other.
- As more competition between capitalists takes place, capitalists will be forced to adopt new technologies just to compete. But at some point even the adoption of new technologies will no longer reduce the costs of production to the capitalist sufficiently to prevent the rate of profit from falling. Eventually this will result in a monumental crisis, exacerbated by the fact that in laying off workers and replacing them with technologies, the capitalists will be losing purchasers for their commodities.

And he made these predictions:

- As capitalism falls more and more into crises, workers will become more conscious of their interests, and band together to overthrow the bourgeoisie.
- Acting together, the workers will wage a revolution that will usher in a new, classless society.
- In this new society the state will eventually wither away, all members of society will act for the common good, and all individual members of society will be equally free to achieve their full potential.

Turner, Beeghley, and Powers (2007) contend that Marx's predictions about the future of capitalism fail on two counts. First, over 150 years after Marx made his predictions, the state has still not 'withered away', nor has the proletariat risen up worldwide to overthrow capitalism. The Russian Revolution and the Chinese Revolution—the two great social revolutions of the twentieth century made in the name of Marx—were peasant revolts and not revolts led by the proletariat. Moreover, in neither case did the state 'wither away'. Instead, in both communist Russia and China, the state became a powerful totalitarian regime. It has only been the recent rise of capitalism in both countries that has brought any hope of a weakening of totalitarianism (Turner, Beeghley, & Powers, 2007, p. 148).

Second, Marx seriously miscalculated the extent to which any given national government is merely the tool of the bourgeoisie. Labour unions, too, have been far more successful than Marx ever envisioned, and in many instances have they gained enough power to force governments to intervene in labour markets in favour of workers (Turner, Beeghley, & Powers, 2007, p. 149). Marx also assumed that a cycle of economic crises, increasing in severity, would bring about an end to capitalism. Witness, however, the global economic crisis that began in 2009, which was met by an unprecedented worldwide effort on the part of national governments to prop up banks and bail out bankrupt multinational companies by putting billions of dollars into the economy—hardly a harbinger of capitalism's decline.

Finally, Marx failed to correctly predict that the state, far from withering away, would turn out to be one of the biggest employers in capitalist societies. As the power of governments to intervene in many facets of life—education, health, infrastructure, communications, policing, the economy, and many more—grew, the requirements of government for employees to administer these areas also grew. It is difficult, indeed, to argue that the interests of these white-collar government employees are the same as either those of capitalists or those of the proletariat.

WHY MARX IS STILL RELEVANT TO SOCIOLOGISTS TODAY

Marx's most enduring contribution is the general theory that is implicit in his work: a theory, to quote Turner (2005, p. 461), 'about the relationships among certain fundamental properties of the social universe—namely, power, production, distribution, inequality ideology, and conflict'. This general theory transcends any specific historical epoch. Unfortunately it has often become lost in Marx's attempts to be historically specific and, of course, in the 'ideological agenda' that he pursued.

MAX WEBER

Introduction

bureaucracy
A form of social organization characterized by (1) a hierarchical chain of command, (2) the allegiance of office holders to a system of impersonal rules and regulations, (3) an absence of personal ties between a bureaucracy's employees and its clients, and (4) decisions made on the basis of documents and files.

Max Weber was the second German scholar trained at the University of Berlin to have lasting influence on the discipline of sociology. Weber, who was in his early twenties when Marx died, rarely cited Marx's work in his own publications, but it is well known that he read Marx and was influenced by his writing. Generally speaking, Marx and Weber do seem to have agreed on the structural factors influencing modern society. Both present conceptual schemes that map the connections between social structures and individual actions. Both recognize that individual freedom of action was limited under capitalism, either through 'alienation' of workers from the 'means of production' (Marx) or, by the 'iron cage' of increasingly rationalized bureaucracies (Weber). Both felt the decision-making process that members of a society were able to engage in was of decisive importance for the developmental direction taken by that society. In writing the slogan 'Workers of the world unite, you have nothing to lose but your chains', Marx looked forward to a worldwide revolution that would herald a new era of social equity and freedom for all. The less-than-optimistic Weber, who characterized the members of capitalist society as trapped within the 'iron cage' of **bureaucracy**, at least granted that they had a wider range of choices available to them than those living in more traditional societies enjoyed (Turner, Beeghley, & Powers, 2007, p. 158).

Despite their similarities, there are many significant differences in both the style and the purpose of the work of these two important German sociologists. Marx never held an academic post, and was not concerned with establishing sociology as an academic discipline. Weber, in contrast, played a central role in establishing sociology as an academic discipline and taught at universities in Germany and elsewhere. Marx was committed to worldwide social revolution and developed his theories of society to support that objective. Weber had no interest in social revolution and rejected Marx's assertions that the central task of social theorists was to change society and that all social theory must be linked to social and political action. Instead, Weber believed that the task of social theory was to promote the gathering of object facts about society and thus to uncover valid, historical truths. Knowledge about societies, Weber felt, was best obtained by comparing different historical periods (Morrison, 1995, p. 215).

Intellectual Influences

Two nineteenth-century German thinkers, Wilhelm Dilthey (1833–1911) and Heinrich Rickert (1863–1936), strongly influenced Weber's ideas about social science methodology. From Dilthey, Weber adapted three ideas:

1. Both nature and human behaviour can be studied scientifically, but with important differences. In the natural sciences, it is enough for a scientist to observe some event or relationship in order to be able to explain it. But explaining social phenomena is quite a different proposition because each person being observed has an inner nature that must be comprehended if the scientist ever hopes to explain what he has observed.
2. The key to producing valid scientific knowledge about social phenomena lies in understanding the subjective meanings that social actors attach to their actions; yet the very background of the scientist doing the observing affects the kinds of explanations she is able to produce. The social scientist must exercise diligence in keeping social scientific statements separate from any kind of value judgements.
3. The key to keeping social scientific statements separate from any kind of value judgements lies in developing a set of abstract concepts (or ideal types) that can be used to classify different kinds of social action, as well as the properties of the social structures within which the social action happens (Turner, Beeghley, & Powers, 2007, p. 165).

Rickert influenced Weber through his interest in *Verstehen*, the process of understanding social phenomena in terms of the subjective understanding that social actors hold about the meaning of their own actions—essentially an empathic approach to understanding human behaviour. Rickert argued that reality presents to the social actor an overwhelming multiplicity of events. In order to navigate such a complex reality, the social actor has to rely on cultural values to lead the way. Weber accepted Rickert's argument that reality, in its entirety, is just too much for any human to comprehend. All that any individual can hope to know about is what gets filtered through a restricted number of cultural values and culturally influenced concepts.

THEMES IN WEBER'S WORK

In spite of illness, Weber wrote a great deal in his lifetime on a wide variety of topics. One authority on Weber, Raymond Awn (1967, pp. 219–20), sees the German sociologist's work as falling into four categories:

1. Studies in methodology, criticism, and philosophy. In these works, Weber considered the relationship between science and human action.
2. Historical works, including a study of the relations of production in agriculture in the ancient world, a general economic history, and studies on specific economic problems in Germany and the rest of Europe.
3. Studies in the sociology of religion, including his most important study on the relationship between Protestantism and capitalism, as well as a comparative analysis of the great religions of the world and the reciprocal influence of economies and religions.

Max Weber, Jr (1864–1920)

Max Weber was the first of seven children born into a well-to-do, cosmopolitan, bourgeois German family

living in the city of Erfurt in Thuringia, Prussia. Weber's maternal great-grandfather, Cornelius Souchay, was an 'adventure capitalist', a man who 'combined speculation carpet baggery, smuggling, and plain old savvy trading and finance into a form of art' (as cited in Roth, 2002, p. 514). It was Souchay's fortune, a part of which was inherited by Max Weber's mother, Helene, that allowed the family to live in 'the grand bourgeois lifestyle' (Roth, 1997, p. 660).

Weber's father, Max, Sr, was an academic and a politician who supported the National Liberalism movement and its party. He served as a city councillor first in Erfurt and then in Berlin, where the family moved in 1869. He was a member of the Prussian Diet (or legislative assembly) for Erfurt and represented several other locations in the Imperial Diet during the 1870s and 1880s.

In 1882 Weber began his university career, eventually finishing his studies at the University of Berlin. During his university career Weber was (like many of the discipline's founders) wild and impetuous, spending much of his free time drinking and brawling. He joined his father's fraternity, engaged in ritual drinking bouts, and (like Karl Marx) acquired fencing scars on his face. But unlike Marx, whose youthful preoccupation with revolutionary ideas had ensured that he would be

4. A treatise on general sociology, entitled *Economy and Society*. Unlike Marx, Weber was not interested in developing a theory of human society. He was more concerned with showing why Western capitalist societies developed in ways that were different from all other types of societies. Unlike Comte, Hegel, and Marx, Weber did not believe that all societies followed general laws of development. He therefore did not develop any general categorizing schema (as Marx did concerning the development of and transitions among different modes of production).

Several important themes appear in Weber's work:

- the nature of methodology and investigation in the social sciences (including ideal types, social action, *Verstehen*, and values)
- rationality
- rationalization
- capitalism and bureaucracy.

given no university post, Max Weber was considered by the authorities to be eminently suitable to teach at a German university. In 1892 he accepted his first academic position, at the University of Berlin.

The young Weber had ambitions to follow his father in a political career. But in 1897, already chronically overworked, he became incapacitated following an argument during which he accused his father of being a tyrant and of mistreating his mother. The elder Weber was ordered out of his son's house and died suddenly a few weeks later. Consumed by guilt and remorse, the younger Max Weber suffered an emotional collapse from which he never fully recovered, effectively ending both his academic and his political careers for close to 20 years.

On a rest-cure trip to the United States in 1904, Weber became intrigued by the pace of life in America and by the country's strange democratic customs. He was convinced that the 'spirit of capitalism' was alive and flourishing in 'ideal-type purity' there. He later wrote that 'with almost lightening speed everything that stands in the way of capitalistic culture in the United States is being crushed.' Much of the inspiration for his book *The Protestant Ethic and the Spirit of Capitalism* *(1905)* came from this visit. By 1908, along with Georg Simmel, Werner Sombart, Ferdinand Tönnies, and Robert Michels, Weber helped organize the first meetings of the German Sociological Society.

Weber, always a strong nationalist, joined the German Democratic Party immediately following World War I. He firmly opposed the 'crazy' left-wing revolutionary elements of the Marxist Social Democratic Party and, concerned for the future of his country, wanted to 'restore Germany to her old glory'. He was critical of the welfare state and its involvement in running the economy. He also strongly opposed the anti-Semitism, anti-Americanism, and Anglophobia that had emerged in post-war Germany (Roth, 2002, p. 517).

In 1920 Weber died suddenly at the age 56, a victim of an influenza epidemic that killed millions following the Great War. Weber is reputed to have once remarked that he became a sociologist because he wanted to see just how much he could stand—just how much he could bear to look directly at the conditions of human existence. The complexities of Weber's life help us to understand the complexities of his thought. He synthesized his national interests with an interest in a global capitalist economy. He championed rationality, yet was able to analyze the role of the irrational in history. Given his psychological problems and his short life, the amount and scope of his sociological writings is truly impressive.

In the following sections we'll look at each of these themes in more detail. We will take up Weber's treatment of class and status in a later chapter.

Methodology and Investigation in the Social Sciences

According to Weber, the methodological foundation of the social sciences includes four elements:

- ideal types
- social action
- *Verstehen* ('interpretive understanding')
- values.

In Chapter 4, on research design and methods, we discussed Weber's concept of *Verstehen* (understanding) and his ideas about the role of values in sociological research. In this chapter we will discuss the two additional concepts central to Weber's approach to sociological thinking and research: ideal types and social action

Ideal Types

ideal type

A methodological construction that summarizes the essential properties common to a number of concrete instances of a given type of social phenomenon in order to help the sociologist identify and categorize the specific social phenomena she studies.

An **ideal type** is a methodological construction. It summarizes the essential properties common to a number of concrete instances of a given type of social phenomenon, and in so doing helps the sociologist identify and categorize the specific social phenomena she studies. Ideal types do not exist in reality; they are heuristic devices used by sociologists to categorize and compare social phenomena. One example of an ideal type is a bureaucracy—any formal, impersonal organization characterized by clear, hierarchically arranged lines of authority. Bureaucracies are made up of salaried officials who are qualified to hold their positions, who follow formalized rules of procedure and goals. Officials usually strive to find ways of efficiently attaining the goals of the organization. Banks, universities, hospitals, government offices, corporations, and even the Girl Guides are all specific examples of the ideal type 'bureaucracy'.

An ideal type can serve the sociologist by helping her formulate hypotheses, determine if a specific type actually exists, and make the characteristics of a specific type clear and understandable. While not a complete description of reality, an ideal type provides the sociologist with an adequate (and therefore meaningful) description of some aspect of reality that she wishes to study.

For Durkheim, as we have seen, sociology was an independent scientific discipline, defined by its unique object of inquiry, 'society'. Much of Durkheim's efforts in establishing sociology as a separate academic discipline were focused on developing a general theory of society. But in Weber's case, all of his sociological inquiries—whether focused on the law, the economy, politics, or religion—took 'social action' as the primary object of sociological inquiry.

Social Action

social action

Any human behaviour that has subjective meaning for an acting individual; an action is a social action when an individual takes into account the meaning his or her actions will have for others observing them, and orients his or her actions accordingly.

Weber was mainly concerned with the meanings that real-life people attached to their social actions. **Social action**, in Weber's words, is 'all human behaviour when and in so far as the acting individual attaches a subjective meaning to it'. As Weber explains it, an action is a 'social action' whenever 'its subjective meaning takes account of the behaviour of others and is thereby oriented in its course' (Weber, 1915/1964, as cited in Swedberg, 1999, p. 573). Sociologist William Tucker gives this example by way of illustration:

> An adult male who is observed kneeling on the floor making hideous faces, thumbing his nose, and making gurgling and cooing noises could, on the exclusive basis of the information just given, be justifiably judged insane by an observer. And this would be the most tenable explanation provided the individual to whom we are referring were alone in the room. However, if we add to this scene one small child seated on the floor in front of the man, watching his antics very intently and reacting by laughing uproariously, it would be quite the opposite of 'tenable' to judge the man insane. On the contrary, he would be called a normal, healthy, good father, or a nice man who likes children very much. (Tucker, 1965, p. 159)

Weber believed that only individuals are capable of meaningful social action. For the purposes of sociology, he argued, 'There is no such thing as a collective personality which "acts". When reference is made in a sociological context,' he continued, 'to a state, a nation, a corporation, a family or an army corps, or to similar collectivities, what is meant is . . . only a certain kind of development of actual or possible social actions of individual persons' (Weber, 1925/1978, p. 14). Weber's point was that only individuals could think, feel, and act. Collectivities were incapable of such things. The objective of a sociologist, then, should be to comprehend the subjective understandings of the individual.

Although he strongly emphasized individual action, Weber was in no way a simple-minded idealist; that is, he did not believe that ideas and beliefs, individually generated and held, determined social action. Especially in his later work, Weber was very clear that the social action of any given individual was affected by both the psychological state of that individual and the external, cultural constraints that surrounded him. The action of the individual, he insisted, is always performed in relationship to some external order. He wrote:

> The satisfaction of our most ideal needs are everywhere confronted with the quantitative limits and the qualitative inadequacy of the necessary external means, so that their satisfaction requires planful provision and work, struggle with nature and the association of human beings. (Weber, 1904/1949, p. 64)

His emphasis on the individual, and the individual's understandings of his actions, contrasts with the kinds of sociology that Durkheim and Marx developed. Weber strongly rejected the 'materialist conception of history', which Marx favoured and which placed the final emphasis on economic factors as the determining factors in human interaction. It was Weber's contention that 'political, religious, climatic, and countless other non-economic determinants' were not accidental, but, rather, that they 'actually follow their own laws.'

For Durkheim, the only unit of study that counted was the collectivity. To make individual motives and subjective understandings of behaviour the central focus of sociology was in direct conflict with Durkheim's ideas about 'society' and 'social facts' having an existence independent of any given individual. For Weber, it is individuals alone who create meaning out of the 'meaningless infinity of the world process'.

Rationality and Social Action

At the core of Weber's interpretive sociology are four distinct *ideal* (or *pure*) *types* of social action of which all humans are capable:

- traditional (or formal): social action motivated by custom or tradition
- affectual (or substantive): social action motivated by emotions
- value-rational (*Wertrationalitat*): social action motivated by cultural values
- instrumental (or means–end) rational (*Zweckrationalitat*): social action motivated by specific goals.

Weber distinguished among these four types of social action based on the degree of **rationality** and meaningfulness he felt characterized each type. 'Rationality' is an important term in Weber's sociology. He used it to mean 'an orientation to reality which systematically weighs up means and ends for purposes of efficacy' (Morrison, 1995, p. 279). In other words, an action is rational (1) if the social actor performing it calculates (within the context of his social and cultural situation) the end he wishes to attain and the means by which he will be able to attain that end, and (2) if both the ends and the means are understandable to (or

rationality
Weber's term for an ideal-type mental state that is characterized by a culturally or emotionally defined, coherent way of thinking, that is goal-oriented and based on a cost–benefit calculation, and that is made within the context of a specific social and cultural situation or within the context of a specific emotional state.

shared by) others who are of the same background. The term rationality, as used by Weber, is always relative to the customs, traditions, and cultural values of the society in which the individual lives, or to the emotional state of the individual.

Weber recognized that although rationality was a trait displayed by individuals, it was a trait that could not be taken out of its social, cultural, and historical context. Different orientations to rationality prevail not only between different societies but also during different historical periods within the same society. For example, between the mid-fifteenth and mid-seventeenth centuries in western Europe a widespread belief in witchcraft and magic resulted in the execution of thousands of women and some men believed to be witches. The social action of identifying women (and, to a lesser extent, men) as witches and subjecting them to trials and to execution was 'rational' in that it was oriented to an existing traditional culture and values and to a shared set of emotional states. By the nineteenth century, however, a different but equally rational (in the sense that Weber uses the term) orientation to science and medicine resulted in very different treatment of women and men who formerly would have been identified as witches and put to death. Scientific thinking led to the identification of oddly behaving men and women not as witches but as people with potentially treatable mental disorders.

Both the earlier practice of burning witches at the stake and the later practice of confining people to mental asylums in order to cure them are examples of instrumental (*Zweckrationalitat*) social action—social action motivated by a clearly defined goal (in the first case of ridding society of a potential danger, and in the second of curing the mentally

How has the rational orientation to identifying and treating mental illness changed since the nineteenth century, when people deemed 'mad' were shut away in asylums?

ill). In Weber's terms, both the thinking that resulted in the death of thousands of women and men as witches and the thinking that resulted in the confinement of the 'mentally ill' in large institutions for treatment by specialists are examples of rationality: both are the result of culturally defined, goal-oriented, and socially shared thought.

Rationalization

Weber distinguished between *rationality* (an ideal-type mental state that motivated individual social action) and **rationalization**, the process by which modern societies develop. Weber used the term to describe 'the process by which nature, society and individual action are increasingly mastered by an orientation to planning, technical procedure and rational action' (Morrison, 1995, p. 218). Rationalization refers to two broad historical trends:

1. the social process whereby societies become more and more reliant on calculation and technical knowledge to gain and maintain control over both natural and social worlds; and
2. the tendency for social actors to free themselves from magical thinking and to replace that with thinking informed by empirical observations.

It was Weber's conclusion that modern Western societies, more than other societies in history, 'reflect the tendency of rationalization in their system of law, politics, science and commercial life' (Morrison, 1995, p. 218). As the economic, political, legal, and religious spheres of Western societies were exposed to rationalization, the monarchies that governed them were replaced by governments based on the principles of legitimate authority and the universal application of legal principles. For Weber, while this was an inevitable development, it was also anxiety-provoking and not always a good thing—hence his commentary on the 'iron cage of bureaucracy' (discussed below).

rationalization
Weber's term for the process by which nature, society, and individual action are increasingly mastered by an orientation to planning, technical procedure, and rational action.

Capitalism and the 'Iron Cage' of Bureaucracy

Weber is often seen as the defender of bourgeois liberalism. But in *The Protestant Ethic and the Spirit of Capitalism* he makes a stinging indictment of capitalism. Protestantism and capitalism, he argues, first went hand in hand in an attempt to 'remodel the world'. Weber famously coined the term 'Protestant (work) ethic' in arguing that the Calvinist emphasis on the importance of individual responsibility to achieve success through hard work and thrift fostered the rise of capitalism. Since that beginning, however, capitalism has emerged victorious and no longer needs the support of the spirit of religious asceticism, characteristic of Protestantism. 'Material goods', Weber asserted, have come to exercise an 'inexorable power over the lives of men as in no previous period in history'.

Weber's target of criticism was not just capitalism but advanced industrialized societies of all forms, including socialist and communist ones. Weber was especially critical of the bureaucratization of all social action, and he coined the famous phrase the 'iron cage of bureaucracy' to describe this. What makes Weber's criticism of capitalism so different from Marx's is that while Marx purported to show the way out of the trap of modern industrial society, Weber believed that there was no way out. In short, in bureaucratic societies, rational action tends to undermine the very ends that motivated it in the first place (McIntosh, 1983, p. 71).

Bureaucracy and Modern Societies

Weber made one of his most important investigations into bureaucratic administration, an ideal type of social organization that he discerned in many societies. Weber was interested in bureaucracies both as a form of administrative rationality and as a form of domination. In formulating bureaucracies as an ideal type, he selected several distinctive features, including the following:

- a hierarchically organized chain of command, with functional specialization of tasks and a well-defined hierarchy of authority
- an organization that follows a clearly defined structure of offices and positions
- a clearly defined and explicitly prescribed list of the positions, rights, and duties of office holders
- allegiance paid by office holders to a system of impersonal rules and regulations, not to the whims of superiors
- reliance on a decision-making process that follows procedure and that is based on considerations of authority, jurisdiction, due process, and correct rulings
- a system of impersonal rules governing the duties and behaviour of office holders
- contractually fixed salaries for office holders, who do not own their positions
- a separation between the private affairs of the official and her administrative responsibilities
- impersonal and uniform rules and procedures to govern the interactions between officials and clients; officials apply these rules and procedures equally to all and discharge their duties 'without regard for persons' (Weber, 1907/1977, p. 310)
- reliance on technical and procedural knowledge, which makes the office holder an expert
- interpersonal relations governed by norms of impersonality: personal ties between employees of a bureaucracy and its clients are discouraged; clients are treated as 'cases'
- the use of documents and 'files' as the basis for legitimate decision making.

It was Weber's opinion that these characteristics gave bureaucracies a certain kind of technical superiority over other forms of organization (Weber, 1907/1977, p. 307). Organized religion traditionally served as one of the first social institutions by which humans were able to make sense out of a messy, overwhelming, infinite reality. Organized religions accomplished this by transforming an indeterminate, menacing non-presence 'into the benevolent presence of the holy' (Cooper, 2003, p. 148). But religion, as the overriding communal force, has been replaced by urban, mass society, which lacks the direction and purpose present in those societies where religion serves as the main sense-making vehicle.

Value-Free Sociology: Is Objectivity Possible?

In his 1904 publication on objectivity in the social sciences, Weber posed this question: 'In what sense are there "objectively valid truths" in those disciplines concerned with the social and cultural phenomena?' (Weber, 1904/1949, p. 51). Most of Weber's subsequent publications were attempts to answer this central question. Weber knew that in studying 'social action', sociologists had to deal with phenomena that have 'subjective meaning' for both the social actors being studied and the sociologist who studied them. Yet, if sociology was to be a true science, its practitioners had to produce 'objective knowledge' about the phenomena they studied.

During Weber's lifetime many social thinkers did not believe that the objective study of society was possible or even desirable. It seemed to them an impossible task to separate the values and morality of the social researcher from the research process. As we have already seen, Karl Marx is an example of a social thinker whose scientific method involved integrating his political and ethical values into his analysis of society. To Weber's way of thinking, however, conducting scientific inquiry meant that statements of facts and statements of value had to be kept separate; the two could not be confused. Sociology, in Weber's opinion, was not a moral science, and the sociologist could not rely on science to either refute or support a specific normative position.

Was Weber therefore advocating that sociologists had to leave their values behind when they did research? The answer is both yes and no. Weber believed that it was impossible for a researcher to be value-free in the sense of having no personal values involved in *choosing* a research subject. But he also believed that values must be put aside once the actual research process was underway. What Weber meant by 'value-free', then, is that the sociologist's personal values should in no way be allowed to affect the actual conduct of research or the use to which the research might be put. Sociology should not try to be a 'moral science' by passing judgement about a particular society or by prescribing how, or for what purpose, the findings of sociologists should be used. (Note that this position is rather different from the one taken by Marx.)

For Weber, the duty of the sociologist was to be open-minded and to never promote one political solution over another. 'Objectivity' means facing up to 'facts', even to uncomfortable ones. An objective sociologist is one who describes 'what is', and who refuses to make value judgements about the 'what is' in terms of what she thinks 'should be'. She is clearly not without personal values, but she is a scientist, and as such she is duty-bound to make sure that her descriptions of what she observes are free from her own ideas about what should be. As sociologists, we frequently are called on to distance ourselves from our own values. To refuse to recognize this and to try instead to impose our own dogma, ideology, or principles within a scientific debate is to be naive or, worse, to act in bad faith. The calling or vocation of a scientist is to be a teacher, not a leader. The duty of a scientist, as a teacher, is to exercise self-restraint and to distance herself from her own values. To do otherwise is to claim an unwarranted moral authority (Scott, 1995, p. 73).

MARX AND WEBER COMPARED

Most frequently, the theoretical contrast between Marxism and academic sociology has been couched in terms of a contrast between, on the one hand, Weber's 'methodological individualism' and commitment to sociology as 'an interpretive perspective on social action', and, on the other, Marx's commitment to 'historical materialism as a science of modes of production' (Hindess & Hirst, 1975; Löwith, 1932/1993, p. 4). Certainly, the sudden collapse of organized communist states in Europe in 1989 and 1990 brought the credibility of Marxism as a theory of society into question.

Despite some very important differences between the intellectual work of Karl Marx and Max Weber—not least among them their respective political attitudes—there are some striking similarities or convergences in their sociological perspectives. Both men identified negative features of bourgeois civilization: Marx wrote about 'alienation', while Weber tackled 'rationalization' and referred to the irrationality of rationalization. Weber was ambivalent about the process of rationalization. On the one hand, he felt that the rationalization of society brought increased knowledge, greater understanding, and ensuing freedom from traditional, illogical social traditions and values. On the other hand, it caused increased impersonality, dehumanization, and the centralization of control over social life. He referred to these latter outcomes as examples of the 'irrationality' of rationalization. This particular theme of Weber's has been taken up recently by American sociologist George Ritzer, who used McDonalds as the paradigmatic case for his analysis of the irrationality of rationalization (1993).

Both Marx and Weber took capitalist society as their object of study and found it to be problematic, but also different from 'traditional' societies in that it opened up new opportunities for change. Marx was eager that these opportunities for change be seized by the proletariat, which he identified as the revolutionary force in capitalist societies. Marx's commitment to revolution was clearly reflected in his theories about social class and social change, and in his lifelong belief in the revolutionary potential of the working class. Weber, by contrast, was at best ambiguous and often pessimistic about the possibility of escape from the 'iron cage' of bureaucracy under capitalism. This was reflected in his sociology, which concentrated on the inexorable march of rationalization, and which offered little by way of prescription or even hope for an escape (Löwith, 1932/1993, p. 7).

Weber believed that with the advance of capitalism the world had become increasingly secular and disenchanted, that scientific ideals of instrumental rationalization had come to pervade all aspects of day-to-day life, and that social activities and authority had become specialized. He became increasingly anxious about the ways in which the process of rationalization had eroded charisma, religion, and enchantment as major forces in people's lives. This erosion involved the rise of bureaucracies, which held people in their thrall and stifled the possibilities of personal autonomy. It made the world predictable, but it destroyed any authoritative purpose and left people without a grand narrative about human existence that religion had previously supplied. From this there was no clear escape; the only answer was stoical resolve (Löwith, 1932/1993, p. 23).

Marx was not afflicted by the same pessimism as Weber. Yes, he saw the world, dominated by bourgeois capitalism, as a place of alienation—alienation from oneself, from the products of one's labour, and from others. But here the similarity ends. Marx, following Hegel's dialectic, presented the proletariat in a world historic role: the proletariat is the means by which the contradictions of bourgeois capitalist society will be resolved. Through struggle with capitalists, the proletariat will bring an end not just to their own exploitation but to the exploitation of all, for all time. Marx held a utopian vision of the end of history, by which he meant the end of all social inequality. It is a powerful vision, and a challenge to all those who would legitimize the permanency of existing social relations.

Weber's sociology was part of his solution to the problems of nineteenth-century Germany and Europe, a solution that was individualistic, inward-looking, and despairing. Marx, by contrast, crafted a solution that was collectivist, external, and hopeful (Löwith, 1932/1993, p. 24). Unfortunately, Marx's complex ideas were quickly transformed into a kind of 'vulgar Marxism', in which an economic base was seen to determine, in a mechanical fashion, all other aspects of any given society. This was certainly Weber's view of Marxism; for Weber, Marxism was dogmatic and simplistic in its economic determinism (Löwith, 1932/1993, p. 24).

WEBER'S SIGNIFICANCE TODAY

There is little doubt that the work of Max Weber continues to have a significant impact on many sociologists, particularly in North America. During the 1940s and 1950s—20 years after his death—Weber was brought into American sociology by Talcott Parsons, Robert Merton, and others who made Weber's ideas the basis of a program of social research, and who used his collective works as a 'quarry for hypotheses to be tested' (Tenbruck, 1980, p. 313). Parsons translated some of Weber's major works from German into English. He also developed his own theory of society, which he called structural functionalism, and which he based on a synthesis of Durkheim's and Weber's work. (Readers will find Parsons' work and the issue of social structure and social agency developed in Chapter 11.)

In 1964, at the Fifteenth German Sociological Congress, held in Heidelberg to commemorate the centenary of Weber's birth, Parsons praised Weber for rising above the 'ideological disputes' of the late nineteenth and early twentieth centuries and for showing how the science of sociology might play a 'major role' in shaping the future of the world. Indeed, Parsons went so far as to claim that Weber's sociology foreshadowed the end of 'ideology'.

A 1911 cartoon featuring the American financier John Pierpont Morgan, one of the wealthiest men in the world. The last two decades of the nineteenth century in the US, marked by rapid industrialization and economic growth, as well as dramatic increases in immigration and urbanization, are known as America's 'Gilded Age'. Why 'gilded' and not 'golden'? What by-products of the 'spirit of capitalism' might Weber have missed or overlooked? Recall the work of Jacob Riis, discussed in the last chapter, which dates to roughly the same period.

That same conference was attended by another American sociologist, Herbert Marcuse. Marcuse, who had fled Hitler's Germany during the 1930s to escape the horrors of anti-Semitism, held a very different perspective on the effects of Weber's sociology. Marcuse argued passionately that Weber's ideas about value-free sociology, far from marking the 'end of ideology', in fact merely supported the domination of one class of people over another (Ashley & Orenstein, 1990, p. 290). Yet even Marcuse used Weber's analysis of bureaucracy and legal-rational modes of thought to help inform his own thinking about social class and class oppression in advanced capitalist societies.

One of the reasons that Weber's work has been so widely adopted stems in part from the fact that he was 'a brilliant and profound apologist for liberal capitalism' (Ashley & Orenstein, 1990, p. 292). His popularity stems, too, from the fact that he seems to have been much more aware than were the many 'Marxists' who followed Marx of the various tensions and contradictions inherent in Western capitalist societies. Yet Weber's work, however dense and divergent, lacks the coherence of Durkheim or Marx. In following Weber's methodology, sociologists are prevented from asking the most important of all scientific questions: are there any social relations so generic that they might constitute sociological laws (Turner, et al., 2007, p. 209)? This question was answered in interesting and affirmative ways in the work of the social interactionists, whose work is the subject of the next chapter.

SUMMARY

This chapter examines the work of two of the most important early sociologists of the nineteenth and twentieth centuries. Taken together, the work of Karl Marx and Max Weber, along with that of Émile Durkheim (whose work was taken up in the previous chapter), is thought by many to constitute classical sociology.

The originators of sociology found much of their inspiration in the liberal and radical extensions of the Enlightenment tradition, with its great hope for the emancipation of all of humanity. However, many social thinkers also realized that with the emergence of industrial capitalism came grave possibilities for exploitation, especially through a bureaucratic system that constantly undermined the conditions necessary for people to enjoy their lives fully.

Those who helped found the discipline of sociology were concerned with what they perceived to be the unsettling consequences of the collapse of traditional society. For Durkheim, as we have seen in the previous chapter, the most significant problem facing modern society was the absence of a morality appropriate to the new social conditions. With old traditions gone and nothing new to replace them, Durkheim contended that normlessness, or anomie, prevailed. It was his opinion that the new discipline of sociology he helped found had an obligation to establish the scientific basis for a new and more appropriate morality.

Karl Marx focused on the material conditions of human existence to develop his dialectical materialist method of studying society. Marx viewed capitalist society as based on social relationships between two very different social classes: workers and owners of the means of production. The interests of these two classes conflict, and the ensuing struggle between them, Marx predicted, would result in capitalism's being replaced by a new kind of society based on socialism.

Like Marx, Max Weber was concerned with showing why Western capitalist societies have developed differently from all other known societies. Unlike Marx, however, Weber rejected a materialist conception of history. Instead he believed that politics, religion, climate, and other determinants followed their own laws, independent of economic considerations that Marx considered central.

According to Weber, the objective of any sociologist should be to comprehend the ways in which social actors understand and conceptualize their own actions, because it is individuals alone who make sense of the world processes. By investigating the consequences of different types of social actions that individuals engage in, along with the conflicts that arise between and among individual members of a society, sociologists can come to understand how individuals reason and act.

DISCUSSION QUESTIONS

1. Compare the political orientations of sociologists who promote positivist (see Comte, previous chapter), interpretive (see Weber, this chapter), and radical (see Marx, this chapter) perspectives on society.
2. Discuss Marx's dialectical materialist method of studying society. How is it different from the dialectic of Hegel?
3. Apply Marx's concept of the capitalist mode of production to analyze Canadian society today.
4. Compare Marx's account of the emergence of capitalism with Weber's explanation.
5. What contributions did Karl Marx and Max Weber each make to establishing sociology as a 'human science'?
6. In what ways has the work of Karl Marx and Max Weber influenced current thinking about society?
7. Discuss Max Weber's concept of bureaucracy. Do you think that his view of 'the iron cage of bureaucracy' is valid today? Explain.
8. What did Weber mean by the concept 'ideal type'? Use examples to help explain your answer.
9. Is value-free sociology ever possible? Explain why you agree or disagree with Weber.

7 The Social-Interactionist Perspective

CHAPTER OUTLINE

LEARNING OBJECTIVES

In this chapter you will:

- consider society as the product of human social interactions
- learn about the social-interactionist perspective
- examine the contributions of George Herbert Mead to social psychology
- reflect on the concept of 'the looking-glass self'
- survey the stages in the social development of the self
- understand the role of the 'I' and the 'Me' as two phases of the self
- consider the links between exotic dancing and the social construction
  of meaning
- think critically about cross-cultural misunderstandings and differences in
  meanings that are ascribed to everyday, commonplace events
- think about the relationship between individual memory and collective
  memory.

INTRODUCTION

Previous chapters have introduced you to three of the four core concepts that make up the sociological perspective:

- the sociological imagination (based on the view that the life of an individual and the history of a society must be understood together)
- the social construction of reality (the belief that all knowledge is knowledge constructed from some point of view)
- science as a way of knowing about the world (the notion that knowledge should be based on empirical evidence).

This chapter introduces a fourth core concept of the sociological perspective: the idea, as it was worked out by twentieth-century American sociologists, social psychologists, and philosophers, that society is the product of human social interactions.

THE SOCIAL-INTERACTIONIST PERSPECTIVE

social interaction
The process by which individuals act, interact, and react to one another in the context of social relations.

During the first half of the twentieth century, pioneering work carried out by sociologists, psychologists, and philosophers (many of them working at the then recently founded University of Chicago) shifted sociological thinking from its focus on large-scale societal processes (characteristic of nineteenth-century social thinkers) to a focus on the ways in which mind, self, and society emerge out of human **social interaction**. The starting point of the social-interactionist perspective 'is the relationships among people as they respond to each other, create shared pasts and futures, and collectively negotiate meaning' (Fine & Beim, 2007).

Social interactionists of the early twentieth century turned their attention to the study of how social reality was produced by and through the collective efforts—that is, the social interactions—of individuals. In addressing the paradoxical relationship between the individual and society, interactionists ascribed primacy neither to the individual nor to society; the individual and society were seen as being mutually (and simultaneously) constituted in the ongoing process of social interaction. George Herbert Mead, whose work we will take up on the next page, was an early advocate of social interactionism. Herbert Blumer (1900–87), another American sociologist and a student of Mead's, later coined the term 'symbolic interactionism' as the name for the study of small-scale social interaction. Blumer's term is currently used to designate the theoretical orientation of a growing number of sociologists who study social interaction using a qualitative research strategy.

Readers will recall from an earlier discussion (see Chapter 5) that Durkheim thought of society as a super-organic 'thing' that existed independent of, and outside of, its individual members. As a 'thing', society exerts pressure on its members to make their conduct conform to society's demands. For social interactionists, in contrast, society is always society-in-the-making; society is best thought of not as some stable thing but as something always evolving, dynamic, and emergent. Thus, while the interactionists accept that society has an important role in producing individuals and independent conscious beings, they also hold that society is at the same time produced by its members. Not only are social interactionists concerned to learn how society is produced by individual actors, they are also concerned to learn how individual actors are, in turn, shaped by society. For them, neither the individual nor society should be taken as the proper unit of analysis for sociological inquiry. Rather, the individual and society are seen as 'different aspects of the same thing' (Park, 1929/1952, p. 203).

Durkheim, who relied on a static, mechanistic model of society, had the problem of explaining irregularities in the behaviour of group members, and the frequent and often extensive changes that societies undergo. Interactionists, in contrast, are faced with the opposite problem: explaining how social order and social structure come about and persist, without losing the insight that reality is both emergent and contingent. You will see later in this chapter, when the issue of time and memory is addressed, that the social interactionists solve the problem of social order and social structure by taking up a version of the dialectical method employed by Hegel and Marx.

SOCIAL INTERACTIONISM AND THE CONTRIBUTIONS OF GEORGE HERBERT MEAD

Philosopher and social psychologist George Herbert Mead brought pragmatist philosophy and social psychology into the fledgling discipline of sociology developing at the University of Chicago. Mead was amongst the first to clearly and extensively theorize social interaction, and his work is considered a key source for conveying the working ideas of social interactionists. His theories place the individual and her experiences, as well as any concept of society, firmly within the context of ongoing social interaction.

Intellectual Influences

Mead was a modest man who underestimated his intellectual abilities and the value of his scholarly contributions. As a result, he published little in his lifetime. Much of what we have from Mead comes to us as compilations of verbatim notes taken by his students during his lectures. Despite his misplaced modesty, Mead stands as one of the founders of sociology, having made significant contributions to our understanding of social interaction. In order to better understand Mead's theories and the importance of his work, it is useful to take a look at the perspectives Mead drew on in developing his own theories about human social interaction and social organization. A survey of some of these sources will give you a sense of the complexity of Mead's thought, and of how his wide-ranging interests enabled him to synthesize a number of different approaches in order to arrive at his own ideas.

Pragmatism

Pragmatism as an intellectual outlook was first articulated by American philosopher and scientist Charles Peirce (1839–1914) in an article published in 1878. It became an acknowledged philosophical school of thought about twenty years later, popularized through the work of the American psychologist and philosopher William James (1842–1910) and the American philosopher John Dewey (1859–1952). Mead was deeply influenced by the pragmatist philosophy of the latter two men in particular.

Pragmatism developed as a reaction to the view of reality presented by rationalist philosophers, who saw the universe as static and predetermined. Pragmatists replaced this view with

pragmatism
A philosophical school of thought that views the social world as dynamic and emergent, brought into being by a variety of social groups that create their own way of talking, acting, and thinking, and of defining what is and is not 'real'.

PROFILES IN SOCIOLOGY

George Herbert Mead (1863–1931)

Mead was born in South Hadley, Massachusetts, in 1863 (for context, just five years after Durkheim was born and a year before Marx). Mead's father, Hiram, was a Puritan clergyman who held the chair in Sacred Rhetoric and Pastoral Theology at the Oberlin Theological Seminary. Between 1890 and 1900, Mead's mother, Elizabeth Storrs Mead, served as president of Mount Holyoke College, one of the oldest and most prestigious women's colleges in the United States. Mead completed undergraduate work at Oberlin College in 1879 and graduated with a master's degree in philosophy from Harvard University in 1888. He then went to study in Leipzig, Germany, where he took courses with Wilhelm Dilthey (whose influence on Weber was noted in the previous chapter) and with the psychologist Wilhelm Wundt, whose experimental psychology later helped Mead develop his own ideas in the area of social psychology.

On his return to the US, Mead took up a teaching post in philosophy at the University of Michigan in Ann Arbour, where he was influenced by his colleagues Charles Horton Cooley and John Dewey. In 1894 both Mead and Dewey moved to Chicago to take up positions in the philosophy department of the recently opened University of Chicago. At that time Chicago was a fast-growing, rapidly industrializing city that had attracted millions of European immigrants. Mead and others like him who taught at the University of Chicago recognized the risk of major social conflict occurring in Chicago. They also shared a belief that science could be used to help better regulate society, and they were committed to applying their research findings to help improve the lives of the poor.

As the offspring of conservative, Protestant parents, Mead was typical of a progressive-era reformer. In early adulthood he rejected his parents' faith while retaining their commitment to improving the lot of others. A strong supporter of Democratic president Woodrow Wilson, Mead advocated for enlightened private and governmental policies to help the less fortunate. Obviously not a supporter of Weber's ideas about the vocation of a scientist, Mead remained a social activist throughout his life with strong radical/democratic sympathies (Da Silva, 2007, p. 297). He believed that the 'study and work' of social and political reform should be done together. To this end, Mead was involved in supporting women's suffrage and other progressive causes, and he helped found the Immigrants' Protective League in 1908. In 1906 he joined the City Club of Chicago, a public affairs forum; as a close friend of the social and political activist Jane Addams, he was involved in the settlement house movement she championed in Chicago. In both his activism and his intellectual work, Mead considered the best approach to the problems of modernity to be social reform that was scientifically grounded in experimental research (Da Silva, 2007, p. 298).

a view of the world as dynamic and emergent. The social universe, the pragmatists held, is pluralistic, and is brought into being by a wide variety of social groups. Each different social group creates its own distinct ways of talking, acting, and thinking, and of defining what is and is not 'real'.

Behaviourism

Mead accepted one of the most general principles of behaviourism, that all behaviours are learned. By adapting and adjusting their behaviours to social situations, individuals achieve gratification. Any behaviour must be understood in the context of its capacity to cause the individual to adjust and adapt to the social environment. However, in so doing, the individual actively and intentionally chooses a line of action; he does not merely passively respond to an environmental stimulus.

Hegelian Dialectics

We have already encountered Hegel's work in Chapter 6, where we reviewed its influence on Karl Marx. Mead took from Hegel an understanding of human history as a dialectical process of change: oppositional forces, inherent in an existing social situation, interact with each other until a new social situation emerges with its own characteristic oppositional forces. Mead used dialectical reasoning in his thinking about consciousness, the self, the group, and scientific methodology, all of which he felt changed through the dialectical process of contradiction and emergence.

The Social Psychology of Wilhelm Wundt

German physician, psychologist, sociologist, and philosopher Wilhelm Wundt (1832–1920) is considered by many to be the 'father of experimental psychology'. Mead studied with Wundt and later cited his work extensively, especially his *Elements of Folk Psychology* (1916), one of the first studies in social psychology. In that work Wundt sets out to demonstrate

Pragmatism—and the idea that the world can be changed through applied effort—got Mead involved in the settlement house movement in Chicago. Mead and his fellow pragmatists hoped to change the way city's poor talked, acted, and thought by bringing them into contact with intellectuals and academics associated with the university. Can you distinguish between the two groups in this photo?

the parallels between what goes on in an individual's body and what goes on in an individual's mind by tying psychological experience to physical gestures. Gestures, Wundt argues, are physical acts that carry social meaning and that serve as stimuli to others involved in the same social situation. Whereas the behaviour of lower animals is guided by instincts, human behaviour is guided by humans' identification with what Wundt termed 'the mental community' (Wundt, 1896/1907, pp. 296–8). As they mature, human children acquire both speech and self-consciousness, along with the ability to create and use 'mental communities' to regulate their social interactions. Following Wundt, Mead designated gestures as the basis for all human communication and social interaction, and language as the most developed of all human gestures to carry common meaning.

The Influence of Charles Horton Cooley

Charles Horton Cooley (1864–1929) was a colleague of Mead's at the University of Michigan, where he taught economics and sociology. Cooley felt that while society is made up of many different kinds of social organizations, what holds everything together—from two-person 'dyads' to large social institutions—is human social interaction. It is only through social interaction that humans share ideas and understandings. Mead accepted Cooley's observation

Can you interpret this scene just by looking at the gestures each of the actors is using? What is each of them communicating?

that social interaction (and social organization) develop out of human communications. Humans see or hear each other's gestures and interpret those gestures by mentally placing themselves in the position of others and then adjusting their own conduct to fit with the conduct of others. From Cooley, Mead adopted the following ideas:

- *The **'looking-glass self'**.* Cooley believed that the self is constructed out of what is reflected back to the individual via other people's gestures. To explain how this works, he used the metaphor of a 'looking glass', or mirror. Just as an individual can get an impression of how she looks to others by reading the image that is reflected back to her in a mirror, so can she get an image of who she is, on a much deeper level, by reading what is reflected back to her in the gestures of others. Humans recognize the gestures of others; they use those gestures as a 'looking glass' to form in their imaginations an image of how they are perceived and judged by others. From this, they can then construct how they should perceive and judge themselves.
- *The self as emergent.* Infants are born with the potential to develop the ability—but not the instinctive ability—to read the gestures of others. Infants and very young children are at first unable to recognize themselves in a mirror, or to see themselves as

looking-glass self
Cooley's metaphor for the sense of self we develop as a result of our propensity to imagine how we appear to others, and how others judge us in any given social situation.

What self-impression is this man likely to have by drawing a crowd of idolizing fans and zealous paparazzi at every public appearance?

objects in the 'looking-glass' provided by the gestures of others. Children must learn to see themselves as others see them, and they do this over a period of time, with practice, through the process of maturation, and through exposure to the gestures of the many others in their social environment. Eventually they are able to form a 'personality'. To this idea of the self as emergent Mead added that as a stable set of self-feelings emerge, the individual is more and more able to act in a stable, predictable fashion, and to co-operate with others (Turner, Beeghley, & Powers, 2007, p. 334).

- *Self-consciousness, social consciousness, and public consciousness.* Cooley saw consciousness as divided into three parts: 'self consciousness', or awareness of oneself; 'social consciousness', or awareness of and attitudes towards other people; and 'public consciousness', or awareness of others as being organized in a 'communicative group' (Cooley, as cited in Turner, Beeghley, & Powers, 2007, p. 335).

- **Primary (or small) groups.** Cooley defined primary (small) groups as human associations characterized by 'intimate face-to-face co-operation'. He saw them as the basic unit of society, 'fundamental in forming the social nature and ideals of individuals'. The primary group offers the first and most important link between the individual and broader social institutions. Past traditions and public morals are given immediate relevance to the individual through the intimacy of the relations between members of primary groups.

primary (or small) groups

Human associations characterized by intimate face-to-face interaction and co-operation, representing the first and most important link between the individual and broader social institutions.

MEAD'S SOCIOLOGY

Mind, Self and Society (1934) is a compilation of verbatim transcripts of Mead's lectures, taken by his students between 1927 and 1930. In these lectures Mead presents his most important social-psychological insights on social interaction, social organization, and the social nature of the self. Underlying Mead's analyses is the view that all observable human activity is an adjustment or adaptation to the social environment.

These are the basic themes of social interactionism:

- *Meaning* is an interactive process, a 'conversation of gestures'. All meaning emerges out of interactions. Humans use 'significant symbols' in their communications with one another.

- *The self* is not present at birth, but is emergent, built out of social interactions and, as a result, endowed with meaning that can shift over time.

- *Societies* emerge out of the social (and symbolic) interactions that occur between the 'selves' and 'others' that make up a myriad of social groupings. Because the individuals who make up a society are involved in many different social groupings, 'society' is emergent, contingent, and always in process.

Meaning Is a 'Conversation of Gestures'

According to Mead, the meaning that any organisms, and especially humans, make of their environment emerges out of interactions. In the process of interaction, the simplest form of communication to take place between two organisms is a 'conversation of gestures'. Here's how a conversation of simple gestures might work between two dogs, 'A' and 'B', who share meaning that is expressed in symbolic gestures:

1. *Organism 1 makes a gesture.* For example, Dog 'A' growls. The gesture (growl) is part of the subjective world of dog 'A': it has a specific meaning for Dog 'A'.
2. *Organism 2 responds.* For example, Dog 'B' growls back. The response (a returned growl) is part of the social world of Dog 'B', who has witnessed and copied the gesture made by Dog 'A'.
3. *Organism 1 makes an 'adjusted response' gesture that takes into account the gesture made by Organism 2.* For example Dog 'A' attacks. The response (attack) is yet another gesture, leading to a subsequent phase of interaction.

Organism 2 might now make another gesture, adjusted yet again, this time in response to the adjusted response gesture of Organism 1. For example Dog 'B' might turn tail and run. This response and adjustment exchange goes on as long as the two organisms continue to communicate and constitutes, in Mead's view, the simplest form of communicative interaction that can exist between two organisms. In both cases the individuals involved act and react without ideas and without deliberating. But what is significant for Mead is that, as the organisms carry on a conversation of gestures, they use each other's gestures as the basis for adjusting their own responses. In so doing they co-operate to coordinate and organize their mutual responses. The result is social interaction.

Human Communication Involves 'Significant Symbols' and Language

In humans, Mead contended, communication involves more than simple gestures; it involves the use of **significant gestures or symbols**. Significant gestures or symbols hold the same meaning for all participants in a conversation. The ability to use significant gestures and symbols distinguishes humans from all other species. A significant gesture or symbol is one that is equally understood by the individual making the gesture and the individual receiving it. Mead used the example of an individual shouting 'Fire!' in a theatre. This is a significant gesture because it evokes the same response (fleeing, escaping) in the individual who made the gesture as it does in those who received the gesture. Significant symbols are the basis for human language, which may be vocal or gestural (i.e. involving gestures, such as a frown, a smile, tears, a clenched fist, and so on). Language, Mead tells us, makes possible the unique human characteristics of 'mind', 'self', and 'society'.

significant gestures or symbols

Gestures or symbols that hold the same meaning for all participants in a social interaction, i.e. any gesture that is equally understood by the individual making it and the individual receiving it.

Mind and 'Taking the Role of the Other'

When first born, Mead tells us, a human infant is similar to a 'lower animal' in that she is capable of making only reflexive responses to the gestures of others. Moreover, her gestures do not produce the same responses in her as they do in others. For example, her cries do not indicate whether she wants milk or feels too cold or has a wet diaper or has gas pains or a myriad of other possibilities that the adult caregiver must intuit.

As the infant matures, however, she gradually acquires the ability to use and interpret her own and others' significant gestures. First she develops the capacity to understand significant symbols; then she acquires the ability to 'role-take'. Finally the young child develops 'mind'— the ability to assume the perspective of others, and to take on the role of others with respect to herself. The child imagines and rehearses possible outcomes of different responses to the behaviour of others, and in so doing she learns to adjust her own behaviour accordingly. 'Mind', according to Mead, is not innate. Rather, it is a behaviour that emerges and grows in the young child as she interacts socially with others and in so doing gradually acquires the capacity to use significant symbols. The acquisition of language makes 'mind' possible; in turn, 'mind' allows the individual to:

- attribute significant symbols to objects in the environment and use the significant symbols as a stimulus in formulating her response to those objects;
- interpret the gestures (significant symbols) of others and use their gestures as a stimulus to her own response; and
- temporarily suspend or inhibit her response to significant symbols, rehearse possible or alternative responses to significant symbols, imagine the consequences of each possible response, and select the response most likely to achieve the best adjustment to the environment (Turner, Beeghley, & Powers, 2007, p. 346).

Mind makes co-operation among individuals possible; it allows them to inhibit initial responses, imaginatively rehearse possible responses, and select out what appears to be the best response. Mind is the foundation or pre-condition for the emergence of 'self'.

The 'Emergent' Self

the self

A sense of identity that each individual possess. According to Mead, it 'arises in the process of social experience and activity' as an outcome of the individual's 'relations to that process as a whole and to other individuals within that process'.

Mead drew on Cooley's idea of the 'looking-glass self' to develop his own analysis. According to Mead, **the self** does not exist at birth. It is, rather, a temporal process (Mead, 1932, p. 12). It has a 'developmental course' and 'arises in the process of social experience and activity' as an outcome of the individual's 'relations to that process as a whole and to other individuals within that process' (Mead, 1934, p. 135).

The self, Mead tells us, emerges out of the individual's capacity to use language, to read the meaning of the gestures and symbolic communications of others, and then to 'take the attitudes that others take towards us' (Mead, 1932, p. 185) and arrive at an image of himself as an object in a particular situation. This image of self informs the individual's own behaviour in response to the initial behaviour of others. The response of the individual in turn causes further reactions on the part of others, and they in turn emit further gestures that cause the individual to adjust his own behaviour in return. Like 'mind', 'self' emerges as the individual interacts with and adjusts his responses to others.

Mead made the significant point that the individual experiences himself only indirectly, through the 'standpoints of other individual members of the same social group, or from the generalized standpoint of the social group as a whole to which he belongs' (Mead, 1934, p. 138). The individual, Mead tells us, 'becomes an object to himself only by taking the attitudes of other individuals toward himself'. Most importantly, the individual accomplishes the task of taking on the attitudes of others only 'within a social environment or context of experience and behaviour in which both he and they are involved' (Mead, 1934, p. 138).

Elementary Selves and the Unified Self

Over time, as the individual derives his sense of self through experiencing many instances of social interaction, a more permanent set of attitudes towards himself emerges and the behaviour of the individual becomes consistent across many social situations. Mead termed the development of a stable attitude towards oneself the *complete* (or *unified*) *self* and felt it was made up of many different *elementary selves*. Depending on the social context, different elementary selves are presented to different audiences (Mead, 1934, p. 140).

The self provides the means by which the behaviour of all the individuals that make up society can be integrated together. The more that the actions of individuals take on consistency, the more their behaviours become predictable to each other, the more they are able to adjust to and co-operate with each other. This happens especially when individuals assess their behaviour with reference to the same generalized others; in so doing, they come to approach situations the same way, with the same underlying understandings, without necessarily having direct contact with each other.

The Two Phases of the Self: The 'I' and the 'Me'

Mead famously divided the 'self' into two phases, **the 'I'** and **the 'Me'**. Mead defined the 'I' as 'the response of the organism to the attitudes of the others'. He defined the 'Me' as 'the organized set of attitudes of others which one himself assumes' (Mead, 1934, p. 173).

The 'I' represents a direct line of action taken by an individual. When an individual acts in any social situation, she does so as the 'I'. For Mead, the 'I' is always associated with becoming, and therefore with novelty and surprise. The 'Me', by contrast, involves looking backward, considering what has already transpired, and then evaluating one's response from the standpoint of the expectation of others. By postulating an 'I' as actor-in-the-present and a 'Me' as actor-looking-back, reflecting on what has taken place in order to evaluate and act again, Mead is able to conceptualize the 'self' not as a 'thing' but rather as a process of adjustment and adaptation. The 'I' of this moment is present in, and reflected on by, the 'Me' of the next moment. The self is 'a constantly flickering alternation' between the two (Flaherty & Fine, 2001, p. 155).

Mead noted that the more intensely an individual is involved in a group, the more likely it will be that her 'I' impulses are shaped by the 'Me' images reflected back to her by other members of the group, and the less likely it will be for the individual's overt behaviour to deviate very much from that of other group members. That said, because humans always interpret 'stimuli' before choosing a response, the future is never set in stone, but is always contingent, and emergent. Indeed, from Mead's perspective, 'there is a constant creation of that which is new'; for that reason, individuals are always 'en route to something' that they cannot foresee. 'We do not know where we are going,' Mead concluded, 'but we are on our way' (Mead, 1936, pp. 295 & 292).

Stages in the Development of the Self: Play, Game, and the 'Generalized Other'

According to Mead, the self develops through three stages, each marked by an increasing capacity for role-taking. In the first stage, the **play stage**, the child has limited capacity to assume the perspective of others and often plays by assuming a single role. For example the child may take on the role of 'doctor' or the role of 'patient' and move between those single roles. Later, when more mature, the child enters the **game stage**, where she has a specific role to play but where she must also assume the role of other players in order to anticipate how they will react.

the 'I'
Mead's term for the response of the organism to the attitudes of the others, representing a direct line of action taken by an individual.

the 'Me'
Mead's term for the organized set of attitudes of others that an individual assumes as part of himself, obtained by looking backward, considering what has already transpired, and then evaluating one's response from the standpoint of the expectation of others. The 'Me' can only be known on reflection.

play stage
According to Mead, the first of three developmental stages of the self, in which the child has limited capacity to assume the perspective of others and often plays by assuming a single role.

game stage
According to Mead, the second of three developmental stages of the self, in which the child has a specific role to play but must also assume the role of other players in order to anticipate how they will react.

the generalized other

According to Mead, the last of three developmental stages of the self, a role taken on by the developing child when she assumes the attitudes held by other members of her community towards her as her own.

All organized team sports, such as basketball, baseball, and hockey, require these kinds of skills. In this stage the child begins to see herself as an object in a larger social organization, and she begins to act in specific ways in order to be able to accurately predict and control the likely behaviour of others towards her. But, Mead tells us, even at this stage the self is not yet complete.

The third and final stage is role-taking with the generalized other. The **generalized other** is the set of 'attitudes' that are held towards an individual by the members of her community.

STUDIES IN SOCIAL RESEARCH

Stripping, Spirituality, and Mead's 'I' and 'Me'

Adopting a qualitative strategy, case study research design, and research methods that included observation, interviews, and focus groups, sociologists Bernadette Barton and Constance Hardesty set out to study 'the linkages between exotic dance (the nudity, music, elaborate body rituals, the black lights) and the meaning informants make of those symbolic resources' (Barton & Hardesty, 2010, pp. 180–1). As Barton and Hardesty note, American morality sharply separates spiritual and sexual worlds, especially when it comes to putting sex up for sale. But in their interviews, Barton and Hardesty found that exotic dancers often describe their time performing onstage in terms of 'spirituality, flow, the loss of self-consciousness'.

Cooley's concept of the 'looking-glass-self' is useful in understanding how exotic dancers feel about themselves, especially as they are viewed by an audience. Barton and Hardesty found that exotic dancers interpret the positive reactions of their audience—the mirror— 'in ways that affirm the self in its physical form' (Barton & Hardesty, 2010, p. 283). They add: 'proudly displaying one's naked body can be a potent act in a culture that repeatedly constrains and degrades women's sexual selves.' They also found that exotic dancers illustrate Mead's theory of the dialectic formation of self (pp. 284–5). In dancing naked for an anonymous audience of appreciative customers, and facing mirrors that force them to look at their own naked bodies, exotic dancers 'begin to perceive of their bodies as beautiful, in some cases goddess-like' (p. 285).

In short, many of these women have found a way to feel good about their bodies and about themselves.

They find themselves 'adored and valued', and they are able to fashion a 'Me'—an internalized perception of themselves drawn from what they perceive are the feelings and attitudes of their customers—that includes being beautiful and desirable. Often, too, the strippers interviewed discussed how they used this new perception of body and self as a means to help them heal 'from the pedestrian abuses of poor body image that almost every woman endures when subjected to increasing unrealistic media images of women's bodies'. Some among them went so far as to talk about how stripping helped them heal spiritually and psychologically from their experiences of childhood sexual abuse and rape (p. 286).

Mead associated the 'I' with creative, spontaneous, and impulsive behaviour. For Mead, the 'I' precedes and works dialectically with the 'Me'. Feeling beautiful and powerful through dancing and overcoming past hurts of sexual abuse all help in creating an 'I' that interprets and responds to the 'Me'-affirming gaze of the audience. Barton and Hardesty liken the 'I' to the spiritual self, which exotic dancers access in part through a combination of elements that strip clubs share with religious congregations, including 'lights, music, sometimes a rhythmic beat and movement, and ritual interactions' and in part through other elements, including 'nudity, intoxicating substances (drugs and alcohol), mirrors, the gaze of others, an elevated platform, and an emotionally charged space' (p. 289).

This 'I', as experienced by exotic dancers, certainly disrupts taken-for-granted constructions of what is and what is not spiritual and challenges our popular assumptions of both the strip club and religiosity

'We appear as selves in our conduct', Mead says, 'in so far as we ourselves take the attitude that others take towards us, in those correlative activities.' In assuming the attitude held by other members of our community towards ourselves we take on the role of the 'generalized other'. In so doing, 'we appear as social objects, as selves' (Mead, 1932, p. 185). In complex societies, Mead noted, individuals must take into consideration a multitude of different 'generalized others', that range from families and friends to social clubs and political groups and even more abstract groups, such as the 'university' or 'the state'.

Located in Toronto's West End, these adjoining buildings make unlikely neighbours of the Bloor Lansdowne Christian Fellowship and Club Paradise strip club. Although he notes that some of the girls occasionally worship at the church, Stephen Mickleson, a member of the Fellowship's board, says the church and the club have different values: 'It's not a show here. . . . We work through kindness and love. The people who work there, many may have had a hard life' (Daubs, 2010). How would you attempt to convince him of the link between spirituality and stripping that Barton and Hardesty have identified?

(p. 294). The way that the exotic dancers interviewed for the study explained their spiritual selves destabilizes our everyday social construction of what a stripper is and what spirituality is. As Barton and Hardesty conclude:

> Exotic dancing can be a more multifaceted experience for women, and the strip bar a more-nuanced environment than most realize, as feminist sexuality researchers have well theorized. . . . Strippers are not only objectified bodies dancing for male desire; at times their sensual movements may be a kind of prayer that connects them, even accidentally, to their own perception of the divine. (Barton & Hardesty, 2010, p. 294).

Here you are, meeting your wife's uncle for the first time. The 'I' reacts and initiates action—shaking hands, saying hello, presenting a bottle of wine. The 'Me', meanwhile, draws on its store of internalized responses from the past—recollections of similar exchanges in comparable social contexts—and provides a running commentary on the results of the actions of the 'I'. The actions of the 'I', which might be quite novel, eventually get incorporated into the 'Me' on sober reflection.

Society Emerges Out of Ongoing Human Social Interactions

Society is the term Mead used to denote the framework that emerges when humans interact with each other via stabilized social relations. This means that, for Mead, society is not some fixed thing (as it was for Durkheim). Rather, society is best conceptualized as the ongoing process of 'mutual adjustment' and 'readjustment' that takes place amongst its members. For Mead, 'society' is possible because its members emit significant gestures, read the significant gestures of others, and use mind and self (both social achievements) to articulate reactions to specific, as well as generalized, others.

A 'society' emerges because of the ability of its members to role-play and to take on the perspective of the generalized other. When we speak of being a member of a specific 'society', we are really referring to the attitudes we use in regulating our own behaviour and the behaviour of others. At any one time, an individual interacts with a combination of close and remote others whose attitudes are all used in the processes of building (or revising) both 'mind' and 'self'. Sometimes the 'generalized other' of an individual's immediate (primary) group diverges from that of other groups to which he also belongs. An individual, for example, who has been raised in a strict Catholic family may also interact in a university class with someone raised as a Buddhist (Mead, 1934, p. 360). In so doing he is exposed to other points of view and to a different 'generalized other'.

Which of Mead's developmental stages does this scene represent?

TWO CURRENT EXAMPLES OF SOCIAL-INTERACTIONIST RESEARCH

apartheid
A policy of racial segregation, especially in South Africa, where, by the 1950s, it consisted of numerous racist laws that allowed a ruling white minority to segregate all non-white persons and to deny them human and political rights (from Afrikaans, lit. 'apartness').

In the following sections we will review two recent studies that have been undertaken from a social-interactionist perspective. In the first example, sociologists Khosro Refaie Shirpak, Eleanor Maticka-Tyndale, and Maryam Chinichian (2007) use symbolic-interactionist theory to examine the differences between foundational Canadian institutions and their views on sexual relations and those of recent immigrants from Iran. The second example involves research done by sociologists Chana Teeger and Vered Vinitzky-Seroussi (2007) on the ways in which the commemoration of **apartheid** in the South African Apartheid Museum actually serves to create collective memories. Both of these examples use a symbolic-interactionist perspective to highlight the complex interactions that take place between individuals and society, as well as the changeable nature of what constitutes 'society'.

Iranian Immigrants' Perception of Sexuality in Canada

The work of early symbolic interactionists, especially George Herbert Mead, has helped researchers today understand the extent to which a sense of self is entrenched in a sense of normalcy and propriety, and how the ways of others can be viewed as strange or deviant. This is illustrated in the research of Shirpak, Maticka-Tyndale, and Chinichian (2007), who have studied how recent Iranian immigrants to Canada interpret and assign meaning to the actions of native-born Canadians, especially around issues of gender relations and sexuality.

Beginning in the 1990s, the chief source of immigration to Canada shifted from Europe (which supplied 90 per cent of immigrants to Canada prior to 1961) to Asia and the Middle East (the source regions of 60 per cent of immigrants to Canada beginning in 1991) (Statistics Canada, 2006, as cited in Shirpak, Maticka-Tyndale, & Chinichian, 2007). One of the largest of the Middle Eastern immigrant groups to Canada consists of Iranians, who come from a country where Islamic worldviews are learned as part of religious teachings and make up an integral part of the laws of the country. As Shirpak, Maticka-Tyndale, and Chinichian (2007) note, the 'norms, roles and expectations' of countries such as Iran regarding sexuality 'may be seen as standing in stark contrast to countries like Canada. As a consequence, the beliefs of Iranian immigrants about sex, sexuality, and the relationships between males and females, as well as between parents and their children, are often starkly different to those held by the majority of Canadians.

In order to understand how Iranian immigrants to Canada interpret 'Canadian sexuality' and ascribe meaning to what they experience while living in Canada, healthcare researchers Shirpak, Maticka-Tyndale, and Chinichian (2007) interviewed 20 adult Iranian immigrants living in Ontario, using symbolic-interactionist theory to frame the research questions they asked.

In traditional Muslim teaching, sexual drives are presented as a natural and necessary aspect of being human, easily aroused and difficult to control. Exposure of a woman's body—whether through absence of clothing or through tight clothing—can easily lead to sexual thoughts and arousal. But the rightful expression of sexual interest can take place only in marriage, and so sexual relations outside of marriage are illegitimate and violate the Iranian criminal code (Shirpak, Maticka-Tyndale, & Chinichian, 2007, p. 114). To prevent illegitimate thoughts or fantasies about anyone but one's spouse, public dress is modest and loose-fitting, covering the entire body. Public segregation of the sexes begins at the primary level of schooling, and interactions between men and women are restricted to parents, siblings, and any other close relatives with whom marriage is forbidden (*maharem*). Men and women who are not related and who appear together in public may be required to provide documents showing that they are related. Conversations with a member of the opposite sex are restricted to 'serious' topics only; casual socializing is inappropriate (Nikzad, 2004, as cited in Shirpak, Maticka-Tyndale, & Chinichian, 2007, p. 114).

In Iran, too, as compared with Canada, the family is privileged over the individual both in law and in custom, and the rights assigned to men are very different from those assigned to women. In Iranian law and in Islamic religious teachings fathers and husbands are the head of the family, while women and girls have limited rights. Men may divorce easily, while women can divorce only under very limited conditions. Men have the right to as many as four permanent wives and to unlimited temporary wives, although to do so they must have the permission of the court and be able to provide for all wives equally.

Canada, in contrast, is a country in which a variety of sexual choices are allowed, and self-fulfillment and self-actualization are often promoted ahead of the interests of the family. Choices about sexuality are left up to the individual, sexual initiation often occurs during the teenage years, and the focus is on individual rights. Women and men are treated equally before the law, and there are no legal restrictions on sexual relations outside of marriage.

As a theoretical approach, symbolic interactionism focuses on the ways in which people actively interpret and create symbols, and on the ways they make sense of, assign meaning

STUDIES IN SOCIAL RESEARCH

Challenging Perceptions of Sexuality in Tehran: Showdown at the Water and Fire Park

'In the 40°C heat of an Iranian summer, what better way to have fun and stay cool than a water fight with friends? In the Islamic republic, however, things are a bit more complicated.

'For one group of boys and girls, their game turned serious when they were arrested for taking part in a water pistol fight in a park in the capital, Tehran. . . .

'[T]he city's police chief confirmed the arrests, blaming the participants for behaving "abnormally" and disobeying Islamic principles. [A] conservative MP, said such events would spread "corruption" and were "shameful". . . .

'Men and women not related by blood or marriage in Iran are not allowed to touch or have relationships outside social norms. However, many youths continue to push the boundaries, despite a crackdown that has targeted certain hairstyles and clothing.'

Source: Saeed Kamali Dehghan. 'Iranian youths arrested for public water pistol fight in Tehran', *The Guardian* (Thursday 4 August 2011).

What symbolic meanings do the actions of the youths who participated in the water fight have for the youths themselves? For the police and other authorities? What kinds of role strain would the youths who participated in this event experience?

role strain

A situation that can occur when there is tension among the various roles attached to a status, or even between the roles attached to different statuses.

to, and communicate about their daily lives and the world in which they live (Shirpak, Maticka-Tyndale, & Chinichian, 2007, p. 116). For Shirpak, Maticka-Tyndale, and Chinichian, symbolic-interactionist theory drew their attention to the symbolic meanings that actions and experiences have for Iranian immigrants to Canada, while pointing to the issue of **role strain** that is experienced by new immigrants transitioning from the symbolic meanings associated with particular actions and experiences in Iran to the very different ones associated with actions and experiences in Canada.

To understand the experiences and actions of Iranian immigrants to Canada and to learn about their interpretations of sexuality in Canada, the three healthcare workers used a qualitative research strategy, a case study design, and in-depth interviews with 10 Iranian men and 10 Iranian women who had recently immigrated to Canada. The interviews were conducted by the two researchers who spoke Farsi, who presented themselves as a male physician and a female midwife. This helped them to deal with cultural sensitivity about speaking to someone of a different gender, and to speaking to someone other than a healthcare professional about sexuality. As the researchers reported, the participants in their research project were not directly asked about their view of the sexuality of Canadians. Rather, the participants were encouraged to frame their views in the context of the personal concerns they had about Canadian ways of dealing with sexuality and parent–child relationships (p. 117). The study's principal findings illuminated the following issues:

1. *Meanings ascribed to Canadian sexuality and sexual relationships.* Most participants spoke positively about the apparent ease with which Canadian men and women interact with each other, and about their knowledge of sexual matters. However, they did not think that Canadian ways would work for them, since they might put their marital and familial relationships in jeopardy.
2. *The symbolic nature of dress.* Most of the interviewees felt that the dress of Canadian women signalled seduction and sexual availability. The Iranian-born women feared their husbands would be seduced, while the Iranian-born men stated that they saw Canadian women's dress as seductive.
3. *Women's rights and freedoms.* The male respondents viewed the freedoms given to Canadian women to make decisions about work, dress, recreation, and whom they wanted to spend time with socially all as threats to the stability of Iranian families. They believed that women's right to petition for divorce on equal footing with men, the availability of state support for single mothers, and the ability of the state to intervene in marital issues (as, for example, in the case of spousal abuse) all encouraged women to leave marriages.
4. *Non-marital interactions and friendships.* Interviewees had difficulty accepting that any social relationship that crossed gender lines (with the exception of familial relationships) could be regarded as non-sexual. The ease of divorce and the number of divorces in Canada all confirmed for them that Canadians put little effort into their marital relationships (p. 120).

A great deal has been written about cross-cultural misunderstandings with differences in meanings ascribed to such things as dress, physical closeness between strangers in public places, physical expression, body language, cultural politeness, and interpersonal interactions. The researchers concluded that differences in interpretation of these and other commonplace events have the potential to create tension and strain and go a long way to undermining inclusive, respectful relations across different ethnic communities. They can create barriers to recognizing commonality of experience and can lead to the perpetuation of stereotypes, ongoing suspicion, and misunderstandings that widen the gulf between people. The authors suggest that because Canada's approach to immigration and nation building is founded on the principle of multiculturalism, the promoting of communication and understanding across cultural divides is an essential ingredient for national unity (Shirpak, Maticka-Tyndale, & Chinichian, 2007, p. 125).

A Social-Interactionist Perspective on Time and Collective Memory

Physicist Albert Einstein once wrote: 'People like us, who believe in physics, know that the distinction between past, present and future is only a stubbornly persistent illusion.' It would appear that Einstein's observation is also shared by social interactionists. Mead said much the same thing when he wrote that the past 'is as hypothetical as the future' and is to be found 'in the present world' (Mead, 1932, p. 31; Mead, 1934, p. 116, as cited in Flaherty & Fine, 2007, p. 153).

Social-interactionist inquiries into collective memory address questions about how individuals and their groups both use the past in their day-to-day, moment-to-moment activities, and have their immediate experiences shaped by the past. Underpinning their research is the conviction that the past is never really past. An interactionist approach to the study of collective memory is characterized by three practices:

1. *It treats collective memory as both a process and a product.* Examining social processes should not preclude considering the outcome of those processes as a product; therefore, any interactionist analysis should include both.
2. *It considers the ways in which collective memories are made effective.* Effectiveness is particularly an issue in divided or contested societies, where strategies that are effective for one audience may fail for others.
3. *It determines how collective memories are tangibly manifested and transmitted in the social sphere* (Flaherty & Fine, 2007).

Sociologist Paul DiMaggio describes collective memory as 'the outcome of processes affecting, respectively, the information to which individuals have access, the schemata by which people understand the past, and the external symbols or messages that prime these schemata' (1997, p. 275). Some sociologists have looked at the interaction between collective memory and individual memory. Chana Teeger and Vered Vinitzky-Seroussi (2007), for example, have shown how the portrayal of historical events by a museum set up to commemorate those events serves to structure the understanding that visitors to the museum take away. Their study of the South African Apartheid Museum is the subject of the section that follows.

Collective Memory: Commemorating Apartheid in South Africa

Opened in 2001, the South African Apartheid Museum stands just off the highway linking Johannesburg and Soweto, near a casino and amusement park. This detail about the location of the museum is important, as you will soon see.

The Apartheid Museum is 'dedicated to telling the story of apartheid in South Africa', and as Teeger and Vinitzky-Seroussi note, it does so not through commemorating 'disagreement and debate' but through 'an over-arching consensus' achieved by a 'large degree of control in terms of both form and content'. Even a difficult past, marked by disputes, tensions, and conflict, can be commemorated consensually.

The term *apartheid* was coined in 1930 from the Afrikaans word for apartness. By the 1950s, apartheid in South Africa consisted of numerous racist laws that allowed a ruling white minority to segregate all non-white persons and to deny them human and political rights. The laws limited the rights of blacks to own land, prohibited social contact between the races, and enforced segregated standards for public facilities, education, jobs, union membership, and political participation. The policy of apartheid produced a system of institutionalized racial discrimination that contravened the United Nations Charter and the Universal Declaration of Human Rights. Opposition to these laws was suppressed by the government, but a growing internal resistance, accompanied by international support, led in 1994 to the country's first multi-racial elections. Nelson Mandela was elected South Africa's first black president, charged with overseeing the transition from minority white rule and apartheid to multi-racial democracy.

Data for Teeger and Vinitzky-Seroussi's study were gathered in 2002–3 from interviews conducted with 18 'relevant agents of memory', including

> . . . the museum's funder, the designer of the museum's initial plan; the curator, filmmakers, historians, archivists, architects, education specialists; representatives of the Gauteng Gambling Board; the curator of a museum in Soweto; and many others. The research also consisted of participant observations of the curatorial team on an 'assessment tour' of the museum, guided tours of the museum, observations of unguided visitors to the museum as well as visits to relevant sites [. . .] and content analysis of artifacts, photographs, and text panels that constitute the museum's narrative as well as documents related to both the construction and the public reception of the museum. (Teeger & Vinitzky-Seroussi, 2007, pp. 59–60)

The Apartheid Museum was built in the context of the country's newly liberalized gaming legislation. Anyone bidding on a casino licence had to offer something to the community as part of the bid. The Apartheid Museum, as it turns out, was the 'winning concept' that tipped the scales in favour of the group that ultimately won the bid for a casino licence. Granted a licence and provided with an Israeli museologist's report to help them along with their ideas for 'The Park of Freedom', the successful bidders began construction on the casino, all but forgetting the museum until they were forcefully reminded of the penalties for noncompliance (Teeger & Vinitzky-Seroussi, 2007, p. 61).

The site on which the museum is located is open, and as one architect involved in the process complained, 'you actually had no control as to what would come, what would happen' (Teeger & Vinitzky-Seroussi, 2007, p. 63). This was partially solved by making the museum into a self-contained 'walled complex', where 'structure, tour guides, security guards and cameras heightened the sensation that control and surveillance are never far away' (p. 63).

As Teeger and Vinitzky-Seroussi explain, the physical structure of the museum presents a carefully controlled beginning, middle, and conclusion. The content presented in the museum is 'carefully controlled to elicit consensus and not conflict'. This is achieved by using four interconnected techniques: 'divorcing the past; legitimizing the present; forgetting through remembering; and experiencing the past' (Teeger & Vinitzky-Seroussi, 2007, p. 64).

In divorcing the past from the present, the museum locates the roots of apartheid in the conflict between the British and Afrikaner settler communities, thus removing the '"original sin" from the hands of the Afrikaners' and controlling for 'expressions of guilt, anger, and accountability that could be directed at this community in the present'. For example, the

Imagine you are a visitor to the Apartheid Museum and you see this sign. How does the juxtaposition of the term 'theme park' affect your experience before you even set foot inside the museum?

orientation film that all visitors are taken to watch fails to explain how early European settlers refused to consider the indigenous groups they encountered as humans and instead hunted them for sport (p. 65).

The Apartheid Museum tells the early history of South Africa in such a way that white settlers are not portrayed as perpetrators of genocide. Instead apartheid in South Africa is presented in terms of British oppression of both blacks and Afrikaners as a result of competition for gold. In this way, the Afrikaners—the descendants of South African Dutch and Hugenot settlers of the seventeenth century—are not 'the evil other' but are made 'part of the newly imagined South African community'. They are portrayed not as villains but as victims of oppression and prejudice who share a common history with black South Africans. Indeed, the museum is designed so that as the visitor moves through the museum's space, towards the post-apartheid area, the corridor becomes narrow, so that 'the apartheid exhibits can no longer be viewed. They are left behind, as is the past' (Teeger & Vinitzky-Seroussi, 2007, p. 67).

Mandela and the ANC are presented as the embodiment of reconciliation in all its aspects—'goodwill, forgiveness and acceptance'—and without 'anger, guilt, vengeance or accountability' (Teeger & Vinitzky-Seroussi, 2007, p. 68). The first image seen by a visitor to the room representing the new South Africa is a picture of Nelson Mandela, 'hero of the story' and 'icon of the nation'. The focus of the museum is on Mandela and his party, the ANC, and not on other efforts, contributions, or alternative visions by others who resisted apartheid. The ANC and its vision of how the past should be resolved are presented as the only, inevitable choice.

Teeger and Vinitzky-Seroussi also comment on the way the technique of 'forgetting through remembering' is employed throughout the museum. The 'agents of memory' who designed the museum did not entirely exclude other versions of events and issues; what they did, though, is treat alternative narratives 'tangentially'. Complete absence serves as a stimulus to remembrance, invoking indignation among those who have an interest in remembering. The marginal presence accorded to white opposition to apartheid, women's resistance, rural resistance, and the role of leaders of the Pan Africanist Congress, for example, may actually serve to 'stimulate forgetting' of alternative visions and ideologies offered by different resistance movements (Teeger & Vinitzky-Seroussi, 2007, p. 69). In much the same way, the issue of violence and the ANC is presented in such a complicated and convoluted way that it 'becomes symbolically absent'. In so doing, potential criticism is preempted, important issues are subsumed under other topics, and forgetting is 'effected through memory' (p. 70).

Similarly, in some installations, visitors to the museum are invited to 'feel what it was like' under apartheid. They enter into a room through doors marked 'white' and 'non-white', their entrance assigned according to cards issued randomly to all visitors at the entrance. They enter cells, hear the cell doors close. Yet, as Teeger and Vinitzky-Seroussi point out, 'apartheid may be "experienced"' but quickly left behind as the 'visitor moves out of the Hall of Segregation, out of the solitary confinement cells' (p. 71).

How do we explain the kinds of memories commemorated in the Apartheid Museum? Teeger and Vinitzky-Seroussi suggest we understand them in the context of 'the political culture of the commemorating society, the relevance of the past to the present agenda and the power of the agents of memory' (p. 72). In South Africa, the Truth and Reconciliation Commission (TRC) operated in a political culture determined to push for a consensus that constructed the past as 'irrelevant for the present agenda'. The TRC was formed to grant amnesty to members of the outgoing apartheid regime during the negotiated transition from white minority rule to non-racial democratic government. With a goal of consensus rather than conflict, the TRC granted amnesty on a case-by-case basis to those who fully disclosed their past. Once disclosed, the past was closed off, no longer salient to present understanding of any social or institutional problems. The work of the TRC, the most powerful agent of memory, helped to define the new nation of South Africa in counterpoint to the 'other', the old South Africa. In an analogous way, the museum's own 'agents of memory', the professionals involved in making the museum's structure and its displays,

> . . . can be seen to have internalized the main messages espoused by the TRC and other powerful people. Rarely did the professionals object to the expected consensual matter. On the contrary, they felt that the museum was a product (as far as content is concerned) of their own autonomy. (Teeger & Vinitzky-Seroussi, 2007, p. 72)

This consensual approach to politics has, over the past three decades, been apparent in South Africa, where there has been little racially motivated political mobilization in spite of the social problems that continue to plague the country. Potentially deeply divisive events are commemorated in ways that both decontextualize and neutralize them. Thus, the Sharpeville massacre of 21 March 1960, where South African police opened fire on black demonstrators, is now commemorated as 'Human Rights Day'. The Soweto Student Uprising of 16 June 1975, where police opened fire on high school students protesting for better education, is celebrated as 'Youth Day'. All South Africans can participate in the celebrations. Like these holidays, the Apartheid Museum makes the present less threatening and constructs consensus through a public memory that moves forward, without looking back.

The 'agents of memory' who were responsible for the Apartheid Museum were explicit in their intent that visitors to the museum leave with only certain kinds of memories. They aimed to ensure that visitors not become divided and 'polarized around race', that the museum 'not open wounds' but rather serve to build consensus and promote a new South Africa, with its 'Rainbow Nation' identity. But Teeger and Vinitzky-Seroussi are quick to remind us that social-interactionist theory is cautious about 'placing the significance of an act in its intended meaning alone'. Significance, rather, is produced in interpretation. Thus, the researchers note, we will have to wait to see if visitors to the Apartheid Museum 'consume the messages' of that museum in the ways intended 'by the individuals who constructed them'.

At present, the interaction between the visitors to the museum and the content they find there is imagined by the 'professionals' who designed the displays to be consensual. The narrative presented about apartheid is carefully controlled to elicit consensus and to discourage conflict. Even the construction of the building promotes this. The words 'Freedom', 'Respect', 'Democracy', 'Equality', 'Reconciliation', 'Diversity', 'Responsibility' are written individually on a series of imposing pillars just inside the front wall of the premises, representing hopes for the present and the future. This is the only part of the museum that is visible from the road, and the words are taken from the core values laid out in the South African Constitution. The rest of the museum is walled off, and the visitor can examine what it contains—the difficult past—then 'sigh in relief' when she exits the museum and leaves it all contained behind her.

SUMMARY

The theme of this chapter, that society is a product of human social interactions, has been taken up in the context of a review of the work of social interactionists. We began with the work of George Herbert Mead, who focused on the ways in which mind, self, and society emerge out of human social interaction.

In the course of this chapter we have seen that social interactionists strive to understand:

- how humans interact with each other and, using symbols, create and build up meanings, define their social situations, and develop (ever-changing) perspectives on the wider social order; and
- how the lives and situations of individuals, social groups, and even societies are in a constant state of evolving and adjusting as individual members of those groups go about interacting with each other.

The accounts of research on civil society and collective memory provided two examples of the process of social interaction through which individual humans organize and understand their lives, and out of which groups, institutions and societies emerge.

By now you should understand the social-interactionist perspective on society: society is an always-emerging process/product. Society is the result of dynamic and ongoing social interactions between its members, which in themselves contain a multitude of contradictions that could, at any moment, result in changes. Social interactionists propose that a continuity runs from individuals (mind/self), through primary groups (community) to larger-scale organizations (society) and that symbolic communication is the means by which all individuals are united together, from intimate and immediate primary groups to large-scale social institutions.

The next chapter introduces the concept of socialization, used by sociologists as a means of explaining how individuals become members of a group and learn to take on the attitudes of others as their own.

DISCUSSION QUESTIONS

1. Discuss the differences between Durkheim's approach to studying society and the approach taken by symbolic interactionists.
2. List the intellectual influences on the work of George Herbert Mead and explain how each influence helped shape Mead's insights into social interaction, social organization, and the social nature of the self.
3. On what basis do the symbolic interactionists argue that the self is not there at birth? What are some of the implications this might have for how the self is conceptualized?
4. What does Mead mean when he says that communication between humans involves the use of significant gestures or symbols?
5. What, according to Mead, is the relationship between the 'I' and the 'Me'? Use the example of exotic dancers to explain how these women fashion a positive view of themselves.
6. Explain what is meant by the 'generalized other', giving examples to illustrate your explanation.
7. How might a symbolic-interactionist perspective help us to deal with the issue of Canadian national unity?

Part IV
Core Concepts

Sociologists, like all other scientists, endeavour to produce knowledge about the world around them. Although the assumed wisdom in the sciences has been that scientists 'discover' reality, that position has been challenged by critical thinkers, who counter that, although we may perceive that the order of whatever we are studying existed prior to our arrival, in fact we impose that order ourselves. Scientists, in other words, don't 'discover' reality; they create it through interpretation.

But if our actual work as social scientists is imputing order and meaning to events or actions, it becomes crucial to understand clearly how we distinguish one set of events and actions from another. It is equally important to understand how we recognize and attribute significance to patterns of relationships that we find among different events and social actions.

In Part IV we explore the use of core concepts in sociological analysis. Learning about the discipline of sociology involves learning to think as a sociologist. We all make sense of the world we live in by using common-sense, taken-for-granted concepts that we have acquired as members of our society. We use those concepts to discern and make sense of all aspects of social life. When we think as sociologists, however, we must put aside taken-for-granted concepts and instead use concepts that are part of the tools of sociological inquiry. These afford us a different perspective on social relations than we have when we use taken-for-granted concepts for day-to-day living.

Becoming a sociologist means learning to make sense of the world in new ways. This involves acknowledging that common-sense ways of thinking about the world are neither 'natural' nor 'common' to everyone. Some of the most fundamental core concepts in sociology are socialization, culture, social structure, and agency. These concepts act as shorthand descriptions of complex social phenomena. By drawing our attention to the existence of complex structures, rules, social practices and process, beliefs, values, and rules, our core sociological concepts allow us to take new and often revealing perspectives on everyday social events and social relationships.

8 Socialization and the Young Child

CHAPTER OUTLINE

LEARNING OBJECTIVES

In this chapter you will:

- gain a clearer understanding of socialization
- examine what is known today about infant cognition
- think critically about how categories of thought are acquired
- consider what cases of feral and abandoned children can tell us about the social roots of human behaviour
- compare what attachment theory and the theory of intersubjectivity have to tell us about early experiences of infants and the process of socialization
- learn about mutual recognition and the intersubjective view of infant–caregiver interaction.

INTRODUCTION

socialization
The process of becoming a member of society, of becoming a social being, or of learning social roles.

The concept of **socialization**, a core concept used by sociologists, anthropologists, and psychologists, has two meanings. First, socialization implies an activity carried out by members of a group: it is the series of active processes group members engage in when they make novices into full members. Second, socialization implies a result or product: through the purposeful actions of group members, the novice (be it a child, an adolescent, or an adult) gradually acquires social and cultural fluency, and becomes both self-aware and skilled in the ways of the social group or the society into which he is being socialized.

Whether an activity or a product, socialization involves three elements:

- *the participants*: the agents of socialization and the novices undergoing socialization
- *the process*: the activities by which members are created/incorporated
- *the requirements*: the conditions that must be met for group membership (Long & Hadden, 1983, pp. 5–7).

Participants in socialization include those doing the socializing—the agents of socialization, or insiders—and the novices being socialized, the outsiders. Depending on whether the

School rituals are instrumental in the socialization of young children. Who are the participants in this scene of socialization? Can you imagine the process and requirements of socialization in this context?

novice is an infant, an adolescent, or an adult, he will already be a member of many social groups—family, work, school, friends, associations, profession, nation, and the like. The precise influence of these other social groups on the novice's socialization into a new group will vary. It will depend on the extent of the individual's commitment to and integration into the other groups and on the ways in which existing commitments and integration will interact with what is being offered by the new group (Long & Hadden, 1983, p. 7).

Incorporating new members into an existing social group involves a variety of processes. As the child or novice adult engages in social interaction, he acquires a sense of self, as well as a body of knowledge and a set of skills that equip him to live as a member of a variety of social groups. Through socialization, group members train newcomers (whether they are children or novices) in the ways of the group: newcomers learn group definitions of the various roles that are available, and how each of those roles is to be played.

Membership in any group, according to Long and Hadden (1983), requires that individuals:

> (1) know and understand the requisites of membership, (2) that they are competent and skilled in their use and application, and (3) that they are committed to following them as guides for action. (Long & Hadden, 1983, p. 6)

Through socialization, those who are to become members of any given group must adopt that group's understandings about behaviour in such a way that group cohesion results. Weber explained that in order for an organization to persist, group members must share 'similar' concepts about that organization (Weber, 1915/1964, p. 14). Group membership is something that is conferred on an individual by others once they are confident that the individual possesses the necessary qualities, whatever they may be, for admission to the group. Group membership is sustained as long as that confidence is sustained, regardless of the individual's actual abilities, knowledge, or skill (Long & Hadden, 1983, p. 6).

Although the process of socialization can be lifelong, we first experience it as an infant and young child. This chapter covers the socialization of infants and children, while the next chapter, Chapter 9, will take up the socialization of adolescents and adults.

THE PRE-SOCIALIZED INFANT

Before we go too far down the path of socialization, we will stop and consider what is known today about infant cognition. What does the literature from the cognitive sciences and infant development tell us about the pre-socialized mental categories that humans are born with? In short, is there anything that is innate about human cognition and subsequent behaviour, or is it all the result of 'socialization'?

Classical sociologist Émile Durkheim believed that there was nothing at all innate about human behaviour. He hypothesized that the basic categories of thought or mental representations we all use are entirely the result of social learning and are passed on from one generation to the next through socialization. In the distant past, Durkheim reasoned, our 'essential ideas', 'categories of understanding', and 'mental representations' first came about as a result of religious activities, particularly those associated with **totemic religions**. According to Durkheim:

> At the roots of all our judgements there are a certain number of essential ideas
> which dominate all our intellectual life; they are what philosophers since

totemic religions
Religions whose members identify with a spiritual totem, typically an animal or other naturalistic figure.

Aristotle have called the categories of understanding: ideas of time, space, class, number, cause, substance, personality etc. They are born in religion and of religion; they are a product of religious thought. (Durkheim, 1912/1965, pp. 21–2)

For Durkheim, the mental categories that each individual possesses are, in fact, collective representations, and he theorized that it is 'experiences in totemic religious rites that instill a sense of group which begins as an externally induced experience and goes on to become a mental representation' (Durkheim, 1912/1965, p. 22). Through social imprinting, or internalization, the external (i.e. culture) becomes internal (i.e. the categories of thought used by an individual). These categories get passed on to subsequent generations via social learning and not through genetic inheritance. In short, according to Durkheim, mental categories are socially generated and not innate, and subsequent generations acquire (and modify) those categories of thought through the process of social learning.

Writing over a century later with the benefit of extensive research on the cognitive functioning of human infants to back him up, sociologist Albert Bergesen (2004) asks if this is really the case. Are all mental categories entirely the result of social learning, or are some categories already present at birth?

ARE HUMANS SOCIAL FROM BIRTH?

Are humans born as 'blank slates' (or *tabula rasa*, as John Locke famously coined the term) on which society, corporate groups, and culture write their messages? Are our 'categories of understanding' acquired only through social interaction? Is, as Durkheim's work suggests, 'society' the single origin of 'mind'? Are humans pre-social at birth and then made into social beings through a process of socialization? Or is there something more that we need to consider—what, in fact, does the pre-socialized infant know?

Here is some of the research that Bergesen (2004) cites to answer these questions:

- Research strongly suggests that babies possess space, depth, and direction perception (Alegria & Noirot, 1978, 1982; Mehler & Dupox, 1994; Walk & Gibson, 1961).
- There is an extensive body of research findings that indicates that infants have pre-socialized representations of numbers and rudimentary addition and subtraction abilities (Feigenson, Carey, & Hauser, 2002; Koechlin, Dehaene, & Mehler, 1998; Lipton & Spelke, 2004; Sharon & Wynn, 1998; Simon, Hespos, & Rochat, 1995; Spelke, 2003; Van de Walle, Carey, & Prevor, 2001; Wynn, 1998).
- Infants seem to possess a rudimentary sense of cause and effect (Baillargeon, 2000; Gopnik, Meltzoff, & Kuhl, 1999; Mehler & Dupoux, 1994).
- Research conducted with infants as young as 3 months of age indicates their capability to represent objects as 'cohesive bodies that maintain both their connectedness and their boundaries as they move', and to understand that 'continuous bodies . . . move only on connected, unobstructed paths' and that 'bodies . . . interact if and only if they come into contact' (Spelke, 2003, p. 282).
- Infants are able to recognize human faces (Bushnell & Sai, 1987; Field, et al., 1984; Johnson & Morton, 1991; Mehler & Dupox, 1994) and can imitate gestures, such as sticking out the tongue, all without the benefit of mirrors. Infants as young as 42 minutes of age were tested, indicating they have an innate mental representation of themselves and

others (Gopnik, Meltzoff, & Kuhl, 1999; Meltzoff & Brooks, 2001). Infants are also able to recognize the outline of the human body (Mehler & Dupoux, 1994).

- Infants, with little socialization, are able to impute motive, intentions, and purpose to adult actions (Baron-Cohen, 1995; Meltzoff & Brooks, 2001; Phillips, Wellmean, & Spelke, 2002; Premack 1990; Woodward 1998, 1999; Woodward, Sommerville, & Guajardo, 2001).
- Infants appear to be able to 'construe a collective entity (a group, organization, community, society, etc.) consisting of multiple objects (different persons) as a unitary individual (a corporate collective, or a group with a life of its own)'. In short 'Infants can individuate collective entities and treat a collection as an individual for enumeration purposes' (Wynn, Bloom, & Chiang, 2002).

These and other recent research studies on infant cognition indicate that human infants are born with:

- mental representations of the substances of objects, along with ideas about cause and effect, number, and so forth;
- a basic theory of the minds of others; and
- some understanding of collective entities, and hence an elementary form of the sociological imagination.

This strongly suggests that the human infant is not born as an entirely blank slate to be written on by society, but that social categories of thought and understanding are already present at birth. It would appear that humans are born already 'social', with rudimentary understandings of such seemingly complex concepts as motives, intentions, and purpose in others. In short, recent research from the cognitive and neurological sciences indicates that humans are born with basic categories of thought already in place, prior to any social interaction (Bergesen, 2004, pp. 406–7). Research also suggests that humans are all born with at least a rudimentary or incipient social 'self' already in place. This can be contrasted with the beliefs of Durkheim, Mead, and Cooley, who felt that all understanding is a direct result of human social interaction.

Children are eager to form social bonds, and are reluctant to break them. Psychologists and anthropologists have noted, for example, the ease with which social bonds are formed among children who are involved in small-group, face-to-face, interpersonal interactions. Sherif, Harvey, White, Hood, and Sherif (1961) conducted an experiment dubbed the 'Robbers Cave' study, in which they randomly assigned previously unacquainted boys to two groups. The researchers were able to show that strong group loyalties and identification quickly emerged, and the two groups became strongly opposed. When the two groups were later re-united into one group and assigned a single, co-operative goal, new emotional and behavioural patterns emerged among the boys to accommodate the new arrangement.

Sociologists, though, are well aware that the 'self', even if incipiently there at birth, requires an enormous amount of interaction with others to become a fully functioning (i.e. socialized) human adult. Abandoned or **feral children**—children who have grown up without the influence of human contact and, thus, without being socialized—are heart-wrenching reminders of this. Studies of the lives and treatment of abandoned and feral children strongly indicate the importance of early social relationships in supporting an individual's development as a social being with a well-integrated sense of self. These studies emphasize the need

feral children
Human children who have lived away from adults from an early age and thus have little experience of human social behaviour or language.

for sustained, supportive, and caring contact with others if the human child is to grow into a socially adept adult.

The point of view developed in the rest of this chapter is that humans are, indeed, born with certain capabilities and set mental categories that favour sociability. But these abilities do not develop by themselves. If the child grows up without frequent enough (and consistent enough) social interaction with others, then her innate sociability (however astonishingly revealed in recent studies) languishes and even atrophies. There are three sources of studies that support this position. The first source consists of case studies of nineteenth- and twentieth-century feral and abandoned children. The second is the work of early attachment theorists (and especially the work of Harry Harlow with rhesus monkeys). The third is the late twentieth-century work of psychoanalysts on the intersubjective nature of infant–caregiver social interactions.

FERAL AND ABANDONED CHILDREN

The theme of abandonment is a very old one in Western mythology. The twin brothers Romulus and Remus, legendary founders of Rome, were believed to be feral children. Set adrift on the Tiber River by enemies of their parents, they were saved, according to legend, by a she-wolf who suckled them and raised them to adulthood. Eighteenth- and nineteenth-century philosophers and social thinkers were fascinated with the issue of feral children because they believed the study of feral children could help them answer the question of what behaviour is innate or natural to the human condition and what behaviour is the result of learning. They were convinced that if feral children could be made to speak, all might be understood. Contemporary writers and thinkers have been equally curious about what children raised in isolation can tell us about what is innate about human behaviour and what can be attributed to socialization.

It is unthinkable for any humane person to keep a child in isolation. However, there have been several cases of abandoned and feral children that have been reported on and studied over the course of the last two centuries. These are sometimes referred to as 'forbidden experiments'. The sections that follow touch on the lives of four of these children—Victor, Genie, Anna, and Isabella—with the cases of Victor and Genie presented in depth. These case studies are offered for two reasons. The first is to illustrate the point, outlined above, that without 'socialization'—that is, without the benefit of close, intense, and deliberate social interaction with adult caregivers—the innate mental categories that we are all born with will remain at best undeveloped, and at worst will atrophy. The second is to illustrate the extent to which scientific theories shape the kinds of questions we can ask, the kinds of evidence we look for in order to be able to answer those questions, and the kinds of explanations we derive from, or apply to, our evidence.

The Wild Boy of Aveyron

On 9 January 1800, a boy who fit Swiss philosopher Jean-Jacques Rousseau's description of an individual in the 'state of nature' was captured in the village of Saint-Serin in the south of France. A few months after his capture, the 'wild boy of Aveyron', or 'Victor', as he was later called, became one of the first feral children to come into contact with the practitioners of the newly emerging human sciences, especially the strain of philosophy known as **sensationalism**. During the eighteenth century, this philosophy (also called **radical empiricism**) won over may converts, who espoused its view that all human beings acquire their ideas, beliefs, knowledge, and experience through sensory experience—touch, smell, taste, sight, and hearing. Among the best-known and most influential philosophers of this genre were the English philosopher John Locke (1632–1704), the French philosopher Étienne Bonnot de Condillac (1715–80), and Rousseau (1712–78).

The 'scientific study' of the boy began with the report written three weeks after his capture by Constant-Saint-Estave, a commissioner in charge of local government. In that report, the commissioner noted that the boy was not toilet-trained, and urinated and defecated whenever he felt the need. Two days after his capture he had been taken—still naked, and known only as the 'wild boy'—to the hospitals in the town of Saint-Afrique, 40 kilometres away. When he was dressed, he had torn off his clothing. He had refused to sleep in a bed and had continually tried to escape. Constant-Saint-Estave concluded that 'from earliest childhood this boy has lived in the woods, a stranger to social needs and habits.'

Stories about the 'wild boy' soon spread throughout France, and the boy was moved once again, this time into the care of a local abbot and biology professor, Pierre-Joseph Bonnaterre, who lived in Rodez. Bonnaterre immediately set about experimenting with his unusual charge, observing and recording his actions and reactions. From Bonnaterre we learn that the boy was about 49 inches (125 cm) tall and appeared to be 12 or 13 years old. His body was covered with scars, including one of almost 4 centimetres in length across the upper end of the tracheal artery, right across the glottis. In his report, Bonnaterre speculated that someone probably had tried to kill the child.

Bonnaterre noted that the boy had no malformation of the tongue or mouth or vocal chords, which might have impeded him from speaking. He further observed that while there was nothing wrong with the boy's senses, he relied on those senses in an order different to the one common to most humans: the sense of smell came first, then taste, and finally touch. While his sense of hearing was acute, he seemed to shut out most of the sounds that people around him made and appeared to be interested only in food and sleep.

When Bonnaterre showed the boy a mirror, he apparently saw a person reflected in it, but did not recognize that reflection as his own. When Bonnaterre held a potato behind the boy's head so he could see it in the mirror, the boy first tried to reach through the mirror to grasp it. When that proved unsuccessful, he reached back over his shoulder without turning around and grasped the potato. But for all his experimenting and efforts to educate the boy, Bonnaterre really did not know what to make of him. The question soon became whether or not the child was simply an 'idiot' (the official term used in the eighteenth and nineteenth centuries to designate a person with a low level of intelligence). Was any effort to educate the child therefore useless? After much observation, Bonnaterre concluded that the child was not without some intelligence, reflection, and reasoning power. However, in every instance that did not concern 'his natural needs or satisfying his appetite', Bonnaterre observed, 'one can perceive in him only animal behavior' (as cited in Shattuck, 1980, p. 18). But like Constant-Saint-Estave before him, Bonnaterre soon lost control of 'the wild boy' to yet another, more powerful group of scientists, the Abeé Sicard and the Society of the Observers of Man.

The Society of the Observers of Man

Roch-Ambroise Cucurron, Abée Sicard (1742–1822), held the position of director of the Institute for Deaf-Mutes in Paris, and it was here that the 'wild boy' was taken. Sicard's approach to the education of deaf-mutes was closely tied to the sensationalist or empiricist ideas of the time.

sensationalism
A theory of human learning, popular in the eighteenth century, that argued that humans acquire beliefs, ideas, and knowledge only through sensory experience (*also called* **radical empiricism**).

The impact of sensationalist theory on the study of human existence was extensive, especially in France. Proponents believed that adherence to sensationalist precepts would not only allow scientific studies of humanity to be undertaken but provide the opportunity to transform the behaviour of certain individuals who had been deprived of normal education. This goal could be achieved through the manipulation of special kinds of sensory input.

Based on this point of view, a whole set of institutions had been created, not 10 years before the 'wild boy' was discovered. The Institute for Deaf-Mutes in Paris was one of these new institutions. While at that school, the 'wild boy', who was then still without a name, was placed under the care of a group of men who called themselves The Society of Observers of Man. Examined by several of the more famous members of the society, including Dr Philippe Pinel (1745–1820), who was widely known for his humane treatment of psychiatric patients, the boy was found to be an 'incurable idiot' who could safely be relegated to an insane asylum and given the minimum of care.

In this scene from *L'enfant sauvage* (1969), a French film based on the story of Victor, Dr Itard holds the 'wild boy' while Dr Pinel examines him to see if he possesses the physical apparatus necessary to speak. Why do you think the emerging scientific community was so fascinated by Victor's case?

Itard and the (Partial) Socialization of Victor

But the story of the 'wild boy' did not end there. His case was taken up by a young medical student, Jean-Marc-Gaspard Itard (1774–1838), who worked with deaf children at the Institute in Paris and who was not convinced by Pinel's finding that there was something organically wrong with the boy. Because he disagreed with Pinel, Itard was willing to go ahead and test John Locke's and Condillac's sensationalist theories on the boy by attempting his socialization. Both Locke and Condillac had argued that all knowledge comes through the senses. Itard extended their work, reasoning that what Victor needed was sensory training and stimulation to help him become more attuned to his social environment. With this goal in mind, Itard developed an educational plan that relied heavily on sensory training. Itard's plan included teaching Victor how to appropriately respond to other people, to use all his senses, to speak, to use other forms of symbolic communication such as pictures and writing, to be more social, and to think clearly (Malson, 1964).

Itard had limited success, and his written accounts of the process—*Memoire of Victor of Aveyron* (1801) and *Report on New Developments in the Case of Victor of Aveyron* (1806)—describe his slow, difficult, and at times frustrating work. Victor learned to wear clothes and to dress himself. He became toilet-trained and was able to recognize and reproduce a few words made out of metal letters. He even learned to say a very few words. Over a period of several years, Victor displayed evidence of both intellectual and emotional growth. He was able to participate in household chores such as setting the table, gardening, and chopping wood. Yet when Victor failed to meet his expectations, Itard, too, quickly tired of his experiments with the boy, leaving him in the care of Mme Guérin, his housekeeper. Victor died in 1828, at the age of about 40. There is nothing in the historical record that describes the cause of his death or gives any hint of what his last years were like.

In spite of Itard's careful work and records, we have little idea of the actual nature of Victor's original condition. Was Victor a normal boy whose isolation from society had made him appear as if he were developmentally delayed? Was Itard's failure to get very far in his attempts to socialize and otherwise train Victor the result of faulty techniques, or did Itard's efforts simply come too late to be effective (Shattuck, 1980, p. 168)? We will never be able to conclusively answer these questions about Victor using the information in the historical record, but we can answer questions about how many scientists of the late eighteenth and early nineteenth centuries thought about human nature and the process of socialization. Victor's capture was important for the members of the Society of the Observers of Man because he afforded them a chance to test out their theories about human nature and social learning. Scientist after scientist who examined Victor and tried to socialize him failed. When their sensationalist theories were not verified by their experiments with Victor, these scientists lost interest and concluded that Victor was 'mentally defective'. Today, we can look back on their efforts knowing much more about what is and what is not innate to humans, and how important social interaction is to the project of 'becoming human'.

Twenty-First-Century Concerns

The research that we reviewed at the beginning of this chapter, carried out by cognitive and neurological scientists, strongly suggests that human infants are, indeed, born with certain mental structures already in place. This research calls into question the sensationalists' view that the human mind at infancy is a *tabula rasa*, without any innate principles, primary notions, or ideas, and that all ideas the developing child acquires are learned solely through social relationships with others. Yet the experiences of children like Victor also point out just how important social interaction with others is in shaping human behaviour. While it is increasingly difficult to deny the findings that humans are born with rudimentary mental structures in place, making us social creatures already at birth, the experience of feral and abandoned children also makes it clear that without sustained social interaction, not much happens in terms of development.

There are several twentieth-century examples of children who were abandoned that we can examine in order to help us better understand what is and is not 'natural' in children who are deprived of social interaction. Like their earlier counterparts, these twentieth-century children also tell us a great deal about the values, beliefs, and ideals of the scientists who study them. Among the most-studied of the twentieth-century children raised in isolation is Genie.

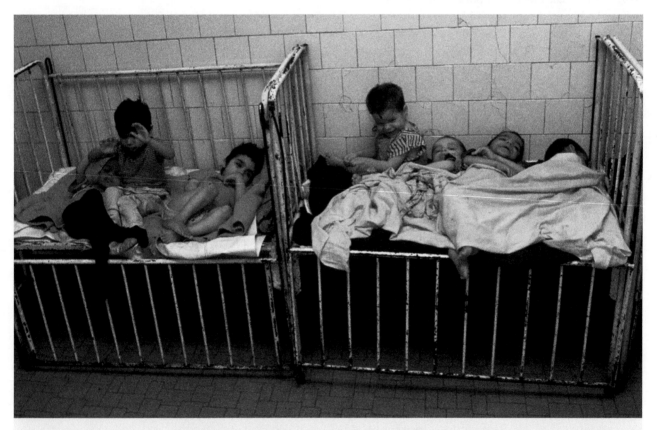

Children lie in a bed in an orphanage in Vulturesti, Romania, May 1990. After the overthrow of the Ceauşescu regime in Romania, Western journalists learned of the deplorable state of the country's orphanages, where abandoned children had, for lack of resources, been crowded together and virtually neglected, many of them from birth. In 2009, a follow-up investigation by the BBC revealed that many child orphans, never having learned even to speak, were later transferred to adult institutions: 'There were dozens of rooms, packed with 160 adults aged up to 80. It was difficult to tell the men and women apart, but they all shared a confined existence. They are all unwanted human beings, abandoned by their impoverished parents at birth and neglected into adulthood by the state' (Rogers, 2009). How does their plight differ from Victor's? What does it suggest about the conditions necessary for the social development of the young child?

Genie

'Genie' is the pseudonym for a California girl who was kept locked up and isolated in her room at her parents' house from about 18 months of age until she was discovered, in 1970, at approximately age 13½ (Curtiss, 1977). Genie's plight was uncovered only after her 50-year-old mother, who was blind and who also had been kept largely confined to the house, took Genie with her and ran away from her abusive, 70-year-old husband after a violent argument. When Genie's mother applied for social assistance, welfare authorities took one look at Genie and called a protective services worker. During the home visit to establish eligibility for assistance, the protective services worker called the police after witnessing Genie's mother attempting to diaper her 13½-year-old daughter. When she was found Genie was a small, withered, stooped girl, who could barely walk (she had flexion contractures at her knees, hips, and elbows) and so held her hands and wrists as though resting them on an invisible rail. She weighed 59 pounds (27 kg) and was 54 inches (137 centimetres) tall, incontinent, unable to chew, barely able to swallow, and unable to focus her eyes beyond 12 feet. She could not cry: her cry was silent and dry, without tears. She masturbated frequently, and salivated and spat out her saliva indiscriminately. She was unable to make any movement that required fully extended arms or legs because of her flexion contractures, and did not seem able to perceive either heat or cold (Rymer, 1992).

Susan Curtiss, a professor of linguistics at UCLA, wrote her doctoral dissertation on Genie. In the following excepts she provides us with the details of Genie's life while living with her parents:

> Genie was confined to a small bedroom, harnessed to an infant's potty seat. Genie's father sewed the harness himself; unclad except for the harness, Genie was left to sit on that chair. Unable to move anything except her fingers and hands, feet and toes, Genie was left to sit, tied up, hour after hour, often into the night, day after day, month after month, year after year. At night, when Genie was not forgotten, she was removed from her harness only to be placed into another restraining garment—a sleeping bag which her father had fashioned to hold Genie's arms stationary (allegedly to prevent her from taking it off). In effect, it was a straightjacket. Therein constrained, Genie was put into an infant's crib with wire mesh sides and a wire mesh cover overhead. Caged by night, harnessed by day, Genie was left to somehow endure the hours and years of her life. . . .
>
> There was little for her to listen to; there was no TV or radio in the house. Genie's bedroom was at the back of the house. . . . Her father had an intolerance for noise, so what little conversation there was between family members in the rest of the house was kept at a low volume. Except for moments of anger, when her father swore, Genie did not hear any language outside her door, and thus received practically no auditory stimulation of any kind. . . .
>
> Hungry and forgotten, Genie would sometimes attempt to attract attention by making noise. Angered, her father would often beat her for doing so. In fact, there was a large piece of wood left in the corner of Genie's room which her father used solely to beat her whenever she made any sound. Genie learned to keep silent and to suppress all vocalization. . . . (as cited in Rymer, 1992, p. 44)

When she was first admitted to hospital, Genie was described by a psychiatrist as 'unsocialized, primitive, and hardly human'; she masturbated frequently and could not be dissuaded from that activity. And she was eerily silent. In her first seven months in the hospital she learned to walk with a jerky motion and became more or less toilet-trained. She also learned hundreds of words and began to speak single words. One month later, she was able to string two words together. One year after she was admitted, she could occasionally form three-word strings such as 'small two cup' or 'white clear block' (Santrack, 1983, p. 207). Genie never learned to ask questions linguistically, and she ultimately developed very little grammar, although not as the result of any congenital disability. Instead, researchers attributed her lack of linguistic skills to the fact that she had passed a critical stage in language and brain development without learning language, and that therefore those parts of her brain that would have been used for language had functionally atrophied (Santrack, 1983, p. 208).

TWO THEORIES OF EARLY SOCIALIZATION: ATTACHMENT THEORY AND INTERSUBJECTIVITY

attachment theory
A theory of early socialization based on the idea that sociability (social stimulation and affection, especially from the mother) is necessary for human growth and development, especially in the early stages of life.

theory of intersubjectivity
An extension of attachment theory, which focuses on the two-way interaction between infants and caregivers in the socialization process, with an emphasis on the role played by subjects other than the maternal figure (*also called* the **intersubjective view**).

Two theories that explain the early experiences of an infant might help us understand how any incipient mental categories and sociability we may be born with are subsequently shaped and developed through the process of socialization. The two theories are **attachment theory** and the **theory of intersubjectivity** (or the **intersubjective view**). Although both have roots in psychiatry, attachment theory is focused on a product (the emotional tie between an infant and her mother), while the theory of intersubjectivity focuses on the process (the social interaction that occurs between a young child and her immediate caregivers).

Since the mid-twentieth century, a great deal of research has been done on the social interactions of infants and very young children with adult caregivers. This research supports the view that infants are active rather than passive participants in the socialization process. Some of the most influential mid-twentieth-century work on the social relationships between infants and their adult caregivers has come from British psychologist John Bowlby. Bowlby's focus on the development of a child's attachment for her mother set him apart from other theorists who saw the mother–infant relationship as little more than a one-way exchange between a passive infant and an active, care-providing parent (usually the mother).

John Bowlby, Mary Ainsworth, and Attachment Theory

John Bowlby (1907–90) served as a psychiatrist in the British army stationed in England during the Second World War. Afterward, he was appointed director of the children's department of the Tavistock Clinic in London. There he established a research unit to study children's responses to separation from their mothers (Eyer, 1992, p. 37). Mary Ainsworth (1913–99) was an American psychologist who joined the team of researchers at the Tavistock Clinic, and whose work contributed to ongoing research on the effects of maternal separation on child development.

As a result of their research carried out during in the 1950s, Bowlby, Ainsworth, and others began arguing that the immature young of all mammals need the protection of a parent, and especially of a mother, in order to survive. Among humans, an attachment must be formed between the infant or young child and her caregiver (usually her mother) in order for normal human emotional and social development to take place. Bowlby turned this observation into a basic thesis called 'attachment theory', which he laid out in a publication, written for the World Health Organization, titled *Maternal Care and Mental Health* (1951). Bowlby defined attachment as the powerful emotional ties between infants and their mothers. The original impetus for the concept came from the research done by Australian ethologist Konrad Lorenz on 'imprinting' in geese. Lorenz observed that immediately after it is hatched, a gosling looks around for a moving object to follow. He found that the newly hatched gosling will eagerly follow any moving, honking, goose-like figure that is present immediately after birth. In a similar way, lambs will follow sheep, and calves will follow cows.

A child who is deprived of close, intimate social interaction with his mother, Bowlby argued, will suffer from all manner of personality disturbances in later life. What is 'essential for mental health', he wrote, 'is that an infant and young child should experience a warm, intimate, and continuous relationship with his mother (or permanent mother-substitute)' (Bowlby, 1965, p. 13). A child who has been even partly deprived of the maternal relationship is prone to suffer. In less severe cases, this suffering ranges from 'anxiety, excessive need for love, powerful feelings of revenge, and arising from these last, guilt and depression'. Complete deprivation has even more far-reaching consequences, and 'may cripple the child's capacity to make relationships with other people' (Bowlby, 1965, p. 14).

A Critique of Attachment Theory

Work on maternal deprivation influenced public policy regarding child welfare and early care of children both in North America and in Europe. Healthcare administrators changed their policies on hospital stays for children, and social workers began to discourage institutional

Konrad Lorenz and his grayleg geese.

placement of children in favour of adoption or stable foster care. Bowlby had claimed that 'full time employment of [a] mother' was equivalent to the 'death of a parent, imprisonment of a parent, war, famine', and other disasters, citing it as a major cause of family failure (Bowlby, 1960, p. 73). It was an argument made also by other attachment researchers and subsequently used to discourage mothers from working or from using daycare centres (Eyer, 1992). Moreover, Bowlby extended his argument by suggesting that an adult's attachments to religious, professional, and other types of organizations ultimately derive from an original attachment to a mother that is then transferred to a religious leader, a supervisor or manager at work, or another person in a position of authority (Bowlby, 1969, p. 207).

In addressing the argument that a mother's employment outside the home is a 'major reason for family failure' we should note that Bowlby did his research and writing in the period immediately following the Second World War. At the time, women who had previously been encouraged to enter the workforce as part of the war effort were actively encouraged to stay at home and resume sole care of their children. This change in attitude allowed soldiers returning home to find employment. The phrasing of Bowlby's research report is important: Bowlby specified that children suffer terribly from *maternal* deprivation (as opposed to deprivation of close emotional ties, regardless of the biological relationship). This argument clearly reflected the belief, current at the time, that women naturally belonged back in the home with their children. In post-war Europe and North America, the presence of a mother, as opposed to a father or some other adult caregiver, was deemed essential to a child's growth and adjustment. Bowlby tried to strengthen his case even further by arguing that not only was the child genetically programmed to give off signals to elicit physical closeness from the mother, the mother was also genetically programmed to respond to her infant's signals. While Bowlby did concede that an overlay of learned responses might occur to interfere with what he thought of as natural, genetically programmed ones, he stuck to the idea that mothering is instinctual, and that it has to be interfered with in order to be suppressed.

Probably the most salient critique of Bowlby and others who concentrate on the mother–infant bond to the exclusion of all other social relations is the extreme narrowness of the focus. Feminist scholars have criticized Bowlby's attachment theory, arguing that it has been used to establish a set of assumptions about the primacy of the mother–infant relationship that incorrectly centres issues of nurturing and child rearing primarily on this relationship (Eyer, 1992). Child rearing and child nurturing, they argue, are not 'naturally' confined to the mother–child relationship, as Bowlby would have it. Rather, they are parts of a social relationship that can be achieved between any adult who takes a caregiver role and the infant (or child) for whom he or she is providing care. There are many different dimensions to the nurturing of children, and this process cannot simply be reduced to maternal attachment and maternal deprivation (Eyer, 1992, pp. 199–200). At the very least, then, we should be speaking of a whole array of social contacts and not just of the mother–child relationship. While the need to belong is a fundamental aspect of human existence, it can be directed towards persons other than a mother. Satisfying relationships with persons other than mother can be formed via the gradual accumulation of intimacy and shared experience (Baumeister & Leary, 1999, pp. 499–500).

But while the term 'maternal deprivation', along with the notion that mothering is instinctive to all women, may be ill conceived as an explanatory framework, attachment theorists' observations that children must make close emotional attachments to at least one other human being in order to develop socially and emotionally have been well documented. Baumeister and Leary (1999) propose that the need to belong in humans requires 'frequent

Detail of the painting *Nativity*, by Martin Schongauer. The primacy of the mother–infant bond has been reinforced in Western society through the Christ story and countless Madonna-and-Child images created over centuries, which cast Mary, the virgin mother, as the primary caregiver, leaving her husband, Joseph, well in the background.

personal contacts or interactions with other persons' that are 'marked by stability, affective concern and continuation into the foreseeable future' (1999, p. 500). Deprivation of these supportive contacts and interactions produces deep and long-term effects. Nowhere is that more effectively illustrated than in the work of Harry Harlow, whose work with monkeys is reviewed in the box below.

THE INTERSUBJECTIVE VIEW OF THE SOCIAL INFANT

Since the 1980s there has been sufficient research to suggest that almost from birth the interaction between an infant and his primary caregiver (who is often, but not necessarily, his mother) is based on mutual recognition. As Jessica Benjamin (1988) describes it, mutual recognition includes 'a number of experiences, commonly described in the research on

STUDIES IN SOCIAL RESEARCH

Harlow's Monkeys

During the period in which theorists like Bowlby and Ainsworth researched and wrote about attachment and maternal deprivation, American experimental psychologist Harry Harlow (1905–81) conducted a series of experiments on rhesus monkeys in the animal laboratory at the University of Wisconsin. His experiments with these monkeys (which today would not pass an ethics review committee) were attempts to prove Bowlby's theories, and they provide disturbing evidence about the effects of social deprivation (Eyer, 1992, pp. 58–9; Harlow, 1958, pp. 673–85).

In order to further explore the ideas he had derived from attachment theory, Harlow separated newborn rhesus monkeys from their mothers and raised them in isolation. Because the babies were separated from other monkeys, Harlow and his fellow researchers were careful to provide for all the baby monkeys' material needs. Harlow reported that the babies were kept in a 'stainless steel chamber where light is diffused, temperature controlled, air flow regulated, and environmental sounds filtered' (Harlow & Harlow, 1974, p. 276). The babies were provided with food and water, and their cages were cleaned by remote control. During the isolation period, the baby monkeys did not see another living creature, 'not even a human hand'.

Harlow found that social deprivation had long-term effects on sexual behaviour. Monkeys isolated beyond 12 months of age totally failed to develop any kind of adult breeding patterns. When females who had been raised in semi-isolation were placed with breeding males, they either engaged in aggressive behaviour or they sat clutching and biting themselves. Isolated females were unable to mate, and when artificially inseminated, they showed no interest in their offspring. Harlow concluded that the sexual inadequacies of the socially deprived adult monkeys did not come from an absence of sex drive but from an absence of the ability to engage in sexual intercourse. 'High arousal was often seen,' he reported, 'but it led to short, intense outbursts of self-clutching and rocking, frenetic, masturbation and violent aggression towards other monkeys (Harlow & Harlow, 1974, p. 278).

In order to test if it was the absence of mothers (as predicted by attachment theory) that produce these behavioural disturbances, or if it was the absence of the company of other monkeys more generally, Harlow raised a group of infant monkeys to adulthood together in the same cage. Unlike the infants raised from birth in isolation, Harlow observed no sexual disturbances in these monkeys (Harlow & Harlow, 1974).

mother–infant interaction: emotional attunement, mutual influence, affective mutuality, sharing of states of mind' (p. 26). But mutual recognition, she argues, is much more than this. It is a crucial category of early experiences. Research increasingly indicates that infants actively participate with the primary adult caregivers in creating this first social bond.

During the latter part of the twentieth century the **intersubjective view**, which is based on the recognition of the two-way interaction between the infant and his caregivers, has gained increasing support. As Benjamin explains, the intersubjective view of the infant maintains that the infant grows in and through the relationship to many others and not just in relationship to a 'maternal figure'.

Daniel Stern and the Interpersonal World of the Infant

In his book *The Interpersonal World of the Infant* (1985), American infant psychiatrist Daniel Stern argues that babies are able to differentiate themselves from their mothers at birth. After their birth, infants progress through increasingly complex modes of social interaction

In another experiment, Harlow raised some of the young monkeys with inanimate surrogate mothers made either from wire mesh or covered with towelling. His research indicated that infant monkeys sought contact more frequently with the towel-covered surrogate, who provided 'contact comfort', than with the mesh surrogate, who provided only milk.

Harlow's research, originally intended to support attachment theorists' beliefs about the innate nature of mothering skills, produced some unexpected results: the ability to nurture is a social skill, one that can be developed equally in males and females. Left from birth in a 'state of nature', without the stimulation of others, (or at least an adequate tactile substitute), adult monkeys will show no signs of a capacity to nurture. Harlow never clearly implied that his findings could be directly applied to human beings, and we, too, should remain cautious about transferring his findings to human behaviour. However, it is fairly safe to conclude that, like the monkeys he studied, humans are social beings and that deprivation of social contact from birth has profound consequences for human sociability and behavioural development.

An infant rhesus monkey clings to its cloth surrogate mother. Compare Harlow's research with monkeys to Lorenz's research, in which he raised baby geese in isolation from their mother and taught them to accept him as a surrogate. Which seems more humane? What does that suggest about maternal attachment and the socialization of the very young?

with others. Stern argues that, far from being passive, infants exert a considerable amount of control over 'the initiation, maintenance, termination, and avoidance of social contact with mother; in other words they help to regulate engagement' (Stern, 1977, p. 21). For example, an infant as young as four months old asserts his independence from his mother by averting his gaze from her. By seven months, that assertion includes gestures and vocalization. At 14 months the child is able to escape the mother by running away, and by two years he expresses his autonomy with language. Interpersonal moments between the child and his caregiver are crucial in 'forming the experiences from which the infant learns how to relate to other people' (Stern, 1977, p. 2).

What follows is a description of the kind of infant–caregiver interaction Stern is talking about. It serves to illustrate the extent to which mutuality plays a central role in the interaction between the child and the caregiver. In this example, Stern describes what happens between a mother and her three-and-a-half-month-old son during a bottle-feeding session:

> During the first half of [the] feeding the baby has been sucking away, working seriously and occasionally looking at his mother, sometimes for long stretches (10 to 15 seconds). At other times he gazed lazily around the room. Mother had been fairly still. She glanced at her baby periodically, sort of checking, and every now and then looked at him with a good long look (20 to 30 seconds) but without talking to him or changing the expression on her face. She rarely said anything when she looked at him. . . .
>
> Until this point, a normal feeding, not a social interaction, was underway. Then a change began. While talking and looking at me [Stern], the mother turned her head and gazed at the infant's face. He was gazing at the ceiling, but out of the corner of his eye he saw her head turned toward him and turned to gaze back at her. . . . He broke rhythm and stopped sucking. He let go of the nipple and the suction around it broke as he eased into the faintest suggestion of a smile. The mother abruptly stopped talking and as she watched his face begin to transform, her eyes opened a little wider and her eyebrows raised a bit. His eyes locked onto hers, and together they held motionless for an instant. The infant did not return to sucking and his mother held frozen her slight expression of anticipation. This silent and almost motionless incident continued to hang on until the mother suddenly shattered that by saying 'Hey!', and simultaneously opening her eyes wider raising her eyebrows further, and throwing her head up and toward the infant. Almost simultaneously, the baby's eyes widened. His head tilted up and, as his smile broadened, the nipple fell out of his mouth. Now she said 'Well hello! . . . hello . . . heeelloooo,' so that her pitch rose and the 'hellos' became longer and more stressed on each successive repetition. The mother then paused and her face relaxed. They watched each other expectantly for a moment. The shared excitement between them ebbed, but before it faded completely, the baby suddenly took an initiative and intervened to rescue it. His head lurched forward, his hands jerked up, and a fuller smile blossomed. His mother was jolted into motion. She moved forward, mouth open and eyes alight, and said, 'oooooh . . . ya wanna play, do ya . . . yeah . . . I didn't know if you were still hungry . . . no . . . noooooo . . . no I didn't . . .' And off they went. (Stern, 1977, pp. 2–3)

Stern goes on to record further exchanges between this mother and her baby in which the mother walks her fingers over the baby's belly and into his neck and armpits, all the while tickling him. Throughout the baby smiles and squirms, but always maintains eye contact with his mother. As each new cycle of play progressed, the mother escalated the level of suspense and excitement using her voice and her facial expressions. The baby became more aroused, and the mounting excitement of both mother and child, as Stern points out, contained elements of both glee and danger of overstimulation. During the second cycle of play the baby slightly averted his face, but kept smiling. By the third cycle of play, the mother and child had still not resumed full face-to-face contact, and the baby had his head slightly turned away. Stern describes what happened next:

> As [the mother] approached, [the baby's] face turned even further but still he kept looking at her. At the same time, his smile flattened. The eyebrows and the corners of his mouth flickered back and forth between a smile and a sober expression. He finally broke gaze with mother, appearing thereby to recompose himself for second, to de-escalate his own level of excitement. Having done so successfully, he returned his gaze to mother and exploded into a big grin. On that queue she began, with gusto, her fourth and most suspenseful cycle, but

Is this nursing infant looking at her mother or at the camera? What would Stern say this indicates about the infant's control over social contact? Do you agree?

this one proved too much for him. . . . He broke gaze immediately, turned away, face averted, and frowned. The mother picked it up immediately. She stopped the game dead in its tracks and said softly, 'Oh honey, maybe you're still hungry, huh . . . let's try some milk again.' He returned gaze. His face eased and he took the nipple again. The 'moment' of social interaction was over. The feeding had resumed. (Stern, 1977, p. 5)

It is from the analysis of moments like these (sometimes called 'free play') that researchers have learned about the crucial significance of the social interactions that take place between caregivers and infants. These interactions are among the most important experiences of the first phase of the infant's life. They teach the infant about how to participate in human events. By the end of the first six months, the infant not only possesses general schemas of the human face, voice, and touch, but also knows the specific face, voice, and touch of her primary caregiver. As Stern explains, by six months of age the infant has 'got' the temporal patterning of human behaviour and the meaning of different changes and variations in tempo and rhythm. She has learned the social cues and conventions that are mutually effective in initiating, maintaining, terminating, and avoiding interactions with her caregiver. She has also learned different discursive modes, such as turn taking. And she now has the foundation of some internal composite picture of her primary caregiver so that, in a few months, after this phase is over, we can speak of her having established object permanence, an enduring representation of the caregiver that she carries around with her, with or without the caregiver's presence (Stern, 1977, pp. 5–6).

By between seven and nine months of age the infant has discovered that different individuals can share the same feelings and intentions. Stern uses the term *intersubjectivity* to designate this dawning awareness on the part of the infant that there are others who think and feel as he does. For example, at seven to nine months, the infant will reach for a toy and at the same time look at his mother to see if she is sharing the excitement. The mother matches not the infant's movement, but the infant's level of excitement, using a different mode of expression (for example, she says 'Wow!').

In work that supports Benjamin's and Stern's view of the intersubjective infant, Colin Trevarthen (1977, 1980) studied the distinct, unequal, but complementary nature of the contributions of infants and caregivers to social exchanges. He analyzed filmed interactions between two-month-old infants and their mothers, and observed how both mother and child played their own parts in establishing coordinated social exchanges. Trevarthen found that the mother structured the communication between herself and her child by responding meaningfully to the infant's initial cue. The infant, in turn, responded to the mother with bodily and vocal signals that matched the rhythms of the mother's communicative activity. In turn, the mother re-responded to the infant, and together the parent and child coordinated their activity by achieving a mutual regulation of expression, gesture, imitation, response, and vocalization.

Jessica Benjamin suggests that intersubjective development is best understood as a spectrum. The awareness that the other is both alike and different is just one moment on that spectrum (Benjamin, 1988, pp. 29–30). The game of peekaboo between mother and child, which is based on the shared tension between expectancy and surprise, produces a sense of mutuality. Mother and child operate together with one intention. The emerging intersubjectivity between mother and child emphasizes how awareness of the separate other, on the part of the infant (and the mother), enhances the feeling of connection: 'this *other* mind can share *my* feeling' (Benjamin, 1988, p. 30). Yet, at the same time, the growing awareness of separate minds and the desire for mutuality can also raise the possibility of conflict. By the age of one, the infant can experience conflict between the desire to assert herself—for example, by pushing all the buttons on the stereo—and the desire to stay attuned to her mother's wishes.

As more research is done based on an intersubjective model of infant–caregiver relations, the model of the infant or young child as a passive being, totally manipulated by outside agents of socialization, is being replaced by a more dynamic one. In this model, infants and their caregivers interact together and co-operate to achieve what was once thought possible only through imposition. Over the last century researchers have moved away from the perception of infants and children as passive lumps of wax or clay to be moulded according to adult intentions. The twenty-first-century infant is an active participant in her own socialization process—a being who is capable of initiating and sustaining social interaction, and of both co-operation and resistance.

NINETEENTH-CENTURY CONCERNS COMPARED WITH CONTEMPORARY CONCERNS

The members of the Society of the Observers of Man, using a sensationalist perspective, developed interests not just in observing and recording human behaviour but also in modifying it. Mid-twentieth-century scholars have taken much from the sensationalists. For example, writing in 1949 about the cases of Anna and Isabella, two young girls who had been raised in isolation and who had come to his attention, American sociologist Kingsley Davis proposed that the study of cases of extreme isolation in children was of great importance to social scientists. Only in such children, Davis wrote, is it possible to observe 'concretely separated' factors of biological and social origin. Davis believed that severely isolated children had grown up without the influence of socialization, and thus their behaviour reflected only those factors that are biologically innate or naturally occurring in all humans.

Davis and other sociologists like him studied feral children in order to support their point of view that, with the exception of isolated and feral children, all human behaviour available for observation is the result of social learning. For Davis and many other mid-twentieth-century sociologists who were without the benefit of early twenty-first-century research from the cognitive sciences on infant cognition, 'social learning' (or socialization) strongly implies that all behaviour normally seen in members of a given society is shaped *only* by external social forces. If there is anything innate in the behavioural patterns of the developing child, society acts to suppress it and to impose in its place behaviour patterns of purely social origin.

We now know that far from suppressing what is naturally there at birth, socialization acts to enhance and develop the incipient social and cognitive attributes all humans are born with. The research of cognitive scientists and neuroscientists has made it difficult to continue to maintain, along with the sensationalists, that humans are all born as blank slates. At the same time, previous research and experiments done by the sensationalists, as well as by attachment theorists and intersubjective theorists, whatever their original objectives, makes it clear that infants and young children require a great deal of social interaction with their adult caregivers in order to become full and participating members of society.

From the vantage point of the twenty-first century, the research on infant–caregiver interactions strongly indicates that human behaviour is the result of the infinite malleability and educability of the human infant, and that an organized mental structure is already present in humans at birth. It is not that this innate mental structure represents a fixed human nature that develops inexorably along certain lines but, more simply, that a basic social-cognitive structure is present in humans from birth. Recent research has now made clear that the socialization process is much more than the simple imposition of external behaviour patterns on an essentially passive and conceptually empty child. We now know that even infants actively engage in social interaction with adults and that they are active participants in their own socialization.

By now you should be aware that socialization is not something that is a once-and-for-all, straightforward or unified process. Rather, the social experience of an individual has a history and is filled with (sometimes irresolvable) misunderstandings, (sometimes irreconcilable) differences, double binds, and conflicting demands. There is a kind of 'tortured complexity' inherent in the process of 'taking on the view' of others (Scott & Thorpe, 2006, p. 335). Individuals participate in many groups, and the differences in the rules and social structures of each of these groups mean that any individual is often exposed to contradictions in the demands made on her. Individuals exposed to different (and sometimes contradictory) demands of a variety of groups have increasing chances to take on new perspectives, or to integrate conflicting expectations into their selves (the 'me'). This in turn will influence their next round of behaviour as 'I'. In this way, the communicative process between individuals who participate in a variety of different groups can lead to new social norms, rules, and institutions.

As the Scottish psychiatrist R.D. Laing argued, no individual can actually experience someone else's experiences of reality. Instead we must all rely on our interpretations of what the other is thinking, and we construct this interpretation from the expressions that they convey. And this often means making a distinction between what the other consciously intends to convey to us—through speech, action, gesture—and the impressions that they do not consciously intend to convey—for example, through non-verbal gestures (Goffman, 1959).

As we will see in the next chapter, socialization is not just confined to childhood but continues throughout life as adolescents and adults struggle with the everyday, ongoing task of presenting themselves, of reacting to the self-presentations of others, and of acquiring the wherewithal to be full members of ever-extending social groups and institutions.

SUMMARY

Socialization is a core concept used by social scientists to designate the active processes group members engage in, making novices into full members. It is also used to designate the result of purposeful actions of group members whereby a novice gradually comes to acquire social and cultural fluency. This chapter has shown that far from being born 'blank slates' on which members of society can then write their messages, infants are already social at birth and have rudimentary understandings of complex social meanings such as motives, intentions, and purpose in others. However, even though there may well be an incipient self present at birth, without an enormous amount of consistent interaction with supportive, caring adults, the human child will not grow into a functioning, socialized human adult.

To help make this point, this chapter has shown how abandoned and feral children, who have grown up with little by way of human care and social interaction, are unable to become fully functioning adults. Victor, the 'wild boy of Aveyron', who was studied by the members of the French Society of the Observers of Man at the beginning of the nineteenth century, and Genie, the young girl who was kept in a cage and who was discovered by social workers in California in the 1970s, both serve as examples of how important adult caregivers are to an individual's development as a functioning human being.

Two theories of early socialization—attachment theory and theories of intersubjectivity—help us understand how, although a human infant is born with incipient mental categories and sociability, those abilities are subsequently shaped and developed through the process of socialization. Attachment theory, developed by the British psychiatrist John Bowlby, focuses on the active mutual relationship that develops between an infant and her caregiver(s). Bowlby's theory revolutionized thinking about the infant–parent relationship, which had previously been treated as a passive infant submitting to an active care-providing parent (usually the mother). American psychologist Harry Harlow's research on attachment between infant rhesus monkeys and their mothers, while at onset intended to support the thesis that mothering skills are innate, actually produced the opposite finding by showing that the ability to nurture is a learned, or socially acquired, skill.

Research by psychiatrists in the last two decades of the twentieth century strongly suggests that there is a two-way interaction between the infant and his caregivers. This is the intersubjective view of infant socialization. Proponents of this view maintain that the infant is not a passive participant in the process of socialization but, rather, exerts a considerable amount of control over interactions with his or her caregivers.

DISCUSSION QUESTIONS

1. In your experience, how are infants and young children socialized into becoming members of society? What are some of the ways that children participate in or resist socialization?

2. Recent research on infant cognition indicates that human infants are born already social, with rudimentary understandings of human motives and purposes. How does this research compare with the view, previously raised by Émile Durkheim, that the mental categories we all possess are purely the result of social imprinting?

3. Bowlby suggests that maternal care is essential to mental health in children and, as a result, should be promoted as part of public policy. Discuss some of the implications of this argument.

4. What are some of the differences between Bowlby's theory of attachment and the intersubjective view proposed by Benjamin and Stern?

5. Compare the research assumptions and research methods of the members of the Society of the Observers of Man (Sicard, Itard) with those used by Daniel Stern, discussed in this chapter.

9 Social Performance and Interaction Rituals

CHAPTER OUTLINE

LEARNING OBJECTIVES

In this chapter you will:

- come to understand socialization as a life-long process
- be introduced to basic concepts sociologists use to understand social interactions, including social status, role, achieved and ascribed statuses, and role strain
- gain a clearer understanding of how social interaction shapes the lives of members of social groups
- consider the transitional steps that adolescent youth go through in being initiated into a downtown drug scene
- study the theories of Erving Goffman on the presentation of self in everyday social interaction
- learn about the notion of social interaction as a performance
- become familiar with the concepts Goffman used to explore the hidden aspects of human social interaction, including *front stage*, *backstage*, *outside*, *impression management*, *teams*, *face work*, and *personal front*
- reflect on the personal transformations that occur during the process of becoming a physician in Canada
- think critically about interaction rituals.

INTRODUCTION

Although a human infant may be born with incipient mental structures that promote sociability, he is not born with a developed social self: he must be socialized in order to become a fully participating member of society. The previous chapter presented socialization as both a process and a product. As a process, socialization is an active one, carried out by members of a group when they work together to make novices into full members. Chapter 8 focused on the socialization of the young child, presenting it as an interactive process and showing how the infant and his caregivers engage with each other in mutual social interaction. Socialization, however, is a life-long process, not limited just to infancy and childhood. To illustrate this point, this chapter looks closely at two cases: young people in Vancouver as they are integrated into the city's drug scene and medical students at a Canadian university as they learn to become full-fledged doctors.

Socialization, as we have seen, is also a product or outcome of an ongoing process. As social products, humans must constantly engage and re-engage with each other, affirming and re-adjusting their self-images, their presentation of self, and their reflections back to others. To help readers understand socialization as a product, this chapter introduces the work of Erving Goffman, Randall Collins, Gary Fines, and others who examine the influence and effects that 'interaction rituals' have on contemporary social life. Of particular concern to these sociologists are the micro-social issues of group solidarity, the creation of symbols and rituals that represent group membership, and the emotional reactions that group members have to these symbols and rituals.

SOCIALIZATION AS AN ACTIVE PROCESS

Few people stop to think about their everyday experiences and the social processes behind the ways that they act towards and react to others. As social actors, we continually present ourselves to others, who are our observers or audience. To be successful, our presentations must refer back to the social world in which we and our observers live. Our presentations must make sense to, and be accepted as legitimate by, the others around us who share our social world. As full members of society we must give social performances that appear to be natural, genuine, and without artifice—performances that conceal the manner in which naturalness is acquired. Sociologist Randal Collins (2004) maintains that our local encounters with others are the foundation of all social life and experiences. Our social institutions work because of the localized interactions that constitute them (Baehr, 2005).

The following are some of the basic concepts sociologists use to help them understand how everyday social interactions and experiences serve to create the reality in which we all live.

Social Actor

social actor
An individual who shares with other social actors a common frame of reference that includes common convictions, beliefs, values, a shared language, activities, and practices

A **social actor** is an individual who shares with other social actors a common frame of reference that includes common convictions, beliefs, values, a shared language, activities, and practices. A social actor possesses specific competencies that allow him to understand and deal with others who share with him a common frame of reference.

Status and Status Set

Status refers to the culturally defined social position that an individual holds in a social interaction. It defines a person's identity and relationship to others. It is a relative concept, and as such it measures a person's importance, or role, in relation to others.

Individuals can hold several different status positions at the same time. For example a given person may be simultaneously a daughter, wife, mother, business partner, best friend, hospital volunteer, and karate instructor, among other things. Prior to this, the statuses that made up her 'status set' might have been daughter, schoolgirl, and karate student.

Our status sets change over time, increasing and decreasing as we become more or less socially active. Any given individual can occupy dozens of statuses over a lifetime. Some of these statuses are **ascribed**, meaning that they are involuntary; 'daughter' is an ascribed status, as is 'teenager'. An **achieved status**, by contrast, is assumed voluntarily, and usually reflects some ability or at least some effort; starting quarterback, business partner, and university student are all achieved statuses. Ascribed and achieved statues are often interconnected. For example, while becoming a doctor is an achieved status, being born into a family

status

The culturally defined social position that an individual holds in a social interaction, defining a person's identity and relationship to others.

ascribed status

A status that is involuntarily assigned to an individual regardless of her abilities or inclinations.

achieved status

A status that is assumed voluntarily, usually reflecting some ability or at least some effort.

Imagine this young woman's status set. What statuses does or might she hold? Which ones are ascribed? Which ones achieved? What might be her master statuses? Pick any one of these statuses and describe the role set attached to it.

master status
A status that has exceptional importance in shaping an individual's identity and life chances.

social role
The behaviour performed by an individual who holds a particular social status.

role set
All of the roles attached to a single status.

with enough money to put you through medical school, or even being born into a family that will support your ambitions, is an ascribed status. Finally, a **master status** is a status that has exceptional importance in shaping an individual's identity and life chances, for better or for worse. Gender, race, and class are all master statuses, and the three that sociologists today tend to focus on.

Role

According to sociologist Ralph Linton, a **social role** is the behaviour performed by an individual who occupies or holds a particular social status. It is the 'dynamic aspect of a status' (Linton, 1936, p. 114). For example, an individual may hold the status of doctor. That status will lead her to perform the role of doctor by seeing patients in her office, attending medical conventions, and referring her patients to specialist colleagues. The concept of **role set** refers to all the social roles attached to a single status. Sociologists know that both the statuses and the roles that people use to define their lives differ from society to society, and even over different historical time periods in the same person's life.

A woman, her child, and her BlackBerry: describe the role strain of a working parent.

STUDIES IN SOCIAL RESEARCH

Initiation into a Local Drug Scene in Vancouver, BC

Our first example of how social interaction shapes the lives of social group members centres on how adolescents become entrenched in a local drug scene. Drug scenes can be described as 'distinctive inner-city areas characterized by high concentrations of drug users and drug dealing within a specific geographical area' (Kerr, Fast, Small, & Wood, 2009, p. 1205). A drug scene can be considered a 'place' in two ways: it includes both a physical location and specific social processes. Together the environment and the social processes operate to isolate newcomers from the outside world and push them toward full integration into the social world of the drug users who congregate at the drug scene. Not only does the geographical area serve as a base for drug use and procurement, it also serves to 'anchor elaborate social and spatial networks, practices associated with the day-to-day realities of securing basic necessities, and wider patterns of income generation activities' (Kerr, et al., 2009, p. 1205).

Background

Adolescents who become drug users go through a series of transitional steps that are often shaped by 'critical moments', or life events. Ethnographers who study adolescent drug users have learned that initiation into injection drug use is often preceded by a number of critical moments (MacDonald & Marsh, 2002; Mayock, 2005, as cited in Kerr, et al., 2009). At some point in their initiation, the stigma around using injection drugs is replaced by curiosity about using the drugs. This occurs in the context of the individual having frequent exposure to injection drug use in a drug-using milieu, where drug use has been made a non-exceptional, normal event, and where the risk associated with injection drug use has been constructed as being acceptable (Kerr, et al., 2009, 1205).

Thomas Kerr and his colleagues studied how adolescents were initiated into the local, street-based drug scene in two neighbourhoods of Vancouver, known as the Downtown Eastside and the Downtown South—areas known to local residents simply as 'down here'.

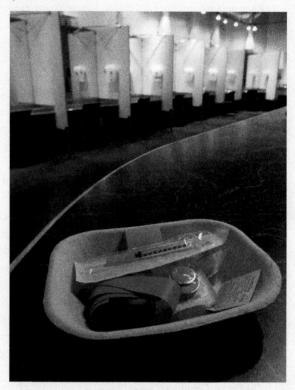

An injection kit sits ready for the next visitor to the Insite clinic in Vancouver. Does the existence of a safe-injection site in a neighbourhood with one of the country's biggest drug problems effectively normalize the use of drugs (i.e. by 'construing' drug use as safe/normal) or help stem the problem by providing resources for overcoming substance abuse?

Vancouver's Downtown Eastside, notoriously known as Skid Row (or Skid Road), is the poorest urban drug and crime scene in North America. Downtown South, a residential and entertainment district with both low-income housing and numerous thriving businesses, is a recent entrant to the drug scene, which focuses primarily on crystal methamphetamine sales and use among youth. The drug trade in the Downtown Eastside has existed for decades and concentrates primarily on crack cocaine, cocaine, and heroin sold primarily to adult users (Kerr, et al., 2009).

Methods

Kerr and his colleagues chose a qualitative research strategy and a case study research design, using interviews as their research method to study how youth transition from the status of 'weekend warrior' to 'street-entrenched' denizen of the local drug scene. The youth they interviewed were deeply involved in the drug scene, their daily lives taken up with the goal of surviving on the streets—coping with homelessness, poverty, and dangerous income-generating activities such as drug-dealing, sex work, theft, and fencing stolen goods. Participants were between 14 and 26 years of age, and included 18 men, 18 women, and 2 transgendered individuals. Sixty-seven per cent identified as Caucasian, 28 per cent as Aboriginal; 5 per cent were black. All had self-reported illicit drug use within the previous 30 days. About half of them reported being homeless, and the majority said that they had experienced being homeless at some time during their involvement in the drug scene. Roughly half reported having been involved in the drug scene for more than three years (Kerr, et al., 2009, p. 1206).

Findings: Coming 'Down Here'

When interviewees described how they became immersed in the drug scene, they spoke both about how they personally chose to become involved and about how their choices were constrained. Many spoke of growing up 'on the streets' and of being introduced to drug use and illegal income-generating activities at a very young age. They described their involvement in the drug scene as an inevitable outcome of their early childhood experiences (Kerr, et al., 2009, p. 1207). They viewed it as a better alternative to the unsafe and unsupportive life situations they grew up in, which were marked by crushing poverty, addiction, criminal involvement, and exclusion from mainstream social opportunities (schooling, supportive families, recreational programs). Moving to downtown Vancouver and into the drug scene gave them a chance to gain what they saw as a sense of belonging, independence, and excitement. It gave them access to street-based social networks of drug users, as well as a chance to learn and engage in illicit income-generating activities (Kerr, et al., 2009, p. 1209).

Participants often reported that they chose to move to downtown Vancouver to escape harassment or arrest at the hands of police in other cities. These youth were aware of Vancouver's reputation as a 'wild place' prior to arriving there, and they emphasized that they 'chose' to be involved in the drug scene to assert their independence, or to escape harmful or repressive family situations. Whether they chose to become involved in the drug scene or simply grew

role strain
A situation that can occur when there is tension among the various roles attached to a status, or even between the roles attached to different statuses.

Role strain can occur when there is tension among the various roles attached to a status, or even between the roles attached to different statuses. The doctor of our example may experience role strain when one of her patients becomes a friend. As readers will see in a later example, brides-to-be can experience role strain during a bridal shower, when trying to juggle their status as daughter, friend, and co-worker.

SOCIALIZATION AS A PRODUCT: THE PRESENTATION OF SELF AND PERFORMANCE

Some of the most important work on the presentation of self in everyday social interaction comes from Erving Goffman (1922–82). Although he spent his professional career teaching at the University of California, Berkeley, and later at the University of Pennsylvania, Goffman up in it, the sense of belonging and independence it afforded ultimately reinforced their exclusion from other, mainstream opportunities such as stable housing, education, and legal employment (Kerr, et al., 2009, p. 1207).

Many of the interviewees reported that they knew others—friends or older siblings—who were already part of the drug scene before they themselves became involved. These friends and siblings were able to provide them with introductions. Many, too, began their involvement in the downtown Vancouver drug scene as 'weekend warriors' or 'twinkies'—they started off by 'hanging out' downtown on weekends, living elsewhere, before moving into the drug scene permanently. They recalled how naive they felt interacting with older, more experienced drug users, and how eager they were to distance themselves from their novice status. They also reported on how quickly and easily they were able to get access to drugs, especially in the Downtown Eastside; drugs are everywhere and easily accessed, and this is an important factor in motivating youths to 'engage in self-identified problematic forms of drug use that were previously "off-limits"' (Kerr, et al., 2009, p. 1208). As one 23-year-old interviewee said, 'On Hastings [in the Downtown Eastside] . . . there's a lot of active drug use, out in the open. And young girls see that, and think that it's glamorous, or they think it's cool, and they'll start to get into it' (Kerr, et al., 2009, p. 1207).

Once the youth arrive on the scene, there is no shortage of peers, drug dealers, and pimps to direct them to the people who can provide illegal drugs and the opportunities for generating illegal income (Kerr, et al., 2009, p. 1209). Many reported that they were introduced to drug dealing shortly after they arrived, and that once they started dealing they also started 'doing' their own product. Drug dependency made it difficult to pay rent. Homelessness and sleeping outside led to a cycle of emotional stress, an escalation in drug use to alleviate the stress, the need to generate more illegal income to support a growing drug habit, more frequent arrests and incarcerations, the destabilization of social networks, further stress, and deeper involvement in illicit income-generating activities.

While Kerr and his colleagues recognize that all participants claimed to have made autonomous decisions to become involved in the drug scene, they note that once there, the 'boundary between safe and destructive action becomes increasingly difficult to navigate, and many young people find themselves suddenly and unexpectedly entrenched within a drug scene of which they want no part' (Kerr, et al., 2009, p. 1209; Mayock, 2005).

was born in Alberta and obtained his undergraduate degree from the University of Toronto. He did graduate work at the University of Chicago and was greatly influenced by Mead's discussion of the tension between the 'I' (the spontaneous self) and the 'me' (the socially constrained self). Goffman is well known for his work on the ways in which people conduct themselves during social encounters. His work helps us to understand the often taken-for-granted aspects of, and conventional views about, human social interaction.

Goffman gained renown for his work on face-to-face social interaction, which he defined as 'the reciprocal influence of individuals upon one another's actions when in one another's immediate physical presence' (Goffman, 1959, p. 15). When two or more people come into contact with each other, solitary action is transformed into 'situated' behaviour. Actors, and 'others', in Goffman's view, are the basic components of any interaction order. As Goffman phrased it, 'there seems to be no agent more effective than another person in bringing a world for oneself alive or, by a glance, a gesture, or a remark, shriveling up the reality in which one is lodged' (Goffman, 1961a, 41).

Dramaturgical Metaphor: Social Interaction as Performance

The metaphor that guided most of Goffman's work was that of dramaturgy. Goffman compared social life to a series of performances given by actors on the stage. The social self is not something that each social actor naturally possesses of his own accord, but is the result of the encounters and interactions between social actors and their audiences. The self, Goffman wrote, 'is a dramatic effect arising from a scene that is presented' (1959, p. 253). It is the outcome (and not the cause) of an interactional performance. It only *appears* to emanate from the actor.

Goffman drew parallels between the everyday activities of a social actor and the performance of a stage actor, presented to an audience. Using a dramaturgical metaphor, Goffman argued that a performance, as presented by an individual social actor on a given occasion, is intended to influence other participants. A performance is often undertaken in order to present the person giving the performance in the best possible light. This usually means that the performer seeks to conform to or exemplify one or more existing social norms. Most performances, therefore, tend to be managed in order to present an idealized view of the situation.

While giving a performance, the social actor believes that the part he is playing is important. He may be sincere or cynical in his portrayal, but in all cases he tries to control how his audience will perceive him. For their part, his audience will try to determine whether the performance he gives is genuine or false.

Any given performance is usually a team effort, as individuals rarely perform strictly for themselves. Groups of individuals work together, co-operating in a performance in order to achieve the expected (desired) outcome.

Developing this metaphor further, Goffman argued that because it is the product of an interaction between a social actor and his or her audience, the self is always vulnerable to disturbances, which must be either prevented or dealt with. Actors need to control their audiences, especially potentially disruptive ones. In making his analysis Goffman used a series of concepts designed to help the sociologist explore hidden aspects of human social interaction that we often overlook in our everyday lives. These concepts include the following:

- **front stage**: the place where the performance takes place, wherever an audience and performers are present.
- **backstage**: the place where whatever is pertinent to the performance but not allowed on the front stage might appear. Backstage behaviour is depicted by Goffman as comfortable and relaxed because while the performers are present, the audience is absent.
- **outside**: the place where neither performers nor audience are involved in the performance.

'Civilized' social interaction places many contradictory and often overwhelmingly complex demands on a social actor. Goffman noted that if we did not have a 'backstage' available to us, we would never be able to relax and be just who we are: the self as a performer might become overwhelmed by the self as it is performed. The back stage provides a safe and bounded area where the harried performer can safely retreat to after her front stage performance.

In his discussion of the backstage, Goffman pointed out that this is an area where social actors can reasonably expect that no members of their audience will appear. This is an area, usually cut off from the front stage, where whatever that was suppressed during a front stage

---

front stage

Goffman's term for the setting where social performances meant to be seen take place. The front stage defines the situation in a general way for both an audience and a performer.

backstage

Goffman's term for the actions or interactions not intended for public view but that support a public role performance.

outside

Goffman's term for those areas irrelevant to the performance of a particular social role or to a particular social situation.

performance is allowed to appear. Actors will go to great lengths to prevent a front stage audience from having access to the backstage. If the front stage/backstage barrier is breached, it is more than likely that the performer can expect to experience problems. With this in mind, however, we should be aware that no one physical area is only front stage or only backstage. For example, a doctor's office may be a front stage when she is examining a patient and a backstage when she is sitting at her desk, eating her lunch. It may become an outside when she is away, at home for the day or attending a medical conference.

Impression Management

Goffman used the term **impression management** for the activity a social actor engages in to guard against the unexpected, such as unintended gestures, improper use of language, and breaches of social etiquette, including dressing inappropriately for an occasion or not knowing the right expression for expressing condolences during a funeral. Goffman was interested in the various methods social actors used to consciously manage the impressions they give others, compared to the impressions they unwittingly give off. Conscious actions used in impression management include keeping a social distance from members of the audience; maintaining self-control, including control over facial expression and the tone of one's voice; and deciding in advance how a performance should take place and then selecting teammates and rehearsing the performance in order to prevent the unforeseen from happening.

In developing the dramaturgical metaphor, Goffman also referred to *settings*, the physical props and scenery that have to be present if a social actor is to give a credible performance. For example, firefighters usually require trucks, hoses, and other equipment to be taken seriously in their work. Doctors usually conduct examinations in an office filled with equipment, medications, and other signs of their profession. In both these cases the social actors go about their business in well-defined settings that are associated with them in everyone's mind.

Goffman used the term **personal front** to refer to the props that an actor needs to make his audience believe that the role he is playing is genuine. Firefighters wear hats, boots, and coats, which identify them as legitimate; doctors wear lab coats and often a stethoscope around their necks, all means of presenting a personal front that identifies them in the role they are playing. Goffman further subdivided the personal front into appearance and manner. *Appearance* refers to all those items or props a social actor uses to indicate her status (the lab coat and stethoscope are examples of these). *Manner* conveys to the audience the kind of role the social actor expects to play. For example an aggressive manner and a meek manner imply different kinds of performances. In general, an audience will expect an actor's manner and appearance to be consistent. We do not expect a doctor, dressed in a lab coat and wearing a stethoscope, to meekly approach us as we lie on an examination table dressed only in a paper gown.

Goffman observed that personal fronts frequently become *institutionalized*. By this he meant that certain fronts become subject to 'collective representations', widely held views about what those fronts are to entail. When a social actor takes on an established role, such as banker or chef or civil engineer, she will find fronts already established for these roles. This means that individual actors learn, rather than create, their social fronts.

During a front stage performances, a social actor will usually try to present the best possible image of herself to her audience; in doing so, she will invariably try to conceal certain aspects of her past or current status from her audience. For example, a university professor who has a drinking problem will try to conceal her alcoholism from her students, as this

impression management
Goffman's term for the activity engaged in by a social actor in order to guard against unintended gestures, improper use of language, and other social faux pas.

personal front
Goffman's term for the props used by a social actor to make others believe that the role being played is genuine.

behaviour is generally considered incompatible with her performance as a lecturer. It may also be necessary for actors to conceal 'dirty work'—those tasks that are 'physically unclean, semi-legal, cruel, and degrading in other ways' (Goffman, 1959, p. 44).

You're at a bar with a couple of friends when this gentleman approaches your table, sits down, and introduces himself as Hector. Describe his social performance. Is it likely to be sincere? What impression is Hector attempting to create? What social norms is he attempting to exemplify? What elements constitute his personal front? What backstage actions and interactions might have preceded this episode?

Teams

To Goffman, focusing on individual actors obscures the most important part about interaction: its social nature. He therefore emphasized the performance of *teams* rather than that of individuals. A team, for Goffman, is a set of individuals who operate together to stage a single performance; each member is reliant on the others to make sure that the performance at hand runs smoothly. A doctor, his patient in a private examining room, a nurse, a receptionist, and the patients in the waiting room might form one team. A university professor, her teaching assistants, and her introductory sociology class might form another team. A successful performance depends on the mutually interdependent participation of all parties involved; all parts of the performance must blend together seamlessly. But performances can vary in the amount of consistency they require. For example, a slip by a surgeon during a delicate organ transplant surgery has the potential to be terribly disruptive. A slip by a grade 5 teacher in naming the Great Lakes by size does not have such potentially disruptive consequences and need not greatly damage the teacher's overall performance.

Goffman points out that the audience often has a stake, as well, in making sure that a given performance is good enough. Audience members will act to 'save the show' by forgiving slip-ups, by not engaging in emotional outbursts, or by giving other special considerations to inexperienced performers. It was Goffman's view that it is rare for actors who play a given role to completely embrace all aspects of that role. Each individual actor usually takes on multiple social roles, and it is for this reason that they are able to engage in what Goffman calls *role distance*. Role distance becomes all the more obvious when there has been a recent transition from one role to another. For example an older child, sent by her parents to supervise the play of younger siblings, may simultaneously engage in the play and also resist doing so, aware of her more senior status.

Face Work and Face-Saving Interchanges

Face, Goffman tells us, is the 'positive social value a person effectively claims for himself'. It is 'an image of self, delineated in terms of approved social attributes—albeit an image that others may share, as when a person makes a good showing for his profession or religion by making a good showing for himself' (Goffman, 1967, p. 5). In order to have 'face', an individual must maintain a certain impression through the performance he gives (Goffman, 1967, p. 6). *Face work* is Goffman's term for the 'actions taken by a person to make whatever he is doing consistent with face'. Maintaining face is precarious work, and an individual has to be constantly wary of spontaneous events or actions he is not prepared for. Face work counteracts those events that might threaten face. Members of 'every social circle may be expected to have some knowledge of face work and some experience in its use', according to Goffman (1967, p. 12).

In order to be able to use 'his repertoire of face-saving practices', Goffman explains, the individual 'must first become aware of the interpretations that others may have placed upon his acts and the interpretations that he ought to place upon theirs' (Goffman, 1967, p. 13). The individual must act both to save his own face and to protect the face of others. He does either by constructing a performance that either avoids situations 'that are expressively incompatible with the judgements of social worth that are being maintained' or by undertaking corrective action if the to-be-avoided event happens.

According to Goffman, when an individual gives a performance, it 'will tend to incorporate and exemplify the officially accredited values of the society' (1959, p. 45). Steps must be taken to maintain or re-establish those officially accredited values, even if the individual 'may privately maintain standards of behaviour which he does not personally believe in . . . because of a lively belief that an unseen audience is present who will punish deviations from these standards' (1959, p. 87).

Officially accredited social interactions tend to be ritualistic. If, somehow, the expected behaviour patterns are disruptive, the individuals involved usually take equally ritualized steps to correct the mistake. This corrective interchange, which Goffman tells us is a model for 'interpersonal ritual behaviour', takes the general form of a challenge, followed by an offering of some sort to correct the mistake, followed by an acceptance of the offered corrective. The exchange ends with a thanks, given by the offender to the one who noticed the offence. Not all parts of the interpersonal corrective ritual need to be present—for example, in the sequence of 'Excuse me' and 'Certainly' (Goffman, 1967, p. 20).

INTERACTION RITUALS

In 1967 Goffman published a book with the title *Interaction Ritual*. Nowhere in that book, however, did he clearly define the term. When a group of people come together during a transition, either to renew some aspect of their association or to face some difficulty, what they usually do involves a limited number of common practices in combination. As Durkheim noted, these practices serve to focus and control their attention (Durkheim, 1912/1915). In many instances, rituals serve as a means for individuals to escape self-awareness and to bond with others. Much of the time, instead of acting consciously and purposively, human action is automatic, and under the influence of pre-conscious social and emotional forces of which a person is largely unaware and unable to control. As Durkheim stated:

> The ordinary observer cannot see where the influences of society come from. [They move] along channels that are too obscure and circuitous, and use psychic mechanisms that are too complex, to be easily traced and sourced. (1912/1915, p. 211, as cited in Marshall, 2002, p. 366)

Sociologist Gary A. Fine (2005) defines *interaction rituals* as routines 'by which individual actions are channelled by historical expectations' (Fine, 2005, p. 1288). They are a 'distinctly recognizable, bounded subclass of the vast bramble of potential action' available to the individual participants. Ritual interactions use symbols to produce a sense of belonging and solidarity amongst the members of a social group or unit. During ritual events, participants are induced to do what they must do even if what they must do is at odds with their normal, everyday behaviour. Randall Collins (2004) considers interaction rituals to form the mechanism that holds society together. If we want to know how large-scale institutions work, we need first to understand the localized interaction rituals that make them up.

Interaction rituals consist of four basic ingredients:

emotional entrainment

A situation in which participants in an interaction ritual become caught up in each other's emotions, leading to a mutual intensification of emotional energy, shared feelings, and common focus of attention.

1. *Two or more persons need to be present.* These individuals need to imagine themselves to be part of a common undertaking. A key micro-mechanism of successful rituals is **emotional entrainment**, which Baehr (2005) defines as 'being caught up in each other's emotions leading to intensification of emotional energy, shared feelings, and a common focus of attention' (Baehr, 2005).

STUDIES IN SOCIAL RESEARCH

Professional Socialization: Becoming a Physician in Canada

For most medical students an important transformation occurs between the time they enter medical school and the time they leave. Over four years they encounter new social norms, a new language, new thought processes, and a new worldview, as they transition from the role of medical layperson to the new role of physician. What process of socialization goes into making a doctor?

To answer this, Canadian sociologist Brenda Beagan (2001) drew on survey and interview data from faculty and students at a Canadian medical school to examine the process of professional identity formation. Until Beagan's study, what sociologists knew about the professional identity formation of student physicians had come from research done at a time when most medical school students were white young men. Many of the students at Canadian medical schools today are women, some of them older, from working-class backgrounds, and/or from visible minority groups. Beagan wanted to know if a professional identity fit these students the same way it had fit their counterparts 40 years earlier.

To conduct her research, Beagan used three research methods. She conducted an initial survey of the third-year class (123 students) at a prominent Canadian school; then she followed up with interviews of 25 students from that class and then with interviews of 23 faculty members from the same school (Beagan, 2001, p. 276). She chose third-year students because the third year traditionally marks an important transition as students move from spending most of their time in the classroom to spending most of their time with patients.

The subjects Beagan interviewed described how they came to think of themselves as medical students. Part of that process required them to learn to experience as normal certain things that, initially, they saw as violations of conventional social norms; examples include touching a patient's body, inquiring about bodily functions, and probing emotional states. As one student stated, 'you have to master the sense that you're imitating somebody, and to feel like it's all right to do that, to invade their personal space' (as cited in Beagan, 2001, p. 277).

Administrators at the medical school helped to make sure that students were properly socialized to adopt a professional appearance. They encouraged the students, implicitly and explicitly, to maintain a professional appearance and not to appear in jeans. Most of the men Beagan surveyed had taken care to appear clean-shaven, wearing collared button-down shirts with ties. Women, likewise, had made an effort to dress well and without conveying any sexual messages. While the men learned not to be too informal, the women learned not to dress too provocatively in order to avoid sexualizing the doctor–patient relationship (Beagan, 2001, p. 279).

The survey participants were conscious that learning the language of medicine was the basis for constructing a new social reality, and they spoke about how they learned to ignore extraneous information about the patients' lives and to focus only on what was clinically relevant. But the key to becoming a successful medical school student and, later, making the transition to being a physician was learning to negotiate the complex hierarchy that positioned students at the bottom. The interviewees had learned that being 'good medical students' meant not challenging anything about the behaviour of those who were teaching them, particularly in front of a patient (Beagan, 2001, p. 281). As one student commented, though they weren't explicitly taught never to critique a professor or attending physician in front of the patient, they quickly learned not to question a superior's decisions. In this way, students developed a sense of alliance with other members of their profession, which trumped any loyalty to patients.

This lesson is a major aspect of the med student's professional socialization and is considered key to becoming a good 'team player' with a well-developed sense of belonging (Beagan, 2001, p. 281). As one student remarked, 'you have to go along with some things . . . in front of the patient. . . . . [I]t wouldn't be good to have the ranks arguing amongst themselves about the best approach to patient care' (Beagan, 2001, p. 282). This lesson extends even to situations in which a colleague or teacher may be violating the ethics and standards of the profession (Beagan, 2001, p. 282).

Aside from learning to defer to those above them in the healthcare system's status hierarchy, the students were taught how to have an appropriate relationship with patients. Although they found themselves at the bottom of the medical hierarchy, they had more status and power than their patients. It is still the case that medical students are taught to keep an emotional distance from their patients, although some faculty do favour treating patients on an egalitarian basis.

Along with emotional distancing, one of the most important skills medical students learn is how to deal with uncertainty, especially uncertainty that arises from lack of experience or insufficient specialized training. Med students learn how to tolerate high levels of uncertainty while facing patients who expect them to know it all. Students learn that impression management is a central aspect of their new identities. They come to understand that in order to be successful physicians they have to adopt, in Beagan's words, a 'cloak of confidence such that audiences are convinced of the legitimacy of claims to competent' (2001,

p. 283). The students Beagan interviewed spoke of how at first it was a matter of playing the role of physician. They talked about 'taking on a role' that at first made them feel like frauds and imposters. They also affirmed the importance of props to help them succeed at their role-playing. These props included white coats, stethoscopes, and name tags. These things—powerful symbols of the profession that make up the personal front of the practising physician—helped students overcome their feelings of fraudulence while demonstrating to faculty, nurses, and patients that they knew something. As one student commented, 'Even if I don't know what I'm doing, I can make it *look* like I know what I'm doing' (Beagan, 2001, p. 283).

Goffman stressed the importance of role-playing to both the socialization process and to identity formation. For Goffman, acquiring an identity was a matter both of doing something and of being something. To be a certain kind of person was not merely to possess the attributes of that person, but also to be able to sustain standards of conduct and an appearance that are acceptable to one's social group (Goffman, 1959, p. 75, as cited in Beagan, 2001, p. 284). What became clear to the medical students was that the more they were treated by others as if they were doctors the more they felt like doctors. For many of them, it was the patients who provided the single most powerful confirmation of their identity as physicians. It was with patients that they felt they could pull off a

2. *Clear boundaries have to be established between insiders and outsiders.* Participants in an interaction ritual have a sense of being included in something from which others are excluded. Participants share common symbols that are assigned importance and that must be defended and reinforced.

3. *The attention of all participants is focused on a common objective or activity.* Participants are not only aware of their own focus but are also aware that other participants are likewise focused.

4. *Participants share a common emotional experience or set of feelings* (Baehr, 2005).

Interaction rituals give individuals a sense of identity and common purpose with others. They marshal resources and prepare participants for activity. According to Collins (2011), individuals who have gone through a successful ritual feel confident, energized, enthusiastic, and proactive. He explains:

convincing performance because they realized they actually did know more than the average person (Beagan, 2001, p. 284). Being addressed as 'Doctor ———' by others was another important indicator for them; however, Beagan's survey indicated that by far more men than women were regularly called 'doctor', and that a significant number of women who participated in the survey had never been called doctor. It would appear that the role of doctor or medical student continues to carry with it an attached assumption of maleness (Beagan, 2001, p. 285).

An interesting side note to the study is that while the students believed they were successfully acquiring the identity of physicians, they believed, almost universally, that they were not doing as well in the roles of spouse, family member, and friend. Beagan's research subjects spoke overwhelmingly about the sacrifices they had made in their relationships with families and friends, as well as in other activities that they had formerly enjoyed—all examples of role strain. Many spoke about having to let go of the other aspects of their identity. Some women felt they had become 'more like men' during their medical training. Others downplayed their sexual or cultural identity in order to enhance their identity as physician-in-training. Relationships with anyone who did not or could not identify with their current identity as a medical student were often dropped. Many students underwent a resocialization process that involved intense

Which of these medical students look most like a physician? Why? What does your answer tell you about the institutionalized personal front of 'doctor'?

interaction with members of the new social group and diminishing contact with other social groups. This was especially the case with younger students.

Beagan's research raised many concerns about the rigorous socialization process that students training to become doctors undergo. However, although her findings exemplify the criticisms that others have made and continue to make about medical training, there seems little effort to change what goes on in medical schools.

> The person who has gone through a successful [interaction] ritual feels energized: more confident, enthusiastic, proactive. Rituals can also fail, if the ingredients do not mesh into collective resonance; a failed ritual drains E[motional] E[nergy], making one depressed, passive, and alienated. Mediocre I[nteraction] R[itual]s result in an average level of EE, bland and unnoticed. (Collins, 2011)

There are many interaction rituals in which some members of a social group act as witnesses while other members of the group undergo a passage from one status to another. The group establishes the moral boundaries that the person undergoing status transition is encouraged to accept through participation in ritual interactions. This might be as simple as the social rituals involving either greetings or farewells, both of which serve to remind others of one's continuing relationship with them. Goffman (1971) notes that greetings directed at close friends or family members are typically used to indicate that the relationship has remained intact since last contact, while farewells are used to indicate that the relationship can be expected to continue until the next meeting. Individuals will often experience distress if the greeting or farewell they receive fails to confirm that the relationship is intact or that it will be continued.

The Bridal Shower as an Interaction Ritual

In most societies getting married is considered a life transition to be celebrated. In Western societies, where the bride and groom know each other prior to getting married, a wedding does not create a new relationship. It does, however, mark an increase in the bride and groom's commitment to maintaining a relationship. The wedding, then, is a ritualized occasion, used to solidify and authenticate a close social bond—and the wedding industry that supports these ritualized occasions is a multi-billion-dollar business. In Canada, it is estimated that the wedding industry garners $4 billion a year. In the US, in 1998, the wedding industry was worth approximately $32 billion (Ingraham, 1999, p. 27); 10 years later, in 2008, the *Wedding Report*, which provides research statistics to those involved in the wedding business, reported that about 2,160,000 weddings had taken place in the US during that year at an estimated cost

Crowds in London gather together to watch the procession of Prince William and Kate Middleton en route to their royal wedding. Although weddings are not uncommon, ones involving the British royal family are. Could you, nevertheless, characterize the event as an interaction ritual, carried out on both a local and an international scale?

of about $19,500 per wedding, or a total cost of around $42.1 billion.

While there is a lot of research literature available on marriages, there are surprisingly few studies of the actual rituals involved. In Western societies the bridal shower is a ritual event, steeped in tradition, which is intended to prepare a woman for marriage. It serves as a marker of a woman's status transition from being an unmarried to a married woman. The basic elements of the ritual used to mark this status transition include gifts, food, the bride herself, and (in sociologist Beth Montemurro's word) 'women who are not always thrilled to be there'. Bridal showers, in fact, are so structured that popular guides for planning these events offer formulas, timetables, and schedules for the activities (Montemurro, 2002, p. 73). Montemurro describes a typical event:

> Quiet, anxious conversation fills the room. About twenty women sit at beautifully decorated tables. Some of the women sip mimosas from champagne flutes. Several flower arrangements in glass vases tied with pastel blue ribbons grace the centre of each table. In the corner, next to the table with the fountain of champagne punch, sits a smaller table for gifts. At this point it already overflows with elaborately wrapped packages, most in white paper, trimmed with ribbons, bows, and flowers. On top of the gifts sits an opened lace umbrella, brought by a friend of the bride's mother. The guests wait for the bride-to-be to arrive, trading opinions on whether the supposed surprise will be successful. The bride's mother has taken on the task of luring the bride to the restaurant where the bridal shower is being held. The women talk about where the couple will go on their honeymoon and if the colour of the ribbon on the flower arrangements resembles that of the bridesmaids' dresses and also discuss another bridal shower held for this bride a few days earlier. Most of the women present are longtime friends of the bride's mother; thus conversation turns to the weddings, engagements, and honeymoons of their own children. It is one-thirty on a Saturday afternoon and we have all gathered to celebrate the wedding that will take place in just one month.
>
> The bride's father and the groom-to-be are present as well. They were responsible for bringing the flowers to the restaurant. They will leave shortly after the bride arrives, as this is a traditional, women-only bridal shower. The bride's father asks, 'Are these things boring? I've heard they're boring.' (Montemurro, 2002, pp. 67–8)

Women often attend bridal showers more out of a sense of duty than out of a willingness to participate in an enjoyable occasion. In fact, many women find bridal showers 'boring, socially awkward, or otherwise uncomfortable'. So why, Montemurro asks, do they continue to participate?

One of the important reasons is that the bridal shower is a ritual event that gives meaning to the social world of its participants by linking past to present and present to future (Kertz, 1988, pp. 9–10, as cited in Montemurro, 2002, p. 69). Although practices are changing, in Western societies bridal showers continue to be a women's ritual: women are the primary hostesses, planners, and guests. Women attend these bridal showers, which serve to highlight family and friendship networks among women at a time of status transition, as a show of social solidarity. Members of the bride's various social groups—her family, friends, and co-workers—all come together in a show of support for the new phase of life she is about to enter.

Failure to attend (and help subsidize) such an event undermines the group's solidarity, and is considered 'deviant and subject to sanctions' (Montemurro, 2002, pp. 70–1).

Montemurro carried out her study of the rituals connected with (mostly) middle-class, white bridal showers by conducting in-depth, face-to-face interviews with 51 women who had been guests of honour at a shower, or who had planned, hosted, or attended a bridal shower within the previous year. Taken together, the women in her sample had attended 288 bridal showers over the five years prior to being interviewed. Montemurro collected her sample using a 'snowball' sampling method (in which Montemurro's research participants referred her to other possible respondents), transcribed her interviews, and then analyzed the transcripts using 'grounded theory': as patterns in the answers she had collected emerged, she organized the data into conceptual themes to build a 'theory'. Montemurro herself also attended five bridal showers, as a participant-observer, and analyzed her field notes using the same methods she used to analyze the interview data (Montemurro, 2002, pp. 72–3).

Stressors

Not only did Montemurro's data indicate a strongly ritualized order to the events of the bridal showers, they also indicated that there are ritual expectations for the behaviour of all those in attendance—brides-to-be, hostesses, and guests. Brides-to-be must appear to be 'thrilled' that they are getting married, and must be duly appreciative of each and every gift they open. Bridesmaids must express joy at the upcoming marriage and delight that they have been chosen to participate in it. Hostesses must convey how thrilled they are to have planned and hosted the shower, and what fun they had—and are having—doing just that. Guests are expected to 'fawn over the bride' and express delight and awe at the 'beauty and taste of the items for which she has registered' (Montemurro, 2002, p. 74).

The interaction that takes place at a bridal shower can be viewed as a 'performance' with dramaturgical elements that incorporate and exemplify the 'officially accredited values of the society' (Goffman, 1959, p. 35). There is an expectation that all participants will strive to give ideal performances, and the women Montemurro interviewed stated that they had attended the shower either 'out of respect' for the bride or so that the bride and others will see them as a 'good' person. But there were many complaints about the experience, ranging from 'boredom' and 'anxiety occasioned by trying to blend families' to the difficulty of merging people from different parts of the bride-to-be's life and the 'ordeal' of planning the event.

Hochschild (1983) has noted that a social role is partly a way of describing what feelings people think are owed to them and what feelings they owe to others. A social role establishes a baseline for which feelings are appropriate to be expressed during specific events (Hochschild, 1983, p. 74, as cited in Montemurro, 2002, p. 76). While all participants at a bridal shower experience stress, the most stress, arguably, is placed on the bride-to-be. Brides-to-be expressed discomfort at being placed 'centre stage', especially during gift opening, where they become the focus of everyone's attention. Unlike other participants in the bridal shower, the bride-to-be has little opportunity to let down her guard and is expected to display the appropriate emotions of delight and gratitude at all times. There are few backstage spaces available to her.

The bride-to-be may also experience stress due to an 'internal conflict about which self to present'. With family, future in-laws, friends, and co-workers all present, the bride may be anxious about which aspects of her 'self' it might be best to present. At her shower, the future bride opens gifts that she cannot reciprocate materially. The only means available to her to 'pay back' the generosity of others is by expressing pleasure and gratitude while opening the gift (and, of course, in the subsequent thank-you note). She is under pressure to give a good performance by individually thanking gift-givers on the spot, using words and expressions carefully chosen to be appropriate to thank each individual. Failing to express the proper (i.e. expected) level of joy and gratitude implies 'lack of connection to the gendered community that has produced [the] event' (Montemurro, 2002, pp. 77–8).

Consider these two rather different comments—one about 'Rose' and another about 'Kelly'—made by bridal shower attendees. 'Rose' is criticized because she did not express gratitude in the appropriate way, while 'Kelly' was praised for her communication of gratitude and thus for strengthening her ties with her gender community:

> I thought that [Rose] was not very enthusiastic or thankful to the people that gave her presents. She was like 'oh, this is nice' and never really—I mean—especially to her mother—we noticed that afterwards—we were talking about that . . . it just seemed a little odd. I don't know if she was in a bad mood that day or what, but she didn't seem overly excited or thankful. I would think if someone threw me a shower I would be like 'thank you so much'. I mean it's nice for someone to do that for you.

> [Kelly] was the most grateful bride I've ever seen. When she stood up and would thank everybody for their gifts, she meant it. And it made your heart feel good that what you did for her, she appreciated. I have never—in all of the showers that I went to—seen someone thank someone for a pillow to put my head on, 'Thank you for getting me this'. . . she appreciated the smallest gift that was given to her. (as cited in Montemurro, 2002, p. 79)

Hostesses experience many stresses as well. Popular etiquette guides say that the hostess should pay for the shower, but often several women will combine their resources. When this happens hostesses face the problem of bringing together several different small groups made up of people who don't normally interact with one another, in order to plan the event. Different generations may have different ideas about what the event should be like, as might individuals from different groups. The hostess and the bride might also disagree about what is expected and how much to spend on the event. Several hostesses expressed concern that their efforts would be evaluated and judged by attendees. Going all out and making a big production out of the food and decoration sends a strong message to the bride about how much the hostess cares. Young hostesses—those in their twenties—expressed feelings of insecurity at hosting their first 'grown-up' party.

Many of the women Montemurro interviewed described bridal showers as boring. As one woman put it, 'it was very like rote. . . . I felt like this is what we're suppose to do. . . . [I]t felt very cookie cutter.' Bridal showers follow 'highly structured, standardized sequences' and are repetitive and redundant, with little variation. The guests take on a passive role. All of this contributes to the lack of enjoyment expressed by the attendees. At the same time, the very thing that makes them boring is what serves to channel emotions and organize the group (Kertzer, 1988, p. 9, as cited in Montemurro, 2002, p. 82).

Finding an appropriate gift that will appeal to the bride while at the same time communicating something about the giver's status is another stressor experienced by guests. Because everyone who consults the registry knows how much each item costs, the gift may be used to present an image of the giver's self: an expensive gift implies generosity; a sentimental one implies a special relationship with the bride; a practical gift implies that the giver is not familiar with the bride and is playing it safe.

Bridal shower guests may also feel uncomfortable because of the social ranking that is part of the ritual. The bride, naturally, occupies the highest status, and other participants are ranked on the basis of the nature of their association with her. To give a shower for a bride-to-be is a declaration of social or familial bonds, and so the hostess is usually ranked next, along with the members of the bridal party who are often enlisted to help with looking after the gifts, organizing games, and serving food and drink. Guests have the lowest status; their relationship to the bride-to-be is unclear and difficult to demonstrate. Symbolically excluded from the bride's intimate circle, their lack of status and power in the ritual is evident to all, and this may make them feel alienated from the ritual. For these guests, both the emotional and material exchange may appear very uneven, and the lack of reciprocity may make showers even less enjoyable (Montemurro, 2002, p. 85).

Why do Bridal Showers Continue?

When Montemurro asked her respondents why they thought bridal showers continue, many responded that it was because of tradition. Women are socialized to be caregivers, and bridal showers offer an institutionalized way in which care for the bride-to-be can be given and received. Men do not easily participate because to do so 'violates the masculine role'. Moreover, at the shower, the bride-to-be is given gifts that will enable her to take care of her future spouse, and thus she is encouraged to take on a traditional feminine identity. Bridal showers reinforce traditional gender roles, and gifts emphasize the traditional wifely duties of cleaning, cooking, and entertaining. Many of young women that Montemurro interviewed rejected or at least expressed ambivalence toward this traditional role. Pursuing careers outside of the home, they experience conflict between their individual achievements and the traditional demands of feminine responsibility that is 'implicitly being called on at the bridal shower' (Montemurro, 2002, p. 89).

Finally, women participate because doing so confirms their connection to their social group, community, and gender. Participation allows them to demonstrate this commitment not only to the bride-to-be but also to the larger community. The social ritual and the emotions expressed during the ritual strengthen social ties and reaffirm the participants' identities as members of a gendered community in which women care for and support each other.

SUMMARY

Socialization is both an active, ongoing process and a product or outcome of that process. In this chapter we have looked at how social interaction, as an ongoing process of socialization, shapes the ways in which adolescents become entrenched in a local drug scene in Vancouver. Areas of downtown Vancouver serve as a focus for drug use and drug procurement, but also serve as a locale that anchors the elaborate social networks and social practices (interaction rituals) associated with the day-to-day lives of those involved in the drug scene.

We have also examined socialization as a product through the work of Erving Goffman, who wrote extensively about how people conduct themselves during face-to-face social encounters. Goffman used the metaphor of dramaturgy extensively in his work, drawing parallels between everyday behaviour of a social actor and a dramatic performance, presented to an audience. Goffman famously argued that the self 'is a dramatic effect arising from a scene that is presented', and that every social actor engages actively in 'impression management'.

Brenda Beagan's work on becoming a physician in Canada illustrates what happens to medical students over the four years from the time they enter medical school to the time they leave. During this period medical students undergo a process of socialization as they encounter new social norms, language, and worldview, and as they take on a new identity as a doctor. Beagan found that impression management was a central aspect to the new role of physician, and that medical students had to learn to adopt a 'cloak of confidence' in order to convince others of their competence.

Interaction rituals—routines through which the actions of individuals are organized into mutually meaningful actions that produce a sense of solidarity among participants—are a central part of all aspects of everyone's life. Interaction rituals affect group solidarity and individual well-being alike. They give individuals a sense of identity and common purpose with others, and are especially important during times of transition, or when people get together to renew some aspect of their association, or to face some difficulty. The bridal shower—which celebrates the important impending social transition of getting married—is an example of an interaction ritual. During a bridal shower the friends and relatives of the bride-to-be can show her their care and support, and at the same time get to demonstrate and reaffirm their commitment not only to the bride-to-be but also to the larger community.

DISCUSSION QUESTIONS

1. Explain in your own words what is meant by the term 'interaction ritual'?
2. List some of the interaction rituals that you are familiar with. How does each ritual affect group solidarity? How does each ritual help shape individual emotional response?
3. Erving Goffman's dramaturgical approach to social interaction implies that we are all actors who perform for an audience. Do you agree with this view? Explain.
4. Role strain can occur when there is tension among the various roles an individual is expected to play. Cite some examples of role strain that you have encountered in your own experience.
5. 'Status' refers to the social position that an individual holds. Social status is a relative concept in that it defines an individual's identity in relationship to others. Cite some examples of ascribed, achieved, and master status.
6. According to Goffman, any performance is usually a team effort, where groups of individuals work together to achieve some expected or desired outcome. Cite some examples of social performances that are team efforts. Describe the front stage, back-stage, and outside of each of the performances you cite.
7. Drawing on an example from your own life, explain how you use impression management to present yourself in a particular light to others. Give an example of how someone might fail impression management and unwittingly 'give off' the wrong impression.

10 Culture

LEARNING OBJECTIVES

In this chapter you will:

- gain insight into how sociologists understand culture
- become familiar with the complexities of the meaning of culture
- compare different approaches to the study of culture taken by anthropologists and sociologists
- learn about the ways in which recent immigrant youths have integrated their traditional culture into mainstream Canadian culture
- gain a clearer understanding of how cultural differences lead to misunderstandings
- learn about the effects of Western media on contemporary Mohawk youth identity
- discover some of the ways that different cultures treat bodily functions and life events.

INTRODUCTION

In 1956, American anthropologist Horace Miner published the results of an ethnographic study of a group of people he called the Nacirema. Miner was particularly interested in the elaborate, strange, and seemingly obsessive daily bodily rituals these people engaged in. He reported his observations in an article published in the journal *American Anthropologist*, and it is worth quoting from that publication:

> The fundamental belief underlying the whole system appears to be that the human body is ugly and that its natural tendency is to debility and disease. Incarcerated in such a body, man's only hope is to avert these characteristics through the use of the powerful influences of ritual and ceremony. Every house-hold has one or more shrines devoted to this purpose. . . .
>
> The focal point of the shrine is a box or chest which is built into the wall. In this chest are kept in the many charms and magical potions without which no native believes he could live. These preparations are secured from a variety of specialized practitioners. The most powerful of these are the medicine men, whose assistance must be rewarded with substantial gifts. However, the medicine men do not provide the curative potions for their clients, but decide what the ingredients should be and then write them down in an ancient and secret language. This writing is understood only by the medicine men and by the herbalists who, for another gift, provide the required charms. . . .
>
> The Nacirema have an almost pathological horror of and fascination with the mouth, the condition of which is believed to have a supernatural influence on all social relationships. Were it not for the rituals of the mouth, they believed that their teeth would fall out, their gums bleed, their jaws shrink, their friends desert them, and their lovers reject them. They also believe that a strong relationship exists between oral and moral characteristics. For example, there is a ritual ablution of the mouth for children, which is supposed to improve their moral fibre.
>
> Daily bodily rituals performed by everyone include a mouth-rite. Despite the fact that these people are so punctilious about care of the mouth, this rite involves a practice which strikes the uninitiated stranger as revolting. It was reported to me that the ritual consists of inserting a small bundle of hog hairs into the mouth, along with certain magical powders, and then moving the bundle in a highly formalized series of gestures. (Miner, 1956, pp. 503–4)

These people, of course, are American (*Nacirema* is 'American' spelled backwards). In his article, Miner (1956) succeeds in making the everyday activities that most North Americans engage in seem strange. Miner accomplishes this by taking an everyday, familiar action—brushing the teeth—out of its familiar context. He observes tooth-brushing as might a person with no 'cultural knowledge' about this daily activity. Indeed, the point of Miner's article is that any activity, including those that we are intimately familiar with, can be made to seem strange and even nonhuman if we interpret it through another 'cultural framework'.

How should a sociologist understand culture? Is culture a set of values and beliefs that we all carry around in our heads—a value system that 'infuses collective life', affecting everyone in the same way at all times? Is it a set of social practices—ways of doing everything from brushing our teeth to burying our dead—that we learn from early childhood? Or is it more analytically useful for sociologists to treat culture as 'complex, rule-like structures that constitute resources that can be put to strategic use' (DiMaggio, 1997; Lizardo, 2006; Swidler, 1986)? One thing is certain: the concept of culture, and its study, is anything but simple.

THE CONCEPT OF CULTURE

'Culture', writes the British sociologist Raymond Williams in his book *Keywords* (1976), 'is one of the two or three most complicated words in the English language' (Williams, 1976/1985, p. 76). And yet it is one of the most widely used concepts in sociology. A large part of the complexity of the word has to do with its history and the meanings that it has come to acquire. In everyday language, the word **culture** is most commonly used to designate static and sometimes elitist notions of the highest achievements of civilization, such as the products of intellectual and artistic activity, including literature, music, theatre, painting, philosophy, and architecture. But, as Williams (1976) writes, even in everyday language the term has not always been used in this way. The first use of the word *culture* as a noun was to describe

culture
Generally, all socially transmitted social practices and knowledge systems, including language, beliefs, values, material objects, and know-how, that are transmitted from one generation to the next, and that enable humans to adapt to and thrive in a given environment.

The earliest sense of *culture*, the cultivation of crops on land, was extended to refer to the cultivation of the mind. Can you trace those early senses to the current scene of popular culture presented here?

certain processes, including the growing and cultivating of crops, the breeding and raising of animals, and then only by extension 'the active cultivation of the human mind' through such pursuits as art, literature, and religious contemplation. By the eighteenth century, however, *culture* had taken on the additional meaning of a distinct, coherent, 'whole way of life', including values, that is manifest in every aspect of social activity.

Social scientists have taken many different approaches to defining the concept of culture and to studying and theorizing the role of culture in human social interactions and social structures. The sections that follow examine four sociological approaches to culture:

- culture as an all-pervasive way of life;
- culture as 'a tool kit';
- the 'production-of-culture' perspective; and
- culture and human embodiment.

CULTURE AS AN ALL-PERVASIVE WAY OF LIFE

During the nineteenth century the term *culture*, in the sense of a distinctive and all-pervasive way of life, was adopted by the fledgling disciplines of comparative anthropology and sociology. In 1871, for example, the British anthropologist E.B. Tylor published his book *Primitive Culture: Researches into the Development of Mythology, Philosophy, Religion, Language, Art, and Custom*, in which he maintained that:

> Culture . . . taken in its wide ethnographic sense is that complex whole which includes knowledge, belief, art, morals, law, custom, and any other capabilities and habits acquired by man as a member of society. The condition of culture among the various societies of mankind, in so far as it is capable of being investigated on general principles, is a subject apt for the study of the laws of human thought and action. (Tylor, 1871/1903, p. 1)

Because most of what humans do is learned and not genetically given (as we saw in chapters 8 and 9), the opportunities for variation in interpreting events and behaviours are almost infinite. The fact that human beings can live together in large social groupings attests to the extent to which having a common culture provides us with a shared set of taken-for-granted understandings about our social world and how we must live in it. The importance of learning culture as a framework for providing all members of a given society with a shared set of skills and understandings was recognized as early as 1917 by American anthropologist Alfred Kroeber (1876–1960). Kroeber, in his book *The Nature of Culture* (1917), proposed the following mental experiment as a way of understanding the difference between the innate, instinctual behaviour of insects and the learned, cultural behaviour of human beings:

> Take a couple of ant eggs of the right sex—unhatched eggs, freshly laid. Blot out every individual and every other egg of the species. Give the pair a little attention as regards warmth, moisture, protection and food. The whole of ant 'society', every one of the abilities, powers, accomplishments and activities of the species . . . , will be reproduced, and reproduced without diminution, in one generation. But place on a desert island . . . two or three hundred human infants

of the best stock from the highest class of the most civilized nation: furnish them the necessities of incubation and nourishment; leave them in total isolation from their kind; and what shall we have? . . . Only a pair or a troop of mutes, without arts, knowledge, fire, without order or religion. Civilization would be blotted out within these confines—not disintegrated, not cut to the quick, but obliterated in one sweep. (Kroeber, 1917/1952, pp. 177–8)

In the same book, Kroeber proposes another mental experiment to illustrate how, at birth, any child is capable of learning any language and acquiring any culture:

> Let's take a French baby, born in France of French parents, themselves descended for numerous generations from French-speaking ancestors. Let us, at once after birth, entrust the infant to a mute nurse, with instructions to let no one handle or see her charge, while she travels by the directest [sic] route to the interior heart of China. There she delivers the child to a Chinese couple, who legally adopt it, and rear it as their son. Now suppose that three or ten or thirty years passed. Is it needful to discuss what the growing or grown Frenchman will speak? Not a word of French; pure Chinese, without a trace of accent and with Chinese fluency; and nothing else. (Kroeber, 1917/1952, p. 29)

Sharing a common culture means that we learn not just a common language but, with that language, a common set of taken-for-granted assumptions about the social world. We use those assumptions as the framework for understanding, explaining, and interpreting all our experiences. Although humans lack the kinds of **instincts** that other animals possess, we have a culture that we share with other members of our society. Having a shared culture enables all members of a given society to access a set of understandings about how and why the world works the way it does. Culture in this sense is vitally important. Humans, as we saw in Chapter 8, cannot grow up to be recognizably human without interacting with others of their kind. A frog, by contrast, can become a frog without any help from others of its species. This is because the frog possesses instincts that tell it how to act as a frog; humans rely instead on social learning to acquire the culture that enables them to act as humans.

In this definition, culture is seen as an entire way of life of a given society that includes both material artifacts and values and beliefs—everything that an individual needs to be a fully functioning member of a given society. This definition, which most sociologists accepted up until the 1970s, portrays culture as being both unitary and internally consistent across all groups and situations comprising a given society. From this perspective, too, individual members of society are thought to acquire their 'culture' through the process of socialization, and to subsequently enact their culture in unproblematic ways (DiMaggio, 1997, p. 264).

But during 1970s and 1980s this definition of culture as an all-pervasive and entire way of life of a given people was challenged by a rather different way of thinking. Instead of viewing culture as an all-pervasive approach to the world that an individual is socialized into, and that thereafter serves as the lens through which to understand the world, critics developed a more dynamic view of culture. According to this view, culture serves as the material out of which peoples' daily lives are constructed, their daily experiences understood and interpreted. From this perspective, culture serves as the 'bricks and mortar' out of which individuals actively construct their interactions with and understandings of the worlds they inhabit (Willis, 1977, p. 185).

instincts
Complex patterns of behaviour that are genetically pre-programmed and that regulate the activities of members of a species; instinctual behaviours tend to be found in all members of a species and are innate.

Culture is a dynamic process that enables us to tailor our responses to specific situations. What are the different cultural requirements in evidence here? Where do you think the photo was taken—Vancouver? Mumbai? London?

Culture has come to be seen as a set of mechanisms that humans actively employ on a moment-by-moment basis, and a means by which their reality is actively defined (Murphy, 1986, p. 14). Culture is no longer viewed as a thing, a static outcome; it is now viewed as a dynamic process—a kind of tool kit we draw on to construct responses to specific situations. For example, Canadian culture values humility, politeness, and consideration of others—unless there's a hockey game on, in which case it values feistiness, combativeness, and even violence. Another example concerns the way that young Canadian Muslim women approach wearing a hijab. Canadians generally, in accordance with Canadian cultural values (and laws), do not insist on female modesty in the way that many traditional Canadian Muslim families do. A Muslim Canadian woman may navigate these difficult and contradictory cultural requirements by wearing a hijab on some occasions and at other times going without, depending on the expectations of the people she is with.

CULTURE AS A 'TOOL KIT'

The shift makes the study of culture much more complicated. Seen from a dynamic point of view, culture is not simply a unified system that people are socialized into from birth and that causes them, uniformly, to act in consistent ways. Culture is more like a 'tool kit' or repertoire from which social actors choose different pieces in order to construct different lines of social action. This means that sociologists should expect individuals to be active, skilled users of culture and not just passive 'cultural dopes'. If we adopt a 'culture as tool kit' perspective, then we also acknowledge that individuals have 'readiness and cultural capacities they rarely employ; and all people know more culture than they use' (Swidler, 1986, p. 277). People consistently use different aspects of culture to accomplish different things depending on circumstances.

As a tool kit, culture consists of 'symbols, stories, rituals, and worldviews, which people may use in varying configurations to solve different kinds of problems' (Swidler, 1986). From this perspective, culture provides social actors with the materials they need to construct their own 'strategies of action' necessary to help them achieve a life goal. Consider, for example, the range of choices available to a Canadian who wishes (as one of many life goals) to find a partner. This person may rely on his network of friends or on an online dating site. He may engage in a number of short-term relationships before finding an ideal partner. He may live with his prospective partner for some time before legally marrying, or he and his partner may live indefinitely in a common-law relationship, as Canadians are demonstrating more and more a comfort with common-law relationships as an alternative to formal marriage. But Canada is a culturally diverse country, and the cultural background of this individual may mean he must rely on family networks as opposed to friends or to his own preferences when he is looking for a partner. He may be limited in his choice of partner because it is important to his family that he seek out someone of the same religion or 'cultural background'. He may not be allowed to consider 'living together' as a reasonable alternative or precursor to formal marriage, and might even have his marriage arranged for him.

In his work on adolescent socialization in a poor neighbourhood in Boston, David Harding (2009) shows how adolescent boys growing up in a disadvantaged neighbourhood came to hold 'unconventional cultural models' about education, work, welfare, and marriage—models clearly at odds with those held by their parents' generation. Harding's study highlighted the influence exercised over adolescent boys by older neighbourhood peers who are from outside the boy's family and school settings.

In his study, Harding notes that poor neighbourhoods are typically culturally hetero-geneous and should not be treated as single, homogeneous entities. Adolescent boys living in the neighbourhood Harding studied are presented with an array of competing cultural models that include community figures whose 'decent values' compete with the 'alternative

STUDIES IN SOCIAL RESEARCH

Chinese Adolescent Immigrants to Canada: Moving Between Two Different Worlds

Jun Li (2009) chose a qualitative research strategy, comparative research design, and semi-structured interviews and narrative essays as research methods to study the ways in which recent Chinese immigrant youths arriving in Vancouver have integrated Chinese traditional culture and mainstream Canadian culture.

Since the start of the twenty-first century, China has been the number-one source of immigrants to Canada. A large number of these immigrants are highly educated professionals, arriving with their families. As a result, Chinese children and adolescents make up the fastest-growing student population in Canada's largest metropolitan areas (Li, 2009, p. 78). But Chinese immigrant adolescents face a number of challenges,

Disney sponsored the 2009 Ice Sculpture Festival held in Harbin, China, demonstrating that popular culture can transcend ethnic and national borders fairly easily. What are the differences between elements of Canadian popular culture—Rick Mercer, K'Naan, the Mounties, three-down football—and the less tangible cultural barriers students from China face upon arriving in Canada?

among them the need to reconcile often profound differences between Chinese traditional and Canadian mainstream cultures. Li wanted to know how Chinese immigrant adolescents cope with the challenge of participating in two different cultures, and how they construct meanings out of their cross-cultural experience.

The Chinese immigrant youths that Li studied encounter on a daily basis significant cultural differences between the traditional culture of their homeland and mainstream Canadian culture. Traditional Chinese culture places value on formal education, hard work, and family, and the parents of Chinese

immigrant adolescents often dedicate themselves to their children's education and future. In return, Chinese children are expected to reciprocate this investment on the part of their parents by living up to parental expectations of high academic achievement and culturally desirable conduct and behaviour (Li, 2009, p. 495).

Most adolescents Li interviewed felt they did well at school because their parents stood behind them and pushed them to succeed. In many cases their parents, although highly educated themselves, could not find professional employment in Canada and so chose to dedicate themselves to making sure their modes of success' presented by the young men held in high regard because their success as drug dealers and hustlers gives them command over economic resources. The boys interact extensively with their older peers in the community, from whom they learn how to navigate the often dangerous streets of their neighbourhood and beyond. These ghetto youths become

children succeeded at school (Li, 2009, p. 488). To help their children achieve this success Chinese parents encouraged their children to socialize only with other 'straight A' students, prohibited them from dating (on the grounds that it would distract them from their studies), and often registered their children in extracurricular activities such as music, languages, art, sports, and social programs. Traditional Chinese parenting style is usually top-down and very strict; participants in the study reported they had little freedom, and that their parents often resorted to corporal punishment.

In dealing with the two, often conflicting, cultures on a daily basis, Chinese immigrant youths found themselves caught between two different worlds: one that demands academic achievement and filial obedience and another that nurtures creativity and independent thinking; one that is restrictive and disciplinary, one that is, by comparison, often friendly and flexible (Li, 2009, p. 497). At home, immigrant Chinese adolescents experience frequent conflicts with their parents' traditional disciplinary practices, which are at odds with mainstream Western liberal and democratic values. The Chinese adolescents Li studied described how they often resisted and resented adult-centred Chinese parenting, yet they had mixed feelings because they knew the kinds of sacrifices their parents had made to bring them to Canada for a chance for success.

As newcomers, immigrant Chinese adolescents at high school are often excluded from circles of both power and popularity because they are seen as 'less desirable' by native-born adolescents. Li's research subjects reported that high school friendship groups develop mainly along racial/ethnic lines—white groups, Chinese groups, South Asian groups, and

so on. The Chinese students were further divided into subgroups: the 'Bananas' (i.e. 'yellow' on the outside, white on the inside—a derogatory term for westernized Chinese), the 'CBC' (Canadian-born Chinese) group, and the 'FOB' ('fresh off the boat') group, comprising the new immigrants (Li, 2009, p. 492). Such complicated groupings make it difficult for the new immigrants to fit in, as they often find themselves unaccepted by any of the established groups, both Chinese and non-Chinese. As one participant reported, when he first immigrated to Canada he was in elementary school and all his classmates were white. He was excluded from playgroups, and it was not until he got to high school that he was able to gradually make friends with other Asians. Although he wanted to make friends with white students, he felt that there was a distance, which he attributed to the fact that 'we have different lifestyles'. This student, who was living at a university residence at the time of the study, reported that he felt that white students' lives were totally different from his:

> [T]hey party a lot, hang out with guys a lot, and they don't seem serious in relationships. When we talk, topics cannot match each other's. They may talk about more relationships, like sex, which I know nothing about. I want to talk about homework, but they are not interested. It is hard to find a common topic. It is weird. (Li, 2009, p. 494)

This student's remarks illustrate the extent to which, even though they participate in the same social setting (in this case, school), Canadian-born and Chinese-born students navigate that shared setting using quite different cultural tool kits.

adept at reading signs of friendship and loyalty, and at recognizing threats to their neighbourhood's public spaces from gangs coming from other neighbourhoods. They come to rely on the protection of their older peers, those who have earned reputations as fighters and who will support them in a conflict. In this neighbourhood, as Harding discovered, many of the adolescent boys grow into young men who place loyalty to their neighbourhood gang above personal achievement in terms of life goals. For these youths, striving for personal achievement over neighbourhood loyalty would require a 'drastic and costly cultural retooling' (Swidler, 1986, p. 277).

If we look at Harding's study from the perspective of culture as a tool kit, we can see that the boys have available to them several different 'cultural' values and strategies for achieving success. Many of these values conflict with each other, and the boys choose from their cultural tool kit those strategies that they believe will provide the most reliable way of achieving a life goal: security on the dangerous streets of their neighbourhood and access to economic resources. In their case, even though their cultural tool kit includes education, work, marriage, and social responsibility—values presented to them by their parents and other members of their parents' generation—many of the youths use other, opposing aspects of their cultural tool kit to set and achieve life goals.

Crossing Cultural Barriers

bride price
A payment of money, cattle, or other goods, made by the family of a man to the family of his wife-to-be.

Sometimes the results of cultural differences and misunderstandings can be quite amusing. For example, while doing fieldwork among the Guajiro Indians living in the northern part of Colombia, an American anthropologist learned that the Guajiro have a custom known as **bride price**. According to this custom, when a man and a woman marry, the family of the husband-to-be is required to pay for his bride with cattle, other goods, or money. This practice upset the anthropologist, who felt that it was an insult to the dignity of women to be bought and sold in such a manner, much like a possession. She confided her feelings to a recent Guajiro bride, and asked the woman if she, too, was offended at being purchased like a cow. The bride didn't answer the question directly. Instead, she asked the anthropologist just how much her own husband had paid for her when they married. Taken aback, the anthropologist proudly announced that her husband had paid nothing for her. Such a practice was not done where she came from. 'Oh what a horrible thing,' came the reply. 'Your husband didn't even give a single cow for you? You must not be worth anything!' (as cited in Whiteford & Friedl, 1992, p. 70).

But sometimes lacking the cultural skills to participate meaningfully in social interactions can have quite unsettling results, as Canadian anthropologist Jean L. Briggs illustrates in her book *Never in Anger* (1970), in which she describes her time spent living among the Utkuhikhalinmiut of the Canadian Arctic. In 1963, Briggs began a 17-month field study of a small group of Utkuhikhalinmiut, or Utku (Inuit to southerners) living at the mouth of the Back River, northwest of Hudson Bay. The nearest settlement was 240 kilometres to the north, in Gjoa Haven, a small mission and trading settlement of perhaps 100 Utku and four or five whites. At the time of Briggs's study, the Utku were mostly self-sufficient and lived largely by hunting and fishing.

When the 34-year-old Briggs first arrived among the Utku, she was adopted as a daughter by a couple, Inuttiaq and Allaq, who had four younger daughters. While living with this family, Briggs found she was often unable to control how she expressed her emotions, and thus she often failed to behave in the culturally appropriate mild and uncomplaining fashion expected by her Utku adoptive family. After many attempts to teach her how to behave, her Utku family resorted to what was, in Briggs's words, the 'ultimate sanction against the display of aggression . . . ostracism':

> The difference between my behavior and that of the Utku could not help but create difficulties, on location, for the latter. . . . It was not only the strangeness of my face and tongue that made me different. I was incongruous in other ways as well. I was an adult, yet as ignorant of simple skills as a child. I was a woman, yet I lacked the usual womanly attributes of husband and children; a 'daughter', yet independently wealthy and accustomed to organizing my own life. In retrospect, my relationship with the Utku seems to divide approximately into three phases, in which from the Utku point of view I was first a stranger and a curiosity, then a recalcitrant child, and finally confirmed irritant. (Briggs, 1970, pp. 225–6)

Briggs's original objective in living among the Utku was to study the social relationships of shamans. She reasoned that because the Utku were so far away from missionary influence, she would find practising shamans among them. But she had been misinformed. The Utku had encountered both Catholic and Anglican missionaries about thirty years before her arrival and were all devout, practising Christians. In the view of the people themselves, their shamans were all 'either in hell or in hiding'.

Briggs found a new direction among the Utku when she lost her temper with some southern sport fishers who had flown into the islands near the Utkus' camp for the summer. Because Briggs was the only bilingual person, she was pressed into service as translator and intermediary between the Utku and the sport fishers, who wished to borrow two canoes. The first round of negotiations ended with the Utku permitting the sport fishers to take their canoes. But now the Utku were stranded on their island and were dependent on the southern visitors to bring them food, which they themselves could no longer fish for, in exchange for carved toys and trinkets. As Briggs recounts:

> I do not know how strongly the Utku felt about the absence of their canoes and their dependence on the foreign visitors. Perhaps none of the alterations in the daily patterns troubled them as much as they did me. Characteristically, the Utku kept well under control whatever negative feelings they may have had. Gratitude was the feeling they expressed openly. . . . Nevertheless, a change was clearly evident in the atmosphere of the Utku camp. . . . Though I have no way of knowing whether the Utku's feelings coincided in detail with mine, there was evidence that the loan of the canoes was to them, as it was to me, a source of strain. (Briggs, 1970, pp. 279–80)

The situation came to a head when Briggs was asked to interpret again for another group of sport fishers who had arrived on the shores and who also wanted to borrow the canoes. At first the Utku complied and lent one canoe, which was subsequently returned because it was damaged. When the fishing guide asked for the loan of the good canoe, Briggs reacted:

> I exploded. And smilingly and in a cold voice I told the kapluna [i.e. white] leader of a variety of things that I thought he should know: that if he borrowed

the second canoe we would be without a fishing boat; that if this boat was also damaged we would be in a very difficult position. . . . I also pointed out the island where our supplies of tea, sugar, and kerosene were cached and mentioned our inability to reach it except by canoe. . . . I told the guy that the owner of the second canoe did not wish to lend it.

The guide was not unreasonable; he agreed at once that if the owner did not wish to lend his canoe, that it was his option: 'It's his canoe, after all.' Slightly soothed, I turned to Inuttiaq, who stood nearby, expressionless like the other Utku. 'Do you want me to tell him you don't want to lend your canoe?' I asked in Eskimo. 'He will not bother with you if you say no.'

Inuttiaq's expression dismayed me, but I did not know how to read it; I knew only that it registered strong feelings, as did his voice which was unusually loud: 'Let him have his will.'

I hoped my voice was calm when I replied to Inuttiaq: 'As you like,' but I was filled with a fury at kapluna and Inuttiaq alike, as well as at myself for having undertaken the futile role of mediator, and my tone was icy when I said to the guide: 'He says you can have it.' Turning abruptly, I strode back to my tent, went to bed, and wept in silence. (Briggs, 1970, pp. 284–5)

Briggs's anger and hostility toward the sport fishers was, for the Utku, the final confirmation of her volatility and inability to control her emotions, attributes that must be strongly avoided in Utku culture. For the next three months, Briggs was socially isolated and subtly shunned. Even though her questions had always been considered rude, the Utku had tried to humour her with answers. Now they simply refused to respond. And yet she was still treated with much care by the people she had so badly offended. 'I was amazed . . . that although my company was an anathema, nevertheless people still took care to give me plentiful amounts of the food I liked best, to warn me away from thin ice, and to caution me when my nose began to freeze'(1970, p. 295).

The experiences of Briggs and other Western anthropologists confirms what most readers already know implicitly: while there are certain similarities between all human cultures—including symbolic communication (i.e. language), conceptualization, and tool making—there is a vast range of differences in how cultural tools are used. Values, norms, and expected and allowable behaviour vary extensively between different cultures. Even within a given culture, there may be large variations in how different members live, experience, and behave in such matters as family organization, work ethics, health and illness, or, as we have just seen in the case of Jean Briggs's attempts at integration into Utku society, even in the expression of feelings.

But what these anthropologists' experiences (along with those of the Chinese immigrant adolescents who took part in Li's study) also confirm is that culture is not a once-and-for-all thing; it is not something that one is socialized into and that then shapes the entirety of the rest of one's life. Participants in new and unfamiliar cultures all report on the ways in which they first try to use the strategies, understandings, and presentations of self available to them through their own cultures and how, eventually, they have to modify what they have acquired via their own culture in order to adjust to what seems at first to be bizarre, inexplicable, or even downright misguided demands.

THE PRODUCTION-OF-CULTURE PERSPECTIVE

In the words of American sociologists R.A. Peterson and N. Anand (2004), the production-of-culture perspective 'focuses on how the symbolic elements of culture are shaped by the systems within which they are created, distributed, evaluated, taught, and preserved' (2004, p. 311). Sociologists using this perspective have traditionally focused on the 'expressive-symbol elements of culture', which include artworks, music, literature, popular culture, and religious practices, as well scientific research reports, legal judgements, newspaper articles, and items from what we now call the cultural industry (video and music recordings, for example). This perspective treats culture not as unchanging but as 'situational and capable of rapid change' (Peterson & Anand, 2004, p. 312).

One focus of studies done from a production-of-culture perspective has been the ways that young people have taken the products made available to them by mainstream cultural industries and 'recombined them in unique ways to show their resistance to the dominant culture and to give expression to their own identities' (Peterson & Anand, 2004, p. 325). The following is an example of the application of this perspective to the study of Canadian Mohawk youth.

Culture and Identity: Canadian Mohawk Youth and Western Pop Culture

Robert Hollands (2004) studied Canadian Mohawk youth living on the Tyendinaga reserve near Belleville, Ontario, to understand the construction of hybrid cultural identity. In his study, he looked at the way Mohawk youths' consumption of Western media and culture intersected with local traditions and customs. Hollands wanted to understand how Western youth culture as it is expressed in film, television, music, and sports gets taken up and moulded into a contemporary Mohawk youth identity. Using a qualitative research strategy, case study design, survey questionnaires, and focus group interviews as his research methods, Hollands learned that young Mohawks actively consume global youth culture and popular media, but they do so strategically in ways that will enforce and extend their Aboriginal identities.

Canadian society is characterized by extensive ethnic diversity in a variety of cultural traditions and 'ways of life'. The Mohawk are the easternmost tribe within the Iroquois/Six Nation Confederacy. They were displaced to their present-day location about 200 years ago, coming from upstate New York. During their time in Canada they have been subjected to gradual colonization and assimilation.

Colonization can be defined as 'an intentional, long-term process' that involves 'replacing the traditional, self-determined lifestyle of indigenous people with a dependent and subordinate status' (Yerbury & Griffiths, 1991, p. 321). Assimilation was a formal policy adopted by the Canadian government to 'civilize' Aboriginal people specifically by 'introducing new values and beliefs as well as new skills such as farming and homemaking' (Fisher & Janetti, 1996, pp. 241–2). As part of this policy, the Canadian government took Native children away from their parents and sent them to residential schools, where, separated from their families and forbidden to speak their language or engage in any traditional customs or practices, these children, it was hoped, would more readily assimilate into Canadian society.

At the 2010 winter Olympics in Vancouver, Russian skaters Oksana Domnina and Maxim Shabalin, in a controversial bid to appeal to the home crowd and pay tribute to Canada's Aboriginal heritage, incorporated elements of Native North American culture in their original dance program. What effect do you think their performance had on Aboriginal viewers? When is cultural borrowing not appropriate?

Among the Tyendinaga Mohawk, the Canadian government's policies of colonization and assimilation, combined with intermarriage with members of the local population and with the general movement of people away from the reserve, helped to undermine any sense of cultural identity (Hollands, 2004, para. 3.5). But since the 1970s, Aboriginal people living in Canada have begun a slow process of trying to regain their lost cultural identity.

To conduct his study, Hollands used a research sample of 35 Mohawk youth (ages 13 to 18) from a local high school, and conducted an in-depth focus group with six of the respondents. Hollands found that Mohawk youth are generally positive about themselves; however, he also found that they preferred American TV programs— ranging in content from cartoons to primetime dramas and soap operas—to Canadian shows. The only Canadian programming that made their lists was *Hockey Night in Canada* (Hollands, 2004, para. 5.11). Although they were aware of the Aboriginal Peoples Television Network (APTN), they found that programming not very exciting, relevant, or even interesting. As one of the interviewees said, 'It didn't really teach us anything. It was worse than the news. . . . There was nothing to keep your attention there' (Hollands, 2004, para. 5:13). In addition to American movies and television, music was an important part of their cultural identity. By far the most preferred type of music among the Mohawk youth was rap (chosen by 60 per cent of the sample), followed by 'alternative' music and dance music (the latter favoured exclusively by females), pop, rock, and metal. Only a very few included traditional Aboriginal music among their favourites (Hollands, 2004, para. 5.17). Commenting on the popularity of rap music among Mohawk youth, Hollands notes that the favourite rapper, Dr Dre, can be classified as a 'gansta rapper', whose songs 'are steeped in the negative consequences of black oppression, but also reflect self-blame, violence and indeed misogyny' (Hollands, 2004, pp. 5.18).

Young men and young women experienced their Mohawk identity differently. Young men were nearly five times as likely as young women to have hunted and to rank hunting as an important activity. While both young men and young women said that they fish, young men rated its importance significantly higher than did the women.

Community leaders have responded to both the loss of ancestral knowledge and Native traditions and to the growing and obvious interest in forms of Western youth culture by initiating a number of programs designed to reintroduce Native youth to their traditional culture. As Hollands reports, these initiatives include 'role model programs, rediscovery camps, healing circles, powwows, Potlatches, sweat lodges, youth justice committees, Native education counsellors, setting up special Native learning and media centers and cultural/language/skill development' (Hollands, 2004, para. 6.4). Many of these programs have been linked to social agency responses to issues such as 'juvenile justice, drug and alcohol abuse, and other social problems experienced by Native youth' (Hollands, 2004, para. 6.4).

Because these programs are aimed typically at 'troubled' Aboriginal youths, the majority of young Mohawk men and women get ignored. Moreover, these programs often talk about Western culture in terms of its distractive aspects, and they all but ignore popular culture as a means of exploring modern identity. Yet, as Hollands' research has pointed out, the majority of Mohawk youth have embraced many aspects of Western youth culture and have developed a 'hybrid' identity. It is clear from their comments that 'traditional culture', if it is to survive it all, has to be updated to reflect contemporary cultural norms (para. 6.5). But, as Hollands also notes, the main obstacles to the development of contemporary Native identity are not just resource-based but have to do with more fundamental issues of power and hegemony. Blatant racism continues to exist. There is general disregard in the wider Canadian culture for what has happened to Aboriginal culture since the time of European contact. Many local non-Native residents feel that the Mohawks have too many 'special rights'. These sentiments, Hollands feels, need to be challenged with reference to the basic historical context and current economic facts. More must be done to help non-Native Canadians understand the importance of preserving Native culture and traditions. But, as Hollands concludes, the exact way in which Mohawk youth will reinvent themselves as modern Aboriginal people is unclear. As one of the youths he interviewed explained,

> It's really hard to say we miss our culture . . . Cos we lost a lot compared to other reserves eh? Like a lot of tradition, we don't have. . . . You just get used to being where you are. So you learn to live with it. You don't really want nothing to change I guess. You want some things to change, but . . . I don't know. (Hollands, 2004, para 6.9)

CULTURE AND HUMAN EMBODIMENT

The final approach to culture to be discussed in this chapter focuses on how culture affects the ways in which we experience a physical condition or an emotion. American anthropologist Mary Douglas (1984) has pointed out that while all humans have the same body, 'with the same number of orifices, using the same energies and seeking the same biological satisfactions', each culture is highly selective in how it views these themes, individually and collectively. Thus, while every human has bodily needs that must be fulfilled, *how* those needs are fulfilled varies widely from culture to culture. There does not seem to be any human physical condition for which cultural treatment is consistent across the globe. In each culture, some bodily functions or life events are viewed as good, while others are viewed as dangerous or 'polluting' (Douglas, 1984, p. 60).

At the beginning of this chapter, we read Horace Miner's tongue-in-cheek account of the mouth-cleansing ritual practised among North Americans, especially after eating. In fact, however, cleansing rituals are common to most cultures, albeit with considerable variation. Among the Mae Enga of the New Guinea Highlands, for instance, ritual cleansing takes place after sexual intercourse to rid participants of sexual pollution. Meanwhile, the Nyakyusa of Tanzania insist on ritualized washing, seclusion, and fumigations after a funeral to make mourners and members of the burial party fit once again for social contact.

There are many other examples involving various physical processes. While all humans need to eliminate bodily wastes, where it is done, in what physical position, and even how often it is done is culturally specific. In Western cultures, it is customary to wash the hands after urinating. Among Arab and other Muslim groups, only the left-hand—considered the profane hand—is used to clean oneself after elimination; the right hand, considered pure, is used for eating. Men of the Chaga tribe of Tanzania wear anal plugs, claiming to have sealed up their anuses to eliminate the need to defecate (Becker, 1973, p. 32).

Eating is essential for survival. As Margaret Visser (1986) writes, although food is part of our everyday lives, it is never just something to eat. In our treatment of food, we 'echo the preferences and principles of our culture'. How, when, where, and even what we eat follow cultural dictates, rules of propriety, and beliefs about what is appropriate food for humans. North Americans, for example, are taught that it is impolite to talk with a full mouth, to eat peas with a knife, or to eat most foods with their hands. The Yurok of California learned to eat with a serious expression on their faces and think about wealth, while the Mundurucu of

Brazil will not behave boisterously while eating in case they offend the spirit-mothers of the animals. As Visser remarks:

> Food choices and presentations are part of every society's tradition and character. An elaborate frozen dessert moulded into the shape of a ruined classic temple can be read as one vivid expression of a society's view of itself and its ideals; so can a round ground hamburger patty between two circular buns. Food shapes us and expresses us even more definitively than our furniture or houses or utensils do. (Visser, 1986, p. 12)

The complex and even convoluted relationships between needs, psychological responses, and culture is illustrated by the following example. American anthropologist Clyde Kluckhohn (1949) tells of an acquaintance in Arizona who took a certain perverse pleasure in causing a cultural response to food. She would frequently serve her luncheon guests sandwiches filled with a light meat that looked and tasted similar to tuna or chicken. After the meal had been served, the hostess would inform her guest that they had lunched on rattlesnake salad sandwiches. Invariably the response of at least one guest would be to vomit (Kluckhohn, 1949, p. 19).

Some public bathrooms are more public than others. How comfortable would you feel using—or walking past—this public toilet on the streets of Varanasi Benares, India? What do you think accounts for cultural differences in how comfortable we feel with human biological processes?

To further illustrate the extent of diversity both within and between different cultures, let's consider the significance of cultural context for understanding two seemingly invariant biological or bodily experiences common to all humans: death and memory. It would appear that both dying and remembering something are, in and of themselves, purely biological processes. While we may want to concede that different cultures specify activities or rituals focusing on death or the use of memory, our everyday experience of the world tells us that the actual acts themselves and their meaning should be fairly consistent for all of humankind. After all, death and memory are bodily undertakings, biologically based and obvious to all. Or are they?

Death and Culture

While death is inescapable for all human beings, it is not the simple and self-evident occurrence that our taken-for-granted, culturally specific understanding might lead us to believe. The reasons for this complexity are not as self-evident as they may first appear, either. For example, we might want to argue that determining when the exact moment of death has occurred is becoming more and more problematic because of advances in modern medical technology and knowledge. What was not so long ago a simple matter of determining whether or not a person continued to breathe and therefore continued to live has now become less straightforward. Moreover, with new technology, it is possible to keep a body alive without there being any brain activity. Thus, it is now possible for a person to be 'brain-dead', even while his body remains alive via technological intervention.

But the problem of defining precisely when death has occurred is not merely a technical one, which can be resolved as we become more technologically proficient; rather, it is very much a cultural issue. Western Christian culture defines death as the opposite of life: there is an instantaneous transformation between one state (life) and the other (death), with nothing in between. But as new medical evidence and practices force us to realize, these matters are not so simple. With the invention of new technologies, our culture may be forcing us to think that perhaps those cultures we previously considered to be 'deluded' and 'primitive' for their failure to accept the instantaneous transportation from life to death might just have a case.

What is considered death, in fact, varies from culture to culture and depends greatly on cultural beliefs and categories. In many societies, death is not thought to occur instantaneously but rather is viewed as a slowly changing condition. Among the seventeenth-century Huron, for example, a body was buried twice: first in an individual grave, and later, when the entire village moved to take up new agricultural land, in a common grave with all individuals who had died between one move and the next. The period between the initial burial and the re-internment in a common grave was marked by a series of changes in the individual's state of being dead.

Today, North Americans usually consider death a private affair. But less than two centuries ago, the dying often said goodbye publicly to as many of their relatives and acquaintances as possible. Even those who were unacquainted with a dying person but were in the vicinity felt free to come and watch the final hours of a stranger's life. In his book *The Hour of Our Death* (1981), French historian Philippe Ariès describes the public nature of death in western Europe during the eighteenth and nineteenth centuries, when a dying person was expected to preside over a group of people gathered to observe his or her passing. Ariès recounts the death of Mme de Montespan, a mistress of Louis XV of France, who, according to one of her biographers, was 'less afraid of dying than she was of dying alone'. Ariès describes her final moments:

On May 27, 1707, when she realized that she was about to die, she was no longer afraid. She summoned all her servants, 'down to the lowest one', asked for their forgiveness, confessed her sins, and presided, as was the custom, over the ceremony of her own death. (Ariès, 1981, pp. 18–19)

Although by the late eighteenth century French doctors had begun to complain about the unhygienic aspects of having so many people invading the bedrooms of the dying, the complaints went unheeded until well into the next century. Quoting from the memoirs of a nineteenth-century French gentlewoman, Mme de La Ferronays, Ariès recounts the following episode:

Walking in the streets of Ischl during the 1830s . . . she heard the church bell and learned that the Holy Sacrament was about to be administered to a young priest whom she knew to be sick. She had not dared to visit him yet, because she had not met him, but the Holy Sacrament 'brought me there quite naturally. I

A recently deceased Indian man is brought to the Ganges River as part of a Hindu funeral ceremony before he is cremated. Hindus believe that the cremated remains must be immersed in a river as part of very strict and complicated funeral rites performed to ensure that the deceased may pass safely to the realm of his ancestors. How does this differ from mainstream Canadian approaches to funerals and cremation services? What do you think accounts for cultural differences in treating the dead?

knelt down by the main entrance along with everyone else, while the priest went by. Then I went upstairs and watched while he received the last Sacrament and Extreme Unction.' (Ariès, 1981, p. 19)

Even the act of going from a state of health to one of decline and ultimate death is not outside the scope of cultural influences. In 1942, W.B. Cannon, a physiologist, published a paper entitled 'Voodoo Death'. In it Cannon contends that death can occur as a result of cultural beliefs in which evil spirits, black magic, and cursed objects can do an intended victim irreparable harm. The belief in the efficacy of such things, Cannon argues, is enough to induce a state of fear in a person who thinks himself or herself to be the target of a curse or of the anger of an offended spirit. The fear and terror experienced by individuals while awaiting their anticipated fate is sufficient to induce a change in their physiological state, something equivalent to severe shock from a wound. The result is a malfunctioning of the circulatory system as the individual's blood pressure drops and he or she falls into a coma. At this point, the victim is beyond the capacity to respond consciously to any intervention and ultimately dies as a result of oxygen starvation to the vital organs. These deaths serve in their turn to reinforce the convictions of others concerning the effectiveness of occult powers and evil spirits (Hirst & Woolley, 1981, pp. 26–7).

What these and many other examples illustrate is the complex relationship between death as a biological experience and death as a cultural experience. The understanding of what constitutes being dead and even the experience of dying are clearly not universal in all human societies. As with all human experiences, it is mediated both by culture and by the embodied nature of human beings. And like all human experiences, the range of cultural diversity in formulating, shaping, and giving meaning to something that, on first examination, appears to be a simple and straightforward biological matter is extensive.

Memory and Culture

Like death, memory is a biological event. But, remembering something is not merely a biologically based, psychological capacity that all humans have independent of any kind of cultural content. A biologically based faculty such as memory is dependent simultaneously on the functioning of the brain and on culturally specific techniques that the individual has acquired. That which at first appears to be purely biological (memory) and that which at first appears to be strictly cultural (technologies to aid memory, such as writing and printing) are in fact closely interwoven, as the following example illustrates.

Printing and Memory

The introduction of printing, which can be defined as 'the mechanical reproduction and duplication of writing by means of movable type', had profound effects on memory and on Western culture in general. Printing transformed techniques of reading, writing, and learning as well as the character of what was read, written, and learned (Hirst & Woolley, 1981, p. 35). Experiments with printing in Europe during the mid-fifteenth century led to the invention of the printing press. By the end of the sixteenth century printing was widespread, and most instruction throughout western Europe was based on the printed word. While 20 million books were printed before 1500, somewhere between 150 and 200 million were put into circulation in the century that followed (Febvre & Martin, 1976).

But why should the introduction of printing into a culture that already used writing transform that culture so profoundly? After all, isn't printing just another way of recording what could already be set down with writing? Not according to Hirst and Woolley, who deliver a very strong response to this question for the following reasons.

First, the labour involved in producing a handwritten manuscript is very different from the labour involved in printing a book. Scribes who produced books engaged in a laborious and time-consuming occupation. They were always struggling with the demand to produce as many books as possible and the need to preserve the integrity of the text from copying errors. As a result, handwritten books were not very common and certainly not in wide circulation. Moreover, books produced in such a fashion were so rare and precious that they were often kept locked away. Personal possession of books was restricted to the wealthy. Individuals such as lawyers and scholars, who relied on books for their profession, usually possessed small, specialized libraries.

Second, without printing—and, therefore, without access to large quantities of books—mass education in a pre-print culture is almost impossible. Our medieval ancestors, if they were illiterate, were not considered uncultured, as they might be today. And a person who could not read in medieval Europe was by no means cut off from popular culture the way one might be today if one couldn't read the latest newsstand offerings or surf the Web. While members of the nobility in many European countries were illiterate, they were nonetheless highly cultured and well aware of the written literature, even if they could not read themselves.

Third, prior to the widespread availability of printed books, university teachers lectured from hand-copied manuscripts. The word *lecturer* means, literally, 'reader of books'. Literacy was not the everyday means of cultured communication; reading and writing skills were ancillary to the spoken language, which dominated medieval culture. Those few who were skilled in reading and writing used those skills in the service of a largely oral culture.

Fourth, the content and style of pre-printed stories and poems were closely tied to an oral tradition. Themes were chosen and composed to hold the interest of a listener, not a reader. Writing, then, was undertaken with listeners, rather than readers, in mind.

So how did the literate but as yet printless cultures of antiquity and the later Middle Ages resolve the problem of sharing complex information in medicine, law, philosophy, and theology? In *The Book of Memory*, social historian Mary Carruthers (1990) writes that for the people of the Middle Ages, it was a matter of training their memories, which not only provided them with the means to converse intelligently when books were not easily available but also provided the means to build character, judgement, citizenship, and piety (Carruthers, 1990, p. 9). A person without memory, she writes, was a 'person without moral character and, in the basic sense, without humanity' (p. 13).

Medieval theologian St Thomas Aquinas wrote about techniques for training memory, which included 'proper preparation of material, rigid order, and complete concentration' (Carruthers, 1990, p. 8). In medieval society a well-trained memory was not just a means for parroting politically correct answers: it was considered a virtue in itself. As such, memory served as a 'condition of prudence that was coextensive with wisdom and knowledge' (Packard & Chen, 2005, p. 1301).

Torture was very much part of medieval society. And it was put to use not only as a punishment, but also as a way of ensuring that children memorized certain rules. Following St Thomas Aquinas's mnemonic techniques of 'proper preparation of material, rigid order, and complete concentration', children were 'reminded' that the volume of any given body equals height times length times width by an illustration of a man with three spears running through different parts of his body, the spears representing, respectively, height, width, and depth. Not only did children receive instruction in calculating volume, but also in what happens to those who deviate from Christian doctrine (Packard & Chen, 2005, p. 1301).

Memory techniques can also affect the form and content of knowledge itself. In the Middle Ages, it was typical for analytical and observational knowledge to be organized into ordered hierarchies of categories. What is significant about these systems of knowledge is that the form of order needed to retain knowledge often restricted growth or change in knowledge. There are certain very powerful, conservative tendencies imposed by a knowledge system that depends on the memory practices of individuals for recalling, storing, and presenting that knowledge. The tendency is to add new knowledge of similar kinds, which is a much simpler and less demanding task than to restructure what is already known.

The development of the kind of critical attitude that many twenty-first-century university teachers think is essential for their students to acquire is possible only when material can be accumulated on a massive scale and when different accounts can be consulted by the same person. Rarely could a medieval scholar place one text beside another for cross-referencing or comparison. Rarely, if at all, could such a medieval scholar afford to do what the German philosopher Friedrich Nietzsche recommended four centuries later: to forget. Nietzsche thought it good that people know both when to forget and when to remember, and saw the benefits of social forgetfulness as a 'way to create openness and freedom in a world derived again and again from highly indirect knowledge of past ages and peoples, not from direct observation of life' (Nietzsche, 1874/1983, p. 118, as cited in Packard & Chen, 2005, p. 1305). French philosopher Henri Bergson (1946) took Nietzchean forgetting and selective remembering a step further, suggesting that all memory is socially constructed. This is an idea that we have already encountered in Chapter 7's discussion of the role of the South African Apartheid Museum in constructing collective memory.

There are, of course, other ways to approach the question of culture than the ones presented in this chapter, and in the next chapter an additional approach to culture—exemplified by Pierre Bourdieu's work on 'habitus'—will be discussed. Chapter 11 will also introduce three additional core sociological concepts: social structure, social agency, and social institutions. Traditionally, sociologists have claimed that while culture provides human social actors with their 'designs for group living', social structure 'defines, regulates, and controls the acceptable modes of achieving these goals' (Merton, 1938, pp. 672–3). This is in contrast to social agency—the subjective aspects of individual experiences—which are often treated as fleeting, short-lived, malleable, and contingent, the expressions of the individual activity and freedom of social actors.

SUMMARY

Culture is one of the most widely used concepts in sociology. As a concept, it encompasses everything that people have, think, and do as members of a given society. To fully function as a member of a society is to be able to communicate with other members of that society in ways that are mutually understandable. A common culture facilitates mutual intelligibility.

There are many different cultures in the world today, with a great deal of diversity among them in social practices, values, norms, and belief systems. One very good reason for studying this diversity is to help reduce ethnocentrism, the tendency to believe that one's own culture is superior to all others.

Sociologists use a number of different perspectives or approaches to study culture. This chapter presented some of those approaches, including culture as an all-pervasive way of life, and culture as a 'tool kit' or repertoire from which social actors choose different pieces in order to construct different lines of social action.

In this chapter we looked at the work of several sociologists who have studied the role of culture. Jun Li's work on recent Chinese immigrant youths arriving in Vancouver focused on the ways in which these youths have integrated traditional Chinese culture with mainstream Canadian culture, and how they construct meaning out of their cross-cultural experiences. Jean Briggs spent 17 months conducting field work among a small group of Utku, living in the Hudson Bay region. Briggs's report on her experiences in a new and unfamiliar culture help us understand some of the ways that experiences are first interpreted through familiar cultural frameworks which are only later modified and adjusted to fit new situations.

Robert Hollands' study of Canadian Mohawk youth living on the Tyendinaga reserve near Belleville, Ontario, serves as an example of how a hybrid cultural identity is constructed. Hollands' research confirms that while Mohawk youth actively consume global youth culture and popular media, they do so strategically in ways that will enforce and extend their Aboriginal identities.

As a final example of the different approaches to culture taken by sociologists we surveyed some of the work of sociologists and anthropologists on the ways in which culture structures how individuals experience a physical condition or an emotion. The work of sociologists Paul Hirst and Penny Woolley show us that even something as common and inevitable as death or memory has different meanings depending on the cultural situation.

DISCUSSION QUESTIONS

1. Discuss the role played by culture in structuring human behaviour and social actions.
2. How can we explain human cultural diversity? In what ways might the study of this diversity reduce ethnocentrism?
3. What is the relationship between human biology and culture? In what ways does human embodiment affect culture? In what ways does culture affect human embodiment?
4. Using Miner's example of brushing teeth, discuss other examples of taken-for-granted aspects of Canadian culture from the point of view of someone unfamiliar with the culture.
5. Jean Briggs's work on the Utku suggests that the expression of emotions such as anger is culturally specific. What are the culturally appropriate ways for Canadians to express other emotions, such as happiness, love, or fear?
6. Robert Hollands' work on Mohawk youth culture shows that while young Mohawks actively consume global youth culture and popular media, they do so strategically in ways that will enforce and extend their native identities. What other examples are there of Canadian youths who use global youth culture and popular media strategically to reinforce their own identities?

11 Social Structure and Social Agency

CHAPTER OUTLINE

LEARNING OBJECTIVES

In this chapter you will:

- be introduced to the concepts of social structure and social agency
- learn about the structural-functionalist perspective
- come to understand the revolt against structural functionalism
- review a well-known study of supermarket shoppers, used as a basis for thinking about the relationship between social structure and social agency
- consider the defining characteristics of structuration theory
- survey Pierre Bourdieu's theory of social structure and social action
- learn about social network analysis
- inquire into structural changes associated with the aging of the Canadian population
- distinguish between bonding social capital and bridging social capital.

INTRODUCTION

social structure

A core sociological concept used to denote the resilient and enduring systematic patterns that order and constrain social life; these patterns are often considered to be non-negotiable.

agency

An individual's capacity for action, inherent in all humans and shaped by a 'specific range of cultural schemas and resources available in a person's particular social milieu' (Mills, 1959/2000).

A little over fifty years ago, C. Wright Mills (1959) wrote *The Sociological Imagination*, in which he issued his famous call to sociologists to locate sociology at the intersection of individual biography and the larger social structures of which the individual was part. **Social structure** is a core sociological concept he used to denote the resilient and enduring systematic patterns of social interaction that order and constrain social life. These patterns are largely non-negotiable. They are often also thought of as being 'objective' (that is, of existing outside the will of individual social actors) and of 'exerting a definite pressure' on individuals. In pointing to social structure in his definition of the sociological imagination, Mills asked sociologists to focus on how social structures shape an individual's capacity for action, or agency. **Agency** is inherent in all humans and is shaped by a 'specific range of cultural schemas and resources available in a person's particular social milieu' (Mills, 1959/2000). This means that the actual forms that agency will take vary enormously from one social milieu to another.

By pointing to an individual's biography and her capacity for action, as well as to the social structures of which she is a part, Mills recognized that sociologists need to account for both agency and structure in order to be able to explain how the lives of individuals develop over time.

More than five decades after C. Wright Mills wrote *The Sociological Imagination* sociologists are still concerned with understanding and explaining the links between the individual's capacity for action and the social structures which help to shape how she will act. Although the concepts that we use to think about this relationship—including social structure and social agency—are among the most important in the sociologist's repertoire, their meanings are surprisingly elusive. Moreover, while some sociologists favour studying agency, others take a social structural approach. This chapter outlines some of the ways that sociologists have dealt with these important, if (sometimes) 'hotly contested', concepts.

Sociologists know that social actors exercise *agency*, or a degree of control over their daily lives. They also know that the extent of this agency or control varies enormously, depending on the nature of the social structures—cultural and historical—that inform their social worlds. It should come as no surprise to learn that in different societies social structures 'are laden with differences in power', that they 'empower agents differently', and that they 'embody the desires, intentions and knowledge' of agents differently as well (Sewell, 1974, p. 21). According to Sewell,

> . . . the scope or extent of agency . . . varies enormously between different social systems, even for occupants of analogous positions. The owner of the biggest art gallery in St Louis has far less influence on American artistic taste than the owner of the biggest gallery in Los Angeles; the president of Chad has far less power over global environmental policy than the president of Russia. . . . Structures, and the human agencies they endow, are laden with differences in power. (Sewell, 1974, p. 21)

As we noted earlier, sociologists, if they don't favour agency in their explanations of social life, tend to focus on social structure. Those who concentrate on social structure, such as the followers of various schools of Marxism, or structural functionalism, make human agency almost irrelevant to their theories of human social organization. Durkheim, a founder of the discipline whose work we took up in Chapter 5, thought that social structures had an underlying logic of their own, so powerful that they were fully reproduced (or only slightly altered) over time. Karl Marx's concept of 'modes of production' (see Chapter 6) points to significant structural differences in the economic relations of members of different societies.

While still in his teens, Free The Children founder Craig Kielburger (left, shown here with his brother and Free The Children co-founder Marc) managed to secure the personal assistance of Prime Minister Jean Chrétien and American media personality and philanthropist Oprah Winfrey to create enormous public awareness about child labour practices in countries like India, where similar efforts by someone of comparable age and position would be impossible. What are some of the factors that diminish or enhance agency in this context?

These differences, he believed, are powerful enough to shape the social organization of an entire society. For structural functionalists, such as Talcott Parsons (whose work is discussed later in this chapter), the acting individual is almost irrelevant to social theory, while the structural elements of society are treated as self-propelling.

Other theoretical schools, including symbolic interactionism (surveyed in Chapter 7), make human agency their main focus, at times reducing social structure to a minor or subordinate role (Archer, 1982, p. 455). However, no matter what their theoretical allegiance, sociologists have never been able to entirely separate the individual from society, preferring instead to see that society is always a 'necessary condition' for any action an individual might initiate. 'Society', says sociologist Roy Bhaskar, 'is both the ever-present condition and the continually reproduced outcome of human agency' (Bhaskar, 1989, p. 34).

Sociologists have developed many different approaches to explaining the relationship between individual agency and social structure. In what follows, we will look at some of these approaches, along with examples of research and case studies to illustrate them.

SOCIAL STRUCTURE

One of the first comprehensive analyses of social structure, which we have already encountered in Chapter 6, was developed by Karl Marx. Recall that Marx divided human societies into one of several different economic stages, or modes of production, which he believed marked the different epochs of human social and economic evolution. During the first half of the twentieth century Marx's work was considered too tainted by political ideology to be used in scientific research. American sociologists rejected anything that Marx had to say— they believed that Marx's ideas conflicted with the ideals of American society. Instead they drew on the work of Durkheim, Weber, and others to develop what came to be known as the structural-functionalist perspective.

Structural Functionalism

structural functionalism

A theoretical paradigm that views society as a large, living organism made up of a number of different but interrelated structures that function together to contribute to a society's survival.

The theoretical paradigm that came to dominate American sociology from the 1930s to well into the 1960s was known as **structural functionalism** or, more briefly, functionalism.

Structural functionalists think in terms of *systems*. A system is a very general concept referring to anything that has parts that are connected to each other. The machine is a system. So is any biological organism or any organized collection of information. Put as simply as possible, the basic metaphor underlying all structural-functional theory is that society is a large, living organism made up of a number of different, interrelated structures. In the same way that the internal organs (i.e. the structures) of a human body work together to contribute to the survival of that body, all the parts of a society also function together to contribute to its survival.

Like a living organism, a society has certain needs that must be met if it is to continue to exist. The structures of any given society, which include its institutions, its culture, and its belief systems, contribute to the overall functioning of that society. All its structures must work harmoniously if the society is to continue to exist.

For a structural functionalist, the answer to the general question *what causes any particular social system to exist?* is that every social structure or regular social pattern of conduct serves a specific function in the system as a whole. The relatively high pay received by physicians, for example, is explained by the need to attract the best possible people to that position. Traditional restrictions on women that confine them to their home while encouraging men to work outside the home is explained by functionalists as serving the joint social needs of socializing children (traditionally the woman's role) and feeding the family (traditionally the man's role).

Structural-functionalist theory comprises four key concepts:

1. *Structure.* Any regular social pattern of conduct. This might be something as complex as a belief system or the institutional structures supporting specific religious practices. It might also be something as simple as the patterns of daily interaction between two people in public spaces—for example, a shopkeeper and her customers. Any given social structure, however, must contribute towards the maintenance of the social system in which it operates if that social system is to continue to survive.

2. *Function.* What any given structure contributes to the smooth operation of the society. While some structural functionalists recognize only the positive contributions of the structure to the functioning of society, others allow for the negative consequences. Robert K. Merton (1949/1968) called these negative functions 'dysfunctions'.

An automobile is a system, a set of parts or structures that operate together to perform a function. In what ways is the manufacturing plant a system? In what ways is the manufacturing sector itself both a system and, at the same time, a structure of a larger system, the national economy?

3. *System.* The relatively stable interaction between two or more persons or two or more social structures. Thus, a married couple might be considered a system, but so might something as large and complex as an entire society.

4. *System need.* Whatever must take place to permit the system to maintain itself. Structural functionalists argue that every system has integration and adaptation as basic needs. All parts of the social system must work together smoothly (i.e. must *integrate*) as well as adapt to the external environment (Zeitlin & Brym, 1991, pp. 82–3).

The example of romance and love in Western societies will give you an idea of how all of these different elements might work together to form a functioning system. From a structural functionalist's perspective, romantic love would be considered a social *structure* of Western society—that is, a relatively stable pattern of social conduct that persists over time. The *function* of romantic love in Western societies might be to prepare young people to leave the security of their families of birth in order to set up their own independent family units. A negative function of romantic love might be that it can lead not to happiness and a strong family unit in marriage but to disappointment and the rejection of a partner once the romantic feelings fade. The basic *system* of romantic love would be the courting relationship of two young lovers, followed by a marriage relationship. The larger societal *system needs* of integration and adaptation are achieved when the young couple moves from dependence on parental units to establishing their own family unit, thus perpetuating the heterosexual family as the basic social structure. From a structural functionalist's perspective, the heterosexual family promotes the emotional and economic well-being of the couple, as well as the biological continuation of society.

By the late 1950s the basic tenets of American structural functionalism could be summarized as follows.

1. Societies are whole systems made up of interrelated parts. Each part has meaning only in relation to the whole. Each part, too, performs a specific function within the system and contributes toward the integration and adaptation of the system as a whole.

2. Each element or part that makes up the whole system is indispensable to that system. Each part performs a specific function that is related to the overall 'need' of the system.

3. Despite the first two points, the integration of all elements of a system into a whole is usually less than perfect. In reality, the system is fragile and unstable. Elements of disharmony and mal-integration are present. These elements necessitate the presence of social control mechanisms.

4. Deviance and other dysfunctional forms of adaptation put strain on existing social structures. Eventually, though, dysfunctional elements are integrated into the mainstream, and equilibrium is restored to the system.

5. Social change is always adaptive and gradual.

6. Social integration is achieved when individual members of a society share common values, including a set of principles that legitimize existing social, economic, and political order.

Probably the best-known of all the American structural functionalists is Talcott Parsons (1902–79), the sociologist who pioneered structural-functionalist theory in the 1930s and who served as its leading architect and proponent through to the 1950s. In developing his grand theory of society, Parsons drew heavily on the work of Durkheim and Weber, especially on their insight into the importance of social integration. It appeared to Parsons that cherished American values were under strain, and social disorganization was rife. The solution, he believed, lay in promoting moral values that would act as a kind of glue capable of holding society together.

The Revolt against Functionalist Theory

By the 1950s, structural functionalism was regarded by many as the only desirable sociological theory available, and sociologists such as Kingsley Davis proclaimed that the methods of functionalism were simply the methods characteristic of any sound, scientific undertaking. However, contemporaries of Davis were already voicing their dissent, claiming that functionalism was anything but a neutral, value-free, objective method of sociological inquiry. One of the most telling criticisms came from those who argued that, due to an over-emphasis on social order and stability, structural functionalism had failed miserably to provide any reasonable analysis of social conflict and social change. Moreover, functional analysis all but excluded the individual from its purview.

Jeffery C. Alexander (1987) has suggested that Parsons' theory of society was linked closely to his hopes for a revitalized post-war America, that he believed his theory of society would better explain social instability and that it would contribute to a process whereby political consensus and social equilibrium could be achieved. Indeed, although Parsons had begun his work in the 1930s by being critical of American society, by the late 1950s a not-too-subtle shift had taken place as he used his theory to highlight what he considered to be the 'stabilizing features of Western society'. Moreover he was by then convinced that the United States was the leading model in the world of what constituted 'the good society'. By the 1950s Parsons had linked his own reputation and stature to that of the United States. As Alexander comments:

> You can easily understand, in light of the strong ideological links, that any significant change in the social environment of the post-war period would greatly affect the reception of Parsons' work. To put the connection crudely and simply, if the prestige of the United States were fundamentally challenged, if it looks less like a model for a good society, then the prestige of Parsons' own theorizing would falter. (Alexander, 1987, p. 13)

When Parsons first began to formulate his functionalist theory he did so within a social atmosphere of hope and belief that a new era had dawned on human social relations. The threat of Nazism had been broken by an alliance of capitalist and communist nations, bringing for many the hope of a future world without strife. In capitalist countries, glaring disparities between the social classes were softened somewhat by social welfare legislation.

Yet by the end of the 1950s, Americans were once again embroiled in class- and race-based conflicts. Developing World nations also began experiencing conflicts. By the 1960s, it was apparent that the American objective of spreading capitalist development in the so-called 'underdeveloped' nations was not going to be easily accomplished. Instead, these nations had become a source of instability and revolution, and not, as had been anticipated, the testing place for American ideals of democracy and economic progress.

During the 1950s and 1960s intellectual and philosophical critiques of Western ideologies and culture also began to appear. The beatniks and then the hippies criticized post-war society for holding up the ideals of individualism, democracy, and personal freedom while at the same time demanding conformity from its youth. Post-war youth, now relatively affluent and independent, were open to what the 'sensual, rebellious culture of rock-and-roll music' had to offer (Alexander, 1987, p. 16).

It can hardly come as a surprise that as early as the 1950s certain sociologists—prominent among them C. Wright Mills—had begun to criticize, not praise, Parsons. Mills wrote that functionalism was an example of a 'grand theory' that reflected the dominant values of American capitalism while failing to address the realities of the division of power in society. Parsons' theories, Mills argued, neglected to consider that the social consent necessary for the functioning of society might have been achieved through manipulation (Mills, 1959/2000, p. 232).

SOCIAL STRUCTURE AND AGENCY

While social structure is often said to exercise objective, external 'constraint' on the subjective experiences of individuals, agency is just as often treated as the unstructured expression of individual, subjective freedom. But just what might this mean? How might we think of the unstructured and free expression of human agency operating in tandem with the constraining, objective, and behaviour-determining force of social structure? Lave, Murtaugh, and de la Rocha's (1984) well-known study of supermarket shoppers provides one way for social scientists to think about the relationship between social structure and agency.

Shoppers and the Supermarket

Lave and associates (1988) set out to 'account for macro-social, political-economic structures'—those aspects of social life that individuals 'neither create nor negotiate directly but which somehow contribute to the public aspect of specific contexts' (Lave, Murtaugh, & de la Roche, 1984, p. 150). In short, they wanted to show how 'objective' social structures—or what Lave has elsewhere called 'macro-structural systems'—might affect the 'subjective' experiences (or agency) of individuals as they negotiate specific social situations. To illustrate the difference between objective social structures and subjective experiences, Lave and colleagues describe the contradiction between the abundance of choice found by a consumer on a trip to the supermarket and the consumer's need to actually make a choice from among all that abundance:

> The supermarket is thought of by consumers as a locus of abundant choices, for which the stock of thousands of items constitutes apparent evidence. But contradicting this view is a different order of circumstances: the shopper cannot provide food for the family if he leaves the supermarket empty-handed, due to attacks of indecision. That is, the shopper, faced with abundant alternatives, nonetheless cannot avoid making choices. Conversely, because the making of choices cannot be avoided, it is to the seller's advantage to proliferate decision criteria in the shopping setting. This contributes to the shopper's experience of abundant choices, helping to maintain the contradiction between choice and the necessity of choosing. This contradiction is not itself generally recognized, much less viewed as problematic, by shoppers. (Lave, Murtaugh, & de la Roche, 1984, pp. 79–80)

The consumer facing a bountiful array of choices is rarely aware that he must make *some* choice if he (and his family) is to eat. Moreover, the notion that there is a great deal of choice is only true in one sense. Indeed, there is an abundance of choices available to the urban consumer, either on the shelves of the local supermarket, or in the myriad of local speciality shops, convenience stores, and farmers' markets that are all easily available. However, in another very important sense, our shopper has very little choice at all. Few urban dwellers are able to choose among hunting and gathering, subsistence farming, and shopping at the local supermarket, farmer's market, or convenience store as their main means of putting food on the table. After all, how many twenty-first-century urban dwellers could realistically consider hunting their own game, apart perhaps fish from a local lake if they're fortunate enough to live by water? External, structural constraints make hunting virtually impossible as a choice.

In the case of our hypothetical shopper's trip to a supermarket to purchase the week's groceries, the trip itself is transient, while the supermarket is more durable and persistent. It was there—physically, socially, and temporally—before our hypothetical shopper arrived, and it remains there after he has completed his weekly grocery shopping 'experience'. It may well be the case that our shopper directly negotiates his individual experience of shopping in the supermarket of his choice, but he does not directly negotiate the social structures that give rise to the phenomenon of supermarket shopping.

Lave and associates make two related points about supermarkets and the experiences of those who shop in them. First, the supermarket business involves two well-differentiated categories

A store this large must offer plenty of choice, right? But what if this were your closest supermarket, and the next closest one was 5 kilometres away? Or what if you lived close to the store but didn't drive—how would that affect your choices? What if you were living on a fixed income?

social institution

Any complex form of social organization that combines a variety of social positions, norms, and values, and that organizes (relatively) stable forms of human social interaction with respect to such fundamental issues as the reproduction of individuals and of the conditions necessary to sustain life (Turner, 1997).

of individuals: shoppers and sellers. Second, the 'supermarket', as a **social institution**, is not controlled by a single individual. Sociologists consider social institutions to be among the 'more enduring features of social life' (Giddens, 1984, p. 31). The supermarket readily imposes itself on the individual shopper's experience, yet the individual shopper is relatively powerless to affect the overall organization of the supermarket. She must comply with well-established procedures for shopping. She chooses from among the goods available, pays for them at the appointed place, removes her groceries from the store, takes them home, and then prepares, serves, and consumes them all within rather strict guidelines. She cannot, for example, bring a propane camp stove with her on her trip to the grocery store, set it up in an aisle, choose food-stuffs from adjacent shelves, cook them on the spot, serve her family a meal, and then exit the store fully expecting that her cooking equipment and dirty dishes will be cleaned and packed up by the staff and sent back to her via the supermarket's delivery truck.

In Western societies there is clearly a strong ideological commitment to treat individual freedom (or *agency*) and social structure as competing or even opposing ideals (Hays, 1994, p. 59). A case in point is US president Barack Obama's recent struggle to pass a bill guaranteeing healthcare to most Americans. Many opponents of the bill are deeply concerned that the introduction of government-sponsored healthcare means the end of their freedom to choose their own doctor, and that universal healthcare will jeopardize their individual right to obtain a higher quality of healthcare for themselves than the state sees fit to offer on a general basis to all Americans. Yet at the same time that people in Western countries have idealized individual freedom, they have also placed considerable value on social order. Witness the strong desire (notably among the same Americans who are so vehemently opposed to socialized healthcare) to have the state act to control crime and punish offenders, or to regulate the individual's expression of sexuality (for example, by prohibiting gay marriages, and, until recently, banning homosexuals from the army).

But many sociologists think that social structure and social agency should not be used as conceptual opposites. For these sociologists, agency always operates within and through social structure. Any action an individual social actor might initiate is always initiated within the context of some set of social relations. Social structure is a pre-existing condition for human agency, but at the same time it is also the continually produced outcome of human agency (Bhaskar, 1989, p. 34). Two sociologists who have tried to theorize the interaction between social structure and social actors are Anthony Giddens and Pierre Bourdieu.

Anthony Giddens and Structuration Theory

social systems

Empirically observable, relatively bounded social practices that link social actors across time and space; examples include global capitalism, a society, a neighbourhood community, or a family.

Structures, says British sociologist Anthony Giddens (1984), are the '[r]ules and resources, recursively implicated in the reproduction of social systems'. By **social systems**, Giddens means the empirically observable, relatively bounded social practices that link social actors across time and space. Social systems include what we often call 'societies' but can also include other kinds of social units, such as global capitalism or, on a smaller scale, a neighbourhood community (Sewell, 1974, p. 6). When he describes rules and resources as 'recursively implicated' Giddens means that the social practices by which social systems are identified are repeatedly re-enacted.

Social structures, then, are the rules and resources that shape the everyday social practices—for example, the daily exchanges of passing neighbours or of school children with the crossing guard in a residential community—that are necessary for the reproduction of a social system (in this example, a neighbourhood community). The important point to remember about any social system is that it is never static. It is always emergent, the outcome of many people interacting simultaneously with one another, following a more-or-less commonly known set of rules and constrained by a common set of resources.

Giddens' **theory of structuration** unites social structure and agency into a single, ongoing process of dynamic interplay between the two elements of structure and agency. According to Giddens, social structures have a 'dual' nature; that is, they are 'both the medium and the outcome of the practices' that constitute them (Giddens, 1981, p. 27). This means that while social structures shape the actions of individuals, the actions of individuals (social systems), in turn, reproduce (or change) social structures; human agency and social structure, far from being oppositional, mutually constitute each other. A chance encounter between neighbours will produce an exchange of civilities—'Hello, how are you today? Hot enough for you?' The social structure guides the actions of these two individuals. If, though, during the course of their exchange they discover a mutual love of books and decide to set up a neighbourhood book club, they have acted independently to establish a new social system (i.e. a new, empirically observable, relatively bounded social practice that links them together across time and space), comprising five or six neighbours discussing a book every Wednesday night.

You will recall from the discussion in Chapter 6 how Max Weber noted that social actors often are stuck in a rut of routine action in bureaucracies, 'where life is constantly breathed into inert regulations which then deaden their animators through routinization' (Archer, 1988/1996, p. 86). Where Weber had little hope that the 'iron cage of bureaucracy' could ever

theory of structuration

A theory that views social structure and agency as two elements in a single, ongoing process of dynamic interplay, in which social structures shape the actions of individuals, while the actions of individuals reproduce or change social structures.

STUDIES IN SOCIAL RESEARCH

Social Structure and Agency in Student Essays

An example of the interplay of agency and social structure can be found in James Wertsch's (1998) study of college student essays on the topic 'The Origins of the United States'. Wertsch analyzed independently written essays by American college students and found that most students used a common cultural framework when asked to explain the motivations of the Americans who founded the United States. Most wrote in their essays that the founding events in American history were motivated by a quest for freedom.

In his analysis of these essays, Wertsch (1998) argues that this shared perspective is an indication of the extent to which cultural tools shape the actions of individuals. In the conclusion to his study he writes:

> One of the most striking facts about the texts [i.e. the student essays] is that all of them were fundamentally grounded in the quest-for-freedom narrative tool. No matter how much or how little the subject seemed to accept and

agree with this narrative tool, they used it in one way or another. . . . [Even] subjects [who] conveyed that they were resisting the quest-for-freedom narrative, in the end still employed it. In fact no student ever attempted to employ another narrative tool in any extended way. . . . In such cases, individuals may try to resist the ways in which such cultural tools shape their actions, but they are often highly constrained in the forms that such resistance can take. (Wertsch, 1998, pp. 107–8)

If we apply Anthony Giddens' theory of structuration to the example cited above, we end up with a kind of perpetual motion machine where the enactment by human social actors of the 'rules of social life' always creates resources that reinforce the rules. Agency draws on social structure, takes certain courses of action, and ends up reproducing the same social structure.

be opened and individuals set free, Anthony Giddens holds out the possibility of new practices appearing and of social change occurring. Unfortunately, Giddens fails to answer vexing questions such as, when can actors be transformative of social structure, and when are they compelled to repeat the 'same old, same old' routinized patterns?

Pierre Bourdieu and 'Habitus'

French sociologist and philosopher Pierre Bourdieu's work has had an enormous impact on sociology in North America. The son of a rural postman, Bourdieu (1930–2002) had an unusual career trajectory, serving as chair of the sociology department at the Collège de France and becoming a 'global public intellectual' whose work has helped to shape scholarship in many disciplines. He began his academic career as a philosopher, before being drafted into the French army during the Algerian War for Independence during the late 1950s. While in the army, Bourdieu conducted his first major study on the experiences of the Kabyle of Algeria as a colonized people. One of his most important works, *Outline of a Theory of Practice* (1972), which he later revised and expanded as *The Logic of Practice* (1980), draws on his study of the Kabyle and offers a theory of social structure and social action that is more complex than Giddens' structuration theory.

Bourdieu became a sociologist not through formal training but through engaging with the work of American sociologists. A friend of Erving Goffman, he translated the Canadian sociologist's works and the work of other North American sociologists into French. Bourdieu was particularly interested in American sociology as a means of breaking out of the 'anti-scientific bent of the French academic field', and he developed his own conceptual systems through sustained empirical research. Yet he was also quite critical of the often mediocre and dry empiricism that he found in much of mainstream American sociology (Postone, LiPuma, & Calhoun, 1993, pp. 1–13; Sallaz & Zavisca, 2007, p. 22).

Bourdieu developed an influential account of human social behaviour, centred around the concept of **habitus,** the intentional but, nonetheless, socially constrained disposition of an individual social actor to act in a certain way and to make a certain kind of sense out of the social world:

> The notion of habitus restores to the agent a generating, unifying, constructing, classifying power, while recalling that this capacity to construct social reality, itself socially constructed, is not that of a transcendental subject but of a socialized body, investing in its practice socially constructed organizing principles that are acquired in the course of a situated and dated social experience. (Bourdieu, 2000a, pp. 136–7)

Social actors are automatically conditioned as a result of the opportunities, necessities, and demands inherent in their social positions. This conditioning, Bourdieu further argues, tends to 'generate dispositions objectively compatible with these conditions and in a sense pre-adapted to their demands' (Bourdieu, 1990b, p. 54). In many ways this conditioning is similar to the concept of socialization that we took up in chapters 8 and 9. Bourdieu maintained that it is particularly powerful in early life as it generates 'a durable attitude toward the world (the primary habitus) that motivates us to see the world in the terms dictated to us by our early social position, and to behave in the ways more or less mandated to us by that position' (Bourdieu, 1990b, p. 53).

habitus
The intentional but, nonetheless, socially constrained disposition of an individual social actor to act a certain way and to make a certain kind of sense out of the social world.

Everyone who is exposed to a similar set of 'opportunities and necessities' tends to develop a similar habitus, and their social practices tend to be 'objectively harmonized without any calculation or conscious reference to a norm and mutually adjusted in the absence of any direct interaction or, a fortiori, explicit co-ordination' (Bourdieu, 1990b, pp. 58–9). In other words, without meaning to, people in shared social positions will develop more-or-less similar ways of viewing their social setting. This does not mean that they all must behave exactly the same way all the time; rather, the concept of habitus takes into account humans' capacity for structured improvisation in their social dealings with each other. But, while the habitus is the outcome of social conditioning, it isn't rigidly determined by social conditioning. It is for this reason that Bourdieu says the habitus *disposes* us to behave in ways that tend to reproduce existing social practices, and thus to reproduce the existing structure of society (Elder-Vass, 2007, p. 327).

For example, an essential part of the social conditioning involved in learning to be either masculine or feminine results in males and females acquiring different dispositions towards

Describe the social structure shown here. Is it natural or deliberate? Is it typical of this kind of social situation? If the body postures and placements were reversed—if, for instance, the man were seated on the couch in this position with the woman perched on the ottoman—would it appear more or less natural?

acts such as 'walking, talking, standing, looking, sitting, etc.' (Bourdieu, 2000b, pp. 141–3). This is not to say that all men of a given society will always walk, sit, and stand in a strictly determined way if presented with the same circumstance; only that the habitus disposes them to certain behaviours. To illustrate how this works, Bourdieu drew on his research on the Kabyle people of Algeria (indigenous peoples of North Africa, called the Moors by medieval and early modern Europeans), who make up about 40 per cent of that country's population. Fundamental to Kabyle culture are several important oppositions, including male/female and high/low, as well as others such as fire/water and light/dark (Bourdieu, 1977, p. 91; Sewell, 1995, p. 14). Kabyle women (female), Bourdieu observed, maintain a bowed comportment (lower), a bodily manifestation of a habitus appropriate to their subordinate status in Kabyle society.

Elder-Vass offers this clarification of Bourdieu's theory: social structures are not 'literally internalized by individuals, but only metaphorically so, through the influence they have on our subjectivity'. Sometimes, he adds, we are able to 'critically evaluate and thus modify our dispositions in the light of our experiences, our reasoning capacities, and our value commitments' (Elder-Vass, 2007, p. 345). So, for example, a Kabyle woman who occupied an important role in her society might be disposed to walk straight, and other members of her society would not find that unseemly behaviour.

An analogy of how social structures are internalized can be made to the accent we all have when we speak any language (whether it's maternal or acquired in later life). It is our disposition to form our mouths into specific shapes that creates certain accents, and we are rarely conscious either of learning to do this or of actually doing it while we speak. Yet the accent we produce when we speak reflects our social origins (Thompson, 1992, p. 17, as cited in Elder-Vass, 2007, p. 327). In the same way, the conditioning of our cultural dispositions is so effective that these cultural dispositions usually remain below the level of consciousness and are often embedded in our physical bodies, having been 'internalized as a second nature and so forgotten as history' (Bourdieu, 1990b, p. 56). The socially influenced dispositions and beliefs that make up the habitus contribute to the reproduction of social structure by supplying us with a range of behaviours that might be activated depending on the situation (Bourdieu, 2000a, p. 149).

SOCIAL NETWORK ANALYSIS

social network analysis
A mathematical method used by sociologists for describing the patterns of social relations among and between individuals, groups, or other social collectivities.

Social network analysis is a promising development in the study of social structure, spurred on in recent years by advancements in computing that have made it possible to analyze large-scale electronic data sets (Watts, 2004, p. 243). It is a mathematical method used by sociologists for describing the patterns of social relations among and between individuals, groups, or other social collectivities. Although it is technically sophisticated, social network analysis has been useful in a wide range of applications. A network can be defined as a set of 'nodes' (technically called 'vertices') and the links between those nodes. The structure of social networks is of interest to sociologists and other social scientists. They provide a visual representation of social structure, and they give an interesting and often instructive view of how individual agency is structured in relation to the agency of other individuals that make up the network.

The metaphor of a social network was introduced through the work of one of the first-generation German sociologists, Georg Simmel (1858–1918). Simmel, who wrote about (among other things) the influence of the city on intellectual life, emphasized the complex interrelationships of parts making up a whole. Beginning in the 1930s, social scientists began to pay attention to the metaphor of social life as a web or interlocking/interwoven fabric that produced a certain structure that in turn organized social life. Social psychologist Jacob Moreno introduced the idea of representing a **social network** as a diagram, with points representing people, and lines representing their social relations.

In the 1950s and 1960s, British social anthropologists John Barnes (1954), Elizabeth Bott (1957), and Clyde Mitchell (1969) all used the idea of social networks in their research. But the most important advancements in network analysis came from a number of sociologists at Harvard University. During the 1970s, Harvard sociologists Harrison White, Scott Boorman, and Ronald Breiger (1976) used the network metaphor to map a variety of social ties existing between members of a population. In doing so they produced different 'block models' of social networks, each serving as a 'picture' of a concrete social structure.

In social network analysis, individuals are treated as the *nodes* of a network structure that are all tied together via some specified connection. These ties have attributes such as strength, frequency, and duration. An absence of ties indicates lack of integration of a node with the rest of the network.

In network analysis:

- Social structure is conceived of as a network of networks.
- The whole pattern of direct and indirect relations between social actors, who might be individuals, firms, or groups, constrains not only the actors' behaviour but also social relations and clusters.
- It is the relations among the nodes of a network, rather than the individual social actors or their attributes, that provide the units of analysis and observation.
- As the whole pattern of relations is relevant, ego-centred (i.e. individual-centred) networks are not the main objects of consideration (Segre, 2004, p. 226; Wellman, 1983).

Network analysis is not a cohesive or unified theory of social structure. Those who use network analysis reject 'explanations of social behavior as the result of individuals' common possession of attributes and norms' and choose instead to view social behaviour as the result of an individual's involvement in structured social relations (Wellman, 1983, p. 165). Individual attributes such as class membership, class consciousness, political party affiliation, age, gender, social status, religious beliefs, ethnicity, sexual orientation, and psychological predispositions are not sufficient, in themselves, to explain why people behave the way they do (Emirbayer & Goodwin, 1994, p. 1415). From the network analysis perspective, individual behaviour must be explained with reference to the networks of social relations that link actors or 'nodes'. The relations between and among the nodes are understood as existing independent of the social actors' beliefs, values, or will. The relations differentially allocate scarce resources—for example, jobs, membership in a club or an ethnic or religious group, income, access to medical care—to the members of a network (Wellman, 1983, p. 176).

In the last decade or so, and especially with the growth of the World Wide Web, social networks have emerged as a frequent and widespread topic of discussion and analysis. Powerful computer software has made it possible to integrate information not just about individual nodes but also about their relationships. With new and extensive data sets and the computing power to analyze them, it is now possible to ask and answer questions about complex social relationships that sociologists were previously unable to address.

social network
A set of individuals or 'nodes' (technically called 'vertices') and the links between them.

Try sketching out some of the possible social networks of this Canadian university student. Consider family, friends, univerity contacts, and others. Try to imagine how some of those relations affect the way she thinks, behaves, and acts.

THE 'GREYING' OF THE CANADIAN POPULATION

A significant structural change that is affecting the Canadian population as a whole is the change taking place in the Canadian age pyramid. From 2001 to 2006 the number of Canadians aged 65 and older increased 11.5 per cent, while the number of children under age 15 declined by 2.5 per cent. The 65-and-older population made up a record 13.7 per cent of the total Canadian population in 2006, while the population under age 15 years fell to 17.7 per cent, its lowest level ever (Statistics Canada, 2006b).

The implications of Canada's 'greying' population are extensive. While Canada has experienced an increase in immigration since 2001, it has not slowed down the aging of the population overall. In 2006, Canada had 1.2 million people aged 80 years and over, nearly two-thirds of them women. The number of people aged 100 years and older increased by more than 22 per cent after 2001, bringing the number of centenarians in Canada to 4,634 in 2006; population projections indicate that by 2031 the number will triple.

There are two factors in particular contributing to the aging of the Canadian population. The first is the baby boom, which began in the late 1940s, following World War II, when young men and women were able to settle into family life and begin producing children. 'Baby boomers' are people born between 1946 and 1965, when the birth rate fell off sharply. You can see the graphic representation of this boom-and-bust cycle of child-bearing in Canada in Figure 11.1, which shows age pyramids of Canada for 1951, 1981, and 2011. If you look at that figure you'll be able to see the wave of population growth of the 1940s and 1950s represented at the bottom of the pyramid for 1951, which moves its way up the pyramid in 1981 and further still in 2011. Statistics Canada projections suggest that by 2016, the number of children under 15 could be outnumbered by the number of adults over 65. The year 2011 is when the first of the baby boomer generation turned 65, so while the growth of the elderly population has been relatively modest up to that point, it will now continue to accelerate as more baby boomers achieve their senior years.

With the exception of the baby boom years, the overall birth rate in Canada has been declining for over a century. This is a trend that is typical of industrialized countries. As more and more children survive to adulthood, fewer children are born. This is because in industrialized societies, unlike agrarian ones, children no longer contribute to their families' economic well-being but instead become an expense. In addition, as women become more educated, and as *patriarchy*—the subjugation of women to the control of men—declines, more women in industrial societies are able to make career choices that do not focus on birthing and raising children. The widespread availability of safe, reliable birth control for women has contributed extensively to their liberation from control by male relatives.

A second factor contributing to the changing structure of Canada's age pyramid has been a remarkable increase in life expectancy. While Canadian women born in 1900 could expect to live to about age 50 and men to about age 47, life expectancy for Canadian women today is over 83 years and for men over 76 years. A rising standard of living has promoted longer life and better health across the entire population. Statistics Canada projects that the proportion of seniors in the Canadian population will have doubled between 2006 and 2031 while the proportion of children will continue to fall. If these demographic changes occur as projected they will have a major impact on the Canadian economy and on Canadian society in general. The Canadian labour force, publicly funded pensions, and publicly funded healthcare will all be affected.

As an increasing number of Canadians reach age 65 they will also live longer on average than Canadians at any other point in our country's history. Immigration to Canada has had an important effect on both the growth and the diversity of the Canadian population and has contributed towards meeting Canada's labour force requirements. However its impact on

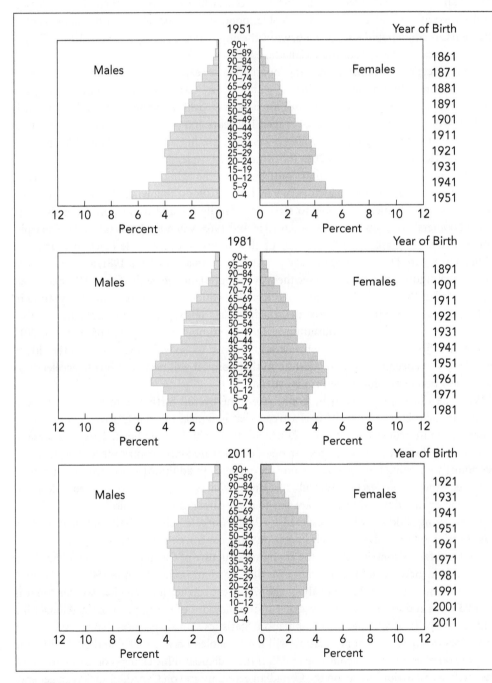

FIGURE 11.1 Age pyramids for Canada, 1951, 1981, 2011

Source: Adapted from Statistics Canada, 1992. *Report on the demographic situations in Canada.* Catalogue no. 91-209.

population aging has been minor. This is because the average age of immigrants to Canada is about 30, and once they arrive they continue to age along with the rest of the population. So while an increase in immigration since 2001 has given Canada a higher rate of population growth, it has not slowed down the aging of the Canadian population. Thus, the median age of the Canadian population (the age that divides the Canadian population into two equal groups) has been steadily rising since 1966. In 2006 the median age was 39.5 years, an increase of almost 2 years from 2001. Statistics Canada projects that the median age of the Canadian population could reach 44 years or more by 2031.

The *working-age population* of Canada is considered to consist of those people between the ages of 15 and 64. In 2006, about 21.7 million Canadians were in the working population. Of all the age groups between 15 and 64 years, the group aged 55–64 grew the fastest between 2001 and 2006, by 28 per cent. This is almost double the rate of growth experienced by the same segment of the working population between 1996 and 2001. About one potential worker

Cuts to seniors' pensions have led many retired seniors to return to the workforce to take up retail and other jobs traditionally held by young people and students. Is this a postive change? Are there any drawbacks? Is Canada's retirement age of 65 too low? How does the label 'senior' for anyone over 65—regardless of how active or capable of working they are—affect our perception of old age?

in six in Canada was between the ages of 55 and 64 in 2006; by 2016, this age category will make up about 20 per cent of the working-age population, or one in five Canadian workers. In general Canadians retire between the ages of 55 and 64; Statistics Canada predicts that by 2016 there will be more people at the age where they can leave the workforce than at the age where they can begin working.

Despite the fact that the baby boomers are aging, they remain the largest population group in Canada. Nearly one out of every three Canadians alive today was born between 1946 and 1965. People born between 1975 and 1995—children of the baby boomers—are considered the 'echo boom'. In 2006 they were between the ages of 11 and 31 and represented 27.5 per cent of all Canadians. Members of the cohort made up of parents of the baby boomers (people born between 1922 and 1938) were between 68 and 84 years of age in 2006. When we take a look at the relative size of the baby boomers' cohort compared with the cohorts of their parents and their children, a number of life cycle issues become apparent. For example, while it is reasonable to assume that the baby boomers' parents' generation, who made up the majority of seniors in 2006, will have several children to rely on for support and companionship in their declining years, things will most likely be very different for the baby boomers. Many baby boomers are 'sandwiched' between the needs of their aging parents and the demands of their children, many of whom still live at home, attend institutions of higher learning, or are unable to find jobs. Moreover, because baby boomers typically limited their fertility more than their parents did, they can expect to have fewer children to rely on in their old age.

The Social Networks of Elderly Canadians

Aging is a complex process that involves adapting to physical as well as social changes, including changes to one's life circumstances. How well individuals are able to adapt depends heavily on the personal and social resources available to them. As people age and live out their later years of life in declining health, faced with chronic illnesses such as cancer, diabetes, lung disease, arthritis, and various forms of dementia, their ability to access resources, as well as their independent capacity to use those resources, often declines.

social capital
Resources developed over time through trust and through the norms of reciprocity amongst members of any given social network, used as a concept by sociologists to help them understand the role of social ties between members of the social network, especially as those ties affect the quality of life of network members.

Social capital, a concept introduced by Pierre Bourdieu, is often used by sociologists to help them understand the role of social ties between members of a social network, especially as those ties affect the quality of life of network members. Social capital can be defined as resources, such as access to government funding, knowledge about where to go to get social services, information about or access to the best schools and daycare centres, and the like, that are developed over time through trust and through the norms of reciprocity amongst members of any given social network. These resources are there for the mutual benefit of the members of the network and can be called upon by individual members when they are in need. By mapping out the connection between members of many different social networks, sociologists have discovered that all networks have certain structural features in common that include the connections among members of any given network, and the connections that some members of a network provide by virtue of being linked into different networks.

bonding social capital
Social capital that reflects relations within a social network.

Sociologists have identified two different types of social capital: bonding social capital and bridging social capital. **Bonding social capital** reflects relations within a social network. The members of a network have strong and often intimate ties to each other. Such ties are well suited to provide for the social and psychological needs of their members and to manage their members' day-to-day activities. Families are an example of a social network tied together through bonding capital. There are strong, intimate ties among family members who spend considerable time with each other, have emotionally intense relationships, and mutually confide in each other. Network members with bonding social capital ties generally expect reciprocal services from each other and share a strong sense of mutual identity (Kavanaugh, et al., 2005, and Reimer, et al., 2008, as cited in Keating & Dosman, 2009).

In contrast, **bridging social capital** is based on weak ties among network members and is better suited to providing access to external resources and information than it is to providing emotional support. Networks made up of friends and neighbours, for example, can be used to provide members with links to community support services, and these types of networks occupy structural positions different to the more intimate networks based on family ties in that the connections they offer members are often more discretionary and individualistic.

bridging social capital
Social capital that is based on weak ties among network members and is better suited to providing access to external resources and information than it is to providing emotional support.

Norah Keating and Donna Dosman (2009) used Bourdieu's concept of social capital to analyze how the families and friends of frail Canadian seniors provide them with care. They undertook an extensive analysis of survey data in order to better understand the structure of social networks of elderly Canadians and how different networks affect the kind of social capital that can be mobilized by elderly, frail network members. Keating and Dosman employed a quantitative research strategy, drawing a sample of 2,407 adults aged 65 and older from the Statistics Canada 2002 General Social Survey on Aging and Social Support who indicated that they had received care from family or friends in the previous 12 months because of long-term health problems or disabilities. As the authors explain, '*Care networks* were operationalized as all family members and/or friends that the respondents said had provided them with help with one or more task in the previous 12 months because of their long-term health problem or disability' (Keating & Dosman, 2009, p. 306). Formal care was operationalized as 'all care provided to the respondent by individuals and nongovernmental organizations, paid employee, or government employee'.

As a result of their research Keating and Dosman were able to identify six care network types. The first three types are based on family ties:

- *the lone spouse*—a husband or wife living alone with a frail spouse
- *children at home*—employed adult, middle-aged children living at home with an elder parent
- *spouse and children*—adult children and a spouse who either live with or in close proximity to the frail adult.

Together these three close family care network types comprise 25 per cent of all care network types (Keating & Dosman, 2009, p. 307).

The second grouping of network care types is based on a broader set of members and includes both family and friends (Keating & Dosman, 2009, p. 309):

- *close kin and friends*—mostly kin (relatives), with some friends who are middle-aged and often employed
- *older diverse*—networks made up largely of older friends (65+) with a few close and/or distant kin
- *younger diverse*—a mix of distant kin and friends aged 45 years or younger.

Describe the care network represented in this photo. Which of Keating and Dosman's types do you think it represents? Which kind of social capital—bonding or bridging— is involved?

The older diverse networks are made up of relatives and friends, most of them over the age of 65, highlighting the presence of same-generation caregivers. Close kin and friend networks are mostly kin with a small portion of middle-aged, unemployed friends. Younger diverse networks are a mix of distant relatives and friends who are middle-aged and younger. Together these three broader-based network types made up 71 per cent of all the care network types Keating and Dosman identified.

These six networks differed considerably in the hours of care that network members were able to provide to a frail, elderly member. The three close family networks provided the highest numbers of hours of care (10–18 hours per week). These networks are close-knit, and most are made up of adult children and spouses who have high normative obligations to give care, and who live with the person requiring care. In contrast, friend and family networks provided between three and seven hours of care per week. In these networks most of the day-to-day care was provided by close kin, while friends provided connections to resources outside the network (Keating & Dosman, 2009, p. 309).

Keating and Dosman's findings indicate that it's not just having connections to relatives that matters when it comes to being able to access bonding social capital. It is close kin who provide frail, elderly Canadians with the key resources they need to get by on a day-to-day basis. But networks consisting only of close relatives were the least likely to provide bridging connections to formal services for the elderly. Networks based on close, nuclear family relationships provided strong, committed care even in the face of limited formal help. But networks that contained more distant kin as well as friends provided the best links to formal community resources. Frail, elderly adults who are members of these types of networks were more likely to receive formal services than were elderly persons whose networks contain only close family members (Keating & Dosman, 2009, p. 312). Recent research indicates that in these situations tensions can emerge between family caregivers over equity in caregiving and these tensions can exacerbate problems in family relationships, even resulting in bitter court battles (312).

In comparison, frail, elderly adults who have social networks with predominantly weak kin ties get linked into formal services much more quickly, because the members of these networks lack the close emotional commitment that is usually required to assume primary responsibility in the ongoing work of caring for frail, elderly adults. By contrast, in family-dominated networks, where there are close ties of kinship and the attending obligations, family members may delay the search for formal help, reluctant to ask for assistance for tasks that they believe they should do themselves. This reluctance to seek professional help, however, may be to the detriment of the elderly person who needs support. Keating and Dosman conclude that while patterns of connections among members of networks of older adults may indeed have positive outcomes for their elderly members, there is also powerful evidence to suggest that 'bonding has its costs'.

For Canadian seniors, having a network that includes *both* strong family ties and ties to friends and neighbours appears to be the best way of gaining access to the kinds of help needed in old age. The different kinds of social relations provided by 'bonding' and 'bridging' networks allow elderly Canadians different ways to realize social capital: close family members provide high levels of care, while distant relatives, friends, and neighbours provide a means to gain access to formal services beyond those needed for day-to-day living.

SUMMARY

Social structure and social agency are two core sociological concepts. Social structure denotes the systematic patterns of organization that shape social life, while social agency is an individual's capacity for action. Sociologists are interested in understanding the links between an individual's capacity for action and the social structures that help to shape the ways an individual can or will act.

Some sociologists favour studying social structure, while others concentrate on agency. Karl Marx was one of the first to offer a comprehensive analysis of social structure. He was followed by others who were likewise interested in social structure but rejected much of what Marx had to say as being too politically motivated. Structural functionalists, led by Talcott Parsons, dominated American sociology from the 1930s to the 1960s, arguing that society was like a biological organism, made up of different, interrelated structures all functioning together to contribute to the society's survival. In the 1980s, British sociologist Anthony Giddens focused on social systems—empirically observable, relatively bounded social practices linking social actors across time and space—including such diverse social units as societies, global capitalism, and neighbourhood communities. Giddens' theory of structuration united social structure and agency into a single, ongoing, dynamic interplay between the two elements.

The work of French sociologist Pierre Bourdieu continues to be relevant for sociologists in North America. Bourdieu developed an influential account of human social behaviour centred on the concept of 'habitus', the intentional but nonetheless socially constrained disposition of an individual social actor to act a certain way and to make a certain kind of sense out of the social world. Social capital, another important concept introduced by Pierre Bourdieu, is often used by sociologists to help them understand the role of social ties between members of a social network, especially as those ties affect the quality of life of network members. Social network analysis is a mathematical method used by sociologists for describing the patterns of social relations among and between individuals, groups, or other social collectivities. Although technically sophisticated, social network analysis is useful in a wide range of applications. The structure of social networks is of interest to sociologists because it provides a visual representation of social structure and gives an interesting and often instructive view of how the agency of one individual is structured in relation to the agency of others who make up a specific social network.

Finally, recent research has examined the 'greying' of the Canadian population, a significant structural change. It is taking place in the Canadian population as a whole and has extensive effects on, and implications for, all Canadians.

DISCUSSION QUESTIONS

1. Construct a structural-functionalist analysis of four or five different social structures (e.g. the family).
2. What are the differences between Marx's view of human society and a structural-functionalist view?
3. Discuss what is meant by the term 'social structure'. Discuss what is meant by the term 'agency'. Provide examples.

4. Use the example of a doctor's office, a university classroom, a restaurant, and/or a shopping mall to discuss the relationship between social structure and agency. In what ways might Giddens' theory of structuration help explain the interplay between agency and structure?

5. Explain Bourdieu's concept of habitus. Use concrete examples drawing from your everyday experiences to illustrate your explanation.

6. Discuss the differences between 'bridging social capital' and 'bonding social capital'. Use concrete examples from your everyday experiences to illustrate your answer.

7. What are some of the implications that you might have to face as a result of the 'greying' of the Canadian population?

12 Social Stratification, Inequality, and Class

CHAPTER OUTLINE

LEARNING OBJECTIVES

In this chapter you will:

- gain a clearer understanding of social inequality in Canada
- analyze issues of social stratification
- study different ways that sociologists use the concept of social class
- reflect on poverty in Canada
- come to understand wealth inequality in Canada
- compare Marx and Weber's approach to social class
- explore the role of social status among prison inmates
- think about the rise of the 'middle class'.

INTRODUCTION

When asked to indicate their social class from among the choices of lower, middle, and upper, most Canadians will choose middle. But Canadian society is anything but egalitarian, and many Canadians do not enjoy the privileges that are commonly thought to go along with being a member of the middle class.

When Canadians do acknowledge inequality, they often think in terms of a single dimension, usually income or wealth. But social inequality in Canada occurs on many different dimensions.

The concept of **social inequality** is used by sociologists to describe how certain attributes that are deemed to be valuable (e.g. wealth, income, education, prestige, occupation, health, life chances) are unevenly distributed across such organizational units as societies, social classes, communities, families, and individuals, and are affected by such factors as race, gender, physical ability, sexual orientation, and age. Sociologists speak of **socioeconomic status** as a composite measure of an individual's social standing that includes a number of these dimensions.

Persistent patterns of inequality in a society are indicative of **social stratification**. Social stratification refers to the organization of members of a given society into hierarchically ranked layers, or 'strata'. When sociologists study social stratification and the social inequality it entails, they seek to explain why valuable attributes are distributed unequally among the members of a society, as well as the consequences of that distribution.

A common-sense perspective on inequality and stratification is that it is the direct result of differences in individual effort, temperament, and/or abilities. According to this view, two individuals pursuing the same occupation, for example, may easily end up with very different amounts of income as a result of differences in individual efforts. As Eric Olin Wright (1994) explains:

> The paradigm case would be two farmers on the adjacent plots of land: one works hard and conscientiously, the other is lazy and irresponsible. At the end of the production cycle one has twice the income of the other. . . . The conscientious farmer saves and reinvests part of the income earned during the first cycle and thus expands production; a lazy farmer does not have anything left over to invest and thus continues production at the same level. (26)

Eventually the conscientious farmer's holdings increase to the point where he must employ others to help him work his farm, while the lazy farmer, having wasted his resources, is unable to support even himself adequately and must go to work for the conscientious farmer as a wage labourer.

Many sociologists, however, are not content to understand social inequalities in the distribution of material wealth and other valuable attributes in this way, or to analyze the resulting hierarchy of social stratification on a case-by-case basis. They look to social-structural causes and not, as in the example above, to differences in personal character, to explain widespread differences. Social forces such as parents' social class, race and/or ethnicity, gender, and sexual orientation are thought by sociologists to exert powerful effects on an individual's life chances and experiences, and are considered to affect social stratification independent of the will, or the conscious understanding, of the individuals involved.

social inequality
A concept used by sociologists to describe how certain attributes deemed to be valuable (e.g. wealth, education, occupation, health, life chances) are unevenly distributed across societies, social classes, communities, families, and individuals, and are affected by socioeconomic status.

socioeconomic status
(SES)
A composite measure of a person's social standing based on a combination of income, education, and occupational prestige rankings.

social stratification
The system by which members of a given society are organized into hierarchically ranked layers, or 'strata'.

When it comes to analyzing issues of social stratification based on inequalities in the distribution of material wealth, social class is among the most discussed theoretical concepts in all of sociology. Sociologists share a common assumption that the concept of social class can be used to construct theories about observable patterns in social behaviour. The concept of social class, they believe, can go a long way to help us explain social stratification and inequalities in the distribution of material resources regardless of what individual members of any given society think about their class position, or even if they understand the social influences that affect their lives. American sociologists H. Gerth and C. Wright Mills (1954/1964) sum up this general application of a sociological imagination to understanding the effects of social class:

> No matter what people believe, class structure as an economic arrangement influences their life chances according to their positions in it. If they do not grasp the cause of their conduct this does not mean that the social analyst must ignore or deny them. (Gerth & Mills, 1954/1964, p. 340)

How would a sociologist use a sociological imagination to understand the root causes of this man's situation? Idleness? Alcoholism? Poor life choices? Childhood abuse? Carelessness with money? Mental illness? Something else? Which of these fit the common-sense perspective? What might be some of the social-structural causes that a sociologist could examine?

Because of the significance of the concept of social class to sociological analyses, it should not be surprising that the concept is used in many different ways and has a wide variety of meanings. Two of the earliest and most influential sociologists to offer insights into how we should conceptualize social class and how it might help in explaining inequalities and social stratification were Karl Marx and Max Weber, whose work we first encountered in Chapter 6. Their ideas continue to bear on many of today's debates on social stratification and inequality in general, and on social class as an economic arrangement in particular, although much of what they originally wrote has been extensively reinterpreted by contemporary sociologists.

This chapter begins with a discussion of social inequalities in the distribution of income and other indicators of material wealth as a social-structural rather than an individual issue. Sociologists have linked inequalities in income (as well as inequalities connected with gender, race and other social indicators) to social class. We then return to the work of Karl Marx and Max Weber by way of addressing social stratification and inequality as societal characteristics rather than individual ones. The next chapter, Chapter 13, expands the discussion to include more contemporary approaches to the analysis of social inequalities, hierarchies, and social class among members of contemporary societies. Later on, you will also be introduced to an ongoing debate around the question *Does social class matter?*

INCOME INEQUALITY IN CANADA

In relation to other countries in the world, Canada can be counted among the wealthy, as Figure 12.1 shows. Yet there are many Canadians who find it difficult to purchase even the basic necessities of life, making poverty one of the 'great unresolved and often overlooked social issues confronting Canadians' (Duffy & Mandell, 2011, p. 125). But just how many Canadians experience poverty? In the midst of so much wealth (relative to most other countries in the world), are income inequality and poverty issues that Canadians need to be concerned about? Aren't they things that governments are 'taking care of'?

The Poverty Line

low-income cutoffs (LICOs)
A set of income thresholds, varying according to community type and family size, used to determine whether a family of specified size and place of residence earns enough to contribute the share of income that the average family devotes to necessities such as food, shelter, and clothing.

As critical-thinking sociologists, one of the first issues we should attend to in order to answer these questions is the concept of poverty and how it is actually defined. In Canada the official measure of poverty is the low-income cutoff, unofficially called the 'poverty line' (see Figure 12.2).

According to Statistics Canada **low-income cutoffs** (or **LICOs**) are 'income thresholds, determined by analyzing family expenditure data, below which families will devote a larger share of income to the necessities of food, shelter and clothing than the average family would'. Notice that the term is plural: not just one but several LICOs are calculated to account for differences in the cost of necessities depending on type of community (e.g. urban or rural) and size of family. LICOs are defined for five categories of community size and seven categories of family size. So, for example, in 2007, for a family of four living in an urban community with a population between 30,000 and 99,999, the LICO was $28,352. A family of four living in, say, Lethbridge, Alberta, with a combined household income (after taxes) of less than $28,352 would be considered poor. For comparison, the 2007 LICO for a single person living in an urban area of the same size was $11,745 (Statistics Canada, 2008a)

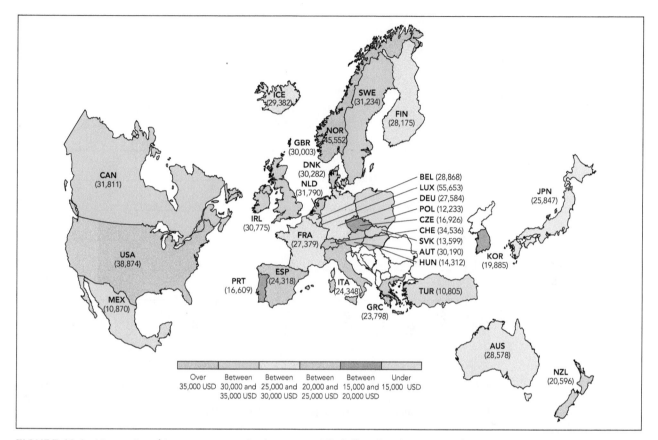

Over 35,000 USD	Between 30,000 and 35,000 USD	Between 25,000 and 30,000 USD	Between 20,000 and 25,000 USD	Between 15,000 and 20,000 USD	Under 15,000 USD

FIGURE 12.1   Net national income per capita in current US dollars (USD) using purchasing power parity (PPP) in 2006
Source: Adapted from *Society at a glance 2009: OECD social-indicators*—OECD © 2009.

In 2007, a total of 2,952,000 individuals (637,000 of them children), representing a little over 9 per cent of the Canadian population, had annual incomes that put them below the Statistics Canada LICO. Most high school and post-secondary students who have worked during the summer or during the school year have first-hand knowledge that the Canadian economy includes numerous low-paid jobs that are not just filled by part-time student workers. In 2004, for example, one in seven full-time employees (1.4 million workers) were paid less than $10 per hour.

International Comparisons

Among similarly industrialized countries, Canada has one of the highest proportions of low-paid workers, with totals higher than European countries and similar to the American rate (LaRochelle-Côté & Dionne, 2009, p. 5). In order to make comparisons between different nations, the OECD has defined low-paid workers as the proportion of full-year, full-time workers who fall below two-thirds of the country's median earnings (OECD, 1996, 1998; as cited in LaRochelle-Côté & Dionne, 2009, p. 6). Canada and the US share the dubious honour of having the highest proportion of low-paid workers among 12 comparable industrialized countries. In both Canada and the US, nearly one-quarter of workers earned less than two-thirds of the median annual earnings in 2000 and again in 2004. Finland had the lowest proportion of low-paid workers, at 7.1 per cent (see Figure 12.3).

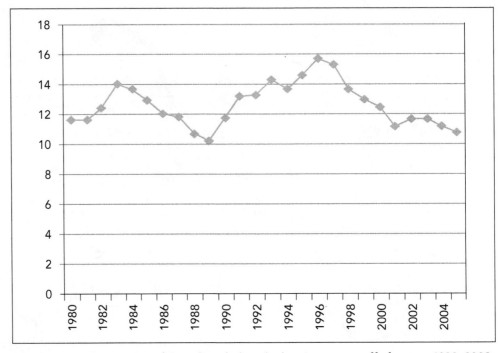

FIGURE 12.2 **Percentage of Canadians below the low-income cutoff after tax, 1980–2009**

Source: Data from Statistics Canada tables 'Persons in low income after tax, 2000 to 2004', retrieved from www40.statcan.gc.ca/l01/cst01/famil19b-eng.htm, and 'Persons in low income after tax, 2005 to 2009', retrieved from www40.statcan.gc.ca/l01/cst01/famil19a-eng.htm.

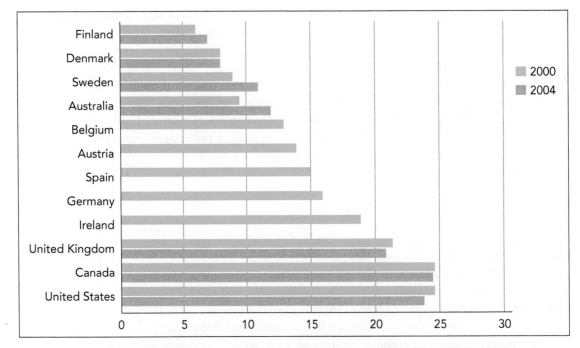

FIGURE 12.3 **International differences in the percentage of low-paid workers, 2000, 2004**

Source: Statistics Canada, 'International differences in low-paid work,' *Perspectives on labour and income*, 75-001-XWE2009106, vol. 10, no. 6, June 2009; http://www.statcan.gc.ca/bsolc/olc-cel/olc-cel?lang=eng&catno=75-001-x.

Child and Family Poverty in Canada

In Canada, child poverty numbers have not improved since 1989, the year the House of Commons unanimously passed a resolution to end child poverty in Canada within a decade; during this time, the federal government has neither adopted an anti-poverty strategy nor undertaken any comprehensive action to address the issue. In 2007, 2.9 million Canadians lived in poverty, more than half-a-million of them children (National Council of Welfare, 2009a). And between 2002 and 2007, around 1.4 million Canadian children lived in poverty for at least one of those six years (National Council of Welfare, 2009b).

Moreover, census data show that poverty rates for certain groups of children are much higher than the average rate. Immigrant children are almost three times more likely to experience poverty than Canadian-born children. Poverty rates calculated for children less than 15 years of age in 2005 show that 33 per cent of immigrant children, compared to 12 per cent of Canadian-born children, lived in poverty.

Among immigrants to Canada, the most recent immigrants had the highest poverty rate of all—39 per cent compared to 19 per cent for those who had arrived between 1991 and 1995. Aboriginal children living off reserves had a poverty rate of 28 per cent; when all Aboriginal children are taken into consideration (i.e. those living both on and off reserves), that rate rises to 34 per cent. Among visible minority children, the highest poverty rates are seen for Koreans (48 per cent), West Asians (44 per cent), Arabs (43 per cent), and blacks (36 per cent). The lowest rates were for Filipino children (12 per cent) and Japanese children (18 per cent) (National Council of Welfare, 2009a).

Poverty rates also vary significantly by family type. Figure 21.4 shows the distribution of household types of people who used food banks in 2011, according to Food Banks Canada's 2011 report, *HungerCount*. As the figure shows, 26.1 per cent of all households using food banks were single-parent families, while 22.9 per cent were two-parent families. Single-person households made up the greatest share, at 39.3 per cent, and couples without children the lowest, at 11.7 per cent.

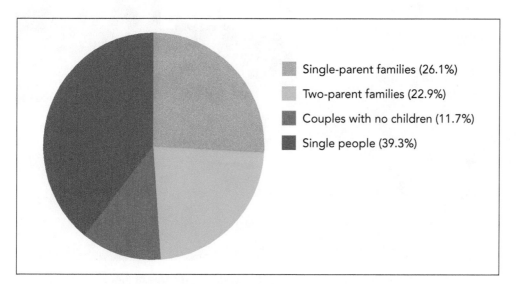

Single-parent families (26.1%)

Two-parent families (22.9%)

Couples with no children (11.7%)

Single people (39.3%)

FIGURE 12.4 Household type of food bank clients, 2011

Source: Based on data from Food Banks Canada (2011). *HungerCount 2011*. Toronto: Food Banks Canada.

Since the 1980s, the majority of Canadians have seen their real incomes either stagnate or decline, and between 2002 and 2007, 40 per cent of Canadians experienced at least one year of low income, while 13 per cent of Canadians experienced at least three years of low income (Statistics Canada, 2007) (see Figure 12.5). Poverty advocates point to a growing reliance on food banks and emergency shelters as an indication of just how badly governments at all levels are failing to help the poorest Canadians, regardless of some arbitrarily set poverty line. Food Banks Canada is the national charitable organization supporting the food bank community across Canada. Each year they publish *HungerCount*, a report based on an annual national survey of food bank use in Canada. In *HungerCount 2009* they reported that 794,738 Canadians 'walked into a food bank looking for help during the month of March 2009—an increase of 18 per cent over March 2008'. Thirty-seven per cent of those assisted were children; 52 per cent were also receiving social assistance, suggesting that 'welfare rates in Canada do not do enough to ensure food security for low-income Canadians' (Food Banks Canada, 2009).

Further Indications of Income Inequality in Canada

Sociologists often divide the population of a given country into *quintiles* (fifths) in order to determine income disparities between the groups at the bottom and the top. How big are the disparities? Are they stable over time, declining, or growing? In Canada income disparities (expressed in 2007 constant dollars) rose between 1995 and 2007. While average after-tax incomes remained roughly the same for families in the bottom quintile (the lowest 20 per cent), as well as for those in the next three quintiles (the middle 60 per cent), they rose for the

A young Cree plays road hockey in the Waswanipi Cree reserve, a Cree/Lynu/Innu reserve of 1,473 people in Quebec. Which are some of the social-structural causes of child poverty among Canada's Aboriginal people?

top quintile, or 20 per cent, of the population (see Figure 12.6). Over that period the gap in average incomes of the top and bottom quintiles rose by 37 per cent, from $87,100 in 1995 to $112,800 in 2007). During the same time, the difference between the average income of the top quintile and that of the middle three quintiles combined increased by 44 per cent, from $54,067 to $77,900.

If we convert the income disparities to ratios (i.e. the top quintile divided by the bottom, or the top quintile divided by the middle three), we see that between 1996 and 2007 the top 20 per cent of income earners in Canada made between 8.4 and 9.1 times more than the families in the bottom quintile and between 2.3 and 2.6 times what those families in the middle three quintiles earned (see Figure 12.7). Income disparities between top and bottom quintiles over this span were among the highest recorded in the previous 31 years. On average, in 2007, for every dollar earned by families in the bottom 20 per cent of earners, families in the top 20 per cent earned $9.11.

Finally, if we compare the distribution of after-tax family income by quintile for 2003, we get yet another snapshot of income disparity in Canada (see Figure 12.7). While the

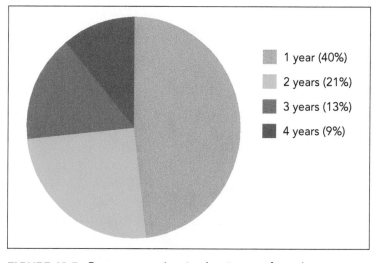

FIGURE 12.5 Persons experiencing low income for at least one year during the six-year period 2002–7

Source: Statistics Canada, *Income in Canada 2007*, 75-202-XWE2007000, June 2010; http://www.statcan.gc.ca/bsolc/olc-cel/olc-cel?catno=75-202-X&cgriog-1&lang=eng.

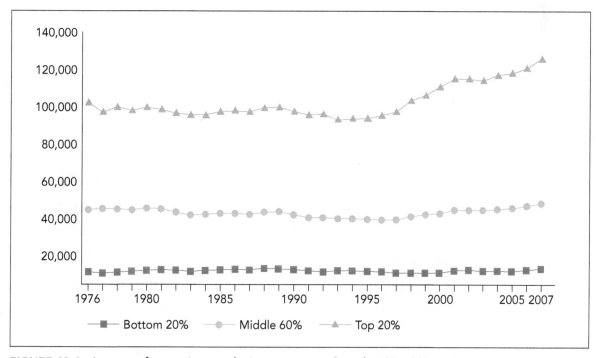

FIGURE 12.6 Average after-tax income, by income group, Canada, 1976–2007

Source: Statistics Canada, 2009, CANSIM Table 202-0706.

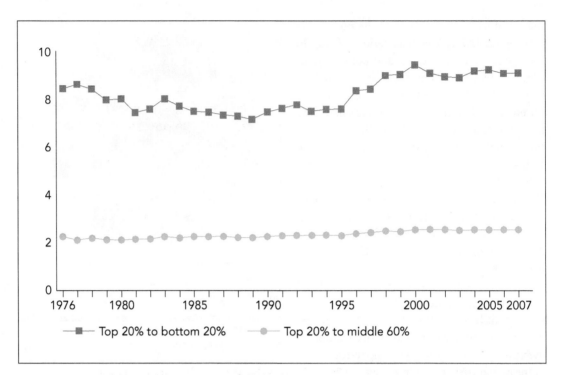

FIGURE 12.7 Relative average income of the top 20 per cent to other groups, Canada, 1976–2007

Source: Statistics Canada, 2009, CANSIM Table 202-0703.

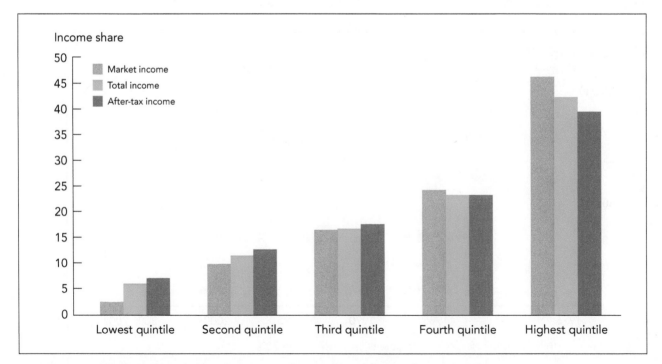

FIGURE 12.8 Family shares of aggregate income, by quintile, after transfers and taxes, 2003

Source: Statistics Canada, *Income in Canada 2003*, 75-202-XWE 2003000, May 2005; http://www.statcan.gc.ca/bsolc/olc-cel/olc-cel?catno=75-202-X&chropg=1&lang=eng.

STUDIES IN SOCIAL RESEARCH

What Poverty Means to a Nine-Year-Old

One way of examining poverty is to consider how it is actually experienced. Here is a list of responses to the question 'What does poverty mean?' from grade 4 and 5 students living in North Bay, Ontario, in the late 1990s.

Poverty Is . . .

Not being able to go to McDonald's
Getting a basket from the Santa Fund
Feeling ashamed when my dad can't get a job
Not buying books at the book fair
Not getting to go to birthday parties
Hearing my mom and dad fight over money
Not ever getting a pet because it costs too much
Wishing you had a nice house
Not being able to go camping
Not getting a hot dog on hot dog day
Not getting pizza on pizza day
Not being able to have your friends sleep over
Pretending that you forgot your lunch
Being afraid to tell your mom that you need gym shoes
Not having breakfast sometimes
Not being able to play hockey
Sometimes really hard because my mom gets scared and she cries
Not being able to go to Cubs or play soccer
Not being able to take swimming lessons
Not being able to afford a holiday
Not having pretty barrettes for your hair
Not having your own private backyard
Being teased for the way you are dressed
Not getting to go on school trips

Source: Interfaith Social Assistance Reform Coalition, 1998, p. 107; as cited in deGroot-Maggetti, 2002, p. 13.

lowest-earning 20 per cent of Canadian families had a little over 6 per cent of the aggregate income earned for that year, the highest-earning quintile of Canadian families had just under 40 per cent of all income earned for that year.

Regional Disparities

If we take the ratio of the top 20 per cent to the bottom 20 per cent average family incomes by province, we can see which provinces have higher ratios—and thus larger disparities—than others (see Figure 12.9). In 2007, income disparities were the lowest in Prince Edward Island

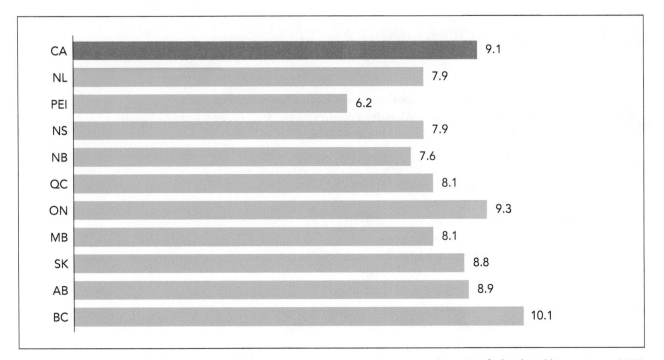

FIGURE 12.9 Relative average income of the top to bottom 20 per cent income groups, federal and by province, 2007
Source: Statistics Canada, 2009, CANSIM Table 202-0703.

and highest in British Columbia. In PEI the top 20 per cent of families had incomes 6.2 times higher than the lowest 20 per cent. In BC the top 20 per cent earned 10.1 times more than the bottom 20 per cent of families in that province.

Highest Income Earners in Canada

Most of the highest income earners in Canada are men. In 2004, of the 1.2 million Canadians who made up the top 5 per cent of income recipients, 75 per cent were men, even though men made up only 48 per cent of all Canadian income recipients (women made up 52 per cent). Moreover, the higher the income, the more skewed the gender composition. Almost 90 per cent of the individuals in the top 0.01 per cent of income earners in Canada in 2004 were men (Murphy, Roberts, & Wolfson, 2007).

Percentage Change in Total Family Income

Income in Canada is becoming more concentrated. In 2004, the top 5 per cent of all income earners saw their share of all income earned in Canada increase by about 25 per cent; the top 1 per cent of income earners saw their share increase by 50 per cent; and the top 0.01 per cent had nearly a 100 per cent increase. As for the bottom 95 per cent of income earners, they actually saw a decrease in their share of the income pie (Murphy, Roberts, & Wolfson, 2007).

Picot and Myles (2005) computed the percentage change in total family income in Canada by *vingtile* (categories of 5 per cent) from 1990 to 2000. Figure 12.10 is based on the Survey of Consumer Finance and its replacement, the Survey of Labour and Income

Dynamics data, after taxes and transfer income, among families in the lowest four and top four vingtiles. It indicates that while the families in the lowest 20 per cent (the bottom 4 vingtiles) saw little change in family income, those in the highest 20 per cent (the top 4) saw increases of between 7 per cent and 16 per cent between 1990 and 2000 (Picot & Myles, 2005, p. 9).

Immigrants and Low Income in Canada

In Canada, low income is concentrated among five groups:

- lone parents
- off-reserve Aboriginal people
- people between the ages of 45 and 64 and not in families
- people with work-limiting disabilities
- recent immigrants. (Hatfield, 2003, as cited in Picot, Lu, & Hou, 2010)

Picot and Myles (2005) note that while the rates of low family income have been falling among Canadian-born groups, they have been rising rapidly among recent immigrants, despite the very high educational qualifications of recent immigrants to Canada (Picot & Myles, 2005, p. 21). Picot, Lu, and Hou (2010) have identified several factors involved in this decline:

The first is the shift in immigrant source countries from Europe and the United States to Asia and Africa, and the associated change in related characteristics, for example, proficiency in official languages, perceived or real differences in educational systems, and cultural differences that may influence labour market

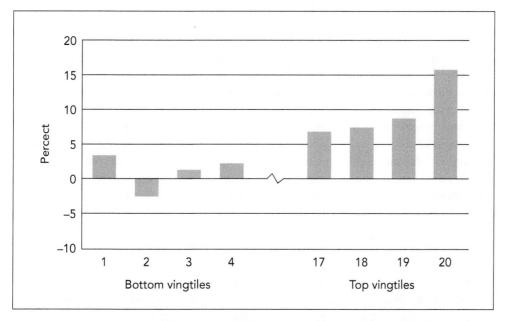

FIGURE 12.10 Percentage change in total family income by vingtile, 1990–2000

Source: Statistics Canada, Analytical Studies Branch Research Paper Series, 11F0019MIE2005240, no. 240, February 2005; http://www.statcan.gc.ca/bsolc/olc-cel/olc-cel?lang=eng&catno=11F0019M2005240.

outcomes. The second factor is the general decline in labour market entry earnings during the 1980s and 1990s that affects both 'recent' immigrants and the Canadian-born alike. The third set of factors relates to the decline in earning returns to foreign work experience and other immigrant specific characteristics. (Picot, Lu, & Hu, 2010)

In 1980, a male immigrant to Canada who had been in the country for five years or less earned on average 85 per cent of what a Canadian-born male would be paid to do the same job; he could have expected his earnings to be on parity with those of a Canadian-born male after 15–20 years. By 2005, the average earnings of a recent male immigrant had fallen to around 65 per cent of the earnings of a Canadian-born male. Male immigrants can now expect to take longer than 20 years to achieve parity with their Canadian-born counterparts. The selection of skilled immigrants to Canada is based on criteria of education, work experience, and knowledge of an official language, with the assumption that an immigrant who possesses these criteria will be more employable. However, the labour market value of these qualifications is less for immigrant workers than it is for Canadian-born workers. For example, the value of an immigrant's foreign-acquired educational qualifications is roughly 'two-thirds of the value of a similar amount of education for the native-born' (Reitz, 2007, p. 18).

WEALTH INEQUALITY IN CANADA

wealth
Total assets less total liabilities, based on marketable assets that are in direct control of families.

Wealth is defined as total assets minus total liabilities, and is based on marketable assets that are in direct control of families. It does not include the crude value of savings held in employer pension plans or future claims on publicly funded, income security programs.

Because accurate data on salaries and wages are widely available, income is probably the most studied indicator of financial well-being. Using income alone as an indicator of financial well-being would be adequate if income and wealth were highly correlated. However, they are not. For example, many wealthy people have low incomes in spite of their wealth, and they support their current levels of consumption with income derived from assets and not employment. Retired people, too, may have low income but substantial net worth, which continues to accumulate after retirement when their income ceases. In contrast, many families have zero or even a negative net worth in spite of also having high incomes. Families who might be counted as living below the poverty line based solely on earned income may live comfortably on assets acquired when their income was higher. In comparison, many families who have incomes that put them well above the poverty line may in reality be carrying considerable debt and have few assets, making them very vulnerable if their current income were to be reduced or to cease. For all these reasons, income is a poor indicator of true financial position.

Statistics Canada's latest *Survey of Financial Security* was conducted in 2005, and it surveyed 9,000 Canadian households. It follows a survey of 23,000 households conducted in 1999. Because the sample of households surveyed in 2005 was so small, Statistics Canada was only able to report on the trends for the top 10 per cent of households (as opposed to the top 1 per cent reported on previously). The top 10 per cent of Canadian households saw their share of wealth rise from 51.8 per cent in 1984, to 55.7 per cent in 1999, and to 58.2 per cent in 2005. In 2005, the bottom 20 per cent of Canadian households was in a debt hole of on average $7,800 (Morissette & Zhang, 2006, as cited in Yalnizyan, 2010, pp. 18–19). The top 20 per cent of families in Canada held 75 per cent of total household wealth in 2005, compared with 73 per cent in 1999 and 69 per cent in 1984 (Statistics Canada, 2006d).

Another source, the financial research institute Investor Economics, identified 544,000 'high-net-worth' households (about 3.8 per cent of all households in Canada) as of December 2009, calculating that this group of households controlled $1.78 trillion in financial wealth, or about 67 per cent of the total financial wealth of Canadian households (as cited in Yalnizyan, 2010, p. 20).

Especially hard hit between 1984 and 2005 were those families in which the major income recipient was between the ages of 25 and 34. While these families had a median wealth holding of $27,000 in 1984, it fell to $17,400 in 1999 and to $13,400 in 2005.

Statistics Canada concludes that:

> The growing inequality in net worth during the past six years followed an increase in inequality in family after-tax income that occurred during the 1990s. This suggests that growing income dispersion over the last decade also contributed to the increase in concentration of wealth. (Statistics Canada, 2006d)

THE INTERNATIONAL PICTURE

Not only are there extreme inequalities in the material welfare among the citizens of any one country, if we compare the overall material welfare of the citizens of one country with those of another we also find extremes. The **Gini coefficient** is a measure of the inequality of a statistical dispersion. It is a real number that can range between 0, if whatever is being measured is equally distributed amongst all members of a population (i.e. total equality), and 1, if a single individual holds all of whatever is being measured (i.e. maximum inequality). The Gini coefficient is commonly used as a measure of inequality in the distribution of income or wealth within a population such as a nation. The Gini coefficients of countries can then be compared to each other. In a country with a Gini coefficient of 0, everyone would have the same income: there would be no disparity. By contrast, in a country with a Gini coefficient of 1, there would be extreme disparity, with one person having all the income. Figure 12.11 shows Gini coefficients for OECD countries calculated for the mid-2000s for all countries. As you can see, Canada is a country characterized by a fair bit of income disparity among its citizens. Canada ranks eighteenth out of 30 countries with a Gini coefficient of about 0.32.

Gini coefficient
A measure of the inequality of a statistical dispersion that can range between 0, if whatever is being measured is equally distributed amongst all members of a population (i.e. total equality), and 1, if a single individual holds all of whatever is being measured (i.e. maximum inequality).

SOCIAL CLASS

In a background document discussing the documentary 'People Like Us', the American Public Broadcasting System (PBS) referred to social class in America as 'the 800-pound gorilla in American life that most Americans don't think about'. Class, they note, 'is a hard subject to talk about in a society like ours, where the ideal is that all people are created equal' (www.pbs.org/peoplelikeus/).

Like Americans, most Canadians think of themselves as middle-class and prefer to leave the matter at that. While many acknowledge inequalities in the distribution of material wealth among their fellow Canadians, they don't connect that with class position, except in the most wide-ranging fashion, as in upper-, middle-, and lower-income categories. With such a crude

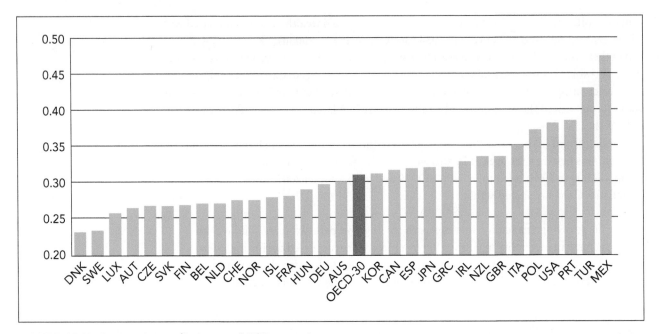

FIGURE 12.11   Income inequality across OECD countries

Note: Countries are ranked, from left to right, in increasing order in the Gini coefficient. Data refer to the mid-2000s for all countries. The income concept used is that of disposable household income in cash, adjusted for household size with an elasticity of 0.5.

Source: OECD Income Distribution questionnaire. Adapted from: http://www.tuac.org/en/public/e-docs/00/00/02/20/document_news.phtml.

conceptual tool, it is not difficult to see why, on a common-sense level, most people in Canada (as well as in the US) consider themselves middle-class.

But given the relevance of social stratification and material inequalities to the quality of life and even the life expectancy of the citizens of any country, it is not hard to understand why the concept of social class is important to social scientists. One of the big issues for sociologists and other social scientists is how social class should be defined. Should it be defined on the basis of income? Occupation? Wealth? Social standing and status? Should we devise some measure that combines all of these? Or do we need to think of social class less as an individual and more as a social-structural phenomenon?

Among the most influential conceptualizations of social class is the one formulated by Karl Marx, who, as we saw in Chapter 6, was both a committed revolutionary and a social theorist. Even in his most theoretically complex writing, Marx's consistent aim was to provide members of the working class (or proletariat) with a comprehensive analysis of capitalist society in order to help them bring about its transformation to a more equitable type of social organization.

Class and the Capitalist Mode of Production in the Work of Karl Marx

capitalist mode of production
A form of social organization characterized by private ownership of the means of production.

Much of Marx's writing was devoted to an analysis of what he termed the **capitalist mode of production**, a form of social organization characterized by private ownership of the means of production. Ultimately Marx expected that societies dominated by the capitalist mode of production would come to be made up of two great, opposing classes: the *proletariat*, also called the working class, and the capitalist class, also called the *bourgeoisie*. Members of the proletariat own nothing except their ability to work (their labour power), which they are obliged to sell to the bourgeoisie, who own and control the material means of production. In the meantime, however, Marx also recognized other classes in capitalist societies, which he variously identified as the petite bourgeoisie, the lumpenproletariat, the financiers, the peasantry, the landed aristocracy, and the middle class. The petite bourgeoisie, for example, was said to be made up of small business owners, and the term *lumpenproletariat* was used to refer to marginalized and often criminal people who lived on the 'crumbs of society'.

Marx pointed out that in all societies, economic activities including the production, exchange, and consumption of goods are always *social* activities. Individuals are never merely isolated producers or consumers. Production, exchange, and consumption all take place under established, well-regulated social relations. Membership in a social class, for Marx, has nothing to do with the possession or lack of individual prestige, income, effort, or even power. Under the capitalist mode of production, class membership is based solely on the social relations that exist between those who own the means of production and those who only own their *labour power*, their ability to work.

The employer pays a wage, by which he purchases exclusive rights over a worker's labour power (and thus rights over everything the worker produces) during those hours that the worker has contracted to work for the employer. Profits are extracted because the capitalist is able to buy the labour power of others at a price that is cheaper than the price realized when the product the worker makes is sold on the market. Even when the worker receives a wage that is entirely 'fair'—that is, even when she receives market value for her labour power and thus has not been cheated—in Marx's view she has still been exploited. This is so because labour power purchased by the capitalist is used only for part of the day to create value that is equivalent to its price (i.e. to the wage). During the rest of the day, the worker creates what Marx called **surplus value**, value over and above the price the capitalist has paid for that day's worth of work. It is the surplus value that is entirely retained by the employer.

surplus value
For Marx, surplus value is the value that a worker creates over and above what is paid to him as a labour cost by the capitalist who employs him.

Social Class and Revolution

Marx was not just interested in providing a description of the economic exploitation of one class by another under the capitalist mode of production. He was also a revolutionary, concerned with understanding and bringing about social change. He believed that social classes played the central role in the transformation of societies. For Marx, then, social classes are actually *social forces*. It was his opinion that, as members of a particular social class, men (and, it should be added, although Marx himself did not mention them, women) make their own history, although not 'just as they please'.

The transition from feudalism to capitalism provided by Marx and Engels in *The Communist Manifesto* illustrates this. The feudal mode of production consists of a system of manorial holdings, held by a lord through the right of inheritance, and the un-free peasants or serfs who are attached to that land and are obliged to render labour and services. In western Europe, this system of hierarchically arranged classes and property holding through birthright was justified by an ideology sanctioned by the Catholic Church: Divine Will had decreed things should be so.

Feudal society was encumbered by a system of customary rights and duties. But, as Marx and Engels point out, ultimately the feudal aristocracy, which benefited greatly from the system, was unable to resist the power of the rising bourgeoisie, who in the context of feudalism constituted the 'revolutionary class'. While the bourgeoisie succeeded in breaking with feudal restrictions and in bringing about the transition to capitalism, it also created another large class of people: peasants who now were 'freed' from the land and as a consequence had no 'property' except their capacity to labour, which they were continually forced to sell in order to gain a livelihood.

In Marx's view, the bourgeoisie, by ushering in capitalism, effectively created the proletariat, and in so doing it also sowed the seeds of its own destruction. As Marx and Engels (1948/1962) wrote, under a capitalist mode of production, 'society as a whole is more and more splitting up into two great hostile camps, into two great classes directly facing each other: Bourgeoisie and Proletariat'. And the proletariat, in their view, was the next revolutionary class, destined to bring about the transition from capitalism to socialism and eventually to advance communism. More importantly, by putting an end to class differences forever, the proletariat was the class destined to finally stop the cycle of human history as the history of class struggle.

Thus, while Marx and Engels recognized that there were more than two antagonistic classes in capitalist societies, they nonetheless contended that as capitalism developed, the two main classes would increase in size and gradually absorb any other subsidiary classes. Ultimately there would come a time when the conflict between the two antagonistic classes would lead to revolution, the outcome of which would be the end of class-based antagonisms and the rise of 'free association' in its place. As Marx and Engels wrote in *The Manifesto of the Communist Party*:

> When, in the course of development, class distinctions have disappeared and all production has been concentrated in the hands of a vast association of the whole nation, the public power will lose its political character. Political power, properly so called, is merely the organized power of one class for oppressing another. If the proletariat during its contact with the bourgeoisie is compelled by the force of circumstances to organize itself into a class; if by means of a

Yan is paid $20 an hour to bake cakes. He works a nine-hour shift and bakes 12 cakes. His employer sells each cake for $44. If the owner's total costs for raw materials, rent, advertising, and other expenses averages $7 per cake, how much surplus value does Yan generate for his employer? What circumstances would allow him to continue to work as a baker without having surplus value extracted?

revolution that makes itself into the ruling class and, as such, sweeps away by force the old conditions of production, then it will along with those conditions have swept away the conditions for existence of class antagonisms and of classes generally, and will thereby have abolished its own supremacy as a class.

In place of the old bourgeois society, with its classes and class antagonisms, we shall have an association in which the free development of each is the condition for the free development of all. (Marx & Engels, 1948/1962, p. 35)

In *A Contribution to the Critique of Hegel's Philosophy of Right: Introduction,* Marx explicitly takes up for the first time the struggle between the working class and the bourgeoisie, and explicitly takes the side of the working class. In this work Marx develops his theory of **hegemony.** The theory of hegemony explains how the interests of one class of people in a society are represented to all members of that society as the universal interests of humanity. The concept is then used to compare these interests with the 'real' interests of the opposing social class in order to demonstrate that what is being presented as 'universal' is in fact the source of all injustice.

Politics for Marx is hegemonic as it involves particular social classes, such as the working class or the bourgeoisie, representing their interests as if those interests were universal. Marx recognized that the interests of the bourgeoisie were hegemonic in capitalist societies, and he set out to do what he could to change that by representing the interests of the working class as the true universal interests of all humanity. As Marx admitted, he did this as part of a revolutionary strategy: 'So that one class *par excellence* may appear as a class of liberation, another class must inversely be the manifest class of oppression' (Marx, 2000, p. 7).

hegemony

A theory used to explain how the interests of one class are represented as the universal interests of humanity, and to compare these interests with the 'real' interests of the opposing social class, in order to demonstrate that what is being presented as 'universal' is in fact the source of all injustice.

A Marxian Analysis of the Toronto Garment Industry

Production, exchange, and consumption under the capitalist mode of production take place primarily on the basis of commodities. Commodities are goods and services that are produced not to meet the immediate needs of those who produce them but to go up for sale on an open market. This means that at both the point of production and the point of consumption, all commodities are evaluated in relation to how well they do on the market. Take the example of buying an article of clothing, such as a coat. To you, the consumer, that coat may represent one way you feel you can express your individuality. You do not consider the coat in any other context than your own use and enjoyment of it. You do not have to think about how that coat was made, or by whom, or how it got to market in the first place, or even why it is that you go to a store to buy your coat. All you are concerned about is whether you can afford it, and if it 'looks good' on you and appeals to your sense of fashion.

But Canadian sociologist Charlene Gannagé (1986), in her now classic study of the Toronto garment industry, *Double Day, Double Blind,* has looked at the coat you have just bought not as the expression of your individual identity, but as a commodity, as one item among many that a particular clothing manufacturer has brought to market to sell. Looked at this way, it is possible to trace many of the social relations that exist among the people who produce clothing for sale in the marketplace, including:

1. those who produce the clothing
2. those who own the factories where the clothing is produced
3. those who sell the clothing
4. the end buyers.

Just how does a piece of clothing get from the producers into the hands of the final consumer? In Toronto during the 1980s, many of the workers in the garment industry were immigrant women and men. Gannagé describes what she saw on a visit to a garment manufacturer one day in 1984, accompanied by 'Matt', a union representative, while conducting research for her doctoral dissertation:

> The next stop was a shop where sections of the garment were made by individual operators. The coats were of poor quality. Matt called them 'garbage'. Because the shop was working at full production, my ears were assaulted by incredible noise. The pace of the work appeared to be very fast. There were no windows, the shop was dimly lit, and material was strewn everywhere. The owner complained about a presser who had walked off the job. According to the owner the presser was a '$26,000 a year man'. The owner's son laughed as his father described the 'crazy' presser. I looked around and noticed a presser with sweat pouring from his face and cheeks puffed as he pushed down the lever of his machine. 'For some reason, all the pressers go crazy,' the owner informed us.
>
> In business for 30 years, the owner had switched from a *conventional* way of production (in which skilled tailors made the whole garment) to a *sectional* method (in which the garment is made in sections by different operators) because it was difficult to find skilled tailors. He showed us the buttonhole machine. (In conventional shops, buttonholes are made by hand). The operator looked up at me and pointed out, 'You just have to make sure you don't lose a finger'.
>
> The owner announced proudly, 'We pay the presser good money.'
>
> 'Why is that?' I asked. 'Because they are more skilled?'
>
> 'No, anyone can be a presser,' he retorted. 'It's the job, especially in the summer, its hard work.'
>
> 'He has lots of trouble with his pressers,' interjected Matt.
>
> 'I don't cause any trouble,' the owner defended himself, 'I don't care if they go to the union.' As we were leaving a woman shouted at Matt to get out of the way because she had to make some money. (Gannagé, 1986, pp. 29–30)

Each worker in this particular garment shop had a social relation with other workers, with the boss, with the union representative, and with people to whom the garments are sold. But none of these relations, with the possible exception of that with the union representative, are based on a concern with the immediate satisfaction of human need.

It might be the case that the 'crazy presser', or the woman who shouted at Matt to get out of her way, contributes to making a product that ultimately ends up satisfying someone's need for a warm winter coat or for a coat that conveys just the right fashion statement. However, the capitalist mode of production under which that coat is produced is insensitive to the need of any individual for a winter coat, except in so far as that need can be translated into the production of a *commodity*.

The relations between the workers and their boss, between the boss and his suppliers, between the boss and the retail stores that buy the finish coats, and between the retail stores and the customers are all based on impersonal exchanges. The relations between people in these exchanges are indifferent to personal qualities, except to the extent that those qualities might determine whether or not a particular commodity is going to have success in the market.

Even when the market brings sellers and buyers together in a face-to-face relationship, as when you enter a retail store and are approached by a sales clerk who wishes to help you choose a coat, this relationship is hardly a personal one. The sales clerk is interested in you only as a customer—as someone who will spend money. It is almost inevitably a desire to make some profit and not a concern that the customer gets the best coat possible, for the best price possible, which motivates the salesperson's interest in the customer. This is especially the case if the salesperson receives a commission for each sale.

It was Marx's point that, with the rise of the capitalist mode of production and the decline of feudalism, personal relations were destroyed and replaced by relations that were to a large extent mutually indifferent. In the capitalist mode of production, he noted, 'personal relations flow purely out of relations of production and exchange.' Under the class system of capitalism, people came to see each other only as a means of satisfying market needs rather than as individual human beings. This state of affairs in turn encourages people to think of themselves as autonomous and independent. Such an ideology of bourgeois individualism, Marx contended, is in fact *false consciousness*. In reality, our life chances are strongly influenced and structured by the pattern of social relations that is predetermined by the market economy.

The logic of production and consumption that operates in the capitalist mode of production is based on the existence of individuals who are separated from one another and from ownership of the means of production, and who strive to accumulate private property, believing that goal to be in their best interests. The illusion of personal independence that many of us living under capitalism hold so dear is based on our ability to own things, including owning our own capacity for work, our labour power. But the real chance of having any control over our identity and existence under capitalism hinges on our ability to own property, especially the means of production. Yan the baker, pictured earlier on page 304 could cease to be a labourer generating surplus value for a capitalist if he went into business for himself and opened up his own cake shop, which would allow him to control the means of production and gain maximum value for his labour. And if he began to hire employees, he would be extracting surplus value from them. But as Marx points out, few are able to achieve such ownership.

It was Marx's firmly held conviction that the capitalist mode of production would eventually be transformed as a result of internal contradictions between social relations of production and the forces of production. He believed that economic crises were opportunities for the proletariat to seize control of the means of production. As capitalism matures, he noted, it becomes more and more unstable, and opportunities for social revolution are more apparent. He predicted that eventually the capitalist mode of production would be entirely replaced by socialism, which in turn would pave the way for advanced communism. When that revolution finally came, all people would be free to enter into very individualized forms of self-expression, not on the basis of their economic status and ability to pay to buy consumer goods, but on their real abilities, needs, and desires.

MAX WEBER ON 'CLASS' AND 'STATUS'

Although Weber was quite critical of the revolutionary intent of Marx's work, there are important similarities in the way both men treated social class. Both Marx and Weber adopted relational concepts of social class: classes for both are derived from the interactions of social actors (and not derived from some graduated hierarchy of individual characteristics, as for example 'amount of income'). Both theorists saw control over economic resources as central to their analysis, although they use different terminology to describe this relationship. Marx calls this 'the relation to the means of production' while Weber refers to 'market capacities'.

Both Marxian and Weberian traditions hold that property rights shape peoples' actions, imposing constraints on what individuals are able to do in order to get what they want. At their core, both Marxian and Weberian class concepts involve the causal connection between social relations to resources and material interests via the way resources shape strategies for acquiring income. However, the main difference between Marx's and Weber's concepts of social class is that while Marx made production and the exploitation of one class by another a central focus of his concept, Weber concentrated on market situation, because it is the market that directly shapes each individual's 'life chances' (Wright, 1997, pp. 30–1).

In a frequently cited passage Weber wrote:

> We may speak of a 'class' when (1) a number of people have in common a specific causal component of their life chances, in so far as (2) this component is represented exclusively by economic interest in the possession of goods and opportunities for income, and (3) is represented under the conditions of the commodity or labor markets. This is the 'class situation'.

Does this pharmacist look like she's personally invested in meeting the needs of human customers, or does she look like she's watching the clock until her shift ends and she can leave to do something she considers more meaningful—like shopping? Is she autonomous or is she governed by social-structural forces of which she might not be quite aware?

> It is the most elemental economic fact that the way in which the disposition over material property is distributed among a plurality of people, meeting competitively in the market for the purpose of exchange, in itself creates specific life chances. . . .
>
> But always this is the generic connotation of the concept of class: that the kind of chance in the *market* is the decisive moment which presents a common condition for the individual's fate. Class situation is, in this sense, ultimately market situation. (Weber, 1925/1978, pp. 927–8)

Like Marx, Weber focused his analysis of social class on the economic sphere. Unlike Marx, however, Weber did not consider ownership (or non-ownership) of the means of production as the defining characteristic of class membership. Rather, Weber talked about class situation in terms of the relationship a person has to a market, the chance a person has of gaining access to 'a supply of goods, external living conditions and personal life experiences' (Gerth & Mills, 1954/1964, p. 181). In Weber's opinion people share a common class situation when they have in common the same life chances, including access to commodity and labour markets.

'Class Situation' and Weber's Structure of Class Categories

Because he focused on the 'action' of individual social actors, Weber preferred to talk about **class situation** by way of referring to an individual social actor's orientations, skills, abilities, and conditions of life, and to the actions that follow from those qualities. Weber defined a common class situation as:

> [t]he typical chance for a supply of goods, external living conditions, and personal life experiences, in so far as this chance is determined by the amount and kind of power, or lack of such, to dispose of goods or skills for the sake of income in a given economic order. (Weber, 1925/1978, p. 181)

But the innumerable potential combinations of conditions, skills, and orientations—all qualities possessed by individual social actors—make for an overwhelming number of potential class categories based on an almost infinite variety of identifiable class situations. So to simplify matters a bit, Weber created a structure of class situations based on two organizing criteria: (1) types of market situation, and (2) possibilities for mobility between class situations.

A market situation, Weber tells us,

> may be said to exist wherever there is competition, even if only unilateral, for opportunities of exchange among a plurality of potential parties. Their physical assemblage in one place, as in the local market square, the fair (the 'long distance market'), or the exchange (the merchants' market), only constitutes the most consistent kind of market formation. (Weber, 1925/1978, p. 635)

Under the rubric of 'market situation' Weber identifies what he feels are two qualitatively different markets: a property market and a market for services. Corresponding to each distinct market are two qualitatively different social classes: 'property classes' and 'acquisition classes' (Barbalet, 1980, p. 408; Weber, 1915/1964, pp. 424–7). These two classes are further divided on the basis of 'privilege'—thus, there are 'positively privileged' and 'negatively privileged' property classes, and 'positively privileged' and 'negatively privileged' acquisition classes.

class situation
An individual social actor's orientations, skills, abilities, and conditions of life, and the actions that follow from those qualities.

Positively privileged property classes consist of owners and direct controllers of property who derive their income from property rents and securities. *Negatively privileged property classes*, by contrast, are made up of those without property—the debtors, the outcasts, the working poor, and slaves (i.e. those who themselves are the property of others).

Positively privileged acquisitions classes are those who control management of productive enterprises and those who are able to influence economic policy in their favour. *Negatively privileged acquisitions classes*, by contrast, consist of skilled, semi-skilled, or unskilled labourers.

Between the two acquisition classes are the *middle classes*, a catch-all class for anyone not fitting into one of the other four classes (see Figure 12.12).

In economic organizations, such as the modern firm, Weber identified three types of social actors: bureaucrats, entrepreneurs, and workers. He considered bureaucrats and entrepreneurs 'positively privileged' members of the acquisition classes, while workers are deemed to be 'negatively privileged' members of the acquisition classes. Bureaucrats run the corporation on a day-to-day basis, workers execute the orders given to them by the bureaucrats, and entrepreneurs represent the spirit of capitalism and possess economic power (Swedberg, 2003, p. 296; Weber, 1925/1978, p. 1108).

Many contemporary sociologists have noted that Weber's classification system is difficult to apply in any empirical research. Especially problematic is his catch-all category of 'middle class', where entrepreneurs, liberal professionals, and labour leaders all rub elbows. As we have already noted, Weber's analysis, unlike Marx's, leaves little room for the analysis of conflict or exploitation between social classes, especially in those situations where the interests of one class are realized only at the expense of the interests of another class.

Status

The concepts of 'property class', 'acquisition class', and 'middle class', along with the more general concept 'social class', are examples of what Weber would call *pure* or *ideal types*. As we saw in Chapter 6, an 'ideal type' is a methodological construction, an abstraction of particular properties drawn from a number of phenomena, which are chosen without regard to historical time or place. The concept of 'status', or 'status group', is another ideal-type concept distilled by Weber out of his examination of feudal estates, Hindu castes, and modern occupational groups. In conceiving of the concept 'status', Weber brought together what he perceived to

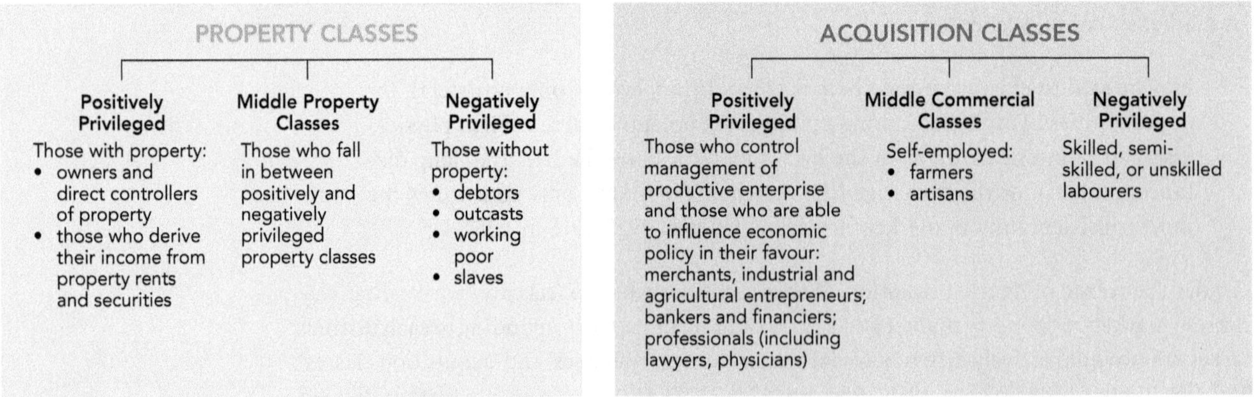

PROPERTY CLASSES			ACQUISITION CLASSES		
Positively Privileged	**Middle Property Classes**	**Negatively Privileged**	**Positively Privileged**	**Middle Commercial Classes**	**Negatively Privileged**
Those with property: • owners and direct controllers of property • those who derive their income from property rents and securities	Those who fall in between positively and negatively privileged property classes	Those without property: • debtors • outcasts • working poor • slaves	Those who control management of productive enterprise and those who are able to influence economic policy in their favour: merchants, industrial and agricultural entrepreneurs; bankers and financiers; professionals (including lawyers, physicians)	Self-employed: • farmers • artisans	Skilled, semi-skilled, or unskilled labourers

FIGURE 12.12   Weber's structure of class categories

be common features of a variety of historical situations. As an ideal type, the concept 'status group' can be applied to the analysis of all societies, yet it refers to none in particular.

Weber defined **status group** as a group of people who claim certain kinds of social esteem for themselves, such as honour and prestige. An elite private club that denies membership to all but a few is an example of a status group. Status groups can be occupational (e.g. doctors, engineers), hereditary (e.g. members of the British nobility), or political (e.g. members of the Liberal Party of Canada). Status group has a very different meaning from social class. While status differences are often associated with class distinctions, especially ones that derive from differences in income or other economic resources, they can also be based on other factors. Whereas social class is a function of market situation and is all about the opportunities an individual has for acquiring possession, status is about consumption patterns, styles of life, and social honour (Barbalet, 1980, pp. 411–12).

status group
A group of people who are accorded the same honour or prestige and who often share the same style of life.

THE 'NEW MIDDLE CLASS'

Classical sociology of both the Marxist and Weberian varieties predicted a gradual erosion of the petite bourgeoisie and their removal from a position of any importance in class relations in advanced capitalist societies. In an attempt to bridge the differences in Marxist and Weberian class analyses, C. Wright Mills held that the consolidation of property and work would put an end to the old middle classes, i.e. the petit bourgeoisie which he claimed had been 'clogging the wheels of progress' (Mills, 1951, pp. 14, 28). As capitalism took off after the Second World War, more and more people were moved out of the petite bourgeoisie and into the ranks of either the working class or the 'new middle class'.

From Mills's perspective, writing in the 1950s, it looked like Marx might have been on the right track when he proposed that, as capitalism advanced, the petit bourgeoisie would gradually disappear and only two opposing classes would remain: the capitalists and the proletariat. Between the late 1950s and the 1980s interest in Marxist theories flourished in American and European universities.

During the 1980s, however, the slide toward only two major classes, predicted by Marx, was halted. Neoconservative governments, in office on anti-labour and pro-business agendas, came to the aid of small businesses, and the decline of the petite bourgeoisie was reversed in countries such as Canada, the United States, the United Kingdom, Italy, Belgium, Finland, and Ireland (Myles & Turegun, 1994, p. 110; OECD, 1992; Stienmetz & Wright, 1989). Even Sweden experienced remarkable growth in self-employment among men, with rates rising from 6.1 per cent to 10.2 per cent between 1985 and 1990, largely in response to the greater emphasis placed on government employment programs and programs supporting small business start-ups (Myles & Turegun, 1994, p. 110; OECD, 1992). As well, by the end of the 1990s, employee downsizing had occurred for large firms in Austria, Belgium, France, Japan, Denmark, Luxembourg, and the UK, as well as in Canada and the United States.

Today there has been a growth in self-employment and in small incorporated businesses, as many of those who were formerly employed by large firms now survive by taking on short-term, temporary contracts or work as 'consultants'. Although the causes of this move from large, vertically integrated corporations with thousands of workers to self-employed contractors and consultants are ambiguous, the consequences for workers are less so: lower income, fewer benefits, and no long-term security.

Don't mistake social class for status group. Middle-class youths will sometimes play down their economic class by donning deliberately torn jeans (very expensive if purchased that way) and vintage store fashions. What kind of status group are they trying to cultivate?

Some of the big questions in contemporary sociology focus around this 'new middle class': Who is in it? What are its boundaries? What are its future prospects?

Following the Second World War, sociologists began classifying workers as either 'white-collar' or 'blue-collar', using conventional and simple occupational classifications: the working class was made up of factory workers and other 'blue-collar' workers who did manual work; non-manual workers included those such as managers, school teachers, clerks, secretaries, and bank tellers, who worked for a salary in offices and stores rather than on the shop floor. It was these workers who made up the new and expanding middle class that C. Wright Mills had written about in *White Collar* (1951), his major study of middle-class life in post-war America.

By the 1970s the followers of Weber and Marx alike had begun to identify two quite broad strata of social classes in their attempt to understand the structure of advanced capitalist societies. On the one hand was a growing class of mid-level corporate officials involved in the day-to-day operation of the modern corporation; on the other hand were the other professional and technical 'knowledge workers' who had become synonymous with post-industrialism (Myles & Turegun, 1994, p. 113). This latter group was variously called the 'professional-managerial class', the 'service class', 'the expert class', or the 'new petite bourgeoisie'. It was also known by the more inclusive label 'the new middle class', a group that now had to be taken seriously.

By the 1980s, administrative, professional, and related occupations made up between one-quarter and one-third of the entire labour force in developed capitalist economies, and these positions continued to grow disproportionately to the rest of the economy. Sociologists began to see the rise of the 'new middle class' as a 'product of the developmental tendencies specific to the advanced stages of monopoly capitalism' (Burris, 1980, p. 136, as cited in Myles & Turegun, 1994, p. 113). By the end of the 1980s, sociologists, whether viewing the question of class from a Marxist or a Weberian perspective, all reached similar conclusions concerning emerging trends in class structure: traditional proletarian jobs in manufacturing and transportation were on the decline, while the shift to service focused on managerial, technical, and professional occupations.

Yet the 'rise' of the new middle class was quite short-lived. In Canada and the United States the patterns of upward economic mobility in place for previous generations had already begun to slow down in the 1960s. The post-war economic boom that served to create the affluent 'middle-class' worker had pretty much come to an end by the 1980s. Downsizing, contracting out, and the use of temporary workers began to affect not just low-wage service personnel but also professional and mid-level managers. Many sociologists turned their attention to analyzing the declining fortunes of the middle class (Myles & Turegun, 1994, p. 119). Today, many of those who were formerly employed by large firms now work on short-term contracts or as marginal self-employed, and there has been a growth in self-employment in small incorporated businesses. Although the reasons behind this movement of people from large, vertically integrated corporations to small firms are unclear, the ramifications are not. Those employed in small firms have 'lower wages, fewer benefits and are less likely to be unionized, and tend to have higher turnover rates', according to Myles and Turegun (1994, p. 112).

The disjuncture between what the classic theories of social class proposed by both Marx and Weber predicted and the actual trends pose a number of theoretical and conceptual problems for sociologists. What is clear is that changes in occupational structure are a poor guide to predicting changes in the distribution of wages and earnings. While classical theories of

STUDIES IN SOCIAL RESEARCH

Social Status and 'Motivations for Assaulting Incarcerated Child Molesters'

Unlike economic class, social status does not necessarily apply to an economic status, but can apply to any position that is obtained through some aspect of social esteem. In the example that follows, Rebecca Trammell and Scott Chenault (2009) interviewed former California prison inmates to examine how these men justified their own violent behaviour, gained respect from their peers, and raised their own social status by assaulting marginalized inmates.

Between 2005 and 2006 Rebecca Trammell interviewed 73 men and women (40 men, 33 women) who had been previously incarcerated in California prisons. Each interview took place within two months of the parolee's release. At the time of the study there were 160,000 inmates in California prisons. Trammell and Chenault did not use a randomized data sample to choose their interviewees. Instead, they created a case study based on 'snowball sampling', where interviewees offer names of other possible research subjects. As a result, it is not possible to generalize the data Trammell and Chenault collected to the entire California prison population. Moreover, although both men and women were interviewed, only the responses of the men could be used in the study, as none of the female parolees interviewed had first-hand knowledge of physical violence against a child molester.

Drawing on Charles Tilly's (2006) work, Trammell and Chenault used storytelling as a research method to encourage the parolees they interviewed to describe justifications for violence. Stories, says Tilly, are verbal accounts that connect group members to each other and to a common culture. They provide simple explanations for the reasons behind deviant behaviour 'even when observers might find the reasons flimsy, contrived or fantastic' (Tilly, 2006, p. 10, as cited in Trammell & Chenault, 2009, p. 337). Stories serve to reassign moral blame for deviant behaviour elsewhere in order to neutralize it.

The male interviewees described a *status hierarchy* of offenders: at the bottom of the hierarchy, lower than other sex offenders, are child molesters.

Interviewees described how they used violence as a way to distance themselves from a child molester and how, in so doing, they raised their own social status in prison. In comparing themselves to child molesters, the interviewees claimed that, unlike the child molesters, they were properly socialized. Yet 83 per cent of the men in the study had gone to prison for committing a violent crime, and five individuals had committed sexual assault against another adult. As the authors explain:

> To lessen the severity of their own crimes, they create a pecking order. To prove that they remain loyal to community standards, they assault child molesters. Their justifications describe a 'good' and 'bad' inmate, and their own social status is elevated by harming others. Aggravated assault is an especially brutal act, which carries serious legal repercussions. However, they argue that not only is this acceptable behavior, it is necessary and accepted by all. (Trammell & Chenault, 2009, p. 348)

The men in the study offered stories as justifications to show that even though they might have been convicted of serious felonies, they were not, and never had been, 'truly deviant' because they still want to protect children. In presenting a tale of justice and revenge, they defined their own behaviour as righteous and just; they assaulted the true deviants because it was the right thing to do. Those who assault child molesters in prison do so publicly, thus reinforcing the prison hierarchy that places child molesters at the bottom while positioning the men who assault them as 'champions of justice' (Trammell & Chenault, 2009, pp. 335–6). As Trammell and Chenault comment: 'the social construction of child molesters is so negative that extreme violence is justified as a way to remove them from the general population.' Assaulting a child molester not only 'reinforces the norm of retributive prison justice', it also 'elevates the social status' of the man who commits the act (p. 336).

social class, whether Marxian or Weberian, have lost some of their cachet, it is hardly the case that social class, stratification, and inequality are no longer significant issues for sociologists. Instead, as readers will see in the next chapter, some new tools and innovative modifications to the foundations set by Marx and Weber have emerged to help us analyze social class, stratification, and social inequality in twenty-first century capitalist societies.

SUMMARY

Whatever way we consider it, Canadian society, although wealthy, is anything but egalitarian, and many Canadians are far removed from the social and economic advantages enjoyed by the 'middle class'. Among similarly industrialized countries, Canada has one of the highest proportions of low-paid workers. Child poverty has not improved since 1989, and over 3 million Canadians (including half-a-million children) live in poverty. Recent immigrants and their children are among the most vulnerable. Internationally, Canada is a country characterized by a fair bit of income disparity among its citizens, ranking eighteenth out of thirty OECD countries.

The persistence and growth of material differences between large numbers of Canadians indicate that class processes identified by social theorists like Marx and Weber are still major factors in shaping the contours of social inequality in Canada and other capitalist societies. Despite many differences in approach, contemporary theorists of social class all agree that class structure in Western industrialized countries can be mapped into hierarchical structures—or social stratification—with proportionally more people in the lower categories than in the higher ones.

Nearly all class theorists, regardless of their chosen perspective, identify a relatively small upper class, which includes the very wealthy and the owners and controllers of industry. They also identify a much larger middle class or classes—those with marketable skills and professions. Finally, all identify a working class or classes, which include both non-manual workers such as office and sales personnel, and manual workers. In Marx's view, the advent of capitalism meant that the bourgeoisie had also created the seeds of its own destruction in the form of the working class or proletariat. Weber did not support Marx's revolutionary analysis and instead produced a theory of class situation based on two organizing criteria: types of market situation and possibility for mobility between class situations.

Despite concerns of some that the classic theories of social class are no longer relevant, the topic of social class has as much if not more significance today than it did in the past when Marx and Weber formulated their different analyses of the problems inherent in capitalist society.

DISCUSSION QUESTIONS

1. What, in your view, does social class really mean?
2. Develop your own model of social class, using whatever criteria you find appropriate. Explain why you chose those criteria.
3. Describe some of the ways in which Canada is an egalitarian society. Describe some of the ways in which Canada is a socially stratified society.

4. What special role in history did Marx and Engels assign to the working class? Is there a chance that the working class will fulfill the role that Marx and Engels expected?

5. Discuss some of the implications that child poverty has for Canadian society.

6. Discuss some of the implications for Canadian society of the trend that has seen a growing concentration of wealth in fewer hands.

7. In what ways does Weber's conceptualization of social class differ from that of Marx's?

Part V
Core Topics of Difference and Inequality

Western society's treatment of differences and inequalities among individuals and populations has followed two often contradictory directions. On the one hand, many people share the concern first expressed during the Enlightenment that institutionalized differentiation of individuals on the basis of parentage, religion, or any other social marker should be eradicated. At the same time, there is a prevailing sense that certain differences, including those based on social class, sexual orientation, gender, physical ability, and biological race, can be considered natural. These differences have been used to justify differential and even discriminatory treatment.

One of the first areas of difference that sociologists focused on was social class. Differences resulting from class played a central role in the work of such heavyweights of the discipline as Karl Marx and Max Weber. Sociological writings in this area have often concentrated on the inequalities that exist, as well as on the principle of social equality and justice for all members of society that should prevail.

While sociologists continue to be interested in differences based on social class, such topics as gender, race, and sexual orientation have lately attracted much attention. In Part V we will look at some of the research and theorizing done by sociologists on these topics.

With the rise of feminist scholarship, sociologists have begun to analyze issues of gender inequality. Western culture provides its members with two sets of acceptable behaviours to emulate: one for males and one for females. Distinctions between the two sets are stereotypical, familiar, and widely shared. Feminist scholarship has pointed out many of the inequalities inherent in these everyday distinctions, foremost of which is the assumption that males are naturally the dominant sex. The distinction between males and females has had profound social, economic, and psychosocial implications for the gender roles and opportunities available to men and women.

Beyond the inequalities that exist between men and women are those based on sexual orientation. Is heterosexuality 'natural' to the human condition as common-sense, Western cultural understandings insist? Are the claims for veritable biological differences legitimate? These are complex issues that continue to be widely debated by social scientists and by the media.

13 Inequality and Social Class: Recent Thinking and Research

CHAPTER OUTLINE

Introduction
Erik Olin Wright on Class and Occupation
Social Mobility
    The Social Reproduction and Transformation of Class Identities
Social Class: The Work of Pierre Bourdieu
    Types of Capital
    Field
    Habitus
    Class Struggle
    Taste, Consumption, and Lifestyle
    Bourdieu's Study of Social Class and Food
Contributing Factors to Social Inequality
Summary
Discussion Questions

LEARNING OBJECTIVES

In this chapter you will:

- review recent thinking by sociologists about social inequalities and social class
- come to understand the concept of 'contradictory class locations'
- learn about social mobility, class, and stratification in China
- reflect on class identity and the transformation of that identity
- be introduced to the work of Pierre Bourdieu on social class
- come to understand four types of capital: economic, social, cultural, and symbolic
- learn about the role of 'field', 'habitus', and differences in taste in distinguishing social class
- gain a clearer understanding of social class as a factor contributing to social inequality.

INTRODUCTION

working class
A social class which is dispossessed of the means of production and sells its labour power to capitalists and is thus exploited and dominated within production.

underclass
The lowest social stratum, consisting of the poor and unemployed.

Today, most sociologists studying social class agree that the basic map of class distribution is hierarchical, and that four very broadly defined divisions are helpful when thinking about inequality and social stratification. Few in number but holding great economic resources is a small but powerful upper class. Beneath the upper class is the middle class, made up of a variety of different groups with assorted marketable skills. The **working class** (beneath the middle class) includes manual labourers, as well as white-collar workers who are employed in sales or clerical positions. The poorest and most disadvantaged, at the bottom of the hierarchy, are often labelled an **underclass**—a concept linked with failure and dependency.

Some sociologists, such as Erik Olin Wright, have drawn up class and occupational typologies that more accurately address the situation found today in well-developed capitalist economies. Others, such as Pierre Bourdieu, expand our analyses of social class by including culture, stratification, and power. In this chapter you will learn about these, and other contemporary modifications to the concept of social class, as well as about the application of the concept of social class to the analysis of social stratification in twentieth and twenty-first century societies.

ERIK OLIN WRIGHT ON CLASS AND OCCUPATION

In response to critiques concerning the limitations of both Marxian and Weberian concepts of social class, Erik Olin Wright (1997) constructed a typology of economic 'class locations', which he set within the framework of class relations. Wright's typology takes into account Marx's criteria of class as a social relationship made up of relations to the means of production, as well as the added factors of 'relations to authority', 'relations to scarce skills', and 'number of employees'. Figure 13.1 lays out Wright's 'basic' typology, while Figure 13.2 illustrates a more 'elaborated typology' of social class that could be used in either a Weberian or a Marxist framework (Wright, 1997, p. 29)

As capitalism matured from the time that Marx and Weber made their analyses, the middle class grew both in size and complexity. Wright and his colleagues (1982) begin with the basic Marxist premise that within any given mode of production there are polarizing class locations, based on the social relations of production. Within the capitalist mode of production, for example, 'the bourgeoisie is defined as that class which owns and controls the means of production and is thus able to exploit and dominate the activities of workers within the production process'. By contrast, the working class 'is defined as that class which is dispossessed of the means of production and sells its labour power to capitalists and is thus exploited and dominated within production' (Wright, et al., 1982, p. 710).

But under mature capitalism this simple division into two completely polarized class positions is absent. Wright and his associates have developed the concept of *contradictory class locations* to help analyze situations in which the complete polarization of social classes predicted by Marx is absent:

> Managers, for example, dominate workers and are dominated by the bourgeoisie, and may even directly exercise certain ownership rights and thus exploit workers, while at the same time being exploited by capital. They are thus in a sense *simultaneously in two classes*: they are workers in that they are exploited and dominated by capital; they are capitalists in that they dominate (and may exploit) workers (Wright, et al., 1982, p. 710).

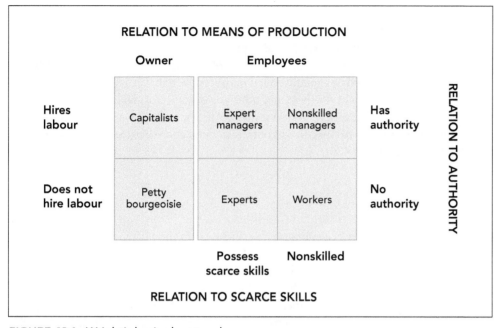

FIGURE 13.1 Wright's basic class typology

Source: Adapted from Wright, 1997, p. 21.

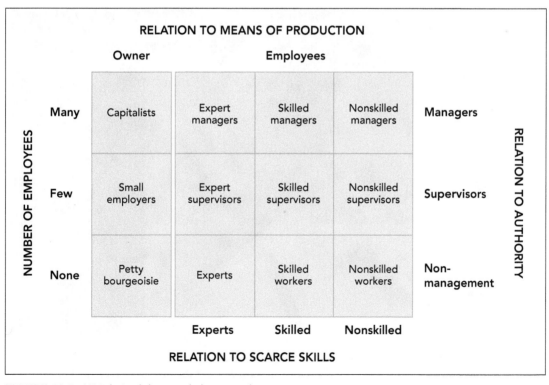

FIGURE 13.2 Wright's elaborated class typology

Source: Adapted from Wright, 1997, p. 22.

Wright and his colleagues add a further complication, noting that several modes of production may be present at the same time in any given society. Capitalist societies always contain 'at least some forms' of non-capitalist production relations, as, for example, when direct producers own and control their own means of production and hire no wage labour. In some societies dominated by capitalist relations of production, vestiges of feudal production relations can also remain. In these and other cases, 'concrete class structures are thus complicated by the fact that certain positions may be determined within these forms of non-capitalist relations' and can be considered 'contradictory locations between modes of production' (Wright, et al., 1982, p. 710).

SOCIAL MOBILITY

ascribed status
The status into which an individual is born.

achieved status
A position in a social hierarchy that has been achieved on the basis of how well an individual performs his or her social role(s).

One of the topics of concern to contemporary sociologists is the shift in the relative balance between ascriptive and achievement mechanisms in the allocation of social status as societies moved from feudal, through industrial, to post-industrial forms of economic organization. As we have already seen, most people born in feudal societies could expect to live lives very similar to those of their parents and their parents' parents before them. For them, intergenerational occupation or status mobility was highly unlikely, and they lived their lives on the basis of **ascribed status**, the status into which they were born.

But such is not the case in contemporary societies dominated by advanced forms of capitalism and industrialization, where **achieved status** is considered to be a viable possibility. Many

This financial adviser makes most of his income on commissions he earns from the products he sells, yet at the same time he's expected to generate revenue for the large investment firm he works for. How does his job keep him in contradictory class locations?

Canadians and Americans share in the vision that if they just apply themselves, get a good education, and work hard, they will be able to achieve upward intergenerational mobility—the upward social mobility of children in relation to their parents. But is this actually the case?

Drawing on survey material from the 1973 *Canadian Mobility Study* and the 1986 and 1994 *Statistics Canada General Social Surveys*, Richard Warner (2005) concluded that the effects of socioeconomic origins, as indicated by fathers' occupational status, on sons' occupational status declined considerably in Canada during the twentieth century. Moreover, education, as a measure of achieved rather than ascribed status, does not appear to have had an increasing effect on the occupational status of either men or women. Warner also found that while the economic returns on a bachelor's degree increased up until the late 1950s, they have declined ever since, especially among men. Returns on an advanced degree beyond the BA, however, have been high since the 1920s for both men and women (although higher for men than for women).

The Social Reproduction and Transformation of Class Identities

The **reproduction of class identity** is the process by which an ascribed social class position is transmitted from one generation to the next. The **transformation of class identity** can be thought of as its opposite: the processes whereby a social actor alters her ascribed social class position in order to achieve a social class position different from the one she acquired from her parents. We have already read about Paul Willis's (1977) classic study of working-class youth in England. In that study Willis offered insights into the ways in which working-class 'lads' rejected middle-class values and goals to prepare themselves to take on working-class jobs. His study is a classic because it helped lay the groundwork for sociologists to understand the reproduction of working-class identity.

Part of Willis's study focused on how the majority of working-class 'lads' contrasted themselves with another, smaller group of working-class youth, whom they called the 'ear'oles'. Unlike their peers who embraced a working-class identity and who later took on working-class jobs, the 'ear'oles' rejected working-class culture and instead tried to get ahead by doing well at school.

While Willis sought to find out how the majority of working-class 'lads' came to take on low-status, low-paying working-class jobs, Peter Kaufman (2003) set out to answer another question: How do individuals from working-class backgrounds, who buy into the education system and attend college or university in pursuit of middle-class jobs, manage to transform their working-class identities into middle-class ones?

To answer this question, Kaufman devised a study of working-class college seniors from a large American public university. Kaufman made the aim of his study to determine if class identity is 'just a de facto process achieved through self declaration' or if individuals must 'actively embrace a particular sense of self and choose with whom they will align themselves'. What is the process, he wanted to know, 'through which individuals embrace specific identities and define themselves accordingly to their actions in hopes of having this identity confirmed by significant others'? In short, how is ascribed class identity transformed into achieved class identity (Kaufman, 2003, pp. 481–2)?

In order to achieve a new class identity, individuals have to be accepted as members of the social class to which they aspire and get significant others to accept and vouch for their new personal identity. In order to be able to embrace and identify with the cultural dispositions of the class to which they aspire, they must become conscious of their existing social identity

reproduction of class identity
The process by which an ascribed social class position is transmitted from one generation to the next.

transformation of class identity
The processes whereby a social actor alters her ascribed status in order to achieve a status different from the one she has acquired from her parents.

and work actively to construct a new social identity. As Kaufman notes, in order to create a new identity, an individual undergoes a kind of metamorphosis, a process of re-socialization. Not only must she reinvent the present, but she must occasionally reinvent the past. Crossing

STUDIES IN SOCIAL RESEARCH

Social Class, Stratification, and Mobility in China

China offers an interesting research location for sociologists to address many questions about social class, stratification, inequality, and social mobility. After Chairman Mao's death in 1976, the new leader, Deng Xiaoping, instituted a wide-ranging reform policy of reversing collectivization in farming and of encouraging commodity production in both rural and urban economies. As a result, the institutional basis of China's pre-reform status hierarchy has been eroded, and in its place a more open class system has evolved (Davis, 1995, as cited in Bian, 2002, p. 92). Between 1978 and 2000 the Chinese economy grew from one of the poorest to the seventh largest in the world, and in 2009 the Chinese economy ranked third in the world in terms of gross domestic product (GDP). Only the United States and Japan had larger economies (Canada ranked tenth, behind Germany, France, the UK, Italy, Brazil, and Spain).

A great deal of research has been conducted on status groups in pre-Mao and post-Mao China. However, very little research has focused on social classes, especially on rural and urban differences, largely because social classes in China are 'in the making', which makes it difficult to discern 'clear class boundaries'. Yanjie Bian (2002), of the Hong Kong University of Science and Technology, has made an important contribution to our understanding of the complex issue of social class in present-day China. In a compelling essay on class stratification, socioeconomic inequalities, and social mobility in the People's Republic of China, Bian argues that Chinese class stratification has been 'transformed from a rigid status hierarchy under Mao' to an open class system that, in the post-Mao period, has altered the distribution of socioeconomic inequalities in that country.

Under Mao, a state socialist economy had eliminated private ownership of productive assets by collectivizing farming and by consolidating urban assets in the hands of the state. All members of Chinese society were classified into qualitatively different status groups along four structural and behavioural dimensions: (a) the rural–urban divide in residential status; (b) the state–collective dualism in economic structure; (c) the cadre–worker dichotomy in occupational classification; and (d) the revolutionary–antirevolutionary split in political characterization (Bian, 2000, pp. 92–3). Under this system it was rare for an individual to be able to change his social position. But economic reforms after 1978 and the rise of labour markets have gone a long way to erode these rigid divisions.

Under Mao's system, those born in rural areas were not usually permitted to move from those locations. Bound to collective farming, they were cut off from many urban privileges such as compulsory education, high-quality schools, healthcare, public housing, and varieties of foodstuffs. As peasants, they were largely forced to remain in the countryside, and only a tiny fraction had the chance to move into towns, whether by military service, marriage, or attainment of higher education.

Meanwhile, city youth could be forced to move to the country for a period of time. The division between privileged state workers and their relatively deprived collective-farm-worker counterparts was far-reaching. State workers received insurance and welfare benefits unavailable to collective workers. Whether urban or rural, though, very few workers were allowed to change jobs during their lifetime.

The crude but official job categories of 'cadre' and 'worker' were considered status groups as well. State cadre, a job classification that included about 5 per cent of the total workforce, occupied prestigious managerial and professional jobs. They received sociocultural boundaries is a kind of 'code switching' (Anderson, 1999), and the interpersonal strategies that one uses to accomplish this go a long way to determining whether or not one will be successful.

above-average compensation packages and training and could be promoted into leadership positions in party and government offices. Those classified as 'workers' were rarely allowed to take on a cadre position. In addition, all households were politically evaluated and categorized as revolutionary ('red') or anti-revolutionary ('black') classes. A pre-revolutionary family class origin of propertylessness automatically made all family members 'red', while a property class origin automatically assigned all family members to the 'black' classes. This categorization could be changed by individual effort. For example, an individual's satisfactory performance in numerous party-led campaigns could reverse a family-derived categorization from 'black' to 'red'. This kind of political labelling reached its high point during the Cultural Revolution (1966–76) (Bian, 2002).

But after Mao's death in 1978 significant economic changes began in the rural areas where, by 1983, collective farming was ended and, after 1992, peasants were allowed to move into the cities. Rural and urban cadres started to turn their attention from the politics of the Communist Party to market opportunities and in some areas even started 'insider privatization', appropriating what had previously been collective assets (Nee & Su 1998, as cited in Bian, 2000, p. 95). This decentralization had the effect of splitting rural peasants into rich and poor peasant classes. Unlike rural reforms, urban reforms came later and under the close guidance of the state. They included an influx of peasants to the cities, decentralization of state industry and the fiscal system, and the

'Cadre schools' were rural farms where recalcitrant students and intellectuals were 'sent down' from the cities to undergo ideological re-education while performing manual farm work. Is class in this context an ascribed or an achieved status?

emergence of labour and financial markets. All of this was accompanied by massive layoffs of state sector workers, who became impoverished while a very few from their ranks managed to gain executive control and income rights over previously state-owned properties.

Bian concludes his study by noting that China's evolving political and economic institutions continue to create 'uncertainties and unpredictable patterns'. Further research is needed, he argues, to help generate new theoretical perspectives to explain 'agents, sources, and mechanisms of change in the system of social stratification and social mobility' (Bian, 2002, p. 109).

Theoretical Context: Presentation of Self and Impression Management

Kaufman drew on the work of Erving Goffman (discussed in Chapter 9) to provide the theoretical context for his study, arguing that the process of social transformation is one of 'interpersonal negotiation'. Any individual who actively sets out to transform his ascribed status must have his achieved status validated by significant others. As Erving Goffman noted, 'if a person wishes to sustain a particular image of himself and trust his feelings to it, he must work hard for the credits that will buy this self enhancement for him' (Goffman, 1967, p. 42).

Impression management, you will recall, is Goffman's term for 'the mostly conscious decisions that individuals make concerning how they can and will display themselves to others' (Goffman, 1959). Goffman noted that individuals try to manage the impressions that others have of them in order to elicit specific kinds of responses from their audience. Impression management is both an individual act and a social requirement, reflecting the intersection between social identity and role identity. In order for working-class students to become accepted members of the middle class and to achieve their desired social identity, they had to engage in behaviour that was acceptable to the members of the social group to which they hoped to belong. Kaufman found that the working-class students he interviewed were well aware of the need for successful self-presentation as a prerequisite for the efforts at constructing a new social identity. They especially focused on two behaviours they thought they would have to change: speech patterns and styles of dress.

Strategies of Identity Formation

About one-quarter of the students Kaufman interviewed were engaged in a process that he labelled 'transformation completion'. These students had parents who had begun the process of social transformation, and the students were aware that it was now up to them to complete the process by going beyond what their parents had already achieved in terms of education, occupation, and income. For example, the father of a girl known as 'Shannon' worked three jobs—as a firefighter, a bus driver, and a dispatcher—while her mother worked as an intake clerk in a social service agency. Neither of Shannon's parents had a college education, but they both worked very hard to achieve an income that could afford them a 'middle-class lifestyle'. Shannon realized that in order to maintain this lifestyle, she had to acquire a university education.

In his study, Kaufman identified a series of personal strategies that the students used in their attempts to transform their social class. These strategies included *associational embrace* (aligning themselves with other individuals who already possessed the professional social class orientation to which they aspired), *associational distancing* (separating themselves from those who held non-professional, working-class orientations), and *behavioural changes* (behaving in ways they believed appropriate for inclusion in a particular social group) (Kaufman, 2003, p. 484).

Kaufman identified associational embrace as the key strategy that students used in taking the first step towards achieving a new class status. Deciding to attend university is an example of this strategy, and as several students whom Kaufman interviewed noted, that decision was often the by-product of the student's interpersonal relations. Having friends who wanted to go to university was often a key reason that the students Kaufman interviewed decided to do the same. The students who sought to change their ascribed social class recognized that they had to consciously embark on strategies of interpersonal relationships, evaluate the resources at their disposal as well as the capabilities for action, and then plan a strategy of social interaction regarding whom they would associate with.

For example, one student, 'Scott', whose father was a tree pruner, decided that he wanted to go to graduate school to study comparative literature. To achieve this new identity, Scott had to begin by engaging in role enactments without knowing whether or not he would be successful. He began by intentionally associating with people who could reflect back to him the identity that he was working hard to achieve. In his interview, Scott described attending a conference organized by the Institute for Postmodern Studies. Scott described feeling 'strange a little bit because I didn't know what they were talking about. . . . I couldn't even comprehend most of what was going on. . . .' He went on to say that he did like the feeling of 'somehow being a participant in that', and he recognized that attending the conference was 'part of the initiation' into an unfamiliar world.

Individuals use associational distancing to set themselves apart from individuals whose values and actions are inconsistent with the social identity they are trying to achieve. For example, in speaking about her former friends, 'Chamique' told Kaufman she realized she no longer shared or embraced the same values they did. Her old friends were 'just into a lot of stuff like drinking a lot' while she wanted to 'start getting involved in activities, networking with people'. But Kaufman notes that the working-class students who seek to transform their social class may find it difficult to distance themselves from their working-class peers and often experience ambivalence. Not only must students such as 'Chamique' separate themselves from their peers, they must also simultaneously leave behind familiar role behaviours that coincided with their membership in their old social group (Kaufman, 2003, p. 493).

Students who came from poor minority backgrounds (and who were typically male) expressed the additional need to distance themselves from the 'hegemonic conception that society holds of their peer group' (Kaufman, 2003, p. 493). In contrast to Willis's 'lads', who rejected mainstream values in order to reproduce their ascribed social class positions, the poor minority males whom Kaufman interviewed had to work hard to overcome the existing dominant ideology in order to avoid reproducing their ascribed social class position. These young men worked hard at legitimizing themselves by repeatedly demonstrating that they should not be associated with the stereotypical portrait current in society. One of the young, poor, urban blacks whom Kaufman interviewed explained how hard he worked to distance himself from the commonly held belief that he and his brothers were lazy troublemakers who wouldn't amount to much. 'Johnny' wanted to have a career in law, and he worked diligently to distance himself from an identity that he believed was unfairly imputed to him and to take on the identity of a professional. As 'Johnny' told Kaufman, 'What I'm saying for me is that it's all about respect. It's all about where people see you. It's all about how other people view you. It's not even in my opinion where you actually are, it's where people consider you, or other people consider you' (Kaufman, 2003, p. 493).

Speech Patterns and Style of Dress

Students in Kaufman's study were aware of the importance of using proper grammar. They were also aware that accent, word choice, and the ways of expressing thoughts were also important class markers. 'Sally' noted that while it feels 'weird', she chose to adopt the speech patterns of her college roommates as opposed to those of her less-educated co-workers back home. Sally recognized that the way she spoke sent a message not just to others but also to her, and so she actively tried to talk like her peers at college. In order to be successful, 'Sally' had to become virtually bilingual, as she moved carefully between two very different social identities and their correspondingly different speech patterns. On the one hand she could be ostracized by her co-workers at home for being 'stuck up'; on the other she could be shunned by her peers at university for being 'lower-class'.

Students also recognized that style of dress was an important identity marker in establishing the parameters of interpersonal relations. Just as there are rules of speech there are also rules of dress and wearing clothes appropriate to a specific interaction setting is a sign that one belongs and knows what is required. This applies equally to both casual and professional settings. One student, 'Steve' commented that he was 'shopping more at Structure and Gap now' because clothes from those stores fit in more with what he perceived to be an 'upper middle-class position' (Kaufman, 2003, p. 497).

SOCIAL CLASS: THE WORK OF PIERRE BOURDIEU

Pierre Bourdieu, whom we encountered in Chapter 11, was especially interested in the role of education in the production and reproduction of social inequality in France. This interest led him to study social class in the context of cultural production and consumption, and to write his most famous book, *Distinction: A Social Critique of the Judgment of Taste* (1979/1984).

We have already seen how Bourdieu combined the analysis of social structure with the analysis of social agency in his work. Bourdieu felt that while social structures instil mental structures in individuals, the mental structures that individuals possess in turn reproduce (or, under certain circumstances, change) social structures. Along with the concept of 'habitus', Bourdieu devised three concepts to facilitate his analyses of the interplay between social structure and agency and their role in the formation of different classes: capital, field, and symbolic power (Sallaz & Zavisca, 2007, p. 23).

Can you recall a social interaction in which you were self-conscious about your social class? What strategies did you adopt to affect a higher or lower class?

Types of Capital

Unlike Marx, who used the term 'capital' to refer to economic capital alone, Bourdieu divided the concept into four main types:

1. economic capital
2. cultural capital
3. social capital
4. symbolic capital.

Each type of capital provides its possessor with a different form of power.

Economic capital does not refer just to monetary income but also to the knowledge to which the accumulation of wealth and the ownership of productive assets gives access. Access to opportunities and expert advice is key to gaining and keeping economic capital.

Cultural capital refers to the capacity to demonstrate competence in some valued area of practice and can take one of three different forms. First, it can take the form of an embodied disposition expressed in tastes and practices; the way you dress, your fashion, is evidence of cultural capital. Second, it can exist as formal certifications given by an educational institution in recognition of the possessors' skills and knowledge; the bachelor's degree you hope to someday earn is a kind of cultural capital. Third, cultural capital can take an object-defined form in the possession of highly valued cultural goods, like the art you hang on your walls, the kind (and age) of carpets you put on your floors, or the million-dollar home that makes you the envy of your poorer neighbours.

Social capital consists of durable networks of social relations that give the individual access to power and resources. Political connections, family connections—any relationships that enable you to get ahead in life are proof of your social capital.

Finally, any form of capital can serve as *symbolic capital* in so far as it is recognized as demarcating the legitimate unequal distribution of whatever is valued. For example, Ken Dryden acquired a lot of prestige as a successful goaltender in the NHL. He was later able to use this symbolic capital when he ran for political office as a candidate for the federal Liberal Party.

Field

Bourdieu argued that the power provided by different forms of capital to their possessors depends on the structure of the *field* in which a particular form of capital is activated. By 'field' Bourdieu meant the local social world in which social actors are embedded and towards which they orient their actions (Sallaz & Zavisca, 2007, p. 24). When speaking about a 'field' Bourdieu frequently used a game metaphor. Like a game, a field has rules, stakes, and strategies; players become invested in and absorbed by it; rules exist that define 'legitimate principles of the field'.

Bourdieu used the concept of field to refer to both the actors and the organizations involved in an area of social or cultural production, and to the dynamic relationships that exist among them. Every field is an arena of potential conflict, and social life is the struggle for a position in one or more fields. A position within any field is achieved via the accumulation and monopolization of different kinds of capital, which are then put into play in a given field, symbolically exchanged, and transformed from one type of capital into another (DiMaggio, 1979, p. 1473). For example, economic capital may be exchanged for cultural capital when a university education is purchased. In the course of acquiring a university degree, the individual may also acquire social capital in the form of networks of contacts with other students, with faculty members, and with alumni, all of which in later life may be indispensable connections in the search for a job. This in turn may generate economic capital, part of which goes to purchase a membership in a high-status golf and country club, leading to the accumulation of further social capital . . . and so on.

While pre-modern societies did not have fields, since most activity occurred in a single social space, modern societies are characterized by a proliferation of fields. In Bourdieu's analysis, in contemporary capitalist societies, all four forms of capital—economic, cultural, social, and symbolic—operate in all fields. The relationships among these fields is governed by the modern state, which Bourdieu characterized as the possessor of a kind of meta-capital through which rules of hierarchies of value are established across fields (Sallaz & Zavisca, 2007, p. 24).

Although his research covered many areas of social life, Bourdieu focused on education as the fundamental institutional means (or field) by which class inequalities in France are reproduced from generation to generation. Children from different class backgrounds enter the school system with differing degrees of cultural capital—that is, with differing capabilities, capacities, and competencies that have been passed on to them through primary socialization in their families. For the children of those classes that are rich in cultural capital, the socialization that takes place in the schools they attend is simply an extension of their primary socialization. For children of the middle classes, school is an arena in which they can persevere in order to better their class position. But for working-class children, school is alien and not intrinsically prized (DiMaggio, 1979, p. 1464).

Schools exacerbate and multiply inequalities already established through primary socialization. They do this by transmitting knowledge in codes that are easily accessible only to those who already possess the kind of cultural capital that is needed to appropriate it. Schooling ensures the continuing success of the well-to-do and channels children of lesser social classes along different paths.

Habitus

'Habitus', the concept through which Bourdieu theorized the relationship between social structure and social agency, is defined as a system of 'durable, transposable dispositions'. As a disposition, habitus is a social actor's embodied sense of the world and her place in it, first instilled via early childhood socialization in her family and other primary groups. This early inculcation makes habitus 'durable', although not unchangeable. And because it is durable, habitus is also transposable in the sense that when a social actor enters a new setting, she carries her dispositions with her.

Bourdieu used the concept of habitus to explain why an arbitrary and discriminatory system, such as the system of education in France, makes sense to those who participate in it. To the extent that members of different social classes differ in their early experiences, each class has its own particular habitus with, of course, certain variations occurring in the experiences of individuals. In situations where the habitus of an individual and that individual's immediate social situation do not completely coincide—and this happens frequently—the individual will often adjust her aspirations to coincide with the probability that they will be satisfied. Thus, from Bourdieu's point of view, the tendency of working-class kids to drop out of school and to have low educational aspirations (as, for example, Willis found among the working-class 'lads' he studied in England) is the product, rather than the cause, of the low statistical probability of their academic success. On the other hand the working-class students in Kaufman's study have adjusted their aspirations to coincide with new probabilities of success in seeking out middle-class careers and class positions, and have begun the process of rebuilding their habitus.

Class Struggle

Bourdieu often discussed the production and reproduction of economic capital, and made frequent references to social class, all of which suggests the strong influence of Karl Marx. But Bourdieu was also concerned about understanding struggles within the dominant class, between those rich in economic capital and those rich in cultural capital. As DiMaggio writes:

> Take, for example, Bourdieu's version of class struggle. There are no classes-for-themselves in his writings. Classes do not seize power. . . . Instead we have aggregates of optimizers, united by habitus, pursuing parallel strategies towards

similar, but not collective ends. Class conflict occurs within fields and organizations or in the misrecognized confrontations and battles of every-day life. The members of Bourdieu's classes are strategists, not strugglers, engaged in practices, not praxis; families, not classes, are the agents of conflict. (DiMaggio, 1979, p. 1470)

For example, in his study of the French class system of the 1960s, Bourdieu identified different factions existing within the French ruling class. Bourdieu ranked these factions on the basis of two opposite and symmetrical hierarchies: one structured by the possession of economic capital, the other by cultural capital. Bourdieu studied, as an example of this, the managerial revolution that occurred in France, focusing on the way in which upper-echelon managers were recruited to their positions. He was particularly interested in how less wealthy factions of the dominant class converted schooling (cultural capital) into high power positions, while the children of wealthy owners—the upper sectors of the dominant class—could rely on their access to economic capital, even if they failed to acquire the cultural capital (i.e. the formal educational certification) needed to secure a high-level position after they graduated.

Bourdieu discovered that the distinction between the less wealthy and the more wealthy factions of the dominant class was blurred over time as the managerial revolution forced the 'children of the upper classes—managers and captains of industry'—to acquire 'credentialed cultural capital' (e.g. to obtain a recognized academic degree) and not just rely on their access to economic capital. For both factions of the dominant class, when cultural capital was supplemented by social capital consisting of 'networks and connections', members of the less wealthy factions as well as those of the wealthier factions were able to convert the entire package into a 'high class position' within a business enterprise. In the course of the managerial revolution, the children of the owners of business, although still advantaged in important ways, were subjected to the same 'rationalized modes of recruitment and selection' as were the children of the less advantaged factions of the dominant class. The result was that, unable to directly transmit their economic wealth, the owners of economic capital were

> . . . forced increasingly to convert a portion of economic capital into cultural capital by sending their children to the proper universities and business schools. These inheritors, in turn, reconvert their cultural and social capital into economic dominance. (DiMaggio, 1979, p. 1466)

Taste, Consumption, and Lifestyle

Sociologist Randall Collins (2000) poses this question: 'Are received sociological theories capable of grasping the realities of contemporary stratification?' We know that since the 1970s the distribution of both income and wealth has become increasingly unequal in Western countries. Yet, says Collins, consider the scenario where wealthy clients go to an expensive restaurant for a meal. The servers greet these customers informally, introduce themselves by name, and assume the manners of an equal invited guest into their home. Furthermore, the servers may interrupt the guests to announce menu specials and advise on what they should order. As an interaction ritual, he points out, 'it is the waiters who command attention for their performance while the customers are constrained to act as polite audience' (Collins, 2000).

Collins provides a second example, this time focusing on celebrities of the entertainment world. On highly ceremonial occasions, movie stars, rock stars, and other celebrities may appear in deliberately casual attire, unshaven, or even dressed in torn clothes. This, says Collins, is 'far from a demeanour giving ritual honour to the occasion'. In appearing this way, the celebrities 'adopt a style that a previous generation would have associated with labourers or beggars'. It is a style, too, that is easily emulated by the general public and 'constitutes a historically unprecedented form of anti-status or reverse snobbery'. Here are a few more examples:

> High ranking government officials, corporate executives, and entertainment celebrities are targets of public scandals involving their sexual lives, employment of housekeepers, uses of intoxicants, and efforts of privacy; social eminence, far from providing immunity for petty derelictions, opens up the high ranking to attacks by the word ranking functionaries. A muscular black youth, wearing baggy pants and a hat turned backwards and carrying a boombox loudly playing angry voiced rap music, dominates the sidewalk space of the public shopping area while middle-class whites publicly shrink back in deference. In public meetings, when women and ethnic minorities take the role of spokesperson and denounce social discrimination against a group, white men of higher social classes sit in embarrassed silence or joined in the chorus of support; and in public opinion expressing and policymaking settings, it is the voice of the underdog that carries moral authority. (Collins, 2000, p. 17)

Collins goes on to note that while in surveys asking respondents to rank occupations in terms of perceived prestige, the occupation 'professor' is consistently accorded a high ranking, once the type of 'professor' is specified—economist, sociologist, chemist, and so on—the occupation 'professor' immediately falls in prestige rating. Similarly the occupations 'scientist' and especially 'physicist' are ranked high on surveys—but most people would not be happy with the prospect of being seated next to a physicist through a dinner party. And while 'plumber' ranks low on surveys on occupation prestige, in practice the income of a plumber is greater than that of many highly educated and credentialed white-collar workers. Plumbers often enjoy an income that may be translated into material resources that no white-collar worker could possibly afford on salary alone.

In many societies, the consumption or display of scarce material goods has been used as a marker of difference, especially of power and domination. In modern capitalist societies, a growth in the capacity for wealth creation since the Second World War has focused attention not on production and acquisition of basic needs but rather on their consumption. 'Consumer culture' rather than economic class is now seen by many people as the most important factor in shaping attitudes and behaviour. In keeping with this, there has been, among social scientists, a growing interest in studying patterns of consumption, taste, and consumer culture. Sociologists who study taste consumption and culture are interested in establishing the ways in which patterns of consumption can be used as a resource to enhance social standing.

One of the forms that 'cultural capital' takes is as 'an embodied disposition that is expressed in tastes and practices'. In his book *Distinction: The Social Critique of the Judgment of Taste* (1979/1984), Bourdieu demonstrates how social differentiation actually takes place. Bourdieu focuses on the way in which differences in **taste**, or the choice of cultural practices and objects that people use in their daily lives, helps to establish class position. Contrary to taken-for-granted understandings, Bourdieu argues, 'taste' is not an individual attribute or something that is achieved but is largely the result of social learning and is highly correlated with social class.

taste
Bourdieu's term for the choice of cultural practices and objects that people use in their daily lives in order to establish and maintain their class position.

According to Bourdieu, a single, dominant middle class existed in France during the 1960s and 1970s. Within that class, however, Bourdieu saw a division between the **bourgeoisie**, who were high in economic capital but low in cultural capital, and the intellectuals, who were low in economic capital but high in cultural capital. Tastes within these two groups differed enormously. While intellectuals displayed a preference for aesthetic modernism, the bourgeoisie preferred the flamboyant and the Baroque. But Bourdieu also noted signs of an amalgamation of the two groups. Members of the bourgeoisie who had previously been able to rely on economic capital alone to secure a good future for their children began to send their children to American business schools or to elite schools in France, as we learned earlier in this chapter. Thus, the children of the bourgeoisie, formerly high in economic capital but low in culture capital, soon became high in both types of capital.

bourgeoisie
A social class that owns and controls the means of production and is thus able to exploit and dominate the activities of workers within the production process.

Perhaps the most talented player ever to step on the greens, an American success story by virtue of his modest roots and mixed black and Asian heritage, Tiger Woods became an object of popular derision and scorn when evidence of his marital infidelity became public. Why is it that people who could never come close to equalling what he has accomplished in his area of expertise—golf—or his wealth not only turn their backs on a once popular sports figure but relish in his downfall?

Bourdieu characterized these young members of the bourgeoisie as a new middle class that grew up in response to a new economy in Europe, one that depended 'as much on the production of needs and consumers as on the production of goods'. Members of this new middle class experienced an economy very different to that of their parents' generation, and as a result, they developed a unique cultural capital. As Bourdieu writes:

> The new logic of the economy reduces the aesthetic ethic of production and accumulation, based on abstinence, sobriety, saving, and calculation, in favour of a hedonistic morality of consumption, based on credit, spending, and enjoyment. (1979/1984, p. 310)

Born into an emerging consumer society, members of the new middle class were bent on acquiring material goods and spending on services, and not out of necessity but for personal benefit or enjoyment. Moreover, Bourdieu argues, this new bourgeoisie made natural allies of the petty bourgeoisie—those working in sales, marketing, advertising, public relations, fashion, interior design, journalism, media, and crafts, as well as those concerned with body and emotional regulation, including dieticians, psychotherapists, marriage counsellors, physiotherapists, fitness trainers, and vocational counsellors. These 'intermediate' positions, Bourdieu argues, are of interest to those individuals who lack cultural and social capital but who want to make the leap into the dominant social classes. They are also of interest to those individuals with a superior family background who have not converted their economic capital into the educational credentials necessary to get themselves into the top positions and who may lack the cultural and social capital to achieve these positions. Thus, the new petty bourgeoisie is made up of those who are downwardly mobile from the bourgeoisie as well as those who are upwardly mobile within the petty bourgeoisie.

In carrying out his research on class and taste, Bourdieu and his associates questioned 1,200 subjects from Paris and Lille and from a small provincial town in France in two separate surveys undertaken in 1963 and again between 1967 and 1968. These large surveys were supplemented with a series of smaller ones. Survey respondents were asked questions designed to gauge their knowledge, preferences, and attitudes concerning a wide variety of topics, including fine art, music, books, film, food, sports, home furnishings, and clothing. Bourdieu was concerned with the relationship between the socioeconomic class of the individual (i.e. their access to economic capital) and their status (i.e. their access to and use of cultural symbolic and social capital). He wanted to discover the nature of the relationship between a person's economic power and the power of the cultural and social symbols with which he or she most identified.

Like Marx, Bourdieu maintained that members of different social classes struggle with one another over resources in order to maximize their interests. In each generation, the members of these social classes are presented with, or acquire, different kinds of economic, social, cultural, and symbolic capital. Each person's engagement in social life is affected by the distribution of these endowments. Bourdieu contended that taste is an important part of the cultural capital that each individual acquires as a result of being a member of a particular social class. Moreover, all people learn their taste (unintentionally), and that taste serves as a powerful means of distinguishing the members of one social class from those of another. Occupying a higher social class does not merely afford a person the capacity to consume more. Nor is class simply a product of the social relations that one has to property and to others in the productive process. An individual's social class, from Bourdieu's point of view, shapes every aspect of that individual's life, including the most seemingly personal and intimate aspects, such as food preferences.

While individuals modify what makes up their habitus as they age, the scope of what is available to them to make those modifications is also circumscribed by what they have inherited, by the social expectations of the groups with which they immediately associate, and by the historical circumstances they encounter. On a day-to-day basis, every action is culturally imbued with meaning, and the practice of day-to-day living reinforces the habitus and the individual's group membership.

Each one of us is a member of formally organized groups, such as clubs and political or religious organizations, or informally organized groups, such as friendship groups. We adopt the identifying marks of these groups—a certain manner of dress, a preference for certain foods, a style of eating, of speaking, or of walking, the kind of music we listen to, the books we read, the movies we watch and even what we have to say about them. By doing all of this and more, we confirm and reconfirm our social identity and our class memberships. We reinforce or adjust our habitus. And we confirm our distinction from those who are part of other groups.

In acquiring cultural and social capital, and in building up the habitus, members of different social classes learn class-specific dispositions towards seemingly personal choices such as music, food, literature, and clothing. These dispositions then serve as a means by which individuals establish their orientation to the rest of society and by which their class membership is recognized.

Bourdieu's Study of Social Class and Food

Common-sense understanding tells us that there is a very simple relationship between the types of food a person consumes and his or her social class. As one goes higher up the socio-economic scale, a smaller portion of total income is spent on food. Moreover, the portion of money spent on more expensive foods such as fresh meats, fruits, and vegetables rises, and the portion spent on cheaper foods such as pasta, beans, and processed meats declines.

But Bourdieu counters this simplified understanding of the relationship between money available to spend on food and taste with the observation that there may be several different consumption patterns possible for the same level of income. In his study, Bourdieu found that those who worked as 'foremen' generally remained attached to popular tastes in food, even though they earned more than clerical and commercial employees. And the food tastes of clerical and commercial employees were closer to those of teachers (well-educated members of French society) and farther from those of manual workers, even though their incomes were closer to those of manual workers that to those of teachers.

In order to account for these patterns, Bourdieu argues, we have to consider the 'tastes of luxury' and the 'tastes of necessity'. The clerical workers in Bourdieu's study spent less money on their food in both absolute and relative terms than did the skilled manual labourers. Instead, they spent their money on 'health and beauty care and clothing, and a slight increase in spending on cultural and leisure activities' (Bourdieu, 1979/1984, p. 180). Bourdieu argues that the manual workers spent more money on food because they embraced an ethic of being in the present, along with a readiness to take advantage of good times and to affirm solidarity with others. Manual workers recognized no reason to give present desires a backseat to future fulfillment. They did not expect that a sacrifice in the present would result in a superior future. For the clerical worker of Bourdieu's study, it was an entirely different matter. By abstaining from having a good time now, the clerical worker 'betrays his ambition of escaping from the common presence' to a future of greater individual self-sufficiency (1979/1984, pp. 180–1).

While 'popular taste' in France during the 1960s was defined by the heavy, the fat, and the coarse, the taste of the professional or senior executive tended towards the light, the refined, and the delicate. As economic constraints disappeared, social constraints took their place, leading those of greater socioeconomic means to forfeit 'coarseness and fatness, in favour of slimness and distinction', a cuisine rich in expensive foods, such as fresh vegetables and meats. Teachers who were richer in cultural capital than in economic capital opted for exoticism—preferring Italian or Chinese cooking—or for populism, eating peasant dishes. As Bourdieu comments, 'They are almost consciously opposed to the new rich with their rich food . . . gross in body and mind, who have the economic means to flaunt, with an arrogance perceived as vulgar, a lifestyle which remains very close to that of the working classes as regards to economic and cultural consumption' (Bourdieu, 1979/1984).

Bourdieu also found that eating habits and the taste for particular kinds of food were associated with a particular domestic economy and the division of labour between men and women. In France during the 1950s and 1960s, traditional, elaborate cooking involved casserole dishes such as *pot-au-feu* (made with inexpensive meat boiled for a long time), *blanquette* (veal stew), or *daube* (beef stew), which required much preparation time and were linked to the traditional role of the wife and mother, especially among the working classes. Higher-class women, Bourdieu tells us, devoted their spare time to 'child care and the transmission of cultural capital', not to cooking. The aim of these women seems to have been to save time and labour in food preparation; they combined this aim with the search for 'light, low-calorie products', such as grilled meat and fish, raw vegetables, frozen foods, and dairy products (Bourdieu, 1979/1984, pp. 185–7).

Tastes in food, too, depend on the ideas that each social class holds about the nature of the body and what it believes are the effects of particular foods on the body's health, strength, and beauty. Working-class people in Bourdieu's survey tended to pay attention to the strength of the male body and were not so concerned with its shape. Professionals in his study, however, were concerned with body image and were interested in eating healthy, non-fattening foods. The body, he concludes, 'is the most indisputable materialization of class taste'.

The differences in the ways different classes regard the body are apparent in many ways, including how the body is fed and cared for, whether or not it is exercised, and what size, shape, and appearance of the body is sought. Bourdieu found that distributions of bodily properties were greatly influenced by class-specific preferences for food, exercise, and maintenance as well as the use of the body in work and leisure.

But body shape has to do with more than just a partially conscious notion of what is or is not a desirable form and condition for the body to take. Distinctions between social classes are more profound, Bourdieu tells us, based on a deeper level of cultural understanding regarding the whole body schema. In particular, Bourdieu cites the actual act of eating, in addition to the selection of foods, as a culturally constructed mark of distinction among social classes. Among the working-class families of the late 1960s and early 1970s, a meal was characterized by the impression of abundance on special occasions, at least for the men, whose plates were always filled twice. Restrictions, however, usually applied to the women, who often shared a plate among themselves or ate leftovers. While a boy's accession to manhood was marked by the privilege of having his plate filled twice, a girl's accession to womanhood was marked by doing without.

Bourdieu noticed a kind of freedom both in the sequencing of the meal and in labour-saving steps in working-class households. For example, dessert might be served on pieces of the cardboard box that it came in; one spoon could be used to stir everyone's coffee, and plates needn't be changed between courses. In a bourgeois household, by contrast, the concern is to eat with 'all due form'. Form is first a matter of rhythm, which implies expectations, pauses, restraints; waiting until the last person is served before starting to eat; taking modest helpings; not appearing overeager, not talking with a full mouth. A strict sequencing of courses is always observed, and all traces of the previous course are removed from the table before the next course is brought to the table. Prior to the dessert, for example, all dishes—even the salt, pepper, and butter—are removed from the table. Rigorous rules of this sort are extended into everyday life, and the distinctions between the home and the exterior world get blurred much more than in the working-class household.

All of this, Bourdieu tells us, is an expression of the bourgeois habitus of order, restraint, and propriety, which cannot be overstepped. Although habits of eating serve as the primary example, all of the bourgeois habitus is permeated with forms and formalisms that are imposed on immediate appetites. There is a 'gentle, indirect, invisible censorship imposed

Is it possible to discern the economic capital and social capital of these diners from their dress, the restaurant, and the kind of food they're eating?

which structures the art of bourgeois living. Correct eating practices, exercised when one is invited out to dinner, are seen as a way of paying homage to one's hosts, as a sort of tribute to the care and effort expended by them' (Bourdieu, 1979/1984, pp. 196–7).

Even with something as seemingly natural as food consumption, we can see how habitus plays a significant role in establishing and maintaining class differences. Bourdieu's study found many similar distinctions between social classes in their approaches to clothing, grooming, beauty, sports, art, and other cultural objects and practices, such as home care and decoration. His work is important because it shows clearly how taken-for-granted knowledge about people's putative 'natural' characteristics, such as tastes in food, clothing, music, art, and even their manners, are really the cumulative results of the socialization process and the kind of habitus that results. An individual's habitus is shaped by previous generations and by ongoing experiences, and it affects almost every aspect of life. Bourdieu showed that, for different social classes, there are very different habitus that dictate both what is desirable in life and how what is desirable is to be achieved, consumed, or displayed. For example, a family meal that would be viewed by the French bourgeoisie as slovenly served and presented, and consisting of 'unhealthy' foods to be avoided if at all possible, is viewed by the working class as unpretentious and filled with delicious, strength-giving foods.

CONTRIBUTING FACTORS TO SOCIAL INEQUALITY

Today the continued material differences among people living in contemporary industrial societies strongly indicates that the analysis of social class has as much significance as it did when Marx and Weber formulated their analyses of the problems inherent in capitalist society. For example, one can still say that social classes in Western societies are characterized by differing means of access to, and participation in, commodity production and consumption, and that this differential access produces varying kinds of advantages and disadvantages for members of a particular class.

Despite many differences in approach, contemporary theorists of social class agree that classes continue to exist in Western industrialized countries, and that they can be mapped into hierarchical structures, with proportionally more people in the lower categories than in the higher ones. (As we have also seen in this chapter, the same can be said for China, which is rapidly emerging as a powerful economy, based on capitalist-like principles of production, distribution, and ownership.)

Almost all class theorists, regardless of their chosen perspective, identify a relatively small upper class, which includes the very wealthy and the owners and controllers of industry. They also identify a much larger middle class or classes, made up of those with marketable skills and professions. Finally, all identify a working class or classes, which include both non-manual workers, such as office and sales personnel, and manual workers. Some even identify an underclass.

But class factors are not alone in contributing to the creation of advantaged or disadvantaged positions. Race, gender, and sexual orientation are also contributors. In the next chapter we take up gender and gender-based inequality.

SUMMARY

In response to critiques about the limitations of classical theories of social class, contemporary sociologists have expanded on, or modified, those theories. American sociologist Erik Olin Wright has laid out an elaborate typology of economic class relations, which takes into account Marx's criteria of class as a social relationship made up of relations to the means of production, as well as the added factors of 'relations to authority', 'relations to scarce skills', and 'number of employees' in a capitalist enterprise. Most interesting, Olin Wright and his colleagues have proposed the concept of 'contradictory class locations' in order to analyze situations in which class polarization has not occurred (as Marx predicted it would).

One topic of interest to contemporary sociologists is that of social mobility, especially as mobility relates to social class, stratification, and inequality. China offers sociologists a challenging research location in which to study social mobility, especially as a more open class system is now emerging in that country while at the same time political and economic institutions continue to change in unpredictable ways.

Yet another topic of interest to sociologists today is class identity and its reproduction and transformation. Classic studies include Paul Willis's study of how working-class 'lads' in England rejected middle-class values and schooling and prepared themselves to take on working-class jobs. His work helped sociologists understand how class identity is produced and reproduced across generations. Kauffman's study of working-class students attending university uses symbolic-interactionist concepts to explain the personal strategies used by working-class students in their attempts to transform their social class. Pierre Bourdieu's justly famous study of the French class system, conducted in the 1960s, helped sociologists to understand just how 'taste' can be used to establish distinctions between different social classes in society. Bourdieu's study showed how distinctions between social classes are maintained and how they are challenged and changed over time.

DISCUSSION QUESTIONS

1. The image at the start of the chapter features actor Margot Kidder portraying Eliza Doolittle in a 1983 television adaptation of George Bernard Shaw's play *Pygmalion*. Find a synopsis of the play or the movie (or the 1964 film *My Fair Lady*, likewise based on the play) online and analyze it in terms of the themes discussed in this chapter.

2. Discuss what is meant by the concept of 'contradictory class location'. Use examples to illustrate your answer.

3. Erik Olin Wright proposed a more elaborate typology of class locations than either Marx or Weber did. In what ways is this an improvement (or not) over the framework originally proposed by Marx?

4. What is the difference between an *achieved* and an *ascribed* status? Is upward mobility truly an option for most Canadians? Explain why or why not.

5. Using Paul Willis's classic study of working-class youths as a model, explain how social class was reproduced or challenged in your high school.

6. Following Bourdieu's example, analyze how 'taste' can be used to define your own class position.

14 Sex and Gender: Nature vs Nurture

CHAPTER OUTLINE

LEARNING OBJECTIVES

In this chapter you will:

- learn to distinguish between social gender and biological sex
- study classical statements about differences between men and women
- learn about the biological basis of sex differences
- think critically about sexual dimorphism
- read about one-sex and two-sex models
- gain an understanding of intersex conditions
- consider cultural differences in the acceptance and treatment of intersexed persons
- review some of the insights from neurological and cognitive studies on sex and gender differences.

INTRODUCTION

In early January of 2005, Lawrence H. Summers, then president of Harvard University, sparked an uproar at an academic conference when he said that innate differences, and not discrimination, play the most important role in the dearth of female professors in science and engineering at elite universities (Bombardieri, 2005). In his talk, President Summers offered three explanations for the small number of women in those high-level positions:

1. Women who have children are reluctant or unable to work 80-hour weeks.
2. Fewer girls than boys do well in science and math in the later years of high school.
3. Women do not have the same 'innate' or 'natural' abilities as men. The 'things people previously attributed to socialization', Summers proclaimed, are now shown not to be 'due to socialization after all' (Bombardieri, 2005).

Among those in the audience who took offence at Summer's comments was Denice D. Denton, then chancellor designate of the University of California, Santa Cruz, and outgoing dean of the College of Engineering at the University of Washington. Denton commented: 'Here was this economist lecturing pompously [to] this room full of the country's most accomplished scholars on women's issues in science and engineering, and he kept saying things we had refuted in the first half of the day' (Bombardieri, 2005).

So who's right? Are there profound emotional, cognitive, and achievement differences between males and females that can be attributed to differences in 'innate' or 'natural' abilities? Or are the differences attributable to the ways in which males and females are socialized? In this chapter you are presented with three interrelated issues:

1. *Biological sex and social gender.* What is the difference between biological sex and social gender? Is there a direct and natural relationship between biological sex and social gender? Are women and men, girls and boys really innately different in their behaviours, psychological profiles, and cognitive abilities?
2. *Sexual dimorphism.* Are there only two sexes, or should we consider categories other than the dichotomous pair 'male/female'?
3. *Different brains?* Do males and females have different brains? Are any brain differences between men and women the result of biological inheritance, or do socialization and culture play the most important roles?

But before dealing with these issues, it is instructive to consider a bit of background information on how social thinkers in the past have addressed questions of sex and gender, nature versus nurture. For most of Western history, men and women have been considered to be fundamentally different. Taken-for-granted understandings about these differences include such beliefs as the following:

- that men and women possess fundamentally different psychological, emotional, and sexual natures
- that males are the naturally dominant, superior sex, while females are the naturally subordinate, inferior sex
- that male domination and female subordination are based on biological differences and are therefore both natural and inevitable (Bem, 1993, p. 1).

What is the basis for these taken-for-granted understandings? And have any of them been borne out by scientific research? In the section that follows we'll look at the history of sociological thinking on sex and gender, and how it has changed over time.

THE CLASSICAL TRADITION IN SOCIOLOGY: A FOCUS ON INNATE DIFFERENCES

During the nineteenth and early twentieth centuries, when sociology was being established as a discipline, an international women's movement was already underway, questioning the taken-for-granted assumptions about women's natural, biologically based subordination to men. However, few of the founders of sociology, with the exception of Engels (1942), expressed much interest in sex and gender issues. Those who did bother to address the issue usually resorted to biological determinism as the best explanation.

Comte, Durkheim, and Engels: Sex and the 'Fathers' of Sociology

According to British sociologists and feminists Pamela Abbott and Claire Wallace (1990), prior to the 1960s, sociologists for the most part ignored the experiences of women and focused instead on those of men. When women appeared at all in sociological studies it was as men saw them and not as they saw themselves.

Auguste Comte found women to be emotionally and spiritually superior to men, making them ideally suited to family and domestic life. But he also judged women, as the intellectual inferiors of males, not suited to anything other than domestic responsibilities.

In *Suicide* (1897), Émile Durkheim discovered what he considered to be an anomaly between the suicide rates of men and women in most western European countries. He found that when a marriage ended either in divorce or in the death of a spouse, men had a much greater tendency to commit suicide than women did. But *during* marriage, women had a higher suicide rate than did their husbands. Durkheim concluded from these empirical observations that marriage affects women and men differently, and that men have more complex and aggressive natures than do women and therefore need more societal bonding. In short, he followed Aristotle's (and Comte's) understanding that women are less developed intellectually. While men commit suicide because they are bereft of social bonds, women commit suicide because those bonds have become too complex and constraining for them to be able to handle.

It was Friedrich Engels who argued that gender relations and especially gender inequalities were the product of social life, and that women's inequality was the result of the development of private property. In *The Origins of the Family, Private Property and the State* (1884), Engels proposed that the solution to gender inequality was the abolition of capitalism. Weber, too, was sensitive to the historically specific nature of the subordination of women, but for the most part remained silent about the issue of gender in the production of inequality.

Functionalism, Parsons, and the Biological Basis of Sex Roles

Sociologists writing about 'sex roles' prior to the 1960s tended to treat masculinity and femininity as necessary and complementary sex-specific, sex-appropriate behavioural and personality traits. Talcott Parsons, whose general theories we encountered in Chapter 11, turned to biology to explain the different roles that men and women took within the family. It was his opinion that the nuclear family—comprising the biological mother and father, living together with their children in their own household—was the family unit most suited to industrial society. It was through the nuclear family that men could be liberated to work outside the home, while women could exercise their maternal destiny and look after home, children, and husband. In Parsons' view, the father was destined to bridge the boundary between the home and the outside world, acting in his capacity as *instrumental* leader of the family unit. The mother, on the other hand, was destined by her biological makeup to take on the *expressive* role.

Parsons and other sociologists influenced by his work thought that the widespread employment of women outside of the family would endanger the 'proper' socialization of children and the 'health' of the family as a social system. Indeed, few male sociologists of the nineteenth and early- to mid-twentieth centuries wrote about women from what might now be considered a liberal feminist position.

Defining Gender

Classical sociologists such as Émile Durkheim and mid-twentieth-century sociologists like Talcott Parsons were not concerned with pursuing the study of 'gender' because they believed that the social roles and behaviours of men and women were (mostly) the results of their biological functions. Indeed, until the 1960s and 1970s, most sociologists were at best 'sex-blind' and at worst sexist. They seldom recognized that women's structural position and experiences in society were different from those of men except in so far as those positions were thought to be biologically determined and therefore 'natural'.

Writing in 1982, British feminist and sociologist Anne Oakley argued that, from its inception, sociology was dominated by men and biased against women. Canadian sociologist Dorothy Smith (1979) expressed a similar view when she pointed out that women had been ignored or treated as inferior by traditional sociology because women's concerns and experiences were considered to be 'subjective', while those of men were thought to be 'objective' and thus (unlike women's) could be relied upon to form the basis upon which scientific knowledge could be founded.

Despite having been dismissed by male sociologists, feminist scholars by the late 1960s and early 1970s had begun to pursue the question of whether or not biological differences between males and females resulted naturally in social, psychological, and behavioural differences. These scholars were careful to distinguish between **sex** and **gender** as different analytical concepts. They argued that an individual's sex is an ascribed status, one determined by biology and present at birth, including anatomy, hormones, and physiology. Gender, on the other hand, is socially constructed; it is an achieved status and not one immediately ascribed to an individual by his or her biology.

Esther Newton's ethnography *Mother Camp: Female Impersonators in America* (1972) was among the first works to analyze gender as a performance and not as a natural result

sex
Either of the two main categories (male and female) into which humans are divided on the basis of their reproductive functions; sex is an ascribed status.

gender
The sense of being male or female, typically with reference to masculine and feminine social and cultural ròles rather than biological differences; gender is an achieved status.

of biological sex. In *Mother Camp*, Newton explored all the intricacies of performing femininity and gender styles in the gay world, including impression management, staging acts, roles, and appearances. Using Goffman's concept of personal front, she discussed 'butch and

Advertising in the 1950s reinforced the ideal social model that featured the father bringing home the bacon (or, in this case, the ice cream) to his wife and children waiting at home. What threat did the liberation of women from their domestic role pose to men?

nellie styles' (1972), explaining how lesbians and gay men managed such styles differently depending on whether they were in a 'straight' or a 'gay' situation. Drag, she argued, calls into question the 'naturalness' of the sex-role system. If sex-role behaviour can be achieved by the 'wrong sex', it follows that all sex-role behaviour is something that is achieved and not inherited by the 'right sex' (Newton, 1972, p. 103).

Thanks to the work of Newton and other scholars, few sociologists by the early 1980s were likely to accept naive biological determinism as an explanation of gender differences and inequalities. Instead, gender studies became a legitimate field of sociological inquiry, with gendered behaviour treated as socially and culturally constructed, rather than merely the natural and inevitable outcome of biologically based differences. By that time, too, gender scholars from many disciplines had started to think more carefully about gender, not as an individual characteristic but as a social process, as something always in question and always in the process of being created. Gender, they argued, was best thought of as the product of social interactions. As such it was never a stable category of being but was open to challenge and to change.

BIOLOGICAL SEX AND SOCIAL GENDER

Over the past several decades there have been numerous published reports in the popular media asserting that biology determines most aspects of male and female behaviour. Everything from differences in parenting styles to sexual orientation and sexual fidelity have been attributed to genetic, heritable factors, while social influences are frequently downplayed. One of the more popular of these publications is John Gray's (1992) *Men Are from Mars, Women Are from Venus*. By 2007 this book had sold over 40 million copies worldwide and had been translated into 40 languages. Gray's writing promotes the understanding that there are enormous and irreconcilable psychological, cognitive, and behavioural differences between males and females. Men and women, Gray holds, think and act differently because they have different brains and bodies. These differences have evolved over millennia as a result of adaptations that were necessary for greater survival success. The sooner we learn to accept and deal with these evolutionary differences the better equipped we will be to manage (and be happy in) our relationships with members of the opposite sex. Of course, Gray's ideas are hardly new, and as readers have already learned, arguments that there are enormous (and significant) differences between the sexes have had a long history in Western culture.

In most societies, being identified as male or female greatly influences the life chances of an individual, including the economic and social roles he or she might expect—or be allowed—to take on. It affects the ways that each person is encouraged to express emotions, and it shapes the quality of relations that individuals might be expected to have with others. Being male or female is so fundamental to the identity of an individual that when we're introduced to someone we haven't met before, the first thing we try to determine is their gender. Our language tells us there are only two sexes; our laws tell us that every birth must be registered as either male or female. For many people, relying on a biological deterministic argument to explain the most complex aspects of human behaviour is both simple and satisfying. Many social scientists, biologists, and neurologists, however, are not so quick to make that simple and straightforward connection.

To answer the question of what connection exists between biology of birth and social behavioural differences we first need to address the issue of biological sex: just what is it, biologically speaking, that makes males and females different?

Biological Sex

An individual's **biological sex** is the outcome of the combination of two specialized reproductive cells, called **gametes**. In females, the gamete is the ovum (large and immobile), which carries only an X-chromosome. In males, it is the sperm (small and mobile), which can carry either an X- or a Y-chromosome. Sperm and egg each have only half the total number of chromosomes needed to form an offspring who inherits traits from both parents.

A **gene** is an encoded protein that regulates some aspect of heredity in a living organism. All living things depend on genes, which hold all the information needed to build and maintain an organism's cells and to pass on genetic traits to offspring. All organisms have genes that correspond to different biological traits. The total complement of genes in an organism is called its **genome**. In humans, genes are bundled together in each cell in 23 pairs of microscopic packages called **chromosomes**, which are long DNA helixes on which many thousands of genes are encoded.

In each of our cells, each member of chromosome pairs 1 to 22 is identical to its partner, although each pair is different from all others. It is only with the sex chromosomes that there is any visible difference between the two members of the pair, and that difference occurs only in males. In females, two X-chromosomes are present, while the members of the twenty-third pair of chromosomes in males are unequal in size and shape: a large X-chromosome is paired with a much smaller Y-chromosome (the 'X' and 'Y' refer to the shape of the sex chromosomes). In the language of biology, the typical human male has a diploid karyotype of the 46 chromosomes, which includes 22 autosomal pairs and an XY-pair of gonosomes, while the typical human female has a diploid karyotype of 46 chromosomes, including an XX-pair of gonosomes in each diploid cell.

Many of the genes found along the sex chromosomes affect traits that are not specifically related to biological sex, such as the ability to distinguish the colours green and red. However, a Y-chromosome carries genes that serve to specify the development of testes. Several weeks after fertilization, the human embryo begins to develop all-purpose gonads that will later become either testes or ovaries. If an X- and a Y-chromosome are present, the all-purpose gonads will begin to develop into testes in the eighth week. If two X-chromosomes are present, the all-purpose gonads will begin to develop into ovaries by the thirteenth week.

The original direction of development of the all-purpose gonads in all embryos is as ovaries. It is necessary for the Y-chromosome to intervene in that development to turn them into testes. To put it more directly, the 'natural' form of the human body is female. It requires a biochemical intervention, instigated by the presence of the Y-chromosome, to change that course of development away from the female form and towards the male form. As developmental biologist Alfred Jost has put it, 'becoming a male is a prolonged, uneasy, and risky venture; it is a kind of struggle against inherited trends towards femaleness' (as cited in Diamond, 1992, p. 73). The presence of a Y-chromosome switches gonad development from the ovarian (female) path to the testicular (male) path.

Of course, being a female is more than having ovaries, just as being male is more than possessing testes. To form a penis, or a vagina and clitoris, the human embryo also possesses other all-purpose sex structures. But unlike the testes, these sex structures do not develop as the direct results of possessing a Y-chromosome. Instead, other primordial sex structures are directed towards the male model of development (and thus away from the female model) because of the secretion of hormones by the testes. In the absence of testicular secretions, or if there is an insensitivity to those secretions, other sex structures continue to develop along the female path.

biological sex
The outcome of the combination of two specialized reproductive cells, called **gametes**. In females, the gamete is the ovum, which carries only an X-chromosome; in males, it is the sperm, which can carry either an X- or a Y-chromosome.

gene
An encoded protein that regulates some aspect of heredity in a living organism. The total complement of genes in an organism is its **genome**.

chromosomes
Long DNA helixes on which many thousands of genes are encoded.

Let's return to the eighth week of gestation of an embryo with X- and Y-chromosomes. At that time testes form, and they in turn begin to produce an *androgenic hormone* (or *androgen*) called testosterone. Some of this testosterone gets converted into another androgen called dihydrotestosterone, or DHT. It is DHT that acts on the other all-purpose sex structures to convert them into the glans, penis shaft, and scrotum. Without the DHT, or in the face of insensitivity to DHT, those all-purpose sex structures would go on to develop into the clitoris, labia minora, and labia majora.

A similar process happens to those structures that will become either fallopian tubes in females or seminal vessels, vas deferens, and epididymis in males. Up to week eight of gestation, the developing embryo has two different sets of ducts, Müllerian ducts and Wolffian ducts. In the absence of testes, the Wolffian ducts atrophy and the Müllerian ducts grow into a female uterus, fallopian tubes, and the inner parts of the vagina. But if a Y-chromosome is present and testes develop, the androgens produced cause the Müllerian ducts to atrophy and the Wolffian ducts to develop into male structures.

Sexual Dimorphism?

sexual dimorphism
The recognition of only two sexes—male and female—per species.

Sexual dimorphism is the recognition of only two sexes—male and female—per species. For most of us, the determination of our maleness or femaleness takes place decisively at the moment of birth, when the attending medical practitioner observes the appearance of our genitals. The fact that almost all infants born with male genitals turn out to accept a masculine role in later life and that almost all infants born with female genitals turn out to accept a feminine role is a powerful common-sense support for the argument that there are two dichotomous

What sex do you think this person is? What gender? Would your answer to the second question be any different if you knew the answer to the first? Are the choices of 'male' or 'female' too limited to represent the gender of this young woman?

sexes, and that the relationship between an individual's biological sex and his or her social gender is both natural and inevitable. But does this hold up to closer sociological scrutiny?

One-Sex and Two-Sex Models

That there are only two 'stable, incommensurable, opposite sexes' and that the political, economic, and social lives of men and women, including both their gender identity and gender roles, are somehow based on these biological 'facts' has been the dominant view in Western culture since the eighteenth century (Laqueur, 1990). It may surprise readers to learn that the notion of males and females as two fundamentally different sexes is of fairly recent vintage. In the history of Western thought there have been some doubts about the existence of only two sexes.

The 'one-sex model' has had a long history in Western thought. According to Galen, the second-century AD Roman court physician to Marcus Aurelius, females were essentially imperfect males who lacked the vital heat necessary to bring about the expulsion of their sexual structures from the body. 'The female is less perfect than the male for one principal reason—she is colder,' Galen wrote, 'for among animals the warm one is the more active, and the colder animal would be less perfect than the warmer' (Galen, 1968, p. 296).

While the female of any species was considered a degenerate or imperfect male, it must be emphasized that she was not thought to possess sex organs that were significantly different from those of the perfect male. Galen invites his readers to try to conceptualize how, turned inwards, the male's external genitalia become a female's, and how, pushed outside, the female's become male:

> Think first, please, of the man's [external genitalia] turned in and extending inward between the rectum and the bladder. If this should happen, the scrotum would necessarily take the place of the uterus with the testes lying outside, next to it on either side. . . .
>
>   Think too, please, of the converse, the uterus turned outward and projecting. Would not the testes [*note*: today we call these the ovaries] then necessarily be inside it? Would it not contain them like a scrotum? Would not the neck [today called the cervix], hitherto concealed inside the perineum but now pendant, be made into the male member? (Galen, 1968, pp. 628–9)

Galen compared the 'degenerate' female organs to the eye of a mole. Like other animals' eyes, the mole's eyes have 'vitreous and crystalline humours and the tunics that surround them'. Yet most do not see. The eyes remain but are left perfect. In the same way, Galen tells us, the uterus is an imperfect version of what would exist if there was enough bodily heat to expel it outward.

This view of the lack of significant differences between male and female sexual parts was reflected in language. What we today distinguish clearly as ovaries and testes, or as semen and ova, were referred to by a single term in Greek and Latin and in early European vernaculars. The shift in how sexual differences were to be understood began in the sixteenth and seventeenth centuries, although this shift at first made little impact on popular thinking (Laqueur, 2003, p. 303). Up until the eighteenth century the most commonly held view was that females and males had the same genitals with the exception that a woman's worked inside her body while a man's were on the outside of his body (and, of course, that the female version was somehow imperfect).

During the eighteenth century, a lengthy transition took place in which the 'one-sex model', where only one archetypical body (male) was considered to exist, was replaced by the 'two-sex model', in which men and women were considered to have distinctly different bodies (Gould, 1991, pp. 11–13). A wide variety of writers promoted the idea of a fundamental distinction between males and females based on discoverable biological differences that ranged from facial features to organs, tissues, and fibres.

Londa Schiebinger (1989) tells us that by the middle of the eighteenth century, physicians in Germany and France had begun to notice that male–female sex differences were present 'in every bone, muscle, nerve, and vein of the human body'. Although anatomists had drawn the human skeleton from observation and dissection since the sixteenth century, it was not until the mid- to late-eighteenth century that those drawings portrayed a marked difference between male and female skeletons. Specifically, the differences emphasized were a smaller skull and a larger pelvis size for females compared to males. That they focused on these and not other parts of the body, says Schiebinger, was not arbitrary. Anatomists focused on the parts of the body that were to become politically significant. Thus, the depiction of female skeletons with smaller skulls and larger pelvises than those of male skeletons was not the result of the growth in realism in anatomy. Rather, as Schiebinger tells us, it was a conscious attempt 'to prove that women's intellectual capabilities were inferior to men's' (1989, p. 43).

Why, we might very well ask, did the two-sex model come to predominate when the one-sex model had lasted for so many centuries? To answer this question requires that we consider the rather contradictory nature of the social reforms that were championed during the Enlightenment, the most prominent of which were appeals to individual freedom and equality. But even as the cause of equality was being promoted, a counter-appeal was being made that in fact not all humans were equal. According to this view, some (Caucasian males in particular) were better suited to producing equality among themselves, while others, including women and non-Caucasians, were of a lesser order, and should therefore be placed under the authority of the superior, Caucasian males.

Ideas of 'nature' played a pivotal role in the development of liberal political thought during the eighteenth century. Philosophers such as Locke and Kant based their ideas about social order on appeals to 'natural reason' and 'natural dignity'. If social inequalities were to be justified, scientific evidence would have to show that human nature varied and was not uniform. The areas of focus were race, sex, and age. Finding sex-based differences between males and females became a priority during the late eighteenth century as a means of prescribing different gender roles for women and men within the social hierarchy.

By the nineteenth century, those differences were being perceived not just in visible bodies but at the microscopic level. Patrick Geddes (1854–1932), a prominent Scottish biologist, argued that the cells that made up males were fundamentally different from those that made up females. Male cells, he maintained, were 'catabolic'—that is, they put out energy. Female cells, by contrast, were 'anabolic', meaning that they stored energy. These differences, he was convinced, demonstrated that women were passive, conservative, and sluggish compared to men, who were more energetic, passionate, and variable (Laqueur, 1990, p. 6).

From the eighteenth century onward, 'scientific discoveries' re-shaped the definition of 'human nature' and were used to justify different social roles for men and women. With a two-sex model, it could be 'scientifically' shown that men should naturally dominate in public spheres and in matters concerning reason and intelligence. Women, on the other hand, could be shown to be 'creatures of feeling', destined by their biology to be mothers and the keepers of tradition and home life.

Intersex

We have already seen that the presence of the Y-chromosome in developing fetuses specifies the development of testes. The presence (or absence) of testes then specifies the remaining male or female structures. Our common-sense understanding tells us that the presence of both an X- and a Y-chromosome should guarantee male organs, while the presence of two X-chromosomes should guarantee female organs. But in fact it's not so simple.

People born with ambiguous sex characteristics (and who thus do not easily fit into either one of the two sex categories recognized in Western thought) are important because they help us understand the relationship between biological sex and social gender. **Intersexed** is a general term used to describe a variety of conditions in which an individual is born with sexual anatomy that does not clearly conform to typical expectations about male and female anatomy. As you will see, the connection between biology, on the one hand, and behaviour and identity as a man or a woman, on the other, is anything but a foregone conclusion. In understanding what happens to people who do not easily fit into either of the two recognized biological sexes, we can gain a new perspective on the relationship between biological sex, gender identity, and social behaviour.

Depending on how the term *ambiguous sex* is defined and on whether that ambiguous sex is discovered at birth or during puberty, estimates of the incidence of 'intersex conditions' vary from 0.0005 per cent (1 child in 2,000) to 4 per cent of all children (Blackless, et al., 2000; Gough, et al., 2008; IPDX, 2008). To put this in perspective, high-end estimates mean that more children are born with ambiguous sex than with Down syndrome (1 in approximately 800 children in Canada are born with Down syndrome—see CDSS, 2009). But while Down syndrome is well known, and an extensive vocabulary exists to discuss and deal with the experience of living with the condition, intersexual phenomena are relatively unfamiliar to the general public and tend to be associated with silence and shame.

As biologist Anne Fausto-Sterling comments, 'sex is a vast, infinitely malleable continuum' (1993, pp. 20–1). Nevertheless, the approach of the medical community to the issue of intersexuality is clearly in keeping with the standard Western view that there are only two 'true' sexes, and that anything else must be made to fit into one of the two categories that nature intended (but somehow, in some cases, neglected to produce). Beginning in the twentieth century and continuing into the twenty-first, the medical community has moved towards completely erasing any form of embodiment that does not strictly conform to the standard two-sex male–female pattern. Today, parents of children with ambiguous sex are expected to quickly make decisions that have far-reaching consequences. Medical professionals world-wide recommend genital surgery at an early phase of the child's life (Roen, 2008; Zeiler & Wickström, 2009, p. 360). Moreover, doctors advise parents not to talk to others about their child's ambiguous sex until the child has been assigned a specific sex, lest they be swayed by the opinions of family and friends rather than being guided in their decision making by the expert opinions of physicians (Zeiler & Wickström, 2009, p. 373). Physicians make every effort to convince parents that what they are doing is revealing the 'true sex' of the child, rather than relying on cultural interpretations of what male or female should mean. But medicine alone cannot determine the 'true sex' of a baby with an intersex condition. Chromosomes do not necessarily dictate gender identity; for example, individuals born with XY-chromosomes but who are insensitive to androgen can lead happy lives as females, and not males.

intersexed
Denoting or affected by any of a variety of conditions in which an individual is born with sexual anatomy that does not clearly conform to typical expectations about male and female anatomy.

As we have learned, there is a long series of biochemical steps—including steps that require the production of a variety of enzymes needed to synthesize DHT from testosterone—that must occur before male genitalia appear. If one of the genes involved in the process is in some way damaged or altered by mutation, the enzyme that it is to produce may be either defective or absent. Some individuals can be born with one X- and one Y-chromosome but also with external genitalia that fail to develop as expected for normal males. In these individuals, some of the male structures develop along the expected line because they are dependent on enzymes and hormones that remain typical. Other male structures—those dependent on altered enzymes—may be completely missing or replaced by female equivalents.

There are a number of cases in recorded medical history of intersexed persons who, as a result of an altered androgen receptor, have grown up to look like normal women. Some of these intersexed individuals have entered careers as fashion models because they conform to standard ideals of feminine beauty—long legs, well-developed breasts, and flawless complexion (Diamond, 1992, p. 73). Because such a child is born with external female genitalia, the condition is usually recognized only when the adolescent consults a doctor when she fails to begin menstruating. At that point, the doctor discovers that the patient has no fallopian tubes or uterus and that the vagina is short and ends abruptly. The patient does have active testes, buried inside the groin, which have been programmed by the Y-chromosome and which actively secrete testosterone. The adolescent develops externally as a female, however, because of the biochemical inability to respond to that testosterone.

What is of interest to sociologists is that most people living with this syndrome, known as hyperandrogenism, view themselves as women in spite of the fact that they have active testes, normal male testosterone levels, and, of course, Y-chromosomes. While they can't bear children, many do get married, adopt children, and are well adjusted to their roles as women. In these cases, not only does having a Y-chromosome, testes, and male testosterone levels fail to make them into men, it also fails to prevent them from living happy and fulfilling lives as women, wives, and mothers.

There are other intersex cases that result from a defect in the enzyme that converts testosterone to DHT. This rare enzyme defect is called 5-alpha-reductase (5AR) deficiency and results in delayed anatomical maleness. Children are born genetically male, with typical Y-chromosomes, testes, and production of Müllerian inhibiting factor. They do not develop fallopian tubes, a uterus, or the internal parts of the vagina. But external male genitalia are very tiny or are entirely absent, and the child is mistaken for a female. The problem may not be detected until puberty, when many of these intersexed children begin to develop external male genitalia.

A child is born with this intersex syndrome only if he inherits the genetic code from both parents. Thus most of the known cases of 5AR intersex children come from parts of the world where marriages between close relatives are common. One such area is a previously remote village in the Dominican Republic. Until 1960 this village had no paved road to the outside world. A total of 38 5AR intersex children, all descendants of a common female ancestor, have been identified by physicians. A second location is a remote area in the New Guinea highlands, also isolated until a few decades ago. A comparison of what happens to children born female but who later become male in each of these societies tells us much about the relationship between biological sex, social gender, gender identity, and social behaviour.

The Treatment of Intersexed Persons in Two Different Cultures

In a certain village in the Dominican Republic, anyone born intersexed prior to the early 1950s was raised unquestioningly as a girl. But by 1950, enough cases had appeared that the

Caster Semenya of South Africa (right) competes in the women's 800-metre semi-finals at the International Association of Athletics Federations world championships in South Korea, where she won a silver medal in September 2011. The 2009 world champion was forced to miss nearly a year of competition while the IAAF investigated allegations that she possessed internal male testes that produced testosterone in levels far greater than those found in most women. The federation reinstated Semenya after approving a new policy on hyperandrogenism, stating that a female athlete is eligible to compete 'if her level of the hormone controlling the development of male sexual characteristics is below the "male range"' (Williams, 2001). Would it be fair to make an intersexed athlete who identifies as female compete against men because of her testosterone levels? Would it be unfair to her opponents to allow her to compete against women?

villagers began paying very close attention to the baby's genitals. Since that time, most inter-sexed individuals have been recognized at birth or in early childhood and have been raised as boys. Among the post-1950 generation of intersexed children, however, 19 were raised as girls, and 18 of those 19 have been studied by scientists. According to Dr Juliane Imperato-McGinley and her associates, who have studied these children, 'of the 18 subjects, 17 have successfully changed to a male gender identity, and 16 to a male gender role' (Imperato-McGinley, et al., 1979, p. 1234). This change occurred around age 16, and was indicated by sexual interest in women.

Only one of the subjects studied was reported to have maintained her original 'gender identity' as a female. This person had an unsuccessful marriage as a teenager and then went to work as a housemaid, wearing false breasts. The others quickly became convinced they were male, and adopted male gender identity and gender roles. At first they and their families were astonished and confused. They were ridiculed in the village, but eventually most married and took on traditional male gender roles, typically working as labourers, while their wives took on the traditional female gender roles of housekeeping, tending the garden, and looking after any children there might have been from a previous marriage.

Writing over 30 years ago, Imperato-McGinley and her colleagues concluded that the inter-sexed children of the Dominican Republic adjusted with such astonishing rapidity to their new gender identities and roles because they were already predisposed to adopt masculine identities and gender roles due to the fact that they had 'masculine' brains. The female gender in which they had been reared had little effect on their development as adolescent males or on their ability to adopt male gender roles and identity in later life because their brain's exposure to testosterone trumped their social conditioning. This conclusion, on first pass, seems to have some merit. However, if we take into consideration the more recent work of anthropologists and neurolo-gists, we have some reason to question Imperato-McGinley and her colleagues' conclusions.

Insights from Anthropology

In Papua New Guinea, highland tribal people began sustained contact with outsiders only about fifty years ago. Among the most feared were the Sambia, a warrior tribe of about 2,400, who lived in an isolated rainforest in the southern part of the highlands (Herdt, 1987). 'Sambia' is a name given to this tribe by anthropologist Gilbert Herdt in order to protect their identity. It is among the 'Sambia' that one of the world's largest concentrations of 5AR-deficient inter-sexed persons are to be found.

Anthropologists Gilbert Herdt (1987, 1993, 1994a, 1994b) and Maurice Godelier (1986) have both remarked that gender role differences between the men and women of the New Guinea highlands are among the sharpest and most rigid to be found anywhere in the world. The male sex is clearly favoured and valued. Men are fighters and hunters, while women's economic and social roles are as gardeners and mothers. The Sambia divide the world into men's space and women's space. Men and women have different footpaths within the villages, and husbands and wives occupy separate living space within their small huts. Children are segregated by sex after about age 7, and boys are eventually forbidden to talk with, or even to look at, women, who, because they possess vaginas, are considered to be 'dirty polluters'.

But only women can grow sweet potatoes (men are considered incapable of such an accom-plishment because they have penises). Only women can secrete milk. Every male infant, therefore, must be entrusted to his mother's care. But at age 7, a boy's care is taken over by the men of the village, and he is forcibly initiated into the life of the communal men's house, where no women are permitted.

Intersexed persons, not unexpectedly, do not fit easily into Sambian life, although the Sambia do recognize three sexual categories; male, female, and *kwolu-aatmwol*, roughly translated as 'transforming into a male thing' (Herdt, 1994b, p. 436). The latter are usually rejected both by their parents and by their peers. In one study of 10 intersexed individuals, only half were married, and one had committed suicide. Of those who had tried to retain their female gender identity, two who had married had been rejected by their husbands after attempts at intercourse. In a separate investigation, Herdt (1994b) identified and studied 14 intersexed individuals over three generations since 1910. In several of the cases known to Herdt, the switch from one gender category to another took place only after marriage, and humiliation. But in these cases the switch was not from female to male, but from female to *kwolu-aatmwol*.

The reported (relative) ease with which gender identity behaviours are changed among the intersexed of the Dominican Republic might suggest that the adoption of male identity and behaviour patterns was easily accomplished because of a true, although previously masked, biological sex. The difference experienced by the intersexed children of New Guinea, however, supports the conclusion that a much more complex relationship exists between biological sex, gender identity, and behaviour than common-sense understanding leads us to believe. As Herdt comments:

> Surely, some elements of sex/gender developments are in turn only motivated or hormonally time-loaded in ways that can influence the outcome of a life. However, we are reminded of the importance of social classification of sexual dimorphism and of the resistance to the creation of a third sex that is so injuring in Western culture. . . . We do not have to alienate human culture and history from biology to accept that, in some places and times, a third sex has emerged as part of human nature: and in this way, it is not merely an illusion of culture, although cultures may go to extreme lengths to make this seem so. (Herdt, 1994b, p. 445)

Further Insights from Neurological and Cognitive Studies

The founding fathers of sociology relied on biological differences as their favoured means of justifying the subordinate position of women in society. For many social scientists today, especially those concerned with the subjugation of women, any arguments based on references to biological differences between males and females as the determinant causes of social differences are roundly rejected. This rejection of biological differences as the determining factor in women's and men's social inequalities is understandable, given the history of using biological differences to justify the subordination of women.

It is difficult, however, to continue to ignore the potential effects of biological differences on gendered behaviour, especially in light of recent research from the neurological sciences. The most recent research from the neurological and cognitive sciences indicates that neither biology nor socialization and culture alone can be relied on to accurately explain male–female differences in behaviour.

Since the late 1980s, many studies investigating differences in cognition and behaviour between males and females have shown that males tend to perform better than females in 'mathematical reasoning and visuospatial tasks, whereas females tend to score higher on tasks involving mathematical calculations, verbal fluency, and perceptual speed' (Christiansen

2001; Hyde & Linn, 1988; Hyde, Fennema, & Lamon, 1990). Studies have also revealed differences in social behaviour and cognition. Psychiatrist Jessica Wood and her colleagues (2008) have recently reported on research showing a complex relationship between social gender, social cognition, and brain morphology. Among their findings:

- Men tend to form larger social groups and be less accepting of non-group members, whereas women tend to prefer dyadic (two-person) interactions and are more compromising (Geary, 2002).
- Men make more frequent displays of physical aggression than women, though women are more likely to participate in relational aggression such as gossiping and backstabbing (Christiansen, 2000; Geary, 2002).
- Women generally perform slightly better in tasks of social cognition (Costanzo & Archer, 1989; Hall, 1984).
- In a study of over 4,000 subjects, including school-aged children and adults in several countries, females consistently were more adept at interpreting nonverbal cues of emotion, such as local intonation, facial expression, and body language (Hall, 1984).
- Girls tend to be more fearful and exhibit more empathy and emotional support than boys, whereas boys demonstrate more impulsivity and physical play (Cote, et al., 2003; Fabes, Martin, & Hanish, 2003; Geary, 2002; Sanchez-Martin, et al., 2000).
- Female infants at three months of age show more interest expressions, such as wide eyes and higher eyebrow placement (Malatesta & Haviland, 1982).
- As young as a few days old, female infants make more eye contact than male infants (Geary, 2002), implying inherent biological differences in social behaviour and cognition (Wood, et al., 2008).

Noting sex differences in cognitive skills along with data that strongly suggest a biological and genetic component to these differences, scientists have also found differences in brain structures that mediate social and cognitive skills. Researchers have discovered that the VFC (ventral frontal cortex) portion of the brain contributes to facial recognition, attribution of intentions, and perception of anger in others, as well as the ability to experience moral emotions. People who have had this part of their brain damaged show lack of concern for others, lack of normal social inhibitions, and impaired reasoning about the mental states of others (Wood, et al., 2008). In order to investigate gender differences in brain morphology and social cognition, Wood and her colleagues compared VFC morphology measures between the sexes and correlated these with tests of social cognition and masculinity/femininity. They hypothesized that because the VFC is larger in women, women would perform better on tests of social cognition given that VFC size correlates with test performance. Their research results supported the hypothesis.

Wood and her colleagues speculate that the origins of gender differences in social cognition in humans might be linked to the fact that the long gestation period coupled with the high degree of postnatal care that an infant requires have resulted in females becoming more adept at the socio-cognitive skills that are required for rearing young, such as interpreting body language, facial expressions, and the early pre-verbal sounds of babies (Wood, et al., 2008).

Other scientists, in addition to Wood, have found male–female differences in brain structure. Welborn and associates (2009) found sex differences in the orbitofrontal cortex structure, indicating that the ventromedial prefrontal cortex (vmPFC) is larger in women. The vmPCF is systematically related to the regulation of emotions and to individual differences in affect (emotion governing behaviour).

It would appear, then, that there are certain differences between the male and female brains. The next question is, are these differences hardwired? Are males destined to behave in one way, and females in another? The short answer is no. Neuroscientist Lise Eliot (2010) has pointed out the crucial but often overlooked fact of **brain plasticity**. Experience (i.e. learning) regularly changes brain structure and function. Brain plasticity is not only the basis of much of children's mental development, it is also the basis of all learning. Even something as simple as the fact of seeing depends on the child's having had normal visual experiences in early life. Without those experiences a young child's visual brain fails to wire up properly, and vision is permanently impaired.

When it comes to the issue of differences in the behaviour of males and females, Eliot agrees that boys and girls are not identical at birth, and that genetic (and hormonal) differences do launch males and females down somewhat different developmental paths. However, as she also points out, early experiences and learning permanently alter the chemistry and function of genes, leading to significant effects on behaviour (Eliot, 2010, p. 23). Thus, biological inheritance, it appears, is only part of the story. Differences in experiences also have profound effects on our brain structures.

Neuroscientist Michael J. Meaney and his colleagues at McGill University discovered significant differences in response to stress and displays of anxiety amongst rat pups whose mothers had vigorously licked and groomed them during the first 10 days of their life compared to those pups whose mothers had rarely licked and groomed them. When exposed to stress, the progeny of the 'low lickers and groomers' showed much higher and more prolonged levels of the stress hormone corticosterone than the progeny of the mothers who licked and groomed their pups more frequently. Meaney and his colleagues (2004) were later able to demonstrate

brain plasticity
A concept used by neurologists to explain why experience (i.e. learning) regularly changes brain structure and function.

From an evolutionary perspective, can you imagine why women might be better than men at interpreting signs of emotion, displaying empathy, and providing emotional support?

that the differences in hormone levels were due to actual structural differences in the brains of highly groomed versus low-groomed rats (thus demonstrating the profound and variable connection between chemistry, brain structures, and social behaviour!).

In her recent book *Pink Brain, Blue Brain* (2009), Lise Eliot argues that while most sex differences between human males and females start out small, they are quickly amplified by our 'gender infused culture'. Infant brains are highly malleable, and small differences, present at birth, are amplified over time by parents and peers in ways that unwittingly (or deliberately) reinforce gender stereotypes. Males and females, she notes, are clearly not identical at birth. There are genetic and hormonal differences, and these differences launch males and females down somewhat different developmental pathways. But while most differences in behaviour start out small—as biases in temperament and play styles—they are soon amplified out of all proportion by environmental influences. Here is Eliot's list of some of the biologically based differences between males and females that scientists have documented, along with the social factors she identifies that exacerbate and reinforce those differences:

1. Boys Are More Active than Girls in Infancy and Childhood

Warren Eaton and his colleagues at the University of Manitoba analyzed more than 100 studies to conclude that the average boy is more physically active than about 69 per cent of girls. This means that 31 per cent of girls are more active than the average boy. Eliot (2010) points out that parenting styles most likely exacerbate this difference: daughters are discouraged from risk-taking more often than sons; in groups, energetic boys tend to encourage each other to higher levels of activity, while energetic girls tend to be discouraged by their more docile friends; girls start playing organized sports at a later age than boys do; they also quit earlier and join fewer teams—differences all influenced by parents and peers.

How great is the role of parenting in a child's style of play? Will the daughter of a more involved father be more likely to take risks on the playground? To play with Lego instead of a doll? To join a hockey league?

2. Boys Do Like Trucks and Girls Like Barbies

Children's gendered toy choice is one of the largest sex differences in behaviour. However, these differences are not nearly as obvious in early infancy. Many studies have found that very young boys like dolls as much as very young girls do. Toy preference, it turns out, emerges towards the end of infancy, grows stronger during preschool years, and then declines somewhat. It is shaped in part by prenatal exposure to testosterone and other androgens. (Researchers have even found gender play preferences amongst monkeys). There is something about vehicles, and moving parts, that appeals to boys and that draws them away from their initial interest in dolls towards toys with which they can interact more physically. Yet as Eliot points out, these preferences are strongly shaped by social interactions. Parents reinforce gender-appropriate play, but even more importantly so do peer groups. Researchers have discovered that by age 3, peer groups play an important role in perpetuating gender norms.

Around age 5, girls will begin to choose 'boy toys' and 'girl toys' equally. Boys, however, rarely make this crossover, a divergence that reflects different societal norms (Eliot, 2010, pp. 25–6). Today, while girls are encouraged to do 'boy' activities, boys are culturally discouraged from 'girl' activities, such as wearing dresses or playing house. Different play preferences shape mental circuits and later abilities. Choosing to play sports or to play with vehicles and building toys tends to exercise physical and spatial skills, while playing with dolls and dress-up clothes stimulates verbal, social, and fine motor circuits.

3. Boys Are More Physically Aggressive

Although both girls and boys compete and fight, there seems to be a difference in whether such behaviour is overt or hidden. Physical aggression is a greater taboo for girls than it is for boys, and girls learn early on to fight in indirect, relational ways: girls use gossip, ostracism, and, more recently, harassing text messages and Facebook sabotage as their means of fighting.

4. Females Are More Empathetic

Girls and women score higher on most measures of empathy or the awareness of other people's emotions, while boys and men score higher on measures of physical and verbal aggression. These differences are not as great as some believe—the average woman is more accurate than just 66 per cent of men in recognizing the emotions of others from photographs. Social learning, Eliot argues, largely shapes the differences between males and females in emotional responses, and while girls start out just a bit more sensitive to other people's faces and their emotions, that advantage grows larger as they age. This is no doubt due to their stronger communication skills and to the practice they get role-playing with dolls and in their more intimate friendships (Eliot, 2010, p. 27).

We can see the importance of social learning when we consider that in very early life baby boys have been shown to cry and fuss more than baby girls. Yet as they grow, boys are taught to hide their expressions of fear, sadness, and tenderness. The training that boys receive makes them not only less expressive but also less attuned to the feelings of others.

5. Females Outscore Males in Language and Literacy

Females outscore males on most measures of speaking, reading, writing, and spelling, beginning in early childhood and continuing throughout life. The gaps are relatively small and change with age. As infants, girls begin to talk sooner than boys do and have an advantage in reading and writing that continues to grow until around Grade 12, when 47 per cent more girls than boys graduate as proficient readers. However, as Eliot points out, schools with strong reading programs have eliminated the differences between boys' and girls' scores, demonstrating that 'this worrisome gap is more a matter of education and practice than inborn literacy potential' (Eliot, 2010, p. 28).

6. Boys Are Better at Visualizing and Handling Objects

Boys have better skills than girls in visualizing and manipulating objects and trajectories in time and three-dimensional space. An average male can perform a mental rotation of an object better than up to 80 per cent of females; an average boy outperforms 60 per cent of girls. Thus, Eliot points out, the skill improves in boys, but not in girls, due to a wide range of visuospatial interests, including targeting, building, throwing, and navigating through video games. Girls' skills in these areas can be improved with training, including playing video games and playing sports like baseball and tennis (Eliot, 2010, p. 29).

Without a doubt, biological sex matters. Boys and girls start out life with slightly different strengths and weaknesses, but these initial differences get greatly amplified by socialization and culture. Boys' brains are 8 to 11 per cent bigger than girls' brains, similar in magnitude to boy–girl differences in height and weight. Girls enter puberty earlier than do boys, and their brains peak in terms of physical growth earlier. Overall, the brains of boys and girls are remarkable for their similarities, not for their differences, yet the differences grow as boys and girls reach adulthood. This plasticity of the brain is quite remarkable, and as Eliot points out, 'your brain is what you do with it. Every task you spend time on—reading, running, laughing, calculating, debating, watching TV, folding laundry, mowing grass, singing, crying, kissing, and so on—reinforces active brain circuits at the expense of other inactive ones' (Eliot, 2009, p. 6).

When we learn something new, or when we repeatedly practise something we have already done before, we 'rewire the human brain'. Considering the different ways that boys and girls spend their time as they are growing up, added to the 'special potency of early experiences in moulding neuronal connections', Eliot concludes that 'it would be shocking if the two sexes' brains *didn't* work differently by the time they were adults' (Eliot, 2009, p. 6).

In the end, of course, the sex differences in behaviour we see reflect sex differences in the brain. But here is the most important point for us to remember: the older the child, the less we can be confident about ascribing his behaviour to genes and hormones. So, as Eliot concludes, there are some truly innate differences between the sexes: maturation rate (quicker for females), sensory processing (quicker for females), activity level (greater for males), fussiness as babies (more in males), and differences in play interests, including toy choices. But the differences that have the most impact, including 'cognitive skills, such as speaking, reading, math and mechanical ability; and interpersonal skills, such as aggression, empathy, risk taking, and competitiveness—are heavily shaped by learning' (Eliot, 2010, pp. 6–7). While these differences 'germinate' from initial biases in brain functioning, they are 'massively amplified by the different sorts of practices, role models, and reinforcement that boys and girls are exposed to from birth onward' (Eliot, 2009, p. 7).

In this chapter you have seen that biological sex does not smoothly or inevitably translate into social gender. It appears that our brains, and thus our behaviour, are highly plastic and responsive to being shaped by social interactions. In the next chapter, we will take a look at how gender-specific practices, role models, and reinforcements shape adolescent and adult gender differences.

SUMMARY

The issue of whether the differences between males and females are based on biology or have social roots generates heated debate. This chapter has presented three interrelated points around which this debate has taken place: the relationship between biological sex and social gender, whether or not there are naturally only two sexes (sexual dimorphism), and whether or not male–female brain differences are the result of biological inheritance alone or the outcome of socialization and cultural factors.

The classical tradition of sociology mostly ignored women, or defined them as the intellectual and social inferiors of men. Structural functionalists of the mid-1900s turned to biology to explain the different roles that men and women took within the family. The biologically different roles assigned to males and to females came together to make up the nuclear family, wherein children were first socialized.

Feminist sociologists of the 1960s and 1970s were the first to distinguish between biological sex and social gender as different analytical concepts, arguing that while sex is an ascribed status, determined by biology that is present at birth, gender is an achieved status and is socially constructed.

Sociologists now recognize that the two-sex model (*sexual dimorphism*) replaced an earlier one-sex model according to which males were considered to represent perfection while females were considered to be degenerate or imperfect males. The two-sex model came to predominate as a result of the contradictory social reforms that were promulgated during the Enlightenment, the most prominent of which were appeals to individual freedom and equality and counter-appeals to a natural hierarchy of humans. By the end of the Enlightenment the prevailing view was that that some humans (Caucasian males, in particular) were better suited to producing equality among themselves, while others, including women and non-Caucasians, were of a lesser order. The two-sex model fit with this ideal.

Finally this chapter has discussed intersexed individuals and their differential treatment across cultures. It has also presented evidence from neurological and cognitive studies to argue that a complex relationship exists between biological sex differences and social gender. Biological sex does not translate directly into gendered behaviour—our brains and our behaviour are very responsive to being shaped by social interaction.

DISCUSSION QUESTIONS

1. What role might biology play in gendered behaviour? What role might socialization play?
2. To what extent might gender identity and gender roles be affected by social and cultural factors?
3. What are the differences between a one-sex model and a two-sex model?
4. Discuss the role of sexual dimorphism in human reproduction. Does sexual dimorphism necessarily mean that sexual relations are meant only for the purpose of reproduction?
5. Consider the differences in life experiences of intersexed persons from the Dominican Republic and from the New Guinea highlands. What might these differences tell us about the role of biology compared with the role of culture in shaping gender roles and gender identity?
6. Discuss the implications that recent research in the neurological and cognitive sciences has for our understanding of the relationship between biological sex and social gender. How might the concept of brain plasticity be used to explain the interaction between biology and social interactions? Use specific examples in your answer.

15 Gender Stratification, Inequalities, and Differences

CHAPTER OUTLINE

LEARNING OBJECTIVES

In this chapter you will:

- explore gender stratification in Canada and other Western industrialized societies
- think critically about gender inequality in Canada
- reflect on women's struggles for political representation
- gain a clearer understanding of the 'gender revolution'
- find out about the relationship between overwork and gender inequality
- examine gender stereotyping
- think critically about 'doing gender'
- learn about feminist contributions to the study of gender relations.

INTRODUCTION

For sociologists, gender is a system of social practices that organize relations of inequality between men and women on the basis of perceived differences. Sociologists emphasize that it is not in-born biological differences but cultural beliefs and confirmatory experiences about the differences between advantaged males and disadvantaged females that perpetuate inequalities between men and women. Moreover, these differences must be sustained in the context of continuous interaction between the two sexes—interactions that are often carried out in the most intimate and familiar spaces, such as the family home (Ridgeway & Smith-Lovin, 1999, p. 192). This chapter investigates the sociological causes and consequences of gender stratification, inequalities, and differences

GENDER STRATIFICATION

gender stratification
The channelling of men and women into different, usually unequal, life situations.

According to an age-old proverb, money talks.

According to a 2008 survey by the Boston Consulting Group, women's annual consumer spending, worldwide, is expected to reach $28 trillion (US) by 2014, while their yearly earnings are expected to exceed $18 trillion. The global market for diet foods will be $20 billion; for facial skin care products, $20 billion; and for apparel (including accessories and shoes), $47364 billion; private wealth held by women is expected to reach $7 trillion ('A woman-owned world', 2010). Women, apparently, have money, make money, and spend a lot more than they make by themselves. Given the amount of money they control worldwide, one would think that women would at least be equal to men in most measures, including economic ones. But this is not the case. **Gender stratification**—the channelling of men and women into different (and usually unequal) life situations—continues to be very much a part of life in Canada as elsewhere in Western industrialized societies.

In spite of gains made over the last several decades, gender stratification remains a fact for Canadian women and men. Men continue to hold more powerful, prestigious, and high-paying jobs than do women, who continue to be overrepresented in low-paying, powerless positions. Canadian women also continue to earn substantially less than men. After narrowing steadily over the previous two decades, the ratio of earnings for men and women aged 25–29 remained unchanged between 2000 and 2005. In 2005, young women entering the Canadian labour market, employed on a full-time, full-year basis, could expect to earn 85 cents for every dollar earned by their male counterparts (Statistics Canada, 2006d).

Gender stratification and inequalities carry over into the home. Although Canadian women do slightly less housework today than they did in the past, they still spend significantly more time at unpaid domestic chores (about 15 hours a week) than do men (who spend about 6.8 hours a week) (Stevens, Kiger, & Riley, 2001). As a result, when we add together both paid and unpaid work time, Canadian women work longer hours than do men, earn less, and have less free time. Finally, Canadian women are much more likely than men to be poor at some point in their lives, either as single parents with sole support of their children or as widows in old age without pensions.

The first part of this chapter presents some of the recent research on gender inequality and stratification. This evidence indicates the extent to which gender inequality exists in Canada and around the world. The first part of this chapter focuses on broad organizational and institutional structures, especially as they result in differences in material well-being between men and women, and discusses the possibility that a gender revolution has indeed occurred. The second part of the chapter turns to an analysis of how gender, as a social identity, is produced and reproduced by men and women in their day-to-day activities.

HOW EQUAL?

Women have struggled for many decades for equality with men, and certainly the laws of Canada support that struggle. But just how 'equal' are Canadian women today?

Employment and Earnings

Recent research on workplace stratification indicates that there are persistent and significant gaps between men's and women's employment experiences and that a gap still exists between what men and women earn—both for doing equivalent jobs and as an overall measure. Significant inequalities persist in the division of both paid and unpaid labour between men and women, as well as in terms of gender-based differences in earnings and in job mobility.

A 2004 Statistics Canada publication, *Women in Canada: A Gender-based Statistical Report* (Statistics Canada, 2004a), and Marcia Almey's *Women in Canada: Work Chapter Updates* (Almey, 2006) indicate that in Canada, the labour force participation of women aged 15 and over), taken as a percentage of total employment, increased from 37.1 per cent in 1976 to 46.8 per cent in 2004. Today, women make up almost 50 per cent of the paid labour force. So, in terms of getting access to the 'public sphere' through being employed outside the home, Canadian women have indeed made progress and are now approaching men's labour force participation rates. There are several important areas, however, where Canadian women and men are unequal:

- Women are much more likely than men to lose work time because of family or personal responsibilities.
- Women are much more likely to work part-time. In 2004, 27 per cent of the total female workforce worked part-time, compared with just 11 per cent of employed men. Women account for about 7 out of 10 part-time workers, a number that has remained stable since the 1970s.
- The majority of women continue work in 'traditionally female' occupations. In 2006, 67 per cent of all working women, compared to 30 per cent of all working men, were employed in teaching, nursing and related healthcare occupations, clerical or administrative positions, and sales and service occupations, with virtually no change from the previous decade. Women made up 87 per cent of nurses and health-related therapists, 75 per cent of clerks and other administrators, 64 per cent of teachers, and 57 per cent of sales and service personnel.
- Women continue to have very low representation in natural sciences, engineering, and maths. In 2006, just 22 per cent of professionals in these fields were women, up slightly from 20 per cent in 1987. It is unlikely that women's representation in these fields will increase in the near future as they continue to make up a small share of the university students enrolled in these fields.

- Women have low representation in goods-producing occupations. In 2006, women made up 31 per cent of workers in manufacturing, 21 per cent of workers in primary industries, and 7 per cent of workers in transportation, trades, and construction work. These percentages are about the same as they were in the 1980s.
- Women's average earnings continue to be substantially lower than those of men. In 2003, women working full-time and full-year earned 71 per cent of what was earned by men working full-time and year-round. This was up from 58.4 per cent in 1967 and 65.8 per cent in 1987 but down from 72.4 per cent in 1995.
- Over the long term women have increased their share of managerial positions, from 30 per cent in 1987 to 36 per cent in 2006. However, this growth occurred between 1987 and 1996, and actually fell slightly from 1997 to 2004. Moreover, women are better represented in the lower-level managerial positions (37 per cent) than they are at more senior levels, where in 2006 only 26 per cent of senior managers were women. Sociologists refer to this situation as the 'glass ceiling'—an unseen barrier keeping women from higher-status management positions (Baxter & Wright, 2000; Cotter, Hermsen, & Vanneman, 2004; Hultin, 2003).

Few women make it to the top, either in terms of income or in terms of positions of power (see Table 15.1). In Canada, although women make up 47 per cent of the workforce, they hold only 17 per cent of the corporate positions in the country's top 500 companies and only 13 per cent of the board seats (Catalyst, 2009). Cohen and Huffman's (2007) study of gender inequality and management indicates that not only does the 'glass ceiling' mean that qualified women are blocked from upper-level managerial positions but their absence has a ripple effect that shapes workplace outcomes for non-managerial women as well. On the other hand, women in non-managerial positions benefit when women do make inroads into upper-status managerial positions. The gender wage gap is smaller under female managers and is much stronger when those managers occupy a high status (Cohen & Huffman, 689–99).

Gender and Politics

At the turn of the twenty-first century, women's struggle for political representation around the world has almost been won. A century previous, women in many countries contested established beliefs that they were unfit to participate in something that was taken to be a man's domain. Women's suffrage in many countries, including Canada, was achieved only after long and bitter struggles. Prior to 1915 women did not have the right to vote in Canada. Between 1916 and 1925 women were enfranchised in all provinces and territories with the exception of Quebec and Northwest Territories. Quebec women gained the right to vote in 1940, while women living in Northwest Territories had to wait until 1951 before they could legally participate in territorial elections. At the federal level, women who were British subjects and who had served in the military were granted voting rights in 1917. A year later, those rights were extended to all women (and men) who were not of Chinese, East Indian, or Japanese ancestry. Men and women of Inuit ancestry were granted the vote in 1950, while registered Indians living on reserves were not enfranchised until 1960 (Maillé, 1990, p. 1).

Today, with the exception of Saudi Arabia, women have the right to vote in all countries where there are legislatures. But while women have the legal right to vote and to stand for election in almost every country in the world, there are significant cultural barriers to their exercise of these rights. In the mid-1970s, fewer than 4 per cent of Canada's members of parliament

TABLE 15.1 Distribution of employment of Canadian women and men, by occupation, 1987, 1996, and 2006

	1987			1996			2006		
	Women (%)	Men (%)	Women as a % of total employed in occupation	Women (%)	Men (%)	Women as a % of total employed in occupation	Women (%)	Men (%)	Women as a % of total employed in occupation
Managerial									
Senior management	0.3	0.8	21.0	0.3	0.7	27.2	0.3	0.8	26.3
Other management	5.7	9.7	30.7	7.8	10.9	37.5	6.7	10.2	36.9
Total management	6.0	10.5	30.1	8.2	11.6	37.0	7.1	11.0	36.3
Professional									
Business and finance	1.9	2.3	38.3	2.8	2.7	46.9	3.3	2.8	51.6
Natural sciences/engineering/mathematics	2.3	7.0	19.6	2.3	8.0	19.1	3.2	10.1	22.0
Social sciences/religion	4.3	2.0	61.4	6.0	2.3	68.8	6.7	2.4	71.3
Teaching	3.8	2.6	52.3	5.1	2.8	60.1	5.6	2.8	63.9
Doctors/dentists/other health	0.9	0.9	43.1	1.2	1.1	48.1	1.4	1.0	55.3
Nursing/therapy/other health-related	8.3	0.9	87.1	8.3	1.0	87.0	8.9	1.1	87.4
Artistic/literary/recreational	2.7	2.1	48.4	3.1	2.4	51.5	3.4	2.6	54.1
Total professional	24.1	18.0	50.4	28.8	20.3	54.2	32.5	22.9	55.9
Clerical and administrative	29.7	7.9	73.9	25.6	7.2	74.9	24.1	7.1	75.0
Sales and service	30.0	18.4	55.2	28.6	19.2	55.4	28.6	19.3	56.8
Primary	2.3	7.2	19.7	2.1	6.5	20.9	1.5	5.3	20.5
Trades, transport, and construction	2.1	28.9	5.2	2.1	26.4	6.1	2.1	26.3	6.5
Processing, manufacturing, and utilities	5.8	9.1	32.4	4.7	8.8	30.6	4.1	8.1	31.1
Total[1]	100.0	100.0	43.0	100.0	100.0	45.4	100.0	100.0	47.1
Total employed (thousands)	5,307.7	7,025.3	...	6,099.0	7,322.4	...	7,757.2	8,727.1	...

1. Includes occupations that are not classified.
Source: Statistics Canada, *Women in Canada: A gender-based statistical report*, 89-503-XWE2005001, March 2006; http://www.statcan.gc.ca/bsolc/olc-cel/olc-cel?lang=eng&catno=89-503-x.

(MPs) were women; currently the figure stands at 22 per cent, a total that places Canada behind Angola, Ecuador, Mozambique, Guyana, and Afghanistan when it comes to the representation of women in parliament (Galloway, 2010). Moreover, once elected, women continue to be underrepresented in cabinet and leadership positions. In the close to 100 years since Canadian women gained the vote federally, only three have been elected as party leaders. Internationally, as of February 2006, only about 10 per cent of sovereign nations have legislatures with better than 30 per cent representation by women (Paxton, Kunovich, & Hughes, 2007, p. 265).

Table 15.2 shows that while the eastern European countries had the highest percentage of women in parliaments between 1955 and 1985, the Scandinavian countries had by 1985 surpassed all other regions in the levels of women's political representation in parliaments. The decline of women in eastern European parliaments parallels those countries' transition from communism to free-market economies. During this transition, women's level of participation declined precipitously. The growth in women's political participation in Latin American countries since 1995 has come as a result of quotas, while armed conflict, which has drawn men into military roles, spurred growth in Africa (Paxton, Kunovich, & Hughes, 2007, p. 266).

Nunavut premier Eva Aariak and Alberta premier Ed Stelmach, August 2010. When Alberta's Alison Redford took over the leadership of the governing PC Party in October 2011, joining Aariak, Christy Clark of BC, and Newfoundland and Labrador's Kathy Dunderdale, it marked the first time that four of Canada's provinces and territories were being governed at the same time by women premiers. Is this a fluke or trend? Are Canadians becoming more willing to accept a woman as leader? What do you think needs to change in order for this to happen?

TABLE 15.2   Historical comparisons of the percentage of women in parliaments across regions, 1955–2055

	1955	1965	1975	1985	1995	2005
Scandinavia	10.4	9.3	16.1	27.5	34.4	38.2
Western Industrial	3.6	4.0	5.5	8.6	12.8	22.7
Eastern Europe	17.0	18.4	24.7	27.0	8.4	15.7
Latin America	2.8	2.7	5.2	8.1	10.0	17.1
Africa	1.0	3.2	5.3	8.0	9.8	16.3
Asia	5.2	5.3	2.8	5.6	8.8	15.3
Middle East	1.2	1.2	2.9	3.5	3.9	8.1

Source: Adapted from Paxton, Kunovich, & Hughes, 2007, p. 266.

One factor that is crucial for understanding who decides to run for office is direct political ambition. In the US, a study by Fox and Lawless (2004) found women much less likely to aspire to political office than men. Comparing four professions most likely to yield political candidates—law, business, education, and politics—Fox and Lawless discovered that women in these professions are much less likely than men to view themselves as qualified to run for office. Other researchers have found that women's low level of political ambition can also be attributed to a lack of female political role models. Additionally, women have less time to participate in politics. Around the world women still perform the majority of domestic tasks, and are primary caregivers for children and other family members. These commitments deprive women of the free time that they need to participate in politics (Paxton, Kunovich, & Hughes, 2007, pp. 266–7).

Women face prejudice as political leaders because of cultural stereotypes that tend to portray them as less capable than men. Moreover, the same stereotypes lead people to evaluate autocratic behaviour in women more negatively than the same behaviour in men. Even in countries like the United States, where women have achieved important gains in both employment and education, 25 per cent of Americans still believe that men are better suited emotionally to govern than are women (Lawless & Theriault, 2005).

Religion, which often argues for women's inferiority to men, has long been used as a reason for excluding women from many aspects of political, as well as social and religious, life, not just in North America but around the world (Paxton, Kunovich, & Hughes, 2007). Of course, major religions differ in terms of their views about the place of women in politics and society, as well as in church hierarchies. Compared to Catholicism and Orthodox Christianity, Protestantism promotes less hierarchy and is more willing to accept women as religious leaders. Islamic law typically interprets women in a manner that constrains their activities. Research has shown that in those countries with large numbers of Protestants there are more female legislators than in countries where Catholics, Orthodox Christians, or Muslims make up the majority (Paxton, Kunovich, & Hughes, 2007). Country-by-country analysis of attitudes about women in politics demonstrates that these attitudes are powerful predictors of women's representation in politics.

What are the qualities you associate with a strong politician? Does your list apply equally to men and to women, or are there some attributes you would expect to find in male politicians but not female ones, or vice versa? Why might we look for different things from male and female political leaders?

A GENDER REVOLUTION?

Anyone living in Western society will be more or less aware of the 'revolution' in women's rights that has taken place since the 1960s. Paula England (2010) deftly summarizes the changes to women's status over that time:

> Women's employment increased dramatically (Cotter, Hermsen, & England, 2008); birth control became widely available (Bailey, 2006); women caught up with and surpassed men in rates of college graduation (Cotter, Hermsen, & Vanneman, 2004, p. 23); undergraduate college majors desegregated substantially (England & Li, 2006); more women than ever got doctorates as well as professional degrees in law, medicine, and business (Cotter, Hermsen, & Vanneman, 2004, pp. 22–3; England, et al., 2007); many kinds of gender discrimination in employment and education became illegal (Burstein, 1989; Hirsh 2009); women entered many previously male-dominated occupations (Cotter, Hermsen, & Vanneman, 2004, pp. 10–14); and more women were elected to political office (Cotter, Hermsen, & Vanneman, 2004, p. 25). (England, 2010, pp. 149–50)

Thanks to these gains, the issue of women's equality is something that is no longer an issue of pressing concern for many young Canadian men and women today. For this reason, it's worth noting some of the significant differences between life today and life a half-century ago for Canadian men and women.

Marriage

In 1950, the average age for first marriage was 28.5 years for men, and 25.9 years for women. Married women were expected to work exclusively in the home and to take responsibility for childcare and other domestic chores. The expected status of most women was that of wife and mother. The expected status of most men was that of breadwinner or provider and head of household. Most women had several children; in 1960 the average number of children per woman in Canada was 3.9.

By the early 1970s, the average age of marriage had risen, and many young women were successfully challenging the belief that women should marry and devote their lives solely to raising families and doing domestic work. The divorce laws had been significantly revised in 1968, when Canada's first unified divorce law was passed, and divorce rates rose steadily. By 2003 almost 40 per cent of marriages ended in divorce before the thirtieth wedding anniversary, and the average duration of a marriage fell to 14.2 years. Approximately 6 per cent of all couples in Canada were living common-law in 1981; by 2000, that rate had risen to 14 per cent. In addition, in 2001, 13 per cent of children under 15 lived in a family headed by unmarried parents, a 25 per cent increase from 1981, indicating that a significant shift had taken place in the view that children should be raised only by married couples.

In 2000, the average age at first marriage was 28 years for women and 30 years for men, and the average number of children per woman had fallen to 1.5. More and more women joined the labour force, while men began to contribute to domestic work and child-rearing. In 2001, when Statistics Canada began collecting information about same-sex partnerships, about 0.5 per cent of all couples reported living in a same-sex union. Two years later, the provinces of Ontario and British Columbia legalized same-sex marriage, and the 2005 federal Civil Marriage Act made same-sex marriage legal across Canada.

For young men and women today, there is still an expectation of getting married and having a family, though marriage may be to a partner of the same or the opposite sex. Young women generally expect to participate in the labour force, and men are more willing to contribute time to domestic chores and child-rearing. But in spite of this, gender inequality in the home remains very much a part of life in Canada. While things have changed, the change has been 'uneven and halting' (England, 2010, p. 150)

Work and Family Roles

During the 1950s, post–World War II prosperity in North America allowed a gender split between male 'breadwinners' and female 'homemakers' in the majority of households. Today, one of the places where changing lives have collided with resistant institutions is in the area of gender and work. Gone are the days when the 'traditional' family included male workers (of all classes, but not all races) with jobs that offered enough economic security to support wives and children. In its place are time-demanding, insecure jobs and women's labour force participation rates that are almost equal to men's. In the US, for example, as of 2000, 60 per cent of all married households had two wage earners, and only 26 per cent were dependent on the husband's income alone. At the same time, single-parent households (headed largely by women) claimed a considerable proportion of American households. Here there is a great deal of variation across ethnic groups: 17 per cent of Asian children, 24 per cent of non-Hispanic white children, 34 per cent of Hispanic children, and 65 per cent of black children (all in the US) live either in a one-parent family or with neither of their biological parents (Blow, 2008; Gerson, 2009).

The institutional ideal of permanent marriage continues to persist despite the social reality of the fluid and uncertain nature of intimate commitment. Tensions between changing personal experiences and resistant institutions have created personal dilemmas for women and men alike. Even though women's labour force participation rates are close to those of men, and children depend more and more on their mother's and not their father's earnings to support them, women remain primarily responsible for childcare. And regardless of whether or not men *wish* to be involved as primary caregivers, their success on the job market remains the most important measure of their social status.

The Effect of the Gender Revolution on Twenty-First-Century Youth: Two Studies

Kathleen Gerson: Young Adults' Views on the Future of Home and Work

Young adults today have come of age in an era of unprecedented change and are faced with building their lives in a world that bears little resemblance to that of their parents and grandparents. They are children of the 'gender revolution' in that they grew up experiencing their parents' own struggles to cope with new family forms and expanding options for women. Now, as they negotiate a transition to adulthood, they are faced with dilemmas about how to craft their own ties to partners, children, and jobs. In order to shed light on the experiences of this generation, Kathleen Gerson (2009) interviewed a group of 18- to 30-year-olds 'about their experiences growing up, their current work and family strategies, and their outlook on the future'. Gerson and her research team interviewed 120 randomly selected respondents from diverse urban and suburban communities around the New York metropolitan area. Her respondents represented the full spectrum of racial and ethnic identities and class backgrounds (Gerson, 2009, p. 737).

Gender flexibility was frequently cited by Gerson's interviewees as the key ingredient of cohesive, egalitarian, and financially secure homes, while gender inflexibility and the threat of getting stuck in a traditional male–female division of responsibilities was thought to weaken family support and lead to a failure to meet children's economic and emotional needs. As Geerson reports:

> Gender inflexibility left them poorly prepared for a host of unavoidable challenges to the traditional division of tasks and responsibilities. Although these challenges were unexpected, they are not random. They reflect widespread and inexorable social shifts that have undermined the 'family wage' and the organized 'male' career, raised expectations for marital happiness and provide new opportunities to remain single or leave unhappy marriages, and fueled woman's growing need and desire to pursue a life beyond domesticity and dead-end jobs. (Gerson, 2009, pp. 741–2)

In spite of their experiences, the young adults Gerson interviewed expressed the desire for a meaningful, lifelong bond with one partner, though this does not mean they expected a traditional relationship. Eighty per cent of the women and 68 per cent of the men aspired to build 'an egalitarian partnership with room for considerable personal autonomy' (p. 742). Three-quarters of those who grew up in dual-earner households, two-thirds of those who grew up in traditional homes, and nine out of ten of those who grew up in single-parent homes wanted their spouses to share breadwinning and caretaking (p. 742). Most young men and women wanted a committed relationship with a partner who would share paid work and family caretaking equitably. But they held 'deep and realistic fears that time-demanding jobs, a dearth of childcare and family-leave options, and their own high standards for an intimate relationship would place their ideal scenarios out of reach' (p. 742).

In the face of this, young men and women pursued 'second-line' strategies. As a second-line strategy to marriage, young women were prepared to fall back on self-reliance. Work was first on their list of life goals, with marriage an option if and when they found the right partner. By contrast, young men worried that equal parenting would cost them promotions

Can you see yourself in this photo? As a young adult, what are your own views on marriage and parenthood? How close is your ideal to the one put forward by the young adults whom Gerson interviewed? What 'second-line' strategies would you consider?

at work—70 per cent of them had a fallback plan for a neo-traditional relationship in which they would reserve the status of primary breadwinner for themselves while leaving open the option for their partners to work.

Gerson predicts that 'despite the shared desire to strike a balance between work and care-taking in the context of an egalitarian relationship, "self-reliant" women and "neotraditional" men are on a collision course' (p. 743). Regardless of race, the young women she interviewed found that the fragility of marriage made it seem foolhardy to rely on a husband for economic security. Danisha, a young African-American woman who grew up in an inner-city, working-class neighbourhood, explains it this way:

> Let's say that my marriage doesn't work. Just in case, I want to establish myself because I don't ever want to end up like, 'what am I going to do?' I want to be able to do what I have to do and still be okay.

The sentiment is echoed by Jennifer, who was raised in a white, middle-class suburb:

> I have to have a job and some kind of stability before considering marriage. Too many of my mother's friends went for that—'let him provide everything'—and they're stuck in a very unhappy relationship, but can't leave because they can't provide for themselves or the children they now have. (p. 743)

These young women felt they didn't have to settle for a marriage that wasn't fully satisfying and mutually supportive. They could postpone making a commitment or get a divorce if they made a poor choice. They would rather be alone than be with a 'jerk'. They also agreed that failing to find a suitable partner wouldn't preclude motherhood or leave them socially disconnected. Just as these young women are redesigning their views on intimate relationships, they are also redesigning motherhood.

It is a different story for the young men Gerson interviewed, who were more inclined to 'fall back on a more traditional relationship, although in modified form'. Faced with 'escalating time pressures, rising insecurities at work, and the cultural paradigm that sees men's earnings as the core measure of their "marriageability" these young men have concluded that equal sharing would be too costly' (p. 744). While they were aware of growing pressures for 'egalitarian sharing in their relationships', this aim ranked behind ensuring their identity as breadwinners.

The young men Gerson interviewed spoke about a woman's 'choice' to work, compared with a man's 'responsibility' or 'right' to do so. From their point of view, women could work but should be the ones to 'fit work in' when there are children (p. 745). As Gerson comments:

> By shifting the meaning of equality for equal sharing to 'women's choice' this outlook makes room for an employed partner without undermining men's position as specialists in breadwinning. Because this strategy frames women's—but not men's—work as 'optional', it converts belief in a child's need for intensive parenting into an injunction for 'intensive mothering'. (p. 745)

This position grants women the ability to work and gain an income that could be used as a buffer against any economic difficulties created by relying on one income without challenging a man's position as the primary earner or imposing the costs of equal parenting on him. However, this approach is in clear conflict with women's expressed desires for equity at home and independence outside the home. The fallback positions of both the young men and the young women, as Gerson points out, are conflicting. 'If a lasting, egalitarian partnership is not possible, most women prefer self-reliance over the perils of traditional marriage, while most men prefer a neotraditional arrangement to the risks and penalties that equal parenting' (p. 746).

Youngjoo Cha: Overwork and Gender Inequality

In an article examining long work hours and gender inequality in the United States, Youngjoo Cha (2010) underscored Gerson's research by showing that the fallback position cited by the men Gerson studied—that is, to be the primary earner—has important consequences among married couples. Cha's research has shown that when a husband works long hours it significantly increases the likelihood that his wife will quit her job, while a wife working long hours does not increase a husband's likelihood of quitting. This effect is strong among workers in professional and managerial occupations and among workers who have children.

Cha (2010) begins by noting that in the US (and the same holds for Canada) working long hours has become increasingly common, especially among men. In 2000, 26.5 per cent of American men, compared with 11.3 per cent of women, worked 50 hours or more per week. This contributes to some of the earning differences between women and men that we noted earlier, especially in high-paying professional jobs where overwork is both common and expected (Jacobs & Gerson, 2004, as cited in Cha, 2010, 303–4). Those who are present at work for long hours are believed to be committed, while those who are not are penalized. This norm of overwork, Cha argues, systematically disadvantages women, who have primary responsibility for domestic work and childcare, with little help from their spouses who are devoting their time to work

Although 78 per cent of all American workers live in dual-earner households, women are disadvantaged by the continued gendered assumptions about women's ultimate responsibility for housework and childcare, and men's ultimate right to focus on their careers. The workplace rewards those who work long hours. However, because women are subject to expectations that they are ultimately responsible for childcare and the family, their ability to work these long hours is often restricted. Moreover, married women whose husbands work long hours and spend little time contributing to domestic chores have their domestic labour time increased, and are less available for overwork. Both situations limit women's ability to work long hours. Thus, when being available for overwork equals having a career, women are clearly disadvantaged, in terms of both promotions and wage growth.

To demonstrate this, Cha examined dual-earner married couples to see how spousal overwork affects women's and men's likelihood of quitting their jobs. In her research, Cha used the 1996 panel of the Survey of Income and Program Participation (SIPP), a longitudinal household survey data set collected by the US Census Bureau, covering the years 1995–2000. The SIPP interviewed individuals every 4 months over a 48-month period. This data allowed Cha to observe changes in men's and women's employment status. Her final sample included 15,205 observations on 23,593 respondents (Cha, 2010, pp. 309–10).

In conducting her study, Cha defined her dependent variable as 'quitting'. This is a **dichotomous variable**, measuring whether an individual's employment status changed from 'working' to 'not working'. Excluded from the sample were workers who quit for 'job displacement, illness, and disability' as well those who quit because they were 'not interested in working'. These exclusions were made in order to 'prevent the possibility that employment

dichotomous variable
A variable that has only two, mutually exclusive categories.

Gerson and Cha conducted their studies in the US, which is one of very few democratic nations with no federal law ensuring paid time off for new parents. A new parent in the US may take up to 12 weeks of job-protected parental leave to care for a newborn, though this period is often without pay. Contrast this with the Canadian situation, where parents may take a combined 12 *months* of job-protected parental leave, during which they may collect employment insurance. (Benefits are even greater in Quebec.) How might Gerson's and Cha's results have differed if they had been focused on the Canadian situation? What incentive is there for governments to create more favourable laws surrounding parental leave?

decisions were driven by non-voluntary, external factors'. The independent variable, 'spousal overwork', was measured using a set of variables based on the work hours of a respondent:

- fewer than 50 hours of work per week
- 50 to 59 hours of work per week
- 60 or more hours of work per week.

The independent variable 'have children' was measured by whether or not the couple had a child under the age of 18 living with the parents (Cha, 2010, pp. 310–12).

Cha (2010) found that having a spouse who works long hours increases women's but not men's likelihood of quitting their job. Having a husband who works 60 hours or more increases women's odds of quitting by 42 per cent; having a wife who works 60 hours or more a week did *not* increase men's odds of quitting. For professional workers, the odds were even higher: 51 per cent for professional women quitting, compared to no increase for professional men quitting. Having children also increased professional women's but not professional men's odds of quitting as a response to spousal overwork: women with children living at home were twice as likely to quit when their husbands worked 50 hours or more, and 3.2 times more likely to quit when their husbands worked 60 hours or more (2010, p. 318).

On the basis of these findings, Cha concludes that 'overwork is a gendered process that results in women's exclusion from the labour market' (2010, p. 315). Cha further addressed the possibility that having wives quit their jobs contributes to husbands having to overwork, but her analyses provided 'convincing evidence that husbands' overwork results in wives' increased quitting, rather than the other way around' (2010, p. 318). Gendered assumptions about who is responsible for which spheres of work mean that overwork reintroduces the separate sphere arrangement into many dual-earner married couples. The results are even more obvious for women with children: odds of quitting are 112 per cent higher for mothers in professional occupations whose husbands work long hours. This, Cha concludes, has important implications for gender equality and contributes to 'the stalled revolution' in which progress toward gender equality 'is hindered by men's limited contributions to household work and childcare' (Cha, 2010, p. 325).

Gerson thinks that we can transcend this impasse by 'creating social intuitions that allow new generations to create the work lives and the families they want rather than those for which they fear they must settle'. She believes that intransigent workplace structures and privatized child-rearing practices are the greatest threats to family and child well-being (Gerson, 2009, p. 751). We need to create flexible workplaces, provide equal economic opportunity for women, stop discrimination against all parents, and build child-friendly communities with affordable, plentiful, and high-quality care. The answer to twenty-first-century work and family conundrums, Gerson concludes, is to finish the gender revolution, and not to turn back the clock to family structures of a previous era, where women were confined to the domestic, and men to the public, spheres (p. 751).

GENDER STEREOTYPING

gender stereotypes
Shared, cultural hegemonic beliefs about how most people 'typically' view men and women

Although we are rarely conscious of it, we use **gender stereotypes**—shared, cultural hegemonic beliefs about how most people 'typically' view men and women—to shape our own actions. Even if we don't consciously condone or agree with them, we think that most people hold the same stereotypical views about gender that we have all learned as part of our culture, and we expect to have our own actions judged accordingly. These shared cultural stereotypes serve as the 'rules' by which public displays of gender differences are coordinated (Ridgeway & Correll, 2004).

Gender stereotypes have long been a source of both comfort and humour. Are jokes that play on gender stereotypes a way of acknowledging the common-sense views we hold but are ashamed to admit, or an attempt to prove them false by ridiculing them?

In the previous chapter, we saw how, in Western societies, it is an acceptable cultural perspective to view 'male' and 'female' as naturally different, biologically defined categories of being, complete with distinctive psychological and behavioural propensities, which are largely the result of differing reproductive functions. Because the behavioural differences between males and females are considered to be rooted in biological differences, they are also considered fundamental and enduring. Moreover, it is a common-sense cultural understanding that these differences support the division of labour between men and women. Men are said to be better equipped, biologically, to be providers, while a woman's biology is said to naturally equip her to bear, care for, and raise children.

Finally, the biological differences between males and females are said to result in different masculine and feminine psychologies and behaviours. Many Canadians believe that we are the way we are, that we think, feel, and behave the way we do, in large part because our genetic makeup makes us so. We tend to conclude that any gender inequalities we observe are, ultimately, the natural outcome of our biological differences (West & Zimmerman, 1987, pp. 127–8).

Sociologist Cecilia Ridgeway (2006) has pointed out that while gender stereotypes do not necessarily imply inequality, they are easily transposed into inequality. For example, a popular gender stereotype held by many in Western societies is that the male gender is the more active and decisive gender. It is an easy step from there to according a higher status to males. Implicit in the belief that men are more decisive is a view of women as more reactive and emotional than males, in need of male guidance, and therefore naturally subordinate to males.

In Chapter 14 we reviewed the work of neurological and cognitive scientists such as Lise Eliot (2009, 2010). Eliot's work, while acknowledging small biologically based differences between males and females that are present at birth, makes it clear that social interaction and culture have important roles to play in either reinforcing or overcoming these differences. In the section that follows we will look at some of the ways in which men and women 'do gender', either consciously or not, in order to present themselves in culturally stereotypical ways as either 'male' or 'female'.

DOING GENDER

In a 1987 article, sociologists Candace West and Don Zimmerman proposed that sociologists stop thinking of gender as a set of individual characteristics and start thinking of gender as a set of cultural practices. Different societies assign individuals to a biological category—the male or the female sex—on the basis of some socially agreed-upon determination of what matters as criteria for membership in one or the other category. The assignment of newborns into the male or female category reflects the belief that males and females already are, or should become, different kinds of people. Those assigned to the category 'male' are subsequently taught to identify themselves not only as biologically male but also (depending on their age) as either boys or men. Those assigned to the category 'female' are taught and expected to identify as biologically female and (depending on their age) as either girls or women.

Being assigned to either the male or female sex category, however, does not naturally result in category-appropriate, gendered behaviour. For any individual to be recognized by others as a 'boy' or a 'man', a 'girl' or a 'woman', he or she must present him- or herself to others (and be accepted by others) as that particular type of being. To be accepted as a boy/man or

'doing gender'
West and Zimmerman's term for the (often unconscious) activity of managing one's conduct in a way that is consistent with what is generally considered appropriate to one's sex category.

girl/woman the individual must master 'a set of conventional signifying practices' through which the identity of 'boy/man' or 'girl/woman' is established and upheld in social interactions (Schrock & Schwalbe, 2009, p. 279). West and Zimmerman (1987) call this '**doing gender**', an active undertaking that involves 'a complex of socially guided perceptual, interactional, and micro-political activities that cast particular pursuits as expressions of masculine and feminine "natures"'. 'Doing gender' is not a 'simple property of individuals'. Instead it is the (often unconscious) activity of managing one's conduct in a way that is consistent with what is generally considered appropriate to one's sex category. The gender activities of individuals simultaneously emerge from and bolster their claims to membership in one or the other sex category. Gender, therefore, is an achieved status, something that must be actively accomplished.

The dramaturgical task of establishing oneself as a boy/man is aided by having a male body. This is because the conventional association of maleness and manhood makes having a male body a symbolic asset, a sign of qualification for inclusion in the category 'men'. However, having a male body is neither necessary nor sufficient to being socially male. Someone with a female body can give a convincing (or at least an adequate) performance as a man, while someone with a male body can fail to establish himself as worthy of being granted manhood status. The same, of course, applies to female bodies and performances as a girl/woman (Schrock & Schwalbe, 2009, p. 279).

A masculine or a feminine self is not acquired directly through biology. Instead, it is a consequence of how an individual's appearance and behaviour are interpreted by others, and it is acquired through psychological, cultural, and social means (Goffman, 1959). As West and Zimmerman (2004) have stated, gender is 'an emergent feature of social situations . . . a means of legitimating one of the most fundamental divisions of society . . .'

Marijuana Use and 'Doing Gender'

Recent research by Rebecca Haines and colleagues (2009) has shown how Canadian adolescents' use of marijuana is connected to gender identity and 'doing gender'. Haines and her team interviewed adolescents, asking them to describe how their experience of smoking marijuana was affected by their gender.

Following the work of Judith Butler (1990/1999, p. 30), Haines and her colleagues characterize gender identity as being constructed out of frequent repetition of stylized acts. Haines summarizes Butler's view of gender as 'sets of socially manipulated codes, internalized images that shift according to context rather than natural identity governed by (biological) bodies' (Haines, et al., 2009, p. 2029). Gender identity is the result of a non-voluntary performance, the 'reiteration of norms which precede, constrain, and exceed, the performer's "will" or "choice"' (Butler, 1993, p. 234, as cited in Haines, et al., 2009, p. 2029). From this point of view, gender is an effect produced by repeat performances of gendered norms.

Paechter (2007) has argued that gender is learned within localized groups such as families, peer groups, and school circles. These groups shape how girls and boys understand what it means to be male or female and provide models of the appropriate ways to enact their masculinity and femininity. Schools, particularly, are gendered institutions in that the academic curriculum, the recreational activities, and the behaviour of students all routinely distinguish and segregate students by gender (Paetchter, 2007).

Haines and her colleagues interviewed 45 adolescents—26 boys and 19 girls between the ages of the 13 and 18—who had volunteered to participate in their study. Because of their legal status and their use of marijuana, students were reassured that their interview material would remain confidential and that the researchers would not speak to parents, teachers, or the police (Haines, et al., 2009, p. 2031). The researchers were interested in the interviewees' history and pattern of marijuana use and their perceived potential benefits and/or consequences of using marijuana. They were also interested in learning about the connection

Do 'nice' girls smoke pot? Do you believe that femininity and marijuana use are mutually exclusive or can a young woman light up without being perceived as a rebel, an attention-seeker, or 'just one of the guys'? If you've been around people who smoke, what gender differences have you observed?

between marijuana use and aspects of adolescent identity, particularly whether there were any male–female differences in the style of use, in gaining access to marijuana, and in concerns over safety, aggression, or violence when smoking. Researchers also wanted to find out if male and female students used different terms to speak about gender and marijuana.

While the 80 students interviewed were generally quite forthcoming about marijuana use, the researchers were surprised that the students 'often appeared uncomfortable with questions specific to gender' (p. 2031). This was especially true when they directly asked about the interviewees' perceptions about gender differences 'in the ways of using, or reasons for using marijuana'. While it was relatively easy for interviewees to reflect on their own use of marijuana, it was difficult for them to reflect on gender as a social category that extended beyond their own personal experiences. Most interviewees claimed that gender was not a significant factor in influencing smoking practices (p. 2031). Comments like 'I really don't notice anything', 'It's probably just a random thing', and 'I really have no idea' were common (p. 2030).

However, when asked about marijuana use in connection to other social activities, the interviewees did identify gender differences in ways marijuana is used and in the reasons for using it (p. 2032). Most students who were interviewed acknowledged that boys smoked greater amounts of marijuana and smoked it more frequently than girls did. Most considered habitual use by girls, but not by boys, to be inappropriate or inauthentic. Several of the male students spoke about using marijuana to enhance outdoor relaxation and male bonding. These interviewees spoke about girls remaining on 'the sidelines giggling' (p. 2033). The males also suggested that smoking reduced the potential for aggressive behaviour that sometimes happens when men get together and party under the influence of alcohol. In fact, being a 'stoner' was often cast by the males as an effective counter to the aggressive masculinity they associated with getting drunk.

Those girls who self-identified as regular and frequent users took pride in their status as being 'just one of the guys'. It was important for them to be able to keep up with the boys and adopt a 'chilled' or relaxed demeanour as opposed to acting 'girly' or 'silly'. Both males and females believed that frequent or flagrant smoking was not typical of 'nice' girls, and that girls who did smoke regularly were rebels. While the boys who regularly smoked marijuana were viewed as cool and natural, girls who smoked regularly were called 'annoying', 'giggly', or too 'immature' to handle being high (p. 2034). Femininity was almost universally viewed as impeding an authentic use of marijuana. Girls who smoked regularly were said to be acting 'heaty'—the opposite of 'cool'—and their peers charged them with being interested more in attracting undue attention to themselves by getting high than in simply getting high to enjoy the state or experience.

Another issue that was raised in discussions about gender, social activities, and marijuana use was concern about the sexual vulnerability of girls, especially in the context of a party. Girls expressed concern that they had to be careful when smoking with guys because they need to remain in control. These girls felt that they not only had to be responsible for their own actions but also for the actions of the boys they were with. They were concerned that smoking a joint might hinder their ability to manage what they considered to be 'natural' risks of male sexuality (p. 2034).

Beyond the girls' acting 'heaty' and being aware of the sexual risk while high, the authors found little evidence of marijuana use as a way of 'doing femininity'. One interesting finding was the number of examples pointing to the use of marijuana to undermine dominant gender norms (p. 2035). Girls who got high acquired status in the masculine way, while boys who were high were allowed to express emotions in ways that would normally be prohibited.

Masculinity, Femininity, and 'Doing Gender' at a Cattle Auction

Watch an old John Wayne western and you get some idea of how ranching and masculinity are intricately tied together in North America. In these movies, the strength of Wayne's character as a man is often pitted against the weather, livestock, and Native North Americans. There is usually a love interest in these films, a woman who is typically portrayed as a 'good-hearted wife' who spends her time keeping the chickens fed and the home fires burning. As often as not, Wayne's character 'left the woman with the wagon train and rode off into the sunset alone to forge his destiny without the weight of a wife' to impede his progress (Pilgeram, 2007, 572–3).

In contrast to this idealized view of gender relations on the ranch, sociologist Ryanne Pilgeram's experiences were quite different. She grew up on a ranch where women were able to 'drive the tractor, castrate a calf, and bake a pie, when necessary' (Pilgeram, 2007, p. 573). Traditionally, operating a farm or ranch in the US is considered a man's role. But the number of women who were principal farm operators increased by 13.4 per cent between 1997 and 2002. The increasing prevalence of women in agriculture, along with an enduring vision of agriculture as a masculine preserve, call out for an examination of the construction of gender in conventional agriculture. In order to do this, Pilgeram examined the ways that 'women in an occupation and daily life that is dominated by men and masculinity perform gender in an effort to secure economic survival while negotiating dominant gender norms' (Pilgeram, 2007, p. 573).

Pilgeram notes that sociologists tend to distinguish between the private, or domestic, sphere (closed and exclusive) and the public sphere (pertaining to the community, where things are open to sight, and are accessible to and shared by all). Sociologists often link the public sphere and men's work, manhood, and representations of masculinity. They have made a similar link between the private sphere, women's work, and representations of womanhood and femininity.

Traditionally women have been portrayed as 'not cut out for farming' (Little, 2002, p. 667). The qualities that make a good farmer are the opposite of the qualities that make a good woman. The ideal type of masculinity specific to farming involves 'being tough enough to handle livestock, strong enough to exert control over Mother Nature, and independent enough to do all this without ever asking for help' (Pilgeram, 2007, p. 577). So how do women ranchers 'do gender' in both the public and private spheres? What are the strategies that they use to succeed in agriculture? Are these strategies a challenge to the masculine world of conventional agriculture, or do they reinforce male dominance in that field (p. 574)?

Between September and November 2005, Pilgeram studied gender in action at local weekly livestock auctions. To collect her data she relied on participant observation and semi-structured, in-depth interviews with four women and three men, varying in age from 21 to 73. Pligeram supplemented her observations with interviews in large part because she was unable to overhear conversations during the auctions: 'It just was not feasible to expect to have a conversation with a cacophony of bleating goats only yards away' (p. 578). Because Pilgeram grew up on a ranch, was the daughter of a rancher, and had a brother in the ranching industry, she gained immediate credibility with her informants. It also helped that she knew how to present herself: 'I made certain that on the days I interviewed and observed I wore sensible shoes, jeans, and no sandals, which farmers and ranchers despise as impractical' (p. 579).

During her initial observations Pilgeram spent most of her time watching the auction and the auction office, noting that both public spaces were 'gendered in very traditional ways with men always in control of the action'. The dangerous, dirty job of bringing animals into the auction ring, complete with 'charging bulls and flying manure', was reserved for men. The job of auctioneer, the person who controls the entire room and has the power to 'drop' something on a novice buyer (by quickly, sometimes artificially, raising the price during the bidding), was also reserved for men. From the auctioneer's opening quip of 'Here we go, boys' to the female clerk's running papers back and forth between the ring and the office while sporting low-slung jeans and manicured fingernails, traditional gender was continually reinforced in the public spaces. Even the female co-owner of the auction, Jackie, confined herself to the office, and jokingly referred to herself as 'the office grunt' (pp. 582–3).

The only time Pilgeram saw women enter the public auction ring was to calm and comfort frightened animals, in a display of traditional femininity. The public sphere of the auction, she concluded, serves to 'reproduce and naturalize traditional concepts of gender', including the idea that the public sphere is a male sphere. However, in the auction audience are female farm operators who complicate these conceptions. Both the farm wives and the female farm operators used 'impression management' to construct different presentations of self and to distinguish themselves from each other. The farm wives sported 'newer jeans, pink sweatshirts and purses', while the female farm operators dressed in 'plaid shirts, old jeans, work boots and often no purse' (p. 584).

The farm wives used subtle messages to signal that they were not actively engaged in the public auctions. They often held children, coats, purses, books, or other articles in their laps, 'suggesting that there was a barrier between themselves and the auction'. Men and female farm operators, on the other hand, rarely did such a thing, choosing to put any bulky item on a spare chair near them. And if a female farm operator did have a purse, she put it on the floor, under her chair. As Pilgeram observes:

> The female farm operators' decision either to bring or not bring a purse, or to place it under their seats, had two consequences. First, it allowed them to disconnect themselves from the femininity associated with a purse, and secondly, it allowed them to assume the less guarded posture, legs slightly apart, that the male operators used. (p. 584)

Although female farm operators appear simultaneously as women and as farm operators, this does not erode gender stereotypes. Instead, female farm operators use masculine stereotypes in order to best present themselves as good farmers, 'even at the expense of their personal identity as women' (p. 585). Both the men and the women interviewed by Pilgeram categorized women either as 'girly-girly' or 'tough'. One of the women farm operators, 'Iris', held out a 'leathery, muscular hand' and told Pilgeram:

> I swear to God, it [farming] makes your hands big and tough and it kind of makes your whole persona tough looking, and I think part of that is because if you go into the group of men and you look like a girly girl, right there they are thinking, 'she has boobs, what can she know?' You kind of have to neuter yourself to look like an 'it', then they respect you more. (p. 586)

STUDIES IN SOCIAL RESEARCH

Feminist Contributions to the Study of Gender Relations

Over the past three decades, feminist studies have gained acceptance within some university systems. However, women's questioning of and struggle against patriarchy and domination by men has a much longer history. Until the mid-nineteenth century in most Western countries, the differences between men and women, including women's subjugation to men, was commonly justified on the grounds that women's position relative to men was part of God's plan for humanity. But beginning in the mid-nineteenth century, the women's rights movement in North America and Europe forced men to see a conflict between their growing commitment to promoting the ideals of equality for all humans on the one hand and their denial of women's equality on the other.

Eighteenth-century writers such as Mary Astell, who published *Some Reflections upon Marriage* (1730), and Mary Wollstonecraft, who wrote *A Vindication of the Rights of Women* (1792), were among the first to call attention to this conflict. In the nineteenth century, suffragists campaigned in the United States, Canada, and Europe for extending the vote to women. In Canada, women were finally given the vote in national elections with the passage of the federal Women's Franchise Act in 1918. But even then, women were still not equal under the law. Under the terms of the British North America Act (1867), women could not be appointed to the Senate because they were not judged to be 'qualified persons' in the legal sense. Judge Emily Murphy appealed to the Supreme Court of Canada and lost her case. She then appealed to the Judicial Committee of the Privy Council of England, and in 1929 that committee overturned the judgement of the Supreme Court of Canada, ruling that the word 'persons' in Section 24 of the British North America Act (BNA) did include women as well as men.

Feminism, as an approach to scholarship, appeared in Canada in the 1970s, a response to the women's liberation movement already underway since the 1960s in the United States. Women were identified as an oppressed group, and feminists across North America demanded equality for women in all social, economic, cultural, judicial, and sexual matters. At the same time, they critically assessed scientific theories, pointing out that while those theories claimed to be neutral and value-free, they actually promoted the oppression of women (Eichler, 1987).

Whether under the banner of feminism, women's suffrage, women's liberation, or no banner at all, many women have refused to accept their unequal position in society as inevitable. In Canada, the United States, and western Europe, there is a long history of women struggling together to make significant changes in women's lives. But even as recently as 1983, a *New York Times*/PBS survey reported that two-thirds of those polled remained unconvinced that their lives had been improved by the women's movement, and many felt that the women's movement had 'led women astray' (Epstein, 1988, pp. 239–40).

As this chapter has shown, significant differences in women's and men's lives still exist. Women continue to work in designated 'female jobs', and men continue to hold more prestigious jobs, earning higher average wages than women do. Women are more likely than men to work part-time and to quit their jobs in order to allow their husbands more time to focus on their careers. Women continue to do more unpaid domestic work than do men, and they have a greater chance of experiencing poverty. Far fewer women than men run for, or are elected to, public office. This segregation cannot be explained away simply by referring to differences in biology or in cognitive processes. As Pat Armstrong and Hugh Armstrong (1993/2010) argue:

> Women's domestic responsibilities, their economic needs, and their integration into larger consumption units mean many women form a cheap and relatively flexible pool of labour. Desegregation of the labour force would require fundamental changes in those sectors that rely on cheap labour

and/or flexible labour force supply. It is therefore in the interests of many employers to maintain the division of labour by sex. Strategies for change, then, must not only take both kinds of women's work into account but must also recognize that employers will resist such change. (Armstrong & Armstrong, 1993/2010, pp. 225–6)

Armstrong and Armstrong called for 'radical alterations in both the structures and ideas that perpetuate the division of labour by sex'. If women's position in Canadian society is to change, they note, strategies for change must be worked out collectively, as people actively 'engage in altering their daily lives' (Armstrong & Armstrong, 1993/2010, p. 228).

Farming didn't just physically transform Iris's body; it tied her ability to find respect and success to a 'neutral' gender presentation of self. 'Iris' felt she was pushed into developing her neutral gender identity in order to be able to gain respect from the men around her, and she wasn't pleased with having to do that.

Pilgeram's work strongly suggests that gender is socially constructed, and that gendered performances change depending on place, audience, and context. An important insight to be drawn from Pillgeram's work is that 'doing gender' is not the same thing as 'undoing gender', which is complicated and often comes at a steep price. Instead of challenging gender ideals, women farm operators adopt a form of masculinity. In so doing they 'actually reinforce the idea that all good farmers are men and that the only way to succeed in agriculture is to conform to the requisite standards of hegemonic masculinity' (p. 575).

UNDERSTANDING GENDER AND SEX

If we wish to understand the complexities of gender, and the relationship of gender and sex, being able to exercise a sociological imagination is a valuable asset. When it comes to gender and sex, the effects of individual biography—including an individual's biology and her individual experiences of being socialized—cannot be understood without reference to what is going on at the level of history and culture. Neither can large-scale structural and organizational processes be properly understood without reference to what is happening at the level of individual biology and biography. Cultural stereotypes link gendered behaviour directly to biology. But if we want to understand the choices individuals make about how to behave in a given situation, we need, simultaneously, to understand how the behaviour of individuals is embedded in structural and institutional contexts and in material arrangements (what Bourdieu calls 'habitus').

As Cecilia Ridgeway (2009) notes, any changes that take place in the gender system we currently experience are 'iterative and may not always proceed smoothly'. Forces for change come from many directions and may include economic, political, and technical factors that alter the taken-for-granted, traditional material arrangements between men and women. The impact of changes to material arrangements may be blunted 'because people interpret the meaning of these changes through the lens of their existing, more conservative gender beliefs'. At the same time, material changes often make it more difficult to hold traditional beliefs about the direct relationship between sex and gender, and make it harder to sustain traditional beliefs as meaningful representations of how women and men should behave in day-to-day life today (Ridgeway, 2009, p. 157). At least we are now aware that there are no insurmountable biological reasons for inequalities between men and women. We can no longer conveniently refer to differences in biology as a compelling reason for denying full humanity, rights, and freedoms to women.

SUMMARY

Gender stratification—a system of social practices that organize relations of inequality between men and women on the basis of perceived differences—is very much a part of Canadian society. Gender stratification and gender inequality have had a long history in Canadian society. Even today Canadian women and men are unequal in terms of earnings, jobs and employment, political participation, and relative amounts contributed to domestic labour. While there have been many important changes in women's position in Canadian society over the last several decades, on average women continue to hold lower-paying jobs with fewer opportunities for promotion. Canadian women are still responsible for the majority of regular household and childcare tasks. Overworked as a result of these additional responsibilities, women are often prevented from advancing at work, reinforcing existing cultural stereotypes.

Gender stereotyping that links gender roles and behaviours to biological differences between men and women continue to be part of the taken-for-granted knowledge of many Canadians. A challenge to that view was raised by feminist scholars West and Zimmerman in the late 1980s, when they proposed that sociologists stop thinking of gender as a set of individual characteristics and start thinking of gender instead as a set of cultural practices. Gender, they argued, is an achieved status, something that must be actively accomplished. Two studies, one on marijuana use by Canadian adolescents and another on the behaviour of women farm owners at cattle auctions, illustrate West and Zimmerman's argument that gender is socially constructed and that 'doing gender' changes depending on place, audience, and context.

DISCUSSION QUESTIONS

1. Why do gender inequalities exist? What sustains those inequalities?
2. What is meant by the term 'doing gender'? Use specific examples to illustrate your answer.
3. Is Canadian society patriarchal? Justify your response.
4. Make a list of the extent to which gender inequality might exist within your family and among your friends and acquaintances.
5. Pat Armstrong and Hugh Armstrong have argued that if women's position in Canadian society is to change strategies must be worked out collectively, as people actively 'engage in altering their daily lives' (Armstrong & Armstrong, 1993/2010, p. 228). What are some examples of changes to daily lives that might be needed in order to change women's position in Canadian society?
6. Is feminism outmoded or does it continue to have an important role to play in Canadian society?

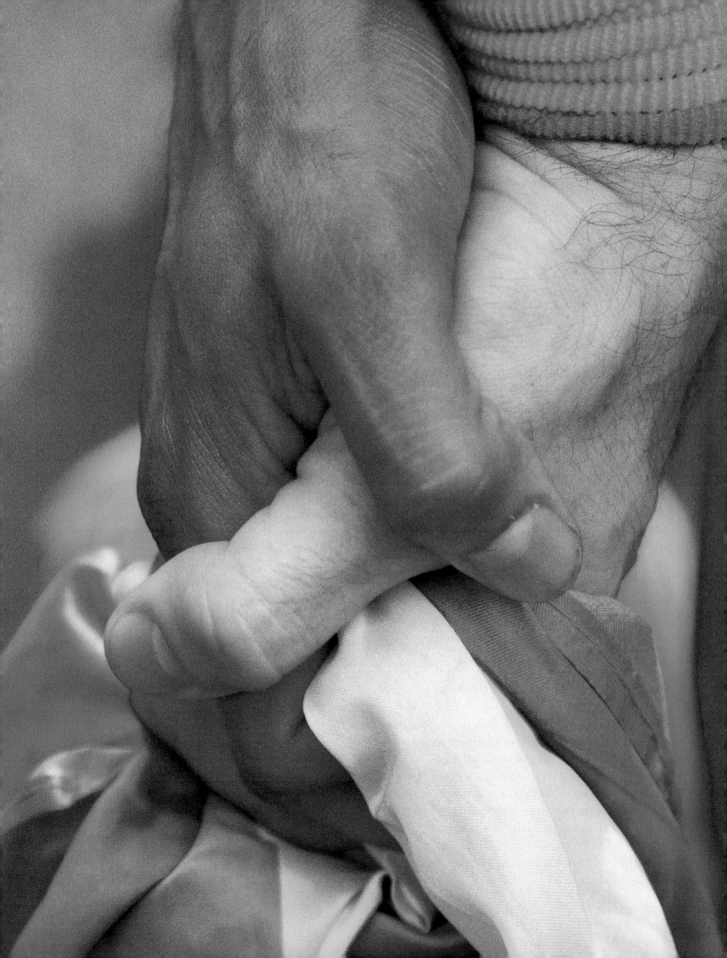

16 Sex, Sexuality, and Sexual Orientation

CHAPTER OUTLINE

LEARNING OBJECTIVES

In this chapter you will:

- think critically about sexual orientation and identity
- learn about the sociology of sexualities
- gain a clearer understanding of sexuality and human rights
- be introduced to the sociology of sex work
- reflect on heteronormativity
- distinguish between heterosexual, homosexual, and bisexual
- gain a clearer understanding of homophobia
- compare human rights in Canada and the United States
- consider same-sex relations in cross-cultural perspective.

INTRODUCTION

Many social scientists today are involved in trying to understand what Jeffrey Weeks (1985) has called 'that bundle of sensual possibilities we know as our sex, and through which we claim to know ourselves'. This chapter takes up four topics of interest to sociologists who study sex, sexuality, and sexual orientation:

1. *Sexual orientation and identity.* Sociologists who study this topic want to know if there is a connection between biological sex, gender identity, and sexual orientation. Are sexual identities something we are born with, they ask, or are they 'discursively produced' and therefore unstable? Is heterosexuality the only sexual orientation that is 'natural', or is a wide spectrum of sexual orientations part of the human condition?
2. *The sociology of sexualities.* Sociologists who work in this field are concerned with the theoretical and methodological influences on the field of sexuality studies. Topics of interest to them include how sexuality has intertwined with culture to create categories of inequality, and what impact globalization has had on 'queer' studies.
3. *Sexuality and human rights.* In this field of study, sociologists focus on the most recent issues with regard to sexual orientation and human rights.
4. *The sociology of sex work.* Some of the issues dealt with in the sociological literature on sex work include determining the main differences between street work and off-street work and between situations where prostitution is legal and regulated and where it is illegal.

SEXUAL ORIENTATION AND IDENTITY

heterosexuality
An expressed preference for a member of the opposite sex as a sexual partner.

In Western industrial societies the positively sanctioned norm for sexual orientation is **heterosexuality**. The term comes from the Greek *hetero*, meaning 'the other of the two'. In contemporary common-sense usage, heterosexuality is considered to be 'normal sexuality' that can be expressed only in terms of sexual practices and orientations that serve to bring together members of the two mutually exclusive categories of male and female, ultimately for the purposes of reproduction.

Other sexual practices that are not directly intended for reproduction but that are practised between two consenting adults of the opposite sex have also received varying degrees of tolerance or approbation, depending on the historical time period and the level of acceptance that is currently in vogue. There are, as British social historian Jeffrey Weeks writes,

heteronormativity
In contemporary common-sense usage, 'normal sexuality' that can be expressed only in terms of sexual practices and orientations that serve to bring together members of the two mutually exclusive categories of male and female, ultimately for the purposes of reproduction.

> . . . a host of sexual practices, falling short of reproductively successful coition, that while incurring ecclesiastical or legal injunctions, are still regarded as 'normal' in heterosexual relations: fellatio, cunnilingus, buggery, biting and so on. They only become 'abnormal', when they substitute themselves for reproductive sexuality, when they become ends in themselves rather than 'fore pleasures'. (Weeks, 1985, p. 85)

The term **heteronormativity** reflects the dominant thinking about sexual orientation in Western culture and refers to the 'the mundane, everyday ways that heterosexuality is privileged and taken for granted as normal and nature'. Heteronormativity includes 'the institutions, practices, and norms that support heterosexuality', especially monogamous, reproductive heterosexuality, and that suppress other forms of sexuality, especially homosexuality (Martin, 2008, p. 190).

Today in Western societies, while the term *heterosexual* applies to people who choose sexual partners of the opposite sex, the term **homosexual** refers to people who choose sexual partners of the same sex, and the term **bisexual** is used to refer to people who choose sexual partners of either sex. Common usage is to call homosexual men *gay* and homosexual women *lesbian*.

homosexual

Denoting people who choose sexual partners of the same sex; it is customary to call homosexual men *gay* and homosexual women *lesbian*.

bisexual

Denoting people who choose sexual partners from either sex.

What factors inform the prevailing common-sense view that heterosexuality is 'normal' and that marriage is natural only when it involves two people of opposite sexes?

While the occurrence of sexual relations between members of the same sex has had a long history in Western cultures, the use of the term *homosexual* is relatively recent. The term was coined in 1869 by K.M. Benkert, who wrote under the pseudonym of Kertbeny. According to Benkert:

> In addition to the normal sexual urge in men and women, Nature in her sovereign mood has endowed at birth of certain males and females individuals with the homosexual urge, thus placing them in a sexual bondage which renders them physically and psychically incapable—even with the best intention—of normal erection. This urge creates in advance a direct horror of the opposite sex, and the victim of this passion finds it impossible to suppress the feeling which individuals of his own sex exercise upon him. (as cited in Money, 1988, p. 9)

By the twentieth century, sexologists such as Havelock Ellis and Sigmund Freud, and later, Alfred Kinsey, developed the concept of sexuality as a continuum, with homosexual and heterosexual at the extremes and varying degrees of homosexual and heterosexual preferences in between. Kinsey went so far as to argue that there was nothing intrinsically perverse or harmful to the human species in any act that was biologically possible. But the scientific findings of Kinsey and other 'sexologists' notwithstanding, until recently in Western society, same-sex sexual relations have been variously defined as a sin, a crime against nature and humanity, a kind of sickness or perversion, and an instance of pathologically deviant behaviour. It has only been within the last half-century that major changes have taken place in the way Westerners understand homosexuality.

During the 1940s medical models dominated both popular understanding and scientific theories about homosexuality. Homosexuals were seen as suffering from a social pathology, and homosexuality was construed as aberrant behaviour, something that could be and had to be 'cured'. In 1948, and again in 1953, Alfred Kinsey published reports that revealed to the American public that the incidence of homosexuality was much higher than had been previously thought. His reports were written in neutral, non-judgemental language and suggested that homosexual behaviour was part of normal human experience. At the same time, another researcher, Evelyn Hooker, conducted tests that showed there were no cognitive differences between homosexuals and heterosexuals. These publications and others helped get the gay rights movement started in the 1950s. By the late 1960s, gay rights activists in the United States had taken to the streets to protest their treatment.

Not surprisingly, how gay and lesbian encounters are defined both by the general public and by researchers, and the ways in which these encounters are experienced in terms of gender roles, has changed enormously over the last century. Research on the Amsterdam gay and lesbian bar culture since the 1930s gives some indication of the ways in which gay relationships have been experienced over time. Until the 1950s, sexual relations between men who participated in the Amsterdam bar scene often involved a man who presented himself as effeminate and another who presented himself as heterosexual. The system here was based on a prostitution model, with the effeminate man submitting to the masculine one. But by the 1960s, many gay men, as well as lesbian women, had discarded the older style of practice based on opposites, and had adopted new possibilities that allowed masculine men to have sex with one another; the same was true of feminine lesbian women. While 'queens' did not entirely disappear from the gay world, they soon became a minority. As Gert Hekma notes:

The revolution in forms of desires and identities that has occurred since the 1950s has meant not a transition from one style to another but the addition of new models to the older ones that were already evolving themselves. The young queen of the 1950s may still be living in the 1990s, but he is quite a different figure from the young queen of the 1990s who may have adopted a punk or Madonna style. (Hekma, 1994, p. 138)

Today, a new model of gay life and sex has emerged, bringing with it legal reform, the de-pathologizing of homosexuality, and gay and lesbian marriages and parenthood.

In Canada, combined data from 2003 and 2005 surveys conducted by Statistics Canada indicate that about 1.9 per cent of the population aged 18 to 59 identify themselves as gay, lesbian, or bisexual (Statistics Canada, 2008b). Other surveys have produced varying results. A survey conducted for the *Toronto Sun* in 2000 indicates that about 6 per cent of Torontonians identified themselves as either homosexual or bisexual. British sociologists C. Bagley and P. Tremblay (1998) surveyed a random sample of 750 Calgary, Alberta, males aged from 18 to 27 and determined that of those surveyed:

- 14 per cent had had voluntary, same-gender sexual contact at some point between the ages of 12 and 27;
- nearly 6 per cent identified themselves as homosexual; and
- slightly over 15 per cent identified themselves as being 'homosexual to some degree'.

The most comprehensive survey of the sexuality of American men and women was conducted by Robert Michaels and colleagues in 1992, with the results published in 1994 (Michaels, Gagnon, Laumann, & Kolata, 1994). 'The public image of sex in America', they wrote 'bears virtually no relationship to the truth.' That image 'consists of myths, and they are not harmless, for they elicit at best unrealistic and at worst dangerous misconceptions of what people do sexually' (Michaels, et al., 1994, p. 1). The researchers found that while 2 per cent of men and 1.4 per cent of women identified themselves as 'homosexual or bisexual', over 10 per cent of men and 8.6 per cent of women reported that they 'had some same-sex desire or experience or identified themselves as homosexual or bisexual'. Some of the results of their survey are summarized in Table 16.1.

CAUSES OF SEXUAL ORIENTATION

There is little consensus about why individuals develop either heterosexual or homosexual orientations, with some scientists arguing that sexual orientation is genetic, others that it is hormonal, and still others that it is the result of early childhood experiences. The American Psychological Association (APA), which represents some of the most current scientific thinking on the topic, concludes that:

[S]exual orientation is most likely the result of a complex interaction of environmental, cognitive and biological factors. In most people, sexual orientation is shaped at an early age. There is also considerable recent evidence to suggest that biology, including genetic or inborn hormonal factors, plays a significant role in a person's sexuality. It's important to recognize that there are probably many

TABLE 16.1 Men's and women's sexual orientation, according to US research by Michaels, et al. (1994)

	Men (%)	Women (%)
Identified themselves as homosexual or bisexual	2.8	1.4
Had sex with a person of the same sex in the previous 12 months	3.4	0.6
Had sex with person of same sex at least once since puberty	5.3	3.5
Felt desire for sex with person of same sex	7.7	7.5
Had some same-sex desire or experience or identified themselves as homosexual or bisexual	10.1	8.6

Source: Michaels, Gagnon, Laumann, & Kolata, 1994, p. 40.

reasons for a person's sexual orientation, and the reasons may be different for different people. (APA, n.d.)

The APA has also has determined that sexual orientation is not a choice. For most people,

> . . . sexual orientation emerges in early adolescence without any prior sexual experience. Although we can choose whether to act on our feelings, psychologists do not consider sexual orientation to be a conscious choice that can be voluntarily changed. (APA, n.d.)

A homosexual sexual orientation, they conclude, is not an 'illness', 'emotional problem', or 'emotional disorder' that can be changed through therapy.

In general, sociologists are less interested in researching the root causes of sexual orientation than in learning about the ways in which sexual orientation is expressed and repressed. In Western societies over the last century, same-sex orientations have become less stigmatized owing in part to scientific research on the normality of sexual diversity and in part to the success of political rights movements. Gay Pride parades, held annually in Canada, the US, and Europe, provide one venue for members of gay and lesbian communities to express their identities publicly and to demand equal rights with the heterosexual majority.

Although scientific knowledge and public opinion about sexual orientation are changing, opposition towards and even hatred of people who don't conform to heterosexual norms remain strong, even in countries where the persecution of homosexuals is no longer legal and where, for the most part, they have won many basic human rights.

HOMOPHOBIA

homophobia

Fear of or antipathy towards persons with non-heteronormative sexual orientations.

Homophobia, or fear of and antipathy towards persons with non-heteronormative sexual orientations, remains strong in many societies. A report sponsored by the International Lesbian and Gay Association (Ottosson, 2010) notes that in 2010, 76 countries in the world continue to prosecute people on the grounds of their sexual orientation. In recent years some important progress has been made in terms of acquiring basic human rights for LGBT (lesbian, gay, bisexual, and transgendered) people throughout the world. In December 2008, the UN General Assembly, with the support of 66 countries, made a declaration supporting the rights of lesbian, gay, bisexual, transgendered, and intersex (LGBTI) people, reaffirming that 'the principle of non-discrimination applies to all human beings regardless of their sexual orientation or gender identity'. The declaration further condemned human rights violations of LGBTI people and urged all states to 'decriminalise consensual adult relations between persons of the same sex' (Ottosson, 2010). A major victory for the human rights of homosexual peoples was achieved in 2009 when the High Court of Delhi, India—a country with one-sixth of the world's population—declared section 377 of the Indian Penal Code invalid as it pertains to sexual activities between consenting adults.

However, there remain five countries—Iran, Mauritania, Saudi Arabia, United Arab Emirates, and Yemen (as well as some regions of Nigeria and Somalia)—where people are

The 2005 movie *Brokeback Mountain*, starring Jake Gyllenhaal and Heath Ledger, generated considerable controversy (in spite of critical acclaim) for featuring two cowboys of ambiguous sexuality who engage in a homosexual relationship. American social conservatives and Christian fundamentalists were especially critical. Is there room for a gay cowboy romance in the canon of American westerns? Or is a gay or bisexual cowboy in a mainstream Hollywood film simply at odds with our heteronormative view of the American frontiersman as a rugged, masculine type?

still put to death for their sexual orientation. The situation is especially grave in Africa, where 38 countries have criminalized homosexuality and where over 50 per cent of the governments of that continent have formally criminalized same-sex unions (Ottosson, 2010).

Anti-homosexual feelings are strong in many people, some of whom are prepared to use violence to back up their beliefs. In a study of approximately 500 young adults in the greater San Francisco Bay area, forensic psychologist Karen Franklin (1998) found that 1 in 10 of her respondents admitted to having used either physical violence or threats against people they believed to be homosexual; another 24 per cent reported that they had engaged in anti-homosexual name-calling. When only the men in her survey were considered, 18 per cent of her respondents admitted to having used physical violence or threats, and 32 per cent admitted to name-calling. One-third of those who said they had never engaged in anti-homosexual aggression confirmed that if a homosexual person flirted with or propositioned them, they would likely respond with assault or harassment.

In Canada, the General Social Survey (GSS) on victimization conducted by Statistics Canada in 2004 found that compared to heterosexuals, 'the odds of being victimized were nearly 2 times greater for gays and lesbians and 4.5 times greater for bisexuals' (Beauchamp, 2004, p. 8). The GSS also found that 44 per cent of gays and lesbians and 41 per cent of bisexuals felt that they had been discriminated against at some time in the previous five years. Fourteen per cent of heterosexuals reported having experienced some form of discrimination. Yet while the majority of gays and lesbians who reported experiencing discrimination (78 per cent) attributed it to their sexual orientation, just 2 per cent of the heterosexuals who reported experiencing discrimination attributed it to their sexual orientation (Beauchamp, 2004, p. 11).

Since 1999 the US-based Gay, Lesbian, and Straight Education Network (GLSEN) has conducted a biennial survey on the experiences of lesbian, gay, bisexual, and transgendered students. Its report on the 2007 National School Climate Survey declares that 'schools nationwide are unsafe environments for a distressing majority of LGBT students who continue to face harassment and even physical assault, often without intervention from school staff.' The survey found that 86.2 per cent of LGBT students had experienced verbal harassment at school during the previous year; 44.1 per cent of respondents reported having been physically harassed, and 22.1 per cent reported having been physically assaulted (punched, kicked, or injured with a weapon). Just over 60 per cent felt unsafe at school because of their sexual orientation. Particularly distressing was the finding that over 60 per cent of those who had been harassed or assaulted at school did not report the incident, believing that little action would be taken. Of those who did report an incident, nearly one-third said that the school staff did nothing in response.

In view of these findings, it is perhaps not surprising that 'many LGBT students are forced to miss class or entire days of school rather than face a hostile environment where they experience continual harassment,' according to the survey. Almost one-third of those who participated in the survey had missed a day of school in the month previous to taking the survey because they felt unsafe, compared to 4.5 per cent of a national sample of secondary school students (GLSEN, 2008).

SAME-SEX MARRIAGE

A recent (2010) Gallup poll in the US indicates that 58 per cent of Americans think that gay or lesbian relations between consenting adults should be legal, and that 57 per cent of Americans feel that homosexuality should be considered an acceptable alternative lifestyle

(Jones, 2010). (By comparison, according to a 2004 poll by the Pew Foundation, 69 per cent of Canadians and 77 per cent of western Europeans were similarly accepting of homosexuality). The Gallup poll reveals that most Americans are willing to allow homosexuals equal rights when it comes to job opportunities (89 per cent) and the chance to serve in the military (70 per cent). However, far fewer Americans are willing to allow homosexuals equal rights when it comes to marriage: only 44 per cent of Americans surveyed would grant same-sex couples the right to marry, and 49 per cent were in favour of 'a constitutional amendment that would define marriage as being between a man and a woman, thus barring marriages between gay or lesbian couples' (Jones, 2010).

In 2001, the Netherlands became the first country in the world to adopt legislation authorizing same-sex marriages. In 2005, the Canadian parliament passed Bill C-38, making Canada the fourth country in the world to recognize same-sex marriage. Acceptance of same-sex marriages among Canadians is strongly influenced both by age and by place of birth. An Environics poll conducted for the CBC in March 2005 showed that while 61 per cent of respondents between the ages of 18 and 29 agreed with redefining marriage to include same-sex couples, more than 71 per cent of those 60 years and older disagreed. And while 65 per cent of Canadians who were born elsewhere disapproved of the bill legalizing

Members of Carleton University Students' Association gather on Parliament Hill to rally against reopening the equal marriage debate in December 2006. Do you think the debate surrounding same-sex marriage in this country is over, or is there a chance it could be reopened?

same-sex marriage, a smaller percentage—50 per cent—of those who were born in Canada disapproved (CBC News, 2005).

The political debate surrounding Bill C-34 provides an interesting study in multiculturalism, religious tolerance, and politics. Canada has a commitment to recognizing and encouraging diversity in its population. In the case of same-sex marriage, some opponents attempted to block the passage of the bill on the grounds of defending minority rights. One of the chief opponents of the legislation was Conservative Party leader (and soon-to-become prime minister) Stephen Harper, who warned parliament that same-sex marriage threatened a social institution fundamental to Canada's minorities. 'New Canadians know that their cultural values are likely to come under attack if this law is passed,' he said (CBC News, 2005). In response, then prime minister Paul Martin pointed out that it was the Charter of Rights that drove the need to change Canadian law, as the Charter protects all minorities, including homosexuals. 'If a prime minister and a national government are willing to take away the rights of one group,' Martin argued, 'what is to say they will stop it?' (CBC News, 2005). Multiculturalism, from his point of view, had to take a backseat to an underlying adherence to the core values laid out in the Charter of Rights and Freedoms.

Human Rights in Canada and the United States: Why Canada Is More Liberal

Canada became a nation in 1867. For the first hundred years, homosexuality was illegal and was considered a mental illness. In 1967, then Liberal Justice minister Pierre Trudeau introduced Bill C-150 in the House of Commons. This bill challenged existing legislation on issues of sexuality, marriage, and abortion by decriminalizing homosexual acts and abortion and making divorce more accessible. It was in introducing this bill that Trudeau famously stated, 'There's no place for the state in the bedrooms of the nation.' The bill passed in spite of enormous opposition, but it was not until 2000, when Bill C-23 became law, that same-sex couples were granted the same rights and obligations as common-law couples. Five years later, in July 2005, the Liberal government passed Bill C-315, the Civil Marriage Act, which recognizes the right of same-sex couples to have access to civil marriage.

There have been many cultural and legal challenges concerning the status of gay and lesbian people in North American over the past forty years. Evidence points to increasing tolerance of homosexuality in both countries. However, Canadian law now guarantees equal rights to gay men and lesbians, including the right to be legally married; no such rights have been given to homosexuals living the United States. In the US, anti-sodomy laws have recently been rescinded by a 2003 Supreme Court decision, and as of December 2010, the US Senate passed a bill allowing gay men and women to serve openly in the military. Yet many states have recently implemented policies prohibiting gay couples from marrying (Adam, 2003). Why is there such a difference in attitudes towards gays and lesbians in the two neighbouring countries?

Research on the social determinants of attitudes towards homosexuality indicates the same patterns found in the determinants of social attitudes in general: women tend to be more accepting (in this case, of homosexuality) than men, and younger generations are more tolerant than older generations. In addition to age and sex, education, social class, and whether or not one is acquainted with a lesbian, a gay man, or a bisexual person all affect the degree of one's acceptance of homosexuality.

In a comparative study of Canadian and American attitudes toward homosexuality, Andersen and Fetner (2008) used a subset of the World Values Survey, or WVS (see www.worldvaluessurvey.org/), focusing only on Canadian and American data collected at three points between 1981 and 2000. Their total sample size was 6,194 respondents, of which 3,004 were from Canada and 3,190 from the United States. They chose as their dependent variable the respondent's attitude towards homosexuality. They determined this attitude with the following question:

> Please tell me for each of the following statements whether you think it can always be justified, never be justified, or something in between. . . .
>
> *Homosexuality*
> Never justifiable   Always justifiable
> 1   2   3   4   5   6   7   8   9   10

Independent variables of interest in their study included country, year the study was conducted, and birth cohort (born before 1920; born 1920–9; born 1940–9; born 1950–9; born 1960–3).

Table 16.2 shows the mean responses to the dependent variable (attitude toward homosexuality) by birth cohort and by country. We can see there are clear generational differences over time in terms of the attitudes towards homosexuality. In both Canada and the United States the views of those in earlier cohorts are less sympathetic to homosexuality than those in later cohorts. What is also evident is that these attitudes change over time in all cohorts. As Andersen and Fetner conclude:

> . . . we have tentative evidence that attitudes towards homosexuality are affected by social influences throughout the life course. This pattern is similar for Canada and the United States, but the mean scores are lower in nearly all cohorts in all years in the US, indicating a lower tolerance of homosexuality. (Andersen & Fetner, 2008, p. 320)

The data in Table 16.2 suggest that while significant social change has occurred in both countries, this change has been more marked in Canada, where by 1990 all cohorts were more permissive in their attitudes towards homosexuality than the corresponding American cohorts, a pattern that continued in 2000. Nevertheless, with evidence of increasingly liberal attitudes about homosexuality in both countries, we can surmise that Canadians and Americans were influenced by widespread cultural and political changes occurring in the two countries (Andersen & Fetner, 2008, p. 325). These changes went hand in hand with increasing media focus on homosexuality, an issue that went from relative obscurity in the 1980s to one with 'significantly high salience in 2000' (Andersen & Fetner, 2008, p. 325). Indeed, it is difficult, Andersen and Fetner comment, to think of another social issue that experienced such dramatic change.

A large part of the reason for the dramatic change in attitudes towards homosexuality is that prior to 1980, many people had uninformed opinions about the issue. The relatively quick rise to prominence of homosexuality as a public issue was brought about in part by the increased visibility of gay men and lesbians as characters in television and film and the 'coming out' of media personalities and other celebrities (Andersen & Fetner, 2008; Walters, 2001).

TABLE 16.2   Results of the World Values Survey on homosexuality: Mean responses to the dependent variable by birth cohort and country (Canada, US)

| Birth cohort | 1981–2 | | | 1990 | | | 2000 | | |
| | Age | Mean | | Age | Mean | | Age | Mean | |
		CAN	US		CAN	US		CAN	US
Before 1920	61+	1.81	1.82	70+	2.71	2.21	80+	3.74	2.41
1920–9	51–60	2.45	2.07	60–69	3.25	2.42	70–79	3.51	4.02
1930–9	41–50	3.18	2.13	50–59	3.81	2.93	60–69	4.77	4.91
1940–9	31–40	3.14	2.61	40–49	4.02	3.08	50–59	5.32	4.66
1950–9	21–30	3.61	2.49	30–39	4.29	3.11	40–49	5.62	4.52
1960–3	18–20	3.54	2.72	27–29	4.44	2.77	37–39	5.98	4.96

Note: High scores indicate greater tolerance of homosexuality.

Source: Andersen & Fetner, 2008, p. 320. 'Cohort differences in tolerance of homosexuality: Attitudinal change in Canada and the United States, 1981–2000'. *Public Opinion Quarterly*, Vol. 72(2): 311–330. © Oxford Journals.

But homosexuality also became a focus of attention as a result of the growing AIDS epidemic in North America. As Andersen and Fetner explain, news stories about the AIDS epidemic:

> . . . gave audiences views into the lives of gay men that were previously hidden, and outpourings of sympathy, as well as charity, grew steadily in both nations over this decade. Cultural symbols in support of AIDS victims, such as the red ribbon, were common through the 1990s. (Andersen & Fetner, p. 325)

But while changes in media representation of gays and lesbians and news stories that aroused sympathy for the plight of AIDS victims might explain a general softening of attitudes over time in Canada and the United States, it does not explain the differences between the two countries. For this we must look at the different social policies regarding gay and lesbian rights. Canada's Charter of Rights and Freedoms, adopted in 1982, has encouraged Canadian courts to make landmark decisions that have extended equal rights to lesbians and gay men on a number of issues, including spousal benefits and marriage (Andersen & Fetner, 2008, p. 326; Herman, 1994). The United States, by contrast, has a narrower definition of constitutional rights, and this has led to mixed results in the courts. US legislators have actually considered amending the American Constitution to prevent same-sex couples from marrying.

Andersen and Fetner conclude that people do respond to national debates on controversy over social issues, and that policy changes affect individual attitudes, even about the most controversial issues (2008, p. 327). But while they have been able to associate differences in the constitutional rights enjoyed by the citizens of the two countries with subsequent differences in public policies, they have been unable to explain why Canadian and American constitutional rights diverged in the first place. Further research is needed to explain why (and how) the Religious Right and other 'pro-family' lobby groups have played such an important role in the US in determining who can and cannot be granted full constitutional protection, while being confined to a less powerful role in Canada.

SAME-SEX RELATIONS IN CROSS-CULTURAL PERSPECTIVE

Same-sex sexual relations occur in all societies. Although the ancient Greeks believed that human nature was characterized by either masculine or feminine attributes, their system of classification was open to other possibilities. In his *Symposium*, Plato proposed that three sexes were originally part of human nature. Greek Hippocratic theory likewise maintained that there were three kinds of men and three kinds of women, depending on the proportions in which the male and female seed was combined. For example, when female seed from a male was overpowered by male seed from a female, the result was an androgynous or 'manly' woman (Lloyd, 1984, p. 91).

Greek polytheism accepted the possibilities of fluid sex categories and a variety of sexual practices, including homosexuality. The later Romans, however, were much more restrictive. Exposed to more diverse cultural standards as a result of their empire building, the Romans became rigid, maintaining that human nature dictated only two sexes (Hoffman, 1984). This strict adherence to two dichotomously opposed sexes still prevails in Western societies. But while contemporary Western culture makes a sharp distinction between males and females and promotes heterosexual relations as the norm (heteronormativity), other cultures do not. In the sections that follow we will examine two cultures where heteronormativity does not prevail.

Two-Spirit People in Native North American Societies

In some non-Western societies, categories of male and female are based not on anatomical or morphological criteria but on gender roles. One example is the 'two-spirit people' found among many Native North American societies and reported on by early travellers and ethnographers (Thayer, 1980, p. 287). **Two-spirit people** (often called **berdaches** in anthropological literature) are either men who adopt women's dress and do women's work or, less commonly, women who adopt men's dress and do men's work. They have been documented in almost 150 Native North American societies (Roscoe, 1987). (There are male two-spirit people in all of these societies and female two-spirit people in about half of them.) According to Roscoe (1994), who uses the anthropological but outmoded term *berdache*, the key features of male and female two-spirit people, in order of importance, are:

- *productive specialization*—crafts and domestic work for male berdaches in warfare, hunting and leadership roles in the case of female berdaches
- *supernatural sanction*—in the form of an authorized and/or bestowal of powers from extra societal sources
- *gender variation*—in relation to normative cultural expectations for male and female genders. (Roscoe, 1994, p. 332)

In many cases cross-dressing (that is, wearing clothing typically worn by members of the opposite sex) is a common and visible marker of two-spirit status, but this is not always the case. Some two-spirit people cross-dress at all times, others on specific occasions (women, traditionally, cross-dressed only when they were hunting or warring), and others not at all. Sexual behaviour also varies. Many two-spirit people prefer sexual relations only with members of the same sex, others with members of the opposite sex, while still others enjoy sexual

two-spirit people
A 'third sex' recognized in many Native North American societies, being either men who adopt women's dress and do women's work or women who adopt men's dress and do men's work. The term is used to indicate a person whose body houses both masculine and feminine spirits. *Formerly called* **berdaches**.

relations with both sexes. In sum, two-spirit status is foremost economic and religious, and not based on gender or sexual differences alone. Commonly, however, such status is associated with exceptional productivity and achievements, and two-spirit people have typically

This postcard photograph, taken in 1877, shows 'Squaw Jim' (left), a two-spirit person of the Crow Nation. In many First Nations circles the anthropological term *berdache*, which derives from a French word for a male prostitute, has been replaced by the term *two-spirit person*. What is the significance of the change? How does the newer term compare in terms of prestige and respect with the words *transgendered or bisexual*?

been well integrated into their communities. And, far from being viewed by members of their societies as 'transvestites' or 'transsexuals', as would be the case in mainstream Western societies, two-spirit people have been recognized as constituting third and sometimes fourth genders (Roscoe, 1994, pp. 335–8).

The religious functions fulfilled by two-spirit people and the life-cycle rituals they undergo are specific to their status. Two-spirit people have not simply exchanged one gender status for another, but have actually entered into an entirely different status. As late as the 1930s among the Navajo, children with two-spirit tendencies were welcomed and encouraged. As adults they were given control of family property, and they acted as heads of households, supervising agricultural and domestic work (Roscoe, 1994, p. 355). According to one Navajo elder, recorded in the early 1930s:

> If there were no *nadle* [the Navajo word for *two-spirit person*] the country would change. They are responsible for all the wealth in the country. If there were no more left, the horses, sheep, and Navajo would all go. They are leaders just like President Roosevelt. A *nadle* around the Hogan [the primary traditional Navajo home] will bring good luck and riches. You must respect a *nadle*. They are, somehow, sacred and holy. (Hill, 1935, p. 274)

Such status, as Roscoe explains, was traditionally neither a 'niche for occasional (and presumably "natural") variation in sexuality and gender, nor was it an accidental by-product of unresolved social contradictions' (1994, p. 370). It was, rather, a 'distinct and autonomous social status, on par with the status of men and women.' A two-spirit gender designation, like that of 'man' or 'woman', entails a specific pattern of behaviour, emotional profile, and social duties and responsibilities. Among Native North Americans, social learning and personal experiences, including religious and supernatural ones, have been just as important as the economy in defining an individual's identity. It would therefore be wrong, Roscoe concludes, to categorize two-spirit people by using Western concepts of cross-dressers, or transvestites, or even as men or women who simply assume the role of the opposite sex.

The Sambia and the Baruya of the New Guinea Highlands

We have already, in Chapter 14, encountered the Sambia people of the eastern highlands of New Guinea. Here we return to the Sambia, and meet the Baruya, another mountain tribe of New Guinea, as illustrations of the point that, as with gendered behaviour, sexual orientation, sexuality, and sexual practices are strongly influenced by social and cultural practices and expectations. This section also aims to reinforce, in yet another way, the fact that heterosexuality and homosexuality have clear, culturally specific meanings. Contrary to common-sense understandings prevalent in Western society, performing certain sexual acts does not invariably reveal an inborn (and therefore immutable) 'true' sex. Even in the area of sex acts and sexual orientation, culture and socialization are enormously powerful forces.

The Sambia have traditionally promoted same-sex relations between pre-pubescent and pubescent boys. Until marriage, all Sambia boys are expected to engage in same-sex relations in order to ensure that they grow to full manhood. At age 7, when they are removed to the man's house, Sambia boys are initiated into sexual relations with older boys. In place of milk from their mothers, the young boys are now told that daily consumption of older boys' semen is essential for their maturation to adulthood.

As Gilbert Herdt (1987) explains, the Sambia are 'pre-occupied' with male–female differences. To the Sambia, femaleness is 'an innate, natural essence' that naturally produces adult femininity. Maleness, by contrast is a 'weak and tenuous essence', and adult masculinity is not its natural product. In order to attain manhood, boys must swallow sperm, and Sambia boys engage in this activity on a daily basis over a period of 10 to 15 years.

The Baruya, another mountain tribe of New Guinea, have institutionalized the same sexual practices as the Sambia. Maurice Godelier, a French anthropologist who lived among the Baruya for many years, tells us that the knowledge that swallowing sperm gives men their strength and the ability to dominate and manage women is 'the holiest of secrets' (Godelier, 1986, p. 52). Any boy who reveals the secret to women or any woman who trespasses in the man's house is punished with the threat of death. The young boys are taught that, at this point in their lives, any heterosexual involvement is unacceptable. Other unacceptable forms of sexual behaviour include masturbation (semen is to be ingested, not expelled) and same-sex anal intercourse.

menarche
The first menstrual period of a woman.

Marriages, however, have been arranged at birth and are expected to be consummated when the girl reaches **menarche**. Just before they are to be married, the young men are told about heterosexual practices. After marriage the young men are expected to have sexual relations with their wives but also to continue ingesting semen. However, once the first child is born, sexual relations between the father and another man is considered as harmful as heterosexual activity is before the birth of the child.

Among the peoples of the New Guinea highlands, the attainment of manhood necessarily entails a period of sexual relations that, in Western culture, would be considered and dealt with as either pedophilia (sexual relations with young boys) or 'enforced' homosexuality or bisexuality. But for the Sambia and Baruya, the omission of a same-sex phase of development would not only stigmatize the young man as deviant but also be clearly detrimental to his health and his ability to become a man.

From the perspective of Western culture, this kind of institutionalized sequence of sexual orientations appears both unnatural and unexplainable. From the perspective of a sociologist who understands the interplay of biology, inheritance, socialization, and cultural imperatives in establishing gender identity and gender behaviours as well as sexuality and sexual orientation, the practices of the Sambia and Baruya are but further examples of the plasticity of the human condition.

THE SOCIOLOGY OF SEXUALITIES: HISTORICAL BACKGROUND

sexuality studies
An interdisciplinary field of study that emerged from the work of scholars and political activists who viewed sexuality not as a biological drive but as something that was socially constructed.

Sexuality studies is the umbrella term used to designate an interdisciplinary field of study that emerged in the 1970s as a result of the work of scholars and political activists such as Jonathan Ned Katz, Ken Plummer, Jeffrey Weeks, and Michel Foucault. Broadly speaking these scholars took a social-constructivist approach and viewed sexuality not as a biological drive but as a 'domain whose meanings change across cultures and history' (Irvine, 2003). While the founders of the discipline of sociology had ignored sexuality, contemporary cross-discipline research into the issue explores the social organization of sexualities along with the history of sexual identity formations as they are affected by race and ethnicity, gender, class, and other factors (Irvine, 2003, p. 451).

During the early decades of the 1900s sociologists interested in the study of sexuality approached the subject through the study of 'deviants'. Sociologists from the University of

So let's say you find yourself sexually attracted to a lonely man wearing a purple hippo suit. Does that make you a sexual deviant? How do we decide what does and does not count as deviance? Is it fair to stigmatize as deviant feelings that are natural, innate, and over which one has no control?

Chicago used that city as a sort of laboratory for their research. Park and Burgess (1925), for example, undertook a study of the 'vice' districts of Chicago, arguing that a city divides into *moral regions*—geographical and social areas organized around specific 'tastes or passions' (Park & Burgess, 1925, p. 45). Other researchers who either taught at or were trained at the Chicago School used diverse methods of inquiry, including life histories, observation, and interviews, combined with the analysis of 'census data, court records, diaries and other documents' to collect their data (Irvine, 2003, p. 433). Homosexuality, pimps, and prostitutes formed most of these early sociologists' subject matter, and the researchers were especially interested in the coping mechanisms used by these sexual 'deviants' (see, for example, Humphreys, 1970/1975; Reiss, 1961).

During the 1960s and 1970s, in the wake of the sexual liberation movement, sociologists became interested in sexuality as the basis of community and community life. These researchers documented life in gay and lesbian communities, the gay and lesbian liberation movements, the impact of sexuality-based discrimination, and the prevalence of anti-gay sentiment. Early scholars of sexuality, such Mary McIntosh (1968), argued that homosexuality was a 'social role' and not an inherent biological condition, while Jeffrey Weeks (1977) examined the history of different sexual categories and belief systems about sexuality. By the late 1960s, influenced by Howard Becker's study *Outsiders* (1963), sociologists who studied deviance turned their attention away from deviance as an inherent characteristic of individuals and toward deviance as an outcome of the interaction between those who made the rules and those who were perceived to be breaking them. The focus of sociological research also shifted from the 'deviants' themselves to the rule-making strategies of social institutions and to those Becker had labelled the 'moral entrepreneurs'.

With Becker's work shaking up the accepted ways of thinking about who and what was 'normal' and who or what was 'deviant', sociologists were now forced to ask questions about who *decides* what is normal, and who *makes up* the rules about what constitutes deviant behaviour. Becker's point was that while an individual could be an 'outsider'—a rule-breaker—with respect to one social group, he could very well be a rule-*maker* with respect to another social group.

The result of this reorientation of focus from the deviant to the rule-maker was a whole spate of sociological case studies that focused on sex offenders, prostitutes, nudists, topless barmaids, gay bars, homosexuals, and transvestites and transsexuals. Sociologists of the 1960s and 1970s sought to understand, and to make visible, the social worlds of a myriad of sexual cultures that they had previously treated only as deviant.

During the 1980s and 1990s sociologists continued to demonstrate that sexual meaning, identities, and practices are intersubjectively negotiated and that sexuality is socially constructed. Some researchers even began to claim that social factors actually *produced* sexuality. For example, sociologists began to treat the concept 'homosexual' as a social category to be analyzed in terms of its relative historical, economic, and political basis, not as a universal category that was fixed and natural. By the mid-1990s, 'queer theory' was making its mark on the study of sexuality. Queer theorists claimed that sexual identity, like any other identity, was arbitrary, unstable, and exclusionary. Today, sociologists who study sexuality, and especially those who identify as 'queer theorists', are sensitive to how sexual identities are socially constructed and are mindful of heteronormativity as a fundamental organizing principle of Western societies (Green, 2002, p. 521).

Just as those interested in studying gender have argued that gender cannot be understood through the presumed 'natural' binary of male–female, queer theorists argue that sexuality cannot be understood through the presumed 'natural' binary of heterosexual–homosexual.

Instead, queer theorists argue that sexual identities, desires, and definitions are fluid and are historically and culturally specific. By the late 1970s, for example, sociologist Martin Weinberg and psychologist Alan Bell had begun speaking of 'homosexualities' (and not homosexuality) as a way of challenging the assumption that sexual categories and the individuals who made up those categories are homogeneous (Bell & Weinberg, 1978; Irvine, 2003, p. 439). In his study of suburban gay men, for example, Brekhus (2003) distinguished several different 'ideal types' of gay male identity:

> The 'lifestylers' or 'peacocks', who live and work in exclusively gay circles, and for whom being gay is a full-time, master identity; the 'commuters' or 'chameleons', who live and work in the suburbs, and commute to hard-core, urban gay lives for sex and socializing; and the 'integrators' or 'centaurs', who live and work in the suburbs and mix that with daily social and sexual activities here and there. Lifestylers treat 'gayness as a noun', commuters treat their identity as a verb, and integrators treated it as an adjective. (Brekhus, 2003, pp. 28–9)

Brekhus's point is that contrary to everyday, taken-for granted opinion, there is no easily identified, single way to be gay. Instead, 'there is considerable complexity within identity categories about how to perform one's identity' (Brekhus, 2003, p. 11). This point was made several decades earlier by sociologist Albert Reiss (1961) in his study of social and sexual transactions between adolescent male 'hustlers' and their adult male 'clients'. It was also made by sociologist Laud Humphreys (1970), who studied men who engaged in 'impersonal sex' in public places. Reiss (1961) was able to show that, in spite of their regular participation in fellatio, the boys in his study did not define themselves as 'homosexuals', claiming that their motives for engaging in sex with older men were economic and not sexual. As one boy stated:

> 'No matter how many queers a guy goes with, if he goes for money, that don't make him queer. You're still straight. It's when you start going for free, with other young guys, that you start growing wings. (Reiss, 1961, pp. 103–4)

Humphreys (1970), in his study of the 'tearoom trade' (gay slang for sex in public washrooms), examined the dehumanizing aspects of having to deal with what was then the 'discreditable identity' of being a homosexual. Humphreys showed a rather mundane side to the men who were, at that time, 'demonized' as engaging in the highly stigmatized behaviour of having sex in a public place. He was able to show that what was then considered to be out-of-the-ordinary sex was in fact a routine accomplishment that took place in the otherwise ordinary lives of otherwise ordinary men (Irvine, 2003, p. 442).

Judith Butler on 'Gender Trouble'

By the beginning of the 1990s, feminist philosopher and social theorist Judith Butler, seeking to 'denaturalize gender' and to find a place for lesbian women in feminist theory, argued that all gender is created through sustained social performances. *Performativity*, as she called it, 'is not a singular act, but a repetition and a ritual'. What we take to be an 'internal essence of gender is manufactured through a sustained set of acts, posited through the gendered stylization of the body'. What we take to be an 'internal feature of ourselves is one that we anticipate and produce through certain bodily acts' (Butler, 1990/1999, pp. xv–xvi).

STUDIES IN SOCIAL RESEARCH

Laud Humphreys and the Ethics of Studying Gay Men in Public

In the 1960s Laud Humphreys, then a PhD candidate at Washington University, conducted one of the most (in)famous studies in the sociology of sex and sexuality: he observed men having brief, and usually impersonal, sexual encounters with other men in public washrooms. Humphreys' PhD dissertation, later published as *The Tearoom Trade: Impersonal Sex in Public Places* (1970), went on to win the prestigious C. Wright Mills Award that year as the book that most effectively addressed an issue of contemporary public importance from a 'fresh, imaginative perspective', and that explicitly or implicitly contained implications for courses of action (http://sssp1.org/index.cfm/m/259). Humphreys, who was a 'closeted' gay man married to a woman, had turned to the study of sociology after serving for many years as an Episcopal clergyman. His personal circumstances clearly influenced the course of his research.

To conduct his research, Humphreys took on the role of a lookout, or 'watchqueen', for the men who had sex. By adopting this role, Humphreys was not only able to observe the behaviour of the men but was also able to record their licence plate numbers and trace them to their homes. Then, posing as a researcher for a general 'social health survey', he visited the men in their homes and had them fill out a questionnaire. On the basis of the data he collected, Humphreys concluded that most of the men he had observed were married (54 per cent), and that they led 'socially respectable' and often 'socially conservative' lives outside of their 'tearoom' encounters. He also found that only 14 per cent of those he observed actually fit with the popular stereotype of homosexuals—men exclusively interested in sexual relationships with other men. Importantly, Humphreys was able to conclude that the men in his study (and by association other 'homosexual men') posed no danger of harassment to straight males or to children.

Humphreys' book was published to a maelstrom of public and academic criticism. Among his fellow academics Humphreys' research methods were roundly criticized as flagrantly violating ethical standards. He had observed his subjects without their prior knowledge or consent. He had followed up his field research with a survey that he administered under false pretences, by neglecting to tell his respondents the actual purpose of his survey. And he went ahead and published his findings without his research subjects' knowledge or consent. Many members of the sociology department at Washington University were so incensed by Humphreys' actions that they petitioned to have his PhD rescinded.

Yet Humphreys is not without his defenders. Sociologist Peter Nardi (1996) has argued that while many continue to debate the methodological and ethical issues raised by Humphreys' research, they often overlook 'its important findings and its early contributions to the emerging field of gay studies' (Nardi, 1996, p. 1). Nardi concludes:

> [A]s we read about periodic raids and arrests for 'lewd behavior' in public places and the strident cries from those who believe their children will be molested and given AIDS by perverts in parks, we must recall Humphreys' descriptions of the ritualized and highly structured encounters and remember how unlikely it is that the unwilling could be seduced. These are the strengths and importance of *Tearoom Trade* that need to be reclaimed from the endless debates about the ethics of its methodology. (Nardi, 1996, p. 9)

Humphreys' research and the subsequent publication of his book revealed important information about homosexuality and sexual behaviour in public places. But his research methods remain controversial, and the publication of his book raises serious questions about research ethics. Do you think that the information Humphreys was able to gather about homosexual behaviour in public places was worth violating the privacy of the people he researched?

In *Gender Trouble: Feminism and the Subversion of Identity* (1990/1999) Butler confronts the taken-for-granted assumptions about the 'naturalness' of using external forms as the markers with which to classify the sex of any given individual. Additionally she raises questions about the naturalness of 'heterosexuality'. The gender and heterosexuality ideals we hold without thinking, she says, very often do violence to those who do not conform. In the preface to the 1999 edition of *Gender Trouble*, Butler states that we need to rethink our use of 'obvious' morphological differences to determine sex, if only on compassionate grounds, so that 'those who fail to approximate the norm are not condemned to a death within life' (p. xx).

We've already seen, in Erving Goffman's work, how important the context of both place and audience is to the presentation of self and the performance of social roles. The performance of gender and of sexual orientation is no exception: an individual's audience must work together with her to produce gender/sexual orientation as part of the social world. Gender and sexual orientation are always done (or performed) in specific social spaces and within the context of certain social norms.

Today, sociologists are aware that thinking about sexual orientation and gendered behaviour as an essential or natural characteristic, born of biology, which is 'naturally occurring' and simply obvious to everyone concerned, does little to advance our understanding of gender and sexual orientation. Sociologists are also aware that neither gender nor sexual orientation is something that one 'is'. Neither is something that an individual chooses to adopt and perform, based on her own preferences, desires, needs, or whims. It is better to think of gender and sexual orientation as things that one *does*, in interaction with others (Fenstermaker & West, 2002, p. 29). Both gender and sexual orientation are 'shifting, malleable and intricately connected to external forces' (Butler, 1999, p. 575).

THE SOCIOLOGY OF SEX WORK

Sex work includes all forms of commercialized sex, including pornography, prostitution, stripping, and telephone sex. Over the past several decades, sociologists have examined the issue of sex work from at least three different perspectives: sex work as a form of deviant behaviour, sex work as a type of gendered relation, and sex work as a distinct occupation (Weitzer, 2000/2009).

Sociologists who see sex work as a form of deviant behaviour employ an analytic framework that stigmatizes sex work and that highlights the ways in which sex workers are subjected to social control and discriminatory treatment. Sociologists who view sex work as a type of gendered relation argue that sex work is an expression of patriarchal gender relations and hold that exploitation, subjugation, and violence against women are intrinsic to all forms of sex work (Dworkin, 1981, 1997; Mackinnon, 1989). These authors see sex work as inherently oppressive of women.

A diametrically opposed perspective is the empowerment paradigm. Sociologists who adopt this paradigm argue that sex commerce is a distinct occupation involving human agency, and that it is potentially empowering for workers (Carmen & Moody, 1985; Delacoste & Alexander, 1987). From this perspective, sex work is simply another routine economic transaction, similar to other kinds of service work such as massage therapy or psychotherapy. Other authors such as Weitzer (2009b) argue that both the oppression and empowerment paradigms are too one-sided; they opt instead for a 'polymorphous paradigm' that holds 'that there is a constellation of occupational arrangements, power relations, and worker

sex work
All forms of commercialized sex, including pornography, prostitution, stripping, and telephone sex.

experiences', and that the polymorphous paradigm is sensitive 'to complexities and to the structural conditions shaping the uneven distribution of agency, subordination, and job satisfaction' within sex work (Weitzer, 2009b, p. 215).

Pornography, one facet of sex work, can hardly be said to be directed towards a fringe market. According to the 2002 General Social Survey, 34 per cent of American men and 16 per cent of women had viewed an X-rated video in the previous year (Weitzer, 2009b, p. 216). In 2009, Simon Lajeuness of the Université de Montréal's Interdisciplinary Research Centre on Family Violence and Violence against Women carried out a study on the effects of pornography on men. Lajeunesse began his research by seeking out men in their twenties who had never consumed pornography. However, he was unable to find any such research subjects and turned his project instead to studying 'the impact of pornography on the sexuality of men and how it shapes their perception of men and women'. In his study, Lajeunesse interviewed 20 heterosexual male university students who had viewed pornography and found that, on average, 'single men watch pornography three times a week for 40 minutes,' while those in committed relationships 'watch it on average 1.7 times a week for 20 minutes'. He also found that most of the pornography consumed by the research subjects (90 per cent) was accessed via the Internet, while 10 per cent came from video stores. Other findings of Lajeunesse's research indicate that his research subjects, on average, began to seek out pornography by age 10, and that they tended to support gender equality, did not want their partners to look like porn stars, and 'felt victimized by the rhetoric demonizing pornography' ('Are the effects of pornography negligible?', 2009).

In spite of the obvious popular appeal of pornography, few sociologists have done research on either the porn industry or telephone sex agencies and their employees. In contrast, stripping has been studied fairly extensively, in large part because of the easy access researchers have to strip clubs. These studies show that the norms enforced in a specific strip club strongly affect the sex workers' job satisfaction and their experiences with clients and managers. Some studies show that exotic dancing can be a coercive experience, with the dancers having little control over their work environment or even their own bodies. Other studies paint a more positive picture, suggesting that 'there is a high degree of agency involved in exotic dance careers' (Bradley-Engen & Ulmer, 2009, p. 30)

Sociologists have found that some clubs are highly exploitive of employees who work as strippers, while other clubs provide strippers with more control over their working conditions. Some strippers find their work exciting, validating, and lucrative; others have experienced repeated violations of personal boundaries, loss of self-esteem, and job burnout (Weitzer, 2009, p. 216). A few studies comparing male and female strip clubs suggest that female audiences are more aggressive towards male dancers than male audiences are towards female dancers. Women who attend strip clubs to view male dancers tend to do so as part of a bonding ritual with other women or as part of some celebratory gathering. Men, on the other hand, usually seek an individualized experience and are more likely to be repeat customers. In all types of clubs, whether with male, female, or homosexual dancers, researchers commonly report on power struggles taking place between performers and clients over personal boundaries.

Weitzer's (2009b) survey of sociological studies of prostitution indicates that prostitutes vary enormously in their reasons for entering into this type of sex work. There is also enormous variation in their access to resources for protection, number and type of clients, freedom to refuse clients and specific sex acts, relationships with colleagues, dependence on and exploitation by third parties, experiences with the authorities, public visibility, and impact on the surrounding community. Although most of the sociological research has been done

Exploited or empowered? Would your opinion vary depending on whether this were part of a photo shoot for a magazine or a live performance? What if this were a man?

on street prostitution, this is the least prevalent type of prostitution. More prostitution in North America, Great Britain, and Australia takes place in 'brothels, massage parlours, bars, casinos, hotels, and private premises' (Weitzer, 2009b, p. 217).

Sociological research has also shown that there are multiple pathways into prostitution, including recruitment by pimps, access through friends, and work in other branches of the sex industry, such as telephone sex or strip clubs. Often, street prostitutes are runaways who have few resources or options but to engage in some kind of criminal activity such as drug dealing, theft, or prostitution. Most report that they began sex work in order to earn money or become independent. Street prostitutes are more likely than off-street workers to use drugs and to engage in unprotected sex. They are more likely to be victimized by others, and they face ongoing dangers such as assault or robbery and rape. Church, et al. (2001), in a study of 115 street prostitutes and 125 off-street prostitutes, found that street prostitutes were more likely to be robbed, beaten, raped, threatened with a weapon, or kidnapped. Moreover, it appears that the safety of indoor prostitution increases if prostitution is legal (Church, et al., 2001, p. 218).

One difference between street work and off-street work is the kind of service each type of sex worker provides to clients. Street workers spend little time with customers and thus have fleeting social interactions. Indoor interactions are usually longer, multifaceted, and more reciprocal. Unlike street workers, indoor workers are much more likely to 'counsel and befriend clients', and their interactions with their clients 'often include elements that are customarily found in romance and dating, such as conversation, hugging, kissing, and gifts' (Church, et al., 2001, p. 220). In a 1986 study, Prince (1986) reported that '75% of call girls, 19% of brothel workers, but none of the street workers frequently had orgasms with customers' (Prince, 1986, p. 42, as cited in Weitzer, 2009b, p. 220). Prince also reported that a comparative study of street walkers and 'call girls' (higher-priced prostitutes belonging to an agency, whose 'dates' are usually arranged in advance over the phone) in California and legal brothel workers in Nevada found that most call girls held positive views about their work, while brothel workers were less positive but generally satisfied, and street prostitutes evaluated their work more negatively (Prince, 1986, p. 497, as cited in Weitzer, 2009b, p. 220).

Although most research on sex work is focused on women in prostitution, there is a growing body of literature that concentrates on male workers, pointing to some basic similarities as well as important differences between female and male prostitution. Like female street prostitutes, male street workers are often runaways or youths who engage in sex work in order to support a drug habit or to survive. Call boys and escorts have regular customers and often develop emotional attachments with some of them in the same way that their female counterparts do. Likewise, upper- and mid-level male prostitutes are more likely than street workers to express job satisfaction. There are, however, some important differences. Male prostitutes are involved in prostitution in a more sporadic way than are female prostitutes. They are less likely to be coerced into prostitution, to have pimps, or to experience violence from customers. They are in greater control of their working conditions, in part because few have pimps and in part because many of them can exercise physical power over their customers. Male prostitutes are less stigmatized within the gay community but more stigmatized in the wider society because of the combination of homosexuality and prostitution (Weitzer, 2009b, p. 223).

In the past, sociologists have paid little attention to the customers of sex workers. In part this is because the women who sell sex, rather than their clients, have been considered 'the problem'; clients are also 'notoriously difficult to contact' (Soothill & Sanders, 2005). The General Social Survey (US), conducted in 2006, reported that 15–18 per cent of American men had had sex with a sex worker at some time in their lives and that 4 per cent had done so in the previous year. Similar figures are reported for Australia and Europe, although the real numbers are probably much higher, given the stigma associated with this kind of conduct and the reluctance of respondents to reply honestly to questions on this subject.

In Great Britain, the National Survey of Sexual Attitudes and Life Styles found that almost 9 per cent of men between the ages of 16 and 44 and living in London had paid for sex in the previous 5 years (Johnson, et al., 2001). Kinnell (2005) estimates that 80,000 sex workers in Britain are visited by on average 20 clients each week. Punternet.com is a popular British website for sex work. The site has hosted 100,502 'Field Reports' between January 1999 and February 2011, which list sexual transactions between 'Registered Ladies' and 'punters'. These transactions represent £12,886,114 in monetary exchanges, at an average cost of £129 per visit (www.punternet.com/frs/fr_stats.php). These are all conservative estimates, and the real number of men who buy sex in Britain is most likely much higher (Soothill & Sanders, 2005).

SUMMARY

This chapter concentrates on how sociologists define, theorize about, and research issues of sex, sexuality, and sexual orientation. Most sociologists today understand these issues in terms of a complex interaction between biological, psychological, social, political, cultural, and historical factors. The study of sex, sexual orientation, and sexuality involves understanding many social institutions and diverse systems of knowledge.

This chapter has presented examples of the diversity of human sexual attitudes and practices and discussions of sexuality and sexual orientation, framed in the context of human rights and equity. Within Canadian society, social patterns involving sexuality have changed considerably over the last century. One of the most recent changes has been legislation allowing homosexual marriages. We have also seen how Canadian parliament, informed by the Charter of Rights and Freedoms, passed this legislation in spite of strong opposition from minority groups.

The question of what determines sexual orientation is no longer simply a question of interest to 'scientists'; it has also become a question with much broader implications in terms of whom we include or exclude as full members of our society. An important human rights issues emerges: can we justify discriminating against people on the basis of their sexual orientation?

DISCUSSION QUESTIONS

1. Is discrimination against people based on their sexual orientation ever justifiable?
2. To what extent might sexual identity and sexual orientation be affected by social and cultural factors?
3. To what extent is sexual orientation a cultural status?
4. Are male and female the only sexes, or is it possible to consider other categories?
5. What is heteronormativity? How does it affect everyday understandings about sexual orientation in Canada?
6. Stephen Harper and Paul Martin, two men who have served as prime minister of Canada, have expressed different opinions about same-sex marriage. Whose opinion do you support? Explain why.

17 Race and Racism

LEARNING OBJECTIVES

In this chapter you will:

*   be introduced to what geneticists who work on human DNA have to say about biologically distinct human groups, or 'races'
*   differentiate between genetic kinship and social kinship
*   learn about the process of 'racialization'
*   become aware of the privileges of 'whiteness'
*   explore the social construction of a multi-racial identity
*   gain a clearer understanding of racism
*   differentiate between institutional racism and individual racism
*   think critically about ethnic and racial discrimination in Canada.

INTRODUCTION

Race, racial segregation, and racism are all pervasive aspects of Western thought and experience. Because of this, the meaning and the reality of these concepts often goes unquestioned in day-to-day living. But what is 'race'? What does it mean to say that Western societies are 'racist', or that most 'whites' live in racially segregated communities and lead racially segregated lives even if they have daily contact with 'blacks'? It should not come as a surprise that in Western society, answers to these questions have varied over time, and that, like 'gender' and 'sex', the concept of 'race' has a long and complicated history.

The 'race scientists' of the late nineteenth and early twentieth century sought to demonstrate that race was a valid, scientific concept, and that included among inheritable racial differences were intelligence and social behaviours such as the propensity for violence. Anti-racist theorists of the mid- to late-twentieth century, in contrast, made the argument that race has nothing to do with inheritable, biological differences and everything to do with the social construction of race as a concept, with distinctly social consequences. Today, most social scientists treat the concept of race as a social construct, that is, as 'a social invention that changes as political, economic and historical contexts change' (American Sociological Association, 2003, p. 7).

This chapter addresses two important issues. First, what is the evidence from the biological sciences that supports the conclusion now commonly held by social scientists that race has no merit as a biological category? Recent research from some of the world's leading geneticists has much to tell us about who we are, where we came from, and why there is no basis for making distinctions between humans based on race. Second, what do sociologists have to say about race as a social concept that changes over time? What does their work tell us about race as a social identity? What does it tell us about the practice of racial segregation and racism in historical perspective and in the context of present-day society? What does it tell us about the consequences of racial inequalities?

RACE: WHAT GENETICISTS HAVE TO SAY

DNA

The hereditary material in all organisms, including humans. Human DNA is made up of about 3 billion base pairs, and more than 99 per cent of them are the same in all people.

Today, geneticists who work on the analysis of human **DNA** (deoxyribonucleic acid) are keenly aware of the ways in which genetics disproves the idea of biologically distinct human groups, or 'races'. DNA is the hereditary material in all organisms, including humans. Almost every cell in our bodies (with the exception of eggs, sperm, and red blood cells) has the same DNA, which is located in the cell's nucleus (nuclear DNA). (We also have another kind of DNA, mitochondrial DNA, found in the cell's mitochondria, which we'll deal with on the following page.) The information contained in everyone's DNA is made up of combinations of only four chemicals: adenine (A), guanine (G), cytosine (C), and thymine (T), (A) combines with (T), and (C) with (G) to make up units called 'base pairs'. Each base pair is also attached to a sugar molecule and to a phosphate molecule. Together, this combination of base pair, sugar, and phosphate is called a *nucleotide*. Nucleotides are arranged in two long strands that form a spiral, also called a double helix (see Figure 17.1). Long strings of nucleotides form genes, and genes are tightly packed together into structures called chromosomes.

Human DNA is made up of about 3 billion base pairs, and more than 99 per cent of them are the same in all people. Spencer Wells explains why DNA is important in understanding an individual's own genetic history, as well as in understanding the genetic differences between two or more individual humans:

> Our DNA carries, hidden in its string of four simple letters, a historical document stretching back to the origin of life and the first self-replicating molecules, through our amoebic ancestors, and down to the present day. We are the end result of over a billion years of evolutionary tinkering, and our genes carry the seams and spot-welds that reveal the story.
>
> It is not the code itself that delivers the message, but rather the differences we see when we compare DNA from two or more individuals. (Wells, 2002, p. xiii)

DNA can make a copy of itself by unwinding, and then each strand becomes a pattern for making a new strand. The two new DNA molecules then have one new strand and one old strand. When DNA replicates, from time to time tiny mistakes are made that produce changes in the DNA sequence. It is these changes that geneticists use to understand genealogical relationships. If two people share a change, they most likely also share an ancestor. Geneticists like Spencer Wells analyze the changes in the Y-chromosome—the piece of DNA that is carried by males all over the world—and in so doing have found that all humans alive today shared a common male ancestor who lived in eastern or southern Africa about 60,000 years ago.

The fact that we all share a common male ancestor does not mean that this man was the only man alive at the time. It does mean, however, that his descendants are the only ones to have survived to the present day, and that all humans alive today can trace their ancestry back him. It means that within the past 60,000 years, or about 2,000 generations, *Homo sapiens* moved out of Africa to populate the entire planet. It also means that the differences between Africans and Europeans are only 'skin deep'. 'We are all African cousins,' says Wells, 'separated by—at most—2,000 generations' (Wells, 2002).

Our most recent female ancestor, traced through mitochondrial DNA, lived about 150,000 years ago. Mitochondrial DNA (MtDNA) is transmitted unchanged only through the female line, from mother to offspring. Mitochondrial DNA exists in the cytoplasm and not the nucleus of the cell. While both human ova and sperm contain nuclear DNA, the ova, but not sperm, also contain large amounts of mitochondrial DNA. Fertilization of an ovum by a sperm results in the recombination of nuclear DNA from both the ovum and the sperm (the parental gambits) and the direct inheritance of mitochondrial DNA from the ovum. The direct

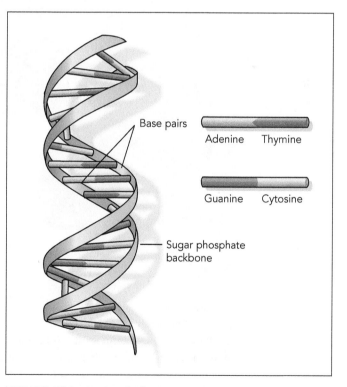

FIGURE 17.1   **A strand of DNA**

Source: US National Library of Medicine, 2011. What is DNA? In *Genetics home reference: Your guide to understanding genetic conditions.*

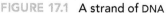

A late nineteenth-century artist's rendering of the five 'human races', as identified by scientists of the day: (clockwise from top left) American, Malayan, Mongolian, Ethiopian, and Caucasian. Although the idea that different biological races exist is now discredited, scientists in the eighteenth and nineteenth centuries argued for the existence of different human races or subspecies to account for differences not just in physical appearance but in intelligence and various aptitudes as well. What role do you imagine social politics might have played in this line of scientific inquiry? What are the implications of concluding that all humans belong to a single, indivisible race?

transmission of mitochondrial DNA from mother to child and onwards via daughters who in turn become mothers serves as a record of relatedness and evolutionary pathways. Genetic analysis of mitochondrial DNA provides no evidence of genetically distinct racial clusters, and indicates a limited and recent amount of genetic variation in human populations.

SOCIAL KINSHIP VERSUS GENETIC KINSHIP

The basis of Western notions of kinship is the making of a family through the shared production of offspring. In Anglo-American culture, however, this belief also coexists with more flexible views. Who is included in family is shaped by complex patterns of sociability and social relatedness along with a sense of alliance and affiliation that is not strictly determined by the crude definition of shared biological descent. The people who make up your extended family may be family friends, godparents and unrelated 'uncles', 'aunts', and 'cousins', and neighbours. This complex definition of kinship is what we call **social kinship**.

Genetic kinship, by contrast, is measured through or read from the genetic material of an individual. This genetic material situates the individual within a line of prehistoric and historical descent. From the point of view of families, those who count as kin are not always those with whom one shares a direct biological relation. Population geneticists, on the other hand, are concerned only with biological relatedness and therefore with genetic kinship (Nash, 2004, p. 5).

Based on their understandings of genetic kinship, present-day geneticists make the argument that genetic research undermines the myth of pure, discrete 'races'. For example, geneticists Bamshad and Olson (2003) note that while there are certain genetic markers that allow geneticists to distinguish between large populations, races as such do not exist from 'a purely genetic standpoint'. Any genetic difference between populations is minimal, and all human populations are 99.9 per cent genetically similar (Olson, 2002).

Evidence of a shared genetic inheritance can certainly be a powerful and emotionally charged event. In a 2003 BBC documentary, *Motherland—A Genetic Journey*, geneticists used MtDNA testing and Y-chromosome testing on 229 British volunteers of Afro-Caribbean origin. The objective of the documentary was to trace the ancestry of the participants and to reconnect them with their historical roots and with relatives about whom they had no previous knowledge. The findings of these tests came as a surprise to many of the participants. Many discovered evidence of European ancestry, something far more prevalent in the paternal lines than in the maternal lines. Also surprising was that a 'white scientist' working on the project who had his own DNA analyzed discovered African ancestry (Skinner, 2007, p. 460).

In this program and others that have taken up the same topic (for example, Discovery Channel's 2002 documentary *The Real Eve*), the science of DNA is shown as a powerful resource for validating (or challenging) identity claims. Many people are now turning to DNA science to understand their genetic links to the past. As David Skinner reports, 'Genetic accounts of "who we really are" are just one of a number of important ways in which contemporary biology is part of changes in how racial differences are presented and lived' (Skinner, 2006, p. 460).

RACE: A SOCIAL CONSTRUCT

In 1998, the American Anthropological Association adopted a 'Statement on "Race"', which acknowledged that while 'both scholars and the general public have been conditioned to viewing human races as natural and separate divisions within the human species based on

social kinship
A notion of kinship or family that is shaped by patterns of sociability and a sense of alliance and affiliation that is not strictly determined by the crude definition of shared biological descent.

genetic kinship
A notion of family or kinship that is measured through or read from the genetic material of an individual.

visible physical differences,' genetic evidence now exists indicating that all humans are 'members of a single species'. Physical variations among humans 'have no meaning except the social ones that humans put on them', and 'inequalities between so-called "racial" groups are not consequences of their biological inheritance but products of historical and contemporary social, economic, educational, and political circumstances' (AAA, 1998).

For their part, the American Sociological Association (2003) published a statement in which they also pointed to the work of geneticists in rejecting **race** as a valid biological concept. At the same time, they claimed that 'race', as a social concept, can be 'the subject of valid scientific investigation at the social level'. This is because social and economic life is 'organized, in part, around race as a social construct'. Like all social constructs, the concept of race is a 'social invention that changes as political, economic, and historical contexts change' (ASA, 2003).

Racialization

Racialization refers to the social and political processes by which racial groups are socially constructed based on perceived physical differences related chiefly to ethnicity. Historically, science has played a significant role in the development of Western beliefs about supposed racial difference. Sociologists understand that there is a dynamic relationship between how science is conducted and the prevailing public discourse on race—over the past two centuries scientists have 'discovered' very different explanations for the diversity found among and between human populations around the globe.

Our present-day, common-sense understanding of race emerged out of the social, political, and intellectual conditions of early modernity. Especially important to the formulation of the concept of race were new social problems—including how to manage growing populations, societies, and states—that western Europeans faced as they expanded their empires, colonized distant lands, and subjugated peoples they found there (Skinner, 2006, p. 463). But it was during the nineteenth and early twentieth centuries that scientific knowledge, techniques, and methods of research established 'race' as an important means of making sense out of human differences. One of the first preoccupations of the biological sciences to emerge during the eighteenth and nineteenth centuries was lineage as it relates to species types. This interest, which got a boost when Carolus Linnaeus introduced his authoritative classification system for plants and, later, animals, extended to humans, especially their presumed inheritance of moral, physical, and mental capabilities from their parents (Skinner, 2006, p. 463). During this period science represented physical, mental, and moral differences between human groups as naturally occurring, fixed, and absolute.

In the nineteenth and twentieth centuries the science of race was closely connected to concerns about the physical and mental health of a nation's citizens and how to preserve and guarantee the competitive strength of the nation as a whole. The **eugenics movement**, founded on a social philosophy dedicated to improving human heredity through selective breeding for 'desirable characteristics', was dedicated to keeping the population of a country healthy and free of disease, as well as preventing collective intelligence, as measured by IQ tests, from deteriorating. These principles were used as the basis for forced sterilization programs instituted by governments around the world, including those of two Canadian provinces—Alberta and British Columbia. The Alberta Sexual Sterilization Act was passed in 1928. Between 1929 and 1972, the board approved 4,725 sterilizations (Historica-Dominion Institute, 2011).

The eugenics movement reflected public consciousness about human differences. 'Experts' writing in both scientific journals and the popular press argued that Caucasians—usually

race
A contested term used in everyday understanding to refer to supposedly inherited biological characteristics that distinguish different human populations.

racialization
The social and political processes by which racial groups are socially constructed based on perceived physical differences related chiefly to ethnicity.

eugenics movement
A social philosophy dedicated to improving human heredity through selective breeding for 'desirable characteristics' in order to preserve and guarantee the competitive strength of the nation as a whole.

identified as the gold standard among humans—were a different species from Africans, Indians, and Asians (in a schema that situated Africans as the least human and therefore closest to apes). But the application of scientific racism was not limited to colonial situations, where nations used the alleged natural inferiority of certain 'races' to justify colonizing them and seizing their land. The eugenics movement grew in popularity during the early decades of the twentieth century and was promoted around the world by governments that intervened to sterilize or euthanize those citizens who were deemed 'unfit', including the 'mentally defective', blind people, women identified as 'promiscuous', homosexuals, and entire 'racial' groups, including the Roma and Jews.

One of the most notorious proponents of the twentieth-century eugenics movement was Nazi leader Adolf Hitler, though it should be noted that several prominent Americans, including presidents Woodrow Wilson and Theodore Roosevelt, also subscribed to eugenicist beliefs. During World War II, Nazi Germany under Hitler took eugenicist ideas about racial purity and racial differences to the point of genocide, exterminating somewhere between 11 million and 17 million people (Jews, Gypsies, and Africans, as well as homosexuals and people with disabilities and political and religious opponents, among others).

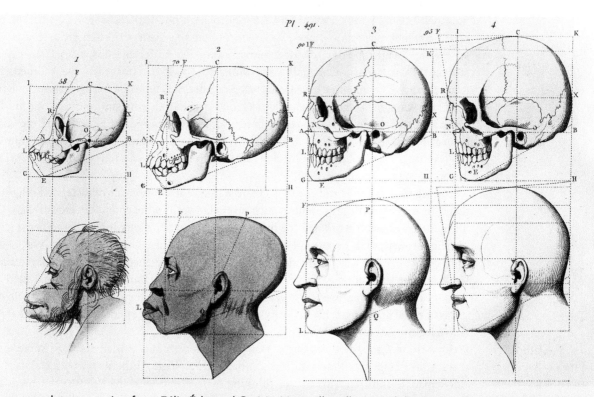

A copperplate engraving from Félix Édouard Guérin-Meneville's illustrated dictionary of natural history (1834), showing Dutch physiologist Petrus Camper's theory of facial angle and beauty. Camper determined that modern humans have a facial angle of between 70 and 90 degrees, while antique Greco-Roman statues had angles near to 100 degrees. Camper claimed that contemporary Europeans had angles of 90 degrees, Asians of 80 degrees, Africans of 70 degrees, and orangutans of 58 degrees. Although Camper intended only to show that Africans were furthest removed from classical notions of beauty, his ideas were later used as scientific evidence to justify racial discrimination.

The eugenics movement, however, was not without strong opposition. Between World War I and World War II, a growing number of critics took aim at the legitimacy of the race concept, with some scientists challenging assumptions about innate biological differences between humans, and arguing instead that new knowledge about heredity and cultural diversity undermined 'traditional' race science (Skinner, 2006, p. 464). From 1930 onwards, anti-racist scientists argued in opposition to the way in which science had been put into service in Nazi Germany as a means for justifying the extermination of millions of people.

After World War II there was a powerful impetus to change outdated beliefs and to replace them with new scientific evidence about the triviality of racial differences and the commonality of features shared by all humankind (Malik, 1996). In the early 1950s the United Nations Educational, Scientific and Cultural Organization (UNESCO) issued statements about the unscientific nature of racism. The first UNESCO statement, written mainly by social scientists, stated that 'the scientific material available to us at present does not justify the conclusion that inherited genetic differences are a major factor in producing the differences between the culture and cultural achievements of different groups.'

The social scientists on the UNESCO committee were trying to manage a socially dangerous concept, but many in the natural sciences were not convinced, and public opinion went with them. For example, in an attempt to align physical anthropology with the natural—and not the social—sciences, Carleton Coon, president of the American Association of Physical Anthropology, divided humans into five different subspecies ('Australoid', 'Capoid', 'Caucasoid', 'Congoid', and 'Mongoloid'). Each subspecies, he claimed, had evolved at a different time and from different ancestral hominids. The earliest to evolve were the Congoids in Africa, and in Coon's estimation, the descendants of this line remained trapped in an evolutionary dead end. The Caucasoids of Europe were the last to appear on the scene, and their dominance was the natural result of their genetic superiority (Wells, 2002, p. 9). Coon published his work in the 1960s, and his theories were widely taken up in the popular media.

During the late 1960s and the 1970s there was another resurgence of racial and other biologically deterministic arguments, which prompted yet another round of fierce debates. One of the scientists who promoted the importance of genetic factors in racial and behavioural differences went so far as to argue that there was a witch hunt going on, and that 'the possible importance of genetic factors in racial and behavioural differences' was largely ignored and in fact had become a taboo subject (Kelves, 1985/1995, p. 270). But by the 1960s, in spite of the re-appearance in some quarters of yet another round of arguments in favour of the biological basis of racial differences, the majority of social scientists were no longer convinced that race was a legitimate biological concept.

ethnicity
The state of belonging to a social group that shares a common cultural heritage that includes language, traditions, food, values, customs and religion.

Interestingly, too, by the 1980s, a new kind of racism had also emerged, as some scientists replaced talk about racial differences based on biological inheritance with claims about incompatible cultures. This line of thinking certainly fit with the UNESCO statement that humanity is biologically unified but culturally diverse. **Ethnicity** became the new 'race', and new forms of discrimination based on ethnicity began to appear. Members of an ethnic group identify with each other and share a common culture. While the atrocities committed in the name of eugenics in Nazi Germany had gone a long way to discrediting biological theories of race, they did not, as Kenan Malik explains, 'destroy the underlying belief that humanity is divided into discrete groups, each defined in some manner by immutable and a-historic characteristics, and that human interaction is determined by the nature of those immutable differences' (Malik, 1996, p. 7).

The 'new racism', as Baker (1981) has called it, provided 'a new vocabulary for discussing "race" without being racist according to the classical formulation' (Skinner, 2006, p. 469). Cultural differences were treated as fixed properties of group members and were, in effect, naturalized as if they were biological (Skinner, 2006, p. 469). However, the arguments of the anti-racist social scientists received a much needed boost in the twenty-first century, when geneticists and other life scientists began presenting new sources of information on human biology and genetics. Advances in human genetics, neurology, reproductive technologies, and molecular medicine have all contributed new evidence with the potential to reframe debates about race and to further correct our common-sense understandings (Skinner, 2007, p. 939).

How Race Is Constructed Socially

While race and racial differences have no basis as biological facts, they certainly continue to be part of the lived experiences of most people. It is for this reason that the concept of race, not as a biological fact but as a social construction, is important to sociologists.

One of the ways that we can track what sociologists mean when they speak about 'the social construction of race' is by looking at the way in which race has been defined and categorized by federal census departments. Here is a copy of the questions on race and ethnicity from the 2000 **census** conducted in the US:

census
A complete enumeration of a population in which information is systematically acquired and recorded about all the members of that population. Censuses are usually conducted by national governments at specific intervals.

→ **NOTE: Please answer BOTH Questions 7 and 8.**

7. **Is Person 1 Spanish/Hispanic/Latino?** *Mark ☒ the "No" box if* **not** *Spanish/Hispanic/Latino.*

 ☐ **No,** not Spanish/Hispanic/Latino   ☐ Yes, Puerto Rican

 ☐ Yes, Mexican, Mexican Am., Chicano   ☐ Yes, Cuban

 ☐ Yes, other Spanish/Hispanic/Latino — *Print group.* ↗

 | | | | | | | | | | | | | | | | | | | |

8. **What is Person 1's race?** *Mark ☒* **one or more races** *to indicate what this person considers himself/herself to be.*

 ☐ White

 ☐ Black, African Am., or Negro

 ☐ American Indian or Alaska Native — *Print name of enrolled or principal tribe.* ↗

 | | | | | | | | | | | | | | | | | | | |

 ☐ Asian Indian   ☐ Japanese   ☐ Native Hawaiian
 ☐ Chinese   ☐ Korean   ☐ Guamanian or Chamorro
 ☐ Filipino   ☐ Vietnamese   ☐ Samoan
 ☐ Other Asian — *Print race.* ↗   ☐ Other Pacific Islander — *Print race.* ↗

 | | | | | | | | | | | | | | | | | | | |

 ☐ Some other race — *Print race.* ↗

 | | | | | | | | | | | | | | | | | | | |

Source: US Department of Commerce, Bureau of the Census, 2000.

In contrast, the Canadian long-form census questionnaire of 2006 asks the following:

17. What were the ethnic or cultural origins of this person's **ancestors**?

An ancestor is usually more distant than a grandparent.

For example, Canadian, English, French, Chinese, Italian, German, Scottish, East Indian, Irish, Cree, Mi'kmaq (Micmac), Métis, Inuit (Eskimo), Ukrainian, Dutch, Filipino, Polish, Portuguese, Jewish, Greek, Jamaican, Vietnamese, Lebanese, Chilean, Salvadorean, Somali, etc.

Specify as many origins as applicable using capital letters.

_____

_____

_____

_____

18. Is this person an Aboriginal person, that is, North American Indian, Métis or Inuit (Eskimo)?

If "Yes", mark the circle(s) that best describe(s) this person now.

○ No ➜   **Continue with the next question**

○ Yes, North American Indian

○ Yes, Métis   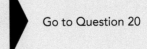 Go to Question 20

○ Yes, Inuit (Eskimo)

19. Is this person:

Mark more than one or specify, if applicable.

This information is collected to support programs that promote equal opportunity for everyone to share in the social, cultural and economic life of Canada.

○ White

○ Chinese

○ South Asian *(e.g., East Indian, Pakistani, Sri Lankan, etc.)*

○ Black

○ Filipino

○ Latin American

○ Southeast Asian *(e.g., Vietnamese, Cambodian, Malaysian, Laotian, etc.)*

○ Arab

○ West Asian *(e.g., Iranian, Afghan, etc.)*

○ Korean

○ Japanese

Other — *Specify*

_____

20. Is this person a member of an Indian band/First Nation?

○ No

○ Yes, member of an Indian band/First Nation

↓

Specify Indian band/First Nation (for example, Musqueam)

_____

21. Is this person a Treaty Indian or a Registered Indian as defined by the *Indian Act* of Canada?

○ No

○ Yes, Treaty Indian or Registered Indian

Source: Statistics Canada, 2006b.

Both Canadian and American censuses allow a fair degree of choice, but whereas the US form asks all respondents to identify their 'race', the Canadian form avoids the term, inviting respondents to identify their 'ethnic or cultural origins', as well as those of their ancestors, in case the respondent identifies as, say, Canadian, but has distant ancestors from the British isles, for example. By way of further comparison, the Irish census form of 2006 asks respondents for information on their 'ethnic or cultural background', but allows a rather limited range of answers:

14. What is your ethnic or cultural background?

Choose ONE section for A to D, then ✓ the appropriate box.

A   White
1   ☐   Irish
2   ☐   Irish Traveler
3   ☐   Any other White background

B   Black or Black Irish
4   ☐   African
5   ☐   Any other Black background

C   Asian or Asian Irish
6   ☐   Chinese
7   ☐   Any other Asian background

D   Other, including mixed background
8   ☐   Other, write in description

Source: Ireland, Central Statistics Office, 2006.

The category of 'Irish Traveler' here is interesting. Irish Travelers are nomadic people of Irish origin who live predominantly in Ireland. Although a small number of Irish Travelers live in the United States, they do not appear as a separate racial or 'ethnic' category in the American census. However, the category 'Irish Traveler' is of great significance to the Irish Central Statistics Office, which offers 33 interactive tables on that group in its published results of the 2006 census (at www.cso.ie/census/Census2006_Volume5.htm).

The census questionnaire used in Singapore explains the intended meaning of the terms 'ethnic group', 'race', and 'mixed parentage', although the definitions are somewhat questionable:

Ethnic group refers to a person's race. Those of mixed parentage are classified under the ethnic group of their fathers. (Department of Statistics Singapore, 2000, p. 16)

And while Canada allows its citizens free choice in defining their ethnic category or categories, in Singapore the choices are limited to four:

1. *Chinese*. This refers to persons of Chinese origin such as Hokkiens, Teochews, Cantonese, Hakkas, Hainanese, Hockchias, Foochows, Henghuas, Shanghainese, etc.
2. *Malays*. This refers to persons of Malay or Indonesian origin, such as Javanese, Boyanese, Bugis, etc.
3. *Indians*. This refers to persons of Indian, Pakistani, Bangladeshi, or Sri Lankan origin such as Tamils, Malayalis, Punjabis, Bengalis, Singhalese, etc.
4. *Other Ethnic Groups*. This comprises all persons other than Chinese, Malays, and Indians. They include Eurasians, Caucasians, Arabs, Japanese, etc. (Department of Statistics Singapore, 2000, p. 16).

The last of these categories, 'Other Ethnic Groups', is a choice that lumps together almost everyone that both American and Canadian censuses try to differentiate.

Not unexpectedly, the statistics offices of different countries will tailor their census questionnaires to the unique ethnic make-up of the countries they represent. It would be wrong to expect the Singapore census questionnaire to ask residents of that country about First Nations band affiliation or 'Irish Traveler' status. But it is also important to realize that census data are used by governments to identify and substantiate demographic trends, including those relating to the extent of ethnic diversity in a country. Not every government will want to promote or encourage multiculturalism among its citizens, and you can see, in looking at the samples provided here, how a census questionnaire might be used to fulfill a political agenda.

STUDIES IN SOCIAL RESEARCH

Census-Taking in South Africa's Apartheid Era

The census form issued by any national government is a political tool. It can be a very useful tool when it generates data that help to shape public policy for the benefit of the country's citizens. But it can also serve more subversive—and in some cases unabashedly racist—political agendas. In this regard, the history of census taking in South Africa, where apartheid was enforced between 1948 and 1996, is instructive.

Between 1911 and 1951, the South African government conducted four censuses distributed among all 'races'. During the same period, they carried out an additional four censuses 'in which only white people were enumerated' (Lehohla, 2007, p. 18). The censuses of 1960 and 1970 contained a full count for 'white,

coloured and Asian people', and a different questionnaire was used for a small sample of 'black people' (remember that 'coloured' and 'black' were separate official categories under apartheid). The 1980 census was the first to use a consistent method of data collection in order to count all population groups, although as Pali Lehohla notes, 'a question on family structure was not asked of the black population' (2007). It was not until the census of 1996 that 'the whole country was covered and all residents of the country were treated equally' (Lehohla, 2007, p. 20). For its 2001 census, Statistics South Africa allows respondents to select from among four racial categories: 'coloured', 'Black African', 'Asian or Indian' and 'White'.

RACE AS A STRATIFYING PRACTICE IN SOCIAL INSTITUTIONS

The concept of race has little validity for geneticists, and most social scientists today agree that as a biological category, race has little merit. However, sociologists and other social scientists continue to do extensive research on the role and consequences of 'race' as a stratifying practice in social institutions such as education, health and healthcare, criminal justice, work, and housing. In Chapter 3, for example, we looked at some sociological studies of racial stratification in the Canadian prison system.

British sociologist Diane Reay and her colleagues (2007) studied the ways in which 'whiteness' is preserved as a privileged identity in London, England. In their research, which is summarized in the section that follows, they discovered a strong cultural desire to privilege whiteness even in the face of a stated desire on the part of white, middle-class parents to break down class and racial barriers by sending their children to multi-racial, multi-class, inner-city schools.

The Privileges of 'Whiteness'

'Whiteness', especially as a privileged identity, is rarely a concern for those who are white and who think about race as a term applied to 'others'—minority groups in general and often blacks in particular. Part of the privilege of 'whiteness' means not having to think about race and its role in day-to-day living. Of course 'whiteness' is only invisible to those who are white; for those who are not, whiteness is everywhere.

British researcher Diane Reay and her colleagues (2007) set out to study 'whiteness' as a privileged identity among a group of middle-class parents living in London, England, who send their children to multi-racial, inner-city schools as part of an effort to tear down ethnic barriers. In conducting their study, Reay and her colleagues used in-depth qualitative research methods to examine choices made by white, middle-class families in relation to urban schooling. Their expressed aim was to understand how such choices 'are related to a wider sense of identity and identification' (Reay, et al., 2007, p. 1043).

Reay and her colleagues interviewed 63 white, middle-class families—a total of 32 fathers and 63 mothers—living in London. They drew their sample in part from those who responded to a newspaper article about the project and who self-identified as white and middle-class. But the authors of the study also assessed middle-class membership in a more conventional way, using the UK's Office for National Statistics classification scheme. In additional, they gathered information on both parents' level of education. The researchers used ethnographic interviewing techniques, including open-ended questioning and 'careful prompting and probing', in order to elicit information from their interviewees, which were designed to help them develop 'theoretical understandings' about the ways in which white social privilege was both maintained and challenged within the context of multi-ethnic urban schooling (p. 1044).

In making their analysis Reay and her colleagues used Bourdieu's concepts of social capital and cultural capital (see Chapter 13). During interviews, parents often reported that inner-city, multi-ethnic schooling was a 'good thing' because it contributed to their children's 'understanding of, and proficiency in, multiculturalist capacities'. These parents were particularly concerned that their children acquire an understanding of different cultures in order to be able to better relate to other people. Many of the parents who were sending their children to multi-ethnic schools in the inner city were professionals working in a variety of social service fields. They were acutely aware that the global economy requires workers 'who can deal with people of other races and nationalities openly and respectfully'. In other words, they wanted their children to be exposed to multiculturalism in order to increase their cultural and social capital. Developing an appreciation for multiculturalism, while expressed by the parents as a positive moral value, was also motivated by self-interest (Reay, et al., 2007, pp. 1045–6).

What does it mean to say that whiteness is invisible?

White, middle-class children who attend inner-city, multi-ethnic, multi-class schools are, indeed, exposed to varying degrees of social mixing with non-white students. But the privileged white, middle-class children of the study—unlike working-class children, many of whom were from other ethnicities—remained 'firmly and primarily anchored' in white, middle-class social networks. Thus, the expressed interest of white, middle-class parents in having their children exposed to 'difference and otherness' could also be understood 'as describing a project of cultural capital'. In attending multi-ethnic, inner-city schools, the children from white, middle-class families acquired liberal credentials that could help them to secure their class position in the workforce. The ability of these children to move in and out of the habitus of those who are marked as 'others' is part of the process in which white, middle-class kids come to understand themselves as both privileged and dominant (Razak, 2002, as cited in Reay, et al., 2007, p. 1047).

White, middle-class parents were aware of the confidence and self-esteem their children gained by attending schools where many other children were far less privileged. As one parent reported:

> Bryony has come out very confident because she was top of the pile as well in that school and she overcame all her fears and worries at the beginning and has come out extremely well adjusted socially and emotionally, very confident and knows where she wants to go. (Reay, et al., 2007, p. 1047)

At the same time, white, middle-class parents also expressed fears about the potential dangers of exposing their children to working-class peers, especially in terms of their own children's attitudes and behaviour. They were particularly concerned about the potential danger from lower-class children whose parents 'had lower aspirations', didn't 'really care about education', and weren't 'really ambitious for their children'. So while the working-class, multi-ethnic 'others' who shared normative values with the white, middle-class parents could be considered 'of value', those who did not share in white, middle-class values were deemed to be of no value at all.

Reay and her colleagues had originally hoped to find that 'altruism and a sense of civic responsibility' were what motivated white, middle-class parents to send their children to inner-city schools, and indeed they did find a few instances of this. However, they also found 'a degree of instrumentalism' that they had not anticipated. The white, middle-class parents did not question their privileged status, even though their privileged position 'was particularly apparent in the multi-ethnic, working-class schools they chose to send their children to'. Most parents were quite content to use their economic, social, and cultural capital in order to get more advantages for their children (p. 1055).

THE SOCIAL CONSTRUCTION OF MULTI-RACIAL IDENTITY

How is it that we go about constructing our own racial identity? On what basis do we ascribe a racial identity to others? Multi-racial identities are of interest to sociologists as an indication of the importance of reflected appraisals. Sociologist Nikki Khanna (2010) examined racial identity formation and negotiation among black/white bi-racial adults. In 2005–6 she conducted in-depth, semi-structured interviews with 40 bi-racial adults living in a large urban area in the American South. Respondents all had one black and one white parent (as identified by the respondents) and were between the ages of 18 and 45. The upper age limit was chosen to include respondents who had grown up during the post–civil rights era. The lower age limit was decided on in order to omit from the study children and adolescents who might not as yet have formed their identities.

Study Background

American slavery ended officially in 1865, and white Southerners, committed to maintaining a strict separation of black and white, implemented legally sanctioned racial segregation in the form of the Jim Crow laws. These laws prohibited marriage between blacks and whites, and defined who was black and who was white. Legislators were afraid that any amount of 'black blood' might taint 'white blood'. It wasn't until almost a hundred years later, with the growing civil rights movement promoting equality and the reversal of Jim Crow subjugation, that new pride in being black emerged, and bi-racial black–white Americans began to strongly embrace black identity (Khanna, 2010, p. 99). In 1967 the Supreme Court of the United States overturned the anti-miscegenation laws, leading to a 'bi-racial baby boom' in the 1970s.

Researchers note that bi-racial people born before the civil rights era of the 1960s are most likely to identify exclusively as black, while those born in the post–civil rights era identified as black, bi-racial, or sometimes as white. Moreover, physical appearance is now an important factor in shaping racial identity amongst black/white bi-racial people

Reflected Appraisals

In Chapter 7, we encountered the work of Charles Horton Cooley (1902) and the concept of 'the looking-glass self', or what symbolic interactionists now call 'reflected appraisals'. To review, individuals form self-conceptions as reflections of the responses they receive from others in their environment. In the process of forming a 'looking-glass self' (i.e. a reflected appraisal) individuals imagine how they appear to others, and they imagine what others' judgements of that appearance might be. Out of this they develop a self-concept. Cooley concluded that individuals come to see themselves as others see them, and that their sense of self and their self-identity are formed by this reflective process.

Khanna (2010) used the concept of reflected appraisals to argue that, in the absence of 'clear-cut and objective criteria for deciding who belongs where, bi-racial and multi-racial individuals may rely on reflected appraisals to decide where they belong racially' (Khanna, 2010, p. 101). Because locating bi-racial individuals within the general population is a difficult task, Khanna relied on **convenience sampling** and **snowball sampling**, which began with her placing flyers in local colleges, universities, and places of worship that asked, 'Do you have one black parent and one white parent?' She then asked interviewees to pass along her information to others with similar backgrounds.

In doing her research, Khanna, who identifies herself as an Asian-Indian/white woman, was conscious of how, in relation to the people she was interviewing, she was both an insider and an outsider. She notes that her 'gender, age, sexuality, status as a researcher, education, racial appearance, and perceptions of my racial identity' positioned her as an outsider for some respondents even while her bi-racial background helped to position her as an insider. Khanna's challenge throughout the project was to be mindful of 'this insider/outsider relationship and of the potential effects on interviewees' responses and my own subsequent analysis' (p. 103).

convenience sampling
A non-probability sampling technique in which research subjects are chosen because they are close at hand.

snowball sampling
A non-probability sampling technique used by researchers when research subjects are difficult to locate, in which the researcher asks initial research subjects to help with finding other research subjects.

'Public' versus 'Internalized' Identities

Khanna measured both *public* and *internalized identities*. 'Public identity' refers to the way in which respondents labelled themselves to others; 'internalized identity' refers to how respondents saw themselves (p. 104). In terms of public identity, 82.5 per cent of respondents labelled themselves using multi-racial descriptors such as 'bi-racial', 'multi-racial', 'mixed', or 'inter-racial'. Only 17.5 per cent labelled themselves exclusively as black or African-American (six respondents) or as exclusively white (one respondent). There was considerably more variation in the internalized identities of the respondents: 60 per cent said they identified more strongly with being black, and 22.5 per cent with being white; just 17.5 per cent claimed to identify with both racial groups equally. Many identified more strongly with being black 'because they believe that it is how they are perceived by others'. Without being prompted by the interviewer, 65 per cent of respondents, when asked about their racial identities, 'describe their identities in relation to how they think "others" or "larger society" perceives them' (p. 108).

One respondent, 'Michael', labelled himself as bi-racial but strongly identified as black. Asked to explain his strong black identity, Michael responded:

> I would say I identify very strongly [as black] only because I think part of how you define yourself is the category that society puts you into. And when people look at me, they're not going to see a white person, you know? And they definitely

Segregated drinking fountains were still a fixture in the American South in the 1960s, when this photograph was taken. Do you think the history of slavery and segregation has an effect on the internalized sense of self of black and non-black North Americans today? What differences might exist for blacks and non-blacks?

see me as a person of color . . . so I definitely feel like I identify more with my black side because that's how I'm perceived rather than being [white]. . . . I think the only reason I identify more with being black is because society's kind of labelled me as that. (Khanna, 2010, p. 108)

Michael's response, like that of many others in the study, confirms the extent to which reflected appraisals are important in shaping racial identity. Many respondents referred to a connection between their physical features and their racial identities. How they saw themselves was strongly influenced by how they thought they appeared to others. Moreover, as Khanna observes, the 'racial reflection they saw in their "looking glass" differed depending upon who was looking at them, for instance, whether their observer was white or black' (p. 110). The experiences of 'Olivia' illustrate this. Olivia told Khanna:

Some people just see me as a black woman. But there's other people who are just like 'what are you?' . . . It depends on the background of the person who's approaching me. (p. 110)

Olivia reported that while blacks often see her as a black woman who's mixed with something else, whites mostly see her only as a black woman. Another respondent, Kirsten, who is bi-racial, commented that because her skin, hair, and eyes are lighter people assume that she is white, but that friends and their parents who learned of her bi-racial background began to see her differently.

In the US, if someone looks black 'according to prevailing social norms', adopting a non-black identity is not acceptable (Waters, 1996, as cited in Khanna, 2010, p. 115). For black–white bi-racial Americans, however, the link between external physical features and racial identity is not clear-cut or straightforward. Having a 'white' physical appearance (as in Oliva's case) does not preclude having a 'black' identity. What is interesting is that it would appear that while possessing a 'white physical appearance' does not conflict with America's image of blackness, having any 'black' physical characteristic automatically rules out a white identity—this is what has come to be known as the 'one drop rule'.

Khanna's study shows that while the 'one drop rule' continues to shape internalized black identities (via reflected appraisals), it does not have the same effect with regard to public identities. The majority of bi-racial respondents in her study publicly identify as bi-racial or multi-racial, an observation confirmed by other research.

RACISM, PREJUDICE, AND DISCRIMINATION

What Is Racism?

In her pioneering study *Race and Racism* (1942), anthologist Ruth Benedict defined **racism** as the 'unproved assumption of the biological and perpetual superiority of one human group over another'. Five decades later, American historian Nell Irwin Painter (2010) defined racism more simply as 'the belief that races exist, and that some are better than others' (p. xii).

Racism is a highly resilient organizing principle that has shaped Western societies both historically and in the present. It is enduring, consistent, and yet, at the same time, variable and flexible. In North America, racial injustice and the oppression of racial minorities have been pervasive aspects of economic, political, and social life.

racism
A set of beliefs about supposedly inherent characteristics pertaining to different human populations, usually involving judgements about the superiority and inferiority of different 'races'.

institutional racism
'Attitudes and practices that lead to racist outcomes through unquestioned bureaucratic procedures' (Carmichael & Hamilton, 1967). *Also called* **systemic racism**.

individual racism
Carmichael and Hamilton's term for the deliberately racist activities and actions by individual people.

The term **institutional** (or **systemic**) **racism** was first introduced by black activists Stokely Carmichael and Charles Hamilton (1967) in their book *Black Power*. They used the term 'to account for attitudes and practices that lead to racist outcomes through unquestioned bureaucratic procedures' (Murji, 2007, p. 844). Carmichael and Hamilton saw institutional racism as *covert*, in contrast to **individual racism**, which they regarded as *overt*.

Individual racism involves deliberate activities and actions by individual people. Institutional racism, by contrast, is more subtle and cannot be reduced to the acts of any individual. Carmichael and Hamilton made it plain that even if white people had no intention of discriminating against blacks, they still collectively benefit from institutional racism. The South African census questionnaire, discussed above, could be viewed as an instrument of institutionalized racism. Institutional racism is a charge currently being levied against the Vancouver police department for its failure to follow up on the reported disappearance of many Native women working in the city's sex trade during the 1990s and 2000s. Police inaction allowed now convicted mass murderer Robert Pickton to continue his killing spree over more than two decades, until his arrest in 2002. A public inquiry was called in October 2011 to investigate why it took police so long to even acknowledge that a serial killer existed, despite the unprecedented number of Vancouver sex workers and drug users (most of them Native women) vanishing without explanation. Yet even the inquiry has been the subject of charges of institutional racism because non-profit advocacy groups representing the kinds of women Pickton made his victims were denied funding for legal counsel to cross-examine witnesses and to present counter-arguments.

There are many interlocking dimensions to institutional, or systemic, racism: the accumulation of resources by coercive means, the use of violence to defend wealth and power, and the rationalization that wealth and positions of privilege are merited as just rewards for natural superiority (Omi & Winant, 2008, p. 121). According to sociologist Joe Feagin (2006) the interlocking dimensions of racism create a 'sustained inability' on the part of whites 'to relate to and understand the suffering of those who are oppressed' (Feagin, 2006, pp. 27–8). Racism, Feagin points out, is more than an individual act: it also relies on a high degree of social consensus. In the US and Canada today, racism rarely takes the form of explicit, legally sanctioned oppression and violence. Instead, white privilege is now about 'whites averting their gaze from the suffering that racism causes, denying it systematically, day after day' (Feagin, 2006, pp. 28).

In his book *Racism without Racists* (2007), Eduardo Bonilla-Silva shows that while whites profess 'colour blindness' and endorse racial equality, they continue to hold prejudiced attitudes and to engage in discriminatory practices. He also shows that minority groups are equally capable of practising colour-blind racism.

What Are Prejudice and Discrimination?

Prejudice, in Gordon Allport's words, is 'antipathy based on a faulty or inflexible generalization' (Allport, 1954). When put in the context of racism, prejudice joins two elements: a negative emotion or affective feeling—*antipathy*—towards one or more target groups, and a poorly founded belief—a *stereotype*—about members of the target group or groups (Quillian, 2006, p. 300). Prejudice is the motivational force behind acts of discrimination. The American National Research Council (2004) defines discrimination as:

> (1) differential treatment on the basis of race that disadvantages a racial group and (2) treatment on the basis of inadequately justified factors other than race that disadvantage a racial group. (as cited in Quillian, 2006)

Racism is both prejudice (a feeling of intense dislike or aversion) and discrimination (the unfair treatment of a person or group). *Racial discrimination* can thus be defined as 'the difference between the treatment that a target group actually receives and the treatment they would receive if they were not members of the target group but were otherwise the same' (Quillian, 2006, pp. 301–2). Using the term 'racist' to refer to an attitude, feeling, or act, signals 'the speaker's unambiguous condemnation of the belief or practice in question' (Quillian, 2006, p. 302).

ETHNIC AND RACIAL DIVERSITY IN CANADA

A 2008 Statistics Canada publication uses 2006 census data to examine the 'ethnic origins of Canada's population' (Statistics Canada, 2008c, p. 6). The 2006 census identified more than 200 different ethnic or cultural origins of respondents' ancestors. Eleven of those ethnic origins had more than 1 million people. Among the most frequently cited ethnic origins reported in the 2006 census were English (6.6 million), French (4.9 million), Scottish (4.7 million), Irish (4.4 million), German (3.2 million), Italian (1.4 million), Chinese (1.3 million), North American Indian (1.3 million), Ukrainian (1.2 million), and Dutch (1.1 million) (Statistics Canada, 2008c).

According to the 2006 census, more than 5 million Canadians—over 16 per cent of the country's total population—identified themselves as members of a visible minority (Statistics Canada, 2008c, p. 6). The Canadian Employment Equity Act defines **visible minority** as 'persons, other than Aboriginal peoples, who are non-Caucasian in race or non-white in colour'. The visible minority population consists mainly of the following groups: Chinese, South Asian, African/Afro-Caribbean, Arab, West Asian, Filipino, Southeast Asian, Latin American, Japanese, and Korean (www.statcan.gc.ca/concepts/definitions/minority-minorite1-eng.htm).

visible minority
An identifiable group of people who are non-white and who, because of some 'visible' characteristic, may experience discrimination.

Between 2001 and 2006 the visible minority population in Canada grew by over 27 per cent, a rate five times greater than the increase of the population as a whole. Fully 75 per cent of the immigrants who arrived in Canada between 2001 and 2006 belong to a visible minority group (Statistics Canada, 2008c, p. 18). At these rates, members of visible minorities could account for 20 per cent of Canada's population by 2017.

There are major regional differences in the distribution of Canada's visible minorities. Only about 2.6 per cent of the people living in Atlantic Canada are visible minorities, while British Columbia is home to over 1 million visible minority persons (24.8 per cent of that province's total population), with almost 87 per cent of them living in Vancouver. Just over 40 per cent of BC's visible minority population are Chinese, while South Asian visible minority groups represent about 6.4 per cent of the province's total population. In Yukon, just over one-quarter of the population reported Aboriginal ancestors, and almost 85 per cent of Nunavut's population reported Inuit ancestral background.

About 96 per cent of the members of Canada's visible minority groups live in metropolitan areas (compared with 68 per cent of the country's population overall), and most of them live in Toronto or Vancouver. Almost 43 per cent of Toronto's population and 42 per cent of Vancouver's population are visible minorities. Between 2001 and 2006, Toronto became home to over 40 per cent of all newcomers to Canada, almost 82 per cent of whom were members of a visible minority group (Statistics Canada, 2008c).

Canada is succeeding at attracting immigrants to this country. Far from 'stealing jobs from hard-working Canadians', as is often claimed, immigrants play a vital role in the country's economy by taking on some jobs that Canadians typically avoid (childcare, home care, housekeeping, for example), and many arrive with excellent professional credentials that make them ideally suited to filling needs in underserviced sectors, such as that of family doctor. But how well are these newcomers integrated into Canadian society once they arrive? The case of employment provides some insights.

Ethnic Discrimination in Canada: The Case of Employment

multiculturalism
An official government policy premised on a 'multiplicity of equal cultures' and highlighting the importance of 'cultural and racial diversity' as a 'fundamental characteristic of the Canadian heritage and identity'.

Canada is a country of immigrants, with one of the highest per capita immigration rates in the world. The official government policy of **multiculturalism**, in force in Canada between 1985 and June 2010, was premised on a 'multiplicity of equal cultures' and highlighted the importance of 'cultural and racial diversity' as a 'fundamental characteristic of the Canadian heritage and identity'. The policy promoted the 'full and equitable participation of individuals and communities of all origins' and ensured that 'all individuals receive equal treatment and equal protection under the law, while respecting and valuing their diversity' (Department of Justice Canada, 1985). But is this the case? Are all Canadians treated equally?

What makes someone a visible minority? Which people in this photo would you say qualify as representing visible minorities? What does it mean that we distinguish between visible minority immigrants and other immigrants? Is one group privileged above the other?

Certainly, according to Section 15.1 of the Canadian Charter of Rights and Freedoms (which came into effect on 17 April 1985):

> Every individual is equal before and under the law and has the right to the equal protection and equal benefit of the law without discrimination and, in particular, without discrimination based on race, national or ethnic origin, colour, sex, age or mental or physical disability.

In addition to the Charter's broad granting of rights to all Canadians, further legislation has been enacted to support the Charter's equality provisions (Lautard & Guppy, 2008, p. 164). Section 2 of The Canadian Employment Equity Act (1995) states that the purpose of the act is:

> to achieve equality in the workplace so that no person shall be denied employment opportunities or benefits for reasons unrelated to ability and, in the fulfilment of that goal, to correct the conditions of disadvantage in employment experienced by women, aboriginal peoples, persons with disabilities and members of visible minorities by giving effect to the principle that employment equity means more than treating persons in the same way but also requires special measures and the accommodation of differences. (Department of Justice Canada, 1995)

The Canadian Employment Equity Act defines visible minorities as 'persons, other than aboriginal peoples, who are non-Caucasian in race or non-white in colour' (Department of Justice Canada, 1995).

Changes in the ethnic composition of Canada have heightened concerns about ethnic and racial inequality, particularly in the area of employment. Studies beginning in the 1980s have indicated that racial inequality does indeed exist in Canada (Baker & Benjamin, 1997; Henry & Ginsberg, 1985; Ornstein, 2000; Pendakur & Pendakur, 1998; Reitz, 2001). Researchers have found that, in Canada, visible minorities perceive themselves to have experienced societal discrimination far more frequently than do whites. One study found that while about 10 per cent of white respondents perceived overall societal discrimination in the previous year, almost 36 per cent of visible minorities reported having experienced discrimination (Reitz & Banerjee, 2005).

Using the 2002 Ethnic Diversity Survey conducted jointly by Statistics Canada and Heritage Canada and based on interviews with 41,666 respondents (of whom 8,622 were members of visible minorities), Banerjee (2006) analyzed the experiences of visible minority workers in Canada and their perception of workplace discrimination. In a previous study using the same data set, Reitz & Banerjee (2005) had found relative household incomes for virtually all visible minority groups in Canada, including Chinese, South Asians, and blacks, to be substantially lower than relative household incomes for almost all white ethnic groups. Nearly all labour force analyses of the earnings of immigrants to Canada have reported that non-European immigrants in Canada earn substantially less than do those of European origin (Reitz & Verma, 2004).

While these findings are important, there is another aspect of discrimination that is not concerned with differences in wage. A number of Canadian studies conducted since the late 1980s have found that visible minorities report significantly greater discrimination and

STUDIES IN SOCIAL RESEARCH

Finding a Place in the Canadian Labour Market: An Immigrant's Challenge

The Toronto Region Immigrant Employment Council (TRIEC) is an organization that helps integrate immigrants to Canada in the labour market through public awareness campaigns, mentorship programs, education and networking, and other initiatives. Its website features stories and testimonials like the one that follows, which highlight some of the obstacles faced by newcomers to Canada.

Micheline Jeanfrancois

Why I left: Because Mexico City was overcrowded with more than 19 million people. I also felt out of place because of my black and white mixed background. That's not as common in Mexico as it is here in Canada. I wanted to live in a city that is ethnically diverse, where uniqueness is embraced.

My first try: I came to Canada a few years ago but couldn't find a job. So I returned to Mexico where I worked as a marketing manager for a US company.

My return: I came back to Canada in March 2005. I started job hunting with my regular resume but was told I was overqualified. Someone suggested I list only my Canadian experience, although I had only worked in jobs outside of my field. I found two jobs this way.

My current position: Through a bilingual job fair, I got hired by Procter & Gamble. I've been promoted three times. Today I'm part of the Americas Knowledge Coordinators team and I use my language skills to focus on projects in Brazil and Argentina. Thankfully, my employer recognizes international talent and experience, and encourages diversity.

Source: TRIEC © 2011

prejudice than do whites in various contexts pertaining to obtaining work, attaining executive positions, earning competitive wage rates, obtaining government jobs and management positions, and being considered for promotion and advancement (Dion, 1989; Dion & Kawakami, 1996).

Using Data from the Ethnic Diversity Survey, Banerjee found that white employees were far less likely to perceive workplace discrimination than visible minority employees were (see Figure 17.2). While just over 5 per cent of white respondents reported workplace discrimination, nearly 35 per cent of black, 25 per cent of South Asian, and about 20 per cent of Chinese employees perceived workplace discrimination (Banerjee, 2006, p. 9).

Survey respondents were asked the following question:

> Discrimination may happen when people are treated unfairly because they are seen as being different from others. In the past five years (or, for recent immigrants, since arriving in Canada), do you feel that you have experienced

discrimination or been treated unfairly by others in Canada because of your ethnicity, race, skin color, language, accident, or religion? (Banerjee, 2006)

Those who answered 'yes' were asked an additional question: 'In which places or situations do you feel you have experienced discrimination or been treated unfairly?' Respondents who answered 'at work', 'while applying for a job', or 'while applying for a promotion' were considered to have experienced workplace discrimination.

Banerjee (2006) found that, overall, 22.5 per cent of members of visible minority groups perceived workplace discrimination (p. 19). Black respondents were most likely and Chinese respondents least likely to have perceived workplace discrimination (p. 20), and immigrants overall were more likely than native-born workers to have perceived discrimination. University education increased the odds of perceiving discrimination, especially for those unable to find work in managerial or professional occupations. To summarize, Banerjee found the following:

1. Immigrant visible minorities are more likely to perceive workplace discrimination than their native-born counterparts.
2. Among immigrants, time spent in Canada increases the likelihood of perceiving workplace discrimination.
3. University-educated immigrants are more likely to perceive workplace discrimination, particularly if they are unable to find work in managerial or professional occupations.
4. Among the native-born, neither education nor occupation affects perception of workplace discrimination.
5. Income discrimination is positively related to perceived workplace discrimination for visible minority men, but not significantly related for visible minority women. (Banerjee, 2006, p. 24)

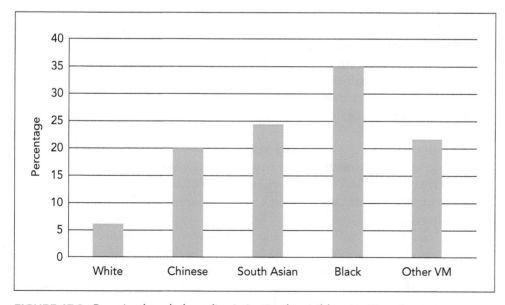

FIGURE 17.2   Perceived workplace discrimination by visible minority category

Source: Adapted from Banerjee, 2006, p. 10.

Banerjee's research findings reaffirm other findings that indicate that workplace discrimination is an ongoing fact of life for many new Canadians, and that members of visible minorities, especially men, experience workplace discrimination and are often unable to find work in the professions for which they trained. Additionally, large earning gaps are prevalent between members of visible minorities who are immigrants and those who are native-born. It seems that regardless of one's level of education attainment, being a member of a visible minority and being a new Canadian make it much more likely that one will experience workplace discrimination and receive a low income.

SUMMARY

In the nineteenth and early twentieth centuries, scientists focused on what sociologists have come to call 'scientific racism'. Today, science, especially genetics, has made important contributions to a re-thinking of 'scientific racism', providing us with new ways of experiencing our deepest identities, challenging our notions of relatedness, personhood, and the nature/culture distinction (Skinner, 2006, p. 462). Recent discoveries by geneticists have provided a new way to bridge the ideas of self, identity, and race.

Today most members of the scientific community accept the notion that 'race' is a social construction. Yet, in spite of the current view that race is a biological myth, race continues to exist as a way of thinking about human biological variation. But as geneticist Alan Goodman (2000) explains, race is 'an inadequate and even harmful way to think about human biological differences'. There are six reasons for this:

1. Race began as a European folk concept from an era when the world was seen as fixed and unchanging; it is incompatible with contemporary evolutionary theory.
2. Human variation is continuous; there is no clear place to designate where one race ends and another begins, as for example with skin colour.
3. Human biological traits vary independently; thus, racial classifications vary by the traits used in the classification. For example, a classification of races based on sickle cell trait would include Africans, Greeks, and Turks together in one category. A classification based on lactase enzyme deficiency would bring together southern and eastern Africans, southern Europeans, Japanese, and Native North Americans. Our current system of race classification, based primarily on skin colour but often correlated with a few other externally visible traits such as hair and eye colour, makes race 'only skin deep'.
4. The variation that exists among populations classified as belonging to the same 'race' category according to our prevailing system is actually much greater than the variation that exists between these race categories once we start to look at genetic variation. Our current system of race categorization statistically explains only a small portion of all human variation.
5. 'Race' cannot be defined in a stable and universal way. Who is defined as a member of any given racial category depends on who is doing the categorizing.
6. There is no clarity as to what race is and what it is not. Some argue that racial differences are the result of genes, others see racial differences as the consequence of the lived experience of those assigned a specific racial category and of racism.

While Goodman (2000) notes that none of these reasons by itself is enough to reject the concept of race as being biologically determined, taken together they form a powerful argument against thinking that race is a valid method for classifying human biological differences (p. 1700).

But, if race has no validity as a biological category, it does have validity as a social construct. As we have seen, the institutional structures of Western societies work to reinforce white privilege. Race identity and solidarity continue to operate, even in the face of a professed 'colour blindness' on the part of most whites, and efforts by the State to guarantee the equality of all citizens regardless of colour.

Racism has a history, consequences, and rationalizations. Sociologists are mindful of the processes that lead to race formation. They study the social, political, and economic contexts, as well as the interpersonal ones, in which racism is practised, and out of which institutional structures supporting racism are built as well as challenged and dismantled.

DISCUSSION QUESTIONS

1. What are some of the broader implications for Western society of the findings of geneticists who are studying human DNA?
2. Discuss the differences between *genetic kinship* and *social kinship*.
3. What does it mean to say that race is a social construct? Discuss the taken-for-granted views of race that are most commonly held by Canadians today.
4. To what extent is Canadian society racist? What are some examples of institutional and individual racism in our society?
5. What is meant by the term 'the new racism'? Explain how ethnicity is used as a basis of discrimination.
6. 'Whiteness' has been called a privileged identity. In what ways might this be the case in Canadian society? Provide examples.
7. What is the difference between *institutional* or *systemic racism* and *individual racism*? Provide examples.
8. Is Canada a multicultural society? Explain your answer.

Part VI
New Topics, New Directions

The final three chapters of this textbook focus on mass media and popular culture (Chapter 18), social media (Chapter 19), and the tools of sociological analysis that sociologists are using today to address (and correct) inequalities across society.

The popular culture we consume for pleasure—via mass media such as television, print media, music recordings, the purchase of cultural artifacts, or attendance at concerts and movies, plays and sporting events—delivers strong statements about underlying cultural values, morals, and accepted social practices. Conversely, it can also deliver messages about how to resist those values, morals, and practices. But, as sociologists have demonstrated, we are not just cultural sponges, consuming popular culture in a vacuum and replicating what we see or hear. Popular culture changes continuously; it is what we informally agree is part of the everyday lives of the majority of a society's members.

One recent development that has had a dramatic effect on the way popular culture is produced, reproduced, and spread is the growth in use of computers and other personal communication devices for facilitating communication among people who do not have to be physically co-present. Social analysts, beginning with Canadian Marshall McLuhan, see that mass media

have made the world a 'global village', a metaphor that is truer than ever since the rise of the Internet. We are living through a 'digital revolution' that has seen vast and growing quantities of information produced and made available to any individual with access to a search engine such as Google or YouTube, often as it is being produced. Social media support digitized social interactions among networked 'community' members. Within a single generation, new technologies have irrevocably changed the way in which most people communicate and keep in touch with friends, family, and the rest of the world. Social media and the new communication technologies are among the newest areas of study for sociologists interested in popular culture and the future of Western society.

Since the inception of sociology, most sociologists have been concerned both with the present moral, social, and political climate of human society and with humanity's future. More particularly, they have been concerned with how a sociological perspective can be best used to understand society and to make a positive impact upon it. This textbook closes with a chapter on sociologists and social activism, and provides some examples of how sociologists today are using the tools of sociological analysis to make a positive impact on our world.

18 Popular Culture and Mass Media

CHAPTER OUTLINE

Introduction
Popular Culture
1. 'Well Liked by Many People'
2. 'Inferior Kinds of Work'
3. 'Work Deliberately Set Out to Win Favour with the People'
4. 'Culture Actually Made by the People Themselves'
Popular Culture and the Industrial Revolution
The Communication of Popular Culture: Many-to-One and Many-to-Many Relations
   One-to-One
   Few-to-Few
   One-to-Many
   Many-to-One
   Many-to-Many

Mass Media and the Communication and Consumption of Cultural 'Goods and Services'
   The Three Screens
Mass Media and Social Behaviour
   Mass Media and Violence
   TV Violence
   Onscreen Violence: Seven 'Research Strands' and Inclusive Results
   Canadian Children's Views About Onscreen Violence
Summary
Discussion Questions

LEARNING OBJECTIVES

In this chapter you will:

- distinguish between popular culture, one-directional mass media, and two-directional user-produced participatory media
- gain a clearer understanding of popular culture
- learn about popular culture and the Industrial Revolution
- examine how popular culture is communicated and shared
- reflect on the role of mass media in communicating entertainment and information
- seek to understand the effects of mass media on consumer behaviour
- think critically about the relationship between onscreen violence and real-world violence.

INTRODUCTION

Popular culture, one-directional mass media, and two-directional user-produced participatory media are closely connected and play increasingly important roles in contemporary Western society. They impact everybody's life on a daily basis. Videos, CDs, DVDs, television and radio broadcasts, the cinema, magazines and newspapers—all are well-known examples of mass media that transmit popular culture. YouTube and mobile phone communications are examples of what we call two- or multi-directional user-produced participatory media. They influence the ways in which popular culture is produced and consumed, created and spread. Not surprisingly, popular culture, mass media, and participatory media have become subjects of intense and often controversial sociological inquiry.

Popular culture, mass media, and participatory media are most often linked in people's minds with entertainment. Very few North Americans have not read newspapers and

STUDIES IN SOCIAL RESEARCH

Graffiti Writing as a Popular Cultural Practice

Graffiti writing is defined by sociologist Maggie Dickinson (2008) as 'a cultural practice that produces a commons and creates a shared, public democratic space' (p. 28). While examples of graffiti have been found on ancient Roman and Mayan architecture, contemporary graffiti writing first made an appearance in the 1960s. Urban youth living in cities such as New York used the sides of subway cars and buildings as canvasses for their commentary on social, economic, and political conditions.

Since the 1970s graffiti writers have faced unrelenting and aggressive prosecution by city officials both in North America and elsewhere. In New York City, officials have made graffiti writing a crime, associating it with out-of-control youth gangs threatening the enjoyment of the city by its more respectable citizens. Others, however, view graffiti as harmless or even valuable, an opinion not shared by the New York Police Department. According to a spokesperson for the NYPD,

before any discussion of graffiti vandalism can commence, one has to understand exactly what is being fought. Apparently there are some who look on graffiti as a type of avant-garde art, which has a place as an expression of social worth. But that view is not only

puerile, it is misguided as well. (NYPD, n.d., as cited in Dickinson, 2008, p. 38)

Among those who hold graffiti to be 'art' are curators of the Brooklyn Museum in New York. In 2006 the Museum hosted a high-profile retrospective of the work of five influential graffiti artists, exploring 'how a genre that began as a form of subversive public communication has become legitimate—moving away from the street and into private collections and galleries' (Brooklyn Museum, 2006, as cited in Dickison, 2008, p. 38).

One graffiti artist who has made the move from the streets to private collections is Banksy, a British artist whose work regularly appears on the streets of London and other cities but also appears for sale at high-end art galleries and auction houses for prices that have at times exceeded $500,000. Banksy uses a combination of free-drawing and stencilling techniques to present an alternative-to-mainstream view of politics and other aspects of contemporary Western life. His work is satirical, subversive, and politically challenging. And like many other graffiti writers he skirts the boundary between art and 'crime'. Local British governments and agencies treat Banksy's work as vandalism, and have it removed from public property. Yet his work has an extensive magazines, watched television or a DVD, downloaded a YouTube video, attended a movie, listened to music on live radio or an iPod. A growing number have posted their own YouTube videos and have played massively multiplayer online games (MMOGs) such as World of Warcraft. Considered this way, it's easy to see how popular culture might appear to be little more than entertainment, requiring only that the viewer or listener sit back and mindlessly consume whatever is put before him. But to take such a limited view of the relationship between popular culture and mass communications would be a mistake.

To begin, engagement with popular culture requires much more than just passively watching a screen or listening to something played through headphones. Popular culture includes all those ways we are organized to interact on a daily basis; it surrounds our lives, and it is something with which we continually and actively engage. Popular culture reflects the accepted values, beliefs, and morality of large numbers of people. People are attracted to elements of popular culture—the *Twilight* series, Santa Claus, printed T-shirts, electronic dance

following, not only among younger, avant-garde artists and musicians, but also among those in the mainstream.

Although he protects his real identity, Banksy is reputed to have done paid work for Greenpeace as well as for big corporations. He has self-published several books containing photographs of his street art and other works and has directed a film about street art, *Exit Through the Gift Shop*, which was nominated for the Academy Award for Best Documentary Feature in 2010.

There are those who claim that once a work of graffiti has been removed from its original context it ceases to be authentic (Miller, 2002, p. 159, as cited in Dickinson, 2008, p. 39). According to Dickinson,

Banksy's work challenges the viewer with political, social, and cultural commentary. How would you interpret the message of this work?

the incorporation of graffiti into high art markets, and as a marketing tool for everything from sodas to video games, also reveals the remarkable flexibility of neoliberalism to incorporate insurgent elements, even if only to a partial degree. (p. 40)

Yet much of graffiti writing that is done today continues to be acts of resistance and disruption on the part of marginalized youth, in spite of ongoing criminalization on the one hand, and co-optation into mainstream culture on the other.

music and hiphop concerts, the nuclear family, mixed martial arts, shopping at the mall, *The Simpsons*, lavish weddings—because they perceive that those elements fulfill a need or want.

Popular culture is not forced on an unwilling population. Rather, individual members of society take elements of popular culture and construct meanings out of them. Often those meanings bear little relation to what the original, commercial producers intended. The fact that North American children recognize Ronald McDonald more often than any other figure with the exception of Santa Claus is an outcome of the ways in which popular culture is delivered via mass media and user-produced participatory media to almost everyone in the world.

POPULAR CULTURE

popular culture
Culture created by masses of people in modern urban-industrial societies. Popular culture is closely related to mass culture and many creations of mass culture become part of popular culture through mass media.

You will recall from an earlier discussion that British sociologist Raymond Williams (1976/1985) called culture 'one of the two or three most complicated words in the English language'. This is so, Williams explained, partly because of the concept's 'intricate historical development, in several European languages, but mainly because it has now come to be used for important concepts in several distinct intellectual disciplines and in several distinct and incompatible systems of thought' (p. 87). The term *popular* is also complex. Originally a 'legal and political term' meaning 'affecting, concerning, or open to the people', it has transitioned to the contemporary meaning of 'widely favoured', 'well liked', or 'from the point of view of the people'. Based on this, Williams suggests four contemporary meanings for **popular culture**:

1. 'well liked by many people'
2. 'inferior kinds of work'
3. 'work deliberately set out to win favour with the people'
4. 'culture actually made by the people themselves'. (Williams, 1976/1985)

Let's look at each of these separate meanings of popular culture.

1. 'Well Liked by Many People'

Popular culture in this sense might be gauged by number of weeks spent at the top of *The New York Times* bestseller book list, number of views on YouTube, number of downloads from iTunes, total print circulation, number of tickets sold, and so on. While it is useful that any definition of popular culture include some kind of quantitative dimension, it is also clear that a quantitative index is not enough for an adequate definition.

2. 'Inferior Kinds of Work'

If popular culture is defined as culture made up by the people themselves, then popular culture is what is left over after we've identified and separated out everything to be classified as 'high culture'. But as sociologist Pierre Bourdieu has shown, distinctions between high culture and popular culture are actually markers of social class. For Bourdieu, the consumption of culture—whether thought of as 'high culture' or as 'popular culture'—has the social function of legitimizing social differences and demarcating the boundaries between social classes.

For most sociologists, the distinction between high culture and popular culture is socially constructed, and not at all 'obvious'. For example, cultural theorist John Storey (2000) points out that 'such distinctions are often supported by claims that popular culture is mass-produced commercial culture whereas high culture is the result of an individual act of creation' (Storey, 2000, p. 6). Yet a look at what constituted 'high culture' a few centuries ago compared to what constitutes 'high culture' today illustrates the point. The work of William Shakespeare is today considered the epitome of high culture, but when Shakespeare wrote his plays they were very much part of popular theatre. The same can be said for the works of Mozart, whose operas are now considered part of high culture, yet when they were composed, Mozart intended them to appeal to the masses. In the 1990s, certain opera singers increased their commercial success (and their incomes) by yet again reversing the high culture/popular culture status of opera when they sang at mass public events and performed duets with pop music stars.

3. 'Work Deliberately Set Out to Win Favour with the People'

Until the 1990s, the work of Luciano Pavarotti (1935–2007) was marketed as high culture. But Pavarotti crossed over into popular music during the latter part of his career to become one of the most commercially successful tenors of all time. In 1990 Pavarotti gave a performance of Puccini's *Nessun Dorma* at the World Cup in Italy. And along with fellow tenors Plácido Domingo and José Carreras, Pavarotti held a concert on the eve of that tournament's final match, bringing operatic highlights to a worldwide audience. Pavarotti made an appearance on *Saturday Night Live* and also appeared in numerous advertisements. He was often seen alongside pop singers and other celebrities, and a free concert he gave in 1991 in London's Hyde Park was covered by a number of British tabloids as a popular culture event. One of the papers, *The Sun,* quoted an audience member as saying, 'I can't afford to go to posh opera houses with toffs and fork out £100 a seat' (as cited in Storey, 2002, p. 7). Another tabloid claimed that the performance 'wasn't for the rich' but for 'the thousands . . . who could never normally afford a night with an operatic star'. The BBC and ITV reported on the event as well, attempting to reintroduce the distinctions between high and popular culture by stating that 'some critics said that the park is no place for an opera' and adding that 'some opera enthusiasts might think it all a bit vulgar' (as cited in Storey, 2002, p. 7).

Another way of defining popular culture is in terms of **mass culture**. Those who use the term mass culture want to make sure that popular culture is identified as 'commercial culture'—that is, culture produced for mass consumption by a mass audience of non-discriminating consumers. And yet cultural consumption is clearly not an automatic or passive activity on the part of a gullible, easily entertained, and fairly stupid population. For example, a large number of the films produced for popular consumption, along with a great deal of music produced in the hope that it will reach a wide (and paying audience), never achieves widespread popularity. One way of approaching all of this is to see mass culture as the product of 'the culture industry'—in other words, culture produced for sale and profit—and popular culture as what people actively make from those products or what they actually do 'with the commodities and commodified practices they consume' (Storey, 2002, p. 12).

Today, there are social theorists who claim that the distinction between popular, high, and mass culture is no longer relevant, at least in Western societies, and that all 'culture'—whether it's a Britney Spears video, a piece of Banksy graffiti, or the Canadian Ballet Company's performance of *Eugene Onegin*—can be recorded, re-packaged, and re-presented for consumption by audiences other than the one for whom it was originally intended.

mass culture
Cultural phenomena (music, dance, symbols, values, consumer goods, etc.) produced for mass consumption by a mass audience (often thought of as non-discriminating consumers).

4. 'Culture Actually Made by the People Themselves'

hegemony
A concept used to refer to the way in which dominant groups in society use 'intellectual and moral leadership' to try to win ascent over subordinate groups.

Popular culture is also viewed as culture that originates from 'the people'. It not something imposed on the people but is the 'authentic' culture of the people. The Italian Marxist Antonio Gramsci used the term **hegemony** to refer to the way in which dominant groups in society use 'intellectual and moral leadership' to try to win ascent over subordinate groups. Cultural theorists who have taken up this concept view popular culture as the site of resistance by subordinate groups against forces of subordination that operate in the interests of dominant groups in the society. In this sense popular culture is not an imposed mass culture nor is it a spontaneously emerging oppositional culture of 'the people'. Gramsci treated popular culture as a place of exchange and negotiation between those who dominate and those who are ruled. Taking a holiday by the sea began first as a privileged activity of the aristocracy, but a century later the vacation down south, the Caribbean cruise, the spring break trip to Fort Lauderdale all became part of popular culture (Storey, 2002, pp. 10–11).

POPULAR CULTURE AND THE INDUSTRIAL REVOLUTION

Popular culture represents 'popular interests and values'. Popular music, street fashion, local restaurants, rap music, sporting events, daytime soap operas, comic books, 'reality television', bridal showers, and backyard barbecues are all examples of popular culture. What the items on this list have in common (and the list could go on) is that they are examples of cultural practices to which almost anyone in society today has access.

Popular culture, as we know it today, emerged during the late eighteenth century, when three key elements came together to support its rise: masses, money, and technological advancements. At that time, the population of Europe and North America was increasing rapidly, and large numbers of people congregated in growing urban areas. The rapid growth of population, the movement away from rural areas, and the increasing mechanization of production and general industrialization disrupted old patterns of culture and called for new ones. In Britain, for example, the Industrial Revolution did three things:

- It changed relationships between owners and non-owners of the means of production. Whereas class relations had previously been based on mutual obligation, they now came to be based largely on the capacity of one class—the capitalists—to purchase the capacity to labour of another class—the proletariat.
- It introduced residential segregation based on social class. With the rise of capitalism came urbanization, and with urbanization came residential segregation. For the first time in British history, towns and cities were divided into sections inhabited only by workers.
- The French Revolution produced a great deal of fear among members of the British government. Worried that the ideals of the French Revolution might be imported into Britain, successive British Governments enacted legislation aimed at repressing and defeating radicalism and trade unionism. Political and trade radicals were driven underground, where they organized beyond the influence of the middle-class.

Together these three factors produced a space for the generation of what became popular culture, outside of the influence and control of the dominant classes. As the Industrial Revolution progressed, new classes emerged that were neither peasant nor aristocrat, but workers and professionals who were paid wages and who, through long struggles, achieved increased levels of pay, better education, and more leisure time. These people were ready for new cultural forms on which to spend time and money.

Time was you'd dress up in your 'Sunday best' to attend a Saturday night hockey game between the Maple Leafs and the Canadiens. Even today, a pair of tickets in the best seats at the Air Canada Centre will cost you $900 (face value)—if you can get them. Is professional hockey a site of negotiation between society's dominant and subordinate groups?

THE COMMUNICATION OF POPULAR CULTURE: MANY-TO-ONE AND MANY-TO-MANY RELATIONS

In order to be 'popular', culture must be shared and communicated among people through interactions. Human interactions can happen in many ways, including the following.

One-to-One

One-to-one relationships are generally two-directional and, therefore, social. In terms of social network analysis (see Chapter 11), these connections are or have the potential to become 'strong ties'. Examples of one-to-one relationships include:

- face-to-face interactions between two people
- telephone calls
- email, instant messaging, text messages.

Few-to-Few

The few-to-few pattern characterizes small, tightly knit groups where strong ties exist among all the members of the group, for example:

- a team
- a family
- a gang
- small-group collaboration.

One-to-Many

One-to-many relationships are generally one-directional and, therefore, not very interactive. Examples include:

- videos, podcasts, documentaries, and general television programs, viewed onscreen (via TV, Internet, or mobile phone)
- newspapers, magazines, and other print periodicals
- radio broadcasts—AM, FM, satellite, or Internet
- email broadcasts, such as newsletters, advertising, and spam.

Many-to-One

'Many-to-one' refers to the communication of input collected from the 'many', distilled and presented to 'one'. These relationships are generally one-directional and, unless a method of sharing the gathered information is in place, not very social. Examples are:

- online social polling/survey tools, feedback forums
- group decision support tools
- crowd-sourcing.

Many-to-Many

Many-to-many relationships are multi-directional and are superficially social because of the short amount of time spent on each relationship. These relationships usually remain as 'weak ties' in a network, although individuals may form one-to-one or small-group connections as 'strong ties'. In networking theory, weak ties are useful for diffusing new ideas. Examples include:

- large-group collaboration
- group chat
- group games, e.g. World of Warcraft
- comments in blogs and online media sites
- shared online meeting platforms
- social media platforms such as Twitter, Facebook, and MySpace (further discussed in Chapter 19).

A flash mob gathers for a pillow fight at a public square in Amsterdam. The flash mob is a pop-cultural event made possible by recent communication technologies that enable a large crowd of people—mostly strangers, though all connected to the originator of the message—to be assembled in short period of time. How would you characterize this form of popular communication?

MASS MEDIA AND THE COMMUNICATION AND CONSUMPTION OF CULTURAL 'GOODS AND SERVICES'

mass media
A term used to refer to one-to-many–type communications in which identical messages are transmitted to large numbers of people (the 'masses') in a very short time. Radio, television, movies, CDs, and DVDs are all examples of media that facilitate one-to-many communication.

At the same time that popular culture was emerging to meet the needs and demands of rising working and professional classes, means of communicating popular cultural goods and services using **mass media** were also developed. Mark Poster (1990) defines mass media as 'systems of communication that structure an unknown group of receivers'. Mass media function as 'centers of information, distributing discourses and images to a broad public'. They are 'systems of cultural transmission without ties to any community'. In the late eighteenth century this was accomplished by the invention of high-speed printing presses. Much later, the means of mass communication expanded to include other media we now associate with 'mass media', including radio, television, movies, CDs, DVDs, MP3s, and the like. These are all examples of media that facilitate the one-to-many type of communication.

Mass media are commonly used to communicate entertainment and information. But as examples of one-to-many communication they also enter into our lives in many other ways. For instance, today most people do their banking via the Internet, which provides the same prompts for each customer: withdrawal or deposit, savings or checking account, amount of transaction. When you deposit money into your bank account via the Internet, the information is transferred from your computer or mobile phone to a central data processor. That data processor connects not just different branches of the same bank but also many different banking systems around the world. Thus, a customer who normally does her banking at a local branch near her home can make transactions from anywhere in the world. Credit cards also link into an equally complex system of electronically stored and transmitted information that allows a user to carry out financial transactions almost anywhere in the world.

Obviously, one-to-many–type communications, achieved via mass media such as TV, radio, the Internet, newspapers, and magazines, are not confined to information that mostly has an entertainment value. Mass media broadcast everything from ads announcing the weekly specials at a local grocery store to local, national, and international weather, the proposed policies of a political candidate in an upcoming election, the latest discoveries in astrophysics, advice about personal relationships, and horoscope predictions, to name just a few things. All this and much more is transmitted locally, nationally, and internationally from one central source to many, many potential readers, viewers, and listeners.

The Three Screens

Most people today access mass communications via a screen, whether it's a TV screen, a computer monitor, or a mobile phone screen. One indication of the ubiquity of screen-accessed communications is that almost two-thirds of the world's entire population (4.4 billion people) viewed coverage of the 2008 Beijing Olympics (Nielsen, 2008a), and an estimated 3.8 billion people watched at least part of the 2010 Vancouver Olympics (Sponsorship Intelligence, 2010).

Data gathered by Nielsen (2008b) indicate that in 2007, the average American home had 2.5 people and 2.8 television sets. In 2010, 292 million American TV viewers spent on average approximately 158 hours and 25 minutes per month watching television, while 134 million Americans spent an average of 3 hours and 10 minutes per month watching video on the Internet, and 20.3 million Americans spent an average of 3 hours and 37 minutes each month watching video on their mobile phones. According to Nielsen, American children aged 2–11 watched the least amount of television—roughly 114 hours per month; adults over 65 watched the most, at almost 219 hours per month. By contrast, teens aged 12–17 watched the most video on a mobile phone (7 hours and 13 minutes, on average), while adults 65 and older watched the least (just 1 hour and 44 minutes, on average) (see Table 18.1).

Canadian data for 2004 (see tables 18.2 and 18.3) show that on average Canadians spent 21.4 hours per week (or almost 93 hours per month) viewing television. Children aged 2–11 averaged 14.1 viewing hours per week, and teens aged 12–17 averaged 12.9 weekly hours. Males aged 18 and over spent 20.9 hours per week viewing television, while females of the same age spent an average of 25.6 hours per week (Statistics Canada). Canadians preferred to watch television dramas (27.3 per cent of total viewing time), news and public affairs (24.4 per cent of viewing time), and variety and game shows (15.2 per cent of viewing time) (Statistics Canada, www40.statcan.gc.ca/l01/cst01/arts22a-eng.htm).

Although most people continue to watch television on traditional TV sets, the popularity of viewing television content via the Internet is growing. A 2008 Nielsen report (2008c) showed that people were spending more time online each week than they had two years earlier. According to Nielsen, 'More than half of the respondents (51%) reported being online for at least three hours a week last year [2007]. In 2005, just 41% of those surveyed said they spent three or more hours online per week.' The same report included the following notes:

- *Viewers are accessing TV content via new media platforms.* A small but significant percentage of respondents reported watching television via desktop computers (14%), laptops (9%), video-enabled mobile phones (6%), or other portable video players (5%).

TABLE 18.1 Monthly time spent watching TV by American viewers, 2010 (first quarter)

Age group	Kids 2–11	Teens 12–17	Adults 18–24	Adults 25–35	Adults 35–49	Adults 50–64	Adults 65+	All 2+
On traditional TV	114:04	108:05	124:22	143:32	161:51	195:17	218:48	58:25
Watching time-shifted TV	6:48	5:54	7:04	13:30	12:36	11:01	5:47	9:36
Using the Internet on a PC	4:28	8:16	22:28	30:16	32:29	28:14	22:53	25:26
Watching video on the Internet	1:24	2:09	5:33	4:30	3:34	2:20	1:27	3:10
Mobile subscribers watching video on a mobile phone	n/a	7:13	5:47	3:15	2:53	2:10	1:44	3:37

Source: The Nielsen Company (1st quarter 2010). Copyrighted information of Nielsen, licensed for use herein.

- *Portable video platforms are slowly gaining popularity.* While a large percentage (82%) of adults in this study own a mobile phone, only 7% subscribe to a video downloading service. Of those respondents who own a video iPod, 35% have never watched a video on it, 16% watch videos two or three times a month, 14% watch videos once a week, and 9% watch videos daily via iPod. (Nielsen, 2008c)

In a study conducted in October 2008, Nielsen researchers found that 'more than 80% of people who watched TV and used the Internet that month had simultaneous sessions—watching TV and being online at the same time' (Nielsen, 2008d). Teens, they found, made up the demographic most likely to have simultaneous TV and Internet usage, but adults aged 35–54 racked up the most minutes watching TV while simultaneously being online.

There is a actually a term for the emerging trend of watching television and using the Internet simultaneously: 'social TV'. People who are in different locations watch the same program and chat with each other about the program using mobile phones, or their computers. For example, a 2011 survey of 1,300 British mobile Internet users under the age of 25 showed that most (80 per cent) used their mobile phones to access Twitter, Facebook, or other mobile applications to instantly communicate with their friends and share comments

TABLE 18.2 Canadians' television viewing by type of program, 2004 (all persons 2 years and older)

	Total	Canadian programmes	Foreign programmes
		% of viewing time	
All programmes	**100.0**	**37.2**	**62.8**
News and public affairs	24.4	18.4	6.0
Documentary	3.2	1.3	1.9
Academic instruction	3.2	1.7	1.5
Social and/or recreational instruction	1.1	0.4	0.6
Religion	0.3	0.2	0.1
Sports	6.5	2.9	3.6
Variety and games	15.2	4.6	10.7
Music and dance	1.0	0.8	0.2
Comedy	10.0	1.6	8.4
Drama	27.3	5.3	22.1
Videocassette recorder (VCR)	4.9	0.0	4.9
Other television programmes	2.9	0.0	2.9

Source: Statistics Canada. Copyrighted information of Nielsen, licensed for use herein.

TABLE 18.3   Average hours per week of television viewing, by province and age/sex groups, fall 2004

	Canada	NL	PEI	NS	NB	Quebec English	Quebec French	Quebec Total	ON	MN	SK	AB	BC
Total population	21.4	22.7	20.0	22.7	23.7	20.6	23.8	23.3	20.6	22.1	21.2	19.4	20.7
Men													
18+	20.9	21.3	19.8	22.4	23.2	19.8	22.9	22.4	20.1	22.0	20.5	18.2	21.5
18–24	12.3	11.4	10.0	11.7	14.8	9.5	12.0	11.6	13.6	12.9	9.7	9.1	13.4
25–34	16.3	15.7	15.6	18.3	19.7	15.7	17.0	16.8	15.2	18.2	16.6	15.0	18.9
35–49	18.3	21.4	20.3	20.6	20.8	16.5	20.0	19.4	17.5	20.5	19.7	16.8	18.1
50–59	23.4	23.6	20.8	24.1	24.4	22.0	25.4	24.7	22.6	23.1	21.7	21.3	24.4
60+	31.1	27.5	26.5	31.2	32.1	29.7	37.0	35.4	29.7	31.5	28.9	28.5	30.3
Women													
18+	25.6	26.8	23.5	27.2	28.4	24.2	29.2	28.5	24.7	26.4	25.7	23.9	23.4
18–24	14.9	17.6	11.7	17.3	15.7	9.9	16.1	15.4	14.6	16.1	15.2	15.3	13.1
25–34	20.8	26.6	20.6	21.2	26.8	18.5	22.4	21.6	20.2	22.0	21.7	20.9	19.1
35–49	22.6	26.6	23.3	25.9	25.4	20.2	24.9	24.2	21.3	24.6	23.6	21.6	22.1
50–59	28.3	25.0	26.0	30.3	29.3	27.7	32.3	31.6	28.3	27.2	26.2	26.9	24.0
60+	35.6	32.2	28.9	33.8	36.9	34.1	42.0	40.7	34.4	35.1	34.2	32.8	32.0
Teens													
12–17	12.9	12.3	12.3	13.8	12.6	13.4	13.7	13.5	13.2	13.0	12.7	12.4	11.7
Children													
2–11	14.1	18.9	14.5	12.9	14.7	14.2	14.3	14.3	13.5	15.5	15.2	14.1	14.4

For Quebec, the language classification is based on the language spoken at home. The total column includes those respondents who did not reply to this question or who indicated a language other than English or French.

Source: Statistics Canada, Television viewing fall 2004, *The Daily*, Friday March 31, 2006; http://www.statcan.gc.ca/daily-quotidien/060331/dq060331b-eng.htm.

in real time about programs they were mutually watching. The study participants said that social TV made watching a program 'fun', or 'more interesting' (Casciato, 2011). According to the report:

> One survey respondent, Ashleigh Foulser, 18, a student in Bournemouth, said, 'I love being able to keep in touch with my mates while I'm at college. They are in different towns to me but it's like having them round to watch TV. We share a lot of jokes and if I comment on something funny or stupid I get replies almost immediately.' ('Under 25's', n.d.)

The use of social media combined with TV viewing means that people can instantly comment—via cellphone, table, or laptop—on what they are viewing and share their comments with friends who aren't physically present. Social media has the potential to turn television viewing from an isolating, individual experience into an integral part of daily social life.

MASS MEDIA AND SOCIAL BEHAVIOUR

Some social science researchers are concerned with the role of mass media in shaping public opinion, especially about political issues, or in determining the fate of public figures, politicians, and government. Some have argued that mass media are totalitarian and undemocratic, that they destroy both individualism and the community. Others, beginning with the late Marshall McLuhan, have taken the opposite approach, arguing that the mass media are in the process of making the world into a 'global village'—a sort of electronic utopia.

There are strong indications that there is a relationship between mass media coverage and consumer behaviour. For example, in November of 2006, media outlets across the US prominently covered a couple of studies from the Harvard Medical School and the National Institute on Aging, which reported favourably on the health benefits of red wine. These studies found that red wine contains resveratrol, a substance that, taken in small amounts daily, had some effect in slowing the aging process. Prior to the release of the studies, the growth in sales of white wine outpaced the growth of sales in red wine. Following the media coverage, red wine sales grew by 8.5 per cent, compared with a growth rate of just 4.8 per cent for white wine. The apparent link between media coverage and consumer spending habits gives a clue as to why the infomercial—essentially a commercial masquerading as a public service bulletin—and pseudo-journalistic talk shows like *The Oprah Winfrey Show* are enormously popular and extremely influential. When the lines between news and entertainment are blurred, it is hard for consumers of mass culture and communication to know whom to trust.

Mass Media and Violence

If mass media can influence consumer behaviour, can the same be said about other behaviours, such as violence and aggression? Many sociologists are interested in investigating the relationship between the representations of violence, crime, and aggressions that are viewed on screens and real-world violent or sexual behaviours, especially among the young. Does watching onscreen violence help shape the subsequent actions of the viewer? Or is the relationship between viewing onscreen violence and individual behaviour less straightforward?

Violence has always played a role in entertainment. Even children's nursery rhymes, such as 'Jack and Jill Went Up the Hill' and 'Humpty-Dumpty Sat on a Wall', are filled with violence. Since the 1960s the issue of onscreen violence and its effects on the behaviour and feelings of children and youths has figured prominently both in public debates and in research studies devoted to this topic. In part, this is because there is an ever-growing concern about increases in the depiction of physical violence in the media. For example, the National Center for Children Exposed to Violence (NCCEV) at the Yale Child Study Center estimates that the average 18-year-old will have viewed 200,000 acts of violence on television (Huston, Donnerstein, & Fairchild, et al., 1992).

In Canada, Guy Paquette and Jacques de Guise (2002) have studied the content of television programming at major Canadian television networks over a seven-year period. Among their findings is that between 1993 and 2001, onscreen incidents of physical violence increased by 378 per cent: in 2001, TV shows averaged 40 acts of violence per hour. Paquette and de Guise also found that onscreen incidents of psychological violence increased by 325 per cent between 1999 and 2001. By 2001, onscreen incidents of psychological violence had outstripped incidents of physical violence on both French- and English-language networks (Paquette & de Guise, 2002).

TV Violence

From its very first commercial appearance in the late 1940s, television, more than any other medium, has been accused of contributing to cultural and political decadence. Television has been viewed as a sort of 'fake magic mirror on the wall forever distracting, and tantalizing, and consequently barbarizing its viewers' (Bratlinger, 1983, p. 252). In its comparatively short history, there have consistently been proposals before governing bodies for television reform and for a reduction in the amount of violence shown, especially to children.

In 1994, the Federation of Women Teachers' Associations of Ontario passed a resolution calling for federal and provincial governments to limit the access of minors to all forms of violence in the media. The Federation singled out television, video games, and music videos as media that glamorize violence. This resolution echoes a policy unveiled by the Ontario Ministry of Education two months earlier to develop anti-violence measures in schools. Educators in Ontario, it appears, were firmly convinced that the blame for violence among young people could be attributed, in large part, to the violence they were watching on television.

When faced with inexplicable acts of violence, commentators frequently point to 'media influence' as part of the explanation. The aforementioned Federation of Women Teachers and a number of other concerned citizens would most likely agree with the sentiments expressed by reporter Martin Kettle in an article published in the *Guardian Weekly* (14 March 1993):

> For years, we have had to listen to the pretentious, ambitious, amoral and above all, cynical cultural hustlers trying to bully us into thinking that the violence and hatred in the heart of modern mass popular culture is something we should admire, even if or even because we don't sympathize with it. Those of us who . . . are ashamed of *The Terminator*, are humiliated by the degenerate, inhuman rubbish of the martial arts movies, who don't find the endless blowing up and mutilation of human beings amusing, trendy, or streetwise, and who want to turn away from all of the baseness that they represent and protect our children's innocent minds, have been mocked mercilessly and opportunistically with any

weapon of abuse that came to hand—as hippies, oldies, lefties, righties, racists, or elitist. Well, who cares what we are, except that we are people? All I know is that these days we're fighting back. . . . Hasta la vista, you bastards. (Kettle, 1993)

Examples of children and youths engaging in unspeakable acts of aggression and violence abound. In Liverpool, England, in February 1993, a two-year old boy, James Bulger, was kidnapped and murdered by two 10-year-old boys. On 20 April 1999, two teenaged boys, Eric Harris and Dylan Klebold, wearing black trench coats and armed with semi-automatic handguns, shotguns, and explosives, walked into Columbine High School in Littleton, Colorado, and killed 12 students, one teacher, and then themselves. Ten days later, a 14-year old Canadian boy shot and killed one student and seriously injured another in a high school in Taber, Alberta.

In his summation of the trial of James Bulger's murderers, Justice Morland suggested that 'exposure to violent videos' could have been partly to blame for the crime. The British press then seized on Justice Morland's comments, claiming that a video rented by the father of one of the killers—*Child's Play 3*—showed 'chilling links' to the murder carried out by the boys. But there was no evidence at all that the boys had seen the video. Although police denied any connection between the video and the murder, the comments of Justice Morland and their subsequent embellishment in the tabloids went a long way to stirring public concerns about onscreen violence, culminating in a proposal for legislation to restrict the availability of videos for home use (Boyle, 2005, pp. 2–7).

The American Psychiatric Association, the Canadian Psychological Association, the American Medical Association, the American Academy of Pediatrics, the American Psychological Association, and the American Academy of Child and Adolescent Psychiatry issued a joint statement stating that it has been proven that media violence causes aggression and probably causes crime. The *Senate Judiciary Committee Staff Report, 1999,* went even further, claiming that television alone is responsible for 10 per cent of youth violence. Yet, as sociologist Jonathan Freedman has pointed out:

> . . . it is almost certain that not one of these organizations conducted a thorough review of the research. They have surely not published or made available any such review. If they made these pronouncements without a scientific review, they are guilty of the worst kind of irresponsible behaviour. If they were in court as expert witnesses, they could be convicted of perjury. It is incredible that these organizations, which purport to be scientific, should act in this manner. (Freedman, 2002, p. 9)

A great deal of controversy remains over the relationship between television viewing and violent or aggressive behaviour. In the next section we will survey some of the research from both sides of the debate.

Onscreen Violence: Seven 'Research Strands' and Inclusive Results

Over 50 years' worth of research on the effects of onscreen violence on children's behaviour has produced two lines of inquiry:

- Does viewing violence onscreen cause children to behave aggressively? That is, does it cause children to imitate the violence or aggression that they see depicted onscreen?
- Does viewing onscreen violence sensitize or desensitize children to violence in real life?

A man reads a memorial to the victims of shootings at Montreal's Dawson College in September 2006. The sign is an apparent response to a comment made by the shooter in his profile on vampirefreaks.com, a website devoted to Goth culture, in which he wrote: 'Life is like a video game, you gotta die sometime' ('Montreal gunman', 2006).

The issue of the effects of media violence on viewer behaviour is hotly contested in social science circles. On the one hand, Huesmann and colleagues (2003) contend that 50 years' worth of evidence shows that there is a link between exposure to media violence and aggressive behaviour. Children who view violent TV programming identify with aggressive TV characters of the same sex. Their perception that television violence is realistic can be linked to aggressive behaviour in later years for both males and females. Freedman (2002), however, asserts that no scientific evidence exists to show that watching TV violence results either in violent behaviour or in a desensitization to violent behaviour.

The Media Awareness Network (MNet) describes itself on its website as 'a Canadian non-profit organization that has been pioneering the development of media literacy and digital literacy programs since its incorporation in 1996'. MNet focuses its efforts on 'equipping adults with information and tools to help young people understand how the media work, how the media may affect their lifestyle choices, and the extent to which they, as consumers and citizens, are being well informed' (MNet, 2010). MNet makes numerous resources publically available on its website (www.media-awareness.ca) and has identified seven 'research strands' on the relationship between violence viewed onscreen and real-world violence and aggression. These seven strands will frame the discussion that follows.

1. Children Who Consume High Levels of Media Violence Are More Likely to Be Aggressive in the Real World

As early as 1956, researchers began comparing the behaviour of children who watched violent programming with those who watched non-violent programming. In 1961, Canadian psychologist Albert Bandura, with colleagues Dorothea Ross and Sheila Ross, studied the effects of exposure to real-world violence, cartoon violence, and television violence on 100 preschool children who had been divided into four groups. The first group 'watched a real person shout insults at an implacable doll while hitting it with a mallet. The second group watched the incident on television. The third group watched a cartoon version of the same scene, and the fourth watched nothing' (Bandura, Ross, & Ross, 1961). All 100 children were then exposed to a frustrating situation. The researchers found that the children in the first three groups responded with more aggression than did the children in the control group. The children who watched a real person use a mallet on a doll, whether on TV or in real life, were more aggressive than those who watched a cartoon. Other laboratory experiments have consistently shown that exposure to violence, whether directly or onscreen, results in increased heart rate, blood pressure, and respiration rate in the laboratory situation.

In a review of literature on children, TV viewing, and aggressive behaviour, Comstock and Strasburger (1990) found that the majority of studies correlate TV viewing with aggressive behaviour. They reviewed a number of studies that used many different research methods—including laboratory experiments, field studies, and longitudinal studies—and concluded that, regardless of the method used, all studies seemed to support the conclusion that television makes a small but significant contribution to violent behaviour in children. But Comstock and Strasburger also found that the effects of TV viewing on aggressive behaviour in children could be reversed if parents and teachers stressed their disapproval of the violence depicted. School-based programs about how to view television critically also helped mitigate the effects of violence.

Rideout, Vandewater, and Wartella (2003) conducted 'a nationally representative random-digit-dial telephone survey' of over a thousand parents of children between 6 months and 6 years of age 'to determine the role of media in the lives of infants, toddlers, and preschoolers in America' (Rideout, Vandewater, & Wartella, 2003, p. 2). Their results, summarized in Table 18.4, include some interesting findings about parents' observations regarding the way their children imitate behaviour from TV. It is interesting to note that parents reported observing their children, across all age categories and both sexes, imitating positive behaviour such as sharing or helping more frequently than negative behaviour such as hitting or kicking.

Other results of the survey, summarized by Rideout, Vandewater, and Wartella, include the following:

- Children six and under spend an average of two hours a day with screen media, mostly TV and videos.
- TV watching begins at a very early age, well before the medical community recommends.
- A high proportion of very young children are using new digital media, including 50% of four- to six-year-olds who have played video games and 70% who have used computers.
- Two out of three zero- to six-year-olds live in homes where the TV is usually left on at least half the time, even if no one is watching, and one-third live in homes where the TV is on 'almost all' or 'most' of the time; and children in the latter group of homes appear to read less than other children and to be slower to learn to read.
- Many parents see media as an important educational tool, beneficial to their children's intellectual development, and parents' attitudes on this issue appear to be related to the amount of time their children spend using each medium.

TABLE 18.4 Percentage of children aged 0–6 whose parents see them imitate behaviour from TV

	Total	Boys	Girls
Aged 0–6			
Positive behaviour (e.g. sharing, helping)	78%	76%	80%
Aggressive behaviour (e.g. hitting, kicking)	36%	45%	28%
Neither	18%	20%	16%
Aged 0–3			
Positive behaviour (e.g. sharing, helping)	70%	68%	72%
Aggressive behaviour (e.g. hitting, kicking)	27%	32%	21%
Neither	26%	29%	23%
Aged 4–6			
Positive behaviour (e.g. sharing, helping)	87%	84%	89%
Aggressive behaviour (e.g. hitting, kicking)	47%	59%	35%
Neither	9%	9%	9%

Source: Rideout et al., 2003:16.

- Parents clearly perceive that their children's TV watching has a direct effect on their behavior, and are more likely to see positive rather than negative behaviors being copied. (Rideout, Vandewater, & Wartella, 2003, p. 12)

2. Children Who Watch High Levels of Media Violence Are at Increased Risk of Aggressive Behaviour as Adults

Eron (1963) studied 856 Grade 3 students living in a semi-rural area in New York State, and found that children who watched violent television at home behaved more aggressively at school. In a follow-up study done when these children were 19 years of age, Eron found that boys who had watched violent television when they were 8 were more likely to get in trouble with the law as teenagers. And, in a further follow-up study done when the subjects were 30 years of age, Eron and Huesmann (1986) reported that those who had watched violent television when they were 8 years old were more likely as adults to be convicted of serious crimes, to use violence to discipline their own children, and to treat their spouses aggressively.

There's a large market in educational videos specifically designed for infants. Their popularity would suggest that parents see a link between what babies watch and what they learn. Do you think parents are more disposed to seeing the benefits of television than to seeing its potential harms? Is it possible that parents' reporting in the study by Rideout, Vandewater, and Wartella was not reliable?

In 2002 Jeffrey Johnson and his colleagues reported on a 17-year interval study of the relationship between television viewing and aggressive behaviour. Their study was conducted in an upstate New York community and included a sample of 707 individuals. Johnson and his colleagues reported

> . . . a significant association between the amount of time spent watching television during adolescence and early adulthood and the likelihood of subsequent aggressive acts against others. This association remained significant after previous aggressive behavior, childhood neglect, family income, neighborhood violence, parental education, and psychiatric disorders were controlled statistically. (Johnson, et al., 2002)

Similarily Huessman's (1986) study of 875 boys living in a semi-rural US county found that the boys' television viewing at age 8 significantly predicted the seriousness of crimes for which they were convicted by age 30.

3. The Introduction of Television into a Community Leads to an Increase in Violent Behaviour

Some researchers have studied the links between media violence and real-life violence and aggression by examining communities before and after the introduction of television. In the 1970s, Tannis MacBeth Williams studied a remote village in British Columbia before and after television was introduced. Williams found violent incidences increased by 60 per cent following the arrival of television. Granzberg and Steinbring (1980) studied three Cree communities in northern Manitoba during the 1970s and found that after the introduction of television, the incidence of aggression and violence among children increased. Centerwall (1989) noted a sharp increase in murder rate in North America in 1955, 8 years after television sets were introduced, and a similar occurrence in South Africa 12 years after the ban on television was lifted in 1975. Joy and colleagues (1986) studied the impact of television on a small Canadian community they called 'Notel'. Because of reception problems, this community did not get television until 1973. Joy's team used two similar communities that already had television as control groups and observed a cohort of 45 first- and second-grade students over a period of two years for incidents of physical aggression. While the rates of physical aggression among the children of the two control groups did not change during the two-year period, the rates of physical aggression among the children of 'Notel' increased by 160 per cent.

While these studies suggest a strong relationship between viewing TV violence and an increase in antisocial behaviour, other studies have failed to demonstrate anything but the weakest relationship. A survey by Steven Messner (1986) of the relationship between exposure to TV violence and the rate of violent crime reported in the *United States FBI Uniform Crime Reports* (1982) failed to confirm the author's hypothesis that populations with higher exposure to television violence would be more likely to display criminal violence. What Messner found, instead, was that high exposure to television violence was consistently related to *lower* levels of reported criminal violence in the populations under study. Likewise, Canadian psychologist Jonathan Freedman (1992) has also pointed out that while violent imagery on Japanese television is more intense, Japan has lower murder rates than both Canada and the United States—two countries with comparatively less violence on television. Freedman has shown that the effects of viewing television violence are short-lived and rarely transferred into the television viewers' everyday social behaviour.

4. Media Violence Stimulates Fear in Some Children

Singer, Slovak, Frierson, and York (1998) surveyed 2,000 Ohio students in Grades 3 through 8 and reported that anxiety, depression, and post-traumatic stress increase with the number of hours of television watched each day. Owens et al (1999) surveyed 500 Rhode Island parents to find that the presence of a television set in a child's bedroom makes it more likely that the child will suffer sleep disturbances. Of the parents surveyed, 9 per cent reported that at least once a week their children had nightmares, which they attributed to watching a specific television show. Cantor and Harrison (1996) studied 138 university students and found that over 90 per cent of them continued to experience fright effects from images they had viewed as children.

5. Media Violence Desensitizes People to Real Violence

Cline, Croft, and Courrier (1973) reported that boys who watch more than 25 hours of television a week are less likely to be concerned by real-world violence than those who watched four hours or less per week. Molitor and Hirsch (1994) confirmed these findings.

Anderson, Carnagey, and Eubanks (2003) ran five experiments examining the effects of songs with violent lyrics on research subjects' thoughts and feelings of aggression and hostility. Based on the responses from 500 college students, their experiments demonstrated that college students 'who heard a violent song felt more hostile than those who heard a similar but non-violent song'. Those who listened to violent lyrics also experienced an increase in aggressive thoughts. The authors speculated that exposure to violent lyrics 'inspired increases in aggressive thoughts and feelings' that, in turn, could 'influence perceptions of ongoing social interactions, coloring them with an aggressive tint', which could then instigate 'a more aggressive response (verbal or physical)' than otherwise would have occurred. All of this, they further speculate, could provoke an 'aggressive escalatory spiral of antisocial exchanges' by increasing aggression in the person's social environment. Individuals close to the person who has listened to violent lyrics (and who is, as a result, feeling and acting more aggressively) will usually respond to that person's aggressive behaviour with aggression of their own. Over time, relationships deteriorate as acquaintances begin to expect aggressive and conflict-ridden interactions (Anderson, Carnagey, & Eubanks, 2003, p. 969). The researchers do note, however, that the hostile thoughts and behaviour, primed by violent songs, may last for only a short time and that listening to non-violent songs may have the effect of dissipating the more aggressive and violent behaviours and feelings elicited by listening to violence.

6. People Who Watch a Lot of Media Violence Tend to Believe that the World Is More Dangerous than It Is in Reality

George Gerbner (1995), in a long-running study of television violence, found that regular TV viewers' perceptions of the world tend to conform to the depictions they see on television. These viewers are more passive, anxious, and fearful than those who view less TV. Those who view greater amounts of television tend to overestimate their risk of being victimized, or feel their neighbourhoods are unsafe. They are also more likely to assume the crime rate is increasing, even when it is not. Gerber calls this the 'mean world syndrome'. Gosselin, de Guise, and Paquette (1997) surveyed 360 university students and found that those who view the most television also believe the world is a more dangerous place. However, contrary to Gerbner's findings, Gosselin and colleagues did not find that heavy viewers were more likely to feel more fearful than those who watched less television.

7. Family Attitudes to Violent Content Are More Important than the Images Themselves

There are a number studies that strongly suggest the media is only one among a number of factors putting children at risk for aggressive behaviour. Research by Huesmann and Bacharach (1988) indicated that parental attitudes towards media violence affect the impact that violence has on their children: 'Family attitudes and social class', they report, 'are stronger determinants of attitudes towards aggression than the amount of exposure to TV' (Huesmann & Bacharach, 1988). In 1992 Andrea Martinez submitted a study to the Canadian Radio-Television and Telecommunications Commission (CRTC) entitled 'Scientific Knowledge about Television Violence'. Martinez began by noting that 'defining the phenomenon of television violence is not an easy task', and identified certain 'grey areas' with respect to research into television violence that have fuelled debate, including:

- methodological problems associated with the instruments used in measuring violence
- different interpretations of the results, centring on the nature and intensity of the link between television violence and aggression for antisocial behaviour
- the significance of the connection between television violence and real-world violence. If, in fact, television violence has negative consequences for behaviour, are those consequences short- or long-term? What is the exact nature of the impact that viewing violence might have on the individual and society? (Martinez, 1992)

For her part, Martinez concluded that 'although television violence is not solely responsible for aggressive tendencies in antisocial behaviour (suicides, homicides, other crimes and distorted perceptions), it is among the risk factors involved' (Martinez, 1992). She found a weak positive relationship between 'exposure to television violence and aggressive behaviour' but also found that 'this bidirectional relation cannot be confirmed systematically in all cultures or even in one particular culture.'

Finally, University of Toronto sociologist Jonathan Freedman (2002) argues that methodological problems with the existing literature limit the validity of findings. Freedman notes that there is no scientific evidence to support the claim that watching onscreen violence either produces violent behaviour in the viewer or desensitizes him to violence. Freedman reviewed the results of 87 laboratory experiments that provided a test of the causal hypothesis 'children who watch more violent programs are more aggressive than those who watch fewer'. He concluded that 'the true correlation between exposure to violent media and aggression is positive for children up to about age ten,' although the evidence is both 'weak and inconsistent' (Freedman, 2002, p. 43). Of the 87 experiments he reviewed, 37 per cent supported the causal hypothesis, 41 per cent did not support the hypothesis, and 22 per cent showed mixed results (that is, some of the results of the study under review supported the hypothesis, while other results were non-supportive). Freedman suggests that we look to societal sources other than TV violence to explain growing rates of violence and crime:

> We have to remember that the availability of television in the United States and Canada coincided with vast changes in our societies. Between 1960 and 1985, the period of the increase in crime, the rate of divorce more than doubled, there were many more single parents and women who worked outside of the home, the use of illegal drugs increased, the gap between rich and poor grew, and

because of the post-war baby boom, there was a sharp increase in the number of young males. Almost all of the experts, including police, criminologists, and sociologists agree that these factors played a crucial role in the increase in crime and no one seriously blames television for these changes in society. It is an accident, a coincidence, that television ownership increased during this same period. These important social changes are certainly some of the causes of the increase in crime—television ownership may be irrelevant. (Freedman, 2002, p. 56)

Canadian Children's Views About Onscreen Violence

In a study of 5,700 Canadian school children, aged 8 to 15 years, George Spears and Kasia Sydegart (2004) examined kids' own views about onscreen violence. They asked the children questions such as:

- Do you see 'violence as an attractive element of entertainment'?
- Do you see 'others imitate violent acts seen in the media'?
- Do you think that 'violence in the media contributes to violence in schools and communities'? (Spears & Sydegart, 2004)

Their survey, administered by teachers, asked school-aged kids to list and rate their favourite television programs according to a list of 10 pre-selected characteristics. Both boys and girls

STUDIES IN SOCIAL RESEARCH

Thelma McCormick: Children's Culture and Onscreen Violence

If we want to understand the relationship between onscreen violence and real-world violence we should be paying attention to children's popular culture. This is the advice of Canadian sociologist Thelma McCormick, who notes that children do not live in isolation. First of all, 'they belong to groups, and second, they share in symbolic culture and language, games, sports, secret passwords, songs, music, rhymes, books, jokes, stories, comic books, slang, codes and private signals, board games, Disney films, ponds and a whole underground of fart jokes, scatological stories and verses' (McCormick, 1993, p. 26). Television, McCormick insists, is only a small part of the larger cultural matrix in which children live. If we only talk about violence on television that children watch and somehow absorbed, we miss what McCormick describes as 'a series of filters between the child and the screen'.

We know that television viewing is a regular part of the activities of most children. But generally they do not watch television alone; they watch with siblings, friends, and adults. By the time children are five, they also understand that television is make-believe. By the time they are seven, they prefer adult programs to those constructed specifically for children. Preschool children enjoy cartoon programs, which are usually very violent. Older children, however, like 'adult violence' but still prefer watching comedy.

What is clear, McCormick insists, is that children do not passively absorb what adults believe to be the 'message' of what they are watching. Moreover, the level of cognitive development attained by the child seems to determine what the child sees and how he or she understands what is being seen (McCormick, 1993, p. 22). McCormick concludes that most studies of the effects of onscreen aggression on children are 'superficial, misleading and adult-centered'. And she insists that such studies 'should not ever, by themselves, be the basis of social policy' (p. 32).

rated their favourite TV programs as 'exciting' and 'funny'. They chose the characteristic 'it has lots of violence' as the last rank in the list of 10 attributes. The attribute 'it has lots of violence' was also the lowest-ranking attribute for video games chosen by girls and near the middle of the set chosen by boys. Among boys, the top 20-ranked games included five 'M'-rated titles (Mature, suitable for persons ages 17 and older), including 'Grand Theft Auto', 'Vice City Counter Strike', 'Halo', 'Medal of Honour', and 'Splinter Cell'. While few girls listed any 'M'-rated games among their favourites, 50 per cent of the boys in grades 8 to 10 included at least one 'M'-rated game as a favourite. However, for these boys, excitement and competition were the primary appeals for choosing 'M'-rated games, while violence was not a strong attraction.

Grade 7–10 students were asked 'if they had ever witnessed someone imitate a violent act that they had learned from a movie or TV show, and if so, whether the act had resulted in injury'. Fifty-one per cent of the respondents said they had, in fact, witnessed such an act. When further questioned, two-thirds of the respondents reported that no one was hurt, while one-third reported that some kind of injury had occurred either to the person who acted violently (12 per cent), to someone else (17 per cent), or to both (5 per cent).

Other findings of Spears and Sydegart's study including the following:

- Forty-eight per cent of Canadian kids aged 8–15 have their own televisions. Twenty-six per cent have their own computer hooked up to the Internet, and by the time they reach Grade 10, 22 per cent have their own cellphones.
- Fifty-one per cent of kids in grades 7 to 10 have witnessed imitation of some violent act (including a dangerous stunt) from a movie or TV show.
- Girls' favourite shows, films, and video and computer games are low in violence. Their media choices tend to be the ones their parents also like.
- A large number of kids say they've experienced no parental guidance on which videos or TV programs they can watch, which video or computer games they can play, or for how long.
- Parents, through supervision and discussion, play a critical role in making their children more aware of the negative impact of media violence. Left to their own devices, kids will tend to regard media violence as benign.
- Kids' top-rated show—*The Simpsons*—is also the program parents think younger children shouldn't be watching.
- Younger children (grades 5 and under) are the ones most frightened by the news, feeling that their personal safety is at risk.
- Lots of kids, though they don't like the news, watch it anyhow and agree that it makes them better informed.
- Frequent news watchers feel more worried about the world but also more motivated to change society for the better.
- One of the top choices of video games for both anglophone and francophone boys in grades 3–6 is 'Grand Theft Auto', an ultra-violent action game aimed at mature audiences, which involves murder, bludgeoning, and prostitution.
- Younger kids are the most frequent video and computer game players. Sixty per cent of boys in grades 3–6 play video or computer games every day. In Grade 10, more than 30 per cent of boys still make this a daily activity.
- Parents supervise children's video and computer games far less than the television shows they watch. Parents' knowledge of the content of the games their children are playing is either very superficial or non-existent.

It appears from Spears and Sydegart's research that empirical evidence linking onscreen violence and real-world aggression in either children or adults is, at best, inconclusive. The direct effects of viewing onscreen violence on real-world behaviour appear to be either very low or nonexistent; moreover,

> the role of kids' emotional response to violent programs and movies is not clear. Those who experience fear when they see violent programs or movies tend to see media violence as having a negative impact on society, but those who say they feel pumped or excited by media violence do not. (Spears & Sydegart, 2004)

Family discussions about social issues presented in the media are important in helping children recognize the potential harm of media violence. Figure 18.1 shows that kids are evenly divided in their opinions about the impact of media violence on violence in schools and communities. Slightly more than half (51 per cent) agreed that there is too much violence in movies and on TV. Over half (53 per cent) reported that they discussed what they watched on TV with other members of their family, and 71 per cent thought that there was too much violence in hockey games on TV.

Some would argue that violent, life-like video games serve a positive social function by providing an outlet for the aggression that young people, especially boys, naturally feel. Do you agree?

Position Statements	Agree	Disagree	Undecided
Violence in media contributes to violence in schools and communities	35	35	33
There is too much violence in movies and on TV	51	28	21
My family often discusses what we watch on TV	53	30	17
There is too much violence in hockey games on TV	71	16	13

FIGURE 18.1 Response to position statements concerning media violence among children in grades 7–10
Source: Spears & Sydegart, 2004.

SUMMARY

The opinion of social scientists about the strength of the connection between viewing media violence and real-life aggression and violence in children (and adults) is mixed. What researchers do agree on, however, is that there has been a change in the nature and pervasiveness of media violence. Violence in traditional media is becoming more explicit, and at the same time children are now exposed to more violence via the digital and online games they play, the music they listen to, and the websites they visit. Much of this exposure 'occurs off the parental radar screen' (MediaPulse, 2003, p. 8). It is to the world of the Internet, social media, and mobile communications that we turn next, in the penultimate chapter of this book.

DISCUSSION QUESTIONS

1. How do mass media affect our social lives and behaviours?
2. What role do mass media play in the construction of popular culture?
3. How do popular cultural meanings get relayed to, interpreted by, and used by individuals?
4. What is the relationship between popular culture, mass culture, and mass media?
5. Analyze a favourite television series for the values, beliefs, and morality it reflects. To what extent do you share that morality? Do the same for a number of rock or pop videos by different recording artists.
6. Do mass media exert an unwarranted influence over the lives of Canadians? Explain.
7. Is there any relationship between viewing violence onscreen and violence in real life? Justify your answer.
8. Should children's viewing of onscreen violence be strictly controlled? Explain your answer.

19 The Internet, Social Media, and Mobile Communications

LEARNING OBJECTIVES

In this chapter you will:

- differentiate between the Internet and social media
- become aware of how social media allow people to gather and share information
- gain a clearer understanding of the implications of social media for social interaction, social networking, and community
- reflect on the changing demographics of the users of social networking sites
- understand more about the relationship between race, social class, and the use of social media
- study the role of the Internet in facilitating the creation of social capital
- distinguish between 'mediated' and 'co-present' social interaction rituals
- learn about 'peep culture', 'oversharing', and 'the sousveillance society'.

INTRODUCTION

Before widespread literacy, information was communicated from person to person through conversations, storytelling, or announcements made by designated individuals, such as the town crier. With the advent of the printing press in the mid-fifteenth century and the growth of reading and literacy rates, news could be nailed to a post (hence, the 'Daily Post' and 'Post Office') or distributed via books, newspapers, journals, and other forms of print.

All of this has changed with the digital revolution. Today vast quantities of information are produced daily, and a myriad of tools for accessing this information is now available to any individual. How much information is available? According to a 2003 study,

> . . . print, film, magnetic, and optical storage media produced about 5 exabytes of new information in 2002. Ninety-two per cent of the new information was stored on magnetic media, mostly in hard disks. *How big is five exabytes?* If digitized, the nineteen million books and other print collections in the Library of Congress would contain about ten terabytes of information; five exabytes of information is equivalent in size to the information contained in half a million new libraries the size of the Library of Congress print collections. (Lyman & Varian, 2003)

That was nine years ago. Since 2003, the situation has only gotten worse (or better, depending on your point of view). EMC Corporation measures and forecasts the vast amounts and diverse types of digital information created and copied annually. Calculated to be 487 billion gigabytes in size, the amount of information created in 2008 is equivalent to more than each of the following:

- 237 billion fully loaded Amazon Kindle wireless reading devices
- 4.8 quadrillion online bank transactions
- 3 quadrillion Twitter feeds
- 162 trillion digital photos
- 30 billion fully loaded Apple iPod Touches
- 19 billion fully loaded Blu-ray discs.

Today, search engines such as Google and YouTube allow us to retrieve information whenever we need and want it, and social media help us sort through the mass of information that comes from the results of a search. For example, asking about the best new restaurant in town on Twitter is likely to produce a slew of recommendations on where to dine (or at least where to get more information) in hours, if not minutes. Just-in-time information is readily available to anyone carrying a smartphone with a Web browser. New tools for filtering and information trapping attempt to help select the most relevant information for our needs.

Sociology is a discipline very much concerned with community: how we connect with each other, form a sense of our place in the world, and develop and maintain our ties to others. The recent explosion in the use of social media has played a significant role in redefining the boundaries of community (no longer confined to close, geographical proximity), how frequently we can reach out to members of that community (now more frequently than ever, via blogs, Twitter, and Facebook), and whom we can include in our social networks (everyone from experts we follow vicariously on Twitter to our closest friends, regardless of the geographical location).

THE INTERNET AND SOCIAL MEDIA

The Internet, as defined from a sociological standpoint by Paul DiMaggio and associates in 2001, is 'the electronic network of networks that links people and information through computers and other digital devices allowing [mediated] person-to-person communication and information retrieval' (DiMaggio, et al, 2001, p. 307). It can trace its lineage back to networks dedicated to scientific and military communications in the late 1960s and early 1970s. The Internet as we know it today emerged around 1982 as an amalgamation of many different networks. But it was not until the early 1990s, when online graphical user interfaces (GUIs) became widely available, the World Wide Web was created, and commercial interests were allowed to participate, that the Internet began its rapid ascent. The launch of the World Wide Web in 1992 allowed users to find each other easily and receive multimedia files from anywhere connected to the Internet. Since that time, the amount of information available on the Web has risen exponentially, from fewer than 2,000 websites in 1995 to over 10 million in 2002 and over 243 million as of December 2009.

Social media refers primarily to the Internet and any mobile media that use accessible, scalable publishing techniques to support mediated social interactions among networked members of a 'community'. Together they form a group of Internet-based applications that allow for the creation and exchange of 'user-generated' information. Social media support 'many-to-many' communications among community members, rather than communications that are dominated by one person or one organization, as is the case in broadcast media. They are part of what is referred to as Web 2.0, although Web 2.0 is actually a broader term that encompasses other aspects of information technologies such as access to databases and distributed content. Recently, social media have been used to facilitate much of human social interaction that is not done on a face-to-face basis. Examples of social media include blogs, microblogs, wikis, podcasts, social networking sites, virtual game worlds, virtual communities, video sharing, music and audio sharing, and social bookmarking.

A study by the Kaiser Family Foundation shows that young people between the ages of 8 and 18 are, on average, spending more than 50 hours each week with digital media (Rideout, Foehr, & Roberts, 2010); Figure 19.1 provides a breakdown, by medium, of how they are spending this time. Erik Qualman (2008), meanwhile, provides the following statistics on the rapid spread of social media:

- Gen Y'ers now outnumber Baby Boomers [in the workplace] and over 96 per cent of them have joined a social network.
- Social media has overtaken porn as the #1 activity on the Web.
- Years to Reach 50 Million Users: Radio (38 years), TV (13 years), Internet (4 years), iPod (3 years) . . . Facebook added 100 million users in less than nine months . . . iPhone applications hit 1 billion in nine months.
- One in six higher education students are enrolled in online curriculum.
- Percentage of companies using LinkedIn as a primary tool to find employees: 80 per cent.
- The fastest growing segment on Facebook is 55–65-year-old females.
- Generation Y and Z consider e-mail passé . . . In 2009 Boston College stopped distributing e-mail addresses to incoming freshmen.
- What happens in Vegas stays on YouTube, Flickr, Twitter, Facebook . . .
- The second-largest search engine in the world is YouTube.
- Successful companies in social media act more like party planners, aggregators, and content providers than traditional advertisers. (Qualman, 2009)

the Internet

As defined by DiMaggio, et al. (2001), 'the electronic network of networks that links people and information through computers and other digital devices allowing [mediated] person-to-person communication and information retrieval' (p. 307).

social media

The Internet and mobile media that use accessible, scalable publishing techniques to support mediated social interactions among networked members of a 'community', including blogs, wikis, podcasts, social networking sites, virtual game worlds, video sharing, and social bookmarking.

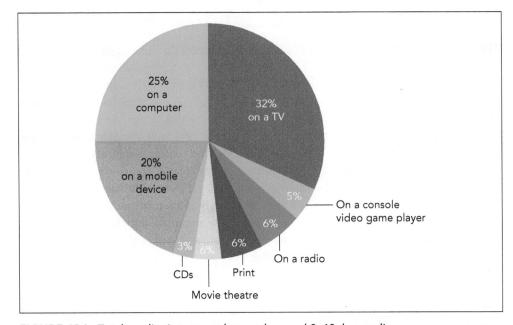

FIGURE 19.1   Total media time spent by youths aged 8–18, by medium

Source: Rideout, Foehr, & Roberts, 2010.

An Ipso Reid survey conducted in March 2010 found that, overall, Canadians' weekly Internet usage—more than 18 hours per week—exceeds television viewing (16.9 hours/week). Internet usage in 2010 was up from 14.9 hours weekly in the previous year, and television viewing was up from 15.8 hours, while the use of other media such as radio, newspapers, and magazines remained stable. The poll found that males spent significantly more time online than females (an average of 20 hours per week compared to 16 hours) and that 18- to 34-year-olds spent an average of 20 hours per week online compared to 18 hours for those 35 and older (Ipsos, 2010).

One big question is whether social media are leading us to become more individualized (a view put forward by Beck & Beck-Gernsheim, 2002; Bugeja, 2005; McPherson, Brasheras, & Smith-Lovin, 2006) or whether they support new forms of social interaction and cohesion (as argued by Boase, et al., 2006; Katz & Rice, 2002; Ling, 2008; MacIntosh & Harwood, 2002). When computer-based technologies were first introduced, many believed they would promote individualizing activities that had the potential to take time away from social interactions with family, friends, and community. However, few social scientists today think that the use of computer-based information technologies necessarily leads to individualism at the expense of social involvement. A study by Veenhof and associates (2005) showed that many Canadians use the Internet 'not to escape social contact or other traditional activities but to enhance them'. For example, in 2005 about 20 per cent of all volunteers in Canada used the Internet to carry out their activities. This is one example of how digital communication technologies create opportunities for social interaction where there previously were none. As Veenhoff and colleagues explain:

> Particularly in Canada, long, cold winters encourage Canadians to stay home and watch television, listen to the radio and read. Thus the advent of the Internet is breeding a more social era, with active communication and information seeking activities compared to the more passive traditional forms of entertainment such as television. (Veenhoff, et al., 2005, p. 23)

How would you describe your own use of social media? Is your time spent online more individualized or does technology actually allow you to be more social than you might be without it?

In a similar vein, Jenkins and associates (2006) developed the concept of 'participatory culture' to speak about opportunities that computer-based technologies afford people, allowing them to participate in social interactions otherwise not available to them, and to develop new 'cultural competencies and social skills' (Jenkins, et al., 2006, p. 4). A research team led by Mizuko Ito (2008) argues that young people today try to establish autonomy and identity through their use of online spaces, where they deal with social norms, explore their interests, develop skills, and experiment with new forms of expression.

Gathering and Sharing Information: Creating Collective Intelligence

Social media have allowed people around the globe to gather their own information and share it with others. This has resulted in a revolutionary and unprecedented reality in which social media facilitate collaboration among partners at geographically distant points all over the world. When this collaboration results in increased knowledge that is accessible to others, the amount of 'collective intelligence' in an organization—or in the world in general—rises dramatically. Even at the turn of the twenty-first century, events organized on the fly, such as the Occupy Wall Street protest movement, which spread to cities around the world during the fall of 2011, or the spontaneous mass gathering of crowds during the pro-democracy movements of the 'Arab Spring' that began late in 2010, would have been difficult if not impossible to organize without the widespread availability of personal mobile communication devices. Up until the turn of this century, the main media of mass communication—newspapers and magazines, radio and television broadcasts—were uni-directional, flowing from publisher or broadcaster to the consumer. The means of information production, to use a Marxist analogy, were in the hands of the few. Today, the advent of mobile communication devices such as cellphones and tablets, combined with social networking sites like Facebook, Twitter, and YouTube, have allowed information to be generated and widely disseminated by anyone with an Internet connection or a smartphone. What is more, anyone with the same technology can add or reply to that information in a way that simply was not possible—certainly not so easily—even twenty years ago.

Small contributions by many individuals can often create a major increase in the store of the world's knowledge. The Internet itself is a phenomenon that was created in a relatively few years by many people building and populating pages with information without any central direction or planning. Similarly, Wikipedia is an example of a major artifact that is crowd-sourced—created by the world's people as a storage space for knowledge. And it's reliable. Wikipedia's early critics denounced it as a tool susceptible to manipulation, bias, propaganda, and misinformation. Yet the speed at which hacked entries, hoaxes, and errors have been corrected testifies to the amount of traffic visiting the website and constantly vetting its accuracy.

Online contributors—from professional journalists to on-the-scene witnesses, and from experts and specialists to dilettantes—share their 'tagged' information with others and thereby add to the storehouse of knowledge available to all. For example, when people in a small village report an outbreak of a particular illness, the multiple reports allow officials and concerned parties outside the village to monitor and track the spread of the disease before it reaches an epidemic. Applications that support 'citizen science' and other forms of 'crowd sourcing' are other examples of data collection that benefits all.

Social media have turned a growing number of us into field researchers, who can report on the details of life that we see around us. Often when we do this we are only acting in our own self-interest, but the accumulated efforts of millions of people results in the astonishing growth of digital information documented above. Social media have facilitated the growth of 'user-generated information' on an unprecedented scale.

Games, Simulations, and Virtual Worlds

Online games, simulations, and virtual worlds are all forms of social media when they involve more than one person. Games designed for learning (also known as 'serious games') represent one of the hottest areas of emerging e-learning technologies. Online gaming and role-playing games took in more than $3 billion in 2007. Major learning management platforms have added simulation or gaming extensions that allow them to launch games and track players' results. Educational games and simulations now appear on smartphones, and traditional educational publishers have announced gaming initiatives in higher education and corporate training markets.

The argument that new media are essential to attracting and retaining young workers is reinforced by the claim that games and other social media help add interest while teaching subjects that are boring to most people, such as compliance training and statistics. Beedle (2004) says that 'playing online games can teach social skills as well as strategy, coordination, multi-tasking and problem-solving,' and that 'many games draw heavily upon important "21st-century skills" such as problem-solving, collaboration, communication, and planning.' For these reasons, there are those who believe that the new generation of employees, brought up in this era of online multiplayer games, will eventually make great leaders.

One psychological benefit to online educational games and simulations is that they help players (or trainees) avoid the embarrassment of social mistakes made in live, face-to-face situations. Games can provide a forum for 'safe failure'. Waller (2006) gives an example:

> Take, for example, diversity training in which you are being personally accused of racism by a person staring right at you out of the computer. What do you say, what do you do? In a live situation, many people would find this desperately uncomfortable, and even among colleagues at a training course the learner may be too nervous to learn effectively. Serious games often create an avatar, which could be of your own design. In the game you could be older or younger and even of the opposite sex if you so wish. Many of the situations where live role play is problematic would be removed, and, instead, we may be seeing a new way of learning difficult subjects. (Waller, 2006)

SOCIAL NETWORKING

Social networking sites (SNSs) are among the most frequented online destinations, and their popularity has been accompanied by a fair amount of coverage in the popular press (Hargitarri, 2007). Since 2009, Canadians without a profile on an online social network site have found themselves in the minority (Ipsos, 2009). Sites such as LinkedIn.com are oriented towards work-related connections. Popular dating sites such as eHarmony.com, PlentyofFish.com, and LavaLife.com focus on finding a romantic connection. AshleyMadison.com is a site intended for married people who are looking for a 'discreet' affair. Social networking sites such as MySpace and Facebook in North America, Orkut in Brazil, Mixi in Japan, and Stayfriends, Wer-kent-wen, and StudiVZ in Germany all allow users to establish and maintain connections with people they already know and who share similar interests. Sites such as Twitter allow people to connect without ever actually making direct contact or getting to know each other, except in a superficial way. For example, a member of the Twitter community can post tweets that are potentially read by thousands, yet not interact individually with any specific reader. That said, social networking sites offer users new opportunities to connect (albeit superficially) with a wide range of people they might otherwise never meet.

social networking

The activity of building and maintaining networks of connections with friends and others who share common interests and activities via special networking websites.

social networking sites (SNSs)

Websites that allow people to build online social networks through online profiles, blogs, and other shared written, audio, or visual information.

Online dating sites have overcome the stigma that surrounded them initially to become a mainstream and popular way of meeting a prospective life partner. Do you think that sites offering adults the opportunity to arrange sexual relationships and extramarital affairs will follow the same path?

In 2009 social networking sites attracted almost 10 per cent of all time spent on the Internet, and about two-thirds of the world's Internet population had visited a social networking site, making these websites a significant aspect of the global online experience. As Nielsen's Charlie Buchwalter (2009) observes:

> [T]he meteoric growth in social media is the single most significant story in the online media space today. . . . Social networking sites ('Member Community' sites [which include both social networks and blogs]) eclipsed e-mail in global reach at 68.4% vs 64.8% in February 2009. And even more significant, in only the first few months of 2009, the reach of these sites is growing at a brisk pace, faster than any other online sector. (Buchwalter, 2009)

One of the most important factors driving the popularity of social networking sites is the growth in the use of mobile devices to access the Internet. In the US, for example, the mobile Internet audience grew by 74 per cent between February 2007 and February 2009. Just over 18 per cent of all mobile subscribers in the US and almost 17 per cent of Canadian subscribers had connected to the Internet via a mobile device by the end of 2008 (see Figure 19.2). Mobile access of social networking sites grew by a whopping 2,060 per cent in 2008, and as of February 2009, 12.3 million subscribers in the US had at some time accessed their social networks over a mobile phone (Nielsen, 2009, p. 13).

One huge (and growing) use of social networking sites is for making romantic connections. Burke and associates (2007) provide these statistics:

- Forty million Americans use online dating services (about 40 per cent of the population of single Americans).
- Match-seekers who post photos receive twice as many emails as those who don't.
- More than 20 million people visit at least one online dating site per month.
- More than 120,000 marriages a year occur because of online dating matches (www.onlinedatingmagazine.com/mediacenter/onlinedatingfacts.html).
- Over 200,000 people met that 'special someone' on Match.com in 2006.
- On average, 90 eHarmony members get married every day.

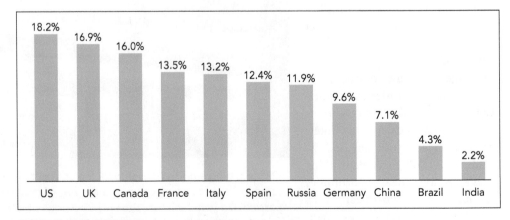

FIGURE 19.2   Mobile Internet penetration by country

Source: Nielsen Mobile. Copyrighted information of Nielsen, licensed for use herein.

- US residents spent over $500 million on online dating and personals services in 2005. (Burke, et al., 2007)

An Ipsos Reid survey conducted in 2008 reported that 16 per cent of Canadians across all age groups had found love online. That number increased to 25 per cent for Canadians between the ages of 18 and 34. Only 7 per cent of those aged 55 and older had started a relationship online ('Technology helps Canadians chase romance', 2008).

Changing Demographics of Facebook Users

Another huge use of social networking sites is to maintain contact with acquaintances, family, and friends. One social networking site that has experienced phenomenal growth is Facebook, a privately owned social networking website launched in 2004 by then Harvard University student Mark Zuckerberg. Facebook started out as a site where college students could connect with each other online. As of August 2010, Facebook had over 500 million active users, half of whom logged on to Facebook in any given day.

Although Facebook started out as a service for university students before expanding to include high school students, as of April 2010 in the US, just slightly less than 75 per cent of users were outside the 18–24 age category (see Figure 19.3). Females make up the greater share of American Facebook users (54.3 per cent versus 42.6 per cent for males; 3.03 per cent of the survey's respondents did not record their sex). Even Canadian university presidents now use Facebook as part of their efforts to be more visible and to stay connected with students, faculty, and staff.

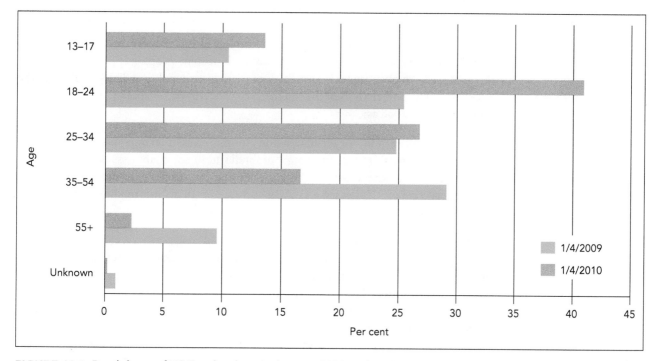

FIGURE 19.3 Breakdown of US Facebook users by age, 2009 and 2010

Source: Adapted from Facebook's Social Ads Platform.

Worldwide, more than 500 million Facebook users spent over 700 billion minutes per month on Facebook, and interacted with over 900 million 'objects' (pages, groups, events, and community pages). The 'average' Facebook user was connected to 80 community pages, groups, and events, had 130 'friends', and created 90 pieces of content each month (for updated statistics, see www.facebook.com/press/info.php?statistics). As of June 2010, 16 million Canadians (almost 48 per cent of the population) were using Facebook, making Canada the fourth-largest market on Facebook (CTV Edmonton, 2010).

Data released in July 2010 by comScore, a US Internet research firm, show that 76 per cent of all women online and 70 per cent of all men online around the world visit a social networking website on a regular basis. Women average 5.5 hours per month on this activity, compared to 3.9 hours for men. This is a significant shift from the early days of Internet use, when men accounted for the majority of time spent online. Indeed, the most prolific users of social networking sites now appear to be new mothers (aged 25–35, with one child at home). These women are 85 per cent more likely than any other demographic group to visit a social networking site, and to publish or own a blog. By comparison, older mothers in the 39–54 age group were only 23 per cent more likely than other demographic groups to post comments on a social networking site (Nielsen, 2009, p. 10).

The gender shift in Internet use can be attributed to the emergence of social networking sites with which women, more than men, are likely to engage. Social networking's reach is highest among Latin American women (94 per cent), followed by North American women (91 per cent). Just 55 per cent of Asian women visited a social networking website. Women also spend about 20 per cent more time on retail websites than men, and are actively visiting online gambling and adult content websites as well (Abraham, Mörn, & Vollman, 2010).

RACE, CLASS, AND SOCIAL MEDIA

When sociologists first started examining the subject of Internet use, they focused on the potential that inequality in Internet access would limit some people's opportunities to find jobs, gain access to government information, or participate in political dialogue. Early in the history of sociological analysis of the Internet, the concern was all about the 'digital divide', commonly understood as:

> the gap between ICT [information and communication technologies] 'haves' and 'have-nots'. [I]t serves as an umbrella term for many issues, including infrastructure and access to ICTs, use and impediments to use, and the crucial role of ICT literacy and skills to function in an information society. (Sciadas, 2002)

The digital divide and the question of unequal access to ICTs remain relevant in a global context, given that there are still parts of the world where the availability of up-to-date computer equipment and the infrastructure required to connect to the Internet are limited. In most of Western society, however, access to ICTs is widespread, if not universal. Most public schools—if not most classrooms—have computers, and in almost any North American city one can go into a public library and sit down at a terminal with access to the Internet. Questions remain, however, about how Internet use differs for North Americans of different social classes, genders, races, and ethnicities, and how their use of it continues to support and reinforce already existing distinctions and inequalities in class, race, and ethnicity.

Class Divisions on Facebook and MySpace

Ethnographer danah boyd (she spells her name without capital letters) has undertaken extensive research on social network sites, having analyzed 'over 10,000 MySpace profiles, clocked over 2,000 hours surfing and observing what happens on MySpace, and formally interviewed 116 teens in 16 states with a variety of different backgrounds and demographics' (boyd, 2007). In order to conduct her research, she has also ridden on buses to observe teen commuter behaviour, hung out at 'fast food joints in malls', and talked to 'parents, teachers, marketers, politicians, pastors, and technology creators' (boyd, 2007a).

While undertaking her research in 2007, Boyd noticed an 'interesting increase' in the number of articles in the popular press about how high school teens were leaving MySpace for Facebook. Intrigued by what the popular press was reporting as a flight of high school students from MySpace, boyd launched her own inquiry. She discovered that what the popular press had to say was only partly true.

> There is indeed a change taking place, but it's not a shift so much as a fragmentation. Until recently, American teenagers were flocking to MySpace. The picture is now being blurred. Some teens are flocking to MySpace. And some teens are flocking to Facebook. Who goes where gets kinda sticky . . . probably because it seems to primarily have to do with socio-economic class. (boyd, 2007a)

Launched in 2003, MySpace was, early on, used primarily by 20- to 30-year-olds; by late 2004, teens started arriving en masse, and by 2005 MySpace was a focal point for youth

How do you account for the fact that women spend more time on social networking sites than men do? What about the fact that new mothers are the biggest users of social networking sites? What are the social implications of these findings?

culture. Facebook, by contrast, was launched in 2004 as a Harvard-only website, and opened its doors to high school students in 2005, but only to those who were 'invited' to join by existing members. Facebook became the place to be if you wanted to go to college, especially a top college or Ivy League school. In September 2006 it was opened to anyone who wanted an account, making it relatively easy for any high school student to join.

Facebook was lauded in the popular press as a college kid 'thing', while at the same time MySpace got press coverage for being a 'dangerous' site, potentially vulnerable to the risk of sexual predators (boyd, 2007a; boyd, 2011). Concerned parents, especially the wealthier and more educated ones, didn't like what they saw on MySpace. They were especially unhappy with what they deemed to be lax moral codes of the urban 20-somethings who were typical users of MySpace. These parents feared that their children might be corrupted through exposure. They didn't see MySpace as 'safe', and they didn't want their children communicating with the kind of people who could be found there.

At the same time, teens on MySpace were having their accounts hacked as a result of security flaws, and many users were inundated with 'friend requests' from scammers. Teens (and their parents) saw these security breaches as evidence of the presence of sexual predators and other 'creepy' people. With their friend networks on MySpace already fractured by the departure of former users forced out by protective parents, and perceiving sexual predators and 'creeps' everywhere, the children of the wealthy and the educated abandoned MySpace in droves. The emergence of Facebook facilitated their mass exit, especially because parents saw Facebook as a 'safe' alternative to MySpace. MySpace was overtaken in popularity by Facebook in 2008, and laid off 30 per cent of its workforce in 2009.

In analyzing the switch from MySpace to Facebook, boyd (2007a) identified a class division—not based on income, but based on other, more subtle characteristics. Facebook, she explains, attracts kids 'from families who emphasize education and going to college'. They are 'primarily, but not exclusively white', and for the most part are honours students. These are the kids who look 'forward to the prom', and who mostly live 'in a world dictated by after-school activities'. boyd labels them 'hegemonic teens' because they 'publically uphold the values of adult society' (boyd, 2007b). MySpace, on the other hand,

> is still home for Latino/Hispanic teens, immigrant teens, 'burnouts', 'alternative kids', 'art fags', punks, emos, goths, gangstas, queer kids, and other kids who didn't play into the dominant high school popularity paradigm. These are kids whose parents didn't go to college, who are expected to get a job when they finish high school. These are the teens who plan to go into the military immediately after school. Teens who are really into music or in a band are also on MySpace. MySpace has most of the kids who are socially ostracized at school because they are geeks, freaks, or queers. (boyd, 2007a)

boyd labels these teens 'subalterns', a term chosen 'to refer to sub-culturally identified and non-hegemonic teens because their expressions are often interpreted by hegemonic mass media in a way that they are always seen as failure' (boyd, 2007b).

Consistent with Pierre Bourdieu's ideas about 'habitus' and distinctions in taste being class markers (see chapters 11 and 13), aesthetics are clearly an issue that separate the teens using Facebook from those using MySpace. boyd reports that when asked why Facebook appeals while MySpace doesn't, most teens who exclusively use Facebook declared MySpace to be 'gaudy' and immature. It was judged to be 'so middle school' and 'lame' compared to the 'clean' and 'mature' look of Facebook. But what boyd's 'hegemonic' teens called 'gaudy' was labelled by the 'subaltern' teens she interviewed as 'glitzy', 'bling' or 'fly':

> Terms like 'bling' come out of hip-hop culture where showy, sparkly, brash visual displays are acceptable and valued. The look and feel of MySpace resonates far better with subaltern communities than it does with the upwardly mobile hegemonic teens. This is even clear in the blogosphere where people talk about how gauche MySpace is while commending Facebook on its aesthetics. . . . That 'clean' or 'modern' look of Facebook is akin to West Elm or Pottery Barn or any poshy Scandinavian design house (that I admit I'm drawn to) while the more flashy look of MySpace resembles the Las Vegas imagery that attracts millions every year. (boyd 2007a)

In 2007, the US military banned MySpace but not Facebook usage. This was an interesting move, as most officers use Facebook, while most enlisted soldiers—'a group that is primarily from poorer, less educated communities'—are on MySpace (boyd, 2007a).

Racial Divisions and Social Media

Boyd (2009, 2011) talks about the migration of users from MySpace to Facebook as an example of 'white flight'. The term 'white flight' has been used elsewhere in the sociological literature on racism to describe the exodus of white people from American urban centres during the twentieth century. Many of those who left did so in order to avoid having to participate in the racial integration of communities and schools. At the same time, many black families were barred from suburban communities either directly by explicit restrictions on housing developments or indirectly by discriminatory practices around mortgages (Massey & Denton, 1993/1998). What followed was urban decay: cities were left in disrepair as they lost their tax base, while powerful street gangs emerged in the areas abandoned by people with money and other resources.

There are intriguing parallels between the 'white flight' from American urban centres to the suburbs and the present-day movement of teens from MySpace to Facebook, as boyd (2007a) observes:

> MySpace has become the 'ghetto' of the digital landscape. The people there are more likely to be brown or black and to have a set of values that terrifies white society. And many of us have habitually crossed the street to avoid what is seen as the riff-raff.
>
> The fact that digital migration is revealing the same social patterns as urban white flight should send warning signals to everyone out there. And if we think back to the language used by teens who use Facebook when talking about MySpace, we should be truly alarmed. (boyd 2007a)

The Internet, as boyd makes clear, is not just divided by class; it is also divided by race, as well as education and many other factors. And while the existence of racial divisions in American (and Canadian) societies is hardly a surprising discovery, the explicitness of such divisions online is.

These divisions were highlighted in an email boyd received after posting her blog essay on the distinction between MySpace and Facebook (boyd 2007a). Anastasia, a 17-year-old New

Yorker, let boyd know that, at least in her school, the split between users of MySpace and users of Facebook had a lot to do with social categories of class and race:

> My school is divided into the 'honors kids', (I think that is self-explanatory, the 'not-so-honors kids', 'wangstas' (they pretend to be tough and black but when you live in a suburb in Westchester you can't claim much hood), the 'latinos/ hispanics' (they tend to band together even though they could fit into any other groups) and the 'emo kids' (whose lives are alllllways filled with woe). We were all in MySpace with our own little social networks but when Facebook opened its doors to high schoolers, guess who moved and guess who's stayed behind . . . the first two groups were the first to go and then the 'wangstas' split with half of them on Facebook and the rest on MySpace . . . I shifted with the rest of my school to Facebook and it became the place where the 'honors kids' got together and discussed how they were procrastinating over the next AP [advanced placement] English essay. (Anastasia, as cited in boyd, 2007a)

The social categories identified by Anastasia reflect the racial, ethnic, and class divisions that structure day-to-day life at her high school. The movement from MySpace to Facebook further exacerbated already existing distinctions.

Other researchers have uncovered similar patterns. Eszter Hargittai's research (2007) reveals that parental education, race, and ethnicity were all significant predictors of the social networking site chosen by first-year students at a diverse midwestern American college. Blogger Chuck Lam (2007a, 2007b) showed that high school students from higher-ranked schools in the San Francisco area were more active on Facebook than were students from lower-ranked schools, who were more active on MySpace. Craig Watkins (2009) also reported on racial and ethnic divisions among college students in their preference for either MySpace or Facebook, along with prevalent anti-MySpace attitudes.

The growing divide between MySpace and Facebook users has some troubling social consequences as people become structurally divided. You can email anyone you like as long as you are both on email and you know the recipient's address—it doesn't matter who your provider or the recipient's provider is. However, a MySpace user cannot 'friend' a Facebook user. As boyd comments, there is no way to communicate across the 'cultural wall' (boyd, 2009). Why does this matter? When cliques form and people are divided, they tend to become intolerant of each other. For example, the best predictor for how someone will side on the issue of gay rights is whether or not they know someone who is gay. As patterns of MySpace and Facebook use become increasingly delineated along class and ethnic lines, there is a risk that social networking sites will reinforce our social differences and threaten social cohesion.

Here are boyd's conclusions about the intersection of social class, race, and social media:

1. Social stratification is pervasive in American society (and around the globe). Social media does not magically eradicate inequality. Rather, it mirrors what is happening in everyday life and makes social divisions visible. What we see online is not the property of these specific sites, but the pattern of adoption and development that emerged as people embraced them. People brought their biases with them to these sites and they got baked in.
2. There is no universal public online. What we see as user 'choice' in social media often has to do with structural forces like homophily in people's social networks. Social stratification in this country is not cleanly linked to race or education or

socio-economic factors, although all are certainly present. More than anything, social stratification is a social networks issue. People connect to people who think like them and they think like the people with whom they are connected. The digital publics that unfold highlight and reinforce structural divisions.

3. If you are trying to connect with the public, where you go online matters. If you choose to make Facebook your platform for civic activity, you are implicitly suggesting that a specific class of people is more worth your time and attention than others. Of course, splitting your attention can also be costly and doesn't necessarily mean that you'll be reaching everyone anyhow. You're damned if you do and damned if you don't. The key to developing a social media strategy is to understand who you're reaching and who you're not and make certain that your perspective is accounting for said choices. Understand your biases and work to counter them.

4. The Internet has enabled many new voices to enter the political fray, but not everyone is sitting at the table. There's a terrible tendency in this country, and especially among politically minded folks, to interpret advancement as a solution. We have not eradicated racism. We have not eradicated sexism. We have not eradicated inequality. While we've made tremendous strides in certain battles, the war is not over. The worst thing we can do is to walk away and congratulate ourselves for all of the good things that have happened. Such attitudes create new breeding grounds for increased stratification. (boyd, 2011)

Those who hold the utopian view that the Internet is a place where inequalities and social divisions are being eradicated should think again. Neither social media nor their users are 'colour-blind'. Rather, the Internet appears to mirror and even intensify what is going on around us in our 'co-present' (i.e. conducted in person—the opposite of 'mediated') interactions. We do not have to look very far to find the same kind of race and class divisions in mediated communications that we find in co-present ones.

SOCIAL CAPITAL AND SOCIAL NETWORKING SITES

Sociologists recently have been examining the role of the Internet in facilitating the formation of social capital, a concept introduced in Chapter 13. Pierre Bourdieu and Loïc Wacquant (1992) define social capital as 'the sum of their resources, actual or virtual, that accrue to an individual or a group by virtue of possessing a durable network of more or less institutionalized relationship of mutual claims and recognition' (Bourdieu & Wacquant, 1992, p. 14). Social capital—the connections within and among those who make up a social network—has value because it affects the life chances of individuals as members of groups. Sociologists have linked increased social capital to a wide variety of positive social outcomes, including better health, lower crime rates, and more efficient financial markets (Adler & Kwon, 2002).

Possessing social capital allows individuals to draw on the resources of the other members of their social networks, resources such as information, personal relationships, and the capacity to organize groups. Social capital also gives individuals access to others outside of their immediate close circle, providing further access to information and resources and, as Mark Granovetter demonstrated (1973, 1982), benefits such as employment opportunities.

Finally, researchers have shown that possessing significant social capital, including ties with friends and neighbours, is related to psychological well-being, including self-esteem and satisfaction with life (Bargh & McKenna, 2004; Helliwell & Putnam, 2004).

Early debates about social capital and Internet use focused on whether the Internet would undercut social relationships as television had, or whether it would serve to reinforce them. When television first appeared in North America, it had far-reaching implications for North Americans' use of other media, such as listening to the radio, attending a movie in the theatre, and reading fiction and general interest magazines; studies documented reductions in all of these activities at the same time that television viewing increased. Later studies also recorded a sharp decline in 'out-of-home socializing, in-home conversation, housework, personal care activities, and even sleep' (Robinson & Godbey, 1999). If a one-to-many broadcast communication medium like television could displace so many activities, researchers reasoned, the Internet, which permits two-way interaction as well as one-way communication, might have even greater effects. But subsequent research has shown this is not the case.

Internet-based personal connections can be important in the formation of 'weak ties', which (as you will recall from Chapter 11) in turn serve as the foundation for bridging social capital. Bridging social capital refers to the value assigned to social networks between socially heterogeneous groups, while bonding social capital refers to the value assigned to social networks between homogeneous groups of people (Putnam, 2000). Wellman and colleagues (2001) have shown that new forms of bridging social capital and relationship building occurred on social networking sites, which often allow users to maintain larger and more diffuse networks of relationships from which they can potentially draw resources.

Ellison, Steinfeld, and Lampe (2007) chose Facebook 'as a research context in order to determine whether off-line social capital can be generated by online tools'. The researchers wanted to know about the effects of participation on Facebook on bridging social capital. Because this form of capital is closely connected to the notion of 'weak ties', it was assessed by 'the extent to which participants were integrated into the Michigan State University community, their willingness to support the community, and the extent to which these experiences broadened their social horizons or worldview' (Ellison, Steinfeld, & Lampe, 2007).

To conduct their study, the researchers drew a random sample of 800 Michigan State University (MSU) undergraduate students, out of which 286 students completed an online survey (a response rate of

The term 'digital divide' is typically used to refer to the unequal access to ICTs among people of different ethnic or socioeconomic classes, but what about as it applies to age? What risks exist for today's seniors—in some ways our most vulnerable population—if they fail to keep up with technology?

35.8 per cent). The survey collected information about demographic and other descriptive variables, including age, gender, year in school, local versus home residence, ethnicity, measured Internet use, and whether or not the respondents were Facebook members. In all, 66 per cent of respondents were female, 87 per cent were white, and 55 per cent lived on campus. On average, respondents used the Internet 2 hours and 56 minutes per day, and 94 per cent of them were Facebook members. The Facebook members reported that they spent between 10 and 30 minutes on average using Facebook each day, and that they had between 150 and 200 friends listed on their profiles.

Facebook enables users to maintain these weak ties cheaply and easily, and certain kinds of Facebook use helped students to accumulate and maintain bridging social capital. This is so because, as Ellison, Steinfeld, and Lamp (2007) comment, 'Facebook serves to lower the barriers to participation' in such a way that students 'who might otherwise shy away from initiating communication with or responding to others are encouraged to do so.' For example, the students reported using Facebook to stay connected to high school friends as well as to the people they knew through an MSU connection, however tenuous that connection might be. The researchers speculate that 'highly engaged users are using Facebook to crystallize relationships that might otherwise remain ephemeral.' Facebook makes it easier to convert latent ties—ties that are 'technically possible but not activated socially'—into weak ties (Haythornthwaite, 2005, p. 137). All of these usages enhance bridging social capital.

Students who reported low satisfaction with MSU life also reported having much lower bridging social capital than those who used Facebook more intensely. The same is true for students with lower self-esteem, suggesting that Facebook may help students to use bridging capital to get better access to information and opportunities and, thus, to get more out of their college experience. Online communities do not necessarily remove people from offline communities and may in fact support relationships and keeping key people in contact even when life changes move them away from each other physically. The strong link between Facebook use and high school connections suggests that social networking sites help maintain relationships as people move from one offline community to another. It may also do the same when these students graduate from college and use Facebook to stay in contact with their college community. These connections could have 'strong payoffs in terms of jobs, internships, and other opportunities', Ellison, Steinfeld, and Lamp (2007) conclude.

MEDIATED AND CO-PRESENT SOCIAL INTERACTION RITUALS

Sociologist Richard Ling (2008) tells about an experience he had involving some friends, a plumber, and a mobile phone. Ling lives in Oslo, Norway, where he works for a telecommunications company. Around 8:30 one morning he was standing outside his home, saying goodbye to friends who had spent the night, when a plumber, with whom he had an appointment, appeared around the corner of his house. In one hand the plumber held a piece of paper that he quickly checked to confirm the address. In his other hand was a mobile phone into which he was talking. The plumber, whom Ling had never met, continued his telephone conversation, re-checked the address on the piece of paper he was holding, walked past Ling and his guests, nodded briefly, and, continuing his mobile phone conversation, went directly into Ling's house through the front door. Ling finished his leave-taking with his guests and retreated to his kitchen, where he was received by the plumber who had by this time had completed his telephone conversation (Ling, 2008, p. 1).

interaction ritual
An event in which participants focus on a common objective or activity and share a common emotional experience or set of feelings.

As Ling points out, the plumber who visited his house had 'made a travesty' of the greeting ritual normally expected between a homeowner and a tradesperson. There was no exchange of hellos, no handshake or small talk, and certainly no extension of an invitation from Ling to the plumber to enter his home. The only residual element of a traditional **interaction ritual** was the plumber's slight nod acknowledging Ling and the fact that he had removed his shoes at the front door (Ling, 2008, p. 2). Ling never learned about the nature of the telephone call. However, it was clear that the plumber's mediated social interaction—the one conducted by phone—was so engrossing that he had judged he could ignore the expected co-present interaction ritual, conducted face-to-face.

How do interaction rituals shape our experience of social solidarity, and how do mediated interactions, such as those that take place via mobile communications devices, play into those rituals? Although Durkheim never spoke about mediated social interactions, he did focus on interaction rituals, especially religious ones, and their implications for social solidarity. Ritual for Durkheim included assembling a group of people together physically, giving them a mutual focus, and inciting in them a commonly shared mood. When taken together, these elements generally lead to the development of a sense of social solidarity.

Durkheim's work on interaction rituals focused on his examination of Australian Aboriginal religions, where there was no opportunity for mediated interaction to be considered. Erving Goffman (1959, 1963, 1967, 1971) also studied ritual interactions in co-present, everyday life, although he focused on day-to-day interactions and not the rituals generally thought to elicit 'oceanic' feelings of oneness, as did Durkheim. For the most part, too, Goffman did not mention mediated interaction (Ling, 2008, pp. 165–6).

Since Goffman wrote his books and articles, the use of mobile telephones and the Internet have exploded. Mediated social interactions have simply become a routine part of daily communication and are regularly used to maintain contacts. And while Goffman himself had little to say about mediated interactions, other sociologists have applied his concepts to mediated contexts. A number of them have observed that those involved in mediated social interactions often experience a sense of co-presence with their interlocutors in a shared social space and have developed a set of social norms to organize those interactions (Ackerman, et al., 1997; Heath & Luff, 1992, as cited in Rettie, 2009, p. 422).

To see someone walk down the street, sit at a bus stop or in a café, stand in a line for a theatre performance, or sit in a university classroom and use a mobile communications device is a very familiar sight. The mobile phone is 'a conduit through which we have physically and often temporally remote contact with others'. It gives us the ability to have mediated contact with whomever we wish from wherever we find ourselves, even in co-presence of others. Because of this, 'we have to pay our interlocutors proper heed just as we have to pay the proper heed to those with whom we are co-present' (Ling, 2008). Goffman had the insight that when we interact with others in the co-present we maintain a 'front stage'.

Goffman's concepts of front and back stages have been of particular use to sociologists analyzing mediated interactions. When we have mediated contact with someone via a mobile communications device and we are in the co-presence of others, we have 'in effect, two front stages upon which to act' (Ling, 2008, p. 169), something that the plumber who arrived at Ling's house failed to acknowledge. A mobile phone call, taken in the co-presence of others, creates 'parallel front stages', blurring boundaries between public and private spaces. Because front and back regions are blurred during mobile phone calls, performances may overlap, role conflict may increase, and interlocutors may become aware of role playing. For example, when a parent talks to her child from the workplace, the call may be overheard by the parent's boss or co-workers. The parent making the call must work to manage the impressions of herself on the part of those in her workplace who overhear her call (Rettie, 2009, p. 423).

Mobile communication has altered the way in which day-to-day interaction rituals take place, develop, and are carried off. Mobile communications are different from other forms of interpersonal mediated interactions such as email and instant messaging (IM) because mobile telephones make us each individually accessible. With mobile telephones the individual and not the location is addressed. When you call someone on a landline you call a location. Hopefully that person is somewhere nearby and is able to 'come to the phone'. But with mobile phones you call the individual wherever he is—sitting in the bathtub, attending a sporting event, chairing a business meeting, or engaging in a sexual tryst (Ling, 2008, p. 3).

Certainly our co-present interactions have familiar interaction rituals attached to them. Even something as simple as greeting a friend entails a different ritual than does greeting someone we're meeting for the first time. Recently micro-level social interaction rituals have also been established for mediated interactions. For example, Japanese teens often begin negotiating a romantic relationship by exchanging mobile phone numbers. Once the preliminaries have been accomplished, the next step is often an SMS-based courtship. The messages that are sent back and forth are highly scripted, carefully written, and edited in order to allow the participants to work through what they want to say and, potentially, to cover over any 'pitfalls' that might emerge (Ling, 2008, p. 170). Teens also use text messaging to prepare for, and then extend, their 'dates'. The couple who is to go out on a date begins by texting each other before the date starts, and then continues their texting after the date is over and they have returned to their respective homes (Ito, 2005). Teens who still live at home with their parents send each other 'goodnight' or 'good morning' greetings. These greetings become part of the obligatory ritualized aspects of their relationship and are ignored at great risk.

Another micro-level social ritual interaction to emerge out of negotiating mediated romantic relationships involves the timing of responses. The amount of time allowed to lapse between receiving and responding to a romantic text message sends a very strong signal. If the receiver waits too long to respond, the wait time can be a signal that she, the recipient, is not all that interested. If she responds too quickly, she could be perceived as being over-eager. Finally, the actual text messages themselves can be made into 'sacred objects' to be 'saved, transcribed, embroidered, and placed into the mythology of the couple' (Ling, 2008, p. 171).

Mediated Communications and 'Being There'

Social interactions—whether of the mediated or of the co-present type—are dynamic, and can often be fraught with problems. While most people try to engineer their social interactions so that they give the correct impression, they also 'give off' unintended signals that alert others to their real intentions. When we slip up—when we give others a peek into the back stage—then there's a need for 'maintenance work'.

In Chapter 9 we looked at the importance of knowing the social status of those with whom we interact. When we know someone else's status, we also know how to properly interact with them; thus, there is always pressure for us as participants to be either clearly in or clearly out of an ongoing social interaction. One of the biggest ways to slip up in a social interaction is to occupy an indeterminate status. Being on the perimeter of an ongoing social interaction—a position of indeterminate status—often causes anxiety, something that can happen when a mediated phone interaction takes place at the same time as a co-present one. This situation places the person having a mediated interaction in a kind of social limbo where those who are co-present can no longer be certain of the true status of the phone user. Is she 'in' or is she 'out'?

Goffman (1971), for example, noted that when a person takes a telephone call in the presence of others, he will often use various gestures and facial expressions to convey to those present that the phone conversation is only a temporary diversion. But with texting and mobile phone conversations taking place so frequently in public, it's all too easy to see the exact opposite occurring, as in the case of Ling's example with the plumber, where the plumber barely acknowledged Ling's presence and walked directly into his house, all the while continuing his mediated conversation. In this case, mediated communication took precedent over co-present communication—a situation that most of us do not expect to happen. As far as the plumber was concerned, his mediated communication took precedence over his co-present communication and allowed him to put what normally is kept backstage on the front stage.

This presents an interesting phenomenon for sociologists to study. From Goffman's point of view, people who share a situation constitute a 'gathering', defined as 'any set of two or more individuals . . . who are at the moment in one another's immediate presence' (Goffman, 1967, p. 144). Such gatherings can occur in front stage and back stage regions. You will recall

Cellphones, the good. How have you used cellphones in your own romantic relationships? Does your willingness to call rather than text a date (or potential date) signify that you are more interested in the person? How long after you've left a date do you wait before making contact? Who texts or calls first?

from the discussion in Chapter 7 that the front region is any physical setting where the main performance takes place. The front region supports the definition of the situation, and defines the interaction's roles. The back region is an area where an individual can drop the role that is being performed on the front stage, prepare her props, converse with other team members, or simply relax in private. Front stage and back stage, of course, are relative terms, and a performance itself takes place equally in both areas. Moreover, an area that is backstage for one performance may be the front stage for another. For example, when a doctor meets with his staff, without a patient present, his office is backstage to his upcoming performance as physician examining a patient. It becomes the front stage when there is a patient actually present to be examined.

Goffman was aware that a person engaged in a focused interaction with someone while in a public space might be momentarily interrupted by someone else, creating an awkward situation for the person who is left out; he referred to this as 'cross-talk' (Goffman, 1971, p. 25). According to Goffman, people in a public space may be either alone ('Singles') or with one or more others ('Withs'). Cross-talk happens when 'one member of a With momentarily sustains exclusive talk with someone who is not in the With', rendering the person who is left out socially vulnerable. Humphreys (2005) has taken this concept and shown how the use of mobile phones creates 'cross-talk' when they are used during a face-to-face interaction. By doing this, the user of a mobile communication device places those with whom he is co-present in an awkward position.

Cellphones, the bad. Imagine this couple is on their first date. Who would have to be on the other end of the line to make taking the call acceptable? How could the gentleman in this picture do a better job of managing his front-stage impression in his co-present situation?

STUDIES IN SOCIAL RESEARCH

'Peep Culture', 'Oversharing', and 'Sousveillance'

Hal Niedzviecki's *The Peep Diaries* (2009) begins with a definition of *overshare*, the word chosen as the 2008 word of the year by the editors of *Webster's New World Dictionary and Thesaurus*, and described by them as 'emerging English':

> **overshare** (verb): to divulge excessive personal information, as in a blog or broadcast interview, prompting reactions ranging from alarmed discomfort to approval. (as cited in Niedzviecki, 2009, p. 1)

The word *overshare*, Niedzviecki goes on to say, might be 'weird' and 'ungainly', but it is also a 'potent marker indicating a major cultural shift'. This, he explains, is because 2008 'was the year we unequivocally and unceremoniously ushered in a new era: The Era of Peep Culture'. Peep culture includes:

> . . . reality TV, YouTube, Twitter, Flickr, MySpace and Facebook. It's blogs, chat rooms, amateur porn sites, virally spread digital movies of a fat kid pretending to be a Jedi Knight, cell phone photos—posted online—of your drunk friend making out with her ex-boyfriend, and citizen surveillance. Peep is the backbone of Web 2.0 and the engine of corporate and government data mining. It's like the famous line about pornography: you know it when you see

it. And you do see it. All the time, every day, everywhere. (Niedzviecki, 2009, p. 1)

'Reality' TV shows such as *American Idol, The X-Factor, Hell's Kitchen, The Apprentice, The Bachelor, Keeping Up with the Kardashians,* and *America's Next Top Model* are all examples, but so are celebrity gossip sites, such as PerezHilton.com and TMZ.com. And the rise of social media means that we can just as easily peek into the 'problems, kinks and lifestyles' of ordinary—i.e. 'not (yet) famous,—people. As Niedzviecki explains:

> Anyone who's ever lost a few hours clicking on the profile pictures of friends and friends' friends knows what Peep is all about. It's about feeling the hours slipping away as you drift wherever the current takes you. It's about wanting to know everything about everyone and, in turn, wanting to make sure that everyone knows everything about you. As with all things Peep, social networks are addictive and instinctual—why wouldn't you want to make 'friends' with the click of button? In an age where parks are replaced by condos and fewer and fewer people know their neighbors, the urge to connect to like-minded people can be incredibly powerful. No wonder there are now social networks for recovering addicts; book

Because they are now so frequent, such disturbances have become 'normalized', along with the repair work that is needed to 'correct' them. It is interesting to note that, compared to a decade ago, we are less and less disturbed by the use of a mobile phone in public, largely because users of mobile communication devices have developed ritualized routines to help them manage the task of managing two front stages simultaneously, or at least to engage in ritualized 'repair work'—something that did not happen in Ling's experience with the plumber.

Other sociologists, such as Gergen (2002), explain that mobile phone conversations typically create an 'inside space', for those who are conversing via phone, and an 'outside space', for those who can hear one-half of the conversation but who are prevented from participating in it. This is similar to co-present interactions taking place between two or more people lovers; divorcees; people with cats, dogs, and kindergartners; people living with chronic illness; and those who aspire to be on reality TV (Niedzviecki, 2009, p. 5)

Social networking sites like Facebook, dedicated to keeping friends connected, and AshleyMadison.com, dedicated to helping married people have affairs, and Twitter, the mini-blogging service, and YouTube, where over 13 hours of video are uploaded each minute, are all examples of 'Peep' culture, in which profiles and posts become fair game as sources of amusement and entertainment for others. This can be considered 'consensual peeping', where information is voluntarily posted for all to consume. Another example is Loopt, which is available on smartphones and allows anyone who uses the service see the whereabouts of any other subscriber. And then there is Google, where over one-third of all Internet users go to conduct a search on someone else's name, often out of curiosity or as something to do.

Less consensual forms of peeping fall under the term *sousveillance*, which was coined by Steve Mann, a professor of computer engineering at the University of Toronto, to describe unofficial forms of watching, such as using a cellphone camera to record events. WikiLeaks, the organization dedicated to releasing classified government communication, engages in a form of sousveillance by publishing documents that otherwise would remain outside of the public record.

Wikipedia identifies one aspect of sousveillance as 'the recording of an activity from the perspective of a participant in the activity'; the online encyclopedia contrasts this form of sousveillance with 'inverse surveillance', defined as 'a subset of sousveillance with a particular emphasis on the "watchful vigilance from underneath", an activity typically undertaken by those who are the subject of surveillance. The Internet contains many instances posted by 'ordinary citizens' of police abuse of authority, schoolyard bullying, anti-gay attacks, and sexual harassment, among other situations. In these cases the 'victims' use mobile technologies to record and publicly report harassment, abuse, and violence. One example is Hollaback! (www.ihollaback.org), a movement (and a website) 'dedicated to ending street harassment using mobile technology'. Hollaback! provides a site where women and LGBTQ people can post about their experiences with the intention of breaking the silence that has perpetuated gender-based violence.

Our growing fascination with, and participation in, peep culture suggests that the more we reveal about ourselves, the more we become used to being constantly under surveillance, and the more convinced we are that we are safer that way.

that may also include bystanders who don't directly participate in the interaction, but who are in a position to observe and hear what is going on. To return to the example of the parent speaking to a child by a mobile phone from her workplace, the parent may deliberately use a child's name to inform her co-workers that she is speaking to her daughter, or she might tell her daughter that she is working hard in order to convey the same message to her boss who is standing nearby (Rettie, 2009, p. 428).

A mobile phone user will often gesture to indicate to people around him that they are what Goffman (1981) called 'ratified participants', who, while they may not be the focus of the telephone interaction, are at least entitled to listen in on the conversation and even to contribute occasional remarks. Mobile phone users will also turn away or even walk away from the face-to-face encounters that the call has interrupted, indicating that the call is private and that they are switching stages. With that gesture, what was previously a front stage now becomes a back stage. This clearly did not happen in Ling's interaction with the plumber, who not only allowed his mediated conversation to take front stage but also violated many interaction rituals associated with co-present social interactions.

A key difference between mobile phone calls and text messaging is the way in which interlocutors are experienced. Respondents in a UK study of heavy mobile phone users (Rettie, 2009) frequently contrasted calls in which they felt as if they and their interlocutors were both 'there', to text messages, in which the interlocutor is perceived to be 'not there' (Rettie, 2009, p. 429). As one respondent put it, during a call both participants are 'together at the same time' because they have '*stopped* to speak to each other'. Most respondents likened phone calls to face-to-face interactions. One respondent commented: 'I know it's . . . not face-to-face on the phone, but it's face-to-face to me.' Explaining why she preferred SMS to a call, the same respondent said 'at least I don't have to talk to them' (Rettie, 2009, p. 429). Several other respondents said similar things: talking on the phone was like being with the person with your eyes shut, whereas with text messaging the other person wasn't experienced as 'being there'. Several respondents explained that text messaging actually 'facilitated intimacy in relationships'. They felt they could take a risk and become more intimate via text messaging because if they were rejected it wouldn't matter so much—they weren't 'really there'. In this context being 'there' doesn't refer to location but to synchronous participation in a shared interaction. In short, for most people, phone calls were much more social than text messages (Rettie, 2009, p. 431).

Goffman (1959) claimed that expressions 'given off' are less controllable and therefore deemed more revealing than expressions given directly. Respondents in Rettie's study (2009) commented that phone calls had more implicit cues than text messages and therefore were more revealing. Although emoticons such as ☺ are used in text messaging to convey emotion, respondents felt that these were only indirectly meaningful and therefore more calculated than expressions given off spontaneously during a phone call. Sending asynchronous text messages makes it easier to control expressions 'given off'. Consequently text messages are deemed to be less revelatory of the true self. This can be useful in certain situations where individuals are concerned about reducing exposure to potential embarrassment, for example, in a new relationship (Rettie, 2009, p. 434). Finally, text messages were not seen as requiring any kind of extended leave-taking; they could be easily ignored or deleted. The closer a text message conversation came to being synchronous, the

Have we become so accepting of cross-talk that we don't realize how it affects the co-present situation?

stronger the impetus to engage in ritualized behaviour closely approximating that of co-present social interactions (Rettie, 2009, p. 432).

SUMMARY

Interaction rituals permeate all aspects of our daily lives, whether those rituals take place in the co-present or are mediated by some communications device. In this chapter we have seen how mediated social interactions, such as those that take place on social networking sites like Facebook and MySpace, are replicating or reinforcing existing divisions of class, race, and ethnicity.

We have also explored how mediated social interaction, such as talking on a mobile phone, during a co-present interaction can disrupt the co-present interaction, and how new kinds of interaction rituals are emerging both to guide mediated interactions and to facilitate situations that involve both mediated and co-present interactions.

It is clear that mediated interactions play an important role in maintaining and even strengthening relations between family members and among friends. They also play an increasingly important role in the process of negotiating and maintaining romantic relationships, especially via short text messages that seem to be less risky than face-to-face communications. Research also shows that small groups benefit from mediated social interactions.

DISCUSSION QUESTIONS

1. Explain how the Internet, social media, and mobile communications are affecting the ways we interact with each other.
2. How have the Internet, social media, and mobile communications transformed our social practices, changed the way we do business, and even affected our most intimate personal relationships? Use specific examples to illustrate your answer.
3. Are we becoming more individualized, or are we finding new ways to be connected as a result of our use of the Internet, social media, and mobile communications? Justify your answer.
4. In what ways do issues such as race, class, gender, and age affect the way we use these new technologies? Explain your answer using examples.
5. In what ways are the new technologies affecting the ways in which politics are conducted locally? Nationally? Internationally? Use concrete examples to illustrate your answers.
6. What are some of the benefits of online games, simulations, and virtual worlds? What are some of the drawbacks?
7. What are some of the differences between 'mediated' and 'co-present' interaction rituals with respect to the ways they promote or fail to promote social solidarity? How has mobile communication altered the way in which day-to-day interaction rituals take place, develop, and are carried off? Use specific examples to illustrate your answer.
8. Describe an example of 'souveillance'. Explain the objective of the example of souveillance you have chosen and explain what effects it had, both intended and unintended.

20 Sociologists and Social Activism

CHAPTER OUTLINE

LEARNING OBJECTIVES

In this chapter you will:

- be introduced to the concept of 'public sociology'
- distinguish between four types of sociological knowledge
- gain a clearer understanding of what sociologists can do to become more relevant
- learn about John Porter's contribution to public sociology in Canada
- learn about public sociology action
- examine the Toronto Teen Survey Report
- reflect on sociologists' contributions to environmental justice
- review the relationship between research and advocacy.

INTRODUCTION

C. Wright Mills, whose ideas about the sociological imagination provide the foundation for this textbook, remarked frequently during the 1940s and 1950s about a crisis in democracy, which he attributed to a 'vanishing public'. Mills had made a study of upper-class individuals who wielded power in the political, military, and economic institutions of America. He published the results of his study as *The Power Elite* (1956), concluding that intellectuals have 'a unique and decisive role in resistance to unbridled corporate power'. In coming to this conclusion Mills followed the lead already set by the American philosopher John Dewey. Dewey (1929) had argued that intellectuals, through books, articles, lectures, and other mass media, could influence public discussion 'by articulating alternative and oppositional values and knowledge to the main conservative drift' (as cited in Aronowitz, 2005, p. 333).

Mills's ideas about, and commitment to, a public role for sociology was consistent with those of the early founders of the discipline. The study of sociology emerged out of the social change and upheavals of the nineteenth century. Its early practitioners looked for order in the violence, tyranny, and inequalities that came in the wake of the early development of capitalism. Some, like Comte, intended sociology to be the 'queen' of the sciences, to play a major role in helping humanity understand, and thus control, the chaotic changes. Durkheim wanted sociology to help humanity turn away from anomie and despair and regain a state of solidarity and moral purpose. Weber, despite pessimism and depression, believed sociology could help humanity find a kind of freedom in rationalization. Karl Marx believed that 'advanced communism', with equality for all, would be the ultimate outcome of the class struggle that threatened to engulf the world.

Since the birth of their discipline, sociologists have debated whether or not the goal of influencing large-scale societal directions is an achievable or even desirable ambition. Some believe it is futile; others are of the opinion that by not pursuing such a goal, sociology has 'lost its critical edge, and in so doing lost its public voice' (Hutter, 2005). In this final chapter we will address the question of the nature and purpose of sociological inquiry.

THE ROLE OF SOCIOLOGICAL INQUIRY TODAY

In 1989, Herbert Gans was elected president of the American Sociological Association. In his presidential address, 'Sociology in America: The Discipline and the Public', Gans introduced the term 'public sociology', and called on sociologists to try to regain some of that critical edge. Gans encouraged sociologists to become 'public intellectuals', revitalize social criticism, and get more sociology into the public media (Gans, 1989, as cited in Brady, 2004, p. 1631).

Almost a decade later, in an article entitled 'The Sociological Eye and Its Blinders', sociologist Randall Collins argued that the sociological eye and social activism were the two core commitments of sociology. Sociology, Collins explained, is a 'distinctive activity' that involves 'looking at the world through . . . the sociological eye'—in other words, seeking the larger social patterns of society. However, Collins saw that many sociologists came to the discipline through the route of social activism, and he noted that there are very few disciplines outside of sociology in which 'activism meshes so directly with one's immediate work' (Collins, 1998b, p. 4). Here however is the potential root of conflict between sociologists of different stripes:

From the activist viewpoint, the judgment on other sociologists' work tends to be 'if you're not part of the solution you're part of the problem'. From the point of view of the voyager with the sociological eye, the activist is just someone who has already made up his or her mind and is no longer open to seeing anything new. (Collins, 1998b, p. 5)

The Occupy Wall Street movement, and its spinoffs across the US and Canada as well as Europe, is evidence that ordinary citizens can be moved to challenge prevailing social, political, and economic ideology. But is it proof that ordinary citizens are capable of shaping or defining public policy?

Collins goes on to say that the two commitments of sociology—the sociological eye and activism—often butt up against each other. 'If we have to choose between them,' Collins advised, 'I say we must choose the sociological eye; if that is lost, all is lost' (p. 6).

Yet other sociologists believe that the problem is not so simply solved. What does it mean for liberal democracy, asks American sociologist Stephen Turner, 'if a significant part of public discourse is false or erroneous' (Turner, 2007, p. 786)? Most people assume that public opinion, when wrong, will eventually correct itself. Yet sociologists often have 'genuine expert knowledge' about pressing public issues that go ignored while erroneous thinking continues to prevail. The problem here, as Turner points out, is that errors in public discourse cannot be easily corrected by members of the public themselves precisely because understanding the nature of those errors requires 'expertise beyond that of ordinary citizens'. Sociologists have that expertise and should actively seek to use it.

In his 2004 presidential address to the American Sociological Association, Michael Burawoy called on sociologists to return sociology to its roots, and in so doing to 'transcend the academy and engage wider audiences' through public sociology. Burawoy directed attention to the uncomfortable and anomalous position that sociologists occupy. On the one hand, sociologists claim to have expert knowledge about 'matters that are in the domain of public discussion in liberal democracies'. At the same time, sociologists are often frustrated with their failure to engage that very public and have their views treated seriously. They are often defeated by the simplistic character of public discussions and by the lack of respect that their profession commands in public forums.

In the sections that follow we'll encounter some of the debates, most recently stimulated by Burawoy's presidential address, around the role of sociologists. Should sociologists maintain a professional detachment from their research and their research subjects? Should they engage in activism only when they can be assured that their 'sociological eye', their unique view on the underlying patterns of society, however unsettling, is not compromised by their commitment to social activism? Or have sociologists spent long enough building professional knowledge? Is it time, as Burawoy tells us, for sociologists to embark on a project of 'taking knowledge back to those from whom it came, making public issues out of private troubles, and thus regenerating sociology's moral fibre' (Burawoy, 2005, p. 5)?

FOUR TYPES OF SOCIOLOGICAL KNOWLEDGE

According to Burawoy (2004), the work of sociologists is devoted to producing four different types of knowledge: professional, critical, policy, and public.

1. *Professional sociology*, consisting of 'multiple intersecting research programs, each with their assumptions, exemplars, defining questions, conceptual apparatuses, and evolving theories', makes both policy sociology and public sociology possible. Professional sociology plays this role because it 'supplies true and tested methods, accumulated bodies of knowledge, orienting questions and conceptual frameworks' (Burawoy, 2004, p. 10).

2. *Critical sociology* has the role of examining 'the foundations—both the explicit and implicit, both normative and descriptive—of the research programs of professional sociology' (p. 10). Critical sociology serves as the conscience of professional sociology, just as public sociology serves as the conscience to policy sociology. It asks the questions 'knowledge for whom?' and 'knowledge for what purpose?'

3. *Policy sociology* is sociology done 'in the service of a goal set by a client'. Examples include serving as an expert witness on a trial or public inquiry, or doing research for a government client on the causes of poverty.

4. *Public sociology* is sociology done as a partnership, where sociologists and public organizations or interest groups each bring their own agenda, and then negotiate the actual direction that research will take.

Each of these four types of sociology has its own legitimation, accountability, politics, and pathologies (see Table 20.1). Burawoy pointed to existing tensions and contradictions between the four 'faces' of sociology, but he also pointed to their interdependency:

> Without a professional sociology, there can be no policy or public sociology, but nor can there be a critical sociology—after all, there would be nothing to criticize. Equally, professional sociology depends for its vitality upon the continual challenge of public issues through the vehicle of public sociology. It was the civil rights movement that transformed sociologists' understanding of politics, it was the feminist movement that gave new direction to so many spheres of sociology. . . . Critical sociology may be a thorn in the side of professional sociology, but it is crucial in forcing awareness of the assumptions we make, so that from time to time we may change those assumptions. . . . Today we might include within the rubric of critical sociology the movement for 'pure sociology', a scientific sociology purged of public engagement. What was professional sociology yesterday can be critical today. Policy sociology, for its part, has reenergized the sociology of inequality with its research into poverty and education. (Burawoy, 2004, pp. 15–16)

TABLE 20.1 Professional, policy, public, and critical sociologies compared

	Professional sociology	Policy sociology	Public sociology	Critical sociology
Legitimation is based on:	scientific norms	effectiveness	relevance	moral vision
Accountability is assured by:	peer review	its clients/patrons	the designated public	a multidisciplinary community of critical intellectuals
Politics are informed by:	defence of professional self-interest	ability to propose policy intervention	democratic public dialogue	internal debate within the discipline of sociology
Pathologies include:	a strong tendency to self-referentiality	servility, as a response to client-imposed contractual limitations	a tendency to pursue fads in order to be popular a tendency to speak down to non-sociologists	a tendency to become dogmatic and no longer relevant either to professional or to public sociology

Source: Adapted from Burawoy, 2004, p. 1607.

In his analysis of sociology as it is practised today, Burawoy drew on Bourdieu's concept of 'field'. For Bourdieu, field is the setting in which social agents are located and in which they interact on the basis of the rules of that field, in conjunction with their habitus, as well as with the social, economic, and cultural capital that each social agent has acquired. Burawoy believes that sociology today is 'a field of power, a more or less stable hierarchy of antagonistic knowledges', with professional and policy sociologies dominating (due to the power of careers and of funding) and with critical and public sociologies taking the subordinate positions (Burawoy, 2004, p. 18). While early sociologists set out to 'change the world', contemporary sociologists 'have too often ended up conserving it'. This is because sociologists who start out in their careers with a 'passion for social justice, economic equality, human rights, sustainable environment, political freedom or simply a better world' often end up being forced to channel that passion into 'the pursuit of academic credentials'—in other words, into what Burawoy calls 'professional sociology' (p. 5). The solution, in Burawoy's view, is that the four divisions of the sociological field should be brought together, and each should allow the other the necessary space to develop.

For Burawoy, public sociology is sociology that reaches beyond its own disciplinary boundaries to involve the larger community in public discussions about the nature of society, its values, and any gap between what a society promises its members and what it delivers (Burawoy, 2004, p. 7). One of the roles of sociology, he notes, is to define human categories. If we do so in collaboration with the people we study, 'we create publics' (p. 8). The category 'women', for example, is a 'public'—a group that is studied by sociologists and that uses sociologists as collaborators in order to advance their interests. This has happened because sociologists have defined women in a way that allows many women to recognize themselves 'as marginalized, left out, oppressed and silenced' (p. 8).

Burawoy's recent challenge to sociologists to make their work relevant to their 'publics' has met with a flurry of responses by other sociologists, some supportive of his vision, some condemning it, and some taking both views. British sociologist John Hall (2005) offered a 'guarded welcome' to Burawoy's plea for public sociology but found Burawoy's ideas 'far too optimistic'. By and large, Hall writes, 'we do not have the capacity to undertake the tasks that Burawoy has in mind. Nor do I detect a groundswell of support for his plea for public sociology' (Hall, 2005, p. 379). Former steel worker and union organizer turned sociology professor Stanley Aronowitz (2005) wrote that 'Michael Burawoy's call for a public sociology is a serious challenge to the prevailing direction of sociology which has joined economics and political science as one of the "servants of power"' (Aronowitz, 2005).

American sociologist Charles Tittle (2004), however, was not so sanguine. To Tittle, public sociology 'involves some false assumptions, endangers what little legitimacy sociology has, thereby helping to undermine the chances of sociological knowledge ever being taken seriously in public arenas, and is in fact, incompatible with good professional sociology' (Tittle, 2004). Tittle concludes that urging public sociology is contrary to 'one of the bases of good society that Burawoy would probably endorse—participation on a more or less equal basis by all citizens' (Tittle, 2004).

MAKING SOCIOLOGY RELEVANT

If public sociology is to be a reality, if the expert knowledge that sociologists possess is to be used in public debate to inform public thinking, it would seem that sociologists need to find better ways to communicate with the general public than the ones they are currently using. Although other disciples, such as medicine and engineering, have been more successful in having the public accept their professional opinions, the North American public routinely disputes or rejects academic claims made by sociologists. What can sociologists do to become more relevant?

Does what sociologists have to offer the general public amount to just one more 'opinion', in the same category, for example, as religious dogma? Is what sociologists have to say nothing more than propaganda? Or is sociology a science based on facts, on par with the natural sciences, and therefore to be granted the same deference received by natural sciences? You should understand by now that in the professional judgement of sociologists, the line between 'fact' and 'opinion' is not at all clear. Sociologists, who understand something about the social construction of reality, are quite cognizant of the struggles that occur around who gets to decide what is 'fact' and what is not (Turner, 2007, p. 791).

On the one hand, sociologists purport to have expert knowledge about matters that are discussed widely in the public domain, such as sex, gender, and race. The value of sociology lies in its ability to use this expert knowledge to make original contributions to public discussions. But what status do these contributions have? Is sociology a means by which liberal democracy 'is supported and improved', or is it 'in fundamental conflict' with liberal democracy because it is an attempt 'to usurp the functions of public discussion by expertizing it' (Turner, 2007)?

No fan of liberal democracy, the founder of sociology, August Comte, believed that the science of sociology would put an end, once and for all, to the cacophony of ill-informed public 'opinion' and replace it with the 'truth of sociology', imposed on citizens by forced education (Comte, 1830–42/1864, as cited in Turner, 2007, p. 786). Sociology, Comte believed, ought to be taught as scientific truth, not as a matter of opinion. Comte's solution about what to do in the face of public ignorance and incompetence was, in Stephen Turner's words, 'draconian', amounting to the abolishment of discussion 'in favour of expert will and indoctrination' (Turner, 2007, p. 786). But do we have to go that far to make sociology relevant today and to ensure that its findings will not be ignored by the public?

Burawoy proposes this solution: sociology, in his opinion, should strive for an organic relationship between sociology as a profession and an activist sociology that serves the interests of a variety of different publics (as cited in Turner, 2007, p. 792). Individual sociologists themselves should decide, as a matter of private value, which social movements and interests to ally themselves with. They should make their decisions on the basis of individual choice so they could, if they choose to, align themselves with the ideals of fundamentalist Christianity, for example, and still be involved in public sociology. Sociology, as a discipline, is not responsible for the commitments and alliances that individual sociologists make. As Turner points out, 'we can recognize a work as a piece of good public sociology while rejecting the values on which it is based' (p. 792).

The success of a piece of sociological research depends in part on the sociologist's relationship to the social movement she is supporting. And this relationship, in turn, provides a constraint on what she does as a sociologist. In this sense the sociologist is compelled to express herself 'in ways that fit with and articulate the experiences and convictions' of the members of the social movement she has chosen to support. In doing this, each sociologist provides expert knowledge of society, although in this case not for society as a whole but rather for 'a society made up of different standpoints'. Women's studies, for example, is a very new discipline, recently added to some (but not all) North American universities. Women's studies was established specifically to represent the standpoint of women, and as Turner points out, it stands in a special relationship to the feminist movement (Turner, 2007, p. 793).

Although sociologists may very well conduct their research from specific standpoints, their research is also held up to professional standards: does the research follow established practices and methods? Is it legitimate, scientific, research? Burawoy supports sociologists engaging in 'advocacy scholarship', which can be defined as conscious attempts to 'understand and articulate the standpoint of some group in society in a way that is intelligible and instructive to the members of the group, as well as to support the standpoint of social research' (Burawoy, 2005). Public sociology takes up the concerns and viewpoints of the partners involved not as topics of research but as a means of defining the problems to be studied. This approach certainly lacks disinterestedness in the sense that research topics are chosen by the people being researched and not by the researchers alone.

By taking up the concerns of community members and by using those concerns to focus their choice of research topics, sociologists contribute to the diversity of political discussion. 'The political meaning of sociology', Turner argues, is to 'contribute to the diversity of political discussion by helping to give voice and support to particular movements and groups' (Turner, 2007, p. 795). Public sociology is a legitimate part of academic scholarship

What's the best way to study the success of Canada's correctional facilities? Is it a topic that should be approached by the sociologist objectively, or is 'advocacy scholarship', in which the sociologist adopts the standpoint of some group (the prisoners, the prison guards, the administration, victims' rights groups, the tough-on-crime government), a better model?

and should be supported because it serves the purpose of improving democratic discussion; however, the findings of such studies are persuasive only if they meet professional standards.

JOHN PORTER AND CLASSIC CANADIAN 'PUBLIC SOCIOLOGY'

Perhaps the best known of all Canadian sociologists, John Porter studied in the late 1940s at the London School of Economics (LSE), where he came under the influence of the British New Liberal sociology of Leonard Hobhouse. Hobhouse was concerned that Britain was an unequal, unjust society. He argued that if the lives of the majority of Britons were to be improved, the British political system of the day, which was based on free-market liberalism, had to be replaced with an interventionist welfare state guided by an applied sociology that was informed by left-leaning liberal and moral principles.

After completing his degree at the LSE, Porter returned to Canada, where he took up a teaching post at Carleton University. The intellectual climate in Canadian universities during the 1950s and 1960s was quite receptive to left-leaning scholarship—much more so than in American universities. It was in this unusual (and transitory) intellectual environment that Porter wrote his most important sociological study, *The Vertical Mosaic* (1965), which combined social science and political advocacy in a classic example of what Burawoy later called public sociology.

Porter's research uncovered evidence of enormous discrepancies between Canadians in terms of wealth, income, and economic opportunity, along with evidence that key Canadian economic and political institutions operated in the interests of a small elite dominated by Anglo-Canadians to the exclusion of most others. Canadian society, Porter charged, was deeply stratified along class and ethnic lines. It was not the egalitarian, equal-opportunity, merit-based society that liberal ideology proclaimed it to be.

Porter was openly critical of the inequalities his research had uncovered, and he took pains to criticize many of his Canadian colleagues for failing to act as social critics and for supporting the status quo (Helmes-Hayes, 2009). These and other charges documented in *The Vertical Mosaic* brought Porter immediate and widespread attention from the media and stimulated a great deal of public debate. The book made bestseller's lists, won American Sociology Association's 1966 MacIver Award, and played a huge role in setting the agenda for English-language sociology in Canada over the next decade.

As a New Liberal thinker, Porter believed that sociology should be practical, and that it should be relevant to public discussion of social issues and useful in formulating and implementing progressive public policy. Porter had three goals for sociology: 'to develop an objective conception of the Good Society, to describe sociology's contribution to realizing that goal, and to develop a method that would allow us to measure societal progress along the way' (Helmes-Hayes, 2009). He spent much of his career as an academic working on research projects that examined the class/opportunity/mobility nexus and attending issues of social justice and inequality. His research projects were intended to contribute to informed debate on social, economic, and political issues and to provide information to guide the decisions of public policy makers, and his work combined all four aspects of sociology—professional, policy, critical, and public—identified by Burawoy. Although in the political climate of today Porter's New Liberal views would be more controversial than they were in the 1960s and 1970s, his work continues to appeal to critical sociologists because of its social democratic values. But his work also appeals to professional and policy sociologists because it is methodologically sophisticated, empirical, and applied (Helmes-Hayes, 2009).

RESEARCH FOR WHOM AND TO WHAT PURPOSE?: SOCIOLOGISTS IN ACTION

By now you should have a lot to think about regarding whom sociological research is done for, and for what purpose. Sociological research is always done in relation to something—whether that something is a goal of simply finding out 'facts', of getting a publication in a prestigious journal, or of using the research findings as a tool to promote the interests of one group or another. For example, many feminist researchers take the stance that their research must be done to promote the well-being of women. From a feminist standpoint, research should be dedicated to exposing women's subjugation, and to ameliorating women's position in society. There is no pretence, here, of value-neutrality. On the contrary, a value-neutral stance is antithetical to the values of feminism.

STUDIES IN SOCIAL RESEARCH

Public Sociology in Action: The Case of Brazil

In an article published in response to Burawoy's call for a 'public sociology', one of Burawoy's former students, sociologist and ethnographer Gianpaolo Baiocchi (2005) talks about the role of critical public sociology in Brazil. What follows is an excerpt from that article. I quote it at length because it illustrates, rather starkly, the differences in the ways in which sociology is practised as a profession in North American and in countries like Brazil.

Baiocchi reports that he was conducting fieldwork among community activists in the city of Porto Alegre, Brazil, when one of his informants during an interview drew him into a debate about the comparative merits of different sociological theories:

> How did, I wonder, someone who did not graduate from high school develop this vocabulary? After much discussion—and promising I'd go back to *Discipline and Punish* to brush up on Foucault—I learned that this theoretical diffusion had come via outside 'advisors' from NGOs who did work in neighborhoods since the 1980s. Very many of these advisors were (and continue to be) sociologists, who often with an undergraduate degree in the discipline, made a livelihood out of this sort of community work through one of the many NGOs that were so important to Brazil's transition to democracy.
>
> . . . In my travels and in my collaborations with colleagues in the academy and in civil society I am often reminded of how different a meaning being a social scientist carries in places like Brazil, South Africa, or India. Brazil is of course famous in this regard. Not only has it recently had a sociologist in its presidency, it currently has a national party in power that, if nothing else, has for two decades defended civil society and today counts many sociologists among its theorists. (Baiocchi, 2005, p. 340)

Baiocchi notes that, in principle, a call for public sociology *per se* is hard to oppose—who, after all, could possibly be against improving 'public debate' and participation? But a call for critical public sociology is another matter, and one more likely to meet with opposition (p. 342).

In North America, institutional pressures within universities discourage sociologists from establishing 'critical connections with civil society' that are seen as 'political'. By comparison, Brazil is a country where critical public sociology has a wide acceptance. In Brazil, sociologists have 'played a

Similarly, other social scientists have conducted their research specifically with the goal of advancing the interests, or bettering the position, of other specified groups in society. As Michael Burawoy (2005) has argued:

> As sociologists we not only invent new categories but also give them normative and political valence. To fail to do so is to give carte blanche to state and market to fill the vacuum with their own needs. We are in the business of fostering such publics as the poor, the delinquent, the incarcerated, women with breast cancer, people with AIDS, single women, gays and so on, not to control them but to expand their powers of self-determination. We should not abandon them to the regulatory state but engage them directly. When we study social movements we simultaneously endorse their presence as a public. We should be more self-conscious about our relation to the people we study, and the effects we produce in the act of research. (Burawoy, 2005, p. 323)

In the sections that follow we will consider three examples of sociologists in action.

comparatively prominent role in public life and in activities of nation-making' (p. 347). Sociologists are not expected to be 'politically neutral'. As a consequence professional sociologists play an important role in societal affairs, although that role has not always been a progressive one. For example, a sociologist formulated the 'racial democracy thesis', which, when codified into state law during the 1930s, became 'an extremely powerful impediment against organizing for racial justice for the following decades' (p. 347).

Baiocchi (2007) suggests that North American sociologists need to learn from the Brazilian example that doing work that is openly political

. . . does not mean compromising in terms of intellectual standards or somehow compromising 'real' sociological work. . . . The records of the generation of scholars who resisted the dictatorship in Brazil point to a sociology that had no option but to be political, and its essays and

Brazil's Rio de Janeiro is a study in socioeconomic contrasts. The popular tourist destination and former capital is an engine of one of the world's fastest growing economies, but it is also known for its widespread poverty, visible in its *favelas*—sprawling shantytowns of fragile, illegally built homes like the ones shown here, perched precariously on the side of one of the city's mountains.

books stand up to any other texts as wonderful sociology. We should follow their cue and engage in work that is too, in its own way, a little heroic. (p. 352)

Public Sociology: The Toronto Teen Survey Report

Another example of Canadian sociological research combining professional, critical, public, and policy sociology is the recent research carried out by Sarah Flicker and her colleagues on the sexual health of Toronto teens. Between December 2006 and August 2007, Flicker, a professor of environmental studies at York University in Toronto, and her colleagues collected 1,216 surveys from a sample of youth living in Toronto. The goal of *Sexpress: The Toronto Teen Survey Report* (2009) was to 'enrich both the quality and quantity of the sexual health information available to Toronto teens and improve the ways in which sexual health promotion and care are delivered' (Flicker, et al., 2009, p. 4).

The research was sponsored by a coalition of Canadian universities and public health and social service agencies, including York University, the University of Toronto, Wilfrid Laurier University, Planned Parenthood Toronto, and Toronto Public Health. It was funded by the Ontario HIV Treatment Network (OHTN), the Canadian Institutes of Health Research, the Centre for Urban Health Initiatives, and the Wellesley Institute. Concerning the large number of public health agencies associated with the study the report authors note:

> Community-based organizations need increased support to provide relevant, inclusive and appropriate programming aimed at improving sexual health outcomes for the youth they serve. The increase in HIV and STI rates, and decrease in knowledge among youth, combined with the multiple and ever-changing needs of Toronto's diverse youth communities demonstrate a need to change the current state of sexual health services and information available to youth. (Flicker, et al., 2009, p. 4)

In conjunction with their community partners, the researchers set out to conduct research that would 'enrich both the quality and quantity of sexual health information' available to Toronto teens, with the objective of improving the effectiveness of both the promotion and the delivery of sexual healthcare. To achieve these goals the researchers adopted a community-based participatory research report. Previous research indicated that peer researchers were effective in sexual health research and prevention strategies. For this reason, the researchers involved Toronto teens in all aspects of the study, and not just as research subjects. Researchers set up a Youth Advisory Committee to help develop research goals, surveys, and protocols, to administer the survey, to conduct post-survey focus group discussions on topics related to healthy sexuality, and to distribute information on local community resources (p. 10).

From December 2006 to August 2007 over 1,200 Toronto teens aged 13–18 and representing a diverse range of ethnic backgrounds and sexual orientations were interviewed about their sexual experiences (Flicker, et al., 2009, p. 4). The sample was selected from 'pre-existing youth groups'; the youth of Toronto were not randomly sampled. Thus, while interviewers made an effort to 'over-sample racialized, sexually diverse and other groups of youth who are often "unheard"' (p. 14), the findings of the survey cannot be generalized to other settings or even to all Toronto youth.

The data were collected via face-to-face interviews conducted by teens in an approach designed to remove some of the inhibitions the interviewees might have felt when talking to older people about sensitive personal matters. The findings include the following:

- 69 per cent of participants reported having kissed a partner
- 25 per cent reported having given or received oral sex

- 27 per cent reported having had vaginal intercourse
- 7 per cent reported having had anal sex
- 24 per cent said they had never engaged in any sexual experiences. (Flicker, et al., 2009, p. 5)

Although 37 per cent of the teens in the survey reported being sexually active, Flicker and her colleagues were surprised to learn that many were 'unsure whether they had had sex or not', even though they had reported engaging in oral, anal, or vaginal sex. Flicker noted that 83 per cent of the respondents had never accessed sexual healthcare from a doctor or a clinic, usually because of concerns over confidentiality. 'The information and services that work for a 14-year-old Asian lesbian', Flicker says, 'are not going to be the same as what works for an 18-year-old straight African male who is a newcomer to Canada' ('Teens want to learn', 2009). Flicker and her colleagues were able to conclude that while young women rated their experiences in accessing sexual health services more highly than young men did, both sexes felt that clinics were not positive towards youth, nor were waiting rooms youth-friendly. The greatest barrier to attending a clinic, experienced by youth of both sexes, was fear of judgement.

Once the data were collected and analysis done, Flicker and her team shared the survey findings with 'service providers who work with youth, such as clinicians, social workers, shelter and group home staff, public health practitioners and community outreach workers' from 55 different agencies (Flicker, et al., 2009, p. 10). They held 13 focus groups with 80 service providers representing 55 service agencies to discuss the findings and to talk about recommendations for change.

One of Flicker and her team's findings was that while both service providers and youth identified many of the same sexual health issues, they frequently differed in what they considered to be the best approach to solving these issues. Flicker and her colleagues offered several recommendations to improve the sexual health of youth, including recommendations to improve sexual health education, clinical care, school-based sexual health education, public health programs and policies, and community-based organizations. They also developed a 'Youth Sexual Bill of Rights', which includes the right to confidential, private, and high-quality care and information, the right to sexual health services without the need for parental permission, and the right to access sexual health clinics for pregnancy tests, birth control pills, condoms, the emergency contraceptive pill, abortion referrals, and free testing and treatment for STIs and HIV (Flicker, et al., 2009).

Environmental Justice

With a growing public awareness of toxic exposures and pollution, new social movements have emerged that focus on environmental issues, including problems of justice in a stratified society. *Environmental justice* is a term that refers to efforts to ensure that humans behave in a way that is environmentally sustainable and that no one group of people—women, minorities, the poor—are exposed to more environmental hazards because of their disadvantaged social status.

Lou Jacobson, who completed a master's degree in sociology, works in California as an energy specialist for the Redwood Coast Energy Authority. As part of his job, Lou provides energy efficiency assessments and project management to companies looking for energy-saving opportunities. Once he has completed his assessment and presented his report, the company decides whether to opt for the changes he has recommended; if they do, he serves as a project manager.

Jacobson has found that while a company's decision to adopt an energy-efficiency approach is often contingent on the bottom line, it isn't always the case that financial considerations play such a large role. Often other social issues act as barriers to energy efficiency. In these cases Lou relies on his sociological training to help him understand why some of his customers are hesitant to take the necessary steps to reduce their companies' energy consumption levels.

In one instance, a local non-profit agency refused a fully funded project because the executive director was skeptical of any government initiative. In this case, Jacobson relied on his sociology training, and used the concept of opinion leadership—seeking input from individuals in a community whose opinion is trusted—to ask the executive directors of other non-profits to provide references. In another instance, Jacobson was able to persuade the executive director of a non-profit organization to install compact fluorescent (CFL) lights. The director was concerned about the potential hazards of CFLs, which contain small amounts of mercury. After reviewing his field notes, Jacobson was able to pinpoint the reasons for the director's reluctance and show him how using CFLs would not only save money but also mitigate climate change. The societal benefits of reduced energy consumption far outweighed individual and community risks, leading the director to finally decide to use the CFLs (Jacobson, 2011, pp. 219–20).

The research and teaching of David Naguib Pellow, a sociologist at the University of Minnesota, focuses on environmental justice issues in communities of colour. Pellow is a member of the Transatlantic Initiative on Environmental Justice (TIEJ), a working group comprising scholars, activists, and lawyers from central and eastern Europe and the US. He is also a member of Global Response, 'an organization that mobilizes letter-writing campaigns to bring attention to human rights and environmental justice abuses around the world' (Pellow, 2011, p. 23). Global Response, he explains, is also a venue 'for creating and disseminating alternative knowledge that seeks to redefine a situation as an injustice'.

Environmentalists often cite the high cost of 'going green' as an obstacle to adopting environmentally friendly policies by governments, corporations, and even individuals. Is this just a common-sense understanding of the situation, or do you think it would stand up to sociological scrutiny? How would you find out?

Of special concern to TIEJ members was the plight of the Roma, one of central and eastern Europe's most despised and targeted ethnic groups. Roma (no longer known by the outdated term 'gypsies') are often forced to live on or near waste dumps, with poor access to clean water and sanitation and exposure to toxics and floods (Pellow, 2011, p. 222). After the Kosovo war in 1999, the Roma living there were relocated by the UN to a toxic waste site, and the children are now suffering from lead poisoning. The letter-writing campaign Pellow initiated prompted the UN to relocate the refugee camp. At the same time Pellow helped create a website where activists could post their case studies of community struggles for environmental justice. TIEJ members became involved in some of these cases and were able to draw on sociological understandings and knowledge to 'disrupt the relations that produced environmental inequality' in the first place, and to turn those practices into general social problems that had to be immediately addressed.

In 2009 Pellow and other fellow activists teamed up to produce a guide for community organizers that tells 'ordinary people' how to confront large mining companies that try to take control of communities to ensure corporate profits, no matter the cost to local communities and ecosystems. Today Pellow regularly uses sociological concepts to help advance the interests of community members around the world. When asked why he became a professor of sociology, he responds: 'because I wanted to change the world. Why else?' (Pellow, 2011, p. 226).

Research and Advocacy in Thunder Bay

As we saw in Chapter 17, race and racism have long been a focus of sociological inquiry. Today, many sociologists in the United States and Canada are using their sociological knowledge to promote social change and social justice by actively working to eliminate racism. Randolph Haluza-DeLay (2003) provides an account of a community-initiated research project on racism that was conducted in Thunder Bay, a city in northwestern Ontario with a population of about 110,000 when the study was conducted in 2003. At the time, about 12 per cent of the population were Aboriginal people, who had already experienced a long history of political disenfranchisement, paternalism, bad faith, and oppression on the part of European colonialists. Thunder Bay itself had experienced a 20-year history of decline in both economic vitality and population.

In 1996 a coalition of organizations with committees on race relations was formed under the name Diversity Thunder Bay. It included representatives from First Nations organizations, multicultural organizations, community agencies, municipal institutions, and police services. The coalition applied for and received federal funding to conduct a study of racism in Thunder Bay. Haluza-DeLay served as the research coordinator and developed a research methodology, prepared a research instrument, pilot-tested the research instrument, sent out 392 surveys (with a 38 per cent response rate), and conducted 45 interviews. Results of that survey were published in a 144-page report, released in March 2002. Findings included extensive evidence of racially motivated incidents of discrimination in the community and racializing social practices in key social locations around Thunder Bay. For example, Haluza-DeLay found that retail establishments and restaurants were by far the most commonly reported sites of racial incidents. The study concluded that racialization was adversely affecting social cohesion in Thunder Bay.

Media attention peaked immediately following the release of the study, then tapered off. But the most interesting reaction came from the members of the Diversity Thunder Bay coalition itself. Institutional reaction to the study, Haluza-DeLay reports, was at first 'cool or dismissive'. The police union immediately disputed the study's findings, complaining that they were based on anecdotes and stories reported from other places and the past. The chamber of commerce took no apparent action 'to acknowledge diversity issues'. Thunder Bay city council, however, undertook an audit of 'diversity-related practices and policies' and reactivated a police committee on race relations (although an insider to that committee felt that 'the police seem to think things are generally OK and they just need to do a little bit') (Haluza-DeLay, 2003). On the other hand, the Nishnawbe Aski Nation (NAN) was able to use the report to follow up on an incident of racism, and succeeded in gaining a formal apology from a store manager for a case of racism. Indeed, anti-racism workers—the most active members of Diversity Thunder Bay—were the most positive about the report, and felt that the study was 'a superb step forward' and that it would be 'extremely beneficial' in the long run, providing much-needed legitimacy to the issue of racism in the city (Haluza-Day, 2003).

One of the most important lessons Haluza-DeLay learned from conducting this research was the value of making research both theoretically sound and at the same time of practical value. Injustice, he points out, has 'certain large-scale structural aspects, but it is played out in personal lives'. A second important lesson, therefore, is that research with a focus on social justice must be contextualized to the specific locale, in this case the need to 'communicate the effects of racism to local and municipal and business authorities'. Haluza-DeLay also notes that while many academics believe in the emancipatory potential of knowledge, this misses the fact that there are power relations at play around which kinds of knowledge get to be reproduced, and what gets suppressed. Simply providing strong and compelling counter-evidence to racist stereotyping is not enough if other knowledge claims are being made by those in dominant, privileged positions. Efforts at social change, he argues, 'must illuminate these unconscious processes, such as those social practices that are experienced as racializing'. It is not knowledge alone that changes social practice but rather the way in which knowledge is taken up and used in a community that promotes change.

EXPLANATORY STORIES: CHARLES TILLY ON MAKING SOCIOLOGY RELEVANT

People usually want to know the reason why something happens. They want understandable answers to the question, 'Why does [did/should] X do Y?' X here can refer to individuals or, just as easily, to 'groups, organizations, categories, forces, or invisible entities' (Tilly, 2004, pp. 446–7). As Charles Tilly explains, reasons can take four general forms: conventions, codified justifications, technical accounts, and explanatory stories.

Conventions, as explanations, do not try to provide adequate causal accounts. If I trip and spill my coffee on your newspaper, I'm not required by convention to go into a detailed explanation of my bad night's sleep, the worries I have about keeping my job, my recently developed hand tremor, and so on. Conventional accounts are expected, and formulaic, on the order of 'Sorry, I'm such a klutz,' or 'Oops—I caught my heel on the carpet' (Tilly, 2004, p. 447). Conventional explanations confirm, repair, or deny social relations and differ greatly depending on the circumstances and the people involved.

Coded justifications include laws, religious prescriptions, and systems of honour, and always involve the people who administer these codes—judges, priests, awards committees, and the like. A coded justification will be used by a judge at a sentencing hearing to explain the lenient sentence given to a first-time offender.

Technical accounts, Tilly explains, 'vary enormously with regard to internal structure and content, but they have in common the claim to identify reliable connections of cause and effect' (Tilly, 2004, p. 449). When the online customer-support technician diagnoses the computer problem you're experiencing, he will do so with a technical account, although a technical account can also come in a parent's simplified warning to a young child that if she touches the hot stove element, she will burn her finger.

Exceptional events, as for example, when a terrible tragedy occurs, when somebody makes a spectacular faux pas, or when something extraordinarily moving happens, call for *explanatory stories*. Explanatory stories are usually shorthand descriptions of cause-and-effect connections (for example, 'I became ill because someone put a spell on me'; 'I was promoted by my boss because she recognized my superior abilities when I saved the Mukherjee account after Bill let the ball drop'). Typically, says Tilly, they 'minimize or ignore the causal role of errors, unanticipated consequences, indirect effects, incremental effects, and environmental effects' (Tilly, 2004, p. 449).

The problem for sociologists, Tilly (2004) points out, is that although most of us have come to accept engineers and physicians as having specialist knowledge within their specific domains, the same cannot be said for sociologists. Sociologists have a special set of problems to deal with when trying to get their findings accepted by the general public. To begin with, sociologists 'commonly are proposing explanations of the very same behaviours and outcomes which people learn early in life to give accounts in the mode of conventions, explanatory stories, and justifications'. To add to the problem, the reasons that sociologists give for why something has occurred often contradict common-sense understandings. Sociologists are often in a position of 'causing offense and cultivating disbelief' as they challenge everyday thinking.

What can be done to improve the ability of sociologists to get their ideas across to the general public? Tilly offers four choices. Sociologists can 'build up records of effective intervention to increase their credibility', 'educate their audiences in the logic of social sciences', 'incorporate their own explanations into widely available explanatory stories', or choose to talk 'only to each other' (Tilly, 2004, pp. 452–3).

Tilly rejects the last of these options out of hand. While the private language that sociologists have developed to speak with each other serves during professional conversations, it is not adequate for use outside of the discipline. True, in fields like demography and survey research sociologists have managed to establish a certain amount of credibility through 'visible and relatively effective interventions: census, election polls, and the like' (p. 453). But, Tilly argues, most other specialties within the discipline have failed to achieve the same success.

The problem, as Tilly sees it, is that dissent affects credibility, and dissent is rife amongst sociologists. In the social sciences in general there are many competing understandings of social processes and what constitutes 'the social good'. The project of creating a common 'sociological voice', or even of 'extracting and teaching a single logic for all social science looks hopeless for the foreseeable future' (Tilly, 2004, p. 453). Tilly does not go as far as Borawoy and Turner in advocating that sociologists actively align themselves with interest groups. But he does have an interesting suggestion for what is needed if sociologists are to have their findings at least considered by those outside of the narrow confines of their profession. Sociologists should couch their findings as readily understandable 'explanatory stories'. This, says Tilly, is the role of a public intellectual: to use mass media and public forums to get a readily understandable message across to the general public.

Tilly cites, as one example of an explanatory story that sociologists have successfully circulated, the argument that if all members of a given category of people suffer the same systematic disadvantages, then 'some combination of discrimination with distinctive life experiences—rather than, say, some crippling incapacity shared in all the category's members—accounts for those disadvantages' (Tilly, 2004, p. 454). Sociologists who get their message out to the public are effective because they have 'recast their technical accounts as readily recognizable explanatory stories'. And while recast technical accounts can never 'encompass all the relevant cause–effect relations' or 'enumerate all the professionals' crucial specifications concerning initial conditions and contingencies', they can at least get right the 'cause–effect relations they do include', in itself a 'valuable sociological contribution' (Tilly, 2004, p. 454).

The news media occasionally broadcast or publish stories that promote an everyday, common-sense view of events that flies in the face of a sociological interpretation. By what other means are common-sense understandings perpetuated and spread?

SUMMARY

Throughout this textbook we have seen that as a group, sociologists use what C. Wright Mills (1959) called the 'sociological imagination' to connect public issues to private concerns and troubles. Sociologists strive to become aware of key, underlying social patterns, and they seek to understand the effects that these patterns have on individuals. American sociologist Randall Collins (1998) identified two core commitments of all sociologists: to use what he called their 'sociological eye' to see beneath the surface of society to the underpinning patterns, and to actively confront social inequities.

The controversy in sociology appears to centre on whether sociologists should ultimately choose to be professionals or activists. Recently sociologists have been reminded of their role as social activists by Michael Burawoy (2004), who argued that it is time for sociologists to engage with members of their communities and to put their expert knowledge to use in those communities. No all sociologists agree—the traditionalists especially still favour objectivity and a professional detachment from research subjects—but more and more sociologists seem to agree that the ideal model for any investigation is one that combines time-honoured, professional methods with the goal of improving the condition of a particular group.

DISCUSSION QUESTIONS

1. What distinguishes Burawoy's four types of sociological knowledge from each other? Give examples of each type.
2. In your opinion, is it possible to engage in public sociology without compromising the legitimacy of professional sociology? Explain your answer.
3. Randall Collins identifies 'the sociological eye' and activism as two core pillars of sociology. But if we have to choose between the two, Randall advocates choosing 'the sociological eye' over activism. Do you agree or disagree? Why?
4. John Porter's three goals for sociology were to develop an objective conception of the 'Good Society', to describe sociology's contribution to realizing that goal, and to develop a method that would allow us to measure societal progress along the way. Do you accept these as the goals for sociology? Why or why not? List any other goals that you think sociologists should strive to achieve and explain why you have chosen those goals.
5. In Brazil sociologists have played an important role in public life and in political policy making. Should sociologists play a similar role in Canada?

Glossary

Aboriginal people   In North America, the Inuit, Métis, and treaty and non-treaty/status and non-status Indians collectively.

achieved status   A position in a social hierarchy that has been achieved on the basis of how well an individual performs his or her social role(s). *Also see* **status**.

agency   An individual's capacity for action, inherent in all humans and shaped by a 'specific range of cultural schemas and resources available in a person's particular social milieu' (Mills, 1959/2000).

alienation   In Marxist theory, a loss of control over, or connection with, some aspect of one's being or activity, particularly as a result of the organization of wage labour. Under capitalism, wage labourers are alienated from their work, from the product of their work, and from their fellow workers because they give up control over their work in return for a wage.

anomie   A term used by Durkheim to describe the weakening or absence of norms governing social life, which allows free rein to destructive (or self-destructive) exercises of will in pursuit of expanding or unrealistic personal goals.

apartheid   A term coined in 1930 from the Afrikaans word for apartness to denote a policy of system of racial segregation and discrimination in South Africa. By the 1950s, apartheid consisted of numerous racist laws that allowed a ruling white minority to segregate all non-white persons and to deny them human and political rights. Apartheid was ended in South Africa in 1994 with the first multi-racial elections and the election of Nelson Mandela as the country's first black president.

ascribed status   The status into which an individual is born. *See* **status**.

attachment theory   A theory of early socialization developed by John Bowlby and based on the idea that sociability (social stimulation and affection) is necessary for human growth and development, especially in the early stages of life. Bowlby emphasized the importance of the mother–infant bond.

backstage   Erving Goffman's term to describe actions or interactions not intended for public view but that support a public role performance (for example, a consultation between doctors for dealing with a particular patient, carried on 'out of earshot' of the patient). *Compare* **front stage**.

berdaches   *See* **two-spirit people**.

biological sex   The outcome of the combination of two specialized reproductive cells, called *gametes*. In females the gamete is the ovum, which carries only an X-chromosome, while in males it is the sperm, which can carry either an X- or a Y-chromosome.

bisexual   Denoting people who choose sexual partners from either sex.

bonding social capital   *See* **social capital**.

bourgeoisie   The social class that owns and controls the means of production and is thus able to exploit and dominate the activities of workers within the production process.

brain plasticity   A concept used by neurologists to explain why experience (i.e. learning) regularly changes brain structure and function.

bride price   A payment—typically of money, cattle, or other goods—made by the family of a man to the family of his wife-to-be.

bridging social capital   *See* **social capital**.

bureaucracy   An ideal type concept used by Weber to designate a form of social organization with the following distinctive features:

- a hierarchically organized chain of command, with functional specialization of tasks and a well-defined hierarchy of authority
- an allegiance on the part of office holders to a system of impersonal rules and regulations rather than to the whims of superiors
- the discouraging of personal ties between employees of a bureaucracy and its clients, who are treated as 'cases'
- the use of documents and 'files' as the basis for legitimate decision making.

burka (*or* burqa)   A loose outer garment, including head covering (*hijab*) and face veil (*niqab*), worn in public by some Muslim women.

capitalist mode of production   In Marxist sociology, the mode of production in which productive property is held privately and used for private gain. Those who own the means of production profit by employing wage labour. Typically, the capitalist mode of production is industrial in nature.

case study   A type of research design that focuses on a detailed analysis of a single case or situation, usually a community or organization, in a specific location.

census   A complete enumeration of a population in which information is systematically acquired and recorded about all the members of that population. Censuses are usually conducted by national governments at specific intervals.

chromosomes   Long DNA helixes on which many thousands of genes are encoded. In humans, genes are bundled together in each cell in 23 pairs of chromosomes.

class situation   A concept used by Weber to refer to an individual social actor's orientations, skills, abilities, and conditions of life and to the actions that follow from those qualities.

comparison (or cross-sectional) study   A research design used to study of the relationship between two or more variables occurring in two or more cases at the same point in time. Cross-cultural research and cross-national research are two typical forms of comparison (cross-sectional) studies.

convenience sampling   A non-probability sampling technique in which research subjects are chosen because they are close at hand (i.e. 'convenient').

core sociological knowledge base   A set of core concepts, skills, and topics that allow us to think differently about the world and to confront its challenges.

corporate crime   Any conduct of a corporation (which exists in law as a 'legal person'), or of the representatives and employees acting on behalf of a corporation, that violates criminal law or that is a civil or administrative violation.

critical thinking   Thinking that is purposeful, deliberate, and self-regulatory, and that arrives at judgements based on well-defined criteria and evidence.

culture   In its broadest usage, all socially transmitted social practices and knowledge systems, including language, beliefs, values, material objects, and know-how, that are transmitted from one generation to the next, and that enable humans to adapt to and thrive in a given environment.

data (sing. datum)   From the Latin past participle of *dare*, 'to give'; literally a thing given or granted. In scientific terms, something known or assumed as fact, and made the basis for reasoning or calculation.

deductive   Denoting research informed by a quantitative research strategy, in which a theory is used to generate hypotheses and to guide and influence the collection of the data needed to confirm or reject the hypothesis. Depending on the conclusions that can be drawn from the data collected, an existing hypothesis is either confirmed and the theory is demonstrated, or the existing theory is revised and a new hypothesis is deduced. *Compare* **inductive**.

dependent variable   *See* **variable**.

dialectical materialism   Marx's term for historical materialism, his theoretical perspective for understanding history, society, and social relations.

dichotomous variable   A variable that has only two, mutually exclusive categories.

disproportionate minority contact   *See* **overrepresentation**.

DNA   The hereditary material in all organisms, including humans. Almost every cell in our bodies (with the exception of eggs, sperm, and red blood cells) has the same DNA, which is located in the cell's nucleus ('nuclear DNA'). Human DNA is made up of about 3 billion base pairs, and more than 99 per cent of them are the same in all people.

'doing gender'   The (often unconscious) activity of managing one's conduct in a way that is consistent with what is generally considered appropriate to one's sex category. This concept was first introduced by Candace West and Don Zimmerman (1987).

emotional entrainment   A situation in which participants in an interaction ritual become caught up in each other's emotions, leading to a mutual intensification of emotional energy, shared feelings, and a common focus of attention.

empirical   Based on, guided by, or employing observation and experiment rather than theory. From the Greek word *empeirikos*, meaning 'experience, skilled'.

empirical evidence   Evidence that has been acquired through direct observation. It is evidence that can be verified or disproved by direct or indirect observation by more than one person. Empirical research bases its findings on empirical evidence, and uses that evidence as its test of reality.

empiricism   A foundation of positivist epistemology, it is an approach to reality that holds that the only valid knowledge is knowledge gained through the process of using the senses to directly observe, record, or monitor social and natural phenomena.

epistemology   The theory of knowledge, a branch of philosophy that deals with the nature, scope, and limitations of knowledge. Epistemological questions such as 'what methods should be used to arrive at an explanation?' and 'What proofs are required?' are about the validity of our knowledge.

ethnicity   The state of belonging to a social group that shares a common cultural heritage that includes language, traditions, food, values, customs, and religion.

eugenics movement   A social philosophy of the nineteenth and twentieth centuries dedicated to improving human heredity through selective breeding for 'desirable characteristics' in order to preserve and guarantee the competitive strength of the nation as a whole. Eugenics theories argue that certain human characteristics or tendencies are genetically inherited, and that those who exhibit negative traits should be kept from having children in order to increase the general 'health' and 'strength' of the population.

feral children   Human children who have lived away from adults from an early age and thus have little experience of human social behaviour or language. Many recorded feral children have been brought up by animals, while others have lived in isolation.

front stage   Erving Goffman's term for social performances meant to be seen and that define the situation in a general way for an audience. *Compare* **back stage**.

functionalism   A general theoretical orientation to the study of society that focuses on large-scale social structures and their role in maintaining or undermining social stability. Functionalists usually maintain that social structures are based on shared values and meanings, that social disorder occurs when shared values and meanings are disrupted, and that social equilibrium is best re-established by restoring old—or establishing new—shared values and preferences. *Also see* **structural functionalism**.

game stage   According to Mead, the second of three developmental stages of the self, during which the child has a specific role to play but must also assume the role of other players in order to anticipate how they will react.

gametes   *See* **biological sex**.

gay   *See* **homosexual**.

gender   The sense of being male or female, typically with reference to masculine and feminine social and cultural roles rather than biological differences; gender is an achieved status.

gender stereotypes   Shared, culturally hegemonic beliefs about how most people 'typically' view men and women.

gender stratification   The channelling of men and women into different (and usually unequal) life situations. Gender stratification is a system of social practices that organize relations of inequality between men and women on the basis of perceived differences.

gene   An encoded protein that regulates some aspect of heredity in a living organism. All living things depend on genes, which hold all the information needed to build and maintain an organism's cells and to pass on genetic traits to offspring.

generalized other   According to Mead, the last of three developmental stages of the self, a role taken on by the developing child as she assumes the attitudes held by other members of her community towards her as her own. In complex societies individuals must take into consideration a multitude of different 'generalized others' that range from families and friends, social clubs, political groups to more abstract groups such as the university or 'the state'.

genetic kinship   A notion of family or kinship that is measured through or read from the genetic material of an individual. This genetic material situates the individual within a line of prehistoric and historical descent. *Compare* **social kinship**.

genome   The total complement of genes in an organism.

Gini coefficient   A measure of the inequality of a statistical dispersion that can range between 0, if whatever is being measured is equally distributed amongst all members of a population (i.e. total equality) and 1, if a single individual holds all of whatever is being measured (i.e. maximum inequality).

habitus   A concept introduced by Pierre Bourdieu to refer to the intentional but nonetheless socially constrained disposition of an individual social actor to behave in a certain way and to make a certain kind of sense out of the social world. It is a durable attitude toward the world that motivates an individual to see the world in ways that are shaped by early social experiences and that are consistent with others who hold the same social position.

hegemony   A concept used to explain the way in which dominant groups in society use intellectual and moral leadership to try to win ascent over subordinate groups by portraying the interests of the dominant class as the universal interests of humanity. The theory is then used to compare these interests with the 'real' interests of the opposing social class in order to demonstrate that what is being presented as 'universal' is in fact the source of all injustice.

hermeneutical   *See* **interpretivism.**

heteronormativity   In contemporary, common-sense usage, heterosexuality as the 'normal sexuality' that can be expressed only in terms of sexual practices and orientations that serve to bring together members of the two mutually exclusive categories of male and female, ultimately for the purposes of reproduction.

hijab   A head covering traditionally worn by Muslim women. The term may also refer to a modest style of dress in general that involves covering everything except the face and hands in public. Traditionally, many different forms of clothing are recognized as satisfying hijab. *Also see* **burka.**

historical materialism   The term used today to describe Marx's theoretical perspective for understanding history, society, and social relations.

homophobia   Fear of and antipathy towards persons with non-heteronormative sexual orientations.

homosexual   Denoting people who choose sexual partners of the same sex. Common usage is to call homosexual men *gay* and homosexual women *lesbian.*

hypothesis   A proposed explanation, carefully expressed, made on the basis of limited evidence as a starting point for further investigation. Hypotheses should not be confused with theories, which are more general explanations based on repeated testing of hypotheses. *Compare* **theory.**

'I' (the 'I')   According to Mead, the response of the organism to the attitudes of the others. The 'I' represents a direct line of action taken by an individual. *Compare* **'Me'.**

ideal type   A methodological construction used by Weber to summarize the essential properties common to a number of concrete instances of a given type of social phenomenon, and in so doing to help

the sociologist in identifying and categorizing the specific social phenomena she studies. The category of 'city economy' is an example of an ideal type category that could be constructed by identifying traits that are common to most city economies.

impression management   Erving Goffman's term for the activity engaged in by a performer in order to guard against the unexpected, such as unintended gestures, improper use of language, and social *faux pas.* Social actors consciously strive to manage the impression they give others, and to control the impressions they unwittingly 'give off'.

independent variable   *See* **variable.**

individualism   A moral stance that stresses the importance of individual self-reliance and independence.

individual racism   A concept introduced by black activists Stokely Carmichael and Charles Hamilton (1967) to describe deliberately racist activities and actions by individual people. *Compare* **institutional racism.**

inductive   Denoting an approach in which theory is the outcome, rather than the starting point, of research (as is the case in deductive theory). *Compare* **deductive.**

instincts   Complex patterns of behaviour that are genetically pre-programmed and that regulate the activities of members of a species. Instinctual behaviours tend to be found in all members of a species and are innate. Instincts differ from reflexes in that instinctual behaviour is complex whereas reflex actions are simple.

institutional racism   A concept introduced by black activists Stokely Carmichael and Charles Hamilton (1967) to 'account for attitudes and practices that lead to racist outcomes through unquestioned bureaucratic procedures'. Carmichael and Hamilton made it plain that even if white people had no intention of discriminating against blacks, they still collectively benefit from institutional racism. *Also called* **systemic racism**; *compare* **individual racism.**

interaction ritual   An event in which participants focus on a common objective or activity and share a common emotional experience or set of feelings. Interaction rituals serve to give individuals a sense of common identity and purpose with others. During interaction rituals participants may use symbols to produce a sense of belonging and solidarity amongst the members of a social group or unit. Participants in an interaction ritual may be induced to do what they must do even if it is at odds with their normal, everyday behaviour.

Internet As defined by DiMaggio, et al. (2001), it is 'the electronic network of networks that links people and information through computers and other digital devices allowing [mediated] person-to-person communication and information retrieval' (p. 307).

interpretive understanding *See* **Verstehen**.

interpretivism An epistemological position associated with qualitative research strategies. An interpretivist (also called a 'hermeneutical') epistemological orientation is based on the assumption that we can learn about the meaning of the actions of people who are separated from us by time or physical space because all humans communicate with one another using some symbolic medium.

intersexed A general term used to describe a variety of conditions in which an individual is born with sexual anatomy that does not clearly conform to typical expectations about male and female anatomy.

intersubjective view *See* **theory of intersubjectivity**.

interview A conversation, usually face-to-face, guided by a series of questions and conducted in order to discover the opinions or experience of someone.

labour power In Marxist sociology, the physical or mental capacity for work that an employee sells to an employer in return for a wage or salary. This sale of labour power was, for Marx, the basis of the exploitation of the worker, and of alienation in the capitalist mode of production.

lesbian *See* **homosexual**.

lifeworld German philosopher Edmund Husserl's term for the entire communal system of meaning that underlies everyday life.

longitudinal (comparison) study A research design that combines the comparison and longitudinal approaches in order to measure and compare the changes in the same variable in two or more groups over time.

looking-glass self A term used by Charles Horton Cooley to stress the view that we become social beings by developing the ability, through socialization, to see ourselves as others might see us in any given social situation. We gain a sense of self only by seeing ourselves reflected in the responses of others in symbolic interactionism.

low-income cutoffs (LICOs) A set of 'income thresholds, determined by analyzing family expenditure data, below which families will devote a larger share of income to the necessities of food, shelter and clothing than the average family would' (Statistics Canada,

2008a). The term is plural because several LICOs are calculated in order to account for differences in community type and family size.

mass culture Cultural phenomena (music, dance, symbols, values, consumer goods, etc.) produced for mass consumption by a mass audience (often thought of as non-discriminating consumers). For mass culture to exist there needs to be a large and concentrated population ('the masses') with money to spend on consumer items and/or technologies of mass communication. As well, there must be transportation to move physical goods or technologies to disseminate electronic ideas or products (the Internet, for example) to this population. *Compare* **popular culture**.

mass media A term used to refer to one-to-many–type communications in which identical messages are transmitted to large numbers of people ('the masses') in a very short time. Mass media are carriers of mass culture, and they transmit that culture without any ties to a specific community. In the previous three centuries this transmission was accomplished via the technology of the printing press. Today, radio, television, movies, CDs, DVDs, and the like are all examples of media that facilitate the one-to-many type of communication.

master status *See* **status**.

'Me' (the 'Me') According to Mead, the organized set of attitudes of others that an individual assumes as part of him- or herself. The 'Me' involves looking backward, considering what has already transpired, and then evaluating one's response from the standpoint of the expectations of others. *Compare* **'I'**.

means of production In Marxist sociology, those things needed for production to take place: in the capitalist mode of production, for example, the means of production include energy, raw materials, tools, facilities, and expertise. Along with labour power, these constitute what Marx called the forces of production.

menarche The first menstrual period of a woman.

mode of production In Marxist sociology, the characteristic way in which human labour is organized and carried out in a given era. The mode of production encompasses both the material and the technological organization of production as well as its social organization (i.e. ownership and control).

multiculturalism The peaceful co-existence within a state of different ethnic and cultural groups. In Canada, multiculturalism was a federal policy in force between 1985 and June 2010, supported by numerous social programs designed to promote and accommodate ethnocultural diversity and highlighting the importance of 'cultural and racial diversity' as a 'fundamental characteristic of the Canadian heritage and identity'.

niqab A veil worn by some Muslim women as part of hijab; it is common in Pakistan and parts of India. *Also see* **burka**.

normlessness *See* **anomie**.

objective knowledge Knowledge purported to be free of bias.

objectivism An ontological position that asserts that all social organizations are independent of the will or ideas of individuals in them.

ontology The study of what there is 'out there'; in other words, the study of what is said to constitute 'reality'.

operationalize Give an operational definition to a concept (or variable) so that it can be measured. For example, the concept 'gender' is operationalized by a choice of 'male', 'female', or 'two-spirit'.

outside Erving Goffman's term for areas irrelevant to the performance of a particular social role or to a particular social situation.

overrepresentation A situation that occurs when a disproportionately large number of people of a particular class or ethnicity is included in a group that is meant to represent the larger population. Overrepresentation can skew the results of a statistical analysis. The term has been used by Canadian researchers and commissions of inquiry to describe a situation in which Aboriginal people are, compared with non-Aboriginal people, disproportionately represented as offenders in the criminal justice system relative to their numbers in the population (Fitzgerald & Carrington, 2008, p. 550). In the American literature, the term *disproportionate minority contact* (or DMC) is used to refer to the phenomenon of minority overrepresentation in the criminal justice system (see e.g. Huizinga, et al., 2007, as cited in Fitzgerald & Carrington, 2008.).

participant observation A type of research design in which a researcher is immersed over a period of time in the social setting under study. During that time the researcher observes and listens in order to gather information on the social life and culture of the people she or he is studying.

personal front Erving Goffman's term for the props needed by an actor in a social situation to make others (the 'audience') believe that the role being played is genuine.

philosophical idealism An approach to philosophy espoused by Hegel, who denied that physical things—trees, houses, people, animals—have 'veritable being' (i.e. that they are real). Instead, following a philosophical tradition that begins with Plato, Hegel emphasized the important role of thought in creating reality. Karl Marx rejected this position, arguing instead that the physical needs and requirements of humans are primary.

play stage According to Mead, the first of three developmental stages of the self, during which the child has limited capacity to assume the perspective of others and often plays by assuming a single role.

popular culture Culture created by masses of people in modern urban-industrial societies. Popular culture is closely related to mass culture, and many creations of mass culture become part of popular culture through mass media. However, popular culture may develop in ways unforeseen by those who market mass culture items. *Compare* **mass culture**.

positivism The epistemological orientation that supports a deductive approach to generating hypotheses. Rationalism and empiricism are considered the 'twin pillars' of positivist epistemology. *See* **rationalism**, **empiricism**.

pragmatism A philosophical school of thought, popularized through the work of William James and John Dewey, in which the social world is viewed as dynamic and emergent, brought into being by a variety of social groups that create their own way of talking, acting, and thinking and of defining what is and is not 'real'.

primary groups Human associations characterized by intimate, face-to-face interaction and co-operation. The primary group offers the first and most important link between the individual and broader social institutions. *Also called* **small groups**.

qualitative data Information that can be measured in terms of quality rather than quantity. A person's place of birth, religious affiliation, and views on same-sex marriage are qualitative data.

qualitative research strategy A research strategy in which a researcher collects data that are rich in description and not easily handled using statistical procedures.

quantitative data Information that can be measured in terms of quantity as opposed to quality. A person's age, height, and weight are quantitative data.

quantitative research strategy   A research strategy in which a researcher focuses on collecting and processing data using statistical procedures.

quartile   In descriptive statistics, each of four equal groups or parts into which a sorted set of measurements has been divided. The term may also refer to each of the three values used to divide the measurement set into four groups: the *second quartile* is the median, which divides the measurement set in two; the *first quartile* is the median of the lower half of the measurement set; the *third quartile* is the median of the upper half of the data set.

questionnaire   A set of questions with a choice of answers, devised and administered to respondents for the purposes of a survey or statistical study.

race   A contested term used in everyday understanding to refer to supposedly inherited biological characteristics that distinguish different human populations.

racialization   The social and political processes by which racially distinct groups are socially constructed.

racism   A set of beliefs concerning supposedly inherent characteristics pertaining to human populations, usually entailing judgements about the superiority and inferiority of different 'races'. Racism often serves to justify exploitation and serves as an underlying belief system expressed in the forms of prejudice.

radical empiricism   *See* **sensationalism**.

rationalism   A foundation of positivist epistemology, it is an approach to reality that has its basis in the work of the ancient Greek philosophers and can best be characterized by the statement, 'What is, is; what is not, is not.'

rationality   Weber's term for an ideal-type mental state that is characterized by a culturally defined, coherent way of thinking. As an ideal type, rationality is any thought that is goal-oriented and based on a cost-benefit calculation and that is made within the context of a specific social and cultural situation.

rationalization   Weber's term for the process by which nature, society, and individual action are increasingly mastered by an orientation to planning, technical procedure, and rational action. Rationalization refers to two broad historical trends: the social process whereby societies become more and more reliant on calculation and technical knowledge to gain and maintain control over both natural and social worlds, and the tendency for social actors to free themselves from magical thinking and to replace that with thinking informed by empirical observations.

reproduction of class identity   The process by which an ascribed social class position is transmitted from one generation to the next.

research methods   The actual techniques a researcher uses to collect data.

research strategy   The general approach or orientation a sociologist takes toward conducting research. A research strategy may be qualitative or quantitative.

role set   All of the roles attached to a single status. *See* **social role**.

role strain   A situation that can occur when there is tension among the various roles attached to a status, or even between the roles attached to different statuses. *See* **social role**.

scientific   Based on or involving science, a 'discipline that collects, weighs, and evaluates the empirical evidence for accepting a particular theory or explanation'. Scientists collect and analyze evidence 'in such a way that others, looking at the same evidence in the same way would draw the same conclusions or at least understand that it is possible to see what the researcher was examining' (Bouma, Ling, & Wilkinson, 2009, p. 7).

self   A sense of identity that each individual possesses. According to Mead, the self is a temporal process that has a 'developmental course' and 'arises in the process of social experience and activity' as an outcome of the individual's 'relations to that process as a whole and to other individuals within that process'.

sensationalism   A theory of human learning, popular in the eighteenth century, that argued that humans acquire beliefs, ideas, and knowledge only through sensory experience. *Also called* **radical empiricism**.

sex   Either of the two main categories (male and female) into which humans are divided on the basis of their reproductive functions; sex is an ascribed status.

sexual dimorphism   The recognition of only two sexes—male and female—in a species.

sexuality studies   An umbrella term used to designate an interdisciplinary field of study that emerged in the 1970s as a result of the work of scholars and political activists who took a social-constructivist approach to sexuality, viewing it not as a biological drive but as something socially constructed.

sex work   All forms of commercialized sex, including pornography, prostitution, stripping, and telephone sex.

significant gestures or symbols   Gestures or symbols that hold the same meaning for all participants in a social interaction. A significant gesture or symbol is one that is understood equally by the individual making and the individual receiving that gesture.

small groups   *See* **primary groups**.

snowball sampling   A non-probability sampling technique used by researchers when research subjects are difficult to locate, in which the researcher asks initial research subjects to help with finding other research subjects. The researcher continues asking research subjects to nominate other potential research subjects until a sufficient number have been sampled.

social action   A concept used by Weber to refer to any human behaviour that has subjective meaning for an acting individual. An action is a social action when the individual takes into account the meaning his or her actions will have for others observing them, and orients his or her actions accordingly.

social actor   An individual who shares with other social actors a common frame of reference that includes common convictions, beliefs, values, activities, practices, and a shared language.

social capital   A concept introduced by Pierre Bourdieu and used by sociologists to help them understand the role of social ties between members of a social network, especially as those ties affect the quality of life of network members. *Bonding social capital* reflects relations within a social network. In contrast, *bridging social capital* is based on weak ties among network members. The latter is better suited to providing access to external resources and information than it is to providing emotional support.

social construction of reality   The belief that the reality experienced by members of any given society is shaped by and shared with other members of the same society. Sociologists maintain that human experiences are social accomplishments or artifices. Because all experience is the product of social interaction, all interpretations of or knowledge about a given experience are open to questions and challenges. The concept was introduced by Peter Berger and Thomas Luckmann (1966).

social dynamics   A term used by Comte to denote the process of social change.

social facts   Durkheim's term for those 'things' that are external to the individual and that are capable of exercising coercive power over him or her. They are independent of, and resistant to, the will of any given individual and, as Durkheim held, 'it is impossible to free ourselves of them'. It is 'social facts' that exercise power over the individual, and not the other way around.

social inequality   A concept used by sociologists to describe how certain attributes that are deemed to be valuable (e.g. wealth, income, education, prestige, occupation, health, life chances) are unevenly distributed across such organizational units as societies, social classes, communities, families, and individuals, and are affected by such factors as race, gender, physical ability, sexual orientation, and age.

social institution   Any complex form of social organization that combines a variety of social positions, norms, and values, and that organizes (relatively) stable forms of human social interaction with respect to such fundamental issues as the reproduction of individuals and of the conditions necessary to sustain life (Turner, 1997).

social interaction   The process by which individuals act, interact, and react to one another in the context of social relations.

socialization   The process of becoming a member of society, of becoming a social being (i.e. gaining a self or an identity), or of learning social roles. Socialization takes place in stages (e.g. primary socialization, secondary socialization).

social kinship   A notion of kinship or family that is shaped by patterns of sociability and a sense of alliance and affiliation that is not strictly determined by the crude definition of shared biological descent. *Compare* **genetic kinship**.

social media   Primarily Internet and mobile media that use accessible, scalable publishing techniques to support mediated social interactions among networked members of a 'community'. They are a group of Internet-based applications that allow for the creation and exchange of 'user-generated' information. Social media support 'many-to-many' communications among community members, rather than communications that are dominated by one person or one organization, as is the case in broadcast media. Examples include blogs, microblogs, wikis, podcasts, social networking sites, virtual game worlds, virtual communities, video sharing, music and audio sharing, and social bookmarking.

social network   A set of individuals or 'nodes' (technically called 'vertices') and the links between them.

social network analysis   A mathematical method used by sociologists for describing the patterns of social relations among and between individuals, groups, or other social collectivities.

social networking The activity of building and maintaining networks of connections with friends and others who share common interests and activities via special networking websites.

social networking sites (SNSs) Websites that allow people to build online social networks through online profiles, blogs, and other shared written, audio, or visual information. Social networking sites have risen in popularity in part because of their ease of use.

social norms A set of rules governing social interaction. Social norms can be prescriptive (they can tell us what to do) or proscriptive (they can forbid us to do certain things). Sumner distinguished between two types of norms: folkways and mores.

social physiology A term coined by Saint-Simon to denote the premise that society could be studied as if it were an organism, demonstrating growth, order, stability, and pathologies.

social relations of production In Marxist sociology, the social relations between individuals in terms of how production is carried out; specifically, the social relations through which control over the productive forces is established and maintained. In their legal form, the social relations of production take the form of property laws.

social role The behaviour performed by an individual who occupies or holds a particular social status. For example, an individual may hold the status of doctor: that status will lead him to perform the role of doctor by seeing patients in his office, attending medical conventions, and referring his patients to specialist colleagues.

social statics A term used by Comte to denote social structure and/or social order.

social stratification The system by which members of a given society are organized into hierarchically ranked layers or strata.

social structure A core sociological concept used to denote the resilient, and enduring, systematic patterns that order and constrain social life; these patterns are largely non-negotiable.

social systems A term introduced by Anthony Giddens to refer to empirically observable, relatively bounded social practices that link social actors across time and space; examples of social systems inlcude a society, global capitalism, a family, and a neighbourhood community.

society The object of sociological study. Society entails the existence of patterned social relations and of shared norms, values, and beliefs. It is best thought of not as made up of individuals but as made up of relationships within which individuals are defined in terms of social categories. Broadly speaking, a society can be defined as a grouping of people who live together and who have developed, through interacting with one another, common interests, institutions, and collective activities.

socioeconomic status A composite measure of a person's social standing based on a combination of income, education, and occupational prestige rankings.

sociological imagination A particular orientation required to understand and draw connections between individual experience and larger social structures. The concept was introduced and defined by C. Wright Mills (1959).

sociology A term coined by Comte for the science by which the laws of the social universe could be discovered. It is the study of all human social experience, whether the chance encounter of two human individuals, the outcome of a highly structured social group, or the result of a worldwide social phenomenon. In the broadest sense, sociology is an interpretation of or commentary on the social experiences that sociologists share with members of the wider society.

standpoint epistemology The view that all research and knowledge production are directly related to the vantage point or social location of the researcher.

status The culturally defined social position that an individual holds in a social interaction, which defines a person's identity and relationship to others. It is a relative concept, and as such it measures a person's importance or role in relation to others. Some of these statuses are *ascribed* (i.e. involuntary; 'daughter' is an ascribed status, as is 'teenager'); *achieved* (i.e. voluntarily, usually reflecting some ability or at least some effort; 'wife', 'mother', 'business partner', and 'university student' are all achieved statuses); and *master* (i.e. one that has considerable bearing on one's life chances; socioeconomic background, race, and gender are examples).

status group a group of people who claim certain kinds of social esteem for themselves such as honour and prestige.

structural functionalism A theoretical paradigm that came to dominate American sociology from the 1930s to well into the 1960s, defined by the basic metaphor of society as a large, living organism made up of a number of different, interrelated structures that function together to contribute to a society's survival.

surplus value Value over and above the price the capitalist has paid for that day's worth of work.

systemic racism *See* **institutional racism**.

tangible *See* **empirical**.

taste A concept used by Pierre Bourdieu to identify the choice of cultural practices and objects that people use in their daily lives, in order to establish and maintain their class position. Taste, according to Bourdieu, is not an individual attribute or something that is achieved, but is largely the result of social learning and is highly correlated with social class.

theory An explanation of observed or regular patterns used to guide research, which directs our attention to certain aspects of people's behaviour, or to certain events or things, and suggests a framework by which we can understand what we observe. Theories are made up of statements and propositions. Robert Merton (1967) distinguished between theories of a more general nature ('grand theories') and theories that pertain to a more limited range of phenomena ('middle-range theories'). *Compare* **hypothesis**.

theory of intersubjectivity An extension of attachment theory, which focuses on the two-way interaction between infants and caregivers in the socialization process. The intersubjective view emphasizes the role played by subjects other than the maternal figure in early socialization. The intersubjective perspective defines individuals in relation to others, not as discrete or isolated units.

theory of structuration Anthony Giddens' theory uniting social structure and agency into a single, ongoing process of dynamic interplay between the two elements of structure and agency: while social structures shape the actions of individuals, the actions of individuals in turn reproduce (or change) social structures.

totemic religions Religions whose members identify with a spiritual totem, typically an animal or other naturalistic figure.

transformation of class identity The processes whereby a social actor alters her ascribed status in order to achieve a different status from the one she has acquired from her parents.

two-spirit people Members of a 'third sex' recognized in many Native North American societies, either men who adopt women's dress and do women's work or women who adopt men's dress and do men's work. They have been documented in almost 150 Native North American societies. The term is used to indicate a person whose body houses both masculine and feminine spirits. *Formerly called* **berdaches**.

underclass The lowest social stratum, consisting of the poor and unemployed.

value relevance The relevance of a problem to a social scientist's own values, especially as the basis for choosing that problem to research.

values The beliefs and feelings that a researcher holds.

variable A concept that is capable of varying in amount or quality, for example income (which varies in amount) or class (which varies in quality). An *independent variable* has a causal impact on a dependent variable. A *dependent variable* is caused or influenced by an independent variable. For example, the decision to attend university (the dependent variable) is influenced by parent's education level, income, and whether or not one's friends are also going to university (all independent variables).

Verstehen Weber's term for 'interpretive understanding', an approach to sociological research in which the researcher employs empathy and imagines what it would be like to relive the experiences of our subjects.

visible minority An identifiable group of people who are non-white and who, because of some 'visible' characteristic, may experience discrimination.

wealth Total assets less total liabilities, based on marketable assets that are in direct control of families. It does not include the crude value of savings held in employer pension plans or future claims on publicly funded income security programs.

working class The social class that is dispossessed of the means of production and sells its labour power to capitalists and is thus exploited and dominated within production.

References

Abada, Teresa, Hou, Feng, & Ram, Bali. (2009). Ethnic differences in educational attainment among the children of Canadian immigrants. *Canadian Journal of Sociology, 34*(1), 1-27.

Abbott, Pamela, & Wallace, Claire. (1990). *An introduction to sociology: Feminist perspectives.* London: Routledge.

Abraham, Linda Boland, Mörn, Marie Pauline, & Vollman, Andrea. (2010, June 30). *Women on the Web: How women are shaping the Internet.* Retrieved from www.comscore.com/Press_Events/ Presentations_Whitepapers/2010/Women_on_the_Web_How_ Women_are_Shaping_the_Internet

Abrams, Philip. (1972). The sense of the past and the origins of sociology. In *Past and Present, 55,* 18–32.

Ackerman, S.M., Starr, B. Hindus, D., & Mainwaring, S.D. (1997). Hanging on the wire: A field study of an audio-only media space. *ACM Transactions on Computer-Human Interaction, 4*(1), 39–66.

Adam, Barry D. (2003). The Defence of Marriage Act and American exceptionalism. The 'gay marriage' panic in the United States. *Journal of the History of Sexuality, 12,* 259–76.

Adler, P., & Kwon, S. (2002). Social capital: Prospects for a new concept. *Academy of Management Review, 27*(1), 17–40.

Alegria, J., & Noirot, E. (1978). Neonate orientation of behavior toward human voice. *International Journal of Behavioral Development, 1,* 291–312.

———, &———. (1982). Oriented mouthing activity in neonates: Early development of differences related to feeding experiences. In J. Mehler, S. Franck, E.C. Walker, & M. Garrett (Eds), *Perspectives on mental representation: Experimental and theoretical studies of cognitive processes and capabilities.* Hillsdale, NJ: Erlbaum.

Alexander, Jeffrey C. (1987). *Twenty lectures: Sociological theory since World War II.* New York: Columbia University Press.

Allport, G. (1954). *The nature of prejudice.* Cambridge, MA: Addison-Wesley.

Almey, Marcia. (2006). Women in Canada: Work chapter updates. Catalogue no. 98-F0133-XWE. Ottawa: Statistics Canada.

American Anthropological Association (AAA). (1998, May 17). American Anthropological Association statement on 'race'. Retrieved from www.aaanet.org/stmts/racepp.htm

American Psychological Association (APA). (n.d.). Sexual orientation and homosexuality. Retrieved from www.apa.org/ helpcenter/sexual-orientation.aspx

American Sociological Association (ASA). (2003). The importance of collecting data and doing social science research on race. Washington, DC: American Sociological Association. Retrieved from www2.asanet.org/media/asa_race_statement.pdf

———. (2005). Teaching resource guides. *American Sociological Association.* Retrieved from www.e-noah.net/ASA/ ASAShopOnlineService/productslist.aspx?CategoryID= ASASS&selection=10

Andersen, Robert, & Fetner, Tina. (2008, Summer). Cohort differences in tolerance of homosexuality: Attitudinal change in Canada and the United States, 1981–2000. *Public Opinion Quarterly, 72*(2), 311–30.

Anderson, Craig A., Carnagey, Nicholas L., & Eubanks, Janie. (2003, May). Exposure to violent media: The effects of songs with violent lyrics on aggressive thoughts and feelings. *Journal of Personality and Social Psychology, 84*(5), 960–71.

Anderson, Elijah. (1999). *Code of the street: Decency, violence, and the moral life of the inner city.* New York: W.W. Norton.

Anderson, Sarah, Cavanagh, John, Klinger, Scott, & Stanton, Liz. (2005). Executive excess 2005: Defense contractors get more bucks for the bang. *United for a Fair Economy.* Retrieved from www.faireconomy.org/press/2005/EE2005_ph.html

Archer, Margaret S. (1982). Morphogenesis versus structuration. *British Journal of Sociology, 33,* 455–83.

———. (1984). *Social origins of educational systems.* London: Sage.

———. (1996). *Culture and agency, the place of culture in social theory.* Press Syndicate of the University of Cambridge: Cambridge. (Original work published 1988)

Are the effects of pornography negligible? (2009, December 1). *UdeMNouvelles.* Retrieved from www.nouvelles.umontreal. ca/udem-news/news-digest/are-the-effects-of-pornography- negligible.html

Ariès, Philippe. (1981). *The hour of our death.* New York: Knopf.

Armstrong, Elizabeth, & Crage, Suzanna. (2006). Movements and memory: The making of the Stonewall myth. *American Sociological Review, 71,* 724–51.

Armstrong, Pat, & Armstrong, Hugh. (2010). *The double ghetto: Canadian women and their segregated work* (3rd edn). Don Mills, ON: Oxford University Press. (Original work published 1993)

Aronowitz, Stanley. (2005). Comments on Michael Burawoy's 'The critical turn to public sociology'. *Critical Sociology, 3,* 333–8.

Ashley, David, & Orenstein, David Michael. (1990). *Sociological theory: Classical statements* (2nd edn). Boston: Allyn & Bacon.

———, & ———. (2005). *Sociological theory: Classical statements* (5th edn). Boston: Pearson.

A women-owned world. Female consumers represent a bigger market than India and China combined. It's time companies recognized their power. (2010, May 8). Special information feature. *The Globe and Mail,* p. L9.

Babooram, Avani. (2008). The changing profile of adults in custody, 2006/07. *Juristat: Canadian Centre for Justice Statistics, 28*(10), 1–56. Retrieved from CBCA Reference. (Document ID: 85-002-X).

Baehr, Peter. (2005, Jan./Feb.). The sociology of almost everything: Four questions to Randall Collins about interaction ritual chains. *Review Forum, Canadian Journal of Sociology Online.* Retrieved from www.cjsonline.ca/reviews/ interactionritual.html

Bagley, C., & Tremblay, P. (1998). On the prevalence of homosexuality and bisexuality, in a random community survey of 750 men aged 18 to 27. *Journal of Homosexuality, 2,* 1–18.

Bailey, B.L. (1988). *From front porch to backseat: Courtship in twentieth-century America.* Baltimore: Johns Hopkins University Press.

Bailey, Martha J. (2006). More power to the pill: The impact of contraceptive freedom on women's life cycle labor supply. *The Quarterly Journal of Economics, 121*(1), 289–320.

Baillargeon, R. (2000). Reply to Bogartz, Shinskey & Schilling; Schilling; and Cashon & Cohen. *Infancy, 1*, 447–62.

Baiocchi, Gianpaolo. (2005). Interrogating connections: From public criticisms to critical publics in Burawoy's public sociology. *Critical Sociology, 31*(3), 339–51.

Baker, M., & Benjamin, D. (1997). Ethnicity, foreign birth and earnings: A Canada/US comparison. In M.G. Abbott, C.M. Beach, & R.P. Chaykowski (Eds), *Transition and structural change in the North American labour market* (pp. 281–313). Kingston: John Deutsch Institute and Industrial Relations Centre, Queen's University.

Baker, Paul J. (1981). Learning sociology and assessing critical thinking. *Teaching Sociology, 8*, 325–63.

Bamshad, Michael J., & Olson, Steve E. (2003, December). Does race exist? *Scientific American*, pp. 78–85.

Bandura, Albert, Ross, Dorothea, & Ross, Sheila A. (1961). Transmission of aggression through imitation of aggressive models. *Journal of Abnormal and Social Psychology, 63*, 575–82.

Banerjee, Rupa. (2006). An examination of factors affecting perception of workplace discrimination. Toronto: Centre for Industrial Relations and Human Resources, University of Toronto. Retrieved from www.cira-acri.ca/docs/workingpapers/StudentPerceptions%20of%20Workplace%20Discrimination_Banerjee_081506.pdf

Barbalet, Jack M. (1980). Principles of stratification in Max Weber: An interpretation and critique. *The British Journal of Sociology, 3*, 401–18.

Barbour, Charles. (2003). Red rhetorics: Politics, polemics and the Marx-machine. PhD Dissertation. University of British Columbia.

Bargh, J., & McKenna, K. (2004). The Internet and social life. *Annual Review of Psychology, 55*(1), 573–90.

Barnes, J.A. (1954). Class and committee in a Norwegian island parish. *Human Relations, 7*.

Baron-Cohen, S. (1995). *Mindblindness: An essay on autism and theory of mind*. Cambridge, MA: MIT Press.

Barton, Bernadette, & Hardesty, Constance L. (2010). Spirituality and stripping: Exotic dancers narrate the body ekstasis. *Symbolic Interaction, 33*(2), 280–95.

Baumeister, Roy F., & Leary, Mark R. (1995). The need to belong: Desire for interpersonal attachments as a fundamental human motivation. *Psychological Bulletin, 3*, 495–529.

Baxter, Janeen, & Wright, Erik Olin. (2000, April). The glass ceiling hypothesis: A comparative study of the United States, Sweden, and Australia. *Gender & Society, 14*(2), 275–94.

Beagan, Brenda L. (2001). 'Even if I don't know what I'm doing I can make it look like I know what I'm doing': Becoming a doctor in the 1990s. *The Canadian Review of Sociology and Anthropology, 38*(3), 275–92.

Beauchamp, Diane L. (2008). *Sexual orientation and victimization 2004*. Canadian Centre for Justice Statistics profile series. Statistics Canada catalogue no. 85F0033M—No. 016. Retrieved from www.statcan.gc.ca/pub/85f0033m/85f0033m2008016-eng.pdf

Beauchamp, Tom L., & Childress, James F. (1989). *Principles of biomedical ethics* (3rd edn). New York: Oxford University Press.

Beck, U., & Beck-Gernsheim, E. (2002). *Individualization: Institutionalized individualism and its social and political consequences*. London: Sage.

Becker, Ernest. (1973). *The denial of death*. New York: Free Press.

Becker, Howard S. (1963). *Outsiders: Studies in the sociology of deviance*. New York: Free Press.

———. (1967). Whose side are we on? *Social Problems, 14*, 239–47.

Beedle, J.B. (2004). What educators can learn from multiplayer computer gaming: A study of who is playing and their perceptions of learning. *Dissertations Abstracts International*, AAT 3155858.

Bell A.P., & Weinberg, M.S. (1978). *Homosexualities: A study of diversity among men & women*. New York: Simon and Schuster.

Bem, Sandra Lipsitz. (1981, July). Gender schema theory: A cognitive account of sex-typing. *Psychological Review, 88*(4), 354–64.

Benedict, Ruth. (1942). *Race and racism*. London: Routledge and Kegan Paul.

Benjamin, Jessica. (1988). *The bonds of love: Psychoanalysis, feminism, and the problem of domination*. New York: Pantheon.

Benton, Ted. (1977). *Philosophical foundations of the three sociologies*. London: Routledge & Keegan Paul.

Berger, Peter. (1963). *Invitation to sociology: A humanistic perspective*. New York: Anchor Books.

Berger, Peter, & Lukmann, Thomas. (1966). The social construction of reality. In Craig J. Calhoun, Joseph Gerteis, & James Moody (Eds), *Contemporary sociological theory* (pp. 43–51). Malden, MA: Blackwell Publishing.

Bergesen, Albert J. (2004). Durkheim's theory of mental categories: A review of the evidence. *Annual Review of Sociology*, pp. 395–408.

Bergson, H. (1946). *The creative mind* (Trans. M.L. Andison). New York: Philosophical Library.

Bhaskar, Roy. (1989). *Reclaiming reality: A critical introduction to contemporary philosophy*. London: Verso.

Bian, Yanjie. (2002). Chinese social stratification and social mobility. *Annual Review of Sociology*, pp. 91–116.

Bianchi, Suzanne M., Milkie, Melissa A., Saye, Liana C., & Robinson, John P. (2000, September). Is anyone doing the housework? Trends in the gender division of household labor. *Social Forces, 79*(1), 191–228.

Black, M. (1962). *Models and metaphors: Studies in language and philosophy*. Philadelphia: University of Pennsylvania Press.

Blackless, M., Charuvastra, A., Derryck, A., Fausto-Sterling, A., Luzanne, K., & Lee, E. (2000). How sexually dimorphic are we? Review and synthesis. *American Journal of Human Biology, 12*, 151–66.

Blow, Charles M. (2008, July 12). Talking down and stepping up. *New York Times*.

Boase, Jeoffrey, Horrigan, John B., Wellman, Barry, & Rainie, Lee. (2006). The strength of Internet ties. Washington: Pew Internet and American Life Project. Retrieved from www.pewinternet.org/~/media//Files/Reports/2006/PIP_Internet_ties.pdf.pdf

Bombardieri, Marcella. (2005, January 17). Summers' remarks on women draw fire. *The Boston Globe*. Retrieved from www.boston.com/news/local/articles/2005/01/17/summers_remarks_on_women_draw_fire/

Bonilla-Silva, Eduardo. (2007). *Racism without racists: Color-blind racism and the persistence of racial inequality in the United States* (2nd edn). Lanham, MD: Rowman and Littlefield.

Borjas, George. (1994). Long run convergence of ethnic skill differential: The children and grandchildren of the Great Migration. *Industrial and Labour Relations Review, 47*(4), 553–73.

Bott, E. (1957). *Family and social network: Roles, norms, and external relationships in ordinary urban families*. London: Tavistock.

Bouma, Gary D., Ling, Rod, & Wilkinson, Lori. (2009). *The research process* (Cdn edn). Don Mills, ON: Oxford University Press.

Bourdieu, Pierre. (1977). Symbolic power. In Dennis Gleason (Ed.), *Identity and structure: Issues in the sociology of education* (pp. 112–19). Dimiffield, UK: Nefferton.

————. (1984). *Distinction: A social critique of the judgement of taste* (Trans. Richard Nice). Cambridge, MA: Harvard. (Original work published 1979)

————. (1990a). *In other words: Essays toward a reflexive sociology.* Stanford, CA: Stanford University Press.

————. (1990b). *The logic of practice.* Stanford, CA: Stanford University Press. (Original work published 1980)

————. (2000a). *Pascalian Meditations.* Stanford, CA: Stanford University Press

————. (2000b). Passport to Duke. In N. Brown & I. Szeman (Eds), *Pierre Bourdieu: Fieldwork in culture* (pp. 241–6). New York: Rowman & Littlefield.

Bourdieu, Pierre, & Wacquant, L. (1992). *An invitation to reflexive sociology.* Chicago: University of Chicago Press.

Bowlby, John. (1951). *Maternal care and mental health.* Geneva: World Health Organisation.

————. (1960). *Maternal care and mental health: A report prepared on behalf of the World Health Organization as a contribution to the United Nations Programme for the Welfare of Homeless Children* (2nd edn). Genevea: World Health Organisation.

————. (1965). *Child care and the growth of love* (2nd edn). Baltimore: Penguin Books.

boyd, danah. (2007a). *Viewing American class divisions through Facebook and MySpace.* Retrieved from www.danah.org/papers/essays/ClassDivisions.html

————. (2007b). Responding to responses to: 'Viewing American class divisions through Facebook and MySpace'. Retrieved from www.danah.org/papers/essays/ResponseToClassDivisions.html

————. (2011). White flight in networked publics? How race and class shaped American teen engagement with MySpace and Facebook. In Lisa Nakamura & Peter Chow-White (Eds), *Race After the Internet.* London: Routledge.

Boyle, Karen. (2005). *Media and violence.* London, UK: Sage Publications Ltd.

Bradley-Engen, Mindy S., & Ulmer, Jeffery T. Social worlds: Contextualizing agency and commitment in adult careers. *The Sociological Quarterly, 50*(1), 29–60.

Brady, David. (2004). Why public sociology may fail. *Social Forces, 4,* 1629–38.

Braithwaite, John. (1984). *Corporate crime in the pharmaceutical industry.* London: Routledge and Kegan Paul.

Bratlinger, Patrick. (1983). *Bread & circuses: Theories of mass culture as social decay.* Ithaca, NY: Cornell University Press.

Brekhus W. (2003). *Peacocks, chameleons, centaurs: Gay suburbia and the grammar of social identity.* Chicago, IL: University of Chicago Press.

Briggs, Jean. (1970). *Never in anger.* Cambridge, MA: Harvard University Press.

Brown, W. (2006). *Regulating aversion: Tolerance in the age of identity and Empire.* Princeton & Oxford: Princeton University Press.

Bryman, Alan. (2004). *Social research methods.* Oxford: Oxford University Press.

Bryman, Alan, & Teevan, James J. (2005). *Social research methods* (Cdn edn). Don Mills, ON: Oxford University Press.

Buchwalter, Charlie. (2009, May 6). The future is bright for online media. *Nielsenwire.* Retrieved from http://blog.nielsen.com/nielsenwire/consumer/the-future-is-bright-for-online-media/

Buechler, Steven M. (1998). Social movements, sociology and the well-Informed citizen. *Sociological Imagination, 35,* 239-64.

————. (2008). *Critical sociology.* Boulder, CO: Paradigm.

Bugeja, M. (2005). *Interpersonal divide: The search for community in a technological age.* London: Oxford University Press.

Burawoy, Michael. (2004). The critical turn to public sociology. In Rhonda Levine (Ed.), *Enriching the sociological imagination: How radical sociology changed the discipline* (pp. 309–22). New York.

————. (2005). For public sociology. *American Sociological Review, 70*(1), 4–28.

Burke, Alanna, Mackin, Rebecca, Romas, Pauline, & Ruff, Michell. (2007). *Algorithms of love: The growing technology and social implications of online dating.* Retrieved from http://anitaborg.org/files/ghc_poster_final.pdf

Burris, V. (1980). Class formation and transformation in advanced capitalist societies: A comparative analysis. *Social Praxis, 7,* 147–79.

Burstein, Paul. (1989). Attacking sex discrimination in the labor market: A study in law and politics. *Social Forces, 67,* 641–65.

Bushnell, I.W.R., & Sai, F. (1987). *Neonate recognition of the mother's face.* Glasgow, UK: University of Glasgow.

Butler, Judith. (1993). *Bodies that matter: On the discursive limits of sex.* New York: Routledge.

————. (1999). *Gender trouble: Feminism and the subversion of identity.* New York: Routledge. (Original work published 1990)

Canada, Minister of Justice. (1988). Canadian Multiculturalism Act (Consolidation). R.S.C., 1985, c. 24 (4th Supp.). Retrieved from http://laws-lois.justice.gc.ca/PDF/C-18.7.pdf

Canada, Parliament, House of Commons. (1883). *Official reports of the debates of the House of Commons of the Dominion of Canada. First session—fifth parliament* (vol. XIV). Ottawa: Maclean, Roger & Co.

Canadian Down Syndrome Society (CDSS). (2009, June 19). What is Down syndrome? Retrieved from www.cdss.ca/information/general-information/what-is-down-syndrome.html

Canadian Sociology and Anthropology Association (CSAA). (1994). *The Canadian Sociology and Anthropology Association statement of professional ethics.* Retrieved from www.csaa.ca/structure/Code.htm

Cantor, J., & Harrison, K. (1996). Ratings and advisories for television programming. In *National Television Violence Study* (vol. 1, pp. 361–410). Thousand Oaks, CA: Sage.

Caplow, Theodore, Chadwick, Bruce A., Bahr, Howard M., & Hill, Reuben. (1982). *Middletown families: Fifty years of change and continuity.* Minneapolis MN: University of Minnesota Press.

Carmen, Arlene, & Moody, Howard. (1985). *Working women: The subterranean world of street prostitution.* New York: Harper and Row.

Carmichael, Stokely, & Hamilton, Charles V. (1967). *Black power: The politics of liberation in America.* New York: Random House.

Carneiro, Pedro, & Heckman, James J. (2002, October). The evidence on credit constraints in post-secondary schooling. *The Economic Journal, 112*(482), 705–34.

Carruthers, Mary. (1990). The book of memory. Cambridge: Cambridge University Press.

Casciato, Paul. (2001, March 12). Television riding social media wave. *Times Colonist* (Victoria). Retrieved from www.timescolonist.com/technology/Television+riding+social+media+wave/4429623/story.htmlCatalyst. (2009). 2009 Catalyst census of the Fortune 500 reveals women missing from critical business leadership. Corporate boards and top executive offices fail to mirror marketplace and talent pool. Retrieved from www.catalyst.org/press-release/161/2009-catalyst-census-of-the-fortune-500-reveals-women-missing-from-critical-business-leadership

Cate, Rodney M., & Lloyd, Sally A. (1992). *Courtship.* Newbury Park, CA: Sage.

CBC News. (2005, April 10). Canadians deeply split on same-sex marriage, poll suggests. Retrieved from www.cbc.ca/canada/story/2005/04/10/gay-marriage-050410.html

Centerwall, B.S. (1989). Exposure to television as a risk factor for violence. *American Journal of Epidemiology, 129,* 643–52.

Cha, Youngjoo. (2010). Reinforcing separate spheres: The effect of spousal overwork on men's and women's employment in dual-earner households. *American Sociological Review, 2*, 303–29.

Charon, Joel M. (2010). *Ten questions: A sociological perspective* (7th edn). Belmont, CA: Wadsworth Cengage Learning.

Christensen, Wendy M., & Ferree, Myra Marx. (2008). Cowboy of the world? Gender discourse and the Iraq War debate. *Qualitative Sociology, 31*, 287–306.

Christiansen, K. (2001). Behavioural effects of androgen. *Journal of Endocrinology, 170*, 39–48.

Church, S., Henderson, M., Barnard, M., & Hart, G. (2001). Violence by clients towards female prostitutes in different work settings. *British Medical Journal, 322*, 524.

Cline, V.B., Croft, R.G., & Courrier, S. (1973). Desensitization of children to television violence. *Journal of Personality and Social Psychology, 27*, 360–5.

Cohen, Mark A. (1989). Corporate crime and punishment: A study of social harm and sentencing practice in the federal courts, 1984–1987. *American Criminal Law Review, 26*, 605–60.

Cohen, Philip N., & Huffman, Matt L. (2007). Working for women? Female managers and the gender wage gap. *American Sociological Review, 72*, 681–704.

Collins, Randall. (1988). *Theoretical sociology*. San Diego: Harcourt, Brace, Jovanovich.

———. (1998a). *The sociology of philosophies: A global theory of intellectual change*. Cambridge, MA: Belknap.

———. (1998b). The sociological eye and its blinders. *Contemporary Sociology, 27*(1), 2–7.

———. (2000). Situational stratification: A micro–macro theory of inequality. *Sociological Theory, 18*, 17–43.

———. (2011, January 25). Interaction rituals and the new electronic media. *The Sociological Eye*. Retrieved from http://sociological-eye.blogspot.com/

Comstock, G., & Strasburger, E. (1990). Deceptive appearances: Television violence and aggressive behavior. *Journal of Adolescent Health Care, 11*(1), 31–44.

Comte, Auguste. (1864). *The positive philosophy of Auguste Comte* (Trans. Harriet Martineau). New York: Calvin Blanchard. (Original work published 1830–42)

———. (1896). *The positive philosophy of Auguste Comte* (3 vols, Trans. H. Martineau). London: George Bell. (Original work published 1830–42)

———. (1966). *System of positive polity* (4 vols). New York: Burt Franklin. (Original work published 1851–4)

Coontz, Stephanie. (1988). *The social origins of private life: A history of American families, 1600–1900*. London: Verso.

Cooper, Robert. (2003). Primary and secondary thinking in social theory: The case of mass society. *Journal of Classical Sociology, 2*, 145–72.

Costanzo M., & Archer, D. (1989). Interpreting the expressive behavior of others: The interpersonal perception task. *Journal of Nonverbal Behaviour, 13*(4), 225–45.

Cote, S., Tremblay, R.E., Nagin, D., Zoccolillo, M., & Vitaro, F. (2003). The development of impulsivity, fearfulness, and helpfulness during childhood: Patterns of consistency and change in the trajectories of boys and girls. *Journal of Child Psychology and Psychiatry, 43*, 609–18.

Cotter, David, Hermsen, Joan, & England, Paula. (2008). Moms and jobs: Trends in mothers' employment and which mothers stay home. In Stephanie Coontz, Maya Parson, & Gabrielle Raley (Eds), *American families: A multicultural reader*. New York: Routledge.

Cotter, David A., Hermsen, Joan M., & Vanneman, Reeve. (2004). *Gender inequality at work*. The American People: Census 2000. New York: Russell Sage Foundation and Population Reference Bureau.

CTV Edmonton. (2010, June 2). Canadian Facebook users now 16 million strong. Retrieved from http://edmonton.ctv.ca/servlet/an/local/CTVNews/20100602/canada-facebook-100602/20100602/?hub=EdmontonHome

Cullen, Francis T., Maakestad, William J., & Cavender, Gray. (1987). *Corporate crime under attack*. Cincinnati, OH: Anderson.

Curtiss, Susan. (1977). *Genie: A psycholinguistic study of a modern-day 'wild child'*. New York: Academic Press.

Dahrendorf, Ralf. (1964). Recent changes in the class structure of European societies. *Daedalus, 93*, 225–70.

Da Silva, Filipe Carreira. (2007). Re-examining Mead. *Journal of Classical Sociology, 3*, 291–313.

Daubs, Katie. (2010, August 2). Toronto's diverse neighbours live in harmony. *The Star* (Toronto).

Davis D.S. (1995). Inequalities and stratification in the nineties. *China Review, 19*, 1–25.

Deegan, Mary Jo. (2003, September). Textbooks, the history of sociology, and the sociological stock of knowledge. *Sociological Theory, 21*, 298–305.

deGroot-Maggetti, Greg. (2002, March). A measure of poverty in Canada: A guide to the debate about poverty lines. Citizens for Public Justice. Retrieved from http://action.web.ca/home/cpj/attach/A_measure_of_poverty.pdf

Delacoste, Frederique, & Alexander, Priscilla. (1987). *Sex work: Writings by women in the sex industry*. San Francisco: Cleis Press.

Delanty, Gerard. (2000). The foundations of social theory. In Bryan S. Turner (Ed.), *The Blackwell companion to social theory*. Malden, MA, and Oxford, UK: Blackwell Publishers.

Department of Justice Canada. (1995). Employment Equity Act 1995, c.4. Retrieved from http://laws.justice.gc.ca/eng/E-5.401/page-1.html#anchorbo-ga:s_2

Department of Statistics Singapore. (2000). Glossary of terms and definitions. In *Census of population 2000 statistical release 1: Demographic characteristics*. Retrieved from www.singstat.gov.sg/pubn/popn/c2000sr1.html

Dewey, John. (1962). *Individualism, old and new*. New York: Capricorn Books. (Original work published 1929)

Diamond, Jared. (1992, June). Turning a man. *Discover*.

Dickinson, Maggie. The making of space, race and place: New York City's war on graffiti, 1970–the Present. *Critique of Anthropology, 28*(1), 27–45.

DiMaggio, Paul. (1979). Review essay: On Pierre Bourdieu. *American Journal of Sociology*, pp. 1460–74.

———. (1997). Culture and cognition. *Annual Review of Sociology*, pp. 263–87.

DiMaggio, Paul, Hargittai, Eszter, Neuman, W. Russell, & Robinson, John P. (2001). Social implications of the Internet. *Annual Review of Sociology*, pp. 307–36.

Dion, K.L. (1989). Ethnicity and perceived discrimination: A comparative survey of six ethnic groups in Toronto. Paper presented at the 10th Biennial Conference of the Canadian Ethnic Studies Association, Calgary, AB.

Dion, K.L., & Kawakami, K. (1996). Ethnicity and perceived discrimination in Toronto: Another look at the personal/group discrimination discrepancy. *Canadian Journal of Behavioural Science, 28*, 203–13.

Donzelot, Jacques. (1979). *The policing of families*. New York: Pantheon Books.

Douglas, Mary. (1984). *Purity and danger: An analysis of the concepts of pollution and taboo.* London: Routledge.

Duffy, Ann, & Mandell, Nancy. (1994). The widening gap: Social inequality and poverty. In Dan Glenday & Ann Duffy (Eds), *Understanding and surviving in the 1990s.* Toronto: McClelland & Stewart.

Durkheim, Émile. (1952). *Suicide. A study in sociology.* (Trans. J.A. Spaulding & G. Simpson). London: Routledge & Kegan Paul. (Original work published in French as *Le suicide: Étude de sociologie,* Paris: Alcan, 1897)

———. (1953). Individual and collective representations. In *Sociology and philosophy* (pp. 1–34). Glenco, IL: Free Press. (Original work published 1898)

———. (1964a). *The Division of Labor in society.* New York: Free Press. (Original work published 1893)

———. (1964b). The dualism of human nature and its social conditions. In Kurt H. Wolff (Ed.), *Essays on sociology and philosophy* (pp. 325–40). New York: Harper & Row. (Original work published in French as *Le dualisme de la nature humaine et ses conditions sociales,* 1914)

———. (1965). *The elementary forms of religious life.* New York: Free Press. (Original work published 1912)

———. (1973). Individualism and the intellectuals. In R. Bellah (Ed.), *On morality and society.* Chicago: University of Chicago Press. (Original work published 1898)

———. (1978). *Rules of the sociological method* (8th edn) (Trans. Sarah A. Solovay & John H. Mueller; Ed. George E.G. Catlin). New York: Free Press. (Original work published in French as *Les règles de la method sociologique,* Paris: Alcan 1895)

———. (1982). *The rules of sociological method and selected texts on sociology and its method* (Steven Lukes, Ed.). New York: Free Press. (Original work published 1895)

Dworkin, Andrea. (1981). *Pornography—Men possessing women.* New York: Perigee.

———. (1997). *Life and death: Unapologetic writings on the continuing war against women.* New York: Free Press.

Elder-Vass, Dave. (2007). Reconciling Archer and Bourdieu in an emergentist theory of action. *Sociological Theory, 4,* 325–46.

Eliot, Lise. (2009). *Pink brain, blue brain: How small differences grow into troublesome gaps.* Boston: Houghton Mifflin Harcourt.

———. (2010, May–June). The truth about boys and girls. *Scientific American,* pp. 22–9.

Ellison, N.B., Steinfeld, C., & Lampe, C. (2007). The benefits of Facebook 'friends': Social capital and college students' use of online social network sites. *Journal of Computer-Mediated Communication, 12*(4), article 1. Retrieved from http://jcmc.indiana.edu/vol12/issue4/ellison.html

Emirbayer, Mustafa, & Goodwin, Jeff. (1994). Network analysis, culture, and the problem of agency. *The American Journal of Sociology,* pp. 1411–54.

Emirbayer, Mustafa, & Mische, A. (1998). What is agency? *American Journal of Sociology, 103,* 962–1023.

Engels, Frederick. (1942). *The origins of the family, private property and the state.* New York: International Publishers. (Original work published 1884)

England, Paula. (2010). The gender revolution: Uneven and stalled. *Gender & Society, 124*(2), 149–66.

England, Paula, Allison, Paul, Li, Su, Mark, Noah, Thompson, Jennifer, Budig, Michelle, & Sun, Han. (2007). Why are some academic fields tipping toward female? The sex composition of US fields of doctoral degree receipt, 1971–2002. *Sociology of Education, 80,* 23–42.

England, Paula, & Li, Su. (2006). Desegregation stalled: The changing gender composition of college majors, 1971–2002. *Gender & Society, 20,* 657–77.

Epstein, Cynthia Fuchs. (1988). *Deceptive distinctions: Sex, gender, and the social order.* New Haven: Yale University Press.

Eron, L.D. (1963). Relationship of TV viewing habits and aggressive behavior in children. *Journal of Abnormal and Social Psychology, 67,* 193–6.

Eron, L.D., & Huesmann, L.R. (1986). The role of television in the development of prosocial and antisocial behavior. In: D. Olweus, J. Block, & M. Radke-Yarrow (Eds), *Development of antisocial and prosocial behavior* (pp. 285–314). New York: Academic Press.

Eyer, Diane E. (1992). *Mother–infant bonding: A scientific fiction.* New Haven: Yale University Press.

Fabes, R.A., Martin, C.L., & Hanish, L.D. (2003).Young children's play qualities in same-, other-, and mixed-sex peer groups. *Child Development, 74,* 921–32.

Facione, P. (1990). *Critical thinking: A statement of expert consensus for purposes of educational assessment and instruction. The American Philosophical Association Delphi Research Report.* Millbrae, CA: The California Academic Press.

Fausto-Sterling, Ann. (1993, March/April). The five sexes. *The Sciences,* pp. 20–1.

Feagin, Joe R. (2006). *Systemic racism: A theory of oppression.* New York: Routledge.

Febvre, L., & Martin, H.J. (1976). *The coming of the book.* London: New Left Books.

Federal Bureau of Investigation (FBI). (1988). *Uniform crime reports for the United States.* Washington, DC. US Government Printing Office.

Feigenson. L., Carey, S., & Hauser. M. (2002). The representations underlying infants' choice of more: Object files vs analog magnitudes. *Psychological Science, 13,* 150–6.

Feigenson, L., Carey, S., & Spelke, E.S. (2002). Infants' discrimination of number vs continuous extent. *Cognitive Psychology, 44,* 33–66.

Fenstermaker, Sarah, & West, Candace. *Doing gender, doing difference: Inequality, power, and institutional change.* New York: Routledge.

Field, T.M., Cohen, D., Garcia, R., & Greenberg, R. (1984). Mother–stranger face discrimination by the newborn. *Infant Behavior and Development, 7,* 19–25.

Fine, Gary A. (2005). Interaction ritual chains (review). *Social Forces, 3,* 1287–8.

Fine, Gary Alan, & Beim, Aaron. (2007). Introduction: Interactionist approaches to collective memory. *Symbolic Interaction, 1,* 1–5.

Fisher, L., & Janetti, H. (1996). Aboriginal youth in the criminal justice system. In John Winterdyk (Ed.), *Issues and perspectives on young offenders in Canada* (pp. 237–56). Toronto: Harcourt Brace & Company.

Fitzgerald, Robin T., & Carrington, Peter. (2008). The neighbourhood context of urban Aboriginal crime. *Canadian Journal of Criminology and Criminal Justice, 50,* 523–57.

Flaherty, Michael G., & Fine, Gary Alan. (2001). Present, past, and future: Conjugating George Herbert Mead's perspective on time. *Time and Society, 10,* 147–61.

Flicker, Sarah, Flynn, Susan, Larkin, June, Travers, Robb, Guta, Adrian, Pole, Jason, & Layne, Crystal. (2009). *Sexpress: The Toronto teen survey report.* Toronto: Planned Parenthood Toronto. Retrieved from www.ppt.on.ca/pdf/reports/TTSreportfinal.pdf

Food Banks Canada. (2009). *HungerCount 2009*: A comprehensive report on hunger and food bank use in Canada, and recommendations for change. Food Banks Canada: Toronto.

Retrieved from www.foodbankscanada.ca/documents/
HungerCount2009.pdf

Foucault, Michel. (1970). *The order of things: An archaeology of the human sciences*. New York: Vintage Books.

Fox, R.L., & Lawless, J.L. (2004). Entering the arena? Gender and the decision to run for office. *American Journal of Political Science, 2*, 264–80.

Franklin, Karen. (1998). Psychosocial motivations of hate crime perpetrators. Paper presented at the annual meeting of the American Psychological Association (San Francisco: August 16). Retrieved from www.scienceblog.com/community/older/1998/A/199800394.html

Freedman, Jonathan L. (2002). *Media violence and its effect on aggression: Assessing the scientific evidence*. Toronto: University of Toronto Press.

Frenette, Marc. (2007, February). *Why are youth from lower-income families less likely to attend university? Evidence from academic abilities, parental influences, and financial constraints.* Ottawa: Statistics Canada. Retrieved from www.statcan.gc.ca/pub/11f0019m/11f0019m2007295-eng.pdf

Gadamer, Hans-Georg. (1986). *Truth and method*. New York: Crossroad.

Gafijczuk, Dariusz. (2005). The way of the social: From Durkheim's society to a post-modern sociality. *History of the Human Sciences, 3*, 17–33.

Galen. (1968). *On the usefulness of parts of the body*. Ithaca, NY: Cornell University Press.

Galloway, Gloria. (2010, October 12). Women: Half the population, and one fifth the seats in Parliament. *The Globe and Mail.*

Gannagé, Charlene. (1986). *Double day, double bind*. Toronto: Women's Press.

Gans, Herbert. (1989). Sociology in America: The discipline and the public. *American Sociological Review, 54*, 1–16.

Gay, Lesbian & Straight Education Network (GLSEN). (2008, October 8). 2007 National school climate survey: Nearly 9 out of 10 LGBT students harassed. Retrieved from www.glsen.org/cgi-bin/iowa/all/news/record/2340.html

Geary, D.C. (2002). Sexual selection and sex differences in social cognition. In A. McGillicuddy-De Lisi & R. De Lisi (Eds), *Biology, society, and behavior: The development of sex differences in cognition* (pp. 23–53). Westport, CT: Ablex Publishing.

Geertsen, Reed. (2003). Rethinking thinking about higher-level thinking. *Teaching Sociology, 31*, 1–19.

Gerbner, George. (1995). Television violence: The power and the peril. In Gail Dines & Jean M. Humez (Eds), *Gender, race and class in media* (pp. 547–57). Sage Publications Inc.

Gergen, K.J. (2002). Cell phone technology and the realm of absent presence. In D. Katz, & M. Aakhus (Eds), *Perpetual contact: Mobile communication, private talk, public performance* (pp. 227–41). New York: Cambridge University Press.

Gershuny, Jonathan I. (2000). Changing times: Work and leisure in post-industrial societies. Oxford: Oxford University Press.

Gershuny, Jonathan I., Godwin, M., & Jones, S. (1994). The domestic labour revolution: A process of lagged adaptation? In M. Andersen, F. Bechhofer, & J. Gershuny (Eds), *The social and political economy of the household* (pp.151–97). Oxford: Oxford University Press.

Gerson, Kathleen. (2009). Changing lives, resistant institutions: A new generation negotiates gender, work, and family change. *Sociological Forum, 4*, 735–53.

Gerth, Hans Heinrich, & Mills, C. Wright (Eds). (1948). *From Max Weber*. London: Routledge & Kegan Paul.

———, & ———. (1964). *Character and social structure: The psychology of social institutions*. New York: Harcourt, Brace & World. (Original work published 1954)

Giddens, Anthony. (1981). *A contemporary critique of historical materialism. Vol. 1: Power, property and the state*. London: Macmillan.

———. (1984). *The constitution of society. Outline of the theory of structuration*. Cambridge: Polity.

Gitlin, Todd. (2000). Afterword. In C. Wright Mills, *The Sociological Imagination*. Oxford: Oxford University Press.

Godelier, Maurice. (1986). *The making of great men: Male domination and power among the New Guinea Baruya* (Trans. Rupert Swyer). New York: Cambridge University Press.

Goffman, E. (1959). *The presentation of self in everyday life*. New York: Doubleday Anchor Books.

———. (1961a). *Asylums: Essays in the social situation of mental patients and other inmates*. New York: Anchor Books.

———. (1961b). *Encounters: Two studies in the sociology of interaction*. Indianapolis: Bobbs-Merrill.

———. (1963). *Behavior in public places: Notes on the social organization of gatherings*. New York: The Free Press.

———. (1967). *Interaction ritual: Essays on face-to-face behavior*. New York: Pantheon.

———. (1971). *Relations in public: Microstudies of the public order*. New York: Harper.

———. (1981). *Forms of talk*. Oxford: Blackwell.

Goodman, Alan H. (2000). Why genes don't count (for racial differences in health). *American Journal of Public Health, 11*, 1699–1702.

Gosselin, A., de Guise, J., & Paquette, G. (1997). Violence on Canadian television and some of its cognitive effects. *Canadian Journal of Communication, 22*, 143–60.

Gough, B., Weyman, N., Alderson, J., Butler, G., & Stoner, M. (2008). 'They did not have a word': The parental quest to locate a 'true sex' for their intersex children. *Psychology and Health, 4*, 493–507.

Gould, Stephen Jay. (1991). The birth of the two-sex world. *New York Review of Books, 38*(11), 11–13.

Granovetter, M.S. (1973). The strength of weak ties. *American Journal of Sociology, 78*(6), 1360–80.

———. (1982). The strength of weak ties: A network theory revisited. In P.V. Mardsen & N. Lin (Eds), *Social structure and network analysis* (pp. 105–30). Thousand Oaks, CA: Sage Publications.

Granzberg, Gary, & Steinbring, Jack (Eds). (1980). *Television and the Canadian Indian: Impact and meaning among Algonkians of central Canada*. Winnipeg: University of Winnipeg Press.

Grauerholz, Liz, & Bouma-Holtrop, Sharon. (2003). Exploring critical sociological thinking. *Teaching Sociology, 31*, 485–96.

Gray, John. (1992). *Men are from Mars, women are from Venus*. New York: HarperCollins.

Green, Adam Isaiah. (2002). Gay but not queer: Toward a post-queer study of sociology. *Theory and Society, 31*(4), 521–45.

Green, Charles S. III, & Klug, Hadley G. (1990). Teaching critical thinking and writing through debates: An experimental evaluation. *Teaching Sociology, 18*, 462–71.

Haines, Rebecca J., Johnson, Joy L., Carter, Connie I., & Arora, Kamal. (2009, June). 'I couldn't say I'm not a girl'—Adolescents talk about gender and marijuana use. *Social Science & Medicine, 68*(11), 2029–36.

Hall, John A. (1984). *Nonverbal sex-differences: Communication accuracy and expressive style*. Baltimore, MD: The Johns Hopkins University Press.

———. (2005). A guarded welcome. *The British Journal of Sociology, 3*, 379–81.

Haluza-DeLay, Randolph. (2003). When the topic is racism: Research and advocacy with a community coalition. *Social Justice, 30*(4), 77–90.

Haque , Eve. (2010). Homegrown, Muslim and other: Tolerance, secularism and the limits of multiculturalism. *Social Identities, 16*(1), 79–101.

Harding, David J. (2009, June). Violence, older peers, and the socialization of adolescent boys in disadvantaged neighborhoods. *American Sociological Review*, pp. 445–64.

Hargittai, Eszter. (2007). Whose space? Differences among users and non-users of social network sites. *Journal of Computer-Mediated Communication, 13*(1), article 14. Retrieved from http://jcmc.indiana.edu/vol13/issue1/hargittai.html

Harlow, Harry. (1958). *Biological and biochemical bases of behavior.* Madison: University of Wisconsin Press.

Harlow, Harry, & Harlow, Margaret Kuenne. (1974). Social deprivation in monkeys. In James B. Maas (Ed.), *Readings in psychology today.* Del Mar, CA: CRM Books.

Harrison, K., & Cantor, J. (1999). Tales from the screen: Enduring fright reactions to scary media. *Media Psychology, 1*, 97–116.

Hartley, Richard D. (2008). *Corporate crime: A reference handbook.* Santa Barbara, CA: ABC-CLIO.

Hartsock, Nancy. (1983). The feminist standpoint: Developing the ground for a specifically feminist historical materialism. In Sandraa Harding & Merrill B. Hintikka (Eds), *Discovering reality* (pp. 283–310). Dordrecht, the Netherlands: D. Reidel Publishing Co.

Hatfield, M. (2003). *Persistent low-income: A key barrier to social inclusions.* Applied Research Branch, Santa Barbara, CA: ABC–CLIO Inc.

Hays, Sharon. (1994). Structure and agency and the sticky problem of culture. *Sociological Theory, 12*, 57–72.

Haythornthwaite, C. (2005). Social networks and Internet connectivity effects. *Information, Communication & Society, 8*(2), 125–47.

Hazelrigg, Lawrence E. (1989). *Social science and the challenge of relativism* (2 vols). Tallahassee: Florida State University Press.

Heath, C.C., & Luff, P. (1992). Media space and asymmetries: Communicative preliminary observations of video-mediated interaction human–computer interaction. *Human Communication Interaction, 7*(3), 315–46.

Heilbron, Johan. (2009). Sociology and positivism in 19th-century France: The vicissitudes of the Société de Sociologie (1872–74). *History of the Human Sciences, 4*, 30–62.

Hekma, Gert. (1994, Autumn). The homosexual, the queen and models of gay history. *Perversions, 1*(3), 119–38.

Helliwell, J.F., & Putnam, R.D. (2004). The social context of well-being. *Philosophical Transactions of the Royal Society, 359*(1449), 1435–46.

Helmes-Hayes, Rick. (2009). Engaged, practical intellectualism: John Porter and 'new liberal' public sociology. *Canadian Journal of Sociology, 34*(3), 831–8.

Hendrick, Susan, & Hendrick, Clyde. (1992). *Romantic love.* Newbury Park, CA: Sage Publications.

Henry, F., & Ginsberg, E. (1985). *Who gets the work? A test of racial discrimination in employment.* Toronto, ON: The Urban Alliance on Race Relations and the Social Planning Council of Metropolitan Toronto.

Herdt, Gilbert. (1987). *The Sambia: Ritual and gender in New Guinea.* New York: Holt, Rinehart and Winston.

———. (1993). Sexual repression, social control, and gender hierarchy in Sambian culture. In Barbara Diane Miller (Ed.), *Sex and gender hierarchies.* Cambridge: Cambridge University Press.

———. (1994a). Introduction: Third sexes and third genders. In Gilbert Herdt (Ed.), *Third sex, third gender.* New York: Zone Books.

———. (1994b). Mistaken sex: Culture, biology and the third sex in New Guinea. In Gilbert Herdt (Ed.), *Third sex, third gender.* New York: Zone Books.

Herman, Didi. (1994). *Rights of passage: Struggles for lesbian and gay legal equality.* Toronto, ON: University of Toronto Press.

Hill, Michael R. (1989). Empiricism and reason in Harriet Martineau's sociology. In Harriet Martineau, *How to observe morals and manners* (sesquicentennial edn, pp. xv–lx). New Brunswick, NJ: Transaction.

Hill, Michael R., & Hoecker-Drysdale, Susan. (2003). Taking Harriet Martineau seriously in the classroom and beyond. In Michael R. Hill & Susan Hoecker-Drysdale (Eds), *Harriet Martineau: Theoretical & methodological perspectives.* New York: Routledge.

Hill, Willard W. (1935). The status of the hermaphrodite and transvestite in Navaho culture. *American Anthropologist, 37.*

Hindness, Barry, & Hirst, Paul Q. (1975). *Pre-capitalist modes of production.* London: Routledge.

Hironimus-Wendt, Robert J., & Wallace, Lora Ebert. (2009). The sociological imagination and social responsibility. *Teaching Sociology 37*, 76–88.

Hirsch, Elizabeth. (2009). The strength of weak enforcement: The impact of discrimination charges on sex and race segregation in the workplace. *American Sociological Review, 74*(2), 245–71.

Hirst, Paul Q., & Woolley, Penny. (1981). *Social relations and human attributes.* London & New York: Tavistock Publications.

Historica-Dominion Institute. (2011). Eugenics: Keeping Canada sane. In James H. Marsh (Ed.), *The Canadian Encyclopedia.* Retrieved from www.thecanadianencyclopedia.com/index.cfm?PgNm=ArchivedFeatures&Params=a2126

Hochschild, Arlie Russell. (1983). *The managed heart: The commercialization of human feeling.* Berkeley: The University of California Press.

Hoffman, Richard. (1984). Vices, gods, and virtues: Cosmology as a mediating factor in attitudes toward male homosexuality. *Journal of Homosexuality, 9*, 27–44.

Hollands, Robert. (2004). Rappin' on the reservation: Canadian Mohawk youth's hybrid cultural identities. *Sociological Research Online, 9*(3). Retrieved from www.socresonline.org.uk/9/3/hollands.html

Hook, Jennifer L. (2006). Care in context: Men's unpaid work in 20 countries, 1965–2003. *American Sociological Review, 71*(4), 639–60.

Hoop, Katrina C. (2009). Students' lived experiences as text in teaching the sociological imagination. *Teaching Sociology, 37*, 47–60.

Huesmann L.R. (1986). Psychological processes promoting the relation between exposure to media violence and aggressive behavior by the viewer. *Journal of Social Issues, 42*(3), 125–39.

Huesmann L.R., & Bachrach, R.S. (1988). Differential effects of television violence in kibbutz and city children. In R. Patterson & P. Drummond (Eds), *Television and its audience: International research perspectives* (pp. 154–76). London: BFI Publishing.

Huesmann, L.R., Moise, J., Podolski, C.P., & Eron, L.D. (2003). Longitudinal relations between children's exposure to television violence and their aggressive and violent behavior in young adulthood: 1977–1992. *Developmental Psychology, 39*(2), 201–21.

Huizinga, David, Thornberry, Terence P., Knight, Kelly E., Lovegrove, Peter J., et al. (2007). Disproportionate minority contact in the juvenile justice system: A study of differential minority arrest/referral to court in three cities. Report to the

Office of Juvenile Justice and Delinquency Prevention. Retrieved from www.ncjrs.gov/pdffiles1/ojjdp/grants/219743.pdf

Hultin, M. (2003). Some take the glass escalator, some hit the glass ceiling. *Work and Occupations, 30*(1), 30–61.

Humphreys, Laud. (1975). *Tearoom trade: Impersonal sex in public places* (enlarged edn). Hawthorne NY: Aldine de Gruyter. (Original work published 1970)

———. (2005). Cellphones in public: Social interactions in a wireless era. *New Media & Society, 17*(6), 810–32.

Huston, A.C., Donnerstein, E., Fairchild, H., et al. (1992). *Big world, small screen: The role of television in American society*. Lincoln, NE: University of Nebraska Press, 1992.

Hyde, J.S., Fennema, E., & Lamon, S.J. (1990). Gender differences in mathematics performance: A meta-analysis. *Psychology Bulletin, 107*, 139–55.

Hyde, J.S., & Linn, M.C. (1988). Gender differences in verbal ability: A meta-analysis. *Psychology Bulletin, 104*, 53–69.

Imperato-McGinley, Julliane, Peterson, R.E., Gautier, T., & Sturla, E. (1979, May 31). Androgens and the evolution of male-gender identity among male pseudohermaphrodites with 5-alpha reductase deficiency. *New England Journal of Medicine, 300*(22), 1233–7.

Ingoldsby, Bron B. (1995). Mate selection and marriage. In Bron B. Ingoldsby & Suzanna Smith (Eds), *Family matters in perspective*. NY: Guilford Press.

Intersex Initiative (IPDX). (2008). Intersex FAQ (frequently asked questions). Retrieved from www.intersexinitiative.org/articles/intersex-faq.html

Ipsos. (2009, June 19). What? You don't have a social network profile? You are now in the minority. Ipsos North America. Retrieved from http://ipsos-na.com/news-polls/pressrelease.aspx?id=4436

———. (2010, March 22). Weekly Internet usage overtakes television watching. Ipsos North America. Retrieved from http://ipsos-na.com/news-polls/pressrelease.aspx?id=4720

Ireland, Central Statistics Office. (2006). Census of Population of Ireland Sunday. Retrieved from www.cso.ie/census/census2006results/volume_5/Appendix_1.pdf

Irvine, Janice M. (2003). The sociologist as voyeur: Social theory and sexuality research, 1910–1978. *Qualitative Sociology, 4*, 429–56.

Interfaith Social Assistance Reform Coalition. (1998). *Our neighbours' voices: Will we listen?* Toronto: James Lorimer & Co. Ltd.

Ito, M. (2005). Mobile phones, Japanese youth and the re-placement of social contact. In R. Ling & P. Pedersen (Eds), *Mobil communication: Re-negotiation of the social sphere*. London: Springer.

Ito, M., Baumer, S., Bittani, M., boyd, d., Cody, R., Herr-Stephenson, B., . . . , & Tripp, L. (2008). *Hanging out, messing around, geeking out: Living and learning with new media*. Report to the MacArthur Foundation.

Jacobs, Jerry A., & Gerson, Kathleen. (2004). *The time divide: Work, family, and gender inequality*. Cambridge, MA: Harvard University Press.

Jacobson, Lou. (2011). Using a sociological tool kit to make energy efficiency happen. In Kathleen Korgen, Jonathan White, & Shelley White (Eds), *Sociologists in action: Sociology, social change, and social justice*. Thousand Oaks, CA: Pine Forge Press.

Jenkins, H., Clinton, Katie, Purushotma, Ravi, Robison, Alice J., & Weigel, Margaret. (2006). Confronting the challenges of participatory culture: Media education for the 21st century. In MacArthur Foundation, *Building the field of digital media and learning*, an occasional paper on digital media and learning.

Jenkins, Richard. (2003, June 6). Bring and buy for a feast of inspiration. *Times Higher Education Supplement*, pp. 30–1.

Johnson, A.M., Mercer, C.H., Erens, B., Copas, A.J., McManus, S., Wellings, K., . . . , & Field, J. Sexual behaviour in Britain: Partnerships, practices, and HIV risk behaviours. *The Lancet, 358*, 1835–42.

Johnson, Jeffrey , Cohen, Patricia, Smailes, Elizabeth, Kasen, Stephanie, & Brook, Judith. (2002, May 29). Television viewing and aggressive behaviour during adolescence and adulthood. *Science Magazine*.

Johnson, M.H., & Morton, J. (1991). *Biology and cognitive development*. Blackwell: Oxford, UK.

Johnson, Sara. (2003, September). Custodial remand in Canada, 1986/87 to 2000/01. *Juristat—Canadian Centre for Justice Statistics, 23*(7). Statistics Canada catalogue no. 85-002-XIE. Retrieved from www.statcan.gc.ca/pub/85-002-x/85-002-x2003007-eng.pdf

Jones, Jeffrey M. (2010, May 24). Americans' opposition to gay marriage easy slightly. Forty-four percent favor legal recognition; 53% are opposed. Gallup Inc. Retrieved from www.gallup.com/poll/128291/americans-opposition-gay-marriage-eases-slightly.aspx

Joy, L.A., Kimball, M.M., & Zabrack, M.L. (1986). Television and children's aggressive behaviour. In T.M. Williams (Ed.), *The impact of television: A natural experiment in three communities* (pp. 303–60). Orlando, FL: Academic Press.

Kappeler, Victor E., Blumberg, Mark, & Potter, Gary W. (2000). *The mythology of crime and criminal justice* (3rd edn). Chicago: Waveland.

Katz, James E., & Rice, Ronald E. (2002). *Social consequences of Internet use: Access, involvement and expression*. Cambridge, MA: MIT Press.

Kaufman, Peter. (2003). Learning to not labour: How working-class individuals construct middle-class identities. *The Sociological Quarterly, 3*, 481–504.

Keating, Norah, & Dosman, Donna. (2009). Social capital and the care networks of frail seniors. *Canadian Review of Sociology, 46*(4), 301–18.

Keesler, Venessa A., Fermin, Baranda J., & Schneider Barbara. (2008, October). Assessing an advanced level introductory sociology course. *Teaching Sociology, 36*, 345–58.

Kelves, D.J. (1995). *In the name of eugenics: Genetics and the uses of human heredity*. Cambridge, MA: Harvard University Press. (Original work published 1985)

Kerr, Thomas, Fast, Danya, Small, Will, & Wood, Evan. (2009, August 21). Coming 'down here': Young people's reflections on becoming entrenched in a local drug scene. *Social Science and Medicine*. 69(8), 1204–10. doi:10.1016/j.socscimed.2009.07.024

Kertzer, David I. (1988). *Ritual, politics, and power*. New Haven: Yale University Press.

Khanna, Nikki. (2010). 'If you're half black, you're just black': Reflected appraisals and the persistence of the one-drop rule. *The Sociological Quarterly*, pp. 96–121.

King, Patricia M., & Kitchener, Karen S. (1994). *Developing reflective judgment: Understanding and promoting intellectual growth and critical thinking in adolescents and adults*. San Francisco: Jossey-Bass.

Kinnell, H. (2005). Demonizing clients: How not to promote sex workers' safety. In R. Matthews, M. O'Neill, & R. Campbell (Eds), *Prostitution now*. Cullumpton, UK: Willan.

Kirby, Sandra, & McKenna, Kate. (1989). *Experience, research, social change: Methods from the Margins*. Toronto: Garamond Press.

Kluckhohn, Clyde. (1949). *Mirror for man*. New York: McGraw-Hill.

Koechlin, E., Dehaene, S., & Mehler, J. (1998). Numerical transformations in five-month-old infants. *Mathematical Cognition, 3*, 89–104.

Koechlin, E., Naccache, L., Block, E., & Dehaene, S. (1999). Primed numbers: Exploring the modularity of numerical representations with masked and unmasked semantic priming. *Journal of Experimental Psychology: Human Perception and Performance*.

Kong, Rebecca, & AuCoin, K. (2008). Female offenders in Canada. *Juristat: Canadian Centre for Justice Statistics, 28*(1), 1–22. Retrieved from CBCA Reference, document ID 1423357601.

Kong, Rebecca, & Beattie, Karen. (2005, May). *Collecting data on Aboriginal people in the criminal justice system: Methods and challenges*. Ottawa: Statistics Canada, Canadian Centre for Justice Statistics. Retrieved from www.statcan.gc.ca/pub/85-564-x/85-564-x2005001-eng.pdf

Kroeber, Alfred Louis. (1952). *The nature of culture*. Chicago: University of Chicago Press. (Original work published 1917)

Lam, Chuck. (2007a, September 14). Analyzing Facebook usage by high school demographic. *Data Strategy*. Retrieved from http://datastrategy.wordpress.com

———. (2007b, September 14). Examining MySpace usage by high school. *Data Strategy*. Retrieved from http://datastrategy.wordpress.com

La Prairie, Carol. (2004). The overrepresentation of Aboriginal offenders in Canadian prisons. In Julian V. Roberts & Michelle G. Grossman (Eds), *Criminal justice in Canada: A reader* (2nd edn). Scarborough, ON: Nelson.

Laqueur, Thomas W. (1990). *Making sex: Body and gender from the Greeks to Freud*.

———. (2003). Sex in the flesh. *Isis, 2*, 300–6.

LaRochelle-Côté, Sébastien, & Dionne, Claude. (2009, June). International differences in low-paid work. *Perspectives*. Statistics Canada catalogue no. 75-001-X. Retrieved from www.statcan.gc.ca/pub/75-001-x/2009106/pdf/10894-eng.pdf

Lautard, H., & Guppy, N. (2008). Multiculturalism or vertical mosaic: Occupational stratification among Canadian ethnic groups. In R. Brym (Ed.), *Society in Question* (5th edn, pp. 120–9). Toronto: Thompson Nelson.

Lave, J., Murtaugh, M., & de la Rocha, O. (1984). The dialectic of arithmetic in grocery shopping. In B. Rogoff & J. Lave (Eds), *Everyday cognition: Its development in social context* (pp. 67–94). Cambridge, MA: Harvard University Press.

Lawless J.L., & Theriault, S.M. (2005). Women in the US Congress: From entry to exit. In L.D. Whitaker (Ed.), *Women in politics: Outsiders or insiders?* (4th edn, ch. 5). New York: Prentice Hall.

Lehohla, Pali. (2007). Knowing how to use information is just as critical as collecting it. In Statistics South Africa, *StatsOnline News Archive*. Retrieved from www.statssa.gov.za/news_archive/20September2007_1.asp

Lettvin, Maturana, McCulloch, & Pitts. (1968). What the frog's eye tells the frog's brain. Retrieved from www.cns.nyu.edu/events/vjclub/classics/lettvinEtAl68.pdf

Li, Jun. (2009). Forging the future between two different worlds: Recent Chinese immigrant adolescents tell their cross-cultural experiences. *Journal of Adolescent Research, 24*, pp. 477–504.

Ling, Richard. (2008). *New tech, new ties: How mobile communication is reshaping social cohesion*. Cambridge MA: MIT Press.

Linton, Ralph. (1936). *The study of man*. New York: Appleton-Century-Crofts.

Lionni, Leo. (1972). *Fish is fish*. New York: Alfred A. Knopf/ Dragonfly Books.

Lipton, J.S, & Spelke, E.S. (2004). Discrimination of large and small numerosities by human infants. *Infancy, 5*(3), 271–90.

Little, Jo. (2002). Rural geography: Rural gender identity and the performance of masculinity and femininity in the countryside. *Progress in Human Geography, 26*(5), 665–70.

Lizardo, Omar. (2006). How cultural tastes shape personal networks. *American Sociological Review, 71*, 778–807.

Lloyd, Genevieve. (1984). *The men of reason: 'Male' and 'female' in Western philosophy*. London: Methuen.

Long, Theodore E., & Hadden, Jeffrey K. (1983). Religious conversion and the concept of socialization: Integrating the brainwashing and drift models. *Journal for the Scientific Study of Religion, 22*, 1–14.

———, & ———. (1985). A reconception of socialization. *Sociological Theory, 3*(1), 39–49.

Löwith, Karl. (1993). *Max Weber and Karl Marx* (Ed. Bryan S. Turner). New York: Routledge. (Original work published 1932)

Lukes, Steven. (1985). *Emile Durkheim: His life and work. A historical and critical study*. Standford: Stanford University Press.

Lyman, P., & Varian, H. (2003). *How much information 2003?* Online paper, University of California at Berkeley. Retrieved from www.sims.berkeley.edu/how-much-info-2003

Lynd, Robert. (1937). *Middletown in transition*. New York: Harcourt, Brace and Co.

Lynd, Robert, & Lynd, Helen. (1929). *Middletown: A study in contemporary American culture*. New York: Harcourt, Brace and Co.

McCormick, Thelma. (1993). Codes, ratings, and rights. Unpublished manuscript.

MacDonald, R., & Marsh, J. (2001). Disconnected youth? *Journal of Youth Studies* 4(4): 373-91.

McDonald, Lynn. (1994). *The women founders of the social sciences*. Ottawa, ON: Carleton University Press.

MacIntosh, W., & Harwood, P. (2002). The Internet and America's changing sense of community. *The Good Society*, pp. 25–8.

McIntosh, Mary. (1968). The homosexual role. *Social Problems, 16*, 182–92.

Mackinnon, Catharine. (1989). *Toward a feminist theory of the state*. Cambridge, MA: Harvard University Press.

McPherson, Miller, Brashears, Mathew E., & Smith-Lovin, Lynne. (2006). Social isolation in America: Changes in core discussion networks over two decades. *American Sociological Review*, pp. 353–75.

Madathil, Jayamala, & Benshoff, James M. (2008). Importance of marital characteristics and marital satisfaction: A comparison of Asian Indians in arranged marriages and Americans in marriages of choice. *The Family Journal, 16*(3), 222–30.

Maillé, Chantal. (1990). Primed for power: Women in Canadian politics. Background paper prepared for the Canadian Advisory Council on the Status of Women. Ottawa.

Malatesta, C.Z., & Haviland, J.M. (1982). Learning display rules: The socialization of emotion expression in infancy. *Child Development, 53*, 991–1003.

Malik, Kenan. (1996). *The meaning of race: Race, history and culture in Western society*. London: Macmillan.

Malson, Lucien. (1964). *Les enfants sauvages: Mythe et réalité*. Paris: Union generale d'éditions.

Marshall, Douglas A. (2006). Explanation or exegesis: Exhuming Durkheim's epistemology. *History of the Human Sciences, 19*, 127–35.

Martin, Karin A. (2008). Normalizing heterosexuality: Mothers' assumptions, talk, and strategies with young children. *American Sociological Review, 74*, 190–207.

Martinez, Andrea. (1992). *Scientific knowledge about television violence*. Ottawa: Canadian Radio-television and Telecommunications Commission.

Marullo, Sam, Moayedi, Roxanna, & Cooke, Deanna. (2009). C. Wright Mills's friendly critique of service learning and an innovative response: Cross-institutional collaborations for community-based research. *Teaching Sociology, 37*, 61–75.

Marx, Karl. (1967). *Capital: A critical analysis of capitalist production* (vol. 1). New York: International. (Original work published 1867)

———. (1970). *A contribution to the critique of political economy*. New York: International Publishers. (Original work published 1859)

———. (2000). *Selected writings* (Ed. David McLennan). Oxford: Oxford University Press.

Marx, Karl, & Engels, Friedrich. (1947). *The German ideology*. New York: International Publishers. (Original work published 1846)

———, & ———. (1956). *The holy family, or critique of critical criticism*. Moscow: Progress Publishers. (Original work published 1854)

———, & ———. (1962). *The manifesto of the Communist Party*. Moscow: Progress Publishers. (Original work published 1848)

Massey, Douglas S., & Denton, Nancy A. (1998). *American apartheid: Segregation and the making of the underclass*. Cambridge, MA: Harvard University Press. (Original work published 1993)

Mayock, Paula. (2005, October). 'Scripting risk': Young people and the construction of drug journeys. *Drugs: Education, Prevention and Policy, 12*(5), 349–68.

Mamdani, Mahmood. (2002). *When victims become killers. Colonialism, nativism, and the genocide in Rwanda*. Princeton, NJ: Princeton University Press.

Mead, George Herbert. (1932). *The philosophy of the present* (Ed. Arthur E. Murphy). Lasalle, IL: Open Court. Retrieved from www.brocku.ca/MeadProject/Mead/pubs2/philpres/Mead_1932_toc.html

———. (1934). *Mind, self and society*. Chicago: University of Chicago Press.

———. (1936). Science raises problems for philosophy—Vitalism; Henri Bergson. In Merritt H. Moore (Ed.), *Movements of thought in the nineteenth century* (ch. 14). Chicago: University of Chicago Press.

———. (1938). *The philosophy of the act* (Ed. A.J. Reck). Indianapolis: Bobbs-Merrill Company Inc.

Meaney, M. (2004) The nature of nurture: Maternal effects and chromatin remodelling. In J.T. Cacioppo & J.T. Bernston (Eds), *Essays in social neuroscience*. Boston: MIT press.

Media Awareness Network (MNet). (2010). Media Awareness Network: About us. Retrieved from www.media-awareness.ca/english/corporate/about_us/index.cfm

Medora, N.P, Larson, J.H., Hortacsu, N., & Dave, P. (2002). Perceived attitudes towards romanticism: A cross cultural study of American, Asian Indian, and Turkish young adults. *Journal of Comparative Family Studies, 33*(2), 155–82.

Mehler, J. & Dupoux, E. (1994). *What infants know: The new cognitive science of early development*. Oxford, Blackwell.

Meltzoff, A.N., & Brooks, R. (2001). 'Like me' as a building block for understanding other minds: Bodily acts, attention, and intention. In B. Malle, L.J. Moses, & D.A. Baldwin (Eds), *Intentions and intentionality: Foundations of social cognition* (pp. 171–91). Cambridge, MA: MIT Press.

Merton, Robert K. (1968). *Social theory and social structure*. New York: Free Press. (Original work published 1949)

Messner, Steven. (1986, February). Television violence and violent crime: An aggregate analysis. *Social Problems, 33*(3), 218–35.

Meyers, Gustavus. (2004). *History of Canadian wealth*. Honolulu, HI: University Press of the Pacific. (Original work published 1914)

Michaels, Robert T., Gagnon, John H., Laumann, Edward O., & Kolata, Gina. (1994). *Sex in America: A definitive survey*. Boston: Little, Brown and Company.

Midgley, Mary. (1992). Science as salvation: A modern myth and its meaning. London: Routledge.

Milgram, Stanley. (1963). Behavioral study of obedience. *Journal of Abnormal and Social Psychology, 67*, 371–8.

———. (1973, December). The perils of obedience. *Harper's Magazine*, pp. 62–77.

———. (1974). *Obedience to authority: An experimental view*. New York: Harper & Row.

Mills, C. Wright. (1951). *White collar: The American middle classes*. New York: Oxford University Press.

———. (1956). *The power elite*. New York: Oxford University Press.

———. (2000). *The sociological imagination*. New York: Oxford University Press. (Original work published 1959)

Miner, Horace. (1956). Body image among the Nacirema. *American Anthropologist, 58*, 503–7.

Mitchell, J. Clyde. (1969). *Social networks in urban situations: Analysis of personal relationships in Central African towns*. Manchester: Manchester University Press.

Molitor, F., & Hirsch, K.W. (1994). Children's toleration of real-life aggression after exposure to media violence: A replication of the Drabman and Thomas studies. *Child Study Journal, 24*, 191–207.

Money, John. (1988). *Gay, straight and in-between*. New York: Oxford University Press.

Montemurro, Beth. (2002). You go 'cause you have to: The bridal shower as a ritual of obligation. *Symbolic Interaction, 1*, 67–92.

Montreal gunman called himself 'angel of death'. (2006, September 14). CBC News. Retrieved from www.cbc.ca/news/canada/story/2006/09/14/gunman-shooting.html

Morrison, Ken. (1995). *Marx, Durkheim, Weber: Formations of modern social thought*. London: Sage Publications Ltd.

Murji, Karim. (2007). Sociological engagements: Institutional racism and beyond. *Sociology, 41*(5), pp. 843–55.

Murphy, Brian, Roberts, Paul, & Wolfson, Michael. (2007, Winter). High-income Canadians. *Perspectives on Labour and Income, 19*(4), pp. 5–17. Statistics Canada Catalogue no. 75-001-XIE. Retrieved from www.statcan.gc.ca/pub/75-001-x/2007109/article/10350-eng.pdf

Myles, John, & Turegun, Adnan. (1994). Comparative studies in class structure. *Annual Review of Sociology*, pp. 103–24.

Nardi, Peter M. (1996). 'The breastplate of righteousness': Twenty-five years after Laud Humphreys' *Tearoom trade: Impersonal sex in public places, Journal of Homosexuality, 30*(2), 1–10.

Nash, Catherine. (2004). Genetic kinship. *Cultural Studies, 18*(1), 1–33.

National Council of Welfare. (2009a, October 2). Poverty profile 2007: Bulletin no. 1—Poverty trends in Canada, 1976–2007. Retrieved from http://www.ncw.gc.ca/l.3bd.2t.1ils@-eng.jsp?lid=8

———. (2009b, November 19). Poverty profile 2007: Bulletin no. 4—A snapshot of children living in poverty. Retrieved from www.ncw.gc.ca/l.3bd.2t.1ils@-eng.jsp?lid=4

Nee, V., & Su, S. (1998). Institutional foundations of robust economic performance: Public sector industrial growth in China. In J. Henderson (Ed.), *Industrial transformation in eastern Europe in the light of the East Asian experience*. London: MacMillan.

Newton, E. (1972). *Mother camp: Female impersonators in America*. Chicago: University of Chicago Press.

Niedzviecki, Hal. (2009). *The peep diaries: How we're learning to love watching ourselves and our neighbors*. City Lights.

Nielsen, Joyce McCarl (Ed.). (1990). *Feminist research methods: Exemplary readings in the social sciences*. Boulder, CO: Westview Press.

Nielsen. (2008a, August). The most viewed Olympics ever—Two thirds of the world's population (4.4 billion) tunes in to Beijing 2008 in the first 10 days of games. Retrieved from http://en-us.nielsen.com/content/nielsen/en_us/news/news_releases/2008/august/the_most_viewed_olympics.html

———. (2008b, June). Average US home now receives a record 118.6 TV channels. Retrieved from http://en-us.nielsen.com/content/nielsen/en_us/news/news_releases/2008/june/average_u_s__home.html

———. (2008c, June). TV websites grow more popular, but viewers still prefer their TV sets, according to Nielsen and CTAM. Retrieved from http://en-us.nielsen.com/content/nielsen/en_us/news/news_releases/2008/june/tv_websites_grow_more.html

———. (2008d, October). TV viewing and Internet use are complementary, Nielsen reports. Retrieved from http://en-us.nielsen.com/content/nielsen/en_us/news/news_releases/2008/october/TV_Viewing_And_Internet_Use_Are_Complementary__Nielsen_Reports.html

———. (2009, April). *The global online media landscape: Identifying opportunities in a challenging market*. Retrieved from http://blog.nielsen.com/nielsenwire/wp-content/uploads/2009/04/nielsen-online-global-lanscapefinal1.pdf

———. (2010). Three screen report, Q1 2010. Retrieved from http://www.nielsen.com/us/en/insights/reports-downloads/2010/three-screen-report-q1-2010.html

Nietzsche, F. (1983). On the uses and disadvantages of history for life (Trans. R.J. Hollingdale). In *Untimely meditations* (pp. 59–123). New York: Cambridge University Press. (Original work published 1874)

Nisbert, Robert. (1966). *The sociological tradition*. New York: Basic Books.

Oakley, Anne. (1982). *Subject women*. London: Fontana.

Organisation for Economic Co-operation and Development (OECD). (1992). *Labour force statistics, 1970–1990*. Paris: OECD.

———. (2008). Growing unequal: Income distribution and poverty in OECD countries. Paris: OECD. Retrieved from www.oecd.org/els/social/inequality

———. (2009). Society at a glance 2009: OECD social indicators. Retrieved from www.oecd.org/document/24/0,3343,en_2649_34637_2671576_1_1_1_1,00.html#press

Olson, Steve E. (2002). *Mapping human history: Discovering the past through our genes*. Boston: Houghton Mifflin.

Omi, Michael, & Winant, Howard. (2009). Thinking through race and racism. *Contemporary Sociology: A Journal of Reviews*, pp. 121–5.

Ornstein, M. (2000). *Ethno-racial inequality in Metropolitan Toronto: Analysis of the 1996 census*. Toronto, ON: Institute for Social Research, York University.

Ottosson, Daniel. (2010). *State-sponsored homophobia. A world survey of laws prohibiting same sex activity between consenting adults*. ILGA, the International Lesbian, Gay, Bisexual, Trans and Intersex Association. Retrieved from http://old.ilga.org/Statehomophobia/ILGA_State_Sponsored_Homophobia_2010.pdf

Owens, J., Maxim, R., Nobile, C., McGuinn, M., Alario, A., & Msall, M. (1999). Television viewing habits and sleep disturbances in school-aged children. *Pediatrics, 104*(3), e 27.

Packard, Noel, & Chen, Christopher. (2005). From medieval mnemonics to a social construction of memory: Thoughts on some early European conceptualizations of memory, morality, and consciousness. *American Behavioral Scientist, 48*(10), 1297–1319. doi:10.11770002764205277-10

Paechter, C. (2007). *Being boys, being girls: Learning masculinities and femininities*. Maidenhead: Open University Press.

Painter, Nell Irwin. (2010). *The history of white people*. New York: W.W. Norton.

Paquette, G., & de Guise, J. (2002). Principaux indicateurs de la violence présentée sur les réseaux généralistes de television au Canada. In N.N. Turgeon (Ed.), *La violence à la télévision et les jeunes* (pp. 25–58). Québec: Centre d'études sur les médias, Université Laval.

Park, Robert. (1952). Sociology, community and society. In Everett Cherrington Hughes, Charles, A. Johnson, Jitsuichi Masuoka, Robert Redfield, & Louis Wirth (Eds), *The Collected Papers of Robert Ezra Park. Vol. 2. Human Communities*. Glencoe, IL: Free Press. (Original work published 1929)

Park, Robert, & Burgess, E.W. (1925). *The city: Suggestions for investigation of human behavior in the urban environment*. Chicago: University of Chicago Press.

Paxton, Pamela, Kunovich, Sheri, & Hughes, Melanie M. (2007). Gender in politics. *Annual Review of Sociology, 33*, 263–84.

Pellow, David N. (2011). Activist scholarship for environmental justice. In Kathleen Korgen, Jonathan White, & Shelley White (Eds), *Sociologists in action: Sociology, social change, and social justice* (pp. 221–6). Thousand Oaks, CA: Pine Forge Press.

Pendakur, K., & Pendakur, R. (1998). The colour of money: Earnings differentials among ethnic groups in Canada. *Canadian Journal of Economics, 31*(3), 518–48.

Peterson, Richard A., & Anand, N. (2004). The production of culture perspective. *Annual Review of Sociology*, pp. 311–34.

Phillips, A.T., Wellman, H.M., & Spelke, E.S. (2002). Infant's ability to connect gaze and emotional expression to intentional action. *Cognition, 85*, 53–78.

Picot, Garnett, Lu, Yugian, & Hou, Feng. (2010). Immigrant low-income rates: The role of the market income and government transfers. *Perspectives on Labour and Income, 22*(1), 13–23.

Picot, Garnett, & Myles, John. (2005). *Income inequality and low income in Canada: An international perspective*. Statistics Canada Catalogue no. 11 FOOl 9MIE – No. 240. Analytical Studies Branch Research Paper Series. Ottawa.

Pilgeram, Ryanne. (2007). 'Ass-kicking' women: Doing and undoing gender in a US livestock auction. *Gender, Work and Organization, 6*, 572–95.

Popper, Karl R. (1969). *Conjectures and refutations: The growth of a scientific knowledge* (3rd edn). London: Routledge & Keegan Paul.

Porter, John. (1965). *The vertical mosaic: An analysis of social class and power in Canada*. Toronto: University of Toronto Press.

Poster, Mark. (1990). *The mode of information: Poststructuralism and social context*. Chicago: University of Chicago Press.

Postone, Moishe, LiPuma, Edward, & Calhoun, Craig. (1993). Introduction: Bourdieu and social theory. In Moishe Postone, Edward LiPuma, & Craig Calhoun (Eds), *Bourdieu: Critical perspectives* (pp. 1–13). Chicago: University of Chicago Press.

Premack, D. (1990). On the coevolution of language and social competence. *Behavioral and Brain Sciences, 13*(4), 754–5.

Prince, D. (1986). *A psychological study of prostitutes in California and Nevada.* Unpublished doctoral dissertation, United States International University, San Diego, CA.

Public Safety Canada Portfolio Corrections Statistics Committee. (2008). *Corrections and conditional release statistical overview.* Ottawa: Public Safety and Emergency Preparedness Canada. Retrieved from www.publicsafety.gc.ca/res/cor/rep/_fl/2008-04-ccrso-eng.pdf

Putnam, R.D. (2000). *Bowling alone.* New York: Simon & Schuster.

Qualman, Erik. (2009, August 11). Statistics show social media is bigger than you think. Socialnomics: World of Mouth for Social Good. Retrieved from www.socialnomics.net/2009/08/11/statistics-show-social-media-is-bigger-than-you-think/

Quillian, Lincoln. (2006). New approaches to understanding racial prejudice and discrimination. *Annual Review of Sociology,* pp. 299–328.

Reay, Diane, Hollingworth, Sumi, Williams, Katya, Crozier, Gill, Jamieson, Fiona, James, David, & Beedell, Phoebe. (2007). 'A darker shade of pale'? Whiteness, the middle classes and multi-ethnic inner city schooling. *Sociology, 6,* 1041–60.

Reiman, J. (2007). *The rich get richer and the poor get prison: Ideology, Class, and Criminal Justice* (9th edn). Boston: Pearson.

Reiss, Albert J. (1961). The social integration of queers and peers. *Social Problems, 9,* 102–20.

Reitz, Jeffrey G. (2001). Immigrant skill utilization in the Canadian labour market: Implications of human capital research. *Journal of International Migration and Integration, 2*(3), 347–78.

———. (2007). Immigrant employment success in Canada, part 1: Individual and contextual causes. *International Immigration & Integration, 8,* pp. 11–36.

Reitz, Jeffrey G., & Banerjee, Rupa. (2005). Racial inequality and social cohesion in Canada: Findings from the Ethnic Diversity Survey. Paper prepared for presentation at the plenary session of the Canadian Ethnic Studies Association Meeting, 'Social Trends and Social Justice: Analysis of the EDS Survey', Ottawa, ON (13–16 October 2005).

Reitz, Jeffrey G., & Verma, A. (2004). Immigration, race, and labor. *Industrial Relations, 43*(4), 835–54.

Renaud, V., & Costa, R. (1999). *1996 Census of population: Certification report, population group.* Ottawa: Housing, Family and Social Statistics Division, Statistics Canada.

Rettie, Ruth. (2009). Mobile phone communication: Extending Goffman to mediated interaction. *Sociology, 3,* 421–38.

Ricoeur, P. (1970). *Freud and philosophy: An essay on interpretation.* New Haven, CT: Yale University Press.

Rideout, Victoria J., Foehr, L., & Roberts, D. (2010). *Generation M²: Media in the lives of 8- to 18-year-olds.* Report, Kaiser Family Foundation Study. Retrieved from www.kff.org/entmedia/upload/8010.pdf

Rideout, Victoria J., Vandewater, Elizabeth A., & Wartella, Ellen A. (2003). *Zero to six: Electronic media in the lives of infants, toddlers and preschoolers.* Menlo Park, CA: The Henry J. Kaiser Family Foundation.

Ridgeway, Cecilia L., & Correll, Shelley J. (2004). Unpacking the gender system: A theoretical perspective on gender beliefs and social relations. *Gender & Society, 18*(4), 510–31.

Ridgeway, Cecilia L., & Smith-Lovin, Lynn. (1999). The gender system and interaction. *Annual Review of Sociology, 25,* 1191–216.

Ritzer, George. (1993). *The McDonaldization of society.* Thousand Oaks, CA: Pine Forge Press.

———. (2000). *Classical sociological theory* (3rd edn). Boston: McGraw Hill.

Robinson, J.P., & Godbey, G. (1999). *Time for life* (2nd edn). State College, PA: Penn State University Press.

Roen, Katrina. (2008). But we have to do something: Surgical 'correction of atypical genitalia'. *Body and Society, 1,* 47–66.

Rogers, Chris. (2009, December 22). What became of Romania's neglected orphans? *BBC News.* Retrieved from http://news.bbc.co.uk/2/hi/8425001.stm

Roscoe, Will. (1987). Bibliography of berdache and alternative gender roles among North American Indians. *Journal of Homosexuality, 14,* 3–4.

Roth, Guenther. (1997). The young Max Weber: Anglo-American religious influences and Protestant social reform in Germany. *International Journal of Politics, Culture, and Society, 4,* 659–71.

———. (2002). Max Weber: Family history, economic policy, exchange reform. *International Journal of Politics, Culture and Society, 3,* 509–20.

Rugge, Tanya. (2006). Risk assessment of male Aboriginal offenders: A 2006 perspective. Ottawa: Public Safety and Emergency Preparedness Canada. (E 98 C87 R844 2006). Retrieved from www.psepc.gc.ca/res/cor/rep/aboriginal_offenders-en.asp

Ruggiero, Vincent Ryan. (1996). *A guide to sociological thinking.* Thousand Oaks, CA: Sage.

Ruminski, Henry J., & Hanks, William E. (1995). Critical thinking lacks definition and uniform evaluation criteria. *Journalism and Mass Communication Educator, 50,* 4–11.

Rymer, Russ. (1992, April 13). *The New Yorker,* pp. 41–81.

Saint-Simon, Henri, Comte de. (1975). *Henri Saint-Simon (1970–1825): Selected writings on science, industry, and social organization* (Trans. Keith Taylor). London: Croom Helm.

Sallaz, Jeffrey J., & Zavisca, Jane. (2007, August). Bourdieu in American Sociology, 1980–2004. *Annual Review of Sociology,* pp. 21–41.

Sampson, Robert J., & Wilson, William Julius. (1995). Toward a theory of race, crime, and urban inequality. In John Hagan & Ruth Peterson (Eds), *Crime and Inequality.* Stanford, CA: Stanford University Press.

Sanchez-Martin, J.R., Fano, E., Ahedo, L., Cardas, J., Brain, P.F., & Azpiroz, A. (2000). Relating testosterone levels and free play social behavior in male and female preschool children. *Psychoneuroendocrinology, 25,* 773–83.

Sawyer, R. Keith. (2002). Durkheim's dilemma: Toward a sociology of emergence. *Sociological Theory, 20,* 227–47.

Schiebinger, Londa. (1989). *The mind has no sex? Women in the origins of modern science.* Cambridge, MA: Harvard University Press.

Schrock, Douglas, & Schwalbe, Michael. (2009). Men, masculinity, and manhood acts. *Annual Review of Sociology,* pp. 277–95.

Sciadas, George. (2002). *The digital divide in Canada.* Ottawa: Statistics Canada. Catalogue no. 56F0009XIE. Retrieved from www.statcan.gc.ca/pub/56f0009x/4193608-eng.pdf

Scott, Alan. (1995). Value freedom and intellectual autonomy. *History of the Human Sciences, 3,* 69–88.

Scott, Susan, & Thorpe, Charles. (2006). The sociological imagination of R.D. Laing. *Sociological Theory, 4,* pp. 331–52.

Segre, Sandro. (2004). A Durkheimian network theory. *Journal of Classical Sociology, 2,* 215–35.

Sewell, William Jr. (1974). Social change and the rise of working-class politics in nineteenth-century Marseille. *Past and Present, 65,* 75–109.

Shattuck, Roger. (1980). *The forbidden experiment: The story of the wild boy of Aveyron.* New York: Farrar, Straus, and Giroux.

Sherif, M., Harvey, O.J., White, B.J., Hood, W.R., & Sherif, C.W. (1961). *Intergroup conflict and cooperation: The Robbers Cave experiment.* Norman: University of Oklahoma Book Exchange.

Shirpak, Khosro Refai, Maticka-Tyndale, Eleanor, & Chinichian, Maryam. (2007, Fall). Iranian immigrants' perceptions of sexuality in Canada: A symbolic interactionist approach. *Canadian Journal of Human Sexuality, 16*(3–4).

Sharon, T., & Wynn, K. (1998). Individuation of actions from continuous motion. *Psychological Science, 9,* 357–62.

Simon, T.J., Hespos, S.J., & Rochat, P. (1995). Do infants understand simple arithmetic? A replication of Wynn (1992). *Cognitive Development, 10,* 253–69.

Simpson, Sally. (2002). *Corporate crime, law, and social control.* London: Cambridge University Press.

Singer, I. (1987). *The nature of love. The modern world* (vol. 3). Chicago: University of Chicago Press.

Singer, M.I., Slovak, K., Frierson, T., & York, P. (1998). Viewing preferences, symptoms of psychological trauma, and violent behaviors among children who watch television. *Journal of the American Academy of Child and Adolescent Psychiatry, 37,* 1041–8.

Skinner, David. (2006). Racialised futures: Biologism and the changing politics of identity. *Social Studies of Science, 36*(3), 459–88.

———. (2007). Groundhog Day? The strange case of sociology, race and 'science'. *Sociology, 41,* 931.

Smith, Dorothy. (1979). A peculiar eclipse: Women's exclusion from men's culture. *Women's Studies International Quarterly, 1,* 281–95.

———. (1990). *The conceptual practices of power: A feminist sociology of knowledge.* Toronto: University of Toronto Press.

Smith, Kenneth. (2004). Marx on the side of the market? *Journal of Classical Sociology, 4*(2), 237–45.

Soothill, K., & Sanders, T. (2005). The geographical mobility, preferences and pleasures of prolific punters: A demonstration study of the activities of prostitutes' clients. *Sociological Research Online, 10*(1).

Spears, George, & Seydegart, Kasia. (2004). Kids' views on violence in the media. *Canadian Child and Adolescent Psychiatric Review, 13*(1), 7–12. Retrieved from www.ncbi.nlm.nih.gov/pmc/articles/PMC2533815/

Spelke, E.S. (2003). What makes us smart? Core knowledge and natural language. In D. Gentner & S. Goldin-Meadow (Eds), *Language in mind: Advances in the investigation of language and thought.* Cambridge, MA: MIT Press.

Sponsorship Intelligence. (2010). Vancouver 2010 Olympic Winter Games global television and online media overview. Report prepared for the International Olympic Committee. Retrieved from www.olympic.org/Documents/IOC_Marketing/Broadcasting/Vancouver2010OlympicWinterGames-BroadcastCoverageAudienceOverview.pdf

Stapleton, John . (2009). Close encounters of the 'thirties' kind. Canadian Centre for Policy Alternatives. Retrieved from www.policyalternatives.ca/sites/default/files/uploads/publications/National_Office_Pubs/2009/Close_Encounters_of_the_Thirties_Kind.pdf

Statistics Canada. (1992). Report on the demographic situations in Canada. Catalogue no. 91-209. Ottawa: Statistics Canada.

———. (2003a). *Aboriginal peoples of Canada: A demographic profile.* Catalogue no. 96F0030XIE2001007. Ottawa: Minister of Industry.

———. (2003b). *Ethnic diversity survey: Portrait of a multicultural society.* Catalogue no. 89-593-XIE. Ottawa: Statistics Canada.

———. (2003c, Autumn). Update on cultural diversity. *Canadian Social Trends, 70,* 19–23. Retrieved from http://dsp-psd.pwgsc.gc.ca/Collection-R/Statcan/11-008-XIE/0020311-008-XIE.pdf

———. (2004a). Women in Canada: A gender-based statistical report. Catalogue no. 89-503-X. Ottawa: Statistics Canada.

———. (2004b). Canadian framework for culture statistics. Catalogue no. 81-595-MIE — No. 021 ISSN: 1711-831X. Ottawa: Statistics Canada.

———. (2006a.) *Appendix C: Comparison of ethnic origins disseminated in 2006, 2001 and 1996.* Ottawa: Statistics Canada. Retrieved from www12.statcan.gc.ca/census-recensement/2006/ref/dict/app-ann003-eng.cfm

———. (2006b). *Census 2006—2B (Long Form).* Ottawa: Statistics Canada. Retrieved from www12.statcan.gc.ca/census-recensement/2006/ref/about-apropos/version-eng.cfm

———. (2006c). *Earnings and incomes of Canadians over the past quarter century, 2006 census.* Catalogue no. 97-563-X. Ottawa: Statistics Canada.

———. (2006d, December 13). Study: Inequality in wealth. *The Daily.* Retrieved from www.statcan.gc.ca/daily-quotidien/061213/dq061213c-eng.htm

———. (2006e, March 31). Television viewing, Fall 2004. *The Daily.* Retrieved from www.statcan.gc.ca/daily-quotidien/060331/dq060331b-eng.htm

———. (2007). Income in Canada. Catalogue no. 75-202-X. Ottawa: Minister of Industry. Retrieved from www.statcan.gc.ca/pub/75-202-x/75-202-x2007000-eng.pdf

———. (2008a). Low income cut-offs for 2007 and low income measures for 2006. *Income Research Paper Series, 2008*(4). Retrieved from www.statcan.gc.ca/pub/75f0002m/75f0002m2008004-eng.htm

———. (2008b, March 9). Health care use among gay, lesbian and bisexual Canadians. *The Daily.* Retrieved from www.statcan.gc.ca/daily-quotidien/080319/dq080319b-eng.htm

———. (2008c). *Canada's ethnocultural mosaic, 2006 census.* Catalogue no. 97-562-X. Ottawa: Statistics Canada. Retrieved from www12.statcan.ca/census-recensement/2006/as-sa/97-562/pdf/97-562-XIE2006001.pdf

———. (2009, June 3). Income of Canadians. *The Daily.* Retrieved from www.statcan.gc.ca/daily-quotidien/090603/dq090603a-eng.htm

Statistics South Africa. 2001. *Census 2001. Census in Brief.* Retrieved from www.statssa.gov.za/census01/html/CInBrief/CIB2001.pdf

Steinmetz. G., & Wright, E.O. (1989). The fall and rise of the petty bourgeoisie: Changing patterns of self-employment in the postwar United States. *American Journal of Sociology, 94,* 973–1018.

Stephens, W. (1963). *The family in cross-cultural perspective.* New York: Holt, Rinehart & Wilson.

Stern, Daniel N. (1977). *The first relationship: Mother and infant.* Cambridge, MA: Harvard University Press.

Stevens, Daphne, Kiger, Gary, & Riley, Pamela J. (2001). Working hard and hardly working: Domestic labour and marital satisfaction among dual-earner couples. *Journal of Marriage and Family,* pp. 514–26.

Storey, John. (2000). *Cultural theory and popular culture: An introduction* (3rd edn). Harlow: Pearson Education Limited.

Struthers, James. 2011. 'Great Depression'. In James H. Marsh (Ed.), *The Canadian encyclopedia.* Retrieved from www.thecanadianencyclopedia.com/index.cfm?PgNm=TCE&Params=a1ARTA0003425

Sullivan, Edmund. (1984). *A critical psychology: Interpretation of the Personal World.* New York: Plenum Press.

Swedberg, Richard. (1999). Max Weber as an economist and as a sociologist: Towards a fuller understanding of Weber's view of economics. *American Journal of Economics and Sociology, 4,* 561–82.

———. (2003). The changing picture of Max Weber's sociology. *Annual Review of Sociology,* pp. 283–306.

Swidler, Ann. (1986). Culture in action: Symbols and strategies. *American Sociological Review, 2,* 273–86.

Swingewood, Alan. (1984). *A short history of sociological thought.* London: Macmillan.

Teeger, Chana, & Vinitzky-Seroussi, Vered. (2007). Controlling for consensus: Commemorating apartheid in South Africa. *Symbolic Interaction, 1,* 57–78.

Technology helps Canadians chase romance. (2008, May 24). *Ottawa Citizen.*

Teens want to learn about healthy sex, not just sexual health. (2009, June 4). *YFile: York's Daily Bulletin.* Retrieved from www.yorku.ca/yfile/archive/index.asp?Article=12729

Tenbruck, Friedrich H. (1980). Prefatory note. *The British Journal of Sociology, 3,* 313–15.

Thayer, James Steele. (1980). The berdache of the Northern Plains: A socioreligious perspective. *Journal of Anthropological Research, 36*(3), 287–93.

Tilly, Charles. (2004). Reasons why. *Sociological Theory, 3,* 445–54.

———. (2006). *Why?* Princeton, NJ: Princeton University Press.

Tiryakian, Edward A. (1975). Neither Marx nor Durkheim . . . perhaps Weber. *The American Journal of Sociology, 1,* 1–33.

Tittle, Charles R. (2004). The arrogance of public sociology. *Social Forces, 4,* 1639–43.Toronto: James Lorimer & Co. Ltd.

Trammel, Rebecca, & Chenault, Scott. (2009). 'We have to take these guys out': Motivations for assaulting incarcerated child molesters. *Symbolic Interaction, 32*(4), 334–50.

Trevarthen, Colin. (1977). Descriptive analyses of infant communicative behavior. In H.R. Schaffer (Ed.), *Studies in mother–infant interaction.* London: Academic Press.

———. (1980). The foundation of intersubjectivity: Development of interpersonal and cooperative understanding in infants. In M. Bullova (Ed.), *The social foundation of language and thought: Essays in honor of Jerome Bruner.* New York: Cambridge University Press.

Trovato, Frank. (1998). The Stanley Cup of hockey and suicide in Quebec, 1951–1992. *Social Forces, 77*(1), 105–27.

Turnbull, Colin M. (1972). *The mountain people.* New York: Simon & Schuster.

Turner, John. (1997). *The institutional order.* New York: Longman.

Turner, Jonathan H., Beeghley, Leonard, & Powers, Charles H. (2007). *The emergence of sociological theory* (6th edn). Belmont CA: Thompson Wadsworth.

Turner, Stephen. (2007). Public sociology and democratic theory. *Sociology,* pp. 785–98.

Tylor, E.B. (1903). *Primitive culture: Researches into the development of mythology, philosophy, religion, language, art, and custom.* London: J. Murray. (Original work published 1871)

Under 25's swap remote controls for phones as 'social TV' trend takes over. (n.d.) *Digital Clarity.* Retrieved from www.digital-clarity.com/press-releases/under-25s-swap-remote-controls-for-iphones-as-social-tv-trend-takes-over

US Department of Commerce, Bureau of the Census. (2000). *United States census 2000.* Retrieved from www.census.gov/dmd/www/pdf/d61a.pdf

US National Library of Medicine. (2011). What is DNA? In *Genetics home reference: Your guide to understanding genetic conditions.* Retrieved from http://ghr.nlm.nih.gov/handbook/basics/dna

Van de Walle, John A. (2001). *Elementary and middle school mathematics: Teaching developmentally* (4th edn). Boston, MA: Addison Wesley Longman.

Van de Walle, J., Carey, S., & Prevor, M. (2001). Bases for object individuation in infancy: Evidence from manual search. *Journal of Cognitive Development, 1,* 249–80.

Van Gyn, Geraldine, Ford, Carol, et al. (2006). *Teaching for critical thinking.* London, ON: Society for Teaching and Learning in Higher Education.

Veenhof, B., Wellman, B., Quell, C., & Hogan, B. (2005). *How Canadians' use of the Internet affects social life and civic participation.* Catalogue no. 56F0004M—no. 016. Ottawa: Statistics Canada.

Visser, Margaret. (1986). *Much depends on dinner: The extraordinary history and mythology, allure and obesssions, perils and taboos of an ordinary meal.* Toronto: McClelland & Stewart.

Wagenaar, T.C. (2004). Is there a core in sociology? Results from a survey. *Teaching Sociology, 32,* 1–18.

Walk, R.D., & Gibson, E.J. (1961). A comparative and analytical study of visual depth perception. *Psychological Monographs, 75*(15).

Waller, Vaughn. (2006, October). Serious games—Fad or opportunity. *Inside Learning Technologies Magazine.* Retrieved from www.cedma-europe.org/newsletter%20articles/LTI%20Mag/Serious%20Games%20-%20Fad%20or%20Opportunity%20(Oct%202006).pdf

Waller, Willard. (1938). *The family: A dynamic interpretation.* New York: Cordon Company.

———. (1951). *The family: A dynamic interpretation* (rev. edn). Reuben Hill, NY: Dryden Press. (Original work published 1938)

Walters, Suzanna Danuta. (2001). *All the rage: The story of gay visibility in America.* Chicago, IL: University of Chicago Press.

Warner, Richard. (2005). Twentieth-century trends in occupational attainment in Canada. *The Canadian Journal of Sociology / Cahiers canadiens de sociologie, 4,* 441–69.

Waters, Mary C. (1996). The social construction of race and ethnicity: Some examples from demography. Presented at the Meetings of the American Sociological Association, New York.

Watkins, S. Craig. (2009). *The young & the digital: What the migration to social-network sites, games, and anytime, anywhere media means for our future.* Boston, MA: Beacon Press.

Watts, Duncan. (2004). The 'new' science of networks. *Annual Review of Sociology,* pp. 243–70.

Weber, Max. (1949). Objectivity in social science and social policy. In E.A. Shils & H. Finch (Eds), *Max Weber: The methodology of the social sciences.* New York: Free Press. (Original work published 1904)

———. (1964). *The theory of social and economic organization.* New York: The Free Press. (Original work published 1915)

———. (1977). *Critique of Stammler* (Trans. Guy Oakes). New York: The Free Press. (Original work published 1907)

———. (1978). *Economy and society* (vols I–III) (Trans. Guenther Roth & Claus Wittich). Berkeley and Los Angeles: University of California Press. (Original work published in German as *Wirtschaft und Gesellschaft,* 1925)

———. (1994). The nation state and economic policy. In Peter Lassman & Ronald Speirs (Eds), *Weber. Political Writings.* Cambridge: Cambridge University Press. (Original work published 1895)

Weeks, Jeffrey. (1977). *Coming out: Homosexual politics in Britain from the nineteenth century to the present.* London: Quartet Books.

———. (1985). *Sexuality and its discontents.* Boston: Routledge & Kegan Paul.

Weitzer, Ronald. (2009a). *Sex for sale: Prostitution, pornography, and the sex industry* (2nd edn). New York & London: Routledge. (Original work published 2000)

———. (2009b). Sociology of sex work. *Annual Review of Sociology, 35*, 213–34.

Welborn, B. Locke, Papademetris, X., Reis, D.L., Rajeevan, N., Loise, S., & Gray, J.R. (2009, December 17). Variation in orbitofrontal cortex volume: Relation to sex, emotion regulation and affect. *Social Cognitive and Affective Neuroscience.* doi:10.1093/scan/nsp028

Wellman, Barry. (1983). Network analysis: Some basic principles. In R. Collins (Ed.), *Sociological Theory 1983* (pp. 155–200). San Francisco: Jossey-Bass.

Wellman, Barry, Haase, A.Q., Witte, J., & Hampton, K. (2001). Does the Internet increase, decrease, or supplement social capital? Social networks, participation, and community commitment. *American Behavioral Scientist, 3*, 436.

Wells, Spencer. (2002). *The journey of man: A genetic odyssey.* Princeton, NJ: Princeton University Press.

West, Candace, & Zimmerman, Don H. (1987). Doing gender. *Gender and Society, 2*, 125–51.

White, Harrison C., Boorman, Scott A., & Breiger, Ronald L. (1976). Social structure from multiple networks. I – Block models of roles and positions. *The American Journal of Sociology, 81*(4), 730–80.

Whiteford, Michael, & Friedl, John. (1992). *The human portrait: Introduction to cultural anthropology.* Englewood Cliffs, NJ: Prentice-Hall.

Wilkins, Kathryn, & Mackenzie, Susan. (2007, August). Work injuries. *Health Reports, 18*(3). Catalogue no. 82-003-X. Ottawa: Statistics Canada.

Williams, Raymond. (1985). *Keywords: A vocabulary of culture and society.* New York: Oxford University Press. (Original work published 1976)

Williams, Richard. (2011, August 26). Oscar Pistorius and Caster Semenya's running battle to reach starting blocks: How the South African athletes forced IAAF to rethink regulations ahead of world championships in Korea. *The Guardian.* Retrieved from www.guardian.co.uk/sport/2011/aug/26/oscar-pistorius-caster-semenya-athletics

Willis, Paul. (1977). *Learning to labour: How working class kids get working class jobs.* New York: Columbia University Press.

Wood, Jessica L., Heitmiller, Dwayne, Andreasen, Nancy C., & Nopoulos, Peg. (2008). Morphology of the ventral frontal cortex: Relationship to femininity and social cognition. *Cerebral Cortex, 18*(3), 534–40. Retrieved from http://cercor.oxfordjournals.org/cgi/content/full/18/3/534

Woodward, A.L. (1998). Infants selectively encode the goal object of an actor's reach. *Cognition, 69*, 1–34.

———. (1999). Infants' ability to distinguish between purposeful and non-purposeful behaviors. *Infant Behavior and Development, 22*, 145–60. doi:10.1016/S0163-6383(99)00007-7

Woodward, A.L., Sommerville, J.A., & Guajardo, J.J. (2001). How infants make sense of intentional action. In B. Malle, L. Moses, & D. Baldwin (Eds), *Intentions and intentionality: Foundations of Social Cognition* (pp. 149–69). Cambridge, MA: MIT Press.

Worsley, Peter. (1982). *Marx and Marxism.* London: Tavistock.

Wright, Erik Olin. (1994). *Interrogating inequality: Essays on class analysis, socialism, and Marxism.* New York: Verso.

———. (1997). *Class counts: Comparative studies in class analysis.* Cambridge: Cambridge University Press.

———. (2002). The shadow of exploitation in Weber's class analysis. *American Sociological Review*, 832–53.

Wright, Erik Olin, Costello, Cynthia, Hachen, David, & Sprauge, Joey. (1982). The American class structure. *American Sociological Review, 47*, 709–26.

Wundt, Wilhelm. (1907). *Outlines of psychology* (7th edn). Leipzig: Engleman. (Original work published 1896)

———. (1916). *Elements of folk psychology. Outlines of a psychological history of the development of mankind* (Trans. Edward Leroy Schaub). New York: Macmillan.

Wynn, K. (1996). Infants' individuation and enumeration of actions. *Psychological Science, 7*, 164–9.

———. (1998). Psychological foundations of number: Numerical competence in human infants. *Trends in Cognitive Science, 2*, 296–303.

Wynn, K., Bloom, P., & Chiang, W.-C. (2002). Enumeration of collective entities by 5-month-old infants. *Cognition, 83*, B55–62.

Yalnizyan, Armine. (2010). *The rise of Canada's richest 1%.* Ottawa: Canadian Centre for Policy Alternatives. Retrieved from www.policyalternatives.ca/sites/default/files/uploads/publications/National%20Office/2010/12/Richest%201%20Percent.pdf

Yerbury, J.C., & Griffiths, C.T. (1991). Minorities, crime and the law. In M.A. Jackson & C.T. Griffiths (Eds), *Canadian criminology: Perspectives on crime and criminology* (pp. 315–46). Toronto: Harcourt Brace Jovanovich.

Zeiler, Kristin, & Wickström, Anette. (2009). Why do 'we' perform surgery on newborn intersexed children? *Feminist Theory, 3*, 359–77.

Credits

Index